The
Technique
of
Television
Production

Twelfth Edition

THE LIBRARY OF COMMUNICATION TECHNIQUES

The Technique of Television Production

Twelfth Edition

Gerald Millerson

Focal Press

London and Boston

Focal Press
is an imprint of Butterworth Scientific

 PART OF REED INTERNATIONAL P.L.C.

First published 1961
Second edition 1963
Third edition 1964
Fourth edition 1966
Fifth edition 1967
Sixth edition 1968
Seventh edition 1969
Eighth edition 1970
Ninth edition 1972
Tenth edition 1979
Eleventh edition 1985
Twelfth edition 1990

© **Gerald Millerson, 1990**

British Library Cataloguing in Publication Data

Millerson, Gerald
   The technique of television production.—12th ed.—(The Library of communication techniques)
   1. Television programmes. Production—Manuals
   I. Title II. Series
   791.45′0232

   ISBN 0-240-51289-8

Library of Congress Cataloging in Publication Data

Millerson, Gerald
   The techniques of television production/Gerald Millerson.—12th ed.
       p.   cm.
   Includes bibliographical references.
   ISBN 0-240-51289-8
   1. Television—Production and direction. I. Title.
   PN1992.75.M5 1990
   791.45′0232—dc20 89-23437

Typesetting and origination by BC Typesetting, Exeter EX2 8PN

Printed and bound by Hartnolls Ltd, Bodmin, Cornwall

Contents

Preface to the Twelfth Edition

No single book can cover the entire field of television production. So, if you are meeting this title for the first time, you will want answers to some important questions:

What are the main aims of this book?

Starting from first principles, it discusses the essentials of successful television production techniques.

This is a practical guide based on a lifetime's personal experience in the medium. It examines the technical operations of television production – the underlying skills involved in camerawork, sound, lighting, etc. You will find guidance on how to use that equipment to professional standards. It discusses associated crafts and their methods.

It analyzes and assesses the work of the television director, and the processes involved in organizing a television production.

What particular features does it have?

Of course, it is important to know how to handle your camera and microphone correctly. We shall be looking at the best methods in detail. But equipment is only a means to an end. It is very easy to become preoccupied with mechanics, and to learn a few routine approaches. This book helps the student to *understand*, not simply *imitate*.

Effective TV production is about *communication*. It is about conveying ideas, influencing an audience, arousing emotions. It is about informing and persuading.

Using the right technique at the right time distinguishes the skilled imaginative craftsperson from the hack.

A major theme running through this book is the effect various techniques have on your audience. When you want to show a close view of a subject, it *matters* whether you choose to zoom in, or to move the camera closer, or cut to another camera. *The audience impact is quite different for each method.* So we shall discuss not only techniques, but why and when to use them.

Will this book suit a range of courses, from introductory to advanced levels?

Yes. The text does not assume previous knowledge. It has been arranged to be used selectively by introductory, intermediary, and advanced study groups.

The book has been designed to provide facts in an interesting, easily digested form. A great deal of information is summarized in straightforward at-a-glance tables and lists. The book is very generously illustrated with figures that concentrate on essentials.

This study encourages the reader to build up a firm foundation of understanding. It encourages the reader to think about the *potentials* of the medium. Knowledge through experience alone can take a long time to acquire. Here that knowledge is encapsulated for you.

Whether you are shooting with a single camera or using a multi-camera crew, whether you are using modest or large-scale facilities, you will find the techniques covered here equally applicable.

What are the changes in this new edition?

It has been extensively revised and augmented, to reflect current practices. As well as extended information about current equipment and the latest techniques, you will find new detailed sections on how to light – step by step, single-camera shooting, using the production switcher (vision mixer), recorded sound effects, postproduction editing and audio sweetening, shooting on location, videotape editing methods, etc. But still the emphasis is on imaginative and creative interpretation, and effective program making.

Because *The Technique of Television Production* is used by a wide range of teaching establishments, the text has been rearranged and developed to be even more 'user friendly'. Detailed technical topics are covered in digests in the extended *Glossary*, to avoid interrupting the flow of the general text. A number of new illustrations have been added.

Acknowledgements

My grateful thanks to the British Broadcasting Corporation, where over the years I have had the widely-based opportunities to develop experience and exchange ideas with many expert colleagues.

Finally, I would like to thank those who have so diligently translated this and my other titles into a variety of languages, yet managed so successfully to preserve the essence of the text.

To those readers who are understandably sensitive to the roles played by women in the medium, I should perhaps explain that the convention of the masculine gender has been used here for many jobs, because it is more widely understood internationally. Having always worked with production teams of differing sex, race and creed, I have no wish to make invidious distinctions.

G.M.

To
my wife, Pamela

Typical development for a complex production

Stage	Activity
PROGRAM IDEA	Subject research
DRAFT SCRIPT	
PRELIMINARY PLANNING	*Preliminary discussion* of production interpretation, initiation of staging designs (sketches, rough plans); perhaps consider lighting, make-up costume, technical facilities.
FINAL SCRIPT	Casting, performer booking.
TECHNICAL PLANNING	*Firming* of production treatment. *Detail planning* of above contributions. *Arrange* graphics, properties, special effects (scenic and video). *Initiate* organizational paperwork (requisitions). *Construction:* scenic, properties, graphics, effects. *Inserts:* obtain library film and graphics; location filming/videotaping.
REHEARSAL SCRIPT	*Make/obtain:* properties, costume, hairwork, models.
PRE-STUDIO REHEARSALS	*Performers practise:* lines, performance, action, business, etc. *Consolidation* of production treatment. *Finalize organization:* lighting, facilities. *Select/devise:* audio effects, background music. *Review/edit* inserts (film, VT) graphics.
CAMERA SCRIPT	*Prepare:* breakdown sheet, show format, camera cards, cue cards, prompters. *Transport:* hired equipment, scenery, props, graphics, costume, etc.
PREPARE STUDIO	*Set up* staging, dress sets, rough light. *Readying services:* telecine, videotape.
* CAMERA BLOCKING	*Adjust:* camera treatment, fine lighting, audio pick-up, make-up, costume, set-dressings, effects.
* RUN THROUGH	Finalize above.
* FINAL REHEARSAL	*Assess:* performance, treatment, operations, etc. Polishing revisions.
* VIDEOTAPING	Record or rehearse/record. Log time-code for required sections (as guide to editing). Check timing, durations. Retakes.
OFF-LINE EDITING DECISIONS	Examine tape (with log/notes from videotaping). Select required shots, shot order and edit points.
ON-LINE EDITING	*Dub off* required shots in order, introduce transitions. *Add* titles, audio sweetening, audio effects, background music, video effects. Post-syncing.
REVIEW	Airing schedule, promotion.
TRANSMISSION	Copying, distribution, archives.

* When 'Rehearse/Record' production techniques are used, these steps merge, as separate shots or sequences are individually blocked . . . rehearsed . . . taped.

1 Television today

For most people, television is just another of those 'taken-for-granted' amenities: part of our everyday life – like radio, films, newspapers. A welcome diversion.

Yet in reality, television is forming the tastes, the opinions, and the aspirations of the world.

A persuasive force

Television provides us with a regular communications channel through which we keep up with the latest news, discover what the weather is likely to be, enjoy games shows, movies, talks and discussions, learn a little more about society and the world we live in. . . . It is there. We accept it all pretty casually.

But as you read through the following chapters, examining the equipment, the techniques, and the processes of television program making, you will begin to see how this 'window on the world' in the corner of the living room is far from the natural extended eye it appears to be.

What seems to the viewer to be a straightforward enough process is really the result of carefully selected techniques. We shall be exploring these techniques, and seeing how they influence our audience's interpretation and response to what they are seeing. There is nothing sinister about this, it is *persuasive craftsmanship*; akin to that used in marketing, advertising, and similar presentational fields.

The medium is inherently persuasive. Even if we use it casually it will still continue to influence. But if we use techniques carelessly or haphazardly the programs will have no coherent form. They will simply be boring to watch.

It's all very technical!

For many coming fresh to the medium the most daunting thing about studying a subject such as television production is the sudden onrush of unfamiliar technical terms. Don't worry. These soon become a familiar part of daily jargon. The technology we shall meet is straightforward enough. And mastering it will leave you free to concentrate on the *creative* aspects of the job.

Video program making

Video program making tends to cover a different subject spectrum from regular television, and is primarily intended for non-broadcast (closed-circuit) use. It is often structured for a restricted audience format.

However, for all practical purposes, one can say that television and video production are identical. Facilities and techniques in the video studio often correspond to those found in broadcast television. More modest video projects working with a limited budget may use less flexible resources, but still produce first-rate presentations, suitable for their particular market.

The tools

We shall be meeting a variety of equipment and discussing how it is used. But in the end, it is **how you use** that equipment that ultimately matters, and **why** you have chosen to use it in that way.

While you need to know how to handle the 'zoom' control on a camera's lens, it is even more important to realize what impact your zooming technique is going to have on your audience.

It is more valuable to develop an instinctive appreciation of *audience response* than to recognize the dozen and one models of cameras or microphones currently available. If you become familiar with equipment basics you can adapt to whatever comes your way. All equipment will have its individual merits and shortcomings.

Ideally, the various techniques we choose to use during a show should arise from the nature of the production itself. The form of setting, the camera treatment, the lighting, the sound, should be selected to suit the occasion.

In a busy schedule it is a temptation, of course, to develop and apply regular 'off-the-peg' routines, rather than a 'tailor-made' approach. But in the end, repetitious routines become as boring to the audience as to the production team.

As you will see, there are many hidden factors that directly affect how a television director can approach a subject, such as:

● The budget,
● The amount of time allocated for rehearsal and recording,
● The studio space available,
● The form and flexibility of the equipment,
● The size and experience of the production team,
● Back-up facilities,
    etc., etc.

All aspects of a production have to be adjusted to suit the situation.

Today's equipment

If equipment has become lighter and lighter, why is so much of the broadcast equipment still quite bulky and heavy? If one can go into a store and purchase a camcorder that produces great pictures and sound on the home recorder, why is all this costly equipment needed for top-grade broadcast and video productions?

Well, to be fair, a great deal of today's professional equipment is much more compact than hitherto, but there are very good reasons for the differences.

Broadcast equipment is invariably heavy duty.

- It has to function to the highest standards.
- It must be extremely stable and reliable.
- Adjusted and maintained to stringent standards, equipment must provide consistent results. A tape recorded on one machine must reproduce identically on another of the same design.
- The equipment must be able to operate hour after hour, and still produce results to a laid-down standard. There should be no noticeable changes in performance; no drifting as the system warms up.
- Broadcast equipment is often used under very trying conditions, having to withstand vibration, bumps and jolts, dust, heat, rain . . .

All facilities have performance weaknesses which are gradually overcome through design and invention. But, generally speaking, state-of-the-art quality performance only comes from equipment that is rigidly constructed, well ventilated, has robust controls, and incorporates sophisticated electronics to ensure precise stable performance.

It is technically unrealistic to expect, for example, that a small low-cost camera will incorporate the various advanced features that ensure precision picture quality. Thanks to skilled design, it will usually produce very good results, but when compared directly with broadcast equipment it will inevitably have limitations.

For many applications, these shortcomings may pass unnoticed, or not matter. But under broadcast conditions, where there are so many links in the transmission chain, deterioration is cumulative, and unacceptable.

Technology influences techniques

In earlier days, when we talked about 'television production' we invariably meant *live* transmissions from a custom-made studio. The audience saw what was happening, as it happened.

There was no method of recording the show, apart from rather primitive kinescope recordings, made by pointing a cine camera at a picture-tube in a TV monitor. If the director needed greater flexibility than the studio TV cameras could offer, then such sequences had to be shot with film cameras, or as slide stills, and switched into the transmission at the appropriate point. Television cameras could operate in a somewhat laborious fashion outside the studio, as 'remotes' ('outside broadcasts'), and minor miracles were achieved by persistent engineers and production teams. But this was communication the hard way! However, this is not simply 'history'. Many of the hazards of those early days are with us still, whenever we transmit any program 'live'; and we shall be discussing the practical problems that live productions bring.

With the invention of videotape systems for recording picture and sound magnetically television production was transformed. It became possible to record an entire television show, transmit it at any convenient hour, and repeat it without having to re-stage the entire production. Now, for the first time, the television director was able to *edit* the television show; to alter, to add, to omit, to correct faulty passages . . . Production techniques could be more flexible. They often became akin to those regularly used in film making. Programs could be made one shot at a time if necessary.

At the same time, many elaborate video effects provided the program maker with ever-increasing visual magic. One could even shoot the action in the studio, and insert the appropriate backgrounds later, when the actors had departed!

Meanwhile, cameras, sound, and videorecording equipment became more compact and much easier to use. The director could now shoot with total freedom on location, under the most adverse conditions. A single operator could move around freely with a single television camera, incorporating its own video and audio recording system. Ever simpler videotape editing arrangements allow the material to be selected and arranged to create the finished program.

Behind the screen

Behind the familiar TV screen lies a complexity of expertise and organization, patient painstaking craftsmanship, ingenious equipment. A fascinating field of study.

Although you will meet certain local differences in terminology or organization, fundamentally all broadcast television throughout the world follows similar program-making processes. These spring from the nature of the medium, and the equipment used.

Emphasis will vary, of course. An organization providing an all-day news service has different requirements from another that is taping 'soap operas'. The facilities needed to televise a golf match are different from those used for a chess tournament. Each type of production has its particular restrictions and opportunities.

Communication is the aim

Television is essentially a *communications medium*. One can lose sight of this, and become preoccupied with the means rather than the intrinsic values of the end product.

When studying television production it is very easy to become intrigued by the bells and whistles of the technology involved; with slick craftsmanship; with the latest electronic gimmicks. One can learn techniques by rote and go on to apply them as a routine.

Program making is an absorbing, extremely satisfying process. But one is always aware of the underlying pressures. The more fully the director understands production principles, the freer he or she is to think about the *significance* of what they are doing. Many find themselves too preoccupied with mechanics to give much thought to such niceties as esthetics, and audience impact.

In the daily program-making process one can become bogged down in the administrative problems of costing, man-hours, regulations, scheduling, and so on. And such factors can strongly influence the form and development of any program. In these circumstances it is easy to lose sight of the value and purpose of the end product itself.

While working on any production it is very difficult to stand back from it all, and assess how your *audience* will respond to it. They are seeing it for the first (and usually the only) time. The production team becomes over familiar with all its aspects. While making the show, everyone is concentrating on their own particular contribution:

While the director is worried about a performer's move . . .
The set designer has noticed where flats do not fit properly . . .
The lighting director is fretting about a boom shadow . . .
The sound engineer finds ventilation noise distracting . . .
The make-up artist is disturbed by a perspiring forehead . . .
The costume designer has noticed creases in a collar . . .
The video engineer is preoccupied with tonal gradation . . .
The producer is concerned with costs of overrunning the scheduled time . . .

A detached viewpoint is difficult to achieve. And when you've put a lot of effort into a project, it is hard to accept that your audience may well be watching the show with less than 100 per cent attention, unaware of any of these problems!

2 The television scene

Not so long ago, most television production was confined to the studio. But today, the television camera is free to shoot virtually anywhere. Programs that once required the coordinated services of a large production group can now be shot by a single person with a hand-held camera/videorecorder!

Shooting on location has its advantages for certain situations. It can provide an authenticity and realism that cannot be attained in the studio. But, as we shall see, location shooting is not without its hazards. For many forms of production the studio has considerable practical advantages.

Although, in practice, studios vary in size from a converted classroom to purpose-built giants around 32 m (100 ft) square, they all have a remarkable affinity. There is a certain atmosphere. It is an unreal world, where performers talking to an unseen audience stand in brightly lit settings, surrounded by a group of silent technicians. One senses the concentration of the team, the highly organized mechanics . . .

But let's visit, in our imagination, a typical TV studio and its associated control areas to see it in action.

The television studio

As you push through the soundproof entry doors the empty TV studio has a strangely inhospitable complexity. The stark expanse of smooth

Fig. 2.1 The television studio
A typical view of the empty studio: with uncluttered staging area, surround safety lane, overhead lighting battens and control-room observation window.

floor with lifeless equipment huddled in one corner. The acoustically padded walls bespattered with technical paraphernalia. A ceiling of dormant lamps clustering above. It has the impersonal silence of a deserted warehouse.

But introduce the scenery, switch on those lamps to bathe the settings in light and shade . . . and the atmosphere becomes expectantly transformed. And with this magic comes a feeling of urgency; a purposeful tension conveyed to performers and crew alike.

A hundred and one jobs converge. The furniture, drapes, and bric-à-brac have been trucked in through the large heavy soundproof studio doors, and now begin to clothe the scene as the sets are dressed. Cameras and sound booms are pushed into their opening positions. Lamps are selectively adjusted. Last-minute rearrangements of sets and props . . . By a daily organizational miracle, the various pieces of the production combine to provide the complete TV show we have been planning and preparing. The cameras set up their shots. Now, on the picture monitor screens, the illusion begins to live!

Yet, within a time span of hours the production will have completed rehearsals; the crew will have learned and practiced the director's treatment; performances hopefully reached their peak . . . and the program has been recorded or transmitted. And then the whole 'magic cave' will be dismantled. Unbelievably quickly, the settings will be 'struck' and tucked away for stock or junking; equipment stored; and floors cleaned off. The original emptiness will return.

Fig. 2.2   Contributory video sources

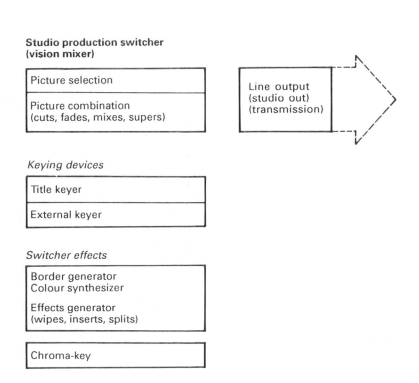

Sources

| Studio cameras |
| Film scanner |
| Slide scanner (caption scanner) |
| Electronic still store |
| Videotape (VT) (VT record/replay) (VT cassette; cart store) |
| Slow motion VT/disc |
| Character generator (graphic titler) |
| Electronic special effects (analogue; digital) |
| Digital art/paint system (computer generated graphics) |
| Weather display |
| Remotes |

Studio production switcher (vision mixer)

| Picture selection |
| Picture combination (cuts, fades, mixes, supers) |

Keying devices

| Title keyer |
| External keyer |

Switcher effects

| Border generator Colour synthesizer |
| Effects generator (wipes, inserts, splits) |

| Chroma-key |

Line output (studio out) (transmission)

Fig. 2.3 Contributory audio sources

These are the conditions in which our theories and hopes become reality. And it is only when we relate our aspirations to the relentless pressure of practical conditions that we see TV production in its true perspective.

The television studio in action

Turn back the clock now, to earlier in the day when camera rehearsal was in progress for a drama production. The illuminated wall signs show that the studio is in closed-circuit rehearsal. So, although all the equipment is *hot* (operating), its output is only being monitored locally. At the scheduled time the studio video (pictures) and audio (sound) signals will

Fig. 2.4 Contributory services

be fed via the coordinating *master control room* (the central switching/ routing control point) to the videotape recorders or immediately to the transmitters for *live* telecasting.

Around the studio you can see examples of the *set designer's* art: the three-walled rooms, a section of a street scene, and a summer garden. After surprise at the colorful realism of these sets the first impression is one of endless lights! Suspended, clamped to sets, on floor stands . . . it is hard to appreciate that each has been placed and angled with precision, for a particular purpose.

At the moment, action is in a 'living room' (an *interior*). Despite the number of people working around, everywhere is surprisingly quiet. Only the dialogue between the actors is audible.

There is little reverberation, thanks to the dampening effect of the acoustically treated walls. A camera dollies gently over the specially leveled floor – where the slightest bumps could judder the picture. Its long cable snakes away to a wall outlet. As we watch, people and equipment move around silently, almost as if choreographed, systematically and smoothly, to an unspoken plan.

But plug your earphones into the studio intercom circuit and you enter a different world! Now you can hear the continuous instructions from the unseen director and his team in the production control room: guiding, assessing, querying, explaining, cuing, warning, correcting . . . coordinating the studio crew through their headsets.

Outside the 'living room' you see the 'sunny garden' (an *exterior*). Close scrutiny reveals that the convincingly flowering trees are really plastic

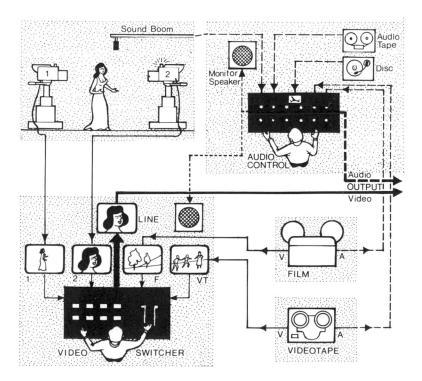

Fig. 2.5 The TV studio system
This simplified diagram shows how video and audio sources are routed to their respective selection points.

blossoms wired to lopped-off branches and the turf is grass matting laid over sandbags. But on camera, the effect is idyllic. Quiet birdsong fills the air from a nearby playback speaker (foldback/program loudspeaker).

The *floor manager* (FM), the director's link with the studio floor, hand cues an actress to enter the garden. The sound boom's telescopic arm swings, its microphone following her as she speaks. The cameras within the room pull away quickly and move to the next set.

The director, from behind the tinted glass of the *production control room*, is watching a series of picture monitors (high-quality TV displays) continuously showing each camera's shot. He hears the *program audio* (all sound sources blended together) on an adjacent hi-fi loudspeaker system. His continuous *intercom* (*talkback*) instructions to the crew's headsets are unheard by the actors or the studio microphones. The FM cues performers, guiding and advising them where necessary; diplomatically relaying the director's instructions and observations.

The director has just seen a bad shot, as a foreground actor *masks* (obscures) another. He asks the FM to stop action. 'Hold it please,' calls the FM. Action pauses while he explains the problem. A slight position change is crayon-marked on the floor (*toe/location marks*). Actors go through the revised moves, and all is well. But the director feels that the shot now looks too close. 'Can you pull back on Two?' Camera Two's cameraman shakes the camera's head to signal 'No.' 'Can you zoom out a little?' And with a wider lens angle, picture composition improves. On the director's go-ahead, the FM calls for silence. 'Right, back to Shot 54, as Joe enters.' He checks the shot on a nearby wheeled floor monitor (*studio monitor*) displaying the program output (*line*). Then with an arm movement, he cues the action, and the game of make-believe springs back to life . . . as if no mere technicalities had interrupted. The rehearsal continues.

The production control room

Here in the production nerve center the director and his staff of specialists control the production. There are two basic approaches to control room design: communal and sectionalized layouts. Each has its merits and shortcomings.

Some have a large soundproof window with tinted glass, providing a good overview of the studio. This helps you to solve at a glance many routine rehearsal problems that are not revealed on camera (e.g. crowded equipment, staging difficulties, lighting faults).

The communal layout

This uses open-plan arrangements in either a single-level or split-level form. Here everyone concerned with production control sits at a long central desk: the *production director*, his *assistant* (who checks program timing, calls shot numbers and stand-by cues), the *switcher* (*vision mixer*),

Fig. 2.6 part 1   The 'communal' production control room
All production operations are concentrated at a central desk. Video and lighting may be controlled locally or elsewhere.

For key to abbreviations, see page 29.

the *technical director* and *audio engineer*; and perhaps the *video control engineer (shader)*. (As you will see, the jobs, titles, and names vary considerably!)

The desk faces a row of picture monitor screens. The *preview (channel) monitors* show the outputs of the various video sources and continuously display each camera's output as well as film, videotape, slide scanners, and remote sources. Any source may be selected and switched (or faded) by the *production switcher* to the *studio output* (line output to master control.) The *master monitor (line, main channel, transmission)* displays the result.

Many production control rooms use small black and white monitors for all previews, and rely on just two large color monitors for assessing color quality. One serves as a general-purpose preview that can be switched to check upcoming shots, video effects, combined sources, etc. The other is the master monitor, showing, in color, the program output (*line, studio out*) from the switcher.

This arrangement is not only more economical than having a large bank of color monitors but overcomes the problem of making all their color pictures match. It can be confusing if monitors drift over a period. On the other hand, one has to switch any picture source onto the preview color monitor before being able to check its color quality, and this is not always convenient.

The director's attention is divided between the various preview monitors, the selected output on the master monitor, and the *program-audio* from a nearby loudspeaker. The director instructs the production team and floor crew (cameras, sound booms) through a headset (earphone and microphone) plugged into the communal intercom circuit (PL – private line). Although this shared-line arrangement is simple, it has the disadvantage that everyone overhears other people's instructions and exchanges, and this can become wearying or confusing in a busy production.

The production director may operate the production switcher (video switching panel, vision mixer) – particularly on remotes (OBs). But for more complex operations a specialist switcher (vision mixer) or the technical director usually does this job, enabling the production director to concentrate on controlling the many other aspects of the show.

The technical director's responsibility can vary between one organization and another. He may direct cameras, actively assisting in production treatment, and he may carry out video switching. As a supervisory engineer, he may oversee the engineering aspects of the production such as aligning effects, checking shots, ensuring source availability, and monitoring quality.

At the far end of the desk the audio specialist (*audio engineer, audio control*) sits at his audio console (board, panel) adjusting and blending the various sound sources.

Depending on the show and its organization, others directly involved in its presentation may include:

1. The *set designer* (*scenic designer*) responsible for the *scenic treatment* (*staging*).
2. The *lighting director* who designs and arranges the studio lighting.
3. The *producer, editors* (script, film, videotape), *sponsor*, special assistants, researchers . . . and so on ad infinitum.
4. Where a program uses elaborate *video effects* these can take some time to prepare. So an extra operator may be needed to devise and control them. Otherwise the person at the production switcher has to arrange these, in addition to the regular inter-source transitions(!).

The technical quality of pictures is controlled by a *video engineer* (*shader, video operator*) who continually monitors and adjusts video equipment, either within the production control room or in a separate technical area (*apparatus room* or in *master control*).

There may be a small adjacent *announce booth* from which announcements and commentaries can be read *out of vision* (*off camera*).

The sectionalized layout

Here the control area is subdivided into separate rooms.

1. Production control – where the director, assistant, switcher and technical director are located.
2. Sound control – audio coordination and control.
3. Vision control – video quality and lighting coordination.

Large glass panels and intercom circuits link these separate rooms. This layout has the advantage that their various activities and discussions do not impinge. No one in these control areas wears headsets and the intercom is of the local mike/loudspeaker type. The director's desk mike relays the general intercom (communal talkback) which is heard over other control rooms' loudspeakers. Individual specialists have their switched *private wire* (*party line*) circuits, for example from audio console to sound-boom operator, as well as being able to break into the general intercom system.

Fig. 2.6 part 2   The 'sectionalized' production control room
Production control, audio control and video/lighting control functions are located in separate rooms to prevent interaction.

Preview picture monitors show:
1, 2, 3, 4   Cameras
F   Film
VT   Videotape
E   Video effects
S   Slides
CG   Character generator/titles
R   Remote source
PV   Switchable preview monitor
L   Line monitor (transmission; program monitor; master monitor)

Personnel:
D   Director
DA   Director's assistant
SW   Switcher (vision mixer)
TD   Technical director/technical manager
LC   Lighting control
VC   Video control
A   Audio control
O   Audio operator (disc/tape)

Equipment:
AI   Audio tape
DT   Disc turntable
MS   Monitor speaker
C   Clock
I   On-air indicator lights

Video control – vision control room

In this area the picture quality of all the local video sources is controlled and matched (cameras, slide/film scanner). Each studio camera's cable is plugged via a studio wall outlet to its main video apparatus – the *camera control unit* (*CCU*). These units, one per camera, are usually housed in an engineering area (master control, apparatus room) where they may be controlled directly by a video engineer.

In a more sophisticated arrangement all the video operational controls are extended to a central console, where a single operator continually monitors and adjusts picture quality from video cameras, slide, film sources. Lighting and pictorial effect are closely interrelated, so the video operator usually sits next to the *lighting console* operator, and shares the same picture monitors. These operators, guided by the lighting director, can therefore work in harmony.

Audio control – sound control room

At his *audio console* (*sound desk, mixer, board*) the *audio engineer* (*sound mixer, sound supervisor*) monitors and adjusts sound dynamics and quality, blending the sources to suit the production's artistic and technical requirements. As well as the studio microphones, he is controlling various additional audio sources including discs, audio tapes (reels, cassettes, carts), film and videotape tracks, announce booth, and remotes.

The audio control man guides by intercom his sound crew on the studio floor. He helps them to avoid mikes or their shadows appearing in shot, warns them of subject moves or shot changes, etc., and assists them in achieving sound perspective to match the pictures. Whether he operates disc and tape recorders himself or is assisted by an operator depends on production complexity and control room layout.

Master control

The *Master Control Room* is the engineering coordination center for a TV station. It provides a master control point where a *routing switcher* interconnects the various production units – e.g. studios, film chains, VTRs, remotes, etc. Because of the technical complexities of source routing, switching is increasingly automated.

The Master Control Room houses such items as synchronizing generators, distribution amplifiers, camera control equipment (CCUs), and may include audio equipment, film chains VTRs, slide scanners, etc., when these are not located in separate areas elsewhere.

Television programs from larger studio centers are often routed to a transmitter via a *Continuity/Presentation suite*. Arranged rather like a production control room, it may have a small studio (and/ or announce booth) for station announcements, newscasts, weather, interviews.

Table 2.1   Typical approximate TV studio sizes

			Typical	*Ceiling*
Local TV/campus studios	Small	150 m² (1600 ft²)	15 × 10 m (50 × 30 ft)	3.5 m (11 ft)
	Medium	216 m² (2400 ft²)	18 × 12 m (60 × 40 ft)	7 m (23 ft)
Network studio center	Small general purpose	330 m² (3500 ft²)	22 × 15 m (70 × 50 ft)	9 m (30 ft)
	Medium	672 m² (7200 ft²)	28 × 24 m (90 × 80 ft)	10 m (33 ft)
	Large	1024 m² (10 000 ft²)	32 × 32 m (100 × 100 ft)	13 m (43 ft)

Continuity control is mainly concerned with providing a smooth-flowing program output from the station: switching between program sources at the scheduled times, inserting commercials, trailers/promos (promotions) for upcoming shows, station idents (channel identification logos), covering breakdowns, etc. In addition, there will be liaison with program sources (studios, remotes, VT and film channels) relative to go-ahead cues, scheduled timing, introductory announcements, etc.

Services and support areas

Most studios have a variety of storage and service facilities nearby that help in the smooth running of day-to-day production. Their size and scale vary, but typically we find:

A *scene dock* – Here the scenery constructed in the *scenic workshop* is temporarily stored, ready for the current production. Either here, or in a nearby *properties (props) storeroom* various items such as furniture, drapes, ornaments, etc. are stored in readiness to dress the settings.

A *technical store* – All the mobile technical equipment is housed here ready for immediate use: camera mountings, lighting equipment, sound booms, picture monitors, cables, etc. This not only helps to protect the equipment but leaves the studio floor clear for scenery to be moved around during the setting period.

Leading off the studio may be:

- *Make-up rooms* (for individual make-up and in-program repairs),
- *Changing rooms* (where clothing/costumes can be changed or valeted),
- A circulation area with rest rooms (*Green Room*) where people can wait during production breaks.
- *Dressing rooms* (where performers can dress, rest, await their calls).

Various technical areas for electronic, electrical, and mechanical maintenance are also located near the studios.

3 How television works

Considering its technical complexity, the basic principles involved in producing a television picture are surprisingly simple.

The video signal

The camera lens focuses an image of the scene onto a light-sensitive surface – this may be either the 'target' in a *camera-tube* or a *solid-state sensor (CCD)* device. There the light image creates a pattern of tiny electrical charges, which correspond to the light and shade in the shot. This electrical pattern is systematically scanned in a series of lines, reading off the strength of each charge in turn. Because the charges depend on the amount of light falling on each point, the fluctuating voltage that results – the *video* – provides us with an electrical replica of the light and shade, and detail in the scene.

In the TV receiver (or *picture monitor*) there is a display screen. This may be part of a picture-tube or a solid-state device. The video is sent along a cable, or via a radio transmitter, and fed to this display system. Here the screen is scanned systematically in a series of identical lines, exactly in step with scanning in the original camera – *in sync*.

As the strength of the video changes, the screen's brightness at the scanning point alters correspondingly. This is all happening so quickly that the eye sees only the overall result – as a complete multi-tone image built up on the screen, which we interpret as a reproduction of the original scene.

3.1 The camera tube (photoconductive types)

The inside of the camera tube's glass face-plate is covered with a fine metallic coating (signal plate), on which a layer of photoconductive material is deposited. The scene's image is focused onto this target (T). The electrical resistance of the layer varies at each surface point, with the light and shade of the scene, so building up a corresponding charge-pattern. The constant electron-beam (E-B) from the tube's gun (G) scans across the target in a series of close parallel lines, neutralizing each point (element) in turn. The resultant re-charging currents constitute the camera's video signal.

Of course, this process sounds a lot simpler than it is in reality, but basically this is the way a monochrome ('black and white') television/video picture is achieved.

In practice, there are many problems. One of these is in ensuring that the entire system, from camera to display screen, is scanning exactly in step. Any *synchronizing* errors would cause the picture to tear, break up, or distort.

Fig. 3.2 The monochrome picture tube

A gun in the picture tube produces an electron beam (E-B), which fluctuates in intensity with the video signal. As the beam scans across the screen in a series of close parallel lines, it causes the fluorescent coating to glow correspondingly, building up the light and shade pattern of the original image. The picture (frame) is scanned in 525 lines (485 active) 30 times each second (Europe – 625 lines, 25 per second). To conserve bandwidth and decrease flicker effects, the odd lines (*odd field*) are scanned, and then the even lines (*even field*) fitted between them (*interlacing*). In simple TV systems, this interlacing varies (*random interlace*) and definition deteriorates.

Color analysis

Looking at the apparently endless range of colors and shades in the world around us, it seems incredible that they can be reproduced on the TV screen simply by mixing appropriate proportions of red, green, and blue light. Yet that is the underlying principle of color television.

The television camera cannot itself respond directly to differences in color. It just detects *brightness* variations. However, if we use a color filter in front of the camera-tube the video signal it produces will then correspond to the amount of that particular color in the scene. Take three camera pick-up tubes, using red, green, and blue filters, respectively, and their video signals represent the three essential primary colors needed to reproduce a picture in full color.

Inside the face of the picture-tube in the TV receiver there is a close pattern of three sets of phosphors. When one set is energized by an electron beam sweeping over it, it glows red. Another set of phosphors glows green, and another blue. When the strength of the beam scanning the red phosphors fluctuates with the 'red' video signal it traces an image there of the scene interpreted by the red camera-tube. At the same time, the separate video outputs of the green and blue camera-tubes are producing their corresponding images on their screen phosphors.

Fig. 3.3 The picture and its video

Showing a typical scanned line and its corresponding video signal.

Color mixtures

Because these phosphor patterns are so tiny, our eyes do not see them as individual dots – although you can do so if you use a magnifying lens. Instead, colors of adjacent dots merge together, and produce a *color mixture*; an effect termed *additive color mixing*.

When you see a similar amount of light from the red, green, and blue dots in an area you experience the sensation of *white light*. Equal amounts of red and blue produce a purplish or *magenta* hue. Blue and green together appear as *cyan*. But, unexpectedly, equal amounts of red and green light produce *yellow* – a strange result until you get used to the idea!

Light and shade

So it's clear enough where the full range of colors comes from in the TV picture. But what about its light and shade, its brightness variations?

Well, as we saw, **R + G + B = white**. If they are all equal but very weak they will result in a very weak white – or what we would call a dark gray. If the signals are stronger, the area on the screen will be brighter. If most parts of the screen are energized by strong video signals, we interpret this as a bright picture; and vice versa.

So, to summarize: the effective *color* (*hue*) results from the actual proportions of red, green, and blue, and the *brightness* of each part of the screen depends on the overall strength of the mixture.

Fig. 3.4 Color TV principles

The focused image is split by a prismatic block (or dichroic filter-mirrors) into three light paths – covering the red, green, and blue regions of the spectrum. Camera tubes (3, 2, or 1) produce corresponding video signals. These signals could be transmitted in this form, and recombined to recreate the original color image (as in color printing processes). However, to provide a *compatible* color TV picture (that will reproduce on monochrome receivers) a complex intermediate system is necessary – NTSC, PAL or SECAM. This involves *coding* to derive special *luminance* (brightness) and *chrominance* (hue, color) video signals. (Monochrome receivers respond to the luminous component of the signal.)

In the color picture-monitor or receiver, the separate RGB components are recovered by a *de-coding matrix* (decoder), each video signal being used to control their respective electron-beam strengths in the picture tube.

Fig. 3.5   Color TV picture-tubes

The tube screen comprises three patterns of phosphors (dots or stripes) that glow red, green, or blue when energized by their associated electron beam. The eye merges these tiny RGB patterns, seeing them as color mixtures; when proportionately activated they appear white to gray.

The color picture tube may take three forms: (1) delta-gun dot mask (shadow mask); (2) self-converging precision in-line (PIL) slot-mask design, or (3) single-gun (three beams) aperture-grille type (Trinitron). The last two avoid the convergence color-fringing problems of 1.

Transmitting color

You could have a color TV/video system that involved sending three separate video signals (R, G, B) from camera to receiver. The sound (audio) signal would be sent separately. This principle would work. But there would be various technical difficulties.

Instead, it is more practical to send a specially *encoded* signal that incorporates all color and brightness information. This encoded signal is *decoded* at the receiver, and reconstituted as separate color signals that drive the picture-tube.

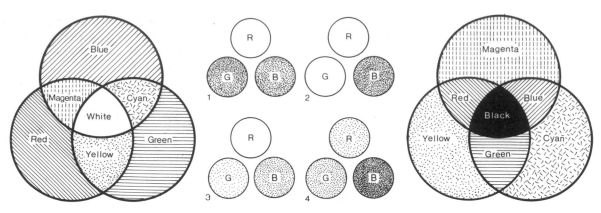

Fig. 3.6 Color mixing

Part 1 Light mixtures – additive primaries

If you project beams of red, blue and green light, these *additive primaries* will blend where they overlap, to produce new *secondary* colors (*subtractive primaries*). In equal proportions,

R + B = magenta (purple)
B + G = cyan (blue-green)
R + G = yellow
R + G + B = white

A secondary color is often termed a 'minus' of the third primary hue: hence yellow is *minus blue*, cyan is *minus red*, and magenta is *minus green*.

Part 2 Hue and luminance

Hue derives from the *proportions* of red, green, and blue present. *Luminance* (brightness) results from their *quantities*.

1. If only one phosphor is activated, the screen appears of primary hue.
2. Two or three phosphors produce additive color mixtures (e.g. R + G = Yellow).
3, 4 If three phosphors are combined, various shades or degrees of color dilution (saturation) result (e.g. diluted red = pink; dim orange or yellow = brown).

Part 3 Pigment mixtures – subtractive primaries

If you print magenta, yellow, cyan pigments onto a white surface (using ink, paint, dyes), new hues appear where they overlap. The surface colors we see are just the remaining part of the visual spectrum, after all other colors have been absorbed by the pigments. So this is termed a *subtractive* process.

It is important, of course, that anyone using a *monochrome* (*black and white*) *receiver* should be able to receive good pictures from color television transmissions. So the encoded color system must be *compatible* with all types of receivers. The ingenious American NTSC method of encoding the signals managed to do just that! It had limitations, but it produced excellent results.

Most TV systems use either 525 or 625 scanning lines to build up the picture. (It is convenient, technically, to relate the scanning rate to the frequency of the public power supplies.) Programs transmitted or recorded on one system will not reproduce on another.

Elsewhere in the world, the NTSC system required changes to suit the different transmission standards in use (625 lines). So organizations introduced improved variations, known as PAL and SECAM. Three incompatible color transmission standards were born, and remain today. Happily, standards converters exist which enable live and recorded programs made on one system to be translated into another.

The television picture

There are times when television engineers may seem to be obsessed with 'picture quality'; with color fidelity, definition, tonal gradation, gamma, and the like. But this preoccupation is not technical pedantry. The quality of the pictures we produce, like that of the accompanying sound, directly affects audience enjoyment. If a camera's picture is not sufficiently sharp the viewer will not be able to see detail or texture clearly. If color varies from one camera to the next, changes will distract when interswitching their shots. If tones are not reproduced successfully, subtle variations will be lost, surfaces will appear flat and unmodeled.

Clearly, picture quality matters, but how good can a TV/video picture be?

Initially it depends on the system used. At best, it can be superb. But there are inevitably various losses between the camera lens and the home screen that degrade the picture.

Picture detail

All electronic and photographic systems have a maximum limit to the amount of detail they can convey. In TV the *definition (resolution)* is initially influenced by the number of picture lines the system uses. But it is also affected by system design. As the image of the scene is scanned in the camera the video should ideally be able to change in strength to correspond with tonal differences. The faster it can change, the finer the detail it can resolve. This rate of change is measured as 'frequency' (4 MHz for a 525-line system; 5 MHz for 625 lines).

Fig. 3.7 Picture detail
The TV system's ability to resolve detail (its resolution) is checked with standard test charts. These contain *gratings* (1) or *resolution wedges* (2). The finest information that can be discerned reveals the system's maximum resolution. (The calibrations indicate the 'number of picture lines' that could be resolved in the picture width.) In a 525-line system, typically '320 lines' (4 Mhz) represents maximum transmitted detail. Maximum closed-circuit resolution may be '640 lines' (8 MHz).

Apart from these technical parameters, many other factors can affect picture clarity, including the lens's performance. It may be dirty or badly focused. Lighting may be producing lens flares. The glass of a prompter attached to the camera can degrade picture quality. Video equipment may have drifted. Or you may be watching a poor videorecording. There can be many reasons for unsharp pictures!

Fig. 3.8 The gray scale
The standard gray scale takes the maximum-to-minimum tonal range readily reproduced by the TV system (overall 20:1 contrast), and divides it into 10 steps. (Relative light reflectance 60–3%.) Each step is √2 times brightness of the next; the logarithmic scale looking linear to the eye. (What appears mid-gray, is only 17½% reflectance; not the 50% you might expect.)

Picture tones

The range of tones a TV system can normally reproduce is restricted; even though this is not very obvious in most pictures. There are limitations in both the camera and the receiver.

Although our eyes can accommodate a tonal range of as much as 1000:1, in which the lightest tone is a thousand times the darkest, the *camera-tube* can only handle around 20:1 to 30:1. Beyond these limits, tones are indistinguishable, and crush into white or black areas. Where details in highlights and shadows are not important in a shot this limitation may not be noticed. Otherwise it may be necessary to adjust the tones of costumes and scenery, and lighting contrast, to try to keep within the camera's tonal limits.

The tonal range that can be reproduced by the *picture-tube* in the TV receiver varies with the receiver's design, and how it is adjusted. A high *contrast* setting coarsens the tones, and restricts the tonal gradation visible. Tones can be reproduced over a range from the tube's maximum brightness (without defocusing) and the 'black' represented by the tube face. Any light falling on the screen reduces available contrast in the picture. Although a tonal contrast of as much as 50:1 may be achievable on a high-grade picture monitor and still reproduce half-tones well, a contrast nearer 20:1 is more likely. Many TV receivers have a range of as little as 10:1 or 15:1 under domestic conditions.

4 What your camera can do

Whether your camera produces color or monochrome pictures, is hand-held, or fitted to a giant crane, the basic operating principles are similar.

Types of television camera

A wide range of television/video cameras are available today, from designs for family video costing a few hundred dollars to sophisticated precision cameras that incorporate current state-of-the-art technology. TV cameras fall into six broad categories:

Studio broadcast cameras

Here we have a market spread of models to suit all categories of studios – closed-circuit training facilities, local access CATV, small production studios, local TV stations, production houses, major studio applications.

As you would expect, camera design and performance vary with cost. While cameras in the lower end of the range can provide very satisfactory picture quality under optimum conditions, the more expensive advanced equipment produces consistently excellent pictures for long periods; even when conditions are poor.

The regular studio camera is quite heavy, for it is fitted with a large zoom lens assembly and a full-size viewfinder for optimum performance. (Cameras of this category are widely used on location, where superior picture quality is essential.) The camera is mounted on a substantial wheeled dolly to enable it to be moved around quickly and silently.

Each camera is cabled, via a studio wall outlet, to its AC (mains) powered *camera control unit (CCU)* located outside the studio. Picture quality is continuously checked and controlled there by an operator/ engineer.

Like other TV camera systems, studio cameras used to rely on careful manual alignment of their circuits to ensure precise color fidelity and high definition. But digital techniques are now used to pre-set all circuit adjustments in modern studio cameras.

Portable broadcast cameras

These cameras provide in a more compact, mobile form a high-quality system suitable for work in both the studio and the field. They are often available in a multi-module form that allows you to choose the most convenient configuration for the occasion. With a larger zoom lens and viewfinder the unit can be used for a range of studio productions. Fitted with smaller units, the camera unit is noticeably more mobile, and suitable for work on location.

Fig. 4.1   Camera design
Television/video cameras today come
in a wide variety of designs, from
compact hand-held forms, to large
studio camera systems.

The portable camera incorporates all its own circuitry, and various
automatic controls are available when required. Its video output can be
cabled direct to a separate portable videotape recorder, or to a CCU or
remote control unit (RCU). Alternatively, the camera may be connected to
a microwave link, which transmits its video to a base station.

The unit is powered from either a 12 V DC (direct current) battery
supply, or household AC power via a suitable adaptor.

The camera will usually include controls that remotely switch the
attached videotape recorder: to record, or to check tape replay (using the
camera viewfinder to monitor the tape).

Lightweight cameras

These self-contained units are designed for work in the field, where
emphasis is on reduced size and weight. They can be hand-held or
attached to a light tripod. Battery powered, they are cabled to a portable
videotape recorder (VTR).

Small hand-held low-cost cameras

Compact hand-held cameras are mainly used for low-cost closed-circuit
video and industrial applications. Again, they are connected by direct
cable to a lightweight VTR.

Combination camera/videotape recorder units: 'Camcorders' – Combo camera – VRC (videorecorder cameras)

This shoulder-mounted camera is self-contained, and incorporates a
recorder which tapes both picture and sound and allows immediate
playback. Designs range from high-grade broadcast systems to the budget
forms used by hobbyists. The popularity of this combined arrangement is
growing daily, for it allows the TV cameraman considerable mobility. It
is increasingly replacing the film camera in news gathering and location
shooting.

Electronic cinematography

This type of television camera is designed to incorporate the characteristic features of a motion-picture camera, and is used by film production units shooting material in video form from which a film print is derived. (See Glossary: Electronic Cinematography; and Index: 'Image transfer'.)

The camera's features (see Table 4.4)

Television cameras are normally designed with features that suit particular applications.

A *studio* camera, for instance, has a large viewfinder that enables the cameraman to adjust focus very accurately as he moves in to take close-ups. A clip at the back of the camera holds a 'shot sheet' showing details of the planned shots.

A *news* cameraman, on the other hand, normally takes more distant shots, so has less difficulty in focusing. He is more concerned with having a lightweight camera to carry around, so welcomes a small compact viewfinder. His work is often unscripted and improvised so he does not use a shot sheet. On the other hand, he has to cope with unexpected changes in lighting conditions that do not arise in the studio, so needs compensatory controls to handle that situation.

Although, as you would expect, there are noticeable variations between the features of individual camera designs, they all have a common format. So let's begin by taking a general overview of the camera.*

■ *A lens system*   This provides a small sharp natural-color image of the scene. The lens usually has adjustable coverage (a 'zoom lens'), but fixed-lens systems are also used.

■ *A beam splitter (with color separation)*   In a color TV system the natural-color image from the lens system has to be split up into three identical versions, corresponding to the proportions of red, green, and blue light reflected from subjects. This can be done by three methods:

● Dichroic mirrors,
● A special prism block,
● Or a striped filter.

(See Glossary: *Beam splitter; Dichroics; Single-tube color.*)

■ *The camera-tubes, or solid-state image sensors (CCDs)*   Traditionally, the highest grade color TV cameras have used three camera-tubes to provide the red, green, and blue components of the color picture. Information on picture details and brightness (luminance) is derived from the combined color channels through ingenious circuitry.

Fig. 4.2   The television camera
The TV camera consists of:

A. The camera head. Z, zoom lens. T, camera tubes. V, viewfinder. C, camera cable (taking technical supplies to the camera, and the resultant video to the camera control unit/CCU). A quick-release *wedge-mount* under the head slides into a corresponding recessed plate on the panning head.

B. The panning head (pan head). This enables the camera head to tilt and turn (*pan*) smoothly. These movements can be restrained by deliberately introduced friction (*drag*), and can be *locked off* to hold the head rigid. *Tilt balance* positions the head horizontally, preventing it being nose- or tail-heavy. One or two attached *pan (panning) handles* (H) enable the cameraman to direct and control the camera head.

C. The camera mounting. This can take many forms, e.g. camera-clamp, monopod, tripod, pedestal, crane.

---

* So that we do not become sidetracked here with technicalities, more complete details of these features are covered in the Glossary.

The best of today's TV/video color camera-tubes and imaging devices are capable of producing extremely attractive picture quality. Although they have their various limitations (Table 21.3), these are not immediately obvious, and only impose slight restrictions on the program maker.

■ *The viewfinder*   This is located on top of the camera. It contains a high-grade *monochrome* picture-tube (cathode ray tube). Normally the viewfinder is fed with the camera's own video, to show the camera operator what the camera lens is seeing. But it can be switched to other sources when necessary (e.g. to display other cameras' pictures, test patterns).

It is essential that the viewfinder on a studio camera has the best possible resolution; otherwise the operator will have difficulty in focusing accurately. Although color picture-tubes are occasionally used in larger viewfinders, they have an inherent 'texture', and cannot resolve such fine detail.

An adjustable *hood* shields the screen, and prevents random light from diluting its picture. The viewfinder can usually be tilted (and perhaps rotated), so that its picture is still visible, whatever the heights of the camera and operator.

The cameraman uses this viewfinder to select and adjust the shot, to compose the picture, and to assess focus adjustments. When working with a single-camera system he may also judge the picture's exposure from the viewfinder image.

Because the viewfinder is a *monitoring* device, any adjustments to it (brightness, contrast, sharpness) will have no effect on the actual picture produced by the camera.

■ *The camera's mounting*   The way the camera is supported can considerably influence its mobility and how smoothly it can be operated. As we shall see, the mounting may be fixed (stationary; static) or wheeled, and the height may be adjustable. The camera is attached to the mounting with a *panning head/mounting head*. (See Glossary.) This device allows the camera head to be tilted and turned ('panned') smoothly and accurately, and held in any fixed position.

The camera's controls

All cameras have three sorts of controls:

● Those you continually adjust during picture making,
● Those you readjust occasionally to allow for changing conditions,
● And those you leave alone! They align the camera's electronics, and should not be 'tweaked' casually.

With *studio cameras*, most controls affecting camera performance are remotely adjusted on a CCU, or RCU, which is located with the main video circuitry in the technical area. The shader/video control operator there adjusts by remote control the exposure, color balance, etc. to get the

Fig. 4.3 part 1   The camera head

1. Lens hood (sun shade, ray shade).
2. Zoom lens.
3. Filter wheel.
4. Prism block (beam splitter) with camera pick-up tubes.
5. Camera cable.
6. Adjustable panning handle (pan handle, pan bar).
7. Twist-grip zoom control.
8. Focus control (many cameras use a control mounted on a panning handle – RHS).
9. Shot box (mounted on the camera head, or on a panning handle – RHS).
10. Monochrome viewfinder (perhaps with magnifying lens).
11. Viewfinder controls (including hi-peaker, crispening image detail).
12. Indicators: mimic tally light, lens-aperture indicator (*f*-stop), zoom lens setting (focal length/lens angle), etc.
13. Camera card clip.
14. Headset jack points (intercom and program) with volume controls. Mixed viewfinder feeds switch.
15. Zoom lens range-extender switch.
16. Call button (contacts shader/video control).
17. Camera mounting head (panning head/pan head), with drag adjustment for tilt and pan action, and tilt/pan locks. Also tilt fore-aft balance adjustment.
18. Tally light with camera number, illuminated when camera selected to line on switcher.

finest picture quality. This leaves the cameraman free to concentrate on skilled camerawork.

But what about the cameraman on location who is using a *lightweight* or a *combo camera*? Who adjusts camera performance in his case? Well, he has the option of

- Leaving adjustments alone, and hoping that results will be satisfactory.
- Adjusting various pre-set controls, until pictures appear optimum.
- Or using special *automatic circuits* that correct/improve performance.

We'll discuss these options when covering *single-camera shooting* in Chapter 22.

Fig. 4.3 part 2   Parts of the camera
Camera designs vary, but the following are typical facilities found in the video
camera:
1. Microphone – electret, unidirectional.
2. Lens hood.
3. Lens aperture (iris) – *f*/1.6 max.
4. Focus control.
5. Manual zoom control.
6. Aperture control.
7. White balance adjust; black adjust.
8. Video gain (0 dB, 6 dB, 12 dB), color bars, camera standy-by/operate switch.
9. Color compensation filter – 3200 K, 5600 K, 5600 K + 12.5% ND, closed.
10. Viewfinder, adjustable – 1.5 in (37 mm) with LED indicators.
11. Power selection, intercom, audio monitoring jack.
12. Camera back: VTR connector, video output, camera cable, monitor video
                output, gen-lock connection for multi-camera set-ups.
13. Eyepiece.
14. Snap-on battery pack.
15. Side of camera: mike input connector, external d.c. socket.
16. Viewfinder controls.
17. Power zoom switch.
18. Auto-iris on/off.

The camera lens

Meet your lens

The lens system is the heart of the camera, as far as the cameraman is
concerned. (See Glossary: *Camera lens*.) Your lens system normally has
three adjustments which can be made manually or semi-automatically:

● *Focus* – adjusting the distance at which the image is sharpest.
● *f-stop* – adjusting a variable iris diaphragm inside the lens system.

- *Zoom* – altering the lens's 'focal length' to adjust how much of the scene the lens covers.

Broadly speaking, how you adjust the *lens controls* will affect:

1. How clear-cut detail is ('focusing'),
2. Exactly what appears sharply defined in the shot ('depth of field'),
3. How much of the scene appears in the shot ('angle of view'),
4. The impression of distance, space and size that the picture conveys,
5. The overall brightness of the picture, the clarity of lighter tones and shadows ('exposure').

Identifying your lens

On the front rim of your lens system you will find two pieces of information:

1. The *maximum available lens aperture* or '*f-stop*'. This indicates how 'fast' the lens is; i.e. how much light it lets through. A 'fast' lens (e.g. $f/1.8$) will still provide good pictures under lower light levels. A 'slow' lens (e.g. $f/3.5$ maximum) would need considerably more light, even at maximum aperture.
2. The *focal length* (Figure 4.4). On a zoom lens, the range of focal lengths is marked either directly (e.g. 9–126 mm) or as a *zoom ratio* (e.g. 9 mm × 14).

Focal length

How large an image you get on the screen will depend on the size of your subject, on how close you are to it, and on the *focal length* of the lens you are using. Knowing its focal length, you can judge what sort of shot it will give you at various distances.

Table 4.1   Typical lens coverages *(see Table 4.3)*

| | Focal length (F) mm | (in) | Horizontal angle | Vertical angle | Horizontal field of view at distances of | | | | | |
					1.5 m (5 ft) m	(ft)	6 m (20 ft) m	(ft)	30 m (100 ft) m	(ft)
25 mm (1 in) camera-tube	12.5	(0.5)	54°	40°	1.53	(5.0)	6.1	(20.0)	30.5	(100.0)
	25	(1.0)	27	20	0.76	(2.5)	3.1	(10.0)	15.3	(50.0)
	50	(2.0)	13.5	10	0.40	(1.3)	1.5	(5.0)	7.6	(25.0)
	75	(3.0)	9	7	0.24	(0.8)	1.0	(3.3)	5.2	(17.0)
	150	(6.0)	4.5	3.5	0.12	(0.4)	0.5	(1.6)	2.5	(8.3)
32 mm (1¼ in) camera-tube	17	(0.6)	50°	37.5°	1.46	(4.8)	5.80	(19.0)	29.0	(95)
	35	(1.5)	26	19	0.64	(2.1)	2.56	(8.4)	12.8	(42)
	52	(2.0)	17	13	0.49	(1.6)	1.95	(6.4)	9.8	(32)
	90	(3.5)	9.5	7	0.28	(0.9)	1.10	(3.6)	5.5	(18)
	135	(5.3)	6.5	5	0.18	(0.6)	0.73	(2.4)	3.7	(12)
	215	(8.5)	4	3	0.12	(0.4)	0.49	(1.6)	2.4	(8)

Table 4.2   Camera-tube sizes

Diameter	Image size	Diagonal of image
1¼ in 30 mm	17.1 × 12.8 mm	21.4 mm
1 in 25 mm	12.8 × 9.6 mm	16 mm
⅔ in 18 mm	8.8 × 6.6 mm	11 mm
½ in 12.5 mm	6.4 × 4.8 mm	8 mm

Typical applications: ENG cameras 18 mm tubes; EFP/OB cameras 25 mm tubes; studio cameras 18 mm to 30 mm tubes.

If, for example, you are using a lens focal length of 20 mm (0.8 in) and then change this to a 40 mm lens the subject will now appear twice as large in the picture; but the shot will only cover half the previous height and width of the scene. If, instead, you had changed from 20 mm to 10 mm focal length, the subject would then appear only half as big on the screen as it first did, but the shot would take in twice the original width and height.

For many years film and TV cameramen have used the focal length of their lenses as a direct guide when planning shots. They knew that they would get a 'waist shot' on a 35 mm lens if the person stood 1.4 m (4 ft 8 in) away. Multiples of this focal length would change the length of shot proportionally.

That was fine, if they continued to shoot with cameras using 35 mm film. But if they used a 16 mm film format these remembered figures failed. Instead, the same focal length lens would give a 'large head' shot at the distance they were used to obtaining 'waist shots'! That is because shot size is affected by the focal length *relative to the size of the camera's film frame*; or, in the case of TV cameras, by the scanned size of the camera-tube's target or image sensor.

Fig. 4.4 part 1   Fixed optics lens (prime lens)
Adjustable focus (distance) and lens stop. Fixed lens angle (focal length).

Fig. 4.4 part 2   Basic lens characteristics
Focal length – the distance from the lens' optical center (rear nodal point) to the tube target when focused at infinity.
Back focus – the distance from the back lens surface to the target, when focused at infinity.

In television, camera-tubes have varied very considerably in size over the years – from 4½-in image orthicon tubes to present-day ⅔-in camera-tubes. So TV cameramen who relied on associating focal lengths of their lenses with particular shot sizes have had to be very adaptable.

To overcome such problems, some TV organizations adopted the practice of referring not to the focal length but to the *horizontal angle of view* of the lens, which can be calculated from it. This convention has very real advantages. The *cameraman* gets used to the shots various lens angles provide. All '25° lenses' give the same shots, whatever the camera-tube's size. For the *director*, too, there are bonuses. You do not need to use tables to estimate shot sizes from different camera positions. You simply draw a 'V' of the chosen lens angle on a scale plan, or, better still, use a protractor. This way you can see exactly what will appear in shot and what will remain outside it. You can see what the relative sizes of subjects will be (Figures 18.6 to 18.8).

Prime and zoom lenses

As you probably know from using photographic cameras, two basic lens forms are generally available: those with *fixed optics* (i.e. having a fixed focal length) and those with an *adjustable focal length* (*zoom* lenses).

Sometimes, where the highest optical standards are necessary, TV cameras are fitted with fixed optics lenses; generally called *prime lenses*, *primary lenses*, or *fixed focus lenses*. But such lenses can only cover a fixed segment of the scene. How wide its coverage is depends on whether it is a *narrow-angle*, *normal*, or *wide-angle* design.

A long focal length lens only covers a narrow segment of the scene – a telescopic effect. A short focal length lens gives you a wide view, but subjects usually appear quite small and far away.

Fig. 4.5 Zoom lens
Adjustable focus, stop, and focal length (lens angle). Altering focal length varies the field of view. Usually set at a pre-selected angle. Changing the angle in shot produces 'zooming in' (as angle narrows, F increases), or 'zooming out' (angle widens, F decreases). Typically 12–120 mm focal length adjustments.

Lightweight zoom lens showing focus (distance) control, zoom lever (focal length/lens angle), *f*-stop (lens aperture).

If you want a closer or more distant shot when using a prime lens you must move the camera or the subject – or change the lens for another with a different focal length. (This is the procedure if a 'turret lens' system is used, which houses a choice of several fixed-optics lenses.)

The invention of the *zoom lens* changed all that. This design has a continuously variable focal length, which the cameraman can adjust to provide any shot size within its range. It is no longer necessary to move or to replace the lens to alter the shot; this can be done by 'zooming'.

Earlier zoom lens designs produced results that were noticeably inferior to fixed lens systems, but advances in optics have considerably improved the performance of even low-cost zoom systems. Because of their operational advantages, most TV/video cameras are now fitted with zoom lenses. They have their drawbacks – but more of that later.

What is a lens angle?

The regular TV screen is a rectangle. Its sides are in 4 by 3 proportions; i.e. if the screen is 40 cm (16 in) across, it will be 30 cm (12 in) high. The TV camera's lens covers a similarly shaped field, stretching away to infinity.

If we draw an imaginary line from the left and right edges of the picture to the camera lens the angle they make at the lens is called the *horizontal lens angle* or, more usually, 'the lens angle'.

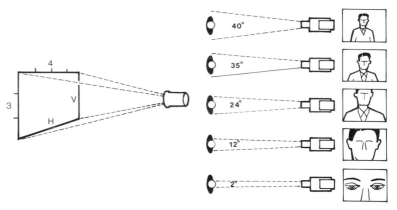

Fig. 4.6 part 1   Angle of view
The TV camera lens 'sees' 4 by 3 proportions. The vertical angle of view is therefore ¾ of its horizontal angle. The angle a lens covers depends on its *focal length* relative to the size of camera-tube used.

For a given camera position, the longer the lens focal length (narrower lens angle) the closer the subject appears; but less of the scene is visible. The shorter the focal length (wider lens angle), the more distant the subject appears.

Fig. 4.6 part 2   Lens angles
Changes are proportional as the lens-angle alters. Using a lens of three times the present angle (i.e. ⅓F), the subject now appears ⅓ of former size and × 3 of scene width is now visible. The effect is that of increasing the camera distance by 3 times. Changing to a narrower angle has the opposite effect.

Fig. 4.7 Viewing distance

Ideally, a photograph should be viewed so that the image subtends a similar angle to that of the original camera lens. The perspective (relative distances, sizes, depths, proportions) will then appear *natural*. Viewing distance, therefore, should really be adjusted to suit the screen size.

Draw a similar angle from the top and bottom of the frame, to the lens, and we have the lens's *vertical angle*. The vertical angle is three-quarters of that value.

Although you can calculate the lens angle from its focal length (see Glossary: *Lens angle*) it is easier to check the manufacturer's figures for the lens, and go from there.

For example, a studio zoom lens may have a focal length varying from 8 to 120 mm, covering an angle from around 57° to 4°. Multiply one focal length limit (e.g. 8) by the angle it provides (57 in this case), and you obtain a factor $8 \times 57 = 456$.

When you want to know the lens angle for any intermediate focal length, divide this factor 456 by that focal length. In this case, a 100 mm setting gives an angle of $456 \div 100 = 45.6°$. Use the factor you have found for your particular lens system.

Figure 18.8 shows how you can make a useful chart to check your lens angles.

Fig. 4.8 Natural perspectives

When the viewing angle equals the camera's lens angle our impression of the picture's perspective will be similar to that of the original scene. Viewing the picture from too far away or using a camera lens of too wide angle for normal viewing conditions gives a false impression of perspective. Depth and distance are exaggerated; distant subjects unduly small. Viewing the picture too closely or using a too narrow angle lens for normal viewing conditions again gives a false impression. Depth and distance are compressed; distant subjects unduly large.

Perspective distortion

Suppose you are viewing a TV screen at home and the angle at your eye is around 20° (Figure 4.8). Then if the camera is using a lens of roughly 20° the picture will appear to have *natural perspective*. That is, distance and proportions will appear as they would to your eye if you were standing in the original scene.

Some scenes contain few clues to perspective (e.g. countryside, deserts, seascapes), while in others perspective changes are very pronounced (e.g. in city streets, within buildings). The exact angle is not at all critical. The lens angle can vary from about 20° to 27° and perspective will still appear very natural.

For general purposes, we can say that the focal length for a 'normal' lens angle

- On an 18 mm (⅔ in) camera-tube is about 11 mm (0.4 in).
- On a 25 mm (1 in) camera-tube is about 16–20 mm (0.6–0.8 in).
- On a 30 mm (1¼ in) camera-tube is about 20–25 mm (0.8–1 in).

But suppose the camera is using a lens angle that is much greater or much less than 'normal'? Then the picture will show *perspective distortion*.

Fig. 4.9 Perspective distortion
(see Glossary)
Reducing the lens angle (increasing
F) provides a magnified image of part
of the scene. This emphasizes
perspective effects normally associated
with distant subjects, and produces
an illusion of space compression.

TOTAL SCENE

Wide Angle Lens   Normal Angle Lens   Narrow Angle Lens

It will convey a very inaccurate impression of distance, space, scale.
Close shots can appear either grotesquely deformed or flattened as if cut
out of board. Vertical columns can appear bowed and bent. Occasionally,
you may want just this sort of distortion for dramatic impact. But you
certainly do not want it to arise through accidentally using an unsuitable
lens angle!

The narrow-angle lens (long-focus lens)

A lens system with a *long focal length* covers only a narrow section of
the scene. It has a limited 'angle of view'. The effect is identical, whether
you are using a narrow-angle prime lens or a zoom lens that has been
zoomed right in to what is often called its 'T' or 'telephoto' position.
(Incidentally, although long-focus lenses are frequently called 'telephoto', the term really refers to a particular, compactly designed lens
system.)

The 'telescopic view' that a narrow-angle ('long-focus') lens provides
enables you to get close shots from a distance. This is the answer –

● When you cannot get the camera near the subject because of
    obstructions,

**Fig. 4.10 Geometrical
(curvilinear) distortion**
Optical distortion in which lines
parallel to the frame edges appear
progressively bent outwards (barrel
distortion) or inwards (pincushion
distortion).

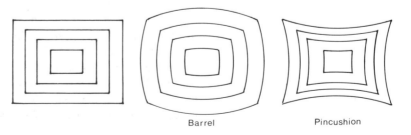

Barrel   Pincushion

- When it is out of reach,
- When there is insufficient time to move,
- When the camera is fixed in position.

Outside the studio, the narrow-angle lens is often the only way you can hope to get shots of distant subjects.

Distortion effects

However, there are drawbacks when using a narrow-angle lens. Depth appears remarkably compressed, and the foreground-to-background distance seems much shorter than it really is. Solid objects look 'depth-squashed'. Distant subjects look surprisingly large and close; they do not seem to diminish with distance, as we would expect.

Anyone moving towards or away from us seems to take an interminable time, even if they are running fast. At the racetrack, horses gallop towards us, but appear to cover little ground despite their efforts.

If the camera shooting with a narrow-angle lens has an end-on viewpoint the subject will look strangely foreshortened:

- A large oil tanker may look only a few meters long.
- In a rowing eight, flat cramped figures squat in a compressed boat.
- Shooting along a piano keyboard, we see considerable depth distortion.

Shooting people with lenses of around 5–10°, you will notice unpleasantly flattened features, flat chests, and generally reduced modeling (contouring). Looking at a face from the front (full face), or a slightly angled face (three-quarters face), the effect can be very obvious.

Camera handling

There are moments when the unexpected happens, and we want to grab a close shot of a fleeting moment – to emphasize someone's reaction perhaps, or show detail in a passing parade. Only a narrow-angle lens can change in an instant, from the wide view it was taking, to get that unplanned shot. The audience will be too interested to notice such niceties as spatial distortion. (It may not be very bad anyway!)

But for the cameraman, narrow-angle lenses spell trouble! Camera handling becomes increasingly harder as the lens's focal length is increased. Even slight camera movement, caused by a wavering hand-grip or dollying over an uneven floor, causes disturbing picture judder. It is no mean feat to follow a fast-moving subject, such as a flying bird, in a close shot with a narrow-angle lens and keep it accurately framed throughout its maneuvers! Apart from handling difficulties, there is the additional hazard of working with a shallow depth of field!

When using a narrow-angle lens it is difficult to hold the camera still for any length of time without a shudder or shake from one's breathing, heartbeat, or tiring muscles. A gust of wind can be a disaster! But it is virtually impossible to hand-hold it when set to a *very narrow* lens angle.

Fig. 4.11 part 1   Lens angles and camera movement
Here we see the effect of moving the camera (positions 1, 2, 3) with wide-angle, normal, narrow-angle lenses.

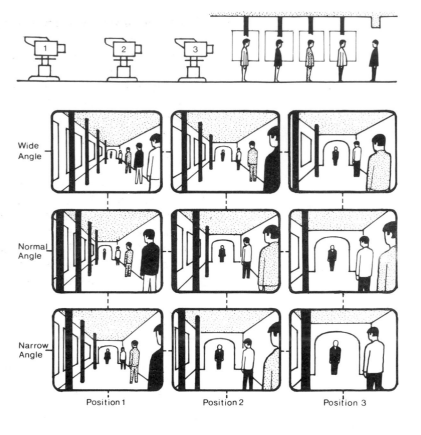

Wide Angle

Normal Angle

Narrow Angle

Position 1   Position 2   Position 3

Fig. 4.11 part 2   Maintaining foreground subject size
If lens is changed, and camera distance altered to maintain the same foreground subject size, proportions change too. (1) Narrow; (2) normal; (3) wide-angle lens.

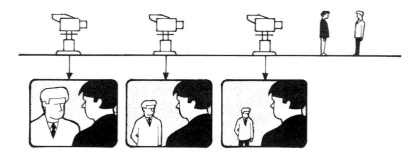

For cameras in the field, lens angles as small as ½° to 5° may be necessary to bring the action close enough. Then the problem is acute. You may even have to *lock-off* the panning head, to keep the picture steady.

In hot weather, close shots of distance subjects taken with a narrow-angle lens can be marred by heat haze rising from the ground. Light diffraction produces an overall shimmering that distorts the picture, and destroys detail. Then there is no remedy except to move nearer to the subject with a wider lens angle.

The wide-angle lens (short-focus lens)

For all practical purposes, we can say that any lens with a horizontal angle of 30° or more has wide-angle characteristics. The shorter the focal length, the wider the lens angle will be.

As you might expect, wide-angle ('short-focus') lenses have exactly opposite characteristics from narrow-angle lenses.

Distortion effects

The wide-angle lens appears to *exaggerate perspective*. Depth and space are overemphasized. Things seem further away than they really are.

If you move the camera while on a wide-angle lens it appears to be traveling faster than it really is. Anyone approaching or walking away from the camera seems to be moving much more quickly than normal.

You can use these various effects to advantage. A short-focus lens can give quite a wide overall view of the scene, even when it is relatively close.

Table 4.3   Lens angles *(see Table 6.2)*

	Advantages	Disadvantages
'Normal' lens (20°–27°)	Perspective appears natural. Space/distance appears consistent when intercutting 'normal' lenses. Camera handling feels natural and is relatively stable. Focused depth is generally satisfactory, even though fairly shallow for closer shots.	Inadequate width-coverage in confined spaces. Camera must move close to subject for detail; so may be seen by other cameras taking longer shots of the same subject.
Narrow-angle long-focus lens (less than 20°)	Brings distant subjects closer. Permits 'closer' shots of inaccessible subjects. Can flatten or reduce emphasis on surface contours. Enable objects spaced-out away from the camera to be compressed into a more cohesive group (e.g. a string of automobiles). Can suggest aborted effort in subjects moving quickly to/from the camera (e.g. running). Defocuses distracting background.	Depth appears compressed. Heat haze may shimmer the picture. Flattening of subject modeling can appear unnatural. Camera handling is considerably more difficult (pan, tilt, smooth dollying). Restricted depth of field makes focusing critical.
Wide-angle short-focus lens (greater than 30°)	Can obtain wide views at closer distances, especially in confined space. Camera handling causes negligible judder. Because of extended depth of field, focusing is less critical. Enables modeling and space to be exaggerated. Impressive spatial effects possible. Useful for grotesque or dramatic shots. Provides considerable depth of field.	Depth appears exaggerated. (Confined spaces cannot be shown in correct proportions.) Pronounced geometric distortion, at widest angles. Susceptible to lens flares. On close-ups, problems with camera shadows falling on subject.

This can be a great help when you are shooting in restricted spaces and shots taken with a normal lens angle look far too close.

Occasionally, when you set up a shot you may find that something nearby is visible as a defocused blur in the foreground. If you move closer until the obstruction is out of shot your subject may appear too large or too close. Moving closer with a wider lens angle can be the answer.

Even a small room can look quite spacious when shot on a wide-angle lens – a very useful deception when you want to emphasize space, or make small settings in the studio appear more impressive.

But there are times when this effect can be an embarrassment. If, for instance, you are shooting within a very confined area such as a cell, only a wide-angle lens will give you a general view of the location. (Any other lens angle would only provide close shots.) But at the same time, the wide-angle lens exaggerates perspective, and makes the surroundings seem very spacious . . . In these circumstances the only alternative is to use a normal lens angle, and move outside the room, shooting in through a window or door.

If you take close shots of people on wide-angle lenses you will get extremely unreal, bizarre distortions: puffed-up bulbous heads, large protruding noses, stumpy legs, and enlarged chests. Fine for grotesques, but totally unacceptable for flattering portraiture!

Never use wide-angle lenses for close shots of geometrical subjects such as pages of print, graph paper, or sheet music. The geometrical distortion can be very pronounced! Better still, try it and see what happens! Panning on a shot containing straight vertical or horizontal lines, you will see them bend as they near the picture edges.

The wider the lens angle (shorter focal length), the more obvious will these effects be. The *fisheye lens*, which has a coverage of from 140° to 360°, can only be used for those odd situations where their gross distortion can be accepted.

Camera handling

On the plus side, camerawork is much easier when using a wide-angle lens. Camera movements appear smoother, and any slight bumps as the camera moves are less likely to cause picture judder. As an extra bonus, focusing is less critical as the available depth of field is much greater.

Summarizing

To summarize these points:
Narrow-angle lenses

- The field of view is restricted. Only a small segment of the scene appears in the shot.
- At the narrowest angles you can get a blow-up 'telescopic' image of the subject.
- Space distance, depth are compressed.
- Camera handling and focusing become difficult.

Wide-angle lenses

● The wide field of view takes in a large segment of the scene.
● The widest lens angles can give a 'wrong end of the telescope' impression.
● Space, distance, depth are exaggerated.
● Camera handling and focusing are easy.

In Table 6.2 you will see the practical features of various lens angles. A typical *zoom lens*, with its adjustable focal length, behaves

● As a narrow-angle or long-focus lens when zoomed fully in,
● As a wide-angle or short-focus lens when zoomed fully out,
● Somewhere about mid-range it has 'normal' lens-angle characteristics.

Supplementary lenses

By adding an extra 'supplementary' lens in front of your lens you can alter its focal length, and hence the lens angle. The power of this 'add-on' lens is quoted in *diopters*. You can use such supplementary lenses with a prime lens or a zoom lens system.

A *positive supplementary lens* reduces the effective focal length, and therefore widens the lens angle. It also allows the lens system to focus on subjects closer than normal. You can identify a positive supplementary lens by holding it at arm's length, when you will see a small *inverted image*.

When you hold a negative supplementary lens the tiny image is *upright*. When placed over the lens the negative lens narrows the lens angle. However, if you position it beyond the main lens's focal length the overall lens angle will *increase*.

The zoom lens

The zoom lens has many practical advantages. You can select any focal length within its range, when it will behave similarly to an equivalent prime lens. You can adjust the focal length while on shot, to alter the image size.

● *Zooming in:* as you increase the focal length the lens angle decreases and the subject image grows larger.
● *Zooming out:* as the focal length is *de*creased the lens angle increases and the subject image grows smaller.

If the focal length of the lens system, when zoomed fully in, is three times that when fully zoomed out, it has a ×3 or 3:1 zoom ratio. So you can change the image size on the screen by a magnification factor of three. With this particular lens you could, for example, zoom out from a close-up to a knee-length shot. The greater the ratio, the bigger the angular change available. A high-ratio zoom lens – e.g. 44:1 – might fill

Fig. 4.12 Zooming
Zooming in progressively fills the
screen with a smaller section of the
scene. (Narrowing lens angle,
increasing focal length.)

Wide Angle
Zoomed Out
ZOOMING OUT
ZOOMING IN
Narrow Angle
Zoomed In

the screen with a person's eye . . . then zoom back until he becomes a dot in the landscape!

Another way of specifying a zoom lens is e.g. *10 × 25*. That simply means that the lens has a zoom ratio of 10, with a minimum focal length of 25 mm (when zoomed right out to the widest angle). Its longest focal length when fully zoomed in is $10 \times 25 = 250$ mm.

Types of zoom lenses

Zoom lens systems are available in high-quality and standard designs, to match all sizes of camera-tube. They range in size from large high-quality studio lenses weighing e.g. 25 kg (55 lb) to lightweight systems weighing e.g. 1.3 kg (3 lb).

■ *Studio application lenses*   These are mainly for use in medium-size studios, and may cover, for example, 5–50°. The narrowest angle is useful for general close-up work, and the widest is not so spread that it easily overshoots settings, and sees lamps.

■ *Field application lenses*   Working away from the studio, in open spaces or public places, you are more likely to need really narrow lens angles (e.g. 1°) in order to get close shots from a considerable distance. This field camera is often isolated way up on a balcony or similar fixed viewpoint, and can only provide a range of shots by changing the lens angle. Although the short-focus end of the range may not cover a particularly wide angle, it will be sufficient for most purposes.

■ *Lenses for ENG use*   These are smaller, lighter, and more compact zoom lens systems. The zoom ratio may be anywhere from e.g. 5:1 to 22:1.

Although lightweight cameras can support larger lens systems when mounted on a tripod or pedestal, hand-held cameras are necessarily restricted. Not only would they add to the overall weight but they would upset the camera's balance. In any case, as we have seen, on narrower lens angles the camera is difficult, if not impossible, to control.

Although zoom systems are intended for specific usage, you will often find units designed for portable cameras being used widely in Studio, Field, and ENG work.

Zoom lens controls

The zoom lens on a lightweight and portable camera may be adjusted directly by a manual zoom level on the lens barrel, or by a nearby two-way switch operating a motor-controlled servo. The latter drives the lens towards the zoomed-out limit (W), or towards the zoomed-in limit (T), stopping when you release the switch.

Larger studio and field zoom lenses are usually adjusted remotely by a control at the rear of the camera (e.g. on the panning bars; Figure 4.13). This may be *direct* flexible-cable control or an electrical *servo* in which a small electric motor adjusts the lens system. Servo control can provide a very smooth even change, particularly during a very slow 'creep-in'.

Unlike direct cable control, servo systems can be designed to give the same 'feel' to the zoom and focus controls, whatever the focal length being used. Servos have the advantage, too, that you cannot inadvertently 'overzoom' (or 'overfocus') and ram the lens against its end stop as it reaches its limits, jerking the picture and even damaging the lens system.

The *hand crank* is a widely used type of zoom control, normally fixed to the right panning handle. Turning the crank adjusts the lens's focal length. Some controls have a speed-selection switch, which allows fast or slow zoom rates.

Another widely used system is a rotating *thumb-lever*, which controls a servo system. Again fixed to the right-hand panning handle, it is turned to the left to zoom out and to the right to zoom in. Light pressure produces slow zooming, with heavy pressure for fast zooms. One soon learns to adjust thumb pressure to control the zoom rate.

The *twist-grip* form of control (like the 'focus' version) is a rotating sleeve which behaves similarly to the thumb-lever. It turns right to zoom in and left to zoom out.

The *push-rod* form of zoom control has been used to a limited extent. This economical design dubiously combines zoom and focus adjustments. *Push–pull* movement zooms the lens, while *turning* the control knob adjusts focus. Smooth control can be very difficult.

The shot box

The *shot box* provides an automated zooming facility. Often attached to larger studio and field cameras, the shot box may be bolted to a panning

Fig. 4.13   Zoom lens controls

Forms of zoom control
On studio cameras:
1. Twist-grip.
2. Hand-crank.
3. Thumb-lever.
4. Push-rod (also focuses).
On lightweight cameras, thumb-operated switches by the handgrip operate the zoom motor.

Panning handle controls. When a camera is fitted to a mounting, the lens is usually adjusted with extension controls: *zoom control* (1–twist grip) fixed to the left panning handle; *focus control* (2–hand crank) to the right.

Shot box (integrated into camera head, or clamped to a pan handle). This provides pre-selected zoom settings; overriden by pan-bar thumb control.
1. Zoom meter shows focal length/lens angle.
2. Buttons select pre-set angles adjusted by knobs at 3.
4. Auto-zoom switch, zooms the lens in/out towards narrowest/widest angles when pressed.
5. Adjusts auto-zoom speed.

Focal length (lens angle) may be adjusted manually (zoom lever on lens barrel), or with a motor system (*power zoom*) operated by a rocker-switch, from Wide-angle to Telephoto (narrow angle). Nearby switches also control the lens *aperture (iris)*: auto, manual, remote control.

handle or fitted within the camera head. This device allows four to six or more pre-set lens angles to be stored, and selected immediately by push-buttons.

● The cameraman can pre-set the actual lens angle (focal length) available at each position.
● A *zoom meter* or *field of view* indicator shows the current focal length/ field of view.

- Another set of buttons will automatically zoom the lens in (narrow) or out (wide).
- The speed of the auto-zoom can be adjusted by a speed control.
- The main zoom control (e.g. thumb-lever) on the panning handle overrides the shot-box controls.

Apart from the convenience of being able to select specific angles rapidly, the shot box can ensure that you use identical lens angles in both rehearsal and taping sessions.

Zoom performance

The zoom lens is more costly, heavier, and more bulky than a prime lens. Its optical performance involves compromises, particularly with less expensive versions. Achieving smooth progressive zooming throughout the range, without the focus drifting, varying image brightness, geometrical distortions, or other aberrations, is indeed a considerable technical challenge.

Zoom advantages

The main advantages of the zoom lens are that:

- You can select any angle within its range very quickly, either manually or by push-button on a *shot box* (Figure 4.13), without losing the picture.
- Zooming can be controlled *manually*, or with a motor-driven *auto-zoom* at various pre-set speeds.
- There are times when one wants to exclude or include a little more of the scene to improve the composition of the shot. Instead of having to move the complete camera mounting a little nearer or further away, you can adjust the lens angle to compensate. Quicker and much less tiring.
- Zooming is easy. (Sometimes *too* easy!) Moving a camera dolly on a shot *smoothly* at an even rate needs experience and skill – particularly if you have to move it fast, or for some distance. Zooming is much more easily controlled.

Zoom disadvantages

Zoom lenses do have their disadvantages:

- The lens behaves differently at different zoom settings.
- It is very easy to use inappropriate lens angles.
- Cameramen may not repeat the rehearsed shots accurately.
- Zooming can be misused, to substitute for camera movement.

Varying performance

Although camera handling and focusing are very easy when the lens is set to a wide angle, things become progressively more difficult as you zoom in to narrower lens settings. Focusing can become very critical. Any camera shake is very obvious.

If you happen to be working on a wide-angle lens setting, and then move in to follow a subject while zooming, some disconcerting things can happen. Concentrating on getting closer and closer, you may fail to notice that you are now moving around on a very narrow lens angle, barely able to hold the shot steady!

Because the depth of field becomes shallow at narrow-angle settings you may find that although the picture appears sharply focused in a long shot, it becomes badly defocused when you zoom in. As we shall see, this often makes it necessary to *pre-focus* before zooming. Having zoomed in, you will probably find it noticeably harder to follow focus due to the restricted depth of field.

When using an *eyepiece viewfinder* some people tend to close one eye to concentrate on the picture. If you do this you may find that when you change from a wide-angle to a narrower-angle zoom setting it upsets your awareness of the space around you. As you move around, nearby obstructions can take you by surprise. Clearly, the safest solution is to cultivate the habit of keeping both eyes open!

Inappropriate lens angles

It is all too easy to select lens angles indiscriminately, so that perspective varies between shots, and people look distorted. Try, as far as possible, to stick to a normal angle, and only alter it for a specific purpose.

Rehearsed shots repeated inaccurately

It is important that the camera set-up during recording should be similar to that during rehearsal. If during taping you are further away from the subject, and zoom in to compensate, the picture will not be the same, even if the shot size is similar. To avoid discrepancies, note (and mark) your floor positions, *and* the lens angle used during rehearsal, to avoid differences in perspective.

If the camera is not fitted with a reliable indicator (or a shot box) the cameraman has to rely entirely on memory to repeat the shot accurately; but even then, floor positions can serve as a useful guide.

Parallactic movement

Why bother to move the camera, when you can simply zoom in and out to change the shot? After all, when you zoom, it looks as if the camera is moving nearer and further away. Or does it?

If you are shooting a *flat surface* such as a photograph or a painting, the effect of zooming is identical with that of dollying – an overall magnification or reduction of the image.

There are important differences though, when shooting *three-dimensional* situations. Suppose the scene contains a person standing behind a tree. From where we stand, they are hidden. If we zoom in on the scene, simply magnifying the image, they remain hidden.

But if instead of zooming we dolly the camera forward, we see quite a different effect. Our viewpoint continually changes. As in everyday life, the picture shows us going *past* different objects in the scene. Their relative positions in the shot alter.

In this example, as we move forward past the tree part of the person comes into sight. Continuing forward, they become increasingly visible . . . until eventually we see them quite clearly, separate from the tree.

This effect, as relative positions change, is known as *parallactic movement*. When the picture zooms, we miss this displacement, and the result looks false, even if one does not recognize why. So zooming is seldom a completely convincing substitute for moving the camera.

Extender lens

Some zoom lens systems include an in-built supplementary lens – a flip-in *extender lens* (*range extender*). Typically this changes the available zoom range by ×1.5 or ×2.

With a ×2 *fixed extender* the basic range of an 8–120 mm zoom lens (57°–4°) would effectively be increased to become a 16–240 mm (28°–2°) system. With the extender lens in, the widest shots available will be limited; but you are able to get closer shots than normal.

Variable extenders (sometimes called 'double zooms') allow the amount of magnification of the basic zoom range to be adjusted (e.g. up to ×2 maximum). To a limited extent, this arrangement minimizes the usual disadvantages of extenders.

There are drawbacks to using any extender lens:

● There is inevitably an overlap between the two ranges.
● The image quality when using the extender is not as high as the normal range; although the softer focus may not be obvious.
● You should not switch the extender lens in/out while on shot, for it will disrupt the picture. So you may need to choose the moment for changeover carefully.
● There can be practical difficulties due to the overlap between the two ranges. Suppose you are on the lower range, and zoomed in to its narrowest angle. Switching to the higher range, you will find that the lens is now *at its narrowest angle* on the high range; a considerable jump in image size! You cannot zoom smoothly from the widest angle (low range) to the narrowest angle (high range).
● There can be a considerable light loss when switching to the extender. A ×2 extender, for example, may require a fourfold light increase for the same exposure! It may not be practicable to open up to a larger lens aperture to compensate.
● The minimum focusing distance can change between the ranges. You may not be able to focus on closer subjects on one range.

Nevertheless, the extender does provide an opportunity to increase the effective range of a zoom lens, and this can be very useful at times.

Focusing

When you focus a camera, you adjust its lens to produce the sharpest possible image of your subject. With a prime lens this involves altering the distance between the lens and the camera-tube target or image sensor. A zoom lens focuses by readjusting internal lens elements.

Focusing methods (Figure 4.14)

Several methods are used to focus the lens system:

1. A *focus ring* on the lens barrel (screwing the lens in/out).
2. A *twist grip* attached to a panning handle.
3. A *focus knob* at the *side* of the camera head.
4. A *focus/zoom* rod at the rear of the camera.
5. *Automatic* focusing.

   1. The *focus ring* is used on all hand-held and lightweight cameras. You turn the manual focus ring until subject details in the viewfinder are as sharp as possible. To make it easier to focus accurately, the viewfinder may have a 'crispening' control, which exaggerates detail.

   2. The panning-handle *twist grip* is very widely used to adjust focusing. Many designs require one complete turn of the grip, to cover the full range from infinity (furthest distance) to the nearest (MFD). Others are less coarse, and take two or three complete turns to cover the range. Focus changes are more gradual. Such controls are very unsuitable if you want to pull focus (throw focus) quickly, e.g. between a subject in the foreground and another in the distance (Figure 5.6).

   Where the focus control is directly linked to the lens by a flexible-cable the result is a simple and trouble-free system. But you may find focusing at narrow lens angles very critical, while at wider angles you can turn the control over an appreciable range before noticing changes in focus.

   Servo systems can be designed to give the same 'feel', whatever the lens angle (focal length).

   3. A *focus knob* fitted to the *side* of the camera is an alternative to the panning handle twist grip on some studio cameras.

   Over the years, cameramen have adopted two basic operating positions, depending on the design of the camera: The commonest approach is to stand upright, holding a panning handle in each hand (focus control on the left handle, the zoom control on the right), looking ahead to the viewfinder.

   Alternatively, he may lean in with forehead touching the viewfinder light-shield to exclude all stray light, and a hand round on a focus control at the side of the camera. In this arrangement the zoom control is fixed to a single panning handle.

   4. In the *combined zoom/focus rod*, turning the control knob adjusts focus (push–pull movement zooms the lens). This is not a particularly effective or convenient system.

   5. *Automatic focusing* is available on an increasing range of cameras. Where a cameraman is moving around with a hand-held camera, and has

Fig. 4.14   Forms of focus control

Typical systems of focus control include:

1. Spoked capstan control
2. Twist-grip
3. Camera-head focus control.

to concentrate on the route and keeping the subject in shot, automatic focusing can be a great help (like *auto-iris*, which adjusts the exposure).

The *auto-focus* system simply sharpens focus on the nearest object in the center of the shot. It sends out a fine infrared beam, which is reflected from the subject and used to adjust the 'distance' setting of the lens. At best, this is a great facility – but there are many surprises!

- If your subject is not in the *center* of the picture auto-focus may sharpen on an unimportant item that is, and leave your subject defocused.
- You may want two subjects at different distances from the camera to look equally sharp. The auto-focus may sharpen on one or neither.
- If you are shooting through a foreground framework of e.g. branches, or a grille, the system will focus on this, rather than your subject beyond.
- If your subject is behind glass (show case, shop window), or beneath the surface of a pool the auto-focus system is fooled.
- Follow a moving subject among others (e.g. someone in a crowd) and the sytem may readjust and focus on other subjects.
- When you zoom to alter the shot size the system may refocus as you recompose the picture.
- If the subject is covered with a black material, focusing may be inaccurate, as black surfaces do not reflect infrared well.
- When shooting in rain or snow, auto-focusing may not be accurate.
- If someone or something moves in front of the camera the system may refocus on it, defocusing your subject. If, for instance, you are panning over a landscape, and a foreground bush or fence comes into shot, the lens may defocus the distant scene and show a well-focused bush.
- Sometimes backgrounds close behind a subject can cause ambiguous focusing.

Where such problems arise the answer is to switch to *manual* focusing instead.

Why focus?

Simple photographic cameras have no focusing control, yet everything in the shot looks reasonably sharp. Why does the TV camera need to be focused continually? There are several reasons:

- A fixed-focus system does not provide maximum sharpness in your subject. The lens is set at the *hyperfocal distance* (see Glossary) so is in 'acceptable focus' from the far distance up to about 2.4 m (8 ft) away. Anything closer is defocused.
- The lens aperture is reduced (small stop), so high light levels are needed for good results.
- Everything in the shot is equally sharp. There is no *differential focusing* in which subjects can be made to stand out against a defocused background.
- The camera cannot focus on close subjects (although a supplementary lens may help).

If, for some reason, you wanted to use your TV camera as a fixed-focus system, so that you were free to move around and concentrate on other things, you could set the lens to the hyperfocal distance. But this is a very limiting technique.

Depth of field

When you focus a lens you are adjusting the *distance* at which it gives maximum sharpness. Anything that is nearer or farther away than this focused distance appears progressively defocused.

The range of distances over which subjects are apparently sharp is called the *depth of field* – not *depth of focus*, which refers to an entirely different thing (focal plane tolerances). The focused area in front of the subject is much shallower than that behind it.

How far sharpness can deteriorate before you notice it depends on the detail in your subject, and how good the system is. If the subject lacks detail, or the system has poor definition, you may have difficulty in seeing exactly what *is* in focus!

Providing a subject remains within this depth of field, you do not need to readjust the focus control. At times, the focused depth may be considerable, especially when the lens is focused at the hyperfocal distance (see Glossary). But it can also become embarrassingly shallow, particularly in close shots. Then when the distance of the subject or the camera changes even slightly you may need to readjust the focus control to maintain sharpness (Figure 4.15).

As you can see in Figure 4.16, the depth of field in a shot alters noticeably when you vary

- The distance at which the lens is focused,
- Or the lens angle (the focal length),
- Or the lens *f-stop*.

Rather than continually following focus as subjects or cameras move around it would seem preferable to stop the lens right down (e.g. *f*/22) to obtain the maximum depth of field. The hard fact of life is that this could necessitate light levels that are anything from eight to 30 times the normal light intensity! (Hardly practicable in a studio.) And as we shall see, all-over focus (*deep focus*) is not always desirable artistically.

Fig. 4.15 Depth of field
Within the depth of field, subjects appear sharp; although definition is optimum at the *focused distance* (FD). Beyond the furthest acceptable distance (Df) and closer than the nearest limits (Dn), subjects are defocused.

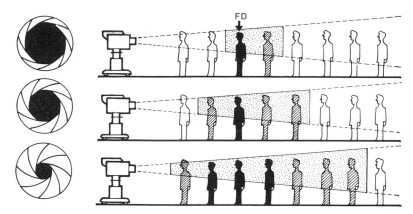

Fig. 4.16 part 1   The effect of aperture on depth of field
Keeping the focal length and focusing distance (FD) constant, the depth of field
increases as lens aperture is reduced (stopped-down).

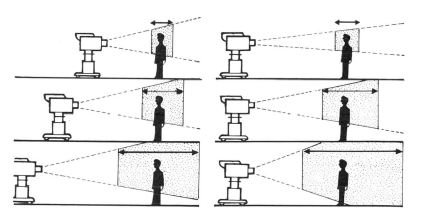

**Fig. 4.16 part 2   The effect of
subject distance on depth of field**
Keeping the focal length and aperture
constant, the depth of field increases as
the camera gets further from the
subject; but image size decreases.

**Fig. 4.16 part 3   The effect of
focal length on depth of field**
Keeping the aperture and subject
distances constant, the depth of field
increases as focal length decreases
(lens angle is widened), but image
size decreases.

If you want to calculate tables showing exactly how the depth of field
changes with your particular lens –

$$\text{The } nearest\ limit = \frac{H \times D}{H + D}$$

$$\text{The } farthest\ limit = \frac{H \times D}{H - D}$$

where H is the hyperfocal distance and D is the distance from lens to the
focused plane.

Focusing problems

If a shot is correctly focused, zooming in or out should have no effect. If focus does vary (tracking error), this may be because the lens needs setting up, or may be due to shortcomings in lens design.

However, even a correctly aligned high-performance zoom lens has a regular operational hazard you should know about (Figure 4.18).

Imagine your lens is fully zoomed out, and the picture sharply focused. You zoom right in to a close shot . . . and find that the picture is now *completely out of focus*. Why?

Fig. 4.18   Zoom lens focusing problems
Unless the camera has been pre-focused, the close-up after zooming it may be unsharp.

Fig. 4.17   Constant depth of field
If the camera distance is adjusted for each lens angle to keep the same subject size, the depth of field will remain the same (for a given *f* stop).

Zoomed out – although the focused distance is incorrect, the subject appears focused due to the considerable depth of field available (wide lens angle).

Zoomed in – without re-adjusting focusing, we zoom in. Now the depth of field has become shallower (narrower lens angle) and it no longer includes subject, which appears defocused.

Focusing with a wide-angle lens setting (short focal length) is so uncritical that whether your lens is actually focused at e.g. 8 m or 10 m (26–32 ft) the shot appears equally sharp. That is because there is a considerable depth of field. The exact focused distance is not easy to see.

However, when you zoom *in*, the focused depth becomes progressively shallower as the lens angle narrows. If you were originally focused at 10 m but your subject is at 8 m, the error will now be very obvious; it will be out of focus!

The only solution is to wait until you are off shot, and *pre-focus* the picture. You zoom in, sharp focus, and then zoom out to the wide-angle shot, ready to start shooting, and zoom in on cue. If you are taken by surprise, or do not have the opportunity to prepare the zoom-in, you have no option but to correct any defocusing during the take. It looks sloppy, but sometimes the lapse can be edited out afterwards.

Minimum focusing distance

Any lens can be focused over a range from *infinity* to a plane a short distance from the lens. Nearer than this *minimum focusing distance (MFD)* the shot remains defocused, the control having reached its limit. This MFD varies with the type and design of the lens. A wide-angle (short-focus) lens can focus down to a few centimeters away. But the MFD for a very narrow-angle (long-focus) lens may be several meters from the camera. For a zoom lens, the minimum focusing distance varies with the angle selected.

Many zoom lenses now have a *macro* setting, which provides a sharp image almost up to the actual lens surface. You can fill the screen with a postage stamp. Whether you can get light on the subject at that distance and avoid camera shadowing is another matter! When you use the macro setting, the lens's zoom action is inoperative.

Setting up a zoom lens

The action of a zoom lens is easier to understand if you regard it as a fixed-focus lens with a telescope of variable magnification in front of it. While its field of view changes, its back-focus distance (rear-lens to tube target) remains constant and sharply focused.

To ensure that the zoom lens maintains focus as you change the focal length (i.e. zoom in and out), the system has to be set up as follows during regular check-outs:

- First zoom in to distant detail and adjust the normal operational *zoom focus* control (*lens focus, front focus, rough* or *coarse focus*) for greatest clarity.
- Then zoom out and adjust the internal pre-set focus control (*camera focus, back* or *fine focus*) for the sharpest image.
- Now you should be able to zoom in/out without focus drift (i.e. correct *focus tracking*). If necessary, repeat this setting-up procedure for optimum results. Once set up, the lens tracking should remain satisfactory for some time.

Lens aperture (*f*-stop)

Looking into a lens system, you will see an adjustable circular *diaphragm* or *iris*, made up of a number of thin overlapping metal blades. The size of the hole formed by these plates is carefully calibrated in graduated stops. These f-*numbers*/f-*stops* (or *transmission* – *T* numbers) are marked around a ring on the lens barrel. Turning the ring alters the effective diameter of the lens opening over a wide range.

Adjusting the lens aperture, two quite separate things happen simultaneously:

1. It changes the brightness of the lens image falling on the camera-tube or image sensor – i.e. the picture's *exposure*.

Fig. 4.19 Lens aperture
Lens aperture is adjustable from a
maximum (e.g. *f/2* for a fast lens
f/5.6 for a slow lens) to a minimum
(e.g. *f/22*). *Large aperture* – small
f-number, shallow depth of field, but
less light needed. *Small aperture* –
large *f*-number, increased depth of
field, but more light needed.

2. It alters *depth of field* in the shot – which, we know, is also affected by
the lens's focused distance and focal length.

f-numbers (f-stops)

The larger its maximum opening, the more light the lens will let through.
Typical maximum stops for a 'fast lens', suitable under lower levels,
would be $f/1.4$ to 1.7 'wide open'. A 'slower lens' with a maximum
opening of e.g. $f/3.5$ would not produce optimum pictures under these
conditions.

As you reduce the lens aperture (stop down) the *f*-stop number
increases. The lens's minimum aperture may be around $f/22$. For
each complete stop you open the lens its image brightness light will
double (halved when stopping down). But a whole stop number is an
inconveniently large calibration, so subdivisions are normally used. The
standard series of lens markings is:

$f/1.4$ 2   2.8   4   5.6   8   11   16   22   32

In practice, intermediate points such as 3.5, 4.5, 6.3 are also used.

You can calculate the difference in the light passed at two apertures
with the formula:

$$\frac{(\text{First}\,f\text{-no.})^2}{(\text{Second}\,f\text{-no.})^2} = \text{light change}$$

So opening up the lens from $f/8$ to $f/4$, the image brightness increases by
four times. Stopping down from $f/4$ to $f/8$, the image brightness changes
to one-quarter. If, for instance, you wanted to increase the depth of field
in a shot, and stopped down to improve focused depth, light levels
(intensity) would need to be increased fourfold to compensate.

Working apertures

The highest grade lenses provide sharp pictures, even at their maximum
aperture (e.g. $f/1.7$). You may be working fully open because lighting is
insufficiently bright to stop down further, or because you want to isolate a
subject, using a shallow depth of field. But clarity (*definition, resolution*)
falls off discernibly towards the edges of the picture at large apertures.

Many lenses only produce optimum picture quality at around $f/5.6$ to
$f/8$. Although stopping down to small apertures (e.g. $f/16$) may make the
subject look sharper (greater depth of field), it does not provide maximum
lens definition.

Exposure

There is a lot of misunderstanding about 'correct exposure'. We might say that a picture is correctly exposed when the subject tones you are most interested in are reproduced convincingly.

As we saw in Chapter 3, the camera-tube can only respond accurately over a relatively restricted range of tones. Brighter areas will crush out above its upper limits; darker tones are lost below its lower limits. The trick is to adjust the lens aperture to suit the prevailing conditions, so that the tones you particularly want to see lie within these limits.

If you want to see more detail in the shadows you will need to open the lens aperture a little to increase exposure. But, of course, this will cause *all* the other tones in the picture to appear brighter, and the lightest might now pale-out badly, or even crush-out to a blank white.

Conversely, if you want to see better tonal gradation in a white dress you may need to reduce exposure by closing down to a slightly smaller stop. This will, however, cause *all* the other tones in the picture to appear darker, and the darkest might now merge, or even crush-out to black.

So exposure is an artistic compromise. But it is also a way in which you can manipulate the image. You might deliberately over- or underexpose the picture to achieve certain effects (e.g. stormy skies). It is quite possible to set the exposure to suit the prevailing light levels, and shoot everything in the scene with that stop. But for more sensitive adjustment of picture tones one really needs to be alert, and continually readjust the exposure (e.g. ± half a stop as camera angles change).

Over- or underexposure can cause visible defects in the picture (Figures 4.20 and 4.21). We'll discuss the subtleties of exposure adjustment in more detail in Chapter 23.

Automatic iris

Lightweight and portable cameras are usually fitted with an *auto-iris*. Switched in, this automatically adjusts the lens aperture to suit the prevailing light levels. At first sight, the auto-iris frees the cameraman from the chore of adjusting exposure for each shot. It is a particularly useful facility when you are very mobile; moving around quickly, concentrating on framing the shot, and not tripping down stairs or bumping into things. Shooting in a sunny exterior, the lens may need to be stopped down to e.g. $f/16$ for correct exposure. But go into a building where light levels are much lower, and the lens now needs to be opened up to perhaps $f/2$ for the camera-tube to receive sufficient light. The auto-iris will make this compensation automatically. Without it, you would have to continually check tonal gradation in the viewfinder picture, and open the iris until the new scene was correctly exposed.

Unfortunately, like any automatic set-up, the auto-iris system cannot make *artistic* judgements, and is easily fooled. Ideally, you want the exposure of your main subject to remain *constant*. But an auto-iris is activated by all other tones in the picture.

Fig. 4.20 Exposure curve
Ideally, as the camera scans various tones in the lens image, its video signal should vary correspondingly. Relative tonal values will then be reproduced accurately in the picture.

Darker tones will only produce a weak video signal; comparable with inherent background noise in the system. We see this noise reproduced as 'snow' or grain in dark areas of the picture.

If tones in the scene reflect more light than the camera tube can handle, the video strength will reach the system's upper limits, and block off to produce a blank white area in the picture.

To avoid the brightest tones clipping-off abruptly, circuitry can make the upper limit more gradual (soft), by introducing a *knee* in the exposure curve; as with photographic film. Highlights are then reproduced more realistically.

The camera tube's overall exposure range can be effectively increased, by beam-enhancement circuits (see Glossary – *Highlight overload*).

Fig. 4.21 Exposure

The camera tube can only reproduce a relatively limited range of tones accurately. This *contrast range* may be as little as 20:1. If scenic tones fall within this range, the *f*-stop can be adjusted to accommodate them. If subject tones or lighting contrast exceed the system's range, detail and tonal gradiation in the lightest and/or darkest areas will appear as solid white or black.

Opening the lens aperture, progressively (e.g. to *f*/2) improves shadow detail, but increasingly *overexposes* the lightest tones, which block off to white.

Reducing the lens aperture progressively (e.g. to *f*/16) improves detail in lightest tones, but increasingly *underexposes* darker tones, which merge to black.

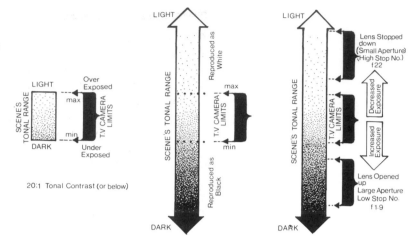

20:1 Tonal Contrast (or below)

- Move in front of a light background, or bring a newspaper into shot, or take off a jacket to reveal a white shirt, and the iris closes and reduces exposure. *All* picture tones now appear darker.
- If a large dark area comes into shot, the iris may open up 'to compensate', and all picture tones appear lighter.
- Walk through trees, where areas of sky and foliage come and go, and exposure can yo-yo up and down quite inappropriately.

Under certain conditions the auto-iris can cause bad underexposure – against a window; very light backgrounds; a shiny background with strong light reflections. Some cameras have a *backlight* control that opens up the lens an arbitrary stop or so above the auto setting, to improve subject exposure.

Summarizing, we can say that at best the auto-iris, like the auto-focus, can be a 'lifesaver'; but at worst the cure is worse than the disease, and results are very uneven. Exposure inaccuracies may be too small to notice; or in news gathering may be unimportant compared with getting clear shots.

Remote iris control

When a camera is connected to a *camera control unit (CCU)* or *remote control unit (RCU)* its lens aperture is usually set up during *camera line-up* to suit prevailing light conditions.

In the studio one aims at reasonably constant light levels (e.g. 1600 lux (150 fc)). During production, the lens aperture of each camera can be remotely controlled, either with coarse adjustment (several stops) or more usually with a fine control (e.g. ± half a stop) to vary exposure subtly for the best picture quality.

Neutral density filters

When the scene is too bright for the aperture you want to work at, a *neutral density filter* is used to cut down the overall intensity. These transparent gray-tinted (neutral) discs are usually fitted in a filter wheel behind the lens (see Glossary). Otherwise they must be clipped over the front of the lens, in a *filter holder*. Typical values range from 1/10 (10 per cent) to 1/100 (1 per cent) transmission. A 10 per cent filter will, for example, cut light down by nearly three stops (e.g. $f/5.6$ to $f/16$).

Neutral density (ND) filters may be used when shooting in very strong sunlight, to prevent overexposure or the need for unduly small apertures. Again, should you want to open up the lens of a particular camera to restrict focused depth for artistic reasons, while perhaps other cameras use smaller stops, a ND filter can be used to compensate exposure.

Camera-tube sensitivity

All TV cameras require a certain minimum general light level to produce clear, crisp pictures with good tonal gradation. The actual intensities needed depend on the camera-tube's inherent sensitivity, scenic tones, the atmospheric effect required, and suitable depth of field (hence the f-stop).

Camera-tube sensitivity varies with design and lineup. High tube sensitivity allows you to get satisfactory pictures under lower light conditions, when otherwise you would have to increase video gain (amplification) despite greater picture noise, to try to strengthen the dim underexposed shot.

In the studio, however, very dim lighting provides depressing and uncomfortable working conditions. Artistic lighting balance becomes difficult, as the eye cannot evaluate light values accurately, or detect extraneous shadows or spill light that are very evident on camera. Instead, when using high-sensitivity tubes we normally find ourselves lighting to comfortable intensities and stopping down or filtering to prevent overexposure.

Cameras are quoted as needing a certain incident-light level at a particular stop. But much depends on the scenic tones (mainly light or dark), light direction, video amplification, lens system, etc. Light levels (intensities) are measured in lux (lumens per square meter) or in foot-candles (lumens per square foot); 1 fc = 10.74 lux. Light levels are only an indication of camera sensitivity when related to the working aperture (f-stop).

Typical light levels required for modern camera systems are around $f/4$ at 805–2700 lux (75–250 fc).

The relative amount of light needed on the scene at various lens apertures (taking $f/4$ as unity) varies:

$f/1.4$	$f/2$	$f/2.8$	$f/3.5$	$f/4$	$f/4.5$	$f/5$	$f/5.6$	$f/6.3$	$f/8$
⅛	¼	½	¾	1	1¼	1½	2	2½	4

<-------------------   ------------------->

Less light   More light

Supporting the camera

Television/video cameras today range from units that can be held in one hand to substantial camera heads that require two persons to lift them onto their mountings.

While you can move anywhere with a *hand-held* camera, over uneven ground, climb stairs, in among a crowd . . . smooth subtle camerawork and rock-steady shots are not at all easy to maintain. Attach your camera to some form of *mounting*, and you have an extremely stable arrangement, allowing you sustained well-controlled camerawork for long periods – but without the mobility and convenience of a hand-held unit.

Obviously, if your camera is heavy you have no choice but to use a mounting.

Lightweight cameras

The smallest video cameras are so light that they can be held in one hand with a molded grip, while the other adjusts focus, zoom, and aperture controls on the lens barrel. The eyepiece held against an eye helps to steady the camera.

By bracing the camera in various ways you can hold it steadier than with the unassisted hands alone; but, wherever possible, a tripod or monopod is preferable.

Portable cameras

Portable cameras have three basic formats:

● Cameras formed from modular units that can be modified to suit different applications.
● Compact camera units weighing about 5 kg (10 lb) that are cabled to a nearby videotape recorder (in a shoulder pack, back pack, or cart).
● Self-contained camcorder units, which include their own VTR system.

These camera units can be shoulder-mounted. How successfully depends on the stamina of the operator. With experience, some camera-

Fig. 4.22 Camera stabilizers
To increase the stability of hand-held cameras:

1. Some form of shoulder-support/ shoulder-pod, brace or body harness may be worn.
2. In the *Steadicam* system, an elaborate spring-stabilized harness (S) is used to hold the camera steady, even during violent movement. A 4-inch electronic viewfinder (adjustable position) is fitted to the support arm (VF).

Fig. 4.23 Hand-held supports
Any camera shake causes the picture to weave and hop about, so it is essential to hold it as rigidly as possible. Grip your camera firmly (but not too tightly) with your eye against the eyepiece and both arms tucked well in. Various techniques help to steady the camera:

1. Stable body positions: (a) legs braced apart; (b) seated, elbow on knees; (c) kneeling; (d) ground support.
2. Nearby supports: (e) back to wall; (f) resting on low wall, fence, railings, car etc.; (g) leaning side against wall; (h) foot on step or box; (i) resting against post.
3. String or chain support (j) attached beneath camera, trapped under one foot and pulled upwards.
4. Monopod: (k) single-leg telescopic tube, or pole.

men can continue shooting for long periods, without pictures that lean to one side, waver, or droop. But arms can tire and backs ache after a while, and it is not easy to sustain high-grade camerawork, particularly when using narrower lens angles.

A U-shaped molded saddle beneath the camera holds it firmly on the shoulder while your right hand fits through the support loop on the zoom lens system. Fingers on this hand are free to operate the *power-zoom* switch (which auto-zooms in or out), and the *iris selection switch.*

The latter may have three positions:

● Manual adjustment,
● Auto-iris,
● Remote iris control.

Your right thumb can press the VTR pause switch and your left hand is free to adjust the *focusing ring* and the *lens aperture (f/stop) ring* on the lens barrel, and the *manual zoom* control lever.

A *body-brace* or *shoulder harness* can help to steady a shoulder-mounted camera. A typical arrangement has a metal prop which fastens beneath the camera and rests in a chest pad, or a belt-support. Some operators contend that body mounts of this sort are restrictive, and that 'breathing bounce' is difficult to avoid.

A simple lightweight adjustable tube, called a *monopod*, can screw to the base of a camera and provide a useful support. You can brace the monopod against your foot, knee, or leg to hold it more firmly. The camera can easily be turned or tilted, but take care to avoid sloping horizons.

A *stabilizing harness* such as the 'Steadicam' or 'Panaglide' stabilizes the camera under the most extreme conditions. An elaborate spring harness 'irons out' violent camera movements, and the operator can walk, run, climb stairs, jump, yet the camera's shot remains remarkably stable. Similarly, it can smooth out movement when shooting in a car, truck, boat, or aircraft. The operator can see the camera's pictures in a small electronic viewfinder attached to the harness. Near-magical results can be achieved at times that are unattainable with other mountings. But underneath it all there is still a vulnerable human operator, and extended work under these conditions can be very tiring.

The panning head (pan head, camera mounting head)

There are times when you can rest your lightweight camera on a handy wall to get rock-steady shots. But makeshift methods are limiting. There might not be a wall nearby! Even the lightest cameras produce smoother, more consistent results if they are fitted to a proper camera mounting or support.

If you simply bolted your camera onto a mounting it would be held firmly enough but quite unable to move around to follow the action. Instead you need a *panning head/camera mounting head*, which goes between the camera head and the top of the camera mounting. It firmly anchors the camera, yet allows it to be turned (*panned*) and tilted, or fixed at any required angle.

The regular method of fastening uses a wedge-shaped plate (*wedge mount/camera wedge*) attached to the underside of the camera head. This slides into a corresponding recessed plate on top of the *panning head*. (Lightweight cameras often use quick-release *wedge mounts*.)

Panning handles are attached to either side of the panning head for the camera operator to support and guide the camera. They may have a center-joint that allows them to be hinged to a convenient angle. (Zoom and focus controls are clipped to the panning handles.)

If the camera head moves around too easily it can be difficult to make smooth, even panning and tilting movements. So *drag* controls allow you to introduce a controlled amount of friction, to steady movements. They should never be overtightened to 'lock-off' the camera. If you want to prevent panning or tilting (e.g. when holding a superimposed graphic, or when leaving or storing the camera) use the separate *head locks*.

Balance adjustments ensure that the camera remains level when it is not being supported by the cameraman. Careful balancing is absolutely essential when you have large zoom lenses, prompting devices, camera lamps attached to the camera, or it will be front-heavy and difficult to operate. In some situations it might even overbalance the mounting!

Fig. 4.24 Camera mounting head (panning head, pan head)
This takes several different forms (*see Glossary*). Attached to the top of a camera mounting (e.g. a tripod), it allows the camera head to be tilted up and down on a central pivot, and turned on a central turntable. Controlled by an attached *panning handle (pan bar)*, friction (*drag*) can be introduced to improve handling. Further controls lock off the head, and adjust balance.

A wedge plate beneath the camera head fits into the quick-release housing on the mounting head.

Choosing the camera mounting

Most TV studios have a complement of two or three *pedestals* or *rolling tripods*, and directors tend to organize their productions to suit the regular mountings available. That is not as restrictive as it seems, because many shows do not require greater shot-flexibility than these mountings provide.

Even when a choice of camera mountings is available, the mechanics of a production can often determine which type you use. Large studio cameras need bigger, more robust mountings. These are inevitably heavier, and require more effort to move around. So a quick camera move might not be practicable. If you are shooting in a small room setting, or a crowded studio, space restrictions must limit your choice. Larger dollies must not only have more room to maneuver but may require more than one operator.

A lot depends on how flexible you need the mounting to be. Is the camera only shooting from a static viewpoint, or has it got to travel quickly, keeping up with a fast-moving subject? Do you need high or low shots? Has the camera to change its viewpoint quickly, to swoop or glide? Does it move around within the scene, round furniture, through door-ways, between trees . . . ? Perhaps you need a mounting that can be taken up and repositioned at a new viewpoint as quickly as possible.

As you will see, each type has its particular features. A point to bear in mind when assessing mountings is that when the camera head is fitted on the pan and tilt head its actual lens height can be some 30–45 cm (12–18 in) higher than their quoted heights.

Types of mounting

Monopod
Camera tripods
    Collapsible tripod
    Pneumatic tripod (Hydro-Ped; PortaPed)
    Rolling tripod/tripod dolly

Camera pedestals
    Lightweight/field pedestal
    Studio pedestal
      Counterweight type
      Pneumatic type

Camera cranes
    Crane-arm
    Lightweight crane
    Motorized dolly
    Large cranes

> *Special mountings*
>> *Low shots*
>>> Low tripod
>>> High hat
>>> Low-angle dolly/camera sled
>> *High shots*
>>> Camera clamp
>>> Hydraulic platforms
>>> SkyCam

Monopod

Although only suitable for the lightest cameras, the *monopod* can be a useful 'just-in-case' device to carry around. It consists of a collapsible metal tube of adjustable length which screws into a socket beneath the camera head. You can brace it against a knee, foot or leg to provide a firm camera support. No camera head is used; you simply swivel around to follow subjects. But remember not to tilt the support accidentally, or horizons will slope. You can carry the camera around with the monopod fitted ready to shoot, but of course it is not self-supporting.

Camera tripods

Collapsible tripod

The *tripod* is only suitable for fixed camera positions, but it does have advantages. It is simple, robust, and can be folded up into an easily transported pack. It can be used in situations where no other could go: on rough, uneven, overgrown surfaces, on staircases, in vehicles . . .

Basically, the tripod has three legs of independently adjustable length. They may be wooden or metal. These are spread apart to form a stable base for the camera. You can screw the camera onto the tripod's panning head and simply close the tripod legs together, when moving to a new position. Better still, use a quick-release *mounting plate* (*wedge*) which allows the camera to be detached in a moment.

Tripods can be preadjusted to various heights (e.g. 500 mm (20 in) to 1600 mm (63 in)) by altering the leg lengths. Some units have a central camera-support column, which can be hand-cranked to adjust height while off shot.

Tripods are a great help if they are used properly, but they are not foolproof. Here are some useful warnings:

● Don't use a flimsy lightweight tripod. It will be flexible and insecure for a video camera.
● Don't be tempted to use the tripod partly open, for it will over-balance! Always adjust camera height by altering leg-length, not by changing the spread.

Fig. 4.25 part 1   The tripod
A simple 3-legged stand with independently extensible legs. Height is preset. Unlike other mountings it can be set up on sloping or uneven ground.

A spider (spreader) may be used to prevent tripod feet slipping.

Fig. 4.25 part 2   Tripod limitations
When a tripod is positioned on a platform or balcony, it has to be set back some distance from the edge. As a result, its downward view is limited; particularly where there is a protective wall. If instead the camera head is fastened to a wall clamp fitting, it will have greater coverage.

Fig. 4.25 part 3   Camera clamps
The panning head may be clamped to a firm tubular-rail structure at a vantage point.

- At maximum height the tripod tends to be unstable. Bottom weighting (e.g. a bag of sand or stones slung under the center of the tripod) or ground-lashings (rope-fastening to a ground-spike) may be a wise precaution – particularly if the ground is sloping, or slippery.
- Don't leave your camera standing unattended on its tripod. People (or animals) may knock it over; a pulled cable may overbalance it.
- Tripods usually have two types of feet: retractable spikes for rough surfaces and rubber pads for smooth ground. (Take care not to use spikes on carpets, wooden floors, etc.!)
- On uneven ground (rocks, stairs) you can fix tripod legs at different lengths, so that the camera remains level as you pan. A level indicator (spirit-level) helps here.
- The feet of a tripod can be fitted onto a Y-shaped *spreader* or *spider* to prevent its feet from slipping. On soft ground, sand, or mud it is best to use a flat triangular wooden base.
- At maximum tripod heights you may have difficulty seeing into the viewfinder (have a step or box handy). Low-angle shots, too, can pose difficulties when following moving subjects.
- If you have a wide panning movement, stand with your body at a midway point, ready to twist from side to side. It may be easier to follow action in a nearby picture monitor than in the viewfinder.

Fig 4.26 Lightweight pneumatic tripod (Hydro-Ped, PortaPed)
A robust tripod mounting, widely used in ENG/EFP production.

Pneumatic tripod (Hydro-Ped; PortaPed)

Although quite portable (e.g. 13 kg (30 lb) in weight) the *pneumatic tripod* provides a very adaptable rigid support for cameras weighing up to e.g. 45 kg (100 lb), even when panning or tilting. It comprises two concentric columns, which can be locked at any point over their 48 cm (18 in) travel. It uses a pneumatic counterbalance system, in which the center column is pumped up and down, before locking off a valve.

The hinged legs at the lower end occupy little spread (40 cm (16 in)), so can be used in very confined spaces. The mounting remains balanced, even when one of the independently adjusted legs is up on a step or curb. It can be used with its legs turned out at right angles to the column (0.69–1.14 m (27–45 in) height), or in a tripod mode (0.94–1.4 m (37–55 in) height).

Although normally a fixed mounting, it can be fitted onto a *crabbing dolly* to provide a very flexible mobile mounting.

Rolling tripod/tripod dolly

This is basically a tripod on wheels. It can be very suitable for simpler studio operations, and its portability makes it extremely useful for remotes.

The tripod fits onto a detachable three-castered base (*skid*; *skate*), which can be folded for transportation. Although the dolly moves around quite easily on a flat level floor, uneven surfaces will judder the picture, especially when you use narrow lens angles. In practice, it is not always easy to control the dolly's direction accurately. It often helps to give the dolly a slight push beforehand, to align the casters in the appropriate direction. Otherwise the picture may jerk as you start to move.

Fig. 4.27 The rolling tripod/tripod dolly
The tripod can be mounted onto a castered base (skid/skate/rolling spider). Height is preset (pneumatic or hand-crank). Easily wheeled on a flat smooth floor (although steering may be imprecise). Caster foot-brakes, and cable guards may be fitted.

Caster Foot Brake

The casters can be left to move in any direction (freewheel), or locked to dolly in a straight line. Cable guards prevent the wheels overrunning floor cables. To hold the mounting immobile, you can either lock off each angled caster or wind down *screw-jacks* (taking care not to damage the floor surface).

In most designs it is necessary to reset the tripod leg lengths to change camera height, and this takes some time and effort.

Camera pedestals

The *pedestal* (*ped*) is the most widely used TV camera mounting. Fundamentally, it consists of a central column of adjustable height, fixed to a three-wheeled base which is guided by a steering wheel and/or a handle (tiller arm).

The rubber-tired wheels can be switched into either

- a *'crab'* mode in which all three wheels are interlinked to move together,
- or a *'steer'/'dolly'* mode where a single wheel steers while the other two remain passive.

Pedestal designs range from pre-set lightweight hydraulic columns on casters to heavyweight monstrosities that can need two people to move them. The ideal pedestal is stable, easy to move, and quickly controlled by one person.

Lightweight/field pedestal

Pedestals for use away from the studio need to be robust but compact, and preferably demountable. Simpler forms have hand-cranked column-height adjustment. (Height-changes are jerky, so have to be made off-shot.) The camera is steered around by its panning handles.

More sophisticated pedestal designs have pneumatically controlled height adjustment. Their height can be changed smoothly while on shot, and the mounting steered accurately by a central surround-ring.

Column and base may be separated for easier transportation. The camera height range is typically around 0.6 m (2 ft) to 1.5 m (5 ft). Where lightweight cameras are used in a studio they have proved very adaptable.

Studio pedestal

The cameraman using a *studio pedestal* needs stamina and dexterity. In a complex production he may need to zoom, focus, pan, tilt, change height, push, and guide simultaneously! So he has to be able to control movements easily and accurately. Shooting at his eye level, this can be a difficult feat. At maximum or minimum column height it becomes impracticable. Just occasionally he may need someone to push the pedestal while he handles the camera head.

Fig. 4.28 The studio pedestal

1. A surround wheel or ring at the top of the column is used to adjust column height (hence the lens height) and to steer the pedestal. A second ring may be tted, to lock-o the column.
2. The lens-height range is typically 1–2 cm (3–6 ft).
3. The camera can be moved around and repositioned in various ways.
4. The rubber-tired tricycle wheels can be steered in either of two ways (foot-pedal selection).
   Dolly (tricycle tracking) mode: single wheel steered, other two fixed. Used for general dolly moves and curved tracks (arcs).
   Crab (parallel) mode: all three wheels interlinked, steered simultaneously. Used for trucking – crabbing, sideways movements, moving into confined spaces.

When using a pedestal the camera height can be adjusted smoothly and precisely, even while on shot, and held firmly in position at heights from about 1–2 m (3–6 ft). A large ring steering wheel around the central telescopic column is used to raise/lower the camera, as well as guide dolly moves. There may be a subsidiary ring to lock off the column height.

The method of adjusting the column height of the pedestal varies. It may be hand-cranked, motor-driven, counterbalanced, hydraulic, or pneumatic. In practical terms the cameraman finds some types are slow to operate, erratic, heavy; others are smooth and easy, but require expert attention.

■ *Counterweight type*   In this widely used type of pedestal a series of traveling weights and springs counter the weight of the central column. These can be adjusted to compensate for the weight of different types of camera. The system is reliable and works smoothly – but the overall weight of the mounting is formidable, particularly when a large zoom lens and a prompter are fitted to the camera head. Fast dolly moves are impracticable. Because its height range is limited to about 1.2–2 m (4–6.5 ft) its productional use is restricted.

■ *Pneumatic type*   The *lightweight ped* is considerably lighter than the counterweighted form. It can be moved around quickly and smoothly, so it allows much more mobile camerawork. It uses compressed air (or an inert gas) from a small tank to control the height of the multiple central column. The mounting has a useful lens–height range – e.g. 1 to 2 m (3 to +6 ft).

One disadvantage of the pneumatic pedestal is that changes in camera weight (e.g. adding or removing a heavy prompter) can require the air-pressure to be readjusted ('re-gassing') by releasing or adding compressed air to the system.

Camera cranes

Crane-arm/boom-arm

The traditional *crane* mounting gives the director considerable freedom. He can move the camera around rapidly or imperceptibly slowly, while changing its viewpoint from near floor level to a high vantage point overlooking the action. But in smaller studios or on location standard cranes are not always practicable. Instead ingenious *crane-arms/ boom-arms* are increasingly used to provide craning action on a static mounting (e.g. 0.3–1.8 m (1–6 ft) with 360° arm turn).

Basically the system consists of a long counterweighted beam, mounted on a central pillar. This is supported on a tripod or pedestal base, or on a four-wheeled platform. In some designs the operator stands beside the camera; in others he controls it remotely, as he watches a picture monitor.

Crane mountings

In traditional camera cranes, the large arm (*jib*; *boom*) that supports the camera on its four-wheeled base can be raised/lowered with smooth precision, while the camera and panning-head remain level, irrespective of its angle.

Not only can the crane cover a greater height-range than the pedestal but it can overreach foreground obstacles. (The pedestal reaches an obstruction, and can go no further.) In many designs the camera, with cameraman, can rotate over a wide arc at any height. Some versions allow the boom to be slewed sideways for *tonguing* movements.

Cranes require two or three operators. The cameraman uses finger movements to coordinate assistants (*dolly operator, grips, pusher, tracker*) in pushing, steering, and elevating the mounting. An attached picture monitor helps them to follow shot development.

Cranes need a fair amount of floor space to move around. For mountings with solid-tired wheels, a level, even floor surface is essential to ensure smooth dollying – although this is less critical for pneumatically tired dollies. Special rails or tracks may be necessary on uneven ground.

The *crab dolly*, which is widely used in film making, can travel in any direction. In one form it has an hydraulically powered vertical column,

Fig. 4.29   The small crane
Lightweight versions of the small
crane are increasingly used.
1. Particularly for remotes, the height
   range (0.6–2 m, 2–7 ft) with
   360° seat and camera-mounting
   rotation offer improved shot flexibility
   (Vinten–'Kestrel').
2. A counterbalanced crane-arm
   attached to a pedestal, tripod, or
   wheeled base again provides a
   variety of viewpoints for portable
   and ENG cameras.

Fig. 4.30   Larger cranes
Heavy-duty cranes are normally used
where extensive camera viewpoint
changes, high-angle or swooping
shots are required for large-scale
action. Thanks to precision
counter-balancing, the boom can be
swung manually by a single operator
(guided by a picture monitor and
cameraman's finger-signals).

Fig. 4.31   Crane movements
Upward/downward movements of
the boom (crane arm, jib) are *craning,
booming, jibbing*. Swinging the
boom sideways is *tonguing left/right*.
Swinging the boom to/from action is
tonguing in/back. The base may be
steered, using a tracking line to/from
action (*dollying, tracking*), or across
the action (*trucking, crabbing*).

Fig. 4.32   Motorized dolly
A 2-man crane in which all operations
are motor-controlled, reducing
crewing requirements and operational
fatigue. Camera height 0.9–2.1 m
(3–7 ft).

but other versions have a motorized boom on which the camera operator
is seated.

Small *lightweight cranes* are useful both inside the studio and on
location, where a height range of 0.6–2 m (2–7 ft) is needed.

Motorized dolly

This type of crane, specially designed for TV studios, uses motorized
control throughout to reduce manual effort. The cameraman has foot
pedals for height control and camera-platform direction. The dolly
operator (*tracker*) on a rear platform controls the dolly's speed and
direction. The cameraman must take care not to depress the crane-arm
onto anything beneath its overhang, or to raise it beneath low overhanging scenery (ceilings, arches).

Larger cranes

These are normally only found in the largest studios, and may be
hired for a particular production. They range in size from the 'Mole'
crane/MPRC crane (Motion Picture Research Council), which covers
heights from e.g. 0.45 to 2.7 m (1½ to 9 ft) to the truck-mounted giants
with heights of 1–8.2 m (3½–27 ft).

Large cranes are unsurpassed in the productional opportunities they
provide in production numbers, large-area displays, and mass spectacle.
But because of the mounting's size, weight, and balance problems, its

three/four-person crew needs to be highly skilled and closely coordinated. The crane needs considerable floor space and ceiling height to maneuver safely, and the wise cameraman takes precautions, wearing a protective helmet and harness. He also needs total confidence in his crew . . . and a good head for heights!

Special mountings

There are situations where more traditional forms of camera mounting cannot get the shot you want. Then various other approaches may solve the problem.

Low shots

■ *Low tripod*   Short fixed tripods, which are considerably more stable than full-size versions, can be effective for many low shots.

■ *High hat*   Surprisingly versatile, the *high hat*, and its smaller *lo-boy* version, can be useful if you need a very low viewpoint. The camera fits onto a short cylindrical base, which is bolted or screwed onto any firm foundation – a platform, a rolling tripod base, or a heavy-duty lighting stand.

■ *Low-angle dolly (sled; creeper)*   Here the cameraman sits on a very low wheeled base, which is pushed by a second operator. The camera may be fitted to a high hat (fixed height) or a short crane-arm (rising from e.g. 0.5 to 1.1 m (1½ to 3½ ft).

■ *Alternative methods*   You can also get low-angle shots by shooting into a low mirror, or using a mirror periscope attached to a pedestal mounting.

High shots

In the studio you might be able to get suitable high-angled shots by shooting up into an overhead mirror, or using a crane at full elevation. But on location the scale of operations changes.

■ *Camera clamp*   If your camera is to be located on a balcony a camera frame/camera tower or some similar structure, the obvious mounting to use is a firmly based tripod. However, there is a major drawback. The camera's vertical field is very limited. It cannot tilt down past the edge of the structure (Figure 4.25 part 2).

Instead, it may be better to fasten its panning head to a tubular steel scaffold framework, with a *camera clamp (scaffold clamp)*. Wire safety bonds ensure that nothing is going to fall down onto unsuspecting passers-by.

Fig. 4.33   Low angle dolly ('sled')
Gives height-mobility for low-angle shots, together with considerable maneuverability.

Fig. 4.34 Hydraulic platform
Considerable platform-height
variation is possible (even while on
shot), giving a high stable viewpoint.

■ *Hydraulic platform (cherry-picker; Simon crane)*   If you need really high shots on location this hired facility can provide staggering viewpoints. It comprises a truck-mounted hydraulic lifting platform, which can raise the camera from 1.8 to 26 m (6 to 85 ft) above the ground. It can also be used to position microwave dishes (radio links) for remote telecasts or ENG work.

If you want to go higher than 26 m you need the services of a helicopter (or a blimp) – with a special camera-stabilizing device to avoid rhythmic vibration.

■ *SkyCam*   This specialized facility has been used successfully over sports fields to provide a 'flying camera'. The remotely controlled camera (which is gyro-balanced) is suspended in the center of an X-pattern of overhead cables. Independent computer-controlled winches simultaneously adjust cable lengths, to rapidly reposition the camera at rates up to 43 kph (27 mph) anywhere over the action area. The camera's wide-ranging aerial views can go from zoomed-out vista shots to zoomed-in detail.

Remotely controlled cameras

Where a production is semi-static (e.g. newscasts, small announce studios, or unmanned reporting studios) the entire studio system can be remotely controlled. Cameras, sound, lights, chroma-key backgrounds, equipment switching, cuing can all be selected and adjusted from a nearby control room, or from a master control room several miles away.

Cameras can be operated directly by desktop joystick controls. Having selected the shots, all information, including pan, tilt, zoom, focus, lens aperture, pedestal height, can be stored for later keyboard selection. Detailed variations of up to 100 shots can be called up from memory.

Table 4.4 Camera and camcorder

This list is a summary of design features and facilities to be found on various types of television/video cameras and camcorders. (*Operational controls)

Zoom lens

● *Focusing**   Maximum sharpness in chosen subject.
  Manual adjustment: Direct (on lens barrel)
                     Cable control (on panning handle)
                     Servo control (on panning handle)
  Auto-focus: Auto-override of manual
  Manual adjustment: Adjustable auto-focus zones
● *Lens aperture (iris)**   Exposure and depth of field control.
  Manual adjustment: Direct (on lens barrel)
                     Remote (servo control at vision control position)
  Auto-iris: Auto-adjusts exposure
                     Backlight override (compensates for false readings due to
                     bright areas)
● *Zoom action**   Alters focal length/lens angle.
  Manual zoom (hand-adjusted lens angle)
  Motorized zoom (switch to zoom in/out)
  Adjustable auto-zoom speed (shot box)
  Switchable zoom positions (shot box)

- *Range extender** Alters zoom coverage.
- *Macro setting** Non-zoom position for very close shots.
- *Fade-out/fade-in facility** Slowly closes lens aperture to 'blackout'. Auto or manual. May be coupled with audio fade.
- *Lens hood (sunshade)* Shades lens from backlight to prevent lens flares.
- *Filter thread* Allows filters or supplementary lenses to be attached to the main lens.
- *Lens mount adapter* Enables alternative lens systems to replace zoom.

*Filter wheel**	Selectable positions: clear, cap-up, neutral density, color correction, effects filters.
Beam splitter	Splits lens image into RGB versions. Prism block or dichroic mirror system.
Imaging device	Converts lens image into video signal. Camera tube (pick-up tube) or image sensor – charge-coupled device.
*Video amplification**	Compensates for low video signal from camera tube. Video gain selection – e.g. 0 dB, 6 dB, 12 dB.

Viewfinder

- *Open monochrome picture tube*, e.g. 115–177 mm (4.5–4.7 in) diagonal. Adjustable position. Light-hood attached. (Color picture tube rarely used, as definition is inferior to black and white tubes.)
or
- *Eyepiece monochrome viewfinder*, e.g. 1½ in. Magnified screen viewed through adjustable eyepiece; eyesight compensation (diopter).
- *Viewfinder adjustments* Brightness, contrast, high peaker (crispening viewfinder detail to aid focusing).
- *Viewfinder indicators* (See *Indicators*) Show selections. Give warning of equipment settings. Display information on set-up/line-up.
- *Viewfinder switching** The V/F can provide various different displays: Show the camera's picture (video output). Show replay picture from VTR. Show other picture sources superimposed on the camera's shot (mixed feeds), e.g. to align mutual graphics. Superimpose the video waveform (or 'zebra-striped pattern') on V/F picture, to show video level/exposure. Display titling from a built-in character generator. Time and date display. Display technical signals for channel adjustment (color bars, tonal sawtooth, auto-white balance, diascope chart). Viewfinder pre-heat switch (warms V/F tube for rapid switch-on).

Camera support

- Hand support (on hand-held cameras).
- Molded shoulder support ('shoulder pod').
- Tripod socket.
- Quick-release adapter plate.
- Accessory shoe: supports small lamp on top of camera (camera light/video light).
- Microphone support bracket.

Program sound

- Attached microphone – rifle mike, with wind shield.
- External microphone socket – for separate microphone.
- Earphone sound monitor jack (to check program audio from mike).
- Face in/fade out – synchronized with lens iris.

Intercom

- Base call – cameraman calls base station to talk on private wire.
- Intercom jack sockets for headset or earpiece.
- Parallel jack sockets – additional intercom output; e.g. for person operating separate VTR.

Cables

- Camera cable to VTR, CCU or base station, **or**
- Video/audio output lead to portable VTR.
- Power cable.
- Radio link to base station.

Power supply

- Portable cameras: 12 V DC.
- Studio cameras: 100/117/220/240 V AC, 60/50 Hz.
- Power on/off* (battery saver auto switch-off if camera is not used for some time).
- Internal battery.
- Clip-on battery pack.
- Battery belt.
- External supply: car battery; AC adapter (household mains).

*Pre-set adjustments**

- Gamma correction. Contrast control. Adjust tonal gradation subtle to coarse. May be fitted as an auto-contrast control, adjusting gamma for better highlight/shadow clarity.
- White balance. Auto or manual. Adapts camera to prevailing light color quality (color temperature).
- Black balance. Auto or manual. Balances system for purity of black.
- Automatic beam optimizer (ABO). Reduces comet-tail or puddling effects on highlights/specular reflections.
- Auto black set. Adjusts darkest tones reproducing as black.
- Auto centering. Auto registration correction. Ensures RGB images accurately registered.
- Auto set-up. Automatic checks and realignment of camera circuits.
- Flare correcting. Reduces effect of internal lens flare.

Indicators

In viewfinder or LCD display on body of camera:

- Tally light (on-air indicator). On top of camera; in viewfinder.
- Manual focus indicator. Shows when the lens image is sharply focused.
- Manual iris/aperture indicator. Shows *f*-stop selected.
- Low light warning when light level is insufficient for full video.
- Backlight compensation switch.
- White balance setting. Adjusts to daylight or artificial light.
- Shutter speed selection. Normally 1/60 (1/50) second. High-speed shutter setting (e.g. 1/1000, 1/1500, or 1/200 second) for improved detail in fast-moving subjects.
- Intercom call light. Base station wishes to contact cameraman.
- Superimpose video waveform (see *Viewfinder*).
- Automatic fault diagnosis. Warnings of circuit performance inaccuracies.
- VTR indicator/warning lights:
  Humidity warning (excess condensation)
  No cassette inserted warning
  Videorecorder on
  Tape position counter
  Running time
  Time remaining
  Tape speed (standard or long play)
  End of tape warning
  Dirty video head warning
  Cassette protected warning (tag has been removed, so cassette cannot be used for recording)
  Erase facility: wipe previous recording
  Battery low warning
  Time and date indication

Additional facilities
- Built-in character generator: set time and date display: lap time counter.
- Superimposed titles facility.
- External character generator input.
- Negative/positive picture reversal (for special effects).
- Auto iris closure on switch-off (to protect pick-up tube).
- Interface adapter:
  Provides camera output in various forms – composite with syncs; separate RGB; separate luminance and chrominance.
  Adjusts to various formats (1 in, U-Matic, VHS).
- Genlock (to synchronize a group of cameras).
- Built-in test pulse circuits, color bar generator.
- Lens error correcting circuits – for registration variations during zooming/focusing.
- Horizontal and vertical scan reversal – to mirro the shot.
- Chroma key signal output.

VTR controls
- On/off button (e.g. on handgrip).
- Record/replay selection.
- Assemble editing (add new shot to end of last take).
- Insert editing (add new shot within recorded material).
- Cassette eject.
- Replay (standard and long play).
- Tape counter reset.
- Tape cue (tape-search for marked cue-point).
- Review (replay last seconds of recorded tape, to check continuity).
- Single frame advance on replay.
- Audio dub – soundtrack replacement.
- Audio and video inputs (allow external sources to be taped/dubbed onto VTR).

5 Handling your camera

From the basic principles of the camera we now turn to the *operational techniques* behind good camerawork.

Studio working conditions

Productions vary considerably in their complexity. Some follow a familiar routine, with cameras taking standard shots from limited viewpoints. In other shows, cameras are very mobile, and follow complicated action. They can require the skilled, highly controlled camerawork that only comes with experience.

Each camera operator is on his own, having to find a way round his particular problems; yet at the same time, he is part of a crew, working together to achieve a coordinated result. In some shows you can help the director by 'offering up shots'; while in others this would be a distraction from a planned treatment. You cannot know what shots other cameras have.

If the production has been planned in meticulous detail the camera-man's role may be to reproduce exactly what the director drew in *storyboard* sketches weeks before. On the other hand, the entire show may be 'off-the-cuff' with the director relying on the camera crew to find the best shots of the action.

Although a senior member of the camera crew may be briefed about the project beforehand, camera operators usually only discover their role on the day, during the actual studio rehearsal. Each camera is issued with a *shot sheet/camera card* showing its main positions and shots throughout the show. From then on, the camera crew relies on intercom instructions during camera rehearsal, to guide their camerawork. During breaks, the director may discuss particular shot problems.

Preparing for rehearsals

You could simply move your camera into the opening position, focus up, and wait for intercom instructions. But don't be caught out! Check over your camera and its mounting beforehand – especially if someone else was using it earlier. In the checkout list you will find the main points you should look at. It takes very little time, and soon becomes a rapid routine.

Pre-rehearsal checkout list

1. Preliminaries
Camera switched on, warmed up, and set up (lined up)?

2. Camera cable
Are the cable plugs at the camera and wall (or equipment) sockets tight?
Is the cable firmly secured to the *camera mounting*? (Don't leave the cable just hanging free from the outlet on the camera head, or when you dolly, it will pull on the head outlet.)
Is there sufficient cable for the camera moves?
Is it suitably routed, and free to move around (e.g. not trapped under scenery)?

3. Camera-head
Is the camera-head firmly attached to the panning head?
Are the *panning handles/pan-bars* firmly attached, and at a comfortable angle?
Unlock the *tilt-lock* and check the camera-head *balance*. Is it nose or back heavy, and needing adjustment?
Check and adjust *vertical drag/tilt friction*.
Unlock the *pan-lock* and check if panning is smooth, with just sufficient resistance. Adjust *horizontal drag/pan friction* if necessary.

4. Mounting
Rolling tripod
Check the tripod's height, fixing, base fittings (brakes, caster movement).

Pedestal
Unlock the column, raise/lower it slowly. Is its movement smooth and easy?
Check that the column does not drift up or down. If it does, it requires re-balancing. (Likely if prompter has been added or taken off since last used.)

5. Steering
Check freedom of movement in all directions.
Check dolly (track) and truck (crab) modes.

6. Cable guards
Adjust cable guards to prevent the dolly from overrunning floor cables (lighting, sound, camera), but avoid guards scraping the floor.

7. Lens cap
Remove the cap from the front of the lens (*lens cap*).
Switch electrical capping out (this may be on the CCU).
Is the lens clean? If not used a compressed-air can, lens brush, or lens-cleaning tissue.

8. Viewfinder
Check focus, brightness, contrast, picture shape (aspect ratio), edge cut-off (you must be able to see right to the edge of the picture frame).
Adjust image sharpening (crispening) for maximum definition.
Are the indicators around the viewfinder working?
Are tally light and indicator cue-lamps OK?
Check mixed viewfinder feeds.

9. Focus
Check the smoothness of focusing action from close-up to the far distance (infinity).
In a servo system, does the focus control tend to overrun or hunt (rhythmical changes)?
Check focus when fully zoomed in, and when zoomed out.
Pre-focus on a distant subject; slowly zoom out checking that focus does not wander (i.e. tracking is correct).

10. The *f*-stop/lens aperture
Check the *f*-stop you will be working at. This lens aperture has been set during camera set-up/line-up to suit standard lighting levels, e.g. 1600 lux (150 fc).

11. Zoom
Is the zoom action smooth throughout the range?
Check any zoom extender lens.
Check any zoom meter or indicator.
Check the *shot box*, and adjust it to the pre-set angles you will be using.

12. Intercom/talkback
Check all intercom circuits (general/production intercom and private-wire circuits) and associated indicators.
Is your headset *one earpiece* (intercom only) or *two earphones* (separate intercom and program sound) OK?
Is the switched intercom to the video engineers/shader/vision control working?

13. Filters
Check the filter wheel, making sure that one is not accidentally left in position.

14. Lock off and cap up
Lock off panning-head and cap up.

15. Prompter
If a prompter is fitted, check that it is secure, connections and cables OK.

16. Shot sheet/camera card
Read through, check camera positions in the studio sets, and clip the card to the camera.

Fig. 5.1 Preliminary camera check
Make it a regular routine to check out your camera before rehearsal.

A   Is it switched on, warmed up, and setup (lined-up)?
B   Cable connections OK at the camera and wall outlets?
C   Camera head security and balance OK?
     Check the panning head (adjust drag).
D   *On a pedestal mounting*, check the vertical column movement.
     On a tripod/rolling tripod, check leg securing screws. Check height/level.
E   Steering OK?
F   Try out both the dolly and truck steering modes.
G   Check that cable guards are not set *too high* (or camera will overrun small
     cables), or *too low* (scraping the floor).
     On *rolling tripods*, check caster brakes, caster movement.
H   Remove lens cap. Is the lens clean?
I   What is the working lens aperture? Are any filters in position?
J   Is the viewfinder correctly adjusted and working efficiently? Check all
     indicators.
K   *Focus*. Check overall focus, and that focus does not vary while zooming.
L   *Zoom*. Check the zoom action throughout its range, and any extender lens.
     Set up the shot box.
M   Intercom, program feeds etc., OK?

During studio rehearsal

Relaxed yet alert

Of course, there are no 'rules' for effective camera operation. But there
are approaches that make life a lot easier, and produce more consistent
results. Other people have found out the hard way, so why not benefit
from it?

You can tell inexperienced camera operators at a glance; standing
poised rigid and tense, eyes glued to the viewfinder, gripping controls
tightly . . . Relax! The best posture is an alert, watchful readiness; very
aware of what is going on around. Not so relaxed as to be casual, but
continually waiting to react.

● In a multi-camera show you need to keep a watchful eye on the *tally
   light* on top of your camera (repeated as a viewfinder indicator). It
   shows that *your* camera has been selected on the production switcher.
   You are 'on-air'. When the light is out, you can move to new positions,
   adjust zooming or focus, check composition, and so on. But do not get

Fig. 5.2 During rehearsal
During rehearsal, make regular checks on:

1. The tally light. It shows whether your camera is on-air.
2. Aim to be relaxed, comfortable yet alert.
3. Be ready for your next shot. When off shot, don't let the camera tilt up onto lights or the sun, and avoid strong specular reflections.
4. Check the viewfinder performance, indicator lights, call-lights, etc.
5. Check your present working lens angle. (It directly affects camera operations.)
6. Check your shot (focus accuracy, depth of field, composition, etc.). *Pre-focus* the zoom.
7. Check for unwanted effects in the shot (e.g. shooting off, lens flares, camera or boom shadows, etc.).
8. Action. Watch the action, to anticipate the need to reframe the shot, refocus, follow action, etc.
9. Be ready to help dolly movements.
10. Continually check intercom (and program sound).
11. Check your shot sheet for moves and camera positions.
12. Is the camera cable free and sufficient for all camera moves?
13. Are there any obstacles that will impede camera moves, or get in the way of the next shot?
14. If any problems develop while the show is on-air, seek help (e.g. tell the FM, call the shader/vision operator), but try not to miss shots.

caught out. Do not move off shot (*clear*) until your tally light goes off. It is useful to check other cameras' lights, when moving around, to ensure that you are not going to get into their shots.

● Is your viewfinder at a comfortable angle, easy to see, and not diluted with spill light? Its tonal adjustment can be critical, to give optimum detail in both the shadows and lightest tones.

● Make it a habit to note the *lens angle (focal length)* at which your lens is set at any time. This helps you to anticipate handling and depth of field problems.

● Another good habit is to *pre-focus* your lens whenever you move to a new position (i.e. zoom right in, focus sharply, zoom out to your present shot). You will then be ready to zoom in from a wide shot to closer detail.

● For most shots, the lens should be around the talent's eye-level – unless the director wants higher or lower angles for some reason. If the camera is slightly lower, at chest height, this tends to give the talent a more imposing look (but they may look down slightly, and develop shadowed eye sockets). A higher camera improves lighting, as the person looks upwards, but they are more likely to be dazzled by lights if they are using a prompter attached to the camera. Items on tables or the floor are usually shot from a height of about 1.2–1.8 m (4–5 ft).

● Continually check your shot sheet/camera card, and be ready to move to your next position once each shot is completed; then prepare for the next shot.

● When you want to match with another camera's picture you will usually switch to *mixed viewfinder feeds*, which shows both shots superimposed. But there are occasions when a *color* floor monitor in the studio can be used instead to check and match the headroom and height of other cameras's shots, and to line up elaborate combined shots (e.g. when using *chroma key*).

● Listen to all intercom/production-talkback instructions, including those for other cameras. Where there is no intercom circuit, or you cannot speak to the director (e.g. when on-air), you may use visual signals such as: '*Yes*' (tilt up and down); '*No*' (pan left and right); '*I've a problem*' (pan/tilt round in circles); '*I've focus problems*' (rapidly rock focus); '*I need to speak on the private wire*' (quick in/out zooms).

● You will meet problems during rehearsal that only the director can solve, by making changes or reorganizing camera treatment. These include such situations as: one subject masking (obscuring) another, insufficient time for dolly moves, compositional problems, focusing difficulties, etc. Let him know, for it may mean stopping rehearsal to work things out. Don't assume that it will be alright next time. It may be worse!

● Be on the lookout for strong specular reflections that may damage the camera-tube, can cause picture defects, and will certainly distract.

● *Occasionally*, an experienced cameraman can help the director by suggesting slight changes in the camera treatment that would improve a sequence, or simplify a complicated situation. What is obvious on the floor may not be evident on monitors in the production control room. But avoid appearing to 'subdirect' the show!

● Sometimes, when there is a difficulty during rehearsal, it can help the director if a neighboring camera turns to give a wide shot of the situation. For example, it might reveal that the on-air dolly is backed against a wall, with no further room to move.

● Avoid the temptation to find odd shots for your own amusement, or 'hint shots' of the studio clock when a break is due.

● Be calm. If you are late on shot, try not to lose it altogether. Do not lose the next! If you misjudge, then try to correct the fault as un-obtrusively as possible.

● Things go wrong during a busy production. What you have to decide quickly is whether:

You can ignore the problem – because you are on-shot, or have a shot coming up, or others know about it and will deal with it.

It would be helpful to inform others (e.g. about a lamp knocked out of position by moving scenery).

You should use your intiative, take immediate action to help.

In most cases the floor manager and his assistants are your on-the-spot contacts. Teamwork is the essence of good production.

Standard shots

A director could explain exactly what he wants to see in a picture by giving the cameraman a mass of detailed instructions. But it is a lot quicker and convenient if, instead, everyone refers to a series of 'standard shots' that immediately pinpoint the required treatment.

Shots of *people* are universally agreed – although unfortunately terms vary (Figure 5.3).

Where there are groups of people, or other subjects, we broadly classify the *length of shot* or *size of shot* according to its *effect*; how much of the screen subject fills – how close it appears to be.

1. *Long shot* or *full shot* is a general, unspecific term for a distant view.
2. *Wide shot* or *cover shot* is a broad view taking in all the action.
3. *Close shot* or *tight shot* is a detailed view, often excluding other subjects nearby.
4. Shooting groups of people, we have the general terms: *single shot, two-shot, three-shot, group shot*, as a guide.

Exactly how you get the shot does not affect the term used. You might, for instance, take a *close shot* on a nearby camera with a wide-angle lens, or with a distant camera on a narrow-angle (long-focus) lens. There will be differences, of course, in perspective, distortion, camera handling, depending on which method you use (but the depth of field will remain the same).

Fig. 5.3 Shots of people
Shots are classified by the amount of a person taken in:

ECU Extreme close-up (detail shot) – isolated detail.
VCU Very close-up (face shot) – from mid-forehead to above chin.
BCU Big close-up (tight CU, full head) – full head height nearly fills screen.
CU Close-up – just above head to upper chest (cuts below neck tie knot).
MCU Medium close-up (bust shot, chest shot) – cuts body at lower chest (breast-pocket, armpit).
MS Medium shot (mid-shot, close medium shot, CMS, waist shot) – cuts body just below waist.
KNEE Knee shot, three-quarter length shot – cuts just below knees.
MLS Medium long-shot (full-length shot, FLS) – entire body plus short distance above/below.
LS Long shot – person occupies ¾ to ⅓ screen height.
ELS Extra long shot (XLS), extreme LS.

Remembering the shot

Most shots or sequences are rehearsed before being recorded. Ideally, during taping you want your shots to be an identical polished version of the rehearsal. There are three ways of ensuring this:

- Look around the shot carefully, and see what is just visible at the edges of the frame.
- Make a note, on a shot sheet/camera card attached to the camera, of shot details (e.g. '*25°; avoid doorway as she enters*'). If you are not given shot sheets, keep your own notes during rehearsal, on a card clipped to the camera. Don't rely on your memory alone.
- For the main camera viewpoints, make a clear but unobtrusive floor mark showing the exact position of one corner of the ped or dolly. Chalk or crayon may be suitable; but no form of permanent marker. (Masking tape or plastic tape is only acceptable *if* it is peeled off afterwards.)

Checking the shot

- Once a shot is established, a quick glance away to the overall scene can warn you of potential problems: e.g. that you are nearly shooting off the setting; that a lamp or another camera will come into shot if you pan right. It will let you know that someone is about to move into the shot, and that you may need to recompose the picture to include them.
- Only lock off the head during breaks, or when pushing the pedestal to a new position, or when shooting titles and graphics on *floor stands*.
- Check your viewfinder picture to see if something is about to move out of shot, or is going to be partly cut off by the edge of the picture.
- Check the composition of your shot (framing, headroom, offset-framing, etc.), subtly correcting for changes that develop (e.g. people moving to different positions in the shot). We shall discuss *composition* in detail in Chapter 7.
- Keep a look-out for the unexpected, such as scenic lines 'growing out' of subjects (Figure 17.23). Are microphones, cameras, lamps, or their shadows just appearing in shot? You can often re-frame the shot slightly to avoid them.

Camera operation

Focusing

Focusing is not always as straightforward as it looks. When the subject has well-defined patterns you can easily detect maximum sharpness – *hard focus*. But with less-defined subjects you may *rock focus* either side of the optimum, and somehow, they still look *soft-focus*.

- The *exact point* at which you focus can matter. As you'll remember, there is more focused depth beyond the actual focused plane than there

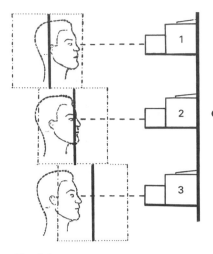

Fig. 5.4 Incorrect focusing
When *accurately focused* (2), the most important part of the subject is sharpest. Even in closer shots the subject can move to some extent, and remain clearly focused (i.e. within the available depth of field).

If you focus beyond the correct distance (i.e. *focused back* (1)), close subjects moving towards the camera are liable to go out of focus.

If you focus nearer than the correct distance (i.e. *focused forward* (3)), close subjects moving away from the camera are liable to go out of focus.

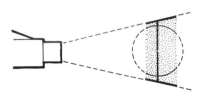

Fig. 5.5 Restricted focus
In close shots, the depth of field may be so restricted, that only parts of the subject are sharply focused.

Fig. 5.6 Throwing and pulling focus
As a dramatic effect, you can deliberately refocus while on shot: from a nearby subject to a more distant one (*throw focus*), or from a distant subject to a nearby one (*pull focus*).

is in front of it. So in closer shots there can be advantages in focusing a little forward of the true focusing point (nearer the camera), to allow for subject movement (Figure 5.4). If you are focused too far back (away from the camera), the problem worsens. When shooting people, the eyes or the necktie are favorite focusing points. Hair-lines can be misleading – especially on thinning hair.

● Many focus controls are quite 'coarse', and the slightest readjustment produces obvious changes. This is great when you need to change focus rapidly (*throw focus/pull focus*); but subtle focus-following can be difficult, and is liable to appear jerky. A control which has 'fine' adjustment needs to turn quite a lot before focus changes are obvious in the picture; so you may have problems keeping up with fast moves to and from the camera. If it takes two to three turns of the control to change focus from *MFD* (minimum focusing distance) to infinity, you may find that you need to readjust your grip midway! Some systems provide coarse/fine selection on the focus control.

● Depth of field is continually changing, as you focus at different distances, select different lens angles, or zoom in or out. This is something you quickly become accustomed to, but it can't be ignored. Focusing is simple in longer shots, but the closer the subject, the greater the focusing problems. You shoot two people speaking, yet can only get a sharp image of one of them at a time. In very large close-ups, focusing can be so critical that only *part of a subject* is sharp, while the rest is completely defocused. In Figure 5.7 are regular solutions to this dilemma.

Moving people

● Watching people in your shot closely, you can anticipate whether they are just about to adjust their position, get up (rise), or move . . . and this alerts you to pan and tilt to follow the action.

● Whenever anyone starts to move, the director has to make a decision that will affect what you do. If people are 'breaking' (moving apart) you need to know how to treat the action.

○ Are they going to remain within the frame? If you are in a long shot there may be room for them. Otherwise you may need to zoom out. If so, how far? Probably just enough to include them.

○ If someone is going to move out of the frame (i.e. you will 'lose them'), you may need to gently re-compose the shot to balance the picture. Perhaps the director is cutting to another camera at that point, and you simply get to your next shot.

Fig. 5.7 The problem of limited depth of field
Where depth of field proves too *limited* (1), the solutions are:

2. *Stop down* – depth of field increases, but higher light intensity necessary.
3. *Focus on one subject* – permitting other(s) to soften.
4. *Split focus* – spread available depth between both subjects (both are now softer than optimum).
5. *Move subjects closer together* – making subjects more equidistant from camera.
6. *Use wider lens angle* – depth of field increases but subjects now appear smaller. (Moving closer for larger image, re-introduces limited depth.)
7. *Pull camera back* – depth increases but shot is smaller.

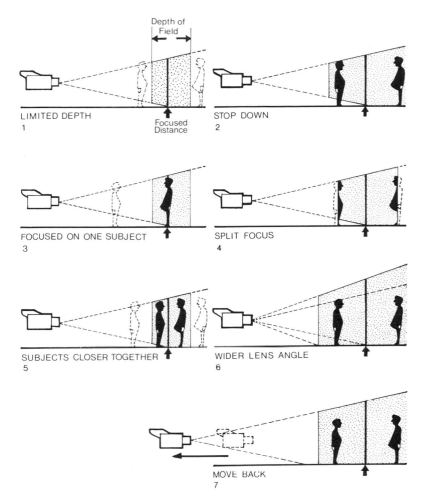

○ Are you going to follow the person? By panning to watch them leaving? Panning and zooming in? Dollying after them? Dollying along with them? Each method has its own audience impact.

● If you are on shot, and then someone moves into frame, is there room for them, or do you need to widen the shot a little (pull back or zoom out)? Avoid overwidening then having to correct.

● When people move towards the camera be prepared to follow focus. The closer they are, the quicker you need to refocus. If they are moving diagonally towards you, you'll need to adjust focus and pan simultaneously.

● If you are panning with a moving subject do not keep it in the center of the frame. Instead, offset it so that it lags behind center-frame. This offset should be greater, the faster the subject. (The offset distance is often called 'looking-room', 'nose-room', or 'lead-room'.)

● Although you can rely on most actors to repeat the moves they made during rehearsal, and to 'hit their marks' every time, never assume this – especially with inexperienced talent. You may need to slightly readjust your previous position or lens angle to get the same shot.

Camera moves

● Whenever you are going to move your camera there are a number of preliminaries. First of all, check your route for obstructions and people. In most studios there are floor cables, scenery, floor lamps, sound booms, picture monitors, loudspeakers, and other cameras to be avoided! Your camera mounting can only run smoothly over the studio floor, so avoid dollying over floor cloths or rugs. During the move, take care not to displace furniture, parts of the set, floor lamps. All very obvious, but in a quick move backwards during a fast-moving show you can overlook the obvious.

● If you are simply moving the mounting *to get to another position* lock off the camera head – preferably pointing slightly downwards, so as not to point it into lights. Then dolly as quietly as possible, causing minimum cable drag noise across the floor. Silence may be more important than speed! Rather than try to pull the stretched cable after you, ensure that you have sufficient slack beforehand (or get help in manhandling it while you dolly). Never pull a cable which has a tight loop in it. You'll damage it.

Fig. 5.8　Checking you camera's angle

1. *To find the angle of your lens.* Place two small objects on a crossline 3 m (10 ft) away, moving them so that they just appear within the left-right frame edges. Measure how far apart they are and check in the table the angle that covers this width.
2. *To set the shot-box to a particular lens-angle.* Look up the *required angle* in the table and find the screen-width it takes in at 3 m (10 ft) away, place them this distance apart (e.g. for 30° they must be 1.61 m (5 ft 5 in) apart). Adjust your lens to just take in the objects at the frame edges, and it is now at the required angle. Adjust shot-box preset, or note zoom setting. You could make up a regular zoom-lens line-up graphic for adjusting all lens angles at this distance.

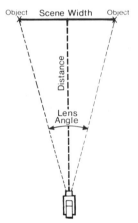

Lens Angle	Width at 3m Distance	Width at 10ft Distance
5° —	0.26 m	10 in
10° —	0.53 m	1 ft 9 in
15° —	0.79 m	2 ft 7 in
20° —	1.06 m	3 ft 6 in
25° —	1.33 m	4 ft 5 in
30° —	1.61 m	5 ft 5 in
35° —	1.89 m	6 ft 4 in
40° —	2.18 m	7 ft 4 in
45° —	2.49 m	8 ft 4 in
50° —	2.80 m	9 ft 4 in
55° —	3.12 m	10 ft 5 in
60° —	3.46 m	11 ft 7 in

● If you are going to change position *to follow a moving subject,* check out the route and cable as before. But now you leave the camera head free. With one hand on the steering ring, and the other on the focus control, push firmly in the appropriate direction. You can push two-handled lightweight tripods by the panning handles for simple moves over short distances.

● If you are using a *rolling tripod,* remember the preliminary push that aligns the wheels. On a *pedestal* you will have selected the dolly (steer/track) mode for the wheels, or the truck (crab) mode. The dolly mode offers precise steering for straight-line moves. The truck mode is best for moving in confined spaces, changing directions, traveling sideways. Cameramen develop their own preferences.

- Start dollying with gentle pressure, and have your foot ready to push the pedestal base.
- At the end of a move, slow the dolly to avoid overrunning the floor marks at your destination, or bringing it to an abrupt halt.

Raising and lowering the camera

- In action, it is best to leave the pedestal column unlocked, ready to 'ped' up or down at any time.
- Particularly from low camera positions, look out for lens flares from light shining towards the camera, degrading picture quality. You can often clear lens flares by raising your viewpoint slightly, or by stretching a piece of masking tape across the top edge of the lens shade (lens hood).
- Whenever you raise or lower the camera-head, take care not to momentarily tilt the lens up or down as you do so. And when changing height quickly, remember it's easy to hit the column's maximum or minimum height limit, and judder the picture. And, of course, there are situations where you can inadvertently crush the camera down onto something just in front of it, or raise the camera and strike something overhead!

Camera shadows

Always be on the look-out for shadows of your camera appearing in shot. This is most likely to occur when you are close in to a subject, and when you are high, looking downwards. You may be able to clear it by moving sideways a little, or pulling out and zooming in (i.e. using a narrower lens angle). Or it may be necessary to relight the subject. Let the lighting director know if the shadow is unavoidable.

After the show

At the end of a production, when any videotaping retakes have been completed and checks made, the director and the technical director will announce on intercom that the studio is cleared. The floor manager will repeat this for everyone in the studio, including performers.

You should then lock off the camera head (tilt and pan), ped down to the lowest column position, and lock it off. If prompters or camera lights have been used, their cables may need to be removed at this stage. Cap up the lens to protect it, and move the dolly to its arranged parking area or a technical store. When the video engineer confirms that the camera has been switched off, remove the cable, and store it either in a neat figure-of-eight pile or on a cable reel. Cable care now avoids a tangle next time! Don't forget to remove your shot sheet (or script), and to clear any masking tape from the studio floor! If the headset is your personal issue, remember to recover it from the camera.

✳ <u>6</u> The persuasive camera

This chapter discusses how you can use the camera to present your subject effectively.

Why do we need techniques?

Shooting style

The simplest way to use a camera is to set it up at a suitable viewpoint, then zoom between overall *cover (covering)* shots showing general action, and closer shots showing detail. But this mechanical, unstimulating routine soon becomes very boring to watch. Good techniques add to the subject's appeal; they arouse our interest. Bald statements are not enough. Rather like listening to a hack pianist who plays the right notes without any sort of expression, our attention falls.

When you point a camera at a scene you are doing much more than simply showing your audience what is going on there. You are selecting particular features in the scene. You are drawing their attention to certain aspects of the action. The way you use your camera will influence the audience impact of the subject.

In an interview, for example, you can shoot the guests from a low viewpoint and give them an air of importance or self-confidence. From a higher viewpoint they might look diminished. Concentrating on detail shots of their nervous finger movements, they may appear insecure or ill at ease.

The camera *interprets* the scene. How you use it will affect your audience's responses. If you use the camera casually you will get haphazard results.

Whenever you point a camera at action you have to make a series of fundamental decisions, such as:

● Which is the best viewpoint? Can the action be seen clearly from there?
● Which features do you want to emphasize at this moment?
● Do you want the audience to concentrate on a particular aspect of the action?
● Do you want to convey a certain impression?

Of course, we seldom analyze in this fashion before deciding on a shot. Instead, we develop an instinctive feeling that a particular type of shot is most suitable for the situation.

Screen size

The size of the screen on which the audience watches the production can influence how they respond to what they see there. It is difficult to distinguish detail on a *small* screen (or a larger screen at a distance). The picture is confined and restricted, and we tend to feel detached as we closely inspect the overall effect. On the other hand, when watching a *large* screen we become more aware of detail. Our eyes have greater freedom to roam around the shot. We feel more closely involved with the action. We are onlookers at the scene.

At typical viewing distances most TV receivers allow us to effectively present a wide range of shot sizes, from vistas to microscopic close-ups. Although wide shots of large-scale events, panoramic views, or spectacular situations are not particularly impressive, this limitation is not too restrictive in practice.

Selecting the shot

Each type of shot has its particular advantages and disadvantages. You can use *longer shots*

- To show where the action is taking place,
- To allow the audience to follow broad movements,
- To show the relative positions of subjects,
- To establish mood.

But long shots do not allow your audience to see details, and you can leave them overaware of what they are missing. For example, in a wide shot of an art gallery they may feel that they are being prevented from seeing individual paintings clearly.

Closer shots are used

- To show detail,
- To emphasize,
- To reveal reactions,
- To dramatize.

Fig. 6.1   Restricted framing
In close shots, action must be kept within the frame area. Avoid moving items in/out of frame (it draws attention to limited viewpoint).

Use too many close shots, and the effect can be very restrictive. You can leave your audience feeling that they are being prevented from looking around the scene; from seeing the responses of other performers, from looking at other aspects of the subject, from following the general action.

Occasionally you may arrange a shot to show both a wide view of the scene and close detail, at the same time, in a combination shot (Figure 6.2).

Of course, any situation can be shot in many different ways. But there are always wrong or inappropriate shots for any given situation.

If action is *incidental* to the purpose of a sequence (e.g. someone speaking about their forthcoming vacation happens to be making an omelette) then shots should concentrate on the people involved, watching

Fig. 6.2 Combined close-up and wide shot
Combined shots can show detail and wider view simultaneously. This can be achieved by *detail insert* (left) or showing foreground detail (right). The latter method requires considerable focused depth.

their interreactions. But if the purpose of the sequence is to show us how to cook, then we need detail shots of the action, with little or no interruption from reaction shots. Obvious enough, but directors do make the wrong choice, and annoy or puzzle the audience.

A shot that is appropriate at one moment could be very unsuitable the next. In fact, there are times when an inappropriate or a badly timed shot can totally destroy an entire sequence.

The very long shot (vista shot)

This is a very distant view of the scene. The environment predominates, and people appear as tiny figures in the landscape. Normally, one can only arrange such shots on location; although it can be achieved in a large studio, using very wide lens angles and electronic insertion.

The *very long shot* enables you to establish broad locale, and to create an overall atmospheric impression. You can use it to cover very widespread action, or to show various activities going on at the same time. It usually takes the form of a high shot from a hilltop, or an aerial view (e.g. a distant view of a battle).

The audience takes a rather detached, impersonal attitude; surveying the scene without any sense of involvement.

Fig. 6.3 Varying the length of shot
1. *Dollying.* Forward dollying can offer a gradual build-up of interest or tension, the importance of the subject growing progressively. Dollying back allows interest, tension or importance to be released gradually. The change can be made imperceptibly or fairly rapidly, the size and rate being controlled throughout. (Zooming has a similar effect for many purposes.) Dollying avoids disruptive editing but can appear laborious when rapid viewpoint changes are needed.
2. *Cutting.* Cutting shock-excites, thrusting the second viewpoint forward forcefully. Cutting to closer shots helps to emphasize momentarily the subject's strength and importance, while cutting to longer shots tends to cause sudden drops in tension and subject-importance.
3. *Mixing* (dissolves). Mixing has something of the transitional smoothness of dollying while taking less time. It enables the viewer to interrelate two viewpoints more readily than cutting, but the double-exposure of slow mixes is highly distracting.

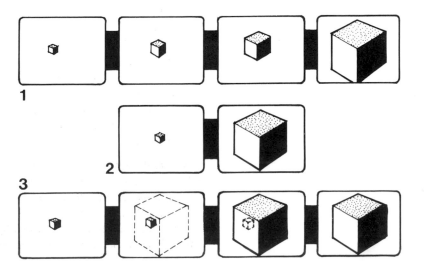

The long shot

Often used at the start of a scene, the long shot immediately shows where it's all happening. This *establishing shot* sets the location and broad atmospheric effect. It allows the audience to follow the purpose or pattern of action.

As you tighten the shot, and show less of the scene, the audience is influenced less by the setting and the lighting. The people within the scene have a greater audience impact, their gestures and facial expressions becoming stronger and more important.

Medium shots

These range from full-length to mid-shots; their value lying somewhere between the environmental strength of the long shot and the scrutiny of closer shots. From *full-length* to *three-quarter shots*, large bodily gestures (outflung arms) can be contained. But they are likely to pass out of shot if the shot becomes tighter. Then you have the option of restricting performer movement, taking a longer shot, or tightening to exclude arm movements entirely.

The close-up

An extremely powerful shot, the close-up concentrates interest. With people, it draws attention to their reactions, response, and emotions. Close-ups can reveal or point out information that might otherwise be overlooked, or only discerned with difficulty. They focus attention, or provide emphasis.

When introducing close-ups, you have to ensure that the viewer wants to look that close, and does not feel that:

1. He has been cheated of the wider view, where something more interesting may be happening.
2. He has been thrust disconcertingly close to the subject – he may become overaware of facial blemishes in overenlarged faces.
3. Detail that is already familiar is being overemphasized.
4. Picture clarity is actually being *reduced*: because there is no fine detail, or irrelevant details have become prominent, or restricted focus has blurred details.
5. Through continually watching close-up fragments, they have forgotten how these relate to the main subject, or have become disorientated.

Where shots do not contain enough detail to sustain continued interest, take care not to hold them so long that they entirely satisfy the curiosity, or encourage attention to wander.

Instead of beginning a sequence with a long *establishing shot*, you can build up impressions gradually, shot by shot; satisfying curiosity a little at a time. This encourages a sense of expectation, speculation.

But take care that delayed piecemeal introductions do not confuse; especially where the locale is unfamiliar. There must be sufficient pointers for our audience to be able to interpret the time, place, and action correctly. Where action has been seen from closer viewpoints for some time, longer shots may be desirable to remind, or re-establish the locale in the viewer's mind.

The prudent director remembers, and allows for, the cameraman's various operational problems when shooting close-ups:

1. Restricted depth of field, which therefore requires critical focusing.
2. Handling difficulties with narrow-angle lenses.
3. Depth compression.
4. The distortions and camera shadowing hazards when using close wide-angle lenses.
5. The difficulties in framing and following close movements.

Sometimes you will need to pan over close-up detail on a large flat surface (map or photograph). Then you must avoid the geometric distortions (keystoning) of a close short-focus (wide-angle) lens, or the restricted focused depth of a long-focus (narrow-angle) lens. It is best to move the lens parallel to the surface by trucking (crabbing) past it; with a long mural this is the only successful solution.

Deep-focus techniques

As you saw earlier, the *depth of field* in a scene varies with the lens *f*-stop, lens angle, and focused distance. You can change it by altering any of these parameters.

Stopping the lens down (e.g. *f*/11), everything from foreground to far distance appears sharply focused. The cameraman has no problems in following focus and there is little danger of subjects becoming soft focused. There is an illusion of spaciousness and depth; enabling shots to

Fig. 6.4 Focus techniques
Deep focus (top illustrations) provides overall clarity. This technique allows the cameraman to compose in depth and also accommodate close shots of three-dimensional subjects. *Shallow focus* (bottom illustrations) isolates subjects from distracting or confusing backgrounds, softens off unwanted detail.

be composed with subjects at various distances from the camera. (But higher light levels are necessary.)

One weakness of this technique is that where there is little camera movement or few progressively distant planes in the picture it can appear unattractively flat. Surfaces or subjects at very different distances can merge or become confused. *Too much* may be sharply and distractingly visible.

Shallow-focus techniques

Using a wider lens aperture (e.g. $f/2$) restricts focused depth. It enables you to *isolate* a subject spatially, keeping it sharp within blurred surroundings; and avoids the distraction of irrelevant subjects. You can display a single sharply focused flower against a detailless background; concentrating attention on the bloom and suppressing the confusion of foliage. Sharply defined detail attracts the eye more readily than defocused areas.

By deliberately restricting depth of field you can 'soften' obtrusive backgrounds, even if these are strongly patterned, so that people stand out from their surroundings.

On the other hand, restricted depth can prove embarrassing when essential details of a close object are badly defocused. The cameraman has the problem of continually refocusing to keep a close moving subject in focus. For instance, close shots along a piano keyboard can demand considerable dexterity of the cameraman when following focus on quickly moving fingers. Where there are two or more subjects in shot, he may not be able to maintain sharp overall focus but have to split focus between them, or select one to focus on.

Occasionally, by changing focus between subjects at different distances (*pulling focus, throwing focus*) you can move the viewer's attention from one to another; however, this trick easily becomes disturbing unless coordinated with action. Blurred color pictures can be frustrating. Whereas in monochrome defocused planes merge, in color the viewer may find himself trying to decipher unsharp detail and the effect can be less acceptable.

Moving the camera head

In everyday life we respond to situations by making particular gestures or movements. These reactions and actions often become very closely associated. We look around with curiosity; move in to inspect an object; withdraw or avert our eyes from a situation that we find embarrassing, distasteful, or boring.

It is not surprising to find, therefore, that certain *camera movements* can evoke associated responses in our audience; causing them to have particular feelings towards what they see on the screen. And these effects underly the impact of persuasive camera techniques.

Table 6.1   Why change the lens angle?

To adjust framing	**A slight change in lens angle:** Where you want to exclude (or include) certain foreground objects, and repositioning camera or subject would spoil proportions; Where a normal lens would not provide the required size or framing, without repositioning the camera or subject.
For otherwise unobtainable shots	**Using a narrow-angle (long-focus) lens:** To shoot remotely situated subjects – where they are separated from the camera by uneven ground or inaccessible; Where the camera is isolated – on a camera platform (tower), shooting through scenic openings; Where the camera cannot be moved – static tripod, obstructions. **Using a wider-angle (shorter-focus) lens:** Where the normal lens does not provide a wide enough shot – space restrictions; To maintain a reasonably close camera position (e.g. so talent can read *prompter*) yet still provide wider shots.
To adjust effective perspective	Altering lens angle and changing camera distance to maintain same subject size, alters relative subject/background proportions and effective distances (Table 6.3). **Using a wider lens angle (short-focus lens)** – enhances spatial impression, increases depth of field; **Using a narrower lens angle (long-focus lens)** – reduces spatial impression, compresses depth, e.g. bunching together a straggling procession.
Insufficient time to change camera distance	**Altering apparent camera distance (shot size) by changing lens angle:** During fast intercutting sequence; When camera repositioning would involve complicated moves.
To provide simpler or more reliable operations	**Zooming in/out instead of dollying** may produce smoother, easier changes in shot size (but perspective and handling effects change). Zooming provides **rapid changes in image size** more safely than fast dollying (for dramatic effect or to suddenly reveal detail). **Zooming in/out on a flat subject** is indistinguishable from dollying, but avoids focus-following problems. Lens angle changes can avoid close-up cameras coming into picture.
To increase production flexibility	Where dollying would distract talent or obscure the camera action from audience. When using only one camera.
To produce distortion	For grotesque close-ups, or to flatten modeling.

Panning the camera

Panning shows us the spatial relationship between two subjects or areas. Cutting between two viewpoints does not provide the same sense of continuity or extent. When panning over a wide arc the intermediate parts of the scene connect together in our minds, helping us to orientate ourselves. We develop an impression of space. But avoid panning across irrelevant areas – such as the 'dead' space between two widely separated people.

Panning should be smooth; neither jerking into action nor juddering to a halt. Erratic or hesitant panning irritates. With a correctly adjusted panning head (suitable drag/friction) and a properly stanced cameraman, such unevenness usually occurs only when using very narrow lens angles or where a subject makes an unpredicted move.

■ *The following pan*   This is the commonest camera movement. The camera pans as it follows a moving subject. In longer shots the viewer becomes aware of the interrelationship between the subject and its surroundings. Visual interaction can develop between the subject and its apparently moving background pattern, creating a dynamic mutual impact (*dynamic composition*). In closer shots the background becomes incidental; often indecipherably blurred.

■ *The surveying pan*   Here the camera slowly searches the scene (a crowd, a landscape), allowing the audience to look around at choice. It can be a restful anticipatory action; providing there is something worth seeing. It is not enough to pan hopefully.

The move can be dramatic, with high expectancy – the shipwrecked survivor scans the horizon, sees a ship . . . but will it notice him? But the surveying pan can build to an anticlimax, too; the fugitive searches to see if he is being followed . . . and finds that his 'pursuer' is a friendly hound.

■ *The interrupted pan*   This pan is a long smooth movement that is suddenly stopped (sometimes reversed) to provide visual contrast. It is normally used to link a series of isolated subjects. In a dance spectacle, the camera might follow a solo dancer from one group to the next, pausing awhile at each as it becomes the new center of interest.

The technique has comic applications: the camera follows a bunch of sailors. They pass a pretty girl. The camera stops in mid-pan to watch her. One sailor comes running back and grimaces to the camera, beckoning it to hurry and catch them up.

In a dramatic application: escaping prisoners slowly stagger over treacherous marshland. One man falls exhausted, but the camera stays with the rest. A moment later it stops and pans back – to see only the last traces of the straggler remain.

Fig. 6.5   Slow panning
To provide a dramatic development. Panning slowly from the sleeping victim . . . along the intruder's shadow . . . then a rapid upward-tilt, revealing the intruder's identity.

■ *Panning speed*   A slow, prolonged pan can create opportunities or disappointments, according to how it is used. If the camera pans slowly over a series of objects that are increasingly interesting or significant the movement will continually hold our attention; even build up to a climax. But a slow pan around without any real points of interest will quickly pall, as the viewer's initial expectancy falls.

■ *The whip pan*   A *fast* pan may produce nothing but a series of broken-up, half-seen images due to stroboscopic effects. But a *whip pan* (*swish, zip, blur pan*) turns so rapidly from one subject to the next that the intermediate scene becomes a brief, streaking blur.

Whether the effect arouses excitement or annoyance largely rests on how the preceding and following shots are developed. As our attention is dragged rapidly to the next shot it gives it transitory importance.

The *whip pan* usually produces a dynamic relational or comparative change:

1. *Joining different viewpoints of the same scene* – the pan *direction* should be compatible with the location of these viewpoints, i.e. panning right to a viewpoint located to camera right.
2. *Providing continuity of interest* – connecting a series of similar subjects or themes.
3. *Changing centers of attention* – from one area of concentration to another, e.g. a golfer drives . . . we whip pan to the awaiting hole.
4. *Showing cause and effect* – a whip pan from a cannon . . . to the demolished castle wall.
5. *Comparing or contrasting* – relating situations, e.g. wealth with poverty, old and new.
6. *Transferring in filmic time and space* – an aircraft takes off . . . whip pan to it landing at the destination.
7. *Dramatic change of direction* – changing the viewpoint with a sudden climax, e.g. the camera subjectively scans the distance, we hear a noise, and it whip pans to see an intruder behind, about to attack.

A whip pan continues the pace between two rapidly moving scenes. It can provide a tempo-bridge between a slow scene and a fast one. But at all times it remains something of a stunt.

A whip pan has to be *accurate* as well as appropriate, to be successful; no fumbling, reframing, refocusing at the end of the pan! To avoid such problems, the effect may be cheated by intercutting a brief separately recorded shot of 'blur' between two static cameras' shots.

Tilting the camera head

Although, strictly speaking, pointing the camera upwards and downwards is *tilting*, most of us talk about '*panning up and down*'. But we'll stick to the correct term here, for the sake of clarity.

Tilting, like panning, allows you to visually connect subjects or areas that are spaced apart. Otherwise, you would need to intercut different shots, or use a longer shot to include both subjects.

Tilting can be used:

1. To emphasize *height* or *depth* – tilting up from a mountaineer . . . to show the steep cliff face to be climed.
2. To show *relationships* – as the camera tilts from the rooftop watcher . . . down to his victim in the street below; or from the victim . . . up to the rooftop, revealing that he is not alone.

Fundamentally, *tilting upward* creates feelings of rising interest and emotion, expectancy, hope, anticipation. Conversely, *tilting downward* is allied to lowering interest and emotion, disappointment, sadness, critical inspection.

Where the viewer is conditioned beforehand by dialogue or action, responses become more complex. The *downward* tilt can become an act of enquiry; the *upward* tilt, a gesture of despair. Again, where a subject no longer holds our interest, the relief of a downward tilt can produce an anticipatory feeling – although the movement is not itself anticipatory.

In practice, of course, you will not stop to hypothesize about each camera movement. You come to recognize the 'feel' of such treatment in a dramatic situation. For example, a woman hears of her son's death, and the camera *tilts down* with her, as she sits. This treatment conveys her grief more convincingly than either a static shot or a depressed viewpoint.

Camera height

The angle from which you shoot can have a considerable influence on the audience's attitude towards it. Intercut high- and low-angle shots of a person demonstrate this immediately. In a drama you may deliberately choose the camera's height to emphasize or diminish a person's dramatic strength, or to control the impact of dialogue. Similarly, if you shoot a piece of sculpture from a low viewpoint it will appear imposing, forceful, and impressive; while shot from above it loses vitality and significance.

How you get that viewpoint is immaterial. Shooting an architect's miniature/model of land development, for example, you could equally well obtain an overhead view from a crane shot, a suspended camera, a mirror shot, or by attaching the subject vertically to the studio wall and shooting straight on to it. The effect is the same, although in some cases camera movement will be very restricted.

Extreme camera angles

Extreme angles have an unhappy knack of drawing attention to the abnormality or ingenuity of the camera's position. If our audience is left wondering how we got that shot, mechanics have intruded over artistic purpose. Similarly, during the now-familiar swooping and climbing of helicopter shots, the viewer can become overaware of wind-beaten grass or telltale shadows of the aircraft on the ground below.

Where extreme angles arise *naturally*, viewers accept them readily: looking down from an upper-storey window; looking up from a seated

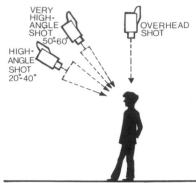

Fig. 6.6 part 1   Level shots
A normal viewpoint, usually around chest height; carries no special significance. Camera height: 1.2–1.8 m (4–5 ft) for a standing person, 1.1 m (3½ ft) for a sitting person.

Fig. 6.6 part 2   Low shots
Low angle shots make most subjects appear stronger, more imposing, overpowering, strange, ominous. A person can seem threatening, pompous, authoritative, determined, dignified, benevolent, according to his attitude and environment. Dialogue and movement become significant and dramatic. The closer we are, the stronger these impressions. In a very-low-angle shot, the subject takes on a strangely distorted, even mystical, appearance. At greater distances, it appears remote and unknown.

Fig. 6.6 part 3   High shots
High angle shots give the audience a sense of strength or superiority, an air of tolerance, even condescension, towards the subject; this feeling increases with distance. Therefore high shots can be used to imply unimportance, inferiority, impotence, etc. Very high angle shots give an attitude of peering down, scrutinizing. From a height of 3–6 m (10–20 ft) surveillance gives way to complete detachment. Overhead shots emphasize pattern and movement in formation (as in ballet and dance spectacle). They reveal isolation or congestion.

position; even an eavesdropper peering through plank flooring to the room below. But an unexplained extreme usually becomes a visual stunt; for example, a bird's-eye view of a prisoner pacing a ceilingless cell, or shooting up through glass floors.

Emotional impact of extreme viewpoints

As you have seen, while *high shots* generally create an audience-strength/subject-weakness relationship, low shots reverse this influence. But the associations are often much more subtle than that. Imagine a high-angle shot of an old man truding through rainswept streets. The audience does not feel 'strength' or 'superiority', but pities him, or feels sorry for his loneliness. But these are, of course, psychological variations on the fundamental theme of 'viewer-strength/subject-weakness' that the high shot provides.

In a very high angle shot, the viewer has an overall view; in fact, more than people on the spot. This underlying response colors our attitude to what we are seeing.

In an *aerial view* we survey the extent of the landscape; we follow the course of a river, seeing houses clustered along its banks, and its toy-like boats. We feel remote, seeing it all at a glance. We see the searchers moving towards the hiding fugitive. We see the magnitude of the

Fig. 6.7   The influence of viewpoint
The viewpoint you choose can influence how your audience responds to the action and to the location.

Part 1   Are we just seeing two people meeting (1), or a confrontation (2), or a challenge (3)? Is the person in white dominant (3), or the person in black (4) (5)? Are we detached observers (6)?

1   2   3

4   5   6

Part 2   Viewpoint can affect how the audience interprets the action, the mood, the dramatic impact. Here an old man sits sleeping. But our first impressions are that (1) he is drunk . . . or (2) just sleeping quietly . . . or (3) lonely, deserted.

1   2   3

invading army. But there is emotional detachment in this inspectional viewpoint; none of the involvement of more normal camera positions. Dynamics are reduced. Some subjects, such as high-wire acts, juggling, balancing feats, can lose their appeal entirely if shot from above, whereas a very low angle position emphasizes their difficulty and suspense.

Portraiture

The camera's height modifies what people look like, too. *Elevated shots* (especially on wide-angle lenses) emphasize baldness and plumpness in women; also through foreshortening and distortion, they can produce a dumpy sawn-off effect.

Low-angle shots can emphasize dilated nostrils, upturned or large noses, heavy jawlines, and scrawny necks. Men with high foreheads or receding hair may look entirely bald. Protruding ears may appear very prominent.

Fig. 6.8   Verticals in overhead shots
In overhead shots, the position of the camera relative to strong verticals in the scene can considerably affect shot impact.
1. Verticals at the bottom of the frame cause tension and instability.
2. This impression is absent where foreground verticals are at the top of the frame.

1   2

Fig. 6.9 Dollying (tracking)
Moving to or from the subject.
Dollying in causes increased interest,
build-up or tension, but the closer
view may result in disappointment,
disillusionment and, consequently,
diminished interest. Dollying back
results in lowered interest, relaxed
tension; unless unseen subjects are
revealed, or when curiosity,
expectation, or hope have been
aroused. Attention tends to be
directed towards the edges of the
picture. Rapid dollying is visually
exciting, but space and safe speed
restrict fast moves. (Controlled
zooming may produce allied effects.)
Dollying (like subject movement to
and from camera) appears faster than
it really is, on a wide-angle lens, and
slower on a narrower lens angle.

Moving the camera

How freely you can move the camera around is determined by the type of
mounting used. Whereas a crane boom shot offers considerable flexibility,
it may not be able to relocate the viewpoint as rapidly as a highly mobile
pedestal. Well-chosen camera moves add visual interest and vitality, as
well as engendering certain audience reactions. The intermovement of
planes (parallactic changes) that takes place as the camera moves provides
an illusion of solidity and depth; a realness that no static zooming camera
can achieve.

But camera movement needs to be motivated, appropriate, smoothly
controlled, and at a suitable speed, or it can become restless and
disturbing.

Prominence of camera movement

The effects of camera movement are most obvious when shooting a static
subject. Movement impact is correspondingly lessened where the camera
moves with the subject; e.g. following it in a *tail-away shot* as the subject
moves away; or dollying out as the subject approaches the camera in a
head-on shot. And if respective direction and speeds match in a *traveling
shot*, the dynamic effect of movement will come largely from the passing
background. Whenever camera and subject are heading toward or away
from each other, the overall impression is considerably heightened.

Move the camera – or the subject?

There are intrinsic differences between the effects of moving the *camera*
or moving the *subject*. You can see this by watching a mute TV screen in a
darkened room. You will feel your peephole vision moved around, almost
physically, as the moving camera *subjectively* examines the scene. Where
the camera is static, the performers will seem to move to and from you; an
objective effect.

Camera movement (or zooming) becomes 'our behavior' by proxy,
towards the subject. *We* the audience are moving; going up to look at or
meet the subject . . . to satisfy our curiosity or to see detail more clearly.
Forward camera movement is strong and exploratory; while dollying back
is usually a weak move.

When a performer moves towards or away from the camera, we the
audience become recipients of 'his attitude towards us'. Our reactions
to his move largely depend upon his demeanour; whether his action
is forceful or casual. Circumstances may alter situations – we may
experience an 'audience superiority' effect as someone walks the length of
a corridor to meet us, but 'inferiority' if they sit while we (the camera)
have to move up to meet them. And remember, the impact of all
movements to and from the camera will be influenced by the lens angle
you are using.

Fig. 6.10 part 2   Craning from a moving dolly
1. Forwards and craning upwards creates an air of freedom, flight, lack of restriction, elevation, joy.
2. Dollying forwards and craning down, implies swooping, power, strength, importance relative to subject when fast; but when done slowly suggests depression, return to normality.
3. Dollying back and craning upwards gives a feeling of complete release; detachment from the subject or action.
4. Dollying back and craning down is a recessive move, often saddening or disillusioning; a return to earth; no longer detached from subject or action.

Fig. 6.10 part 1   Craning from a static dolly
1. When craning up from level, audience response is elation, superiority, eventual detachment as height increases; while the subject becomes less significant, even unimportant.
2. When craning down from level, the response is depression, inferiority, even a feeling of being dominated; and the subject becomes more important, impressive, significant.
3. Craning down from an elevated height with superior viewpoint will produce an effect of return to normality, with some sense of depression.
4. Craning up from low-level to level produces the same effect, but with a slight feeling of elation.

Fig. 6.11   Arcing
1. Circling round a subject to see it from a different viewpoint, tends to be a self-conscious move, drawing attention to the action. Spurious side-slip effects can arise.
2. Slight position changes can help when one performer masks (obscures) another.

Fig. 6.13 part 1   Following the subject – long shot throughout
Audience impact comes chiefly from the moving environment; subject importance
being limited. The pace of action is relatively slow. Varying composition or tone
during the pan, can produce emotional changes – e.g. the 'uplift' on panning from
low to high key. Sudden mood changes are achieved by, for example, having the
actor raise window blind to let in daylight, or switching room lights.

Fig. 6.13 part 2   Following the subject – close shot throughout
The subject dominates, its strength depending on camera height. The influence of
the environment is limited, and pace varies with dynamic composition. Slightly
off-centering the subject in the direction of movement creates a feeling of
anticipation, expectancy.
1. Profile – weak against a plain background, but an impression of speed and
    urgency against a detailed background.
2. Three-quarter frontal – can be dramatically strong. By preventing us from seeing
    the subject's route or destination, marked curiosity can be encouraged.
3. Elevated frontal – although himself weakened, the subject dominates his
    environment.
4. Depressed frontal – the subject is especially forceful, dominating his
    environment. *Rear shots introduce a subjective effect.*
5. Three-quarter rear – partially subjective; the viewer moves with the subject
    expectancy developing during movement.
6. High rear shot – almost entirely subjective; produces increased anticipation;
    searching.
7, 8. In level and low shots there is a striking sense of depth. The subject is strongly
linked to the setting and other people, yet remains separate from them.

Fig. 6.13 part 3   Following the subject – long shot to close-up
The subject walks up to the camera. Environment predominates at first, but the
subject grows increasingly stronger as it approaches. The impact can be modified by
dollying or zooming as the subject approaches.

Fig. 6.13 part 4   Following the subject – close-up to long shot
A weak, recessive movement, generally accompanied by lowering tension as the
subject's strength falls and that of the environment increases. Used to depict
pathos, anticlimax.

**Fig. 6.13 part 5   Following the subject – then arriving at his destination
before him**
1. The camera moves more quickly than the subject, to his destination – the
    quickening pace providing an exciting introduction to the new position; but it
    must be sustained to be effective. The shot shows spatial relationships and gives
    the viewer time to assimilate the destination before the subject arrives.
2. Here the person begins to move, you cut to his destination, and he then arrives.
    Often mechanically convenient, the cut gives the destination shot impact.
    Audience-superiority can arise through foreknowledge of the subject's
    destination, and provide pathos, bathos, stage irony, climactic effects. It avoids
    lengthy dollying shots, and can imply non-existent spatial relationships.
    Irrelevant intermediate movement is eliminated and pseudo-filmic-time effect
    achieved, but interest and tension can flag while awaiting the subject.

**Fig. 6.13 part 6   Following the subject – cutting from the static subject
to his destination**
A simple but weak treatment, unless dialog or gesture has indicated that he is
going to move. Spatial relationship or significance may not be clear to the viewer.
Static action cuts of this kind can make the viewer over-conscious of the time taken
for the subject's move. On commenced-action cuts, as in part 5 above, this is less
pronounced.

**Fig. 6.12   Camera and subject
movement**
Someone enters a room (in long shot)
and crosses to a table (arriving in
close-up). There are two methods of
single-camera treatment, each
providing a different audience impact.
1. The entrance and walk are taken
    in long shot. When the subject has
    stopped, the camera dollies in to
    close-up.
2. The camera pans and trucks
    throughout the walk, with subject
    and camera arriving
    simultaneously in a close-up.

Subjective treatment

When you use the camera *subjectively*, it is as if the viewer is actually walking about within the scene, following the action. The camera pushes through a crowd, moves up to inspect something, glances up at nearby detail. We encounter this approach regularly, of course, when shoulder-mounted cameras are used, instead of shooting from the static viewpoint of a fixed tripod.

Subjective camera movement creates a participatory effect for the audience. But if a director moves us when we do not want to do so, or fails to show us something we wish to see, we feel resentful or frustrated. The skilled director persuades his audience to want a change in viewpoint, or a move. The unskilled director thrusts it upon them.

Imitative camera movement

Apart from the familiar ploy of moving cameras to suggest jogging vehicles or rolling ships, camera movements can provide subjective comments on the action itself. Staggering as it dollies after a drunk; copying the bounce of a dandy's gait; swaying in waltztime as we follow a girl home from her first dance.

Drawing attention to itself quite openly, the camera movement becomes a tongue-in-cheek observation between the director and his audience. When it comes off, this device has persuasive appeal.

Fig. 6.14   The canted shot
1. Canting is most pronounced with subjects inherently associated with horizontal or vertical stability. Left: slight slanting (about 10°) is ineffectual. Centre: typical tilt around 20–30° is used to convey instability, abnormality, dynamism. Right: excessively canted (50–60°) the effect is excessive overbalancing.
2. From low-angle (or high-angle) positions, canting causes subjects to lean into, or out of frame.

Table 6.2   Productional uses of lens angles

About 50°

The widest lens angle generally used in the studio.

Used for wide shots at close camera distances.

Used to exaggerate setting size, space, distance, scale.

Exaggerates dolly movements and speed.

Exaggerates performer movements to and from the camera.

Used to frame fast on erratically moving subjects.

Allows very smooth camera handling.

Provides considerable depth of field. (It may be excessive.) Used to create deliberate grotesque geometric (barrel) distortion – e.g. of CU faces, forward arm movements.

But camera is liable to *overshoot* (*shoot-off*), and get lens flares.

About 35°

Frequently used for close shots of small objects, but camera shadows may arise.

Enhances the impression of space and distance; but without the extreme exaggeration of wider lens angles.

Generally emphasizes dolly movements and speed.

Provides easy camera handling.

Greater depth of field makes focusing much easier.

Appreciable camera movement may be necessary to correct framing.

About 25°

The 'normal' lens angle, used for most purposes and providing natural perspective in the picture.

A generally effective lens angle for good camera handling.

Allows convenient working distances when shooting close-ups, title cards, etc.

The associated depth of field suits most shots. It is sufficient for longer shots (deep focus), yet allows closer subjects to be isolated from their defocused background.

About 15°

Useful narrow angle for 'close shots' from a distance – whether due to subject inaccessibility, or to avoid other cameras coming in shot.

Isolates individuals from a group.

Noticeable compression of depth and perspective distortion.

Camera handling is not easy.

The lens angle is only really suitable for slight dolly movements.

Depth of field is somewhat restricted.

About 10°

Achieves close-ups from around 3.5 m (11½ ft) but depth compression is considerable.

Very 'compressed' perspective.

Depth of field is very limited for close shots.

Camera handling becomes coarse; needs skilled operation, even for limited movements.

Movement of close subjects is often hard to follow accurately.

About 5°

Used for static close shots on a distant camera.

Considerable depth compression.

Mainly suitable for flat subjects, where perspective distortion is absent.

Most unsuitable for close-ups of people, because of extreme perspective distortion.

Camera handling is extremely coarse.

Subject movement is very difficult to follow.

Depth of field is extremely limited.

Focal lengths (mm)

Approx. Angle	Camera-tube size			
	12.5 mm ½ in	18 mm ⅔ in	25 mm 1 in	30 mm 1¼ in
50°	7.5	10	15	17
35°	10	14	20	27
25°	15	20	30	38
15°	25	33	50	62
10°	37	50	75	94
5°	75	100	150	188

Dollying

Zooming

Fig. 6.15   Comparing dollying and zooming

1. *Dollying:* when a camera moves through a scene, relative sizes and spacing of subjects change proportionately. This continual parallactic movement causes planes to become visible and disappear with position changes. Perspective remains constant.

2. *Zooming:* as the field of view alters with lens angle, the shot is simply enlarged or diminished. There is no parallactic movement, no planes appear/disappear, or change relative proportions. So effective perspective appears to change (unless the viewer adjust his viewing distance to compensate) and visible 'depth-stretching' or compression results.

Fig. 6.16   Trucking (crabbing)

Moving across the scene, parallel with it. Trucking becomes associated with an attitude of inspection, critical observation, expectancy, intolerant appraisal. The lateral displacement of planes (*parallactic movement*) introduces a strong illusion of depth and solidity, but the restriction of the picture's frame becomes over-apparent if trucking stops abruptly.

Using the zoom lens

As you saw in Chapter 4, the zoom lens brings both advantages and pitfalls for the unwary. It is too easy to use lens angles indiscriminately, just to change subject image size.

There is a great temptation to stand and zoom, rather than move around with a normal lens angle. It is an easy operation, demands little of the cameraman or director, and avoids problems such as keeping close cameras out of long shots. There is just the need for a pre-zoom focus check, before zooming in.

Zooming is extremely convenient. But it only simulates camera movement. There are no natural parallactic changes; and scale, distance, and shape become distorted through zooming. A slow zoom made during panning, tilting, or subject movement may disguise these discrepancies.

Fig. 6.17　The need to pre-focus

1. The considerable depth of field available with a wide lens angle broadens focusing, so that subjects may appear sharp although not at the focused plane.
2. However, on zooming in to a narrow lens angle (without re-focusing) depth of field becomes restricted, and the subject now falls outside the available depth of field.

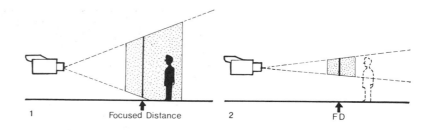

1　　　　　Focused Distance　　　　2　　　　　FD

Required Shot

1　　　2　　　3a　　　3b

Fig. 6.18　Adjusting proportions

Altering relative subject proportions in the picture can be achieved by changing to a different lens-angle and readjusting camera distance (see Fig. 4.11 Pt 2).

1. A distant narrow-angle lens provides the required subject/foreground proportions.
2. A closer position using a normal lens angle, shows required foreground proportions, but the subject appears too small.
3a. Dollying-in will correct the subject size but loses the foregound fence.
3b. Widening the lens angle now will bring the fence into shot again, but the subject image appears small and the subject foreground distance increased.

Table 6.3　Adjusting picture proportions

Subject size	Background appears	Lens angle correction	Camera position
Too large	Too large*	Use wider lens angle (zoom out)	Keep camera still
Too small	Too small*	Use narrower lens angle (zoom in)	Keep camera still
Satisfactory	Too distant	Use narrower lens angle	Increase camera distance
Satisfactory	Too near	Use wider lens angle	Move camera closer
Too large	Satisfactory	Use narrower lens angle	Increase camera distance
Too small	Satisfactory	Use wider lens angle	Move camera closer

But relative subject/background proportions satisfactory.

A rapid zoom during an exciting fast-moving ball game would scarcely disturb even the pedant. Much depends on the occasion.

Zooming can provide a visual bridge from the wide view to the close-up, without the time and effort involved in dollying or the interruption (and possible disorientation) of *cutting*. A *rapid zoom-in* produces a highly dramatic swoop onto the subject. An instant *crash (snap) zoom-in* flings subject detail at the audience. Such effects can be fantastically forceful – or plain annoying!

All zooming should be decisive. Avoid the nauseous results of rhythmical or jerky in–out zooms, or quick *slight* angular changes that look like an operational error.

Zooming on *flat surfaces* (maps, illustrations) avoids the need to *follow focus* that dollying would entail. On title cards you can produce carefully controlled size changes (titling growth or shrinkage) by zooming.

Use zoom-ins to direct attention, to increase tension, to give powerful emphasis, or to restrict the coverage. But the zooming action itself should be used discriminately for particular occasions – like wipes, star filters, diffusion discs, and similar productional tinsel. Certain effects, like that of zooming in and dollying back simultaneously (keeping the subject-size constant), are bewildering, to say the least!

⚹ <u>7</u> Effective picture making

Why do some pictures look very attractive, while the eye passes over others disinterestedly? Why do some draw the eye to a particular subject, while in others we look around? Why are some pictures so atmospheric, while others appear so 'ordinary'? The answers lie in effective picture making.

Behind the picture

One tends to think of picture making as the prerogative of the cameraman. For the camera on location that is largely true. But in the studio, where the entire environment is *contrived*, it is the culmination of many combined talents.

The design of the setting, the way it has been lit, the viewpoint selected by the director, can all be controlled to provide appropriate conditions for the occasion. The tonal quality of the picture, too, can be adjusted electronically over a wide range.

The cameraman's opportunities to create a meaningful composition depend directly on the way the scene in front of him has been developed, how action has been arranged. Stand someone in front of a flatly lit plain background, and the prospects for interesting shots are very limited. Sit the same person in a well-designed, attractively lit setting, and the camera can explore the situation, producing arresting shots.

Persuasive picture making is the result of successful teamwork. If the lighting is inappropriate, or the director selects an ineffective camera position, the result will be inferior pictures – and lost opportunities.

Fig. 7.1 Why compose the picture?
The unguided eye wanders around the scene, finding its own centers of interest.

Composing the picture

What is *composition*? Some people think that it is the idea of arranging pictures to provide an attractive harmonious effect. It is much more than that. It is a way of arranging pictures so that the viewer is directly attracted to certain features. You can influence how he responds to what

121

he is seeing. You can compose a picture to create anticipation, unease, apprehension, excitement, restful calm. The mood can be depressed, or expansive.

The principles we shall explore here are guides, rather than 'rules' to be slavishly copied, but they are essentially *practical*.

Practical composition

Under everyday working conditions you will meet three basic approaches to composition:

1. Composition by **design.**
2. Composition by **arrangement.**
3. Composition by **selection.**

Composition by design

This occurs where you have an *entirely free hand* in composing your picture. The artist approaching his blank canvas can arrange line, tone, and color in any way he chooses, without concern for accuracy or feasibility. The physical limitations are minimal and are inherent in his medium. Canaletto 'improved' his paintings of London by actually repositioning entire buildings for effect, whatever the resulting topographical errors. Only occasionally does this freedom exist for the camera (e.g. in process work).

Composition by arrangement

Here you *deliberately position subjects* before the camera to produce an appealing, meaningful result. A set designer dressing a setting does this by placing furniture, flowers, and ornaments to form appropriate arrangements. Sometimes even a single carefully introduced foreground object (a leafy branch, perhaps), will help the cameraman to devise appropriate composition.

More usually, a designer creates *potential* rather than specific composition opportunities; an environmental package suiting the mood and mechanics of the occasion, rather than calculated composition arrangements.

There is always the danger when arranging natural situations that the resultant effect will look deliberately contrived. You can become over-aware of how 'cleverly' the picture has been manipulated.

Composition by selection

This is the situation most cameramen encounter. The camera is positioned at a certain viewpoint chosen by the director (or the cameraman himself) and he composes the shot *using what is there*, to show the subject most effectively. In this situation you can adjust the picture's composition in several ways:

- *Adjust framing.* Positioning the shot to deliberately include/exclude parts of the scene, or to alter subjects' positions in the frame (balance).
- *Increasing/decreasing the lens angle.* The lens angle of view will determine how much of the scene appears in the picture from that viewpoint.
- *Adjusting the camera position.* As the camera moves up/down or sideways, foreground objects change position in the frame more noticeably than distant ones. So even slight readjustments can considerably alter the compositional relationships.
- *Proportions.* By altering the lens angle, and changing the camera distance to compensate, you can keep the same sized shot but adjust proportions within it.

The director and composition

The director's attitude to pictorial composition varies between individuals, and with the type of production. For many shows, the director is so preoccupied with what is being said, with performance, continuity, and mechanics, that he does not arrange the composition of shots specifically. Instead, he indicates the shot size required (CU, singles, two-shots, group shots) and leaves details of lens angle, framing, etc. to the cameraman.

In other types of production (primarily drama), the director deliberately groups actors to provide particular compositional arrangements – for dramatic effect, or to direct audience attention. In some cases, he (or the set designer) may have prepared a *storyboard sketch,* showing the detailed composition of certain *keyshots.*

Composition principles

Composition principles are not laws. They are indications of how people respond to distribution of line and tone. Whether you put that tone into the scene, or are selecting from whatever is already there, is not important. What *is* important is that if you do not organize pictures appropriately, your audience may well react by looking at the wrong things, interpret the picture inappropriately, or become bored by unattractive shots. *Composing shots* is not just a matter of 'pictorial packaging' but a method of controlling continuity of thought.

Fig. 7.2 Subjective lines
The mind tends to seek pattern and to see relationships, even where none really exist. Individual subjects seem to combine or interact to form patterns.

Fig. 7.3 Illusory attraction

1. A disc in the center of the frame appears at rest, surrounded by empty areas of equal tension. A change in subject size alters this reaction between the subject and its frame. An over-large subject bulges the frame, squeezing-out the surrounding space, while a too-small subject becomes compressed by the large area of empty space surrounding it.
2. This compression effect gives way to a forceful thrusting as the intermediate space lessens.
3. Tension is built up between subjects in a picture. The two close subjects convey a feeling of mutual interlinking – illusory attraction. In a more complex example, the isolated subject appears to be attracted towards the more stable supported group.

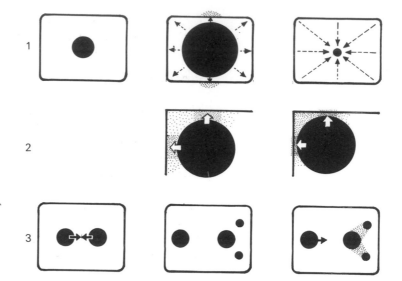

The effect of the picture frame

The camera does much more than 'put a frame' round a segment of the scene. *It inherently modifies whatever it shows.* Because the screen *totally isolates* its subjects (the viewer cannot see whatever else is happening), and because the resultant picture is flat (and cannot reproduce stereoscopic depth) unique relationships develop within it that are not present in the actual scene.

No shot directly portrays *reality.* In many cases our own experience enables us to rationalize and interpret, so that we make a pretty accurate assessment of what we are seeing, e.g. a tourist photograph composed to make the Statue of Liberty rest on someone's outstretched hand . . . or is it a model after all? But this does not always happen; particularly where the viewer is not familiar with the situation.

The subjective effects that arise in the flat framed picture take several forms:

1. Although one plane may be some distance behind another, they can appear conjoined or even merge in the shot.
2. Spatially unrelated areas of tone and color are often juxtaposed in the picture; interacting and influencing pictorial balance. Simultaneous contrast effects result.
3. Seen in perspective on the flat screen, the shapes of objects and composition lines can change with camera angle.
4. A series of quite unrelated subjects at varying distances can combine pictorially to form a composition group.
5. Within the picture, *imaginary* composition relationships can seem to develop between subjects, and visual tensions form between them.
6. As subjects approach the edge of the screen, impressions of tension or compression can develop; particularly in screen-filling shots.

7. The lateral position of subjects influences their composition impact.
8. Various dynamic effects arise (dynamic composition).

Proportions

There are no formulae for beauty. But centuries ago, artists discovered a widely accepted principle guiding harmonic proportions – the Golden Section or Golden Mean. Great painters, sculptors, architects, have used these ratios in many ways (often unwittingly, perhaps) when expressing their concepts of beauty.

If you cut a straight line into sections that provide the most pleasing relationship, you will find with incredible regularity that the line lengths are divided according to the Golden Section, in a constant ratio, so that the small part is to the larger, as the larger is to the whole. These proportions work out in practice to about 8:13 (often quoted as 3:5).

Fig. 7.4 Proportions
The Golden Section. Dividing for ideal proportions tends to produce YZ:XY in the same proportions as XY:XZ. Making several such divisions, a series appears, and this ratio of division, the Golden Section, is about 3:5.

Dividing the frame. An equally divided frame allows only formal balance – usually dull and monotonous. Thirds can lead to quickly recognized mechanical proportions. Dividing the screen in a 2:3, or a 3:5 ratio achieves a far more pleasing balance.

Such proportioning has quite far-reaching applications, for it gives us a guide to ratios that most readily please the eye. Be suspicious of such formulae; but see how often they seem to validate themselves.

Rule of thirds

When composing a shot, you should avoid mechanically dividing the screen into regular sections. A screen cut into halves or quarters can produce a dull, monotonous balance.

You will find the 'rule of thirds' often advocated when selecting proportions. Main subjects are placed at the intersections of lines dividing the screen vertically and horizontally into three equal parts. A useful enough mechanical concept to guide in composing pictures, it should not be followed overslavishly for it can develop a recognizable sameness.

Framing

As you frame or line up a shot, you are doing several important things:

1. First of all, you are choosing *exactly* what the viewer is going to see; what is to be included within the picture (*on-frame, in-frame*); and

Fig. 7.5 part 1   Safety margins
As TV screen edges are usually masked off, avoid placing important action or titling near the frame edges. Some monitors and camera viewfinders indicate the safe area (engraved, or from a special generator).

Fig. 7.5 part 2   Framing people
1. Avoid frame-cutting people at natural joints; as shown intermediate cutting-points appear more attractive. Similarly avoid framing so that they touch the screen edge as in 2.

Fig. 7.5 part 3   Framing – frame positions
1. Center screen is generally the weakest area for holding the viewer's attention. Continual or sustained use of picture-center becomes monotonous.

2. Positions near frame edges seldom give good balance (particularly scenic lines running parallel with them). Frame corners exert an outward pull on subjects placed there. Subject strength and importance tends to increase higher in the frame and towards the right.

Fig. 7.5 part 4   Relevant framing
Do not just frame the subject for an attractive effect, but to suit the program purpose.

Fig. 7.5 part 5   Tight framing
Close shots of people bring problems such as arm gestures, or explanatory items remaining unseen out of shot. Tight framing emphasizes the screen's confines. Head movements can pass out of frame, leaving it empty; thus requiring catch-up panning, which is a fidgety and obtrusive operation.

Fig. 7.5 part 6 Offset framing – still subjects
For side or ¾ views, center-frame positions (*a*) provide an unattractive balance. Slight offsetting (*b*), sometimes referred to as 'looking room', is usually preferable; although this must not be overdone (*c*) unless you want to draw attention to that side of the frame, or imply isolation.

Horizontal framing can affect significance too. Notice when the door is included in the shot, someone's entry is expected (*d*).

what is to be excluded from it (*off-frame, out-of-frame, out-of-shot*). You may be selecting to concentrate attention and avoid distractions, or to show more subject detail. You might omit information deliberately – or reveal it in another shot.

2. As you alter a shot's framing, you are repositioning line and tone within the picture, and modifying its audience impact.

All parts of the frame do not have equal pictorial value. The effect changes, depending on where you place the main subject.

How you frame a shot will not only alter compositional balance but can influence the viewer's interpretation of events. Framed in a certain way, a two-shot might lead him to expect someone is about to enter the room, or that an eavesdropper is outside a door.

Headroom changes proportionally with the length of shot; lessening as the shot tightens. In a multi-camera production the headroom can vary considerably between different cameras. So it is as well for the director to check that comparable shots match.

Fig. 7.5 part 7 Offset framing – moving subjects
When a subject moves, keep it slightly lagging behind the center of the frame. The amount of offset needed increases slightly with the speed of movement.

Fig. 7.5 part 8 Headroom
1. For good vertical balance, people should be framed with appropriate headroom (*a*). Avoid the cramping effect of insufficient headroom (*b*), or the bottom-heavy effect of excess (*c*).
2. Whether compositional elements become an incidental border, or oppressively overhang the action, largely depends on how they are framed.

Fig. 7.5 part 9 Reframing
As subjects leave or enter frame, the cameraman normally readjusts framing unobtrusively for the next situation. For dramatic purposes you may deliberately NOT reframe; the tension from the unbalanced composition emphasizing the second subject's departure or absence.

Pictorial balance

For most purposes you will want *balanced* composition. Not the equal balance of formal symmetry, for that is uninteresting, but a picture with *equilibrium*.

Balance in a picture is affected by:

1. The *size* of a subject within the frame.
2. Its *tone*.
3. Its *position within the frame*.
4. The *interrelationship* of subjects in the shot.

Fig. 7.6 part 1   Adjusting balance

1. Balance pivots about the picture center.
2. Unbalanced shots are visually unstable and unattractive.
3. But formal *symmetrical* arrangements usually prove monotonous and uninteresting.
4. Certain compositional grouping has considerable stability, but must be correctly framed to appear balanced.
5. To reduce symmetry, you may *angle* subjects (avoiding head-on positions); for balance can change with shape.
6. Or you can adjust relative *sizes* of subjects.
7. Altering the subject's relative *distances* from center-frame changes pictorial balance. (Try adjusting positions of cut-out card shapes.)
8. Isolation gives a subject weight.
9. By *grouping* individual subjects, they have greater collective 'weight'. (See *UNITY*.)
10. *Size and tone* combine to affect overall balance. Larger areas and darker tones should be framed carefully. Dark tones towards the top of the frame produce a strong downward thrust – top-heaviness, a depressed closed-in feeling. At the bottom of the frame, they provide a firm base for composition, lending it solidity. (See Fig. 7.12.)

Fig. 7.6 part 2   Changing balance
Balance and emphasis can be altered in several ways.
1. By changing the lens-angle (zooming) – size change.
2. By altering the camera-distance – proportions change.
3. Readjusting subject height.
4. Altering subject grouping.
5. Changing camera height.
6. Changing viewpoint – different tones, masses come into shot.
7. Lighting changes – altering tones or colors of areas.

A balanced picture has a coordinated, structured look. Balance unifies the subjects within a shot. Occasionally, you may deliberately arrange the picture so that it is *unbalanced*, to create a dynamic restlessness or tension. But use this effect sparingly. A balanced arrangement does not have to be static. You can continually readjust the balance of a shot – by moving a person, altering the framing, etc. – so as to redirect attention to a different subject, or to alter the picture's impact. *Balance* is a very subjective effect. You cannot measure it. But there are number of useful guiding principles:

1. A center-frame position is satisfactory; safe but dull to watch.
2. As a subject moves from picture center, the shot feels progressively unbalanced.
3. This effect arises more strongly with bigger and/or darker objects; especially if high in the frame.
4. A subject or tonal mass to one side of the frame usually requires compensatory counterbalancing in the remainder of the shot. This could be an equal opposite mass (symmetrical balance), or a series of smaller areas that together counterbalance the main offset region.
5. Tone influences visual *weight*: darker tone subjects look heavier and smaller than light-toned ones.
6. A small darker area, slightly offset, can balance a larger light-toned one further from picture center.
7. Darker tones towards the top of the frame produce a strong downward thrust – top-heaviness, a depressed closed-in effect. At bottom frame they introduce stability and solidity.
8. Balance is more influenced by vertical elements than horizontals; although the overall horizontal effect determines the final balance.
9. Regularly shaped subjects have greater visual weight than irregular ones.

Fig. 7.7 Unity (order)
Unity is cohesion; interrelationship of masses. A picture can be balanced, yet not be unified (1), or a group unified without overall balance (2). Real or imaginary compositional lines create visual unification. Lines or tones that divide the screen (3) disrupt unity.

10. Warmer colors (red, orange) appear heavier than cooler ones (blue, green), bright (saturated) hues looking heavier than desaturated or darker ones.

Unity (order)

When the composition of a shot is *unified* all its component parts appear to hang together, and form part of a complete pattern. Without unity, one has the impression of randomness; of items being scattered around the frame.

Wherever possible, try to group subjects (either across the screen or in depth) so that they appear interrelated – by real or imaginary compositional lines (Figures 7.19 and 7.20).

Fig. 7.8 Visual rhythm
1. Pictorial arrangements can produce a monotonous repetitive effect, or interesting variety of emphasis in shape or tone; a visual rhythm.
2. While verticals and diagonals give an emphatic rhythm, horizontals and slow curves convey a restful rhythm.
3. Although identical repetition is dull, used as a progressive visual development, repetition can build and strengthen a theme.

If you intercut between shots of a scene that give a very different impression from various viewpoints this can destroy *inter-shot unity*. So aim for visual continuity in style and tonal balance between successive shots.

Visual rhythm

In music and poetry the ear prefers a recognizable, but not too elementary, rhythmical beat; the eye also is attracted by a variety of pattern. *Visual rhythm* is a pattern term; a variation of visual emphasis, of outline. While a solemn, quiet mood is suited by slow, smooth-flowing lines; a rapid, spiky staccato would match an exciting, dramatic situation.

The emotional influence of tone

The set designer and the lighting director use light and shade to create the picture's emotional key.

Fig. 7.9 part 1 Tonal impressions
Sharply-defined tonal contrast (left) is used to isolate and define areas, suggest crispness, hardness, vitality, dynamism.
Graded tone (right) blends areas together, guiding the eye from darker to lighter regions. It suggests softness, beauty, restfulness, vagueness, lack of vigor, mystery.

Fig. 7.9 part 2 Tonal emphasis
Tonal contrast emphasizes shape and mass. A small dark area becomes subjugated within a large white background, whereas a small light area stands prominently from a dark tone.

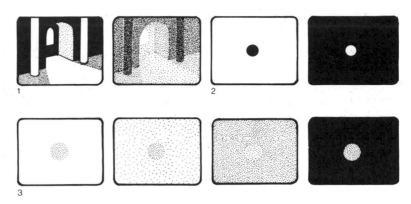

Fig. 7.9 part 3 Simultaneous contrast (spatial induction)
Adjacent tones interact. A light tone can make a nearby one look darker; while a dark area apparently lightens a light tone further. The same central tone here appears different as its background changes. The sharper the contrast and borders, the stronger this effect.

Large areas of contrasting tone can give a picture strength, vigor, significance. And in practice, most attractive shots usually include a wide variety of tones.

Where tones in a picture are predominantly light, the effect is open, simple, perhaps weak. Add small distinct areas of dark tone, and the picture develops a liveliness, cheerfulness, delicacy. Darker tones give a shot strength and significance. They can add force and dignity.

But pictures with large areas of unrelieved dark tone can look somber, heavy, or sordid. The overall impression can be disappointingly dull and uninteresting. Little detail or tonal gradation is generally visible, and video noise is often prominent. When there are smaller distinct light areas within the dark tones the overall effect tends to be mysterious, dramatic, or solemn.

Scale

We judge how large or small a things is by comparing its size and proportions with familiar items we recognize in the picture. Without a comparative scale, we can only guess. A finger moves into shot, and we realize that a chair we are looking at is a skilfully made miniature. The eye is easily fooled, as you can see in Figures 7.10, 10.26 and 10.27.

Fig. 7.10 Scale
The viewer judges scale subjectively; by how fully the subject fills the screen and by the presence of other objects of known size.
If size-references are omitted (absent or obscured by viewpoint) accurate interpretation of scale may be impossible.

Fig. 7.11 Foreground and scale
Foregrounds influence our impression of scale and distance; particularly for isolated and remote subjects. Try to include foreground and perspective clues to define and unify depth; but avoid over-emphasized, stylized, and artificial relationships.

Perspective lines can influence our impression of scale and relative size.

Again, although there is no relationship between shot size and the size of the subject, we often assume when an unfamiliar subject fills most of the frame that it is larger than it really is.

Subject prominence

A subject's *surroundings* have a considerable influence on our attitude towards it. Consider the difference between a coin imposingly displayed on a velvet cushion . . . or heaped with others in a rusty junk box. Depending on how you present a subject, it can appear important or trivial. It can look powerful or weak; interesting or incidental. It may even be overlooked altogether!

Isolation gives a subject emphasis. You can create this emphasis in many ways:

- By the subject's attitude,
- By contrasting tones,
- By the camera height,
- By the composition of the picture,
- By the subject's position and size relative to its surroundings,
- By using background pattern or form to make the subject look more prominent.

You will find typical methods summarized in Figure 7.12.

Subject attitude

A performer's associative attitudes can modify his effective strength, whether he looks forceful, cowed, submissive.

His general *posture* is significant too. *Weak attitudes* include side or rear views, lying down, looking down, bowed, stooping, clasped hands, and slow movements. *Strong attitudes* include frontal view, uptilted head, hands clenched, stamping feet, and fast movement.

Camera treatment can have a considerable influence on our reactions to a subject. Shooting a ranting dictator in a high-angle long shot would make his gestures appear futile, weak, and ineffective. However, a low-angle mid-shot would give them a powerfully dramatic force.

Where you use a strong camera treatment for weak performance attitudes you strengthen them; so that an old woman making weak submissive gestures could seem to have a dignity and an inner strength against adversity when shot from a depressed viewpoint.

Fig. 7.12 part 1   How subject strength is influenced by viewpoint
1. Unsuitably arranged, a subject's strength is diminished.
2. Low-angle shots emphasize subject strength and importance; while high-angle shorts suggest weakness, unimportance.
3. Subject-strength grows as the shot gets closer.

Fig. 7.12 part 2   Subject strength – frame position
Set higher in the frame, the subject gains strength.

Fig. 7.12 part 3   Subject strength – size proportions
Relative proportions of subject size and surroundings will affect the subject's 'power'.

Fig. 7.12 part 4   Surroundings influence subject strength
1. A supported subject appears weaker than an unsupported one.
2. A subject can be dominated by dynamic scenic lines, or by other stronger subjects.
3. Background line and tone can strengthen or weaken the subject.

Picture shape

A picture's shape can affect the viewer's feelings towards the scene. A *horizontal* format can give it stability, restfulness, extent . . . A *vertical* format can imply height, balance, hope . . .

The original motion picture screen shape (aspect ratio) had 4:3

Fig. 7.13 Picture shape
The effective picture shape can be modified by (1) electronic wipes, camera mattes (vignettes); or (2) by using a scenic opening as a border; or (3) by restricted lighting.

(1.33 : 1) proportions. But subsequently, to enhance big-screen presentation, several others were developed (1.65 to 2.55 : 1). Television adopted the original 4 : 3 format; and while this cannot be intrinsically altered, you can change its *effective shape* by introducing mattes (wipes), masks, scenic restriction or by lighting restriction.

Unifying interest

You should normally arrange a picture so that the eye can find satisfaction within the frame; concentrating on certain features, while the rest become a subordinate background. Avoid three-ring circus techniques, with several things happening simultaneously. They divide attention, creating ambiguity and confusion. One picture – one focal point.

Fig. 7.14 Split interest
Aim to localize interest. Avoid split centers of attention, except for dramatic purposes.

Unifying the center of interest does not prevent you moving it around freely. This continual flow, linking together parts of the picture, is often termed *transition* or *continuity*. The eye moves naturally from one area to the next.

Speed of compositional lines

The eye scans some shapes at a leisurely rate (gently curved lines), while others are appreciated quickly (straight lines, zig-zags). Through suitable selection, you can adjust the picture's vitality and the speed with which the eye examines it. Faster lines move attention quickly and would allow fast intercutting.

Simple lines and shapes direct attention more readily than complex or disjointed ones. Interest is strongly attracted by clear-cut geometrical shapes, particularly when they seem to arise accidentally. An excess of simple line soon palls though, and leads to a stark unsympathetic atmosphere.

Fig. 7.15 Speed of composition lines
1. A pattern or direction-of-line over which the eye lingers is termed 'slow'. Predominating curved lines suggest leisure, beauty, deliberation.
2. 'Fast' lines are usually straight or angular, creating an impression of speed and vitality.
3. Unbroken lines are faster than broken ones.
4. Direction of movement will affect 'speed'; the first three directions being generally faster than the remaining four directions.

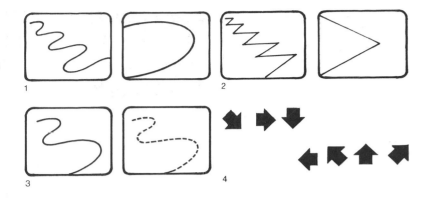

Continuity of centers of interest

Although our eyes continually move around the picture, we usually find that interest is localized at any given moment to about one-twelfth of the screen area. You can divide the 4 by 3 frame into twelve equal segments.

Where successive centers of interest are widely spaced, the viewer's concentration must be disrupted to some extent while he seeks each new spot. Fast interlinking composition lines help here. This situation particularly arises, of course, whenever you cut to another shot. If the new picture presents an entirely different interest location, the audience becomes overaware of the transition; so the points should be reasonably matched.

Poorly matched transitions, especially between numerous brief-duration shots, can accelerate mild audience resentment into marked hostility. This situation arises all too regularly where editors demonstrate

Fig. 7.16 Related shots
The compositional arrangements and action can move the eye about the picture. On cutting to another shot, a new center of interest presents itself. If the centers are too dissimilar, as in the first pair of illustrations, the viewer becomes over-aware of the change. But where reasonably matched, the transition may be almost unnoticed.

Fig. 7.17 Movement of interest
Good visual continuity between shots does not necessitate static arrangements. Composition and action can introduce unlimited interest-movement, providing successive shots match at the transition.

their prowess by rapid cutting to the beat of fast music. Even if synchronism is perfect, inept matching of centers of interest (often with too little time to examine each shot) becomes totally frustrating.

In certain types of program (e.g. pop videos, program trailers) a vogue has developed for fast cutting between a series of completely unrelated shots. The result can be an exciting montage, as one unexpected image after another hits the screen, and the eye searches for points of interest. Or it can be a haphazard, meaningless confusion. Clearly, a technique to be handled carefully!

Composition continuity in multi-camera production

A regular problem in multi-camera production is that a composition set-up that looks great from one viewpoint may be quite disappointing from another. On cutting, you find that the new shot is unbalanced, or lacks unity. It may draw attention to the wrong subject. The more complex the set-up, the greater is the chance of this happening.

Fig. 7.18 Cross-cut shots
1. If successive pictures are matched accurately, some visual confusion can arise when inter-switching between cameras.
2. Where alternative foci are continually being intercut, it may be less disturbing to space (offset) centers of interest.

There are several ways of overcoming this problem and controlling compositional continuity:

1. You might rely on the well-composed main shot, and just accept the shortcomings of the other brief shots.
2. You can arrange subjects so that they suit all shooting angles – as in most interviews.
3. If shooting is *discontinuous*, you might slightly rearrange the composition of each shot in turn (*cheat*) – people's positions, set dressing, lighting. This is a regular practice during filming, for it produces optimum results. But it can be very time consuming, and cause continuity errors.
4. You can recompose the first shot so that it is still satisfactory . . . but more suitable for the next shot's composition.

Fig. 7.19   Care in grouping
Cameras shooting actuality, have to select from available grouping. But by attention to people's positions a wider range of shots becomes possible.

1. People must normally work closer together than in everyday life, to avoid widely spaced shots.
2. Where close spacing is inappropriate. cross-shooting groups them.
3. Although parallel face-to-face conversation may seem more natural, slight angling improves shot-opportunity.
4. Similarly, closed groups are better opened up.

Fig. 7.20 part 1   Continuity of composition – two shot
The subject can be arranged to provide appropriate composition from several viewpoints.

Fig. 7.20 part 2   Continuity of composition – three shot
Although composition continuity becomes more difficult with larger groups, a variety of shots is available with careful grouping.

5. You can reposition performers just at the moment of the transition. So having delivered a line, the actor turns away . . . on the cut . . . to a new position.

Color impact

Most of us take color for granted. We accept that a surface is a particular shade of green, for example. But in fact, what we are interpreting as 'green' can vary considerably: with the color of the light falling on the surface, its angle, any other nearby color, and various other factors.

Surface effect

The color of a smooth surface generally looks 'purer' (more saturated) than a rough-textured one of identical color; its brightness, too, will change more noticeably with the light direction. The color of a surface can seem to vary with the quality of the incidental light, appearing brighter and more saturated under hard light than under diffused lighting. A color surface may reflect light onto a nearby subject – so the face of a person wearing a yellow sweater may be tinged yellow by its reflected light.

Fine color detail

Our eyes cannot readily detect fine detail in color. Where a scene contains tiny areas of color (whether small patterns or distant subjects) these will seem to get paler as they grow smaller. The actual color of fine detail can become difficult to identify. Yellow, for instance, tends to become indistinguishable from light gray, and blue detail can become confused with dark gray. Similarly, bright areas of green, blue-green, and blue appear identical when very small. Eventually, as detail size diminishes, even strong reds and blue-greens become indistinguishable, so that you can only detect differences in brightness between them.

Warm and cold colors

Colors are often associated unconsciously with warmth and distance. Red, yellow, and brown seem 'warm', and areas of these colors tend to look bigger and nearer than the 'cool' hues such as blue and green. You will find, too, that darker and more saturated colors seem nearer than lighter or desaturated ones.

Subjectively, the pictorial 'weight' of a color is often affected by its 'warmth': warmer tones seem heavier than cooler ones, saturated colors look heavier than duller desaturated ones. For these reasons, it is desirable when composing masses in a picture to keep areas of saturated color small, for they can easily balance much larger ones of desaturated color.

Simultaneous color contrast (lateral color adaptation)

The appearance of any color can be considerably affected by the background against which it appears; an effect known as *simultaneous contrast*. A green dress against gray drapes will not only look greener than normal, but the gray background itself may tend to take on the complementary hue (magenta) and appear 'warmer'. If you place a white object in white surroundings, and illuminate it with both white and magenta light, its shadow appears to be green! Clearly, the eye and the brain can play strange tricks!

The same turquoise object may look lighter, darker, bluer, greener, according to its background colors. When a strong color appears against a pale version of the same hue the background seems grayer. A strong color will appear more vibrant when backed by white, than against black. Conversely, a darker color is more pronounced against a black background. Any color will look brightest and strongest against its complementary color.

Even *neutral tonal values* (white, grays, black) are modified by their background. The darker the background, the lighter will the subject tones appear to be (and vice versa). Light tonal areas look larger. Darker tones look heavier. All these factors can strongly influence our impressions of size, distance, and pictorial balance.

Separation of color

Although color surfaces may in reality be some distance away from each other, they can appear adjacent when seen together within the shot. So there is a mutual interaction between them.

Bright colors

Bright colors hold the attention – particularly scarlets, bright yellows, and orange. But their prominence can become embarrassing when they are defocused, for the eye turns to them yet cannot see detail there. Pastel (desaturated) hues do not pose this problem – but they, on the other hand, can lack vigor and visual appeal if widely used.

Where there are reasonably equal areas of strong color a disharmonious tension can develop between them, particularly where they are not complementary. So it is preferable to have one or more of them desaturated (i.e. grayed-off, less vivid).

Approximate color constancy

This illusory effect continually influences our evaluation of color. We experience it when looking at a picture containing a familiar subject of known color – a mailbox, perhaps. Having fixed on this item, we go on to judge other colors in the picture accordingly. Even where the reproduced color of this subject is considerably different from that of the real thing, the brain adjusts its interpretation, so that we are predisposed to see it as 'correct'; perhaps regarding others nearby as inaccurate, although they are actually satisfactory.

All interpretation is subjective. We regularly misinterpret as 'white' areas that in reality are quite blue or yellow. Blue puddles on the sidewalk may look unnatural, although they truly reflect a blue sky. A 'black' object in bright sunlight may actually be reflecting more light than a dimly illuminated 'white' – although our brain, making a comparative judgement, refuses to believe this.

After-images

After looking at a color for some time you will often experience a brief color 'hang-over' on switching to the next shot. Following exposure to red, you will see a blue-green (cyan) ghostly after-image on a black screen. After orange, a peacock-blue after-image follows. Yellow gives blue; green gives purple (magenta); while after blue an orange-yellow image is seen.

Bearing this in mind, you would expect some interaction between a succession of colors. Such *successive contrast* causes white to appear bluish-green after looking at a red screen. Similarly, yellow appears bright green; blue appears more intense and greenish; while repeated red has a grayed appearance.

Admittedly, these are extreme situations, but color distortion on quick cuts and the visual fatigue that follows overexposure to a strong color are not to be disregarded.

Color associations

Color and emotion are inextricably interlinked. Color associations are legion. For example:

Red – with warmth, anger, crudity, excitement, power, strength.
Green – with spring, macabre, freshness.
Yellow – with sunlight, the Orient, treachery, brilliance.
White – with snow, delicacy, purity, cold.

Dynamic composition

So far, we have been discussing the composition of *still* pictures, or pictures with little movement – principles that have long been widely accepted. But what happens when the subject and/or the camera *moves*? Then a series of interesting dynamic effects develop that offer us exciting opportunities. We have termed this previously unexplored field *dynamic composition*.

The still picture

Still photographs have become such a regular part of our daily life –
in newspapers, magazines, books, our own snapshots – that we accept
them as perfectly natural. Yet these 'frozen moments' really have
interestingly different characteristics from the real world we experience.
They encapsulate what something looked like at a particular *instant*.
It may not even be typical. The picture shows a segment of the world, and
puts a frame around it. This frame affects our impression of the subjects
within it.

Look at a video of any interview and examine a person's expressions
frame by frame! An animated face will appear to switch instantly,
appearing coy, surprised, bored, threatening, asleep, wistful . . . The brief
glimpses produce totally uncharacteristic effects that are not there when
seen at normal speed.

In everyday life we see a solid three-dimensional world. We do
not think about the 'composition' of the scene we are looking at.
Arrangements change continually as we move around.

In a still picture, whether it is a photograph or a painting, subjects
within the frame become part of an enclosed pattern. We become aware of
the *tonal masses*, *directional lines*, *perspective*. In the real world, we do not
respond to this degree.

Part of the attraction of a still picture lies in the fact that we can study
its details at leisure. We can concentrate on any aspects that interest us.
Action that is intriguing when we catch only a fragmentary glimpse may
prove uninteresting when we watch it in its entirety. A situation that is
effectively composed in a still may become less attractive when movement
rearranges its component parts. The underlying appeal of many great
paintings and sculptures lies in this indefinable feeling of 'suspended
animation about to commence'.

Compositional balance that appears so forceful in a still often goes
unnoticed during motion. Take a photograph of a horse leaping a fence,
and the shot can look dynamic, strong, graceful. Show a moving picture
of the same action, and the result may seem quite commonplace and
unexciting.

Certain production techniques spring from this idea of *uncompleted
action* in order to savor and emphasize the dynamics:

● During a fight scene the director cuts to a *freeze frame*, or a sequence
   of stills showing people flying through the air, or crashing to the ground.
● Intercutting between brief shots of action without showing us
   the results of the action. The executioner's hand moves forward . . .
   a bystander starts to speak . . . a head turns . . .
● Showing an action sequence, then fading out before it ends. The hero
   walks into the distance . . . the picture fades.

Such methods create a *climax* – which, if left to follow through, would
often lead to an anticlimax.

Potentials of the moving picture

A still picture seldom holds the attention for long. The moving picture offers *continued interest*. Movement attracts. Through change, the director can introduce variety in the picture, and hold the audience's attention concentrated on the particular subject he chooses. Changes enable him, for example, to:

- Alter a subject's prominence,
- Redirect the viewer's attention,
- Add or remove information as the audience watches,
- Transform the mood of the scene,
- Show movement, growth, development.

Even this brief list reminds us of the potential persuasive power of the moving picture.

The *still picture* allows the viewer freedom to scrutinize and assess. The *moving picture* often gives him time to grasp only the essentials, before it is replaced by the next; particularly if action is fast or brief.

If the information in a succession of pictures is obvious, simple, or familiar to the audience, changes can be rapid. (A sophisticated or informed audience may actually find the fast pace stimulating, as they rapidly assess each new shot.) But if the pace is too great for your audience, they are likely to build up resentment as you snatch away each shot before they have finished looking at it. In the end their attention and interest can lapse.

Movement can be dynamic and stimulating – or confusing and tiring. It depends on the subject, and your audience.

Fig. 7.21 part 1   Representing movement
Symbols can represent many different dynamic situations – the subjects, their direction, and their path within the TV frame.

Fig. 7.21 part 2   Dynamic effects
As the symbol moves within the frame and approaches other symbols, we sense dynamic changes in relationships. Similar effects occur as subjects move around within a real picture.

Fig. 7.22 Gravity
There is a tendency to interpret movement within the picture as if gravity were always involved. So in these illustrations movement is seen as:
1. Normal progress.
2. Moving uphill; climbing.
3. Moving downhill; descending.
4. Rising.
5. Falling.
Such movement is regarded as difficult, easy, forceful, weak, etc.

A theory of dynamic composition

In daily life we continually make very subjective judgements as we assess the movements and speed of things around us. As we drive through flat, featureless country we feel that the car is traveling at a much slower speed than the speedometer shows. Driving along a tree-lined road, the reverse happens, and we tend to overestimate speed.

Fig. 7.23 The impression of movement
1. Our impressions of movement in a picture often depend on the way the subject is framed, on the apparent speed of other subjects, and on the passing background. Firmly framed against a plain background, there is no sense of movement. If the subject's position wavers and it is known to be moving, the movement is assumed to be so fast as to be difficult to follow. Add signs of a background racing past (e.g. aircraft in clouds) and the sense of movement and speed grows considerably.
2. To this there can be added four general axioms. Movement across the screen tends to appear exaggeratedly fast. Movement to or from the lens seems slower for narrow-angle, faster for wide-angle lenses. Camera movement in the direction of subject movement reduces its speed. Camera and subject moving in opposite directions increase their mutual speed and impact.
3. The flat screen can cause the viewer to misinterpret spatial movements. On camera the people seem to be running to meet – but the plan view shows otherwise!

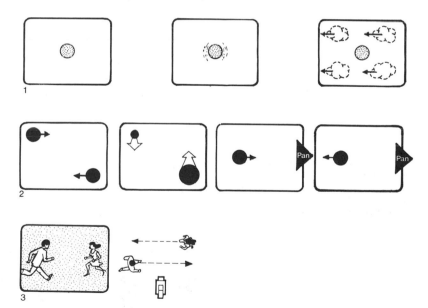

Watching moving pictures, we carry over these arbitrary interpretations. Because the image is within a frame, and two-dimensional, there are further influences.

We cannot *see* speed and movement in the picture, we can only interpret from clues that are there. Against a plain white sky, a fast-moving aircraft appears stationary. When we see the landscape beneath streaking past, we have an impression of speed.

Fig. 7.24 Restriction of movement by the frame

1. When we see movement *in free space* (e.g. a flying bird), it appears to have total freedom. But when we see the same action within the frame of a picture, an illusion of *restriction* develops. The frame subjectively 'inhibits movement'. If we hold the subject center-frame as it moves, this sense of restriction is limited. But in closer shots, the frame appears to impede movement.
2. When we frame the picture to keep the moving subject near the *lagging edge* of the picture, restriction is much less.
3. But when we frame the subject near the leading edge, its restriction becomes emphasized.

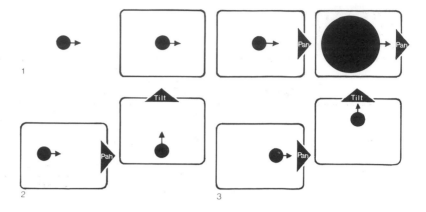

Here are a few typical ways in which we react to movement in a picture:

1. *Effort.* Slower speeds can suggest effort; that a movement is difficult; especially if it is accompanied by sounds that are similarly associated (e.g. low pitched, forceful, percussive). If we replay a normal action in slow motion, this can increase the impression of effort involved. We also interpret the amount of effort, from signs of strain, tension, slipping, etc., even when these have been faked.
2. *Relative speeds.* We assess the speed at which someone is running towards us by the rate at which their image size grows. (Shot on a narrow-angle lens, this increase is slow, so we lose a sense of speed.)

Fig. 7.25 Restriction of movement by masses

The shape and position of masses (moving or still) in the picture can alter the interpretation of events.

1. The mass in the path of the moving subject suggests imminent impact or arrest.
2. Converging, encircling, crushing, as when a crowd presses in on a central figure.
3. Expansion, new freedom, isolation, as when using an iris-out wipe.

Even complicated situations can be arranged to emerge quite naturally.

4. The restricted feeling aroused by the traveler moving at dusk between darkened sky and ground.
5. The compression effect as the camera pans left (following the pursuer), and the wall moving frame-right create a pincers compression movement towards the distant victim.
6. As the camera dollies down the alley, the distant light area grows – creating an expansive effect.

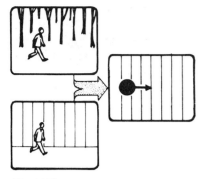

Fig. 7.26 Background patterns
As subjects move past them, background patterns can exert strong effects upon picture impact.

Fig. 7.27 Background and subject movement
Where movement is in the direction of background pattern, the movement will appear unimpeded if slightly restricted. The line emphasizes direction. Where the subject moves across (against) the pattern, effort is emphasized; movement appears stronger. Subject shape may modify these effects.

Fig. 7.28 Moving background and subject 'strength'
Against a plain background, the effect of this low-angle shot remains constant as the subject walks and the camera dollies back. But if a series of horizontals move downwards (crossboards in a ceiling) during the move, *it is considerably strengthened.*

3. *Space.* When there is a lot of space (border) around a subject in the picture it can modify our impression of speed, compared with a closer shot.
4. *Relative movement.* Where more than one plane is moving within the frame we sense an underlying pattern of *compression* (impact, collision), or *expansion* (parting, stretching, strain).

1

2

Fig. 7.29 Background and directions
1. When the subject moves across a static patterned background, the viewer feels an undertow of movement. Where the subject is held in frame and the background passes the direction of this undertow changes.
2. As the subject moves over the upward-sweeping background, an upward force seems to be exerted on the subject. In addition, background tones modify its apparent size and importance.

1   2

Fig. 7.30 Speed
The subject's shape can affect its apparent speed.
1. Although moving at the same speed the 'tall' object appears to be moving faster than the 'flat' object.
2. The apparent speed is also increased as the background becomes more detailed. Shot-size will modify how much of the background is visible and hence effective speed-impact.

Fig. 7.31   Rhythm
Visual rhythm from the passing background will seldom be as regular as these examples, although quite strong rhythmical patterns can be built up naturally from passing flags, trees, palings, etc.

5. *Gravity*. Although gravity is irrelevant, we subconsciously associate movement and position within the frame with gravitational forces. Something moving from top to bottom appears to be moving downwards, sinking, falling, collapsing. Moving from bottom to top of the shot, it is rising against gravity, floating, climbing.

6. *Fixation point*. The visual impact of movement can depend on where we happen to fix our attention. Looking skyward, we see moving clouds and static buildings . . . or static clouds and toppling buildings.

7. *Power*. Slower movements tend to suggest greater power and force. If a car hits a wall in fast-motion, the wall simply falls down. We judge

Fig. 7.32 part 1   Patterns of movement
Some movement patterns have widely accepted associative feelings.
1. Continuity.   2. Vigor; excitement, indecision.   3. Beauty, charm.
4. Expansion.   5. Contraction, collapse.
Smooth action suggests control, evenness, simplicity; while *jerky* irregular motion suggests the clumsy, erratic, uncontrollable.

Fig. 7.32 part 2   Patterns of movement
In massed dance and marching, the viewer sees simple pattern formations from group movement, and individual movements.

that the wall was weak. In a slow-motion replay the car seems to crash into the wall, which breaks apart under great force. The dynamics are changed.

8. *Strength*. Something that is large in the frame, and is moving towards the camera, appears to grow stronger and more threatening. Seen from a side viewpoint, the same action (e.g. a truck backing) can seem quite incidental.

Using dynamic composition

As you can see in Figure 7.21, we can represent subjects and their movement within the picture by symbols. These provide a convenient 'shorthand' method of showing complicated effects. You could test these effects for yourself by drawing a succession of frames at the edge of these pages, and flicking through them to animate an example.

Whether we are looking at symbols or real subjects, the effects of movement can considerably affect the way we interpret what we are seeing:

● The apparent effects of gravity (Figure 7.22).
● Our impressions of movement (Figure 7.23).
● The frame appears to restrict movement (Figure 7.24).
● Tonal masses appear to restrict movement (Figure 7.25).

Fig. 7.33   The dynamic effect of tone
The effective strength of static and moving masses varies with tone.
1. When a dark subject moves through converging dark areas, the mutual impact is powerful.
2. For lighter tones the 'crushing' effect is lightweight against a heavy substantial subject.
3. The *apparently* larger but lightweight subject suggests less resistance to approaching forces. There is a hint of destruction.
4. Both subject and approaching forces are lightweight, so the effect is less dynamic than in the first example.
5. Dynamic pursuit.
6. Ineffectual pursuit of strong subject.
7. Annihilation of vulnerable subject.
8. Undramatic. Following rather than pursuing.

Fig. 7.34 Changing visual significance
You can alter the strength of a subject by changing its *position*, its *size*, or its *background*.

1. The upward movement and higher position strengthens the left-hand person.
2. Striped object is approaching. At first it is insignificant, but with increasing size, its importance and interest exceed that of the static subject.
3. As the subject passes from the dark background to the light one, there is an emotional uplift.
4. Passing from a region of restrictive verticals to a plain background produces a sense of freedom, and an effective speed change (fast to slow).
5. As the shot cants off the horizontal, pictorial balance becomes unstable.
6. The camera tilts upwards, and the verticals in this background converge into diagonals.

Fig. 7.35 Dynamic effects between pictures
Seeing a rapid succession of shots (still or moving), the viewer subconsciously compares or contrasts them.

1. Cutting between scenes with similar movement-form or shape, emphasizes this effect.
2. The vigorous verticals of one scene contrasts effectively with the restful horizontals of the next.
3. The successive size differences here produce expansive jumps.

Fig. 7.36   Area of interest
1. With a slope to the right, the eye tends to favour the distance and so run out of frame.
2. With the reverse slope, the eye tends to favor the foreground.

Fig. 7.37   Concentration of interest
1. Placed on the left, the window is just part of the scene; the foreground person dominates. When it is on the right, the viewer anticipates important action through the window; the person becomes less important.
2. The viewer is very conscious of the watcher on the right, but only half-aware of his victims. Placed on the left, the watcher is nearly overlooked, attention focusing on his victims.

- Background patterns can affect our impression of movement (Figure 7.26).
- Background patterns can affect the effort of movement (Figure 7.27).
- Background patterns can affect apparent subject strength (Figure 7.28).
- Changes in the background can appear to interrelate with the moving subject (Figure 7.29).
- The apparent speed of a subject can be affected by its shape, and by the background pattern (Figure 7.30).
- The passing background can build up a visual rhythm (Figure 7.31).
- Patterns of movement can create an emotional response (Figure 7.32).
- The tones involved can affect a picture's dynamics (Figure 7.33).
- Movement can change the visual significance of a picture (Figure 7.34).
- Dynamic effects can result from a succession of shots (Figure 7.35).

Fig. 7.38   Direction of slope
Direction of the slope can alter a picture's attractiveness, there being a tendency for version 1 to seem more dynamic than 2.

Accepted maxims

You see the principles of dynamic composition applied daily; and from experience, some excellent widely accepted working axioms have emerged.

■ *Direction of movement*   Like vertical lines, vertical movement is stronger than horizontal, which is the least arresting.

Table 7.1   Lateral reversal effects

Pictorial balance	Subjects tend to look heavier (affecting balance more markedly) on frame *right*. So frame left can support more weight (i.e. greater density or mass) than right. A predominant mass on frame right can make the picture unbalanced or lopsided. The space between subject and left frame may appear excessive where masses predominate on frame right.
Pictorial stability	The picture may look more stable one way round than another; dormant in one version – but dynamic when reversed.
Apparent proportions	Large dark foreground areas on frame right may produce a crowded, shut-in, or heavy feeling; while the reverse gives a more open impression.
Subject strength	A composition element that seems unimportant when located on the left can become obtrusive on frame right (although the reverse seldom holds). A subject overlooked on left frame may become compositionally or dramatically significant on the right.
Area of interest	Our reaction to diagonal lines can vary with their slope direction. So our attention center can be directed in depth within the scene.
Concentration of interest	The eye tends to wander towards frame right (even with a predominant frame left subject). Where strong subjects are positioned frame right, left-hand subject may go almost unregarded.
Picture significance	Part of the scene may take on an implied significance in a mirrored version.
Visual interpretation	Our interpretation of what is happening or what the picture depicts may be modified by left–right disposition.
Direction of slope	A down-slope to the right tends to be interpreted as downhill; and an up-slope as uphill. This influences how difficult or forceful lateral movements along such slopes appear to be as they move in an 'uphill' or 'downhill' version. Similarly, a vertical object leaning or falling to the right tends to 'fall forward', rather than backward.

A left–right move is stronger than a right–left action.

A rising action is stronger than a downward one. Hence a rise from a seated position has greater attraction than a downward sitting movement.

An upward move generally looks faster than a horizontal one.

■ *Diagonal movement*   Like diagonal lines, this is the most dynamic movement direction.

■ *Movement towards the camera*   All forward gestures or movements are more powerful than recessive action away from the camera: a glance, a turned head, a pointing hand. Similarly, a shot moving towards a subject (dolly/zoom in) arouses greater interest than one withdrawing from it (dolly back/zoom out).

Where someone moves in front of another person (or scenery) they attract more attention than when moving behind them. Avoid such cross-moves in shots closer than mid-shot.

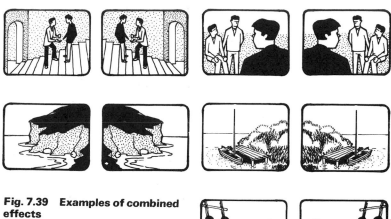

Fig. 7.39 Examples of combined effects
Check these examples, and see what differences you notice in the feel of the left and right-handed versions. (See Table 7.1.)

■ *Continuity of movement* While a moving subject attracts attention more readily than a static one, continuous movement at constant speed does not maintain maximum interest. Where action is momentarily interrupted or changes direction, the impact is greater than one carried straight through. Converging movements are usually more forceful than expanding ones.

Mirror images

If you look at any collection of photographs direct and then in a mirror you invariably find a difference in the appeal of the two versions. Differences may be great or slight; but they do modify the picture's impact.

The various effects that arise regularly through 'right-handedness' in composition treatment can influence which way round you arrange your picture to suit any particular purpose.

8 Editing

Editing can too easily degenerate into routine switching between shots. But skilful editing can make a vital creative contribution to production.

Editing in television production

In television production you will meet editing in three forms:

1. *Video switching* in real-time, using a *production switcher* (*vision mixer*).
2. Postproduction *videotape editing* (Chapter 14).
3. *Film editing* (Figure 13.1).

Although each of these processes is mechanically quite different, the *artistic effects* of editing in each case can be identical as far as your audience is concerned.

The nature of editing

In purely *mechanical* terms editing is concerned with:

1. The *moment* you choose to change from one shot to another (the *cutting point*).
2. *How* you make that change (*cut, mix,* etc.), and the *speed* of this transition.
3. The *order of shots* (*sequence*), and their *duration* (*cutting rhythm*).
4. Maintaining good picture and audio *continuity*. Combining action that was shot at different times and places, perhaps by a single camera.

At a purely *practical* level, editing allows you to create a smooth-flowing picture development. You can omit moments that are irrelevant, or distracting, or contain errors. You can shorten or lengthen the duration of action.

Editing overcomes mechanical problems. If a subject is just about to move out of shot . . . you can cut to a new viewpoint, and show the action continuing, apparently uninterrupted. Editing can bridge space and time.

Artistically, the potentials of editing are far-reaching. Editing decisions have a direct influence on how your audience responds to the program material; their interpretation, their emotional reactions.

Even where it is possible to shoot action in one continuous unbroken take, it is often preferable to introduce changes in camera position, shot coverage, composition, or to interrupt action. By doing so, you can influence audience response, change dramatic impact.

1. Editing can shift the centre of interest, redirect attention to another aspect of the subject or the scene.
2. Editing can emphasize, or hold back information.

3. Editing is selective. The order and duration of shots can affect how an audience interprets and reacts to them.
4. Editing can given an audience a sense of freedom: of being able to move rapidly in space and time. It can juxtapose events occurring at quite different times and places.
5. Editing can create interrelationships that may or may not have existed.
6. Editing can change the entire significance of an action in an instant – to create tension, humor, horror . . .

Editing and the TV director

In *film making*, a specialist editor and his assistants are responsible for the mechanics and techniques of the editing process; submitting the product for the director's critical appraisal in review. From the rough-cut, the final fine-cut version is developed.

In most TV shows the director does his own editing – either making spontaneous decisions, or working to a detailed script. He may operate the *production switcher* (*vision mixer*) himself. But usually a *technical director* or specialist *switcher* (*vision mixer*) operates the equipment under his instruction. For multi-camera productions most of the inter-shot switching is completed 'on the hoof' during the original recording.

Postproduction VT editing mainly involves: joining separate 'takes', inserting corrections, cutting overmatter. During VT editing, video effects may also be added, and audio sweetening carried out.

Whether a director works from a marked-up camera script showing all his planned intershot transitions; arranges editing during rehearsal; or makes spontaneous decisions during taping largely depends on the type of program.

Watching the preview picture monitors continuously showing his various video sources, the director selects at the required moment, switching the chosen source(s) onto line (transmission, main channel, studio output). The shots may have been planned precisely, approximately, or offered up by the cameramen and modified as necessary. Pre-recorded videotape or film are played in on cue. (These inserts may be separate segments, or excerpted from longer recordings.)

Each preview monitor *continually* displays all the pictures from its particular source: not only the shots that have been set up ready to be switched to line (transmission) but the endless random pictures. So a bank of monitors will show off-shot cameras moving into position, film channels running up to their next cue, graphics being set up, lighting adjustments, VT shuttling through . . . With this background, the director is busy concentrating on the sources of the moment, guiding the production team, instructing, correcting, selecting, coordinating their work. All this is in addition to checking performance, keeping on schedule, and coping with various contingencies. It is little wonder that under these conditions, 'editing' can degenerate into mechanical switching!

Videotape editing

As videotape recording developed, various production methods became possible that were quite impracticable during *live* transmissions. The elaboration of these techniques depends largely on the sophistication of the videotape editing facilities available.

Basically, videotape editing involves selecting and playing the sections of tape you want and recording the results on another videotape recorder; rather as one dubs sound from one audio tape recorder to another. But, as you will see later, in practice this can be a sophisticated, highly mechanized process!

The program sound is usually recorded alongside the video, on one track of the videotape. When the *picture* is edited, its associated sound will need to be dubbed off, and may require separate treatment. This will be done by an *audio engineer (sound supervisor)*.

The problems and opportunities of videotape editing begin with the way the director has decided to record the show (see Chapter 19, Table 19.3). The regular methods are:

- Live-on-tape,
- Basic retakes,
- Discontinuous recording,
- Dedicated VTRs,
- Isolated camera (ISO),
- Single-camera recording.

Live on tape

The program is recorded continuously in its entirety, as if it were a live transmission. The videotape is used here as a straightforward recording medium to provide more convenient scheduling of facilities and transmission, repeat transmissions, later analysis, etc. All editing is carried out on the studio production switcher during performance, and the show is ready for transmission at the conclusion of the recording session. A single videotape recorder (VTR) may be used; perhaps with a parallel VTR channel recording a duplicate version, in case of recording faults (*back-up copy, backing, insurance copy*). A very worthwhile practice, particularly when repeats are not possible!

Basic retakes

Here the production is recorded continuously as for transmission, but any errors (performers, production, technical) are re-recorded and the corrected sections substituted. *Duration trimming* may require some editing cuts – often covered by introducing *cutaways/nod shots/reaction shots*. As most programs can be improved by such editing, this method is widely used.

Discontinuous recording

The show may be taped in a series of sequences or scenes, each retaken as necessary to correct or improve. These *takes* can be shortened, action removed, or their order changed. Sometimes several versions are shot; the preferred one being selected later. The production switcher is used for most intershot transitions.

During later videotape editing, sections (containing their own intrinsic editing) are dubbed off in their final order to form an edited composite tape. Further audio treatment (audio sweetening) can be added at this stage (background music, audio effects) from unsynchronized audio disc or tape. Various video effects may be introduced during post-production editing (wipes, multi-images, color synthesizer treatment, detail insertions, etc.).

Dedicated VTRs

Here each camera's output is separately recorded on its own dedicated VTR. No production switcher is used during recording; all transitions and selections being made during a postproduction dubbing session to form a composite tape.

Videotape editing is carried out using complex computer-controlled facilities incorporating digital editing techniques, all guided by time-code shot identification. As a one-hour program may involve 300–400 individual edits, the operation clearly requires systematic organization of sophisticated postproduction facilities.

Isolated camera (ISO)

Here the production, which may be live or 'live-on-tape', is edited 'on the hoof' with the studio production switcher, and taped by the *main VTR*. However, throughout the show, pictures from one of the cameras are *also* being recorded on a separate isolated VTR. (The camera chosen for the 'ISO' can be varied at any time.)

Pictures from the ISO camera can be selected on the switcher whenever they are needed, but all its shots (on-air and off-air) are taped on the isolated VTR. This arrangement provides several useful opportunities:

1. *Replay inserts.* A regular use for the isolated VTR is to provide *instant replay in slow motion* during a live or live-on-tape production. At any chosen moment (e.g. after a goal has been scored in a game) the ISO tape is stopped, rewound, and replayed into the program. (This tape may also be used for later videotape editing.)
2. *Cover shots.* The ISO camera may concentrate on one subject (e.g. always taking shots of the visiting nabob), so that no important action is missed when the director cuts away to another shot.
3. *Stand-by shots.* During a closed-circuit recording session you have the opportunity to take extra or alternative shots that can be used later to facilitate editing. But when you record a once-only situation (e.g. a

public event), this single program tape contains all the shots you have available. This can make any subsequent editing difficult.

If parts of the recording need to be replaced for any reason the only solution is to copy portions of the program tape, and re-insert them as 'repeat shots'. However, if the ISO camera records separate *additional* shots during the event (e.g. crowd shots, an overall view, or action seen from a different viewpoint) this extra material can be edited into the program tape wherever necessary, and allow editing changes or corrections to be made.

Single-camera recording

Here the production is shot in any convenient order, on a single camera. The portable VTR may be incorporated within the camera unit (*combo camera*), or carried separately. The VT editor receives a collection of tapes (cassettes or reels) containing everything that has been shot.

Types of editing

Three types of editing are widely used: *continuity cutting, relational cutting*, and *dynamic cutting*.

Continuity cutting

In *film editing* the editor may spend considerable time and thought in deciding on the final shot order, the exact cutting points, cutting rhythm, etc. Although this is possible with more sophisticated VT editing systems, time usually precludes this precision.

In most TV productions editing is simplistic, serving the practical purpose of interrelating viewpoints, creating a feeling of consecutiveness and order, interlinking dialog and action. At best, the technique provides a clear straightforward narrative, a smooth pictorial flow, and unobtrusive transitions. At worst, such *continuity cutting* becomes a purely functional routine.

Example
Mr Brown speaks – cut to CU of Brown.
Mr Smith speaks – cut to CU of Smith.
Anchorman speaks – cut to three-shot of group.

Relational cutting

Here, through intercutting, shots that have no direct connection in reality are deliberately given an implied relationship.

Examples

Woman seen walking up to house, *cut* to woman in a room. We assume she entered house, and is now in a room there. (Actually shot with different women in similar costume, at different locations).

Shot of aircraft in flight, *cut* to pilot at controls. (A library model shot has been intercut with a studio mock-up. Neither is real.)

Man approaches foot of stairs, *cut* to him coming upstairs. (Action may have been shot on different occasions.)

In *parallel cutting (parallel action)*, shots from two different locations or action groups are repeatedly intercut; usually as a dramatic development to heighten tension, e.g. fast intercutting between fugitive and pursuers. *Cross-cutting*, on the other hand, intercuts between different viewpoints of the same subject, usually for visual variety.

Whenever you join two shots together by a *cut* you immediately establish a relationship between them. This juxtaposition is both *physical* and *intellectual*.

Physically, the viewer's eyes become aware of the change, and begin tracing a fresh interest pattern in the new picture.

Intellectually, the viewer has to interpret the new picture. (Where are we now? What is this? What is happening?).

These responses are, of course interrelated. Where the shots are compositionally matched (matched cuts) and the significance of the second shot obvious, it will be a *smooth cut*.

Where shots are pictorially unmatched (jump cut, mismatched cut) the effect can be very disturbing, as the audience has to search around for the subject in the new shot. Similarly, their attention is disrupted if they do not instantly realize how the second shot relates to the first, or what it is all about.

Dynamic cutting

Sophisticated intercutting can create dramatic emphasis, convey moods or abstract ideas that are not readily expressed in more direct terms. The ideas themselves may not be implicit in the component shots. Cause–effect relationships are often interpreted.

Examples

Shot of broken window, *cut* to small boy crying. (A lost ball? Punished after breaking the window?)

Intercut shots symbolically suggesting 'Spring', 'Progress', 'Terror', etc.

The cut

The cut is the simplest transition. It is dynamic, instantly associated two situations. Sudden change has a more powerful audience impact than a gradual one, and here lies the cut's strength.

Fig. 9.1   The cut
The mechanics of picture transitions can be shown graphically. Here the *cut* (straight cut, flat cut) is shown – from one shot or scene to another.

Fig 8.2   Intercut shots of the same subject
1. Avoid cutting between similar or near-similar shots.
2. Extreme changes in shot size (e.g. over 5:1) are distracting, unless explained by dialogue or story-line (see Fig. 17.1).
3. Viewpoint angle cuts of less than 20° or over 60° can be visually disturbing.

Fig. 8.3   Visual continuity
1. The viewer can lose sense of direction where there are dissimilar backgrounds.
2. This is unlikely to happen where there is background continuity, or (3) compositional links between pictures.

Cutting, like all production treatment, should be purposeful. An unmotivated cut interrupts continuity and can create false relationships between shots. Cutting is not akin to repositioning the eyes as we glance around a scene, for we move our eyes with a full knowledge of our surroundings and always remain correctly orientated. On the screen, we know only what the camera show us; although guesses or previous knowledge may fill out the environment in our minds.

Cutting jumps attention between new viewpoints or locations, so the viewer has continually to relocate and interpret each new shot. This is a problem during fast intercutting between different locations.

Where quite dissimilar shots are intercut, your audience may have some difficulty in appreciating continuity or relationships. But you can establish an immediate connection through:

1. *Dialog* – introducing or implying the next shot's substance.
2. *Action* – establishing a cause–effect relationship.
3. *Common reference points* (a person) in both shots.
4. *Audio continuity*.

Occasionally, and *only* occasionally, you may want to mislead the viewer's continuity deliberately for a comic or dramatic purpose.

Where a quick viewpoint change seems obtrusive it has usually not been clearly *related*, and has not fulfilled the *purposes* outlined earlier. It is a change that the viewer has no reason to want or expect. Unmotivated changes rarely satisfy.

It is generally inadvisable to intercut between shots of widely differing size (LS to BCU), or over a wide angle unless the attention is tightly localized.

■ *The moment for the cut*   Cut should preferably be made on an *action* or *reaction* – turning head, gasp of astonishment, a rise. However, there are two philosophies about the moment to make the cut. Some editors contend that the cutting moment should be *just before* or *after* an action.

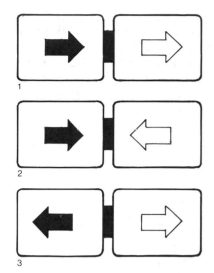

Fig. 8.4 Cutting between moving pictures
Cuts during movement create strong subjective effects.
1. *Directional* cuts between subjects moving in the same direction, suggests continuity of action or direction, pursuit, similar purpose.
2. *Reverse* cuts between opposite directions can suggest converging forces, impending meeting or collision, or (3) diverging forces, parting, expansion.

A transition during a movement can disrupt it and create a spurious cutting rhythm. Others maintain that by cutting *during* a movement you avoid the illusion of its being jerked into action or suddenly halted (from an in-motion shot to a static one). Where the aim is to transfer attention rather than create a visual shock, the cut can be hidden within action, as the audience is preoccupied with the movement itself.

■ *The delayed cut*   A *late* cut is frustrating. Badly timed, it has missed the optimum moment for change. But the *delayed cut* has exciting possibilities. It deliberately withholds the new shot until after the expected moment – in order to create audience suspense, interest, and anticipation. For example:

1. *Cutting on a reaction:*
   Knock at door. Writer looks up –
   Cut – Door opens. Woman enters. 'May I come in?'

2. *Delaying the cut:*
   Knock at door. Writer looks up. Door heard opening.
   Woman's voice, 'May I come in?'
   Cut – To woman at door, who enters.

■ *Cutting between moving pictures*   When moving shots are intercut, you invariably create spatial interactions between them, even when none exists. Intercutting such shots suggests:

1. Moving together (meeting, collision).
2. Moving apart (parting, expansion).
3. Moving in the same direction (following, chasing, similar destination).

To avoid these effects, cutaway shots or intermediate movement directions (to or from camera) can be introduced. Where the viewer is watching a single moving subject any direction changes should be obvious or deducible. Otherwise he will see distracting direction-jumps or may lose orientation.

■ *Cutting between static and moving pictures*   Cutting from a static scene to a moving one suddenly accelerates audience interest. The new shot springs into action; its speed, energy, or violence being accentuated by its sudden appearance.

Cutting from a moving scene to a static shot causes a sudden collapse in tension; which, if unsatisfied, can lead to a rapid fall-off in interest. Or it

Fig. 8.5 Avoiding directional reversal
Where a subject appears in successive shots showing movement in opposite directions, you can avoid accidental subjective effects by introducing an intermediate buffer shot showing a head-on view (perhaps including the actual change in direction).

Fig. 8.6 part 1   Matched and mismatched cutting

Mismatching on cutting can take several forms, but in each case results in visual disruption.

1. *Height changes* – mismatched lens-heights (for no dramatic purpose).
2. *Headroom changes* – mismatched headroom.
3. *Size jumps* – instantaneous growth or shrinkage occurs if subject size changes only slightly on the cut (e.g. a–b, or b–c). A difference of at least a–c (4:3 previous size) is desirable.
4. *Transformations* – if too closely matched, the viewer may see 'magical transformations' on the cut!

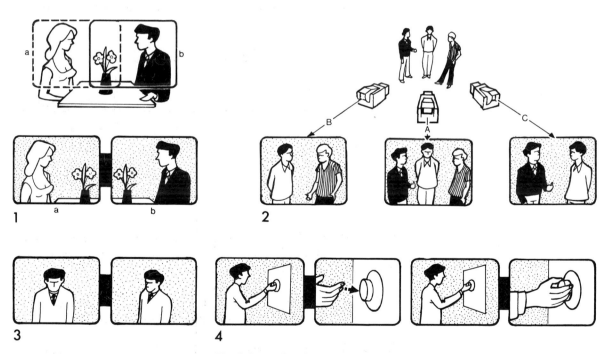

Fig. 8.2 part 2   Matched and mismatched cutting

1. *Jump cuts* – if the same subject is included iin successive shots, it may jump frame-position on the cut – a common dilemma in table shots.
2. It can arise also in group shots. Cameras A–B or A–C intercut, but not B–C.
3. *Twists* – a slight difference in the viewpoint can produce a turn or twist on cutting. Hopefully, the disruption may be disguised by 'motivating' the change (e.g. a singer turns to face the new camera), or by a slow dissolve.
4. *Continuity matching* – when shooting *discontinuously*, you must match shot detail and action for each cut, during editing; e.g. the moment of turning a knob, opening a door, lifting a glass. Otherwise continuity is disrupted.

Fig. 8.7 Rediscovery on a cut
Camera 1 pans, following the action. The black pillar passes out of shot (frame left). *Cut* to Camera 2 (to prevent shooting off) and the pillar is rediscovered on frame right again! A similar situation arises when someone who has just entered a shot is seen, after a cut, to re-enter the next.

Panning

can produce a highly dramatic interruption. For example, panning with a searcher around an empty room . . . and then *cut* – to a static shot of someone watching his actions.

■ *Cut to begin or end action*   These devices must be used with caution. They can too easily look like operational errors!

The cut-in: a shock introduction to vigorous action, catastrophe, chaos.
The cut-out: a severe, definite conclusive action as you cut to a blank screen at the end of a shot. An emphatic gesture or comment of finality.

Fig. 8.8 part 1   The cut-in

Fig. 8.8 part 2   The cut-out

The fade

■ *The fade-in*   This provides a quiet introduction to action. A slow fade-in suggests the forming of an idea. A fast fade-in has rather less vitality and shock value than the cut.

■ *The fade-out*   A quick fade-out has rather less finality and suspense than the cut-out. A slow fade-out is a peaceful cessation of action.

■ *The fade-out/in*   Linking two sequences, the fade-out/in introduces a pause in the flow of action. Mood and pace vary with their relative speeds and the pause time between them. You can use this transition to connect slow-tempo sequences, where a change in time or place is involved. Between two fasting-moving scenes it may act as a momentary pause, emphasizing the activity of the second shot.

A cut-out/in with a pause between shots is valueless. It always looks like a lost shot – or a mistake.

Fig. 8.9   The fade-in and fade-out
1. Fast fade-in.
2. Slow fade-in.
3. Fast fade-out.
4. Slow fade-out.
The fade-out and fade-in may be combined in permutation (slow-out, fast-in etc.) to link two shots producing a fade out-in.

Fig. 8.10   Combinations of fade and cut
1. The cut/fade-in results in a surge, a visual crescendo, strongly introducing the new shot.
2. The fade-out/cut-in produces a visual punch; used between a succession of static shots (e.g. of captions, paintings), provides a dynamic introduction to each.

The mix (dissolve, lap dissolve)

The *mix* is produced by fading out one picture while fading in the next. The two images are momentarily superimposed; the first gradually disappears being replaced by the second.

Mixing between shots provides a smooth restful transition, with minimum interruption of the visual flow (except when a confusing intermixture is used).

A *quick-mix* usually implies that their action is concurrent (parallel action).

A *slow-mix* suggests differences in time or place.

Mixes are generally comparative:

1. Pointing similarities or differences.
2. Comparing time (especially time passing).

Fig. 8.11   The mix (dissolve)
The mix usually compares successive shots.
1. Fast mix.
2. Slow mix.

3. Comparing space or position (mixing a series of shots showing progress).
4. Helping to relate areas visually (when transferring attention from the whole subject to a localized part).

Mixes are widely used as 'softened-off' cuts, to provide an unobtrusive transition for slow-tempo occasions where the violence of a cut would be disruptive. Unfortunately, they are used also to hide an absence of motivation when changing to a new shot!

A very slow mix produces sustained intermingled images that can be tediously confusing. Between different viewpoints of the same subject, they result in twin images.

■ *Matched dissolves*   By mixing between carefully matched shots with similarly framed subjects you can obtain a transformation effect. Its main applications are to suggest time changes (boy to man, seasonal change), or *flashbacks* (reversed time), or magical changes (pumpkin to Cinderella's coach).

■ *Mixes on movement*   Mixes during movement are usually only completely satisfactory when their relative directions are similar. Mixing opposite directions can arouse feelings of confusion, impact, or expansion, without necessarily indicating that these subjects are involved. But it is a transition to be used cautiously.

■ *Defocus dissolve*   The first camera gradually defocuses, while you mix to a second completely defocused shot which then sharpens. Normally used for *flashbacks*, but sometimes introduced for transformation effects, or decorative interscene transitions.

■ *Ripple dissolve*   Here the first shot becomes increasingly broken up by horizontal rippling (weave), during which you mix to a second rippling shot . . . which steadies to a normal image. Generally introduced for flashback effects.

The wipe

The wipe is a visual effect, mainly used for decorative transitions. It can be produced by several methods, but most production switchers include electronic wipe facilities. It had a particular vogue in early movies, and is now mainly used in trailers and commercials. There the visual impact of the wipes tends to disguise the raw edges of compositionally unrelated fragments.

The effect of the wipe is to uncover, reveal, conceal, fragment; according to how it is applied. In all forms it draws attention to the flat nature of the screen, destroying any three-dimensional illusion.

The wipe direction can aid or oppose the subject's movement, modifying its vigor accordingly. The edge may be sharp (hard-edged/hard wipe)

Fig. 8.12 part 1   Uncover wipe
Second image is progressively uncovered.

Fig. 8.12 part 2   Pushover wipe
Second image pushes over, displacing original one. (Push-off/pull-off/push-on wipe).

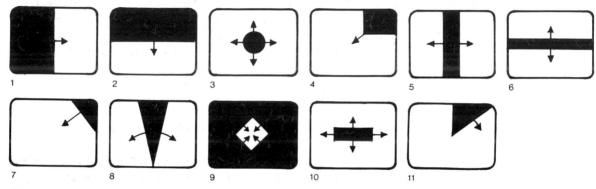

Fig. 8.12 part 3   Common wipe patterns
1. Horizontal wipe/line-split. (When static, this provides a split-screen).
2. Downwards vertical wipe.
3. Iris/circle wipe (out or in, expanding or contracting).
4. Corner wipe – top right. (When static, this provides a *corner inset*).
5. Barndoors/line bar/horizontal split wipe (expanding or converging).
6. Vertical split wipe/field bar (wipes out or in).
7. Diagonal (top right).
8. Fan wipe (in or out).
9. Diamond wipe-in.
10. Box wipe-out.
11. Rotary/clock wipe.

Fig. 8.12 part 4   Multiple and complex wipes
1. Multiple iris (out).
2. Blind wipe (out).
3. Cross wipe.
4. Explosion.
5. Multiple wipe with ripple (only the wipe-pattern ripples, not the pictures involved).
6. Hard-edge wipe.
7. Soft-edge wipe.

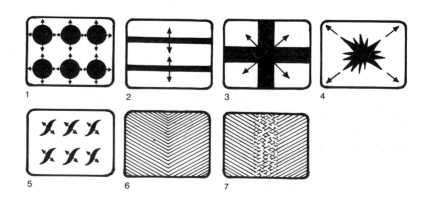

or diffused (soft-edged/soft wipe), the latter being much less distracting. Broad soft-edged versions can have the unobtrusiveness of a mix.

Wipes take many geometric forms with a variety of applications. A circular (*iris*) wipe, for example, may be used as a transition between close-up detail (a soloist musician) and a wider viewpoint (the full orchestra).

The split screen

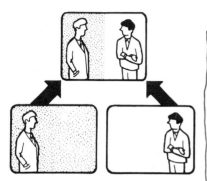

Fig. 8.13   Split screen
The screen is split into two or more segments, showing a series of pictures or respective portions of these components.

If a *wipe* is stopped during its travel, the screen remains divided; showing part of both shots. In this way you can produce a localized *inset*, revealing a small part of a second shot, or where the proportions are more comparable, a *split screen*.

The split screen can show us simultaneously:

1. Events taking place at the same time,
2. The interaction of events in separate locations (phone conversations),
3. A comparison of appearance, behavior, etc. of two or more subjects,
4. A comparison of before and after (developments, growth, etc.),
5. A comparison of different versions (comparing a relief map with its aerial photograph).

Superimpositions (half-lap dissolves, supers)

In film, superimposition necessitates exposing each frame twice or more (double exposure) in the camera, or more usually in the laboratory's optical printer. In television, you simply fade up two or more picture channels simultaneously.

Because the tones of superimposed pictures are additive, the light areas of any picture generally break through the darker tones of other shots with which it is superimposed.

Whether superimposed subjects appear solid or transparent will, therefore, depend on relative picture tones. Where a lighter-toned subject is superimposed on a *black background*, it will appear solid. On lighter-toned backgrounds, it will be proportionately diluted. Superimposed over multi-tones, the result appears 'transparent'.

But you must always guard against messy confused images, particularly where multi-colored or multi-tone shots are combined (color mixtures and lightness variations result). You should also avoid any movements (or zooms) of superimposed cameras where supers are being used to provide subject inserts, unless you want growth, shrinkage, or side-slip effects.

Superimposition can be used productionally to convey several ideas:

Fig. 8.14   Superimposition
Two or more pictures faded up at the same time; their relative strengths being controlled by video faders.

1. *Spatial montage:* suggesting that two or more events are occurring concurrently in different places.
2. *Comparison:* showing the similarity or difference between the subjects juxtaposed. (Bringing together action, events, locale, having parallel significance.)

3. *Development:* displaying stages in a process. (A half-built house with architectural sketches superimposed.)
4. *Relationship:* showing subjects' interrelationships, how components are positioned. (A mechanism superimposed on a faint image of the entire machine.)
5. *Thoughts:* a close shot of a person, with images of his thoughts superimposed.

Superimposition has a number of practical mechanical applications:

1. To obtain transparent-looking images (ghosts).
2. To achieve larger or smaller proportions (giants, dwarfs), by 'solid' superimposition.
3. To permit appearances and disappearances.
4. To combine titling with another picture.
5. To insert subjects (solid or transparent) into a separate background shot.
6. To add 'surface texture' (e.g. canvas), or a decorative border.
7. To emphasize or identify detail (map route, selected area pointer).

Order of shots

It is a characteristic of the human mind that we continually seek meaningful relationships in what we see and hear – even where none exists. In any rapid succession of shots we subconsciously try to establish a connection between them (slow mixes between them reduce this effect).

We can interpret a succession of shots in several ways:

1. Shot A may cause (or lead to) Shot B's situation.
2. Shot A may be explained by Shot B.
3. Shots A and B together may give rise to Shot C.
4. Shots A and B together may be explained by Shot C.
5. Shot A juxtaposed with Shot B may imply an idea 'X' that is not implicit in either A or B alone.

In various circumstances you may find that the order in which you present a series of shots will influence your audience's interpretation of them.

Even a simple example shows the nuances that easily arise. *A burning building – a violent explosion – men running towards an automobile.*

Altering the order of these shots, can modify what seems to be happening:

1. Fire – automobile – explosion:
   Men killed while trying to escape from fire.
2. Fire – explosion – automobile:
   Running from fire, men escaped despite explosion.
3. Automobile – explosion – fire:
   Running men caused explosion, firing the building.

Not only is the imagination stimulated more effectively by *implication* rather than direct statements but indirect techniques overcome many practical difficulties.

Suppose you join two shots: *A boy looking upward . . . tree falling towards camera*. One's impression is that a boy is watching a tree being felled. Reverse the shots and the viewer could assume that the tree is falling towards the boy who, sensing danger, looks up. The actual pictures might be totally unrelated; a couple of library shots.

Cause–effect relationships

Sometimes pictures convey practically the same idea, whichever way they are combined: *woman screaming* and *lion leaping*. But there is usually some distinction, especially where any cause–effect relationship is suggestible.

Cause–effect or effect–cause relationships are a common link between successive shots. Someone turns his head – the director cuts to show the reason. The viewer has become accustomed to this concept. Occasionally, you may deliberately show an unexpected outcome:

1. A bore and his victim are walking along a street.
2. Close-up of bore . . . who eventually turns to his companion.
3. *Cut* to shot of companion far behind, window gazing.

The result here is an amusingly sardonic comment.

But sometimes the viewer expects an outcome that does not develop and he feels frustrated or mystified, having jumped to wrong conclusions:

1. A lecturer in long-shot beside a wall-map.
2. *Cut* to a close-up of map.
3. Lecturer now in an entirely different setting.

The director used the map-shot to relocate the speaker for the next sequence, but the viewer expected to find the lecturer beside the map, and became disorientated.

Even more disturbing are situations where there is no visual continuity, although action has implied one:

1. Hearing a knock at the door, the girl turns . . .
2. *Cut* to a shot of a train speeding through the night.

The director thought that he would create tension by withholding who was outside the door, but he inadvertently created a false relationship instead. Even where dialog or action explains the second shot, this is an unsuitable transition. A mix or fade-out/in would have prevented misunderstandings.

Quite often, in an attempt to shorten scene duration and to create filmic time, directors cut from one shot to another in which the same person appears in different costume at a different time and place. Whether the technique is acceptable or confusing is challengeable.

Montage

In a montage we present a series of images which combine to produce an associative effect. These pictures can be displayed sequentially, as a multi-image screen, or superimposed.

1. *Sequential montage.* One brief shot follows another in rapid succession, usually to convey an abstract concept, such as 'Development, Prosperity, Civilization, Industry'.
2. *Multi-image montage.* We can show several images at the same time by dividing the screen into two, four, eight or 16 segments. Any smaller, and each section loses its impact and becomes part of an overall pattern. These images may be of the same subject, or of several different subjects. They can be *stills* (e.g. showing various stages as an athlete clears a pole vault) or *moving pictures* (e.g. showing different people using the same product).

    You can use a multi-image montage series for many purposes – to show steps in a process, to compare, to combine different viewpoints, to show action taking place at different places, to demonstrate different applications of a tool, to show variety, and so on.
3. *Superimposed images.* This form of montage is less used nowadays, for as images overlap each other the color picture quickly becomes confused; particularly where there is a lot of detail (see *Superimpositions*).

Fig. 8.15 Montage
1. A rapid succession of related images, or (2) juxtaposed images (quad split/segmented shot) or (3) superimposed images developing a common theme.

Duration of shots

If a shot is too brief the viewer will have insufficient time to appreciate its intended information. Held too long, and attention wanders. Thoughts dwell on the sound, eventually giving way to rumination – or channel switching! The limit for most subjects is probably around 15–30 seconds; and for a static shot, much less. For a mute shot, it could be as little as 5–10 seconds. The belief that a close shot can sustain interest longer is arguable.

Fig. 8.16 Response to cuts
1. The viewer's response to a cut is not instantaneous. When the cut is made, the audience-impact is slightly delayed; building to a peak and dying away gradually.
2. A series of cuts may achieve individual impacts; there being sufficient time for each reaction to subside.
3. Faster cutting may produce a cumulative build-up.
4. Through repetition, surprise may diminish with each cut, resulting in declining tension.

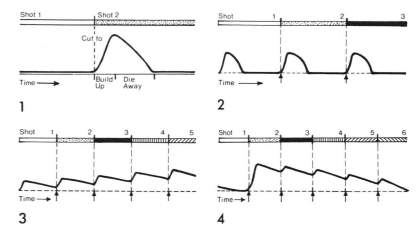

The 'correct' duration for a shot depends on its purpose. We may show a hand holding a coin for half a minute as its features are described by a lecturer; whereas in a drama, a one-second shot would tell us that the thief has successfully stolen it from the owner's pocket. Given the right occasion, even a single subliminal frame (1/30 or 1/25 second) can be seen and responded to!

Many factors influence how long you can usefully hold a shot:

1. The amount of information you want the viewer to assimilate (general impression, minute detail).
2. How obvious and easily discerned the information is.
3. Subject familiarity (its appearance, viewpoint, associations, etc.).
4. How much action, change, or movement the shot contains.
5. Picture quality (marked contrast, detail, strong composition, all hold most interest).

Audience attention is normally keyed to production pace. A short flash of information during a slow-tempo sequence may pass unnoticed, while in a fast-moving sequence it would have been fully comprehended.

Cutting rate

The frequency with which you can cut within a series of shots depends initially on successful shot matching, continuity, whether the transitions are motivated, and their purpose. Cuts may be used relatively unobtrusively; or as deliberate interruptions to shock, surprise, emphasize, accentuate. With the latter, you have to judge carefully the borderline between pleasurable shock and distracting annoyance.

Where the picture contains fast action, the cutting rate can be high; whereas in a slow-moving scene, fast cutting would usually be intrusive – unless perhaps the accompanying sound has a rapid tempo.

Although fast cutting is simple enough on the switcher, it may not be so easy for the cameras to get onto new shots between each cut. Unless you are repeat-intercutting the same set of pictures you may quickly run out of shots!

In a live program a fast average cutting rate during continuous action imposes considerable strain on the entire crew, as cameras rapidly readjust positions and compose their next shots. Unless the production treatment is straightforward, camera moves limited, and action reliable, operation standards are liable to deteriorate. A half-hour live telecast may contain some 200 shot changes; but figures tell us little, unless we know details of the camerawork involved.

Videotape recording, like filming, permits any cutting rate we choose. But clearly the briefer the shots to be selected and inserted into the program, the more exacting and time consuming the VT editing will be.

Cutting rhythm

Within a picture sequence we can become aware of certain intrinsic rhythms:

1. Subject movement – rhythm of moving machinery.
2. Composition changes – the dynamic effects of passing backgrounds (a line of trees).
3. Superimposed movement – regularly flashing street sign.

If you take two pictures (each with its own internal rhythms) and intercut them, a comparative effect results.

A *cutting rhythm* can be set up according to the durations of successive shots. Shot duration might, for example, be progressively shortened as tension rises – an increasing cutting rate. Long and short durations might be contrasted to compare leisurely and urgent paces. Similarly, you can use cutting rhythm to emphasize audio rhythm, or vice versa.

Picture monitor facilities

As you will remember, there is a bank of picture monitors (*channel monitors*) in the production control room, each displaying pictures from a particular source: Cam. 1, Cam. 2, Cam. 3, slides scanner, replay videotape, film . . . etc. In addition, there are two larger monitors. The *MASTER MONITOR* and the *SWITCHABLE PREVIEW MONITOR*.

The *MASTER MONITOR* (*line, main channel, program, transmission*) displays whatever you have selected on the production switcher to go to *line*. The *SWITCHABLE (SELECTABLE) PREVIEW MONITOR* displays whatever is switched to it by the *PREVIEW* bus on the switcher unit.

Quite often, the *MASTER MONITOR* and the *SWITCHABLE PREVIEW MONITOR* are the only **color** monitors. The rest are monochrome. If the studio uses digital video effects there may be an additional color monitor to display these.

Camera 2   1   2   1   2   1

Duration 8   8   5   5   3   3
in Seconds

**Fig. 8.17 Sequential
inter-cutting**
Each subject accuses the other of
treachery, tension is rising. The
camera dollies closer and closer, shots
become larger and larger, and of
increasingly shorter duration.

The production switcher

You can do several things with the production switcher:

1. *Select and interlink shots.* You can select one or more of the various picture sources and send your choice to line to be recorded or transmitted (*studio output, main channel, program, transmission*). You can *cut* between channels (i.e. by switching), *mix* (*dissolve*), *fade*, or superimpose pictures.

   When you select any channel, that switcher button lights up, indicators are illuminated beside the corresponding picture monitor, and at the camera (a main tally light and an on-air warning light in the viewfinder).

2. *Wipes.* Another group of controls on the switcher enables you to wipe from one picture to another, in a wide range of patterns. This facility can also be used to segment the screen (e.g. split screen), or to combine parts of different shots.

3. *Titles.* Titles from any type of source (title card, slide, character generator) can be adjusted in outline, tone, and color, and inserted into a picture.

4. *Picture manipulation.* Some switchers include controls that can change the appearance of the picture in several ways – e.g. make it negative, ripple, invert, mirror.

5. *Special video effects.* There are usually controls enabling you to insert a selected subject or section from one picture into another (e.g. chroma key). More elaborate digital video effects are usually controlled by a separate *effects unit*; operated, perhaps, by a second person.

6. *Preview facilities.* Larger switchers include a row (*bus; bank*) of *PREVIEW* buttons. When you select any of the incoming picture sources here, it appears on the *SWITCHABLE PREVIEW MONITOR*. (This is a picture-checking facility; it does not affect the studio output at all.)

   Suppose you have only four preview monitors available but five or more sources. How can you check the extra incoming channels before

'A' Bus

'B' Bus

CAM 2 – On·Air
CAM 3 – Prepared for Mix

1   **2**

Fig. 8.18 part 1   The production switcher – principles of the A–B switcher

There are two identical rows of push buttons called *buses* or *banks*, labelled A and B (or BUS-1, BUS-2). Each pair of A and B buttons selects a particular video source (typically 6 to 20 sources per bus: cameras, film VTR, slide scanner, etc.). The *BUS fader lever(s)* position determines which bus is in use.
1. A single fader may be fitted (mixing or superimposing between A and B buses).
2. If twin faders are included, they may be operated together, or 'split' to fade A and B buses separately.
With the fader moved to the top, A-bus is active.
Switching buttons on A-BUS cuts the chosen source (e.g. Cam 1) to the studio's line output (main channel; on-air). (B-bus switching produces no visible result, unless connected to a preview monitor; when it becomes a preparatory bus.)

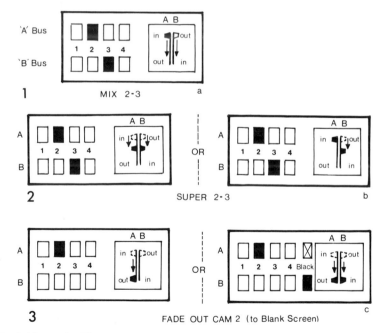

Fig. 8.18 part 2   The production switcher – basic operations

1. MIX (DISSOLVE) between Cams 2 and 3.
Select 2 on A-bus. It is now on line (on-air) as the bus fader is at A. Prepare for a Mix, by pressing 3 on B-bus.
Push down bus fader(s) from A to B, and output mixes from Cam 2 to 3. Move fader to A-bus: output mixes back from Cam 3 to 2.

2. SUPER CAMERAS 2 and 3.
Either as for a Mix; stopping when superimposition strength is as required. Or split faders, moving appropriate lever towards the bus to be added.

3. FADE OUT CAM 2 (to blank screen).
Either split faders, pushing A-bus lever to OUT (B-bus is already faded out); or where the system would lose chroma using this method, select special *black-level* button in the other bus and mix to black.

Preview Monitor Switching

'A' BUS

'B' BUS

Program Bus   (Switching Bus)

Switches over
to A/B Panel

Mode Switch

Fig. 8.18 part 3   The 'A-B-C' switcher

A separate program bus is used only for *cutting* (switching to line). The A/B buses
are used for setting up *mixes and effects* (supers, split-screen, wipes, chroma-key,
inserts).

The A/B fader lever can be used in either of two ways: (a) *Mix mode*, to provide
mixes/dissolves/superimpositions between buses. (b) *Mask key mode*, in which it
fades in a keying signal, or makes a pattern *transition*, or operates a wipe-pattern
movement.

A *take* button or bar may interswitch between A and B buses. Preview buttons
switch chosen channels onto preview monitor for checking before use. (Do not
affect output to line.)

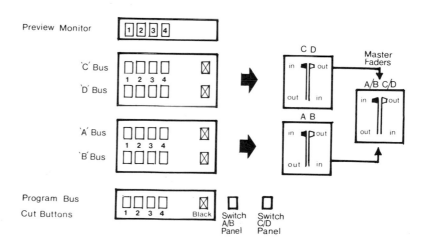

Preview Monitor

'C' Bus

'D' Bus

'A' Bus

'B' Bus

Program Bus
Cut Buttons

Master
Faders

Switch
A/B
Panel

Switch
C/D
Panel

Fig. 8.18 part 4   The 'A-B-C-D' switcher

An elaboration, providing two duplicate pairs of buses – A/B and C/D. Now a
prearranged combination of cameras can be set up on one pair of buses (e.g. for
titling or effects), while the other pair is used for cuts and/or mixes.

Master fader levers select the entire A/B and/or C/D combinations are required. A
pair of buses (A/B or C/D) is called a MIX/EFFECTS (M/E) BANK.

Channel 2 selected on 'A' Bank

Fig. 8.18 part 5   The fader-per-chanel mixer
This European switcher (also known as 'knob-a-channel mixer') includes two identical independent banks (A and B), in which each video channel has its own individual fader and cut-button. So any group of sources can be chosen and mixed together in any proportions, on either bank.
The central master control panel can select either bank as a prearranged group, or combine the two banks. The flexibility of this system makes it particularly useful when creating complex video effects.

switching them 'on-air'? You use the *PREVIEW BUS* to switch them onto the *SWITCHABLE PREVIEW MONITOR* beforehand. Similarly, if you have any shots that combine several sources (supers, inserts), or any video effects, you select the *MIX* button on the preview bus to check them on this monitor. If you use a *flip–flop* facility to intercut between two cameras, whichever is off-air will be displayed on the *SWITCHABLE PREVIEW MONITOR*.

7. *Remote controls*. Extra switches may be located at the switcher to remotely operate a slide scanner, film scanner, VTR channel, etc. (e.g. remote start, stop, change).

Switching conditions

People using production switchers for the first time are often puzzled to find that

- Some controls have an obvious effect, while others apparently do nothing!
- At one moment a control appears to be working, while shortly afterwards it seem inoperative!

This situation is easier to understand if you think of most controls as having three different conditions, which we might call:

'*ON-AIR*', '*PREPARATION*', '*AVAILABLE*'.

The condition of any given control will depend how you have set up the switcher board.

- *ON-AIR*. If you operate any control that is selected for on-air use, you will see the result immediately on the *MASTER MONITOR* (line monitor).
- *PREPARATION*. Before putting any pictures on-air you want to be able to preview and adjust them. Any straightforward shot will appear on the channel preview monitors. But suppose you have a *combination*

shot, involving two or more sources. It might be a superimposition, a split screen with an inserted title, or a special effect. This will need to be prepared beforehand. The switcher enables you to adjust the associated controls while checking the effect on preview, then switch this prepared picture to line at the right moment. Instead of using the *SWITCHABLE PREVIEW MONITOR* for this purpose (it can be distracting for the director, and prevent his using it for program previews), some organizations have a separate additional monitor for shot preparation.

● *AVAILABLE*. Finally, there will be a number of controls that have not yet been selected for any purpose. They are available but inactive. They do nothing until you actually *route* them to preview or line.

Operating the switcher

At first sight, the switcher seems to be a mass of switches and levers. But things are not as complicated as they look. The answer to mastering any switcher is to take each function a step at a time.

The switcher is laid out systematically. At the top is the row of **PREVIEW** buttons for the *SWITCHABLE PREVIEW MONITOR*. Its buttons can be routed as you wish, but typically, they will be arranged in order (left–right): CAM 1, CAM 2, VTR, FILM, SLIDES, C-G (character generator), etc. The more sources/channels you have, the more switches you need. All the buses below it follow a similar order.

To help the operator to see which parts of the switcher are in use at a glance, push-buttons often light up *dimly* when selected and *brightly* when the function controlled by that button is on-air.

Cutting (switching)

Let's begin with straightforward cutting (switching) between sources. This is normally done on a row of push-button switches marked **PROGRAM**. As with the **PREVIEW** buttons, each key on this *PROGRAM BUS (BANK)* is connected to a corresponding picture source.

Press **CAM-1** button on the program bus. The key lights, Camera 1's shot is switched 'on-air' to be videotaped or transmitted, and it appears on the *LINE MONITOR (TRANSMISSION)*. Press **CAM-2** switch, and the switcher output cuts to Camera 2's picture.

Faders

The video fader is similar in principle to the gain control (volume pot) on an audio amplifier or radio. Certain designs of production switcher do the obvious, and have a video fader associated with each picture channel (Figure 8.18 part 5). But this arrangement has drawbacks where you want to combine and manipulate pictures. Instead, most switchers use a different, ingenious system that provides considerable flexibility.

As well as the **PROGRAM BUS** which cuts between channels, you will see two more identical horizontal rows of switch-buttons, marked **MIX A** and **MIX B**. (Again, each button corresponds with the picture source in that vertical line.) At the end of these twin rows is a communal T-shaped control lever – the **fader bar (T-bar)**. You move this up and down to select which of the rows of switches is active.

A nearby push-button switch marked **MIX** selects whether the **PROGRAM** bus or the **FADER BAR** selection affects what is happening on-air. This fader bar actually consists of two separate faders that are normally used locked (ganged) together. The left-hand **A-FADER** operates on whichever channel is selected on the bus **MIX-A**; and the right-hand **B-FADER** controls the channel on **MIX-B** bus.

If you separate ('split') the fader levers, and push the **A** lever up, it fades up the channel switched on in **MIX-A**. Push downwards, and the **A** channel fades out. Fader lever **B** does the *opposite* for the **MIX-B** bus. (Down for max. **B**; up for min. **B**.) So when you move the *combined* levers upwards you will fade up the channel selected on **A**, and fade out the different channel on **B** at the same time. The result is a **MIX**.

At the end of each row of source buttons is one marked **VIDEO BLACK**. If you select this button on one of the banks and fade over to it . . . the result is a *fade to black*.

When you have the fader bar right up to the **MIX-A** bus, then any switching on the **MIX-B** bus will not have any visible effect on-air (although you can check what is happening by watching on **PREVIEW**). You can switch **MIX-B** bus to another channel, ready for the next mix.

Suppose, for example, you are taking *CAM-1* on **A** bus, then mix to *CAM-2* on **B** bus. The studio output mixes from *CAM-1* to *CAM-2*. You are now free to switch **A** bus to a different source (e.g. **FILM**) ready for the next transition. Later, when you mix back from **B** to **A**, you will see Camera 2's picture mix to the film channel. (A lot more straightforward in practice than it sounds.)

Superimpositions

To superimpose two shots you simply set up one source on the **A** bus and the other on **B** bus, then move the combined fader bar part way. In the middle, both pictures will be of equal strength. Move the control lever a little nearer **A** bus, and that picture becomes stronger while **B** weakens.

Any *switching* on either bus during the superimposition will show on-air. So whenever you use combined pictures, avoid switching on those buses, unless that is exactly the effect you want (e.g. to switch a superimposed title).

Alternative methods

There are often alternative ways of doing the same thing. For example, you would normally switch between channels on the **PROGRAM** bus.

But suppose that you have been using the **MIX (MIX/EFF)** buses, and have just mixed to a camera on the **MIX-A** bus. You now want to *switch* to another camera. Do you have to move over to the **PROGRAM** bus to do so?

No. You can interswitch between the channel buttons on your present **MIX-A** bus. People using simpler switchers do that all the time, for they have no separate **PROGRAM** bus. However, it is better practice to use the **PROGRAM** bus for switching wherever possible, so that the **MIX-A/MIX-B** buses are always available for mixes, fades, and supers.

One quickly learns various tricks. Suppose you have been interswitching on the **PROGRAM** bus. You are on *CAM-1*, but want to *mix* to *CAM-2*. A typical solution is to set up **MIX-A** with *CAM-1* (fader bar to **A**) and transfer to it (**MIX** button). There will be no effect on the transmitted picture, for you've changed to the same channel. But now you are on the **MIX** buses, you can *mix* to *CAM-2* whenever you're ready.

To get back from the **MIX** buses to the **PROGRAM** bus, do the reverse. With *CAM-2* on a **MIX** bus, punch up the same channel on the **PROGRAM** bank, and go to it with the **MIX** button.

So here you have the basics. You now know how to *CUT, MIX, FADE,* and *SUPER.* And how to move between the **PROGRAM** and **MIX** buses. From now on, much depends on the design of your particular switcher.

Additional switcher features

Today's switchers contain an ever-increasing range of facilities, to make operation easier and to allow more elaborate treatment. They also incorporate various *video effects* that we shall discuss in detail later, in Chapter 21 (Table 21.3).

Most of the regular features found in production switchers are summarized in Table 8.1. But let us look in more detail at some particularly useful facilities.

- Wipes
- Re-entry
- Downstream keyer
- Take bar (cut bar)

Wipes

Most switchers have a facility for *wiping* between pictures, creating split screens and inserts. In some you press an appropriate **EFFECTS** switch and are routed into a side-chain, consisting of two more **EFFECTS** buses. A separate control bar (looking like another fader-bar) selects between them. If you put *CAM-1* on **EFFECTS-A** bus and *CAM-2* on **EFFECTS-B** bus, adjusting the control lever will cause one camera's shot to wipe out the other.

Table 8.1   Production switcher terms
For terms associated with *electronic insertion*, see Table 19.4.

Audio-follow-video	Facility providing mike-channel switching to correspond with video switching (e.g. intercutting between both ends of a phone conversation).
Auto-switching	Provides automatic interchannel switching at an adjustable rate.
Black input/black buttons	On some switchers, one simply fades out the channel or line fader to obtain a black screen. On others, this would result in a loss of color (chroma) during the fade-out, so a 'black-level' channel button is selected to fade to. (Fade-out is caused by loss of 'color-burst' when fading out a composite video signal.)
Border generator	A narrow line (tone or color) of adjustable width and sharpness, around a picture segment or lettering.
Bus/bank	A series of selector cut buttons (one for each source) associated with a particular function.
Cascading re-entry	An arrangement in which a composite picture (e.g. a quad-split screen derived from several sources) can be further treated (e.g. title insert), by re-entering it at a later point in the switcher routing/chain.
Composite/coded signal	The combined NTSC (PAL or SECAM) signal including picture and sync pulses.
Cut buttons	Push-buttons used to intercut sources (*Program bus*).
Decoded signal	The individual red, green, blue video signals of the total TV picture.
Double-take/double-cut	Switching the foreground subject shot, and the background scene shot simultaneously, in a combined picture.
Downstream keyer	Switching arrangement that enables graphics/titling to be inserted over the main program output from the main switcher unit, without involving a mix/effects system (so leaving that section available for wipes or chroma-key use).
Effects bus/mix-effects bus	A bus used for intersource mixes (dissolves), or for combined-source effects.
Flip-flop controls	A circuit that interswitches the line output between a channel selected on the *program* bus, and a channel selected on the *preview (pre-set)* bus. On operating the *take* switch, the previewed channel is transferred to program bus and put on-air. Simultaneously, the channel that was on-air switches away to the preview bus and its monitor. This arrangement provides an automatic preview display of each upcoming shot (on a single-*line preview monitor*) before transferring it to line.
Flip-flop mix	The system mixes from program to a pre-set selection, for either direction of the fader lever.
Channel fader	Individual video fader for each picture source.
Group fader	Fader controlling a group of sources (e.g. a bus/bank).
Inputs	Switches routing selected video sources to each channel on the switcher.
Joystick	A vertical stick (or roll-ball) controlling the movement, position, direction of wipes, mattes, etc. around the screen.

Table 8.1 (cont.)

Knob-a-channel mixer	A vision mixer favored in some European studios, in which each video channel has its own independent fader. A switch bus facilitates cutting. Its simplicity eases operation for many types of program; particularly when mixing/dissolving fully modulated pictures.
Linear key	A system used for keying in titles without extraneous edge effects. (When used to key in video, can provide color to monochrome dissolves, negative monochrome pictures, and tinting effects – e.g. 'sepia toning'.)
Lock-out	With some switchers, a 'lock-out' situation can develop when you arrange a succession of picture treatments (series insertion; cascade). No intermediate stage can be altered without disrupting the entire composite. (For instance, having combined mattes, titles, chroma key, colorized background, you cannot then decide to put borders around titling.)
Mix-effects (M/E)	A switcher arrangement in which a subfader enables sources on two separate buses to be combined (super, inset, wipe), then selected simultaneously in this form by the master fader.
Non-composite signal	A composite video signal with sync pulses removed (station sync being re-added after processing).
Preview bus/pre-set bus	Switch buttons enabling any picture source(s) to be selected on a single preview monitor (to check effects, supers, split screen, insertions, etc.).
Program bus	Cut buttons interswitching program sources. The result is seen on the line output (studio output, transmission)
Re-entry	A facility allowing a picture treated in one part of a switcher to be fed into another section; e.g. the output from one **M/E bank** can be switched into another **M/E bank** for further treatment.
Sync/non-sync mode	Adjusts switcher to accept video-sources that are *in-sync* or *out-of-sync* with local synchronizing pulses.
Take-bar/cut-bar	A facility in some switchers that enables you to record a program's transitions (cut/mix/wipe, etc.) and composite effects in a memory/file/store and play them out to line as required, simply by pressing a *take-bar*. (Similarly *AUTO-TAKE, AUTO-DISSOLVE, AUTO-WIPE*.)
Wipe	A picture transition in which one shot progressively displaces another, usually in a decorative pattern; automatically, or by moving a control lever. A wide range of different patterns can be selected by thumbwheel switches or push-buttons (tablet switches).

The *direction* of the wipe will depend on which way you move the lever. You can move it at any speed, stopping mid-way if you wish to produce a split or divided screen. The actual form of the wipe depends on which pattern you have selected from the menu.

Smaller switchers do not have these extra **EFFECTS** buses. For economy and compactness, they have just the one pair of **MIX** buses. When you press the **EFFECTS** button your regular **MIX** bank is transformed into an **EFFECTS** bank. Now, when you move the 'fader bar' it no longer mixes but *wipes* instead – between the channels selected on the two sides **A** and **B**. In this switcher design the system is termed a **MIX/EFFECTS** bus or bank.

Some switchers extend this idea of multi-use, and, for example, the **PREVIEW** bus can double as an **EFFECTS KEYING** bus and the **PROGRAM** bus as a **MIX** bus.

Similarly, it may be possible to have a mix-effects set-up on the **PROGRAM** output and a different set-up on the **PREVIEW** output. Pushing a **TAKE PREVIEW** button switches the **PREVIEW** arrangement over to the **PROGRAM** output. Whether such ingenuity proves to be helpful or limiting mainly depends on what you want to do.

Re-entry

The *re-entry* or *cascading* facility allows you to combine two or more sources in one part of the switcher (e.g. a person with a chroma-key insert), and then take this prepared 'package' as if it were a single source and route it to a different **MIX** or **EFFECTS** bank, where it can be combined with a *further* source.

This *double re-entry* technique is regularly used in newscasts, sports programs, demonstrations, where you have a simulated display screen behind the speaker (Figure 21.20), and want to *fade* a series of titles or insets in/out without affecting the composite. (Using other methods, they would have to be abruptly *switched* in/out.)

Some switcher designs allow you to take *that* 'composite plus re-entry package' and enter it into yet another section of the switcher for further treatment – a process termed *cascading*. ('Cascade' simply means connected in a series; one after another.) This circuitry enables you to create and intercut multi-source images.

Downstream keyer

When you have set up various effects, wipes, supers, chroma-key combinations, it may not be particularly convenient or easy to key in subtitles or graphics in addition. That is where the downstream keyer is particularly useful. This feeds into a point at the *output* of the main switcher unit (*line-out*), so is quite independent and does not involve any controls set up on the main board, leaving them free for other functions.

The downstream keyer unit normally includes a **MASTER FADER BAR**, which controls the entire switcher output, allowing the transmission picture to be faded to black.

Take button (cut bar)

The **TAKE BUTTON/CUT BAR** enables you to switch from one set-up to another simply by pressing a single button. You can use this facility to continually interswitch between two cameras. After pressing a **FLIP–FLOP** key, you punch them ·up on the **PROGRAM** and the **PREVIEW/PRESET** buses, respectively. One will appear on the

MASTER MONITOR (LINE/TRANSMISSION) and go to line, while the other appears on the *SWITCHABLE PREVIEW* monitor. (Their corresponding indicator lights are illuminated on the switcher and beside the monitors.) Press the **TAKE** button, and they change over; the on-air camera switches to preview, and the camera that was previewed is now on-air. (The indicators, too, will change.) Press **TAKE**, and they switch back. Although the result is the same as when using the **PROGRAM** bus alone for switching, it reduces the danger of hitting the wrong button during repeated interswitching, and one's reaction time is faster.

The **TAKE BUTTON** is most valuable, however, when you want to interswitch between a series of complex combined pictures.

In the most advanced switchers the operator can organize and set up elaborate transitions or multi-source effects at any time, and store all details (including the direction, speed, and position of wipes) in a *file/memory* ready for the moment they are required. These pre-set effects can then be selected in any chosen order, and introduced simply by pressing a *TAKE BUTTON/CUT BAR*.

Switcher design in practice

Some switchers are very easy to use, but are limited in the number of things they can do at the same time. Others have extensive facilities; but it can take patience and a quick mind to work out how to set them up to achieve complex results.

Operators develop their particular loves and hates in switcher design. But much depends on the circumstances in which you are using the switcher. Is the show spontaneous, or meticulously planned? Are transitions simple, or between complex combined shots? A live transmission of the Olympics, with many cameras, time inserts, inlays of commentators, detail shots, interswitching between events, and so on is a far cry from cosy studio interviews where any errors can be retaken! Different pressures; different needs. And again, where most of the editing is carried out during postproduction work, using computerized selection, problems are of a different order.

9 Lighting

Effective lighting makes a vital contribution to a television production. We quickly recognize bad lighting when we see it, but good lighting is so unobtrusive and 'natural' that we take it for granted. In this chapter, we shall discuss the secrets of successful lighting techniques.

The aims of lighting

Lighting in television and film is about much more than just making things *visible*. It has to satisfy a number of often conflicting objectives:

- *The lighting must enable all the TV cameras to produce pictures of the highest quality.* This means that the light levels (light intensity) must be appropriate for the camera lens aperture (*f*-stop) being used so that the picture can be exposed correctly.
- *The lighting must be consistent.* It must suit all camera positions.
- *The lighting treatment must take into account the mechanics of the production.* It must fit in with the scenery, the camera treatment, the sound boom's positions, etc. Badly positioned lamps can prevent talent from reading the prompter, cause flares in a camera lens, result in boom shadows, spoil a skilfully designed setting, degrade make-up . . .
- *Good lighting creates a three-dimensional illusion in the flat picture.* It imparts an impression of solidity and depth in subjects and surroundings.
- *Lighting should usually produce an attractive visual impact.* It should enhance the appearance of people.
- *Lighting must be appropriate.* It should create the right sort of atmosphere for the occasion. The lighting in realistic settings should look natural, not seem contrived. It can suggest the time of day, or weather conditions.
- *Successful lighting guides the audience's interest.* It directs their attention towards important features.
- *Lighting can create compositional opportunities for the cameraman.*
- *Lighting should not make us aware of staging defects.* For example, the viewer's attention should not be drawn to wrinkles in a cyclorama, joins in sets, strong reflections, cables shadows . . . through unsuitable lighting.

Why is lighting necessary?

The technical reasons.

As you know (Chapter 4), the TV/video camera needs a certain amount of light reflected from the scene to be able to produce a good tonal range in the picture, without various distracting defects (such as noise and picture lag).

If there is too little light, the lens aperture has to be opened up to compensate, and the available depth of field is considerably reduced. Too much light, and pictures become overexposed, unless you stop down the lens (depth may now be too great), or use neutral density filters. In the studio, excess light wastes power, causes ventilation problems, and is unpleasant to work in. Light levels need to be related, wherever possible, to the preferred working *f*-stop.

The TV camera can only handle and reproduce relatively limited tonal contrasts. If the lighting is contrasty, details in the lightest and darkest tones will be lost.

On location, the existing lighting may not be suitable. From the camera position, it may prove to be

● Too bright – e.g. strong sunlight causing performers to squint their eyes.
● Too dim – e.g. insufficient for well-exposed shots.
● Too flat – e.g. diffuse light, in which subjects lack form or definition.
● Too contrasty – e.g. lighter tones burned out, and shadows clogged.

Under these conditions we need to augment or replace the natural lighting . . . or tolerate the results. Sometimes the only solution is to alter the camera position.

The artistic reasons

Our impressions of space and form when looking at a picture depend on a number of factors, such as perspective, scale, the way planes overlap, comparative details, relative sizes, and so on. But lighting, too, plays a major part in how we interpret what we see. Even when structure and outline give us leading clues, the play of light and shade strongly influences our judgements of size, shape, distance, surface texture, contours.

Lighting is strongly associated with mood. Through carefully chosen light direction and contrast you can change a scene's entire atmospheric impact. It can impart fun or fantasy, mystery or dramatic tension. Lighting can enhance a setting, and create pictorial beauty, or it can deliberately create a harsh, unattractive, sordid effect. Lighting can transform a rich imposing environment into a garish tasteless display, or reduce it to a boringly dull characterless emptiness.

You can use light selectively, to emphasize certain aspects of the scene while subduing others; avoiding or reducing distracting features. You can exaggerate form; draw attention to texture, or suppress it. You can merge planes, or cause one to stand out prominently from another. Through shadow formations, lighting can suggest structures that do not exist, or hide what is there.

You *can* illuminate the action and the setting simply by spreading enough light around to ensure that the cameras get good pictures. Some people do that! But if you want pictures in which subjects stand out solidly from their backgrounds, which have an attractive appropriate atmosphere, and which are free from distracting shadows and hot spots, it is necessary to apply systematic lighting techniques.

The nature of light

When you use light you can apply it with large 'brush strokes', or with fine delicate attention to detail. You can wash it across the scene, or pick out and emphasize certain features. But to exercise this control you need to appreciate the subtleties of light itself. So we begin by looking at the practical basics of illumination.

1. *Light intensity*. The strength of light we require on the subject and the surroundings will determine how powerful the lamps need to be, relative to the area they have to cover. (In practical terms this will affect the sizes of fittings, the power required, ventilation, etc.)
2. The *color quality* of the light (its *color temperature*). Light and camera performance need to be matched to avoid inaccurate color quality.
3. *The light dispersion*. Some light sources produce *hard light* which casts strong shadows, while others create *soft light* which is diffused and shadowless. This range of fittings offers us the choice of bold brush strokes or subtly graded half-tones.
4. *Light direction*. The direction of light affects the way light and shade falls on a subject. It determines which features are highlighted, and which fall into shadow.

Light intensity

The amount of light needed to illuminate a setting and the action within it is partly a technical decision, and partly an artistic one. You might, for example, use one strong keylight to cover both the action and the background, or a series of restricted lamps, each lighting a carefully chosen area.

Camera systems are usually quoted as having a particular sensitivity – requiring a certain light level (intensity) for a given *f*-stop. But this is only a general guide. Much depends on the nature of the surroundings. To reveal detail in the walls of a dark-paneled room will require much more light than would be needed with light-toned walls.

Lighting intensities can be influenced by the surface finish; whether walls are smooth or rough textured; whether they are plain or strongly contoured. The contrast range of the set dressings used can also affect the amount of light needed to illuminate a situation effectively.

Paradoxically, a spacious light-toned setting may require less intense lighting than much more confined dark-toned surroundings. Lighting quality cannot be judged in kilowatts!

Of course, ultimately light intensity from various directions must be adjusted to suit the atmospheric effect and mood you are aiming for (*lighting balance*).

When using a TV/video camera we have one great advantage. Unlike the *film* lighting-cameraman, who has to wait for film to be processed, we can immediately see the result of our lighting treatment. We can assess its artistic effect, and judge its technical suitability.

When first lighting, or when lighting under unfamiliar conditions (e.g.

Table 9.1 Methods of light measurement

Incident light method	Reflected light method	Surface brightness method
Meter positioned beside the subject, pointing at light sources.	*Meter positioned* beside the camera, pointing at the subject.	*Meter positioned* beside the camera, pointing at the subject.
Measures light intensity falling upon subject from each lamp direction in turn.	*Measures* average amount of light reflected from scene and received at camera lens.	*Measures* brightness of surface at which the instrument is directed.
Providing for (average) subjects of fairly restricted tonal range, typical incident light intensities and balance suitable to camera can be assessed. Base light, key light, fill light, and back light measured in turn.	*Providing* average, reflected light levels suitable to camera's sensitivity. Measure lightest and darkest tones separately, and use midway reading for guide exposure.	*Provides* readings by measuring surfaces of known reflectance (skin, 'standard' white, black). You can then deduce the suitability of light intensities falling upon them. *Also* allows scenic tonal contrasts to be measured to prevent overcontrasty lighting, overlit highlights, underlit shadows.
Ease of operation: method is simple and consistent. Does not require experienced interpolation. Widely used in motion-picture lighting.	*Ease of operation:* readings vary with meter angling, and experience is needed to make allowance for subject tones and contrast. Large dark areas cause readings to be falsely low, encouraging overexposure of highlights. Large light areas give high readings, which may cause underexposed shadows.	*Ease of operation:* method requires some experience in judging the *importance* of individual surfaces' brightness relative to overall exposure.
Advantages: when a show is to be repeated original levels can be duplicated readily. Balance between various light directions readily checked.	*Advantages:* method provides a quick rough check of average light levels. Can facilitate evenness of lighting.	*Advantages:* method is capable of assessing surface brightness and contrast very accurately.
Disadvantages: arbitrary allowance has to be made for subject tones. The amount of light required depends upon the subject – which this method cannot assess. Method only directly useful for 'average' subject tones. Does not take into account tonal values, proportion of tones, and tonal contrast.	*Disadvantages:* meter readings are only of an 'average' nature; which varies considerably with tonal values and proportions. Method does not indicate contrast range of subject or lighting. Meter's 'angle-of-view' seldom identical with the camera-lens's. Where a single surface (e.g. a face), is to be equally exposed in a variety of settings, measured exposure *should* be constant; but will vary as adjacent tones change.	*Disadvantages:* several separate readings are necessary to check evenness of lighting and contrast. Method measures scenic tones, but does not distinguish their relative importance; and hence the desired exposure. Tonal contrast measurements may not signify: if the tones measured do not appear together in picture; if their proportions are small and unimportant; if they *may* be acceptably 'crushed out' without injuring pictorial quality.

Note: Where meter is held close to subject, measuring individual surface brightness, method becomes as for surface brightness method.

Fig. 9.1 Light measurement
Light measurements avoid gross over or under exposure. Basic methods:
1. Incident light falling on subject.
2. Average light reflected from scene at camera.
3. Measuring surface brightnesses (tonal values and contrast).

on location), it is advisable to make careful measurements of light levels. With experience, one becomes accustomed to lamp performance at various distances, and only occasionally needs to make light checks. Any slight variations are readily compensated by dimmer or lens aperture adjustments.

- *Incident light* measurement helps to assess the relative intensities of lighting from various directions.
- *Reflected light* measurements provide a general indication of the amount of reflected light reaching the camera.
- *Surface brightness* checks help to assess the contrast range within the scene (Table 9.1).

Color quality of light

Eye and brain are astonishingly adaptable. We appear to see effects that are not really there (as in optical illusions), and we overlook effects that can clearly be measured by suitable instruments. An everyday example of the latter is the way we accept a very wide range of quite different light qualities as representing 'white' light.

If we analyze 'white' light we find that it is really a mixture of a range of colors. The spectrum is red, orange, yellow, green, blue, indigo, violet light in similar proportions. In many forms of illumination some parts of the spectrum are much more prominent than others, and the result is far from true white. For example, light from candles or dimmed tungsten lamps actually has a warm yellowish-red color quality; or, as we say, a *low color temperature*. Daylight can vary considerably, from cold bluish north sky light (a *high color temperature*) to the low color quality of light around sunset. Yet our brains compensate, and accept all these luminants as 'white light'. (See Glossary: *Color temperature*.)

Television and film cameras are not fooled in this way. They do not self-compensate. If the illumination has bluish or yellowish characteristics the pictures would show this as a pronounced color cast. To avoid such coloration, we have two solutions:

- *Adjust the* **camera** *to compensate for variations in the color temperature of the prevailing light*. Either by using a suitable color-correction filter (in the filter wheel) and/or altering the relative gains of the camera's RGB channels – the *color balance*. On many cameras we electronically readjust the system's color balance by pressing the camera's WHITE BALANCE button while shooting a white surface.
- *Adjust the color temperature of the* **light** *to suit the camera's color balance*. If you are using tungsten lamps when shooting in daylight (e.g. to illuminate shadows) you can place compensatory blue filter material or special dichroic filters over them, to raise their effective color temperature (e.g. from 3200 K to 4500–7500 K).

Conversely, if daylight is illuminating a room in which you are using quartz or tungsten lamps a large sheet of filter medium (amber-orange) can be stretched over the window to reduce the effective color temperature of the daylight to match the interior lighting.

Cameras are usually set up to suit the prevailing light quality; e.g. 2950 K. But this varies between different types of luminant. Tungsten-halogen lamps ('quartz lights') burn at 3200 K, while tungsten lamps can have a noticeably lower color temperature of e.g. 3000 K. High-powered HMI lamps produce light of 5600 K, which blends well with daylight but does not mix with tungsten sources.

As tungsten and quartz lamps are dimmed their color temperature falls – the light lacks blue, and develops a 'warmer' yellowish-red quality.

Light dispersion

Soft light

Soft light is the scattered diffused shadowless illumination that in nature comes from a cloudy overcast sky, and is reflected from rough surfaces of all kinds (walls, sand, snow). You can create soft light artificially, by using:

- Large-area light fittings (e.g. multi-lamp banks),
- Heavy diffusion in front of light sources,
- Internal reflection within large light fittings,
- Or by bouncing light from large white surfaces (e.g. matte reflector boards, or a white ceiling).

Only large areas produce really diffuse light quality. Many so-called soft light sources cast discernible shadows.

We use *soft* light when we want:

- To illuminate shadows without creating additional shadows,
- To avoid emphasizing modeling and texture (e.g. for flattering portraiture),
- To provide delicate tonal gradations. (They may be too subtle to register on many TV screens.)

However, *soft light* does have practical disadvantages:

- Really diffused light can be difficult to control, for it spreads around and is not easy to restrict.
- Badly used, soft light can produce flat unmodeled illumination. Texture and form can be difficult to see in the picture. If used as an overall *baselight* it can reduce the impression of depth, overlight the walls of settings, destroy atmosphere, and produce flat, uninteresting pictures.
- The intensity of soft light falls off rapidly with distance, and very approximately follows an 'inverse square law'.★

Hard light

Hard light is the directional illumination that produces sharp shadows, and in nature comes from direct, unobscured sunlight. This light comes

★ The *inverse square law* strictly applies only to point sources. The light intensity at 1 m falls to 0.25 (1/4) at 2 m, 0.06 (1/16) at 4 m, 0.016 (1/64) at 8 m.

from any concentrated small-area source. (Although the sun is large, it behaves as a 'point source', because it is so far away.) Compact light sources such as candles, small spotlights, open-bulb fittings, gas-discharge lamps (e.g. HMI), and arc lamps all produce well-defined shadows.

We use *hard light* when we want:

- To create bold well-defined modeling; a sharp clear-cut vigorous effect.
- To cast pronounced shadows (e.g. tree-branch shadows).
- To localize light to specific areas.
- To produce coarse shading; an abrupt brightness fall-off.
- To project light over some distance, at a reasonably constant intensity. (The light rays from focused spotlights are roughly parallel and do not 'fall off' quickly with distance.)

However, *hard light* does have practical disadvantages:

- The shadows from hard light may prove to be unattractive, inappropriate, distracting.
- Hard light can overemphasize texture and surface modeling.
- High contrast can produce crude, harsh, unsubtle tones.
- Multiple shadows arise when the subject is lit by more than one hard light source.

Clearly, for effective lighting treatment you need a suitable blend of *hard* directional light and *soft* diffused light. Usually the hard light reveals the subject's contours and textures, while the soft light reduces undue contrast or harshness, and makes shadow detail visible. You may deliberately emphasize contour and texture; or minimize them, depending on the blend and direction of the illumination.

The direction of the light (Figure 9.2)

The effects of lighting will vary as you alter the angle at which it strikes the subject. Raising or lowering a lamp, or moving it round the subject, will change which parts are lit, which are thrown into shadow. It will

Table 9.2   Light direction

Direct-frontal (from camera position)	Direct frontal lighting along the *lens axis* reduces texture and modeling to minimum. Valuable for disguising wrinkles or avoiding confusing shadows.
Edge lighting (side lighting)	Light skimming along a surface (from above, side, or beneath) emphasizes texture and surface contours. Ideal for revealing shallow relief such as in coins, embossing, wood grain, fabric, and stonework. Produces poor portraiture on full-face shots (ugly facial contouring).
Back lighting	Light directly behind the subject and along the camera lens axis is largely ineffectual unless the subject is translucent or has edge-detail (fur, hair, feathers). Slightly offset back light illuminates the subject's outline, modeling its borders and helping to distinguish it tonally from its background.

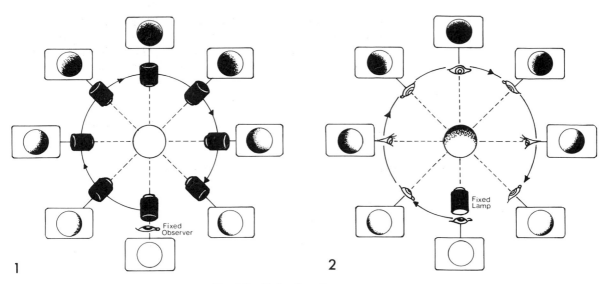

Fig. 9.2   Light direction
1. From a fixed viewpoint, the effect of the lighting changes as *the source* moves round the subject (shading develops on the side opposite the illumination).
2. Using a fixed lamp, appearance alters as *our viewpoint* changes.

affect how contours and texture are reproduced. Surface markings and decoration become more or less obvious. If you reposition the light, or alter the camera's viewpoint, the appearance of various features of the subject can change.

The technique of lighting

Let us turn now from the way light behaves, and the general effects it can have, to basic lighting techniques. At this stage, the actual *types* of equipment you use to provide the 'hard' light and the 'soft' light are unimportant. Each will have its particular advantages and disadvantages.

Lighting a flat surface

You might think that you couldn't go wrong when simply lighting a flat surface. But there can be problems.

There are situations when you want patchy, uneven lighting to create a more interesting, dramatic effect. But at others, the surface must be lit evenly overall. Any shading or patchiness would be quite unacceptable – e.g. on a title card, graphic, photo blow-up, or skycloth.

The *edge lighting* that is great when we want to emphasize texture in a brick wall would show up wrinkles, bumps, and creases in the backdrop or cyc! The frontal lighting that can produce a flatly lit cyclorama can cause hot spots of reflected light on an oil painting, making it difficult to see properly.

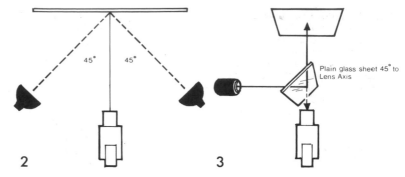

Fig. 9.3   Lighting a flat surface

1. Light from a frontal position near the camera (B), may reflect to produce hotspots, flares. Offset at (A) will overcome reflections, but may cause uneven illumination.
2. For critical work, dual lighting from either side (30–45° offset) is preferable. Soft light sources reduce spurious surface texture or irregularities (blisters, wrinkles).
3. Shadowless lighting (along the lens axis) is necessary for multi-layer graphics (Pepper's ghost).

Hard light can exaggerate texture and surface undulations. And it can be difficult to blend adjacent spotlight beams together, without light fall-off or patchiness. Soft light provides more even lighting, but it shades off with distance, and can spill around uncontrollably. The greater the angle at which the light falls on the flat surface, the more uneven its illumination.

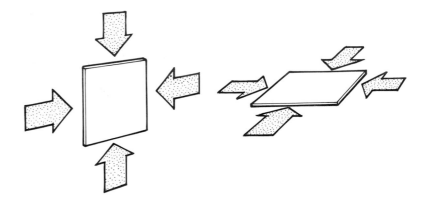

Fig. 9.4   Edge-lighting
Whatever the position of a surface, if light skims along it at an acute angle, any texture or unevenness will be emphasized.

Lighting an object

Most solid subjects require three basic light-source directions – referred to as *three-point lighting*. The exact angles depend on the subject and the aspects you want to emphasize.

■ *Key light*   This is a predominant hard light, normally in a cross-frontal position – for example, up to around 45° vertical, 45° horizontal from

Fig. 9.5 Lighting an object

Effective lighting treatment usually involves four basic lighting functions:

Key light. Usually one lamp (spotlight) in a cross-frontal position.

Fill light. Usually a soft light source illuminating shadows and reducing lighting contrast. But may not be required, or alternatively a reflected hard light is used (rarely a direct spotlight).

Back light. Usually a spotlight (or two) behind the subject, pointing towards the camera. (Occasionally soft light is used.)

Background (setting) light. Backgrounds are preferably lit by specific lighting, but they may be illuminated by the key or fill-light spill.

the lens axis. This lamp creates the principal shadows; reveals form, surface formation, and texture; and largely determines the exposure. Only one key light should normally be used for a subject.

■ *Fill light (fill-in, filler)* This soft shadowless illumination reduces tonal contrast between highlights and shadows, revealing shadow detail. It should not modify the exposure nor create additional shadows or modeling. The fill light is usually located 0–30° from the lens axis and on the opposite side from the key light.

■ *Back light* This is a hard rimming light behind the subject, separating it from the background. It helps reveal edge contours, transparency, and tracery. A single lamp or two spaced back lights may be used.

There is nothing mandatory about these arrangements. The key light is positioned to suit the object's particular features. If a single *side key* is sufficient, neither back light nor fill light may be needed. If the object is transparent or translucent you may only back light it, or even rest it on an illuminated panel for the best effect (e.g. engraved glass).

Fig. 9.6 Surface brightness

1. Apparent surface brightness depends on both surface tone and incident light intensity. Each of these examples would appear equally bright. The surface texture and finish, affect how brightness changes with light direction and the viewing angle.
2. Complete absorption (e.g. black velvet). Little or no reflection. Surface appears dark from all viewpoints.
3. Diffuse reflection (rough irregular surface). Light scatters in all directions, fairly bright from all viewpoints.
4. Spread reflection (glossy surface). Fairly dark at a; fairly bright at b; bright at c.
5. Specular reflection (shiny surface). Fairly dark at a, b. Very bright at c.

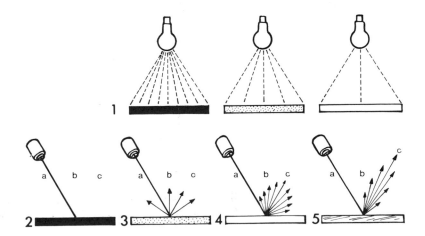

Table 9.3   Lighting terms

Base light or foundation light	Diffuse light flooding the entire setting uniformly – used to prevent underexposure of shadows or excessive contrast.
Rim light or rimming	Illumination of subject edges by back light.
Modeling light or accent light	Loose term for any hard light revealing texture and form.
Cross light, counter key or balance light	An occasional second frontal key – positioned 30–60° horizontally from lens axis. Not used for portraiture.
Kicker, cross-back, or ¾ back light	Back light some 30° off lens axis.
Effects light	Light producing specific highlight areas on backgrounds – e.g. around a light fitting.
Bounce light	Diffuse illumination obtained by reflection from a strongly lit surface such as a ceiling or a *reflector board*.
Set light or background light	Light illuminating the background alone.
Eye light or catch light	Eye reflection (preferably one only) of a light source, giving lively expression. Sometimes from a low-powered camera light.
Camera light, basher, headlamp, camera fill light, or spot bar	Small light source mounted on camera to reduce contrast for closer shots, improve/correct modeling, and for localized illumination (e.g. title card).
Hair light	Lamp localized to reveal hair detail.
Clothes light	Hard light revealing texture and form in clothing.
Top light	Vertical overhead lighting (edge lighting from above). Undesirable for portraiture.
Underlighting	Lamp below lens axis used to illuminate, relieve, or disguise downward shadows. Also used to create uncanny effects.
Side light	Light located at right-angles to the lens axis. Reveals subject's contours. Creates ugly portraiture for full-face shots, but effective for profiles.
Contrast control light	Soft fill light from camera position illuminating shadows and reducing lighting contrast.
Edge light	Light skimming along a surface, revealing its texture and contours.

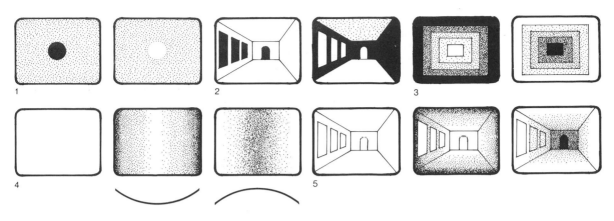

Fig. 9.7   The effects of surface tones

1. A subject's tones affect its prominence (relative to background and other adjacent tones), its apparent size, and its apparent distance. Lighter tones generally appear more prominent, larger, and more distant than darker ones.
2. While our eye stops at the black openings, the white ones suggest space beyond.
3. Progressively lighter planes recede. Progressively darker ones advance.
4. Tonal gradation (shading) affects our impression of form. If a flat plain area is shaded, it appears to have shape.
5. Pictorial perspective conveys an impression of space, which is enhanced by appropriate tonal change – and largely destroyed by unsuitable treatment.

Lighting people

Although facial details vary between individuals, the basic head formation remains similar enough, so that the unattractive effects produced by poor lighting are much the same for most people.

Fig. 9.8   Pitfalls in portrait lighting

Various unattractive effects can arise from unsuitable portrait lighting.

1. *Steep frontal key light.* Black eyes, harsh modeling, long nose shadow.
2. *Two frontal keys.* Twin nose-shadows and shoulder shadows (latter can also arise from two backlights).
3. *Steep backlight.* Hot head-top; bright nose-tip, and eartips; long bib-shadow on chest.
4. *Oblique frontal key.* Talking profile seen on shoulder. Bisected face.
5. *Side key.* In full face bisects the face. Half of it crudely edge-lit, half unlit.
6. *Dual side-keys.* Create central 'badger' shadow effect, and coarse modeling.

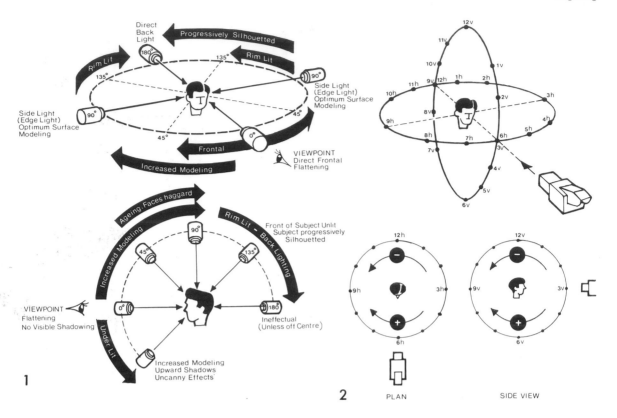

Fig. 9.9 Lighting angles

1. The lighting angle chosen depends on the particular features you want to emphasize or suppress.
2. Using two imaginary clock faces, lamps' positions are easily designated. The camera is always shown as at 3 o'clock V (3V), 6 o'clock H (6H). (Hours are 30° steps, minutes are 6° each.) Intermediate positions between hours are shown by + (clockwise) or − (anticlockwise) signs.

General maxims

There are a number of generally accepted principles when lighting people:

1. Place the key light within about 10–30° of a person's nose direction.
2. Have them look *toward* rather than away from the key light, if re-angling their position.
3. Avoid *steep* lighting (above 40–45°) or oblique angles.
4. Avoid a very wide horizontal or vertical angle between the fill light and the key light.
5. Do not have more than one key light for each viewpoint.
6. Use properly placed soft light to fill shadows.
7. Avoid sidelight on full-face shots.
8. For profiles it is generally best to place the key light on the far side of the face (upstage). This gives improved solidity and avoids casting shadows of the sound boom.

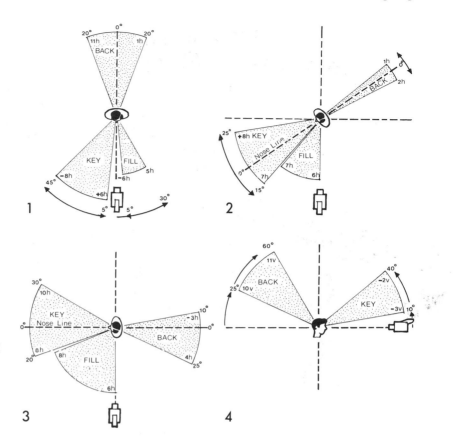

Fig. 9.10   Lighting a single person
The plans and elevations show typical range of lighting angles within which good portraiture is achieved.
1. Full face.
2. Offset head (¾ front, 45° turn).
3. Profile.
4. Vertical angles for each are shown.

Lighting groups of people

Check the direction in which each person is looking, and arrange their key/back/fill lights to fit (Figure 9.10). One appropriate lamp may suit a whole group, but problems can arise if there are big differences in the relative tones of their costumes, skin, and hair. Light intensity may be too strong for one; too weak for another. Then localized reduction with diffusers or shading off light with a barndoor or flag may be the solution.

Where subjects are close, or you have few lamps, one light may have to serve two different purposes – e.g. as a key for one and a back light for someone else (Figure 9.11).

Fig. 9.11   Lighting two people
1. Several arrangements are effective (each has particular advantages) with keys at A and B, C and D, A and D, or C and B.
2. The lamps here may be shared, as Key A/back B, and Key B/back A. Or used specifically as keys, with extra backlights.

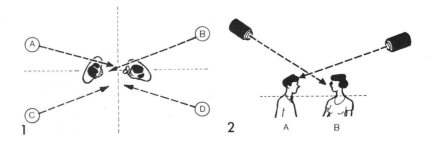

Where there are groups of people (audience, orchestra) you can either light them as a whole or in subdivided sections, still using three-point lighting principles and keeping overlaps to a minimum.

Table 9.4　Lighting people

	Front light	*Back light*
Lamp's vertical angle too steep	Harsh modeling which gives a haggard and ageing appearance. Gives black eyes, black neck, and long vertical nose shadow. *Emphasizes:* forehead size, baldness, and deep eyes. Figure appears busty. Casts hair shadows onto forehead. Hat brims and spectacles produce large shadows.	Nose becomes lit while face in shadow ('white nose'). Effect most marked when head tilted back. 'Hot top' to forehead and shoulders.
Lamp's vertical angle too shallow	Picture flat and subject lacks modeling. Produces shadows on background.	Lens flares or lamp actually in shot.
Underlighting	Inverted facial modeling. Shadows of movement beneath head level (e.g. of hands) appear on faces. Shadows may be cast up over background. 'Mysterious' atmosphere when underlighting used alone. Useful to soften harsh modeling from steep lighting. Reduces age lines in face and neck.	Largely ineffectual but can be used for back lighting women's hair. Shadows from ears and shoulders cast on face.
Light too far off camera axis	In full face, long nose shadow across opposite cheek. An asymmetric face can be further unbalanced if lit on wider side. One ear lighter than the other.	Ear and hair shadows are cast on cheek. One side of nose is 'hot'. Eye on same side as back light appears black – being left in shadow while temple is lit.

Note: All lamp positions are relative to camera viewpoint.

Table 9.5　Lighting balance

	Too bright	*Too dim*
Frontal light	Back light less effective. Skin tones are high and facial modeling lost. Lightest tones tend to be overexposed. Gives a harsh pictorial effect.	Back light predominates and often becomes excessive. Darker tones are underexposed. Can lead to muddy, lifeless pictorial effect.
Back light	Excessive rim light. Hot shoulder and top of heads. Exposing for areas lit by excess back light causes frontal light to appear inadequate.	Two-dimensional picture which lacks solidity. Subject and background tend to merge. Picture appears undynamic.
Filler	Modeling from key light reduced and flattened.	Produces excessive contrast and subject too harshly modeled.

Lighting areas

It is best to avoid flooding areas with light; e.g. spreading high-intensity soft *base* or *foundation light* and superimposing spotlights for modeling and intensity variations; unless you are seeking a really high-key effect.

Except for high-key pictures, the visual appeal of intense soft light is limited – although it does make key light positioning less critical, as ugly modeling is strongly diluted (*lit out*). Such treatments flatten modeling and produce overlit backgrounds.

Dynamic lighting requires appropriately positioned spotlights, relieved by suitably placed and carefully controlled fill light. (The amount of fill light due to random reflections from floor and scenery is usually minimal.)

Fig. 9.12 Lighting areas
Where action is localized, the three-point lighting technique (1) can be applied at specic positions throughout the setting (2).
One lamp may be used for several positions. Overall three-point treatment can be used for general action (3) or the area can be sectionalized (4).
5. For cross-shooting cameras, lamps over the set's side-walls can be used as key/backlights, with suitable positioned soft ll-light.

The most attractive picture quality usually comes from analyzing the performance area into a series of *locating points* (by the table, at the door, looking out the window) and tailoring the three-point lighting at each to suit the action. One lighting arrangement will often suit other shots or action in that area (perhaps with slight lighting rebalance).

Given sufficient lighting facilities (enough lamps, dimmers, etc.) and adequate time to readjust lamps, you could light to suit each individual shot. But such elaboration is not normally feasible.

Where action is more general or widespread you must cover the area in a systematic pattern of lamps.

Light fittings

Light sources (luminants)

Several kinds of luminant are used in TV lighting: regular tungsten lamps, tungsten-halogen lamps ('quartz lamps'), gas-discharge lamps (metal halide, HMI, CSI, linear light sources), and fluorescent tubes. Carbon arcs are now only used on some remotes (OBs) and location filming – to a decreasing extent.

■ *Regular tungsten lamps* Confusingly also called 'incandescent' (which *all* TV luminants inherently are!) or 'tungsten' (used in quartz lamps too!). Still extensively used, the regular tungsten filament lamp is relatively cheap, has a reasonably long life, exists in a wide range of intensities (power ratings), is generally reliable, and can be mounted in many types of fittings.

Against this, tungsten lamps waste much electrical energy as heat. Their relatively large filaments prevent them being true point sources and providing crisp, clear-cut shadows. Their color temperature is normally relatively low and decreases as they get older. The light output also decreases due to the bulb (globe) envelope blackening.
Typical color temperatures 3000–3200 K.

■ *Overrun lamps* These tungsten lamps are deliberately designed for a supply voltage that slightly exceeds the filament's normal rating. By this means, you achieve a much greater light output and a higher color temperature – but at the expense of a considerably shortened life. *Photoflood* and *Nitraphot* are widely used versions.

Such lamps can be used in *practical fittings* (wall brackets, table lamps) on sets, or location interiors.

Portable lightweight systems make use of overrun lamps in traditional tungsten or quartz form. For example, a *Colortran* unit using only 3 kW of power can provide the light output of a regular 10 kW tungsten rig. So, too, *Sunguns* run from belt-batteries can offer intense hand-held illumination on location.
Typical color temperatures 3400–3500 K.

■ *Tungsten-halogen (quartz lamps, halogen lamps, quartz iodine)* Here the tungsten filament is enclosed within a quartz or silica envelope filled with a halogen gas. This restricts the normal filament evaporation and bulb blackening, so providing a longer lamp life and/or a higher, more constant light output of increased color temperature (e.g. 3200 K) that is ideal for color television.

The bulb must not be handled since body acid attacks the surface, and the lamp becomes brittle and extremely hot in use. Tubular strip and compact designs are available, making lighter and much smaller fittings possible. Twin-filament lamps are produced which provide three intensities of similar color temperature by switching.
Typical color temperatures 3200 K.

CID compact iodide daylight
CSI compact source iodide
HMI hydrargyrum medium arc-length iodide

Fig. 9.13 Internal reflector lamp (sealed beam)
Available in regular tungsten and quartz (tungsten halogen) forms. Used individually in clamps or grouped (Fig. 9.14 part 1, section 3). The glass front may be clear, ribbed or frosted, to give a wide, medium or spot beam, *hard* or 'softened' quality. A color compensating filter (integrated, or attached) matches the luminant to daylight. Widely used *PAR lights* incorporate a parabolic aluminized reflector (650–1000 W, 3200 K).

■ *Gas discharge lamps*   These lamps are compact, extremely efficient sources, using a mercury arc ignited within argon gas. Special 'rare-earth additives' result in near-daylight illumination (5600–6000 K). Luminants of this type are found in CSI, CID and HMI lamps, and are increasingly used for effects/pattern projectors, follow spotlights, high-intensity interior and exterior lighting.

Discharge lamps necessarily require auxiliary circuitry (ignitors and ballast units), and there is usually a 1.5–3-minute build-up time from switch-on (striking) to full light. Dimming methods are restricted and a lamp cannot usually be restruck quickly after switch-off; a disadvantage for 'shoot-and-run' types of production (documentaries, ENG).

Film shot with an HMI light source may exhibit flicker problems (visible beat, dark-frame) unless special equipment is used.

The highly efficient HMI lamp is particularly convenient for use on location to fill shadows in exteriors and to light within large daylit interiors, for its color temperature blends well with daylight. It provides some three to five times as much light as a quartz light of equivalent power, while producing less heat. A single 2.5 kW HMI lamp can give as much light as *two* color-corrected 10 kW tungsten lamps; while a 6 kW HMI unit has a similar output to a 225 A carbon arc but uses only half the power. Typical power ratings range from 200 W (with a light output similar to a 1 kW quartz light) through to 1200 W (equivalent to 6 kW quartz light), and can be run from normal 120-V 60-cycle household supplies (mains). Larger units of e.g. 2.5 to 4 kW are valuable for single-source large-area lighting, especially at night.

Most HMI sources are fitted with a Fresnel lens, and are remarkably compact, notwithstanding the need for an associated ballast unit or ignitor (starter).

■ *Fluorescent tubes*   The ubiquitous fluorescent tube has been used as a soft light source for base light, cycloramas, etc., but the color quality of the light is very uneven, and does not match well with other sources. Economical but bulky and fragile, this low-intensity non-directional light source has limited use; mainly in portable form as a fill light, when shooting in locations illuminated only by fluorescent fittings.

Types of light fitting (luminaires)

Four basic forms of light fitting are used in TV:

1. Soft lights/floodlights.
2. Spotlights/Fresnel spots.
3. Effects projectors/pattern projectors.
4. Follow spots.

■ *Soft light fittings*   These include *scoops, broads, floodlight, banks, internally reflected units, striplights, cyclorama lights*. They are used mainly for fill light and for broad lighting of backgrounds. They can be hung,

Fig. 9.14 part 1   Soft-light sources – open-lamp types

1. *Scoop* (1–1½ kW) has spun aluminium bowl of diameter 0.3–0.46 m
   (1–1½ ft). Emergent light is not particularly soft (or controllable) where an
   open lamp is used (tungsten or quartz). Spun-glass scrim fits into supports,
   aiding diffusion. The lamp is obtainable in fixed-focus and adjustable (ring-focus)
   forms; the latter has adjustable light-spread. (Versions with lamp-shields are
   available to prevent direct light emergence.)
2. *Small broad* (½–1 kW) is a tubular quartz light. Flaps or barndoors restrict the
   light spread. The emergent light from an open bulb is fairly hard. That from
   versions using a light shield is softer. Broads of 1 kW, 2 kW, 5 kW are widely
   used.
3. *Floodlight bank (nine-light, cluster)* consists of groups of internal reflector lamps
   (650–1000 W each). They create soft-light through multi-source light overlap.
   Its sections may be switchable and adjustable. Widely used for location lighting.
4. *Fluorescent bank* is a group of fluorescent tubes providing diffuse illumination.

Fig. 9.14 part 2   Soft-light sources – internal reflection types

1. Internal reflection from shielded
   tubular quartz-lights, produces
   diffused high-intensity
   illumination.
2. *Large broad* 'Softlight' (1–6 kW
   typical) has reflected internal
   lamps (tubular quartz or
   fluorescent).
   A diffuser may also be attached.

Fig. 9.14 part 3   Soft-light sources – cyclorama lighting

Special fittings used to provide an
even spread of light over a vertical
surface (cyc, backdrop). Fitted with
color medium where colored
illumination is required.

1. *Ground-row* (*trough*) containing
   tubular quartz units
   (625 W–1500 W).
2. *Strip-light* (*border light*) consists
   of a row of internal-reflector
   lamps.
3. *Suspended cyc* light is a single or
   multi-unit fitting (for color mixing)
   with strip quartz-lights.

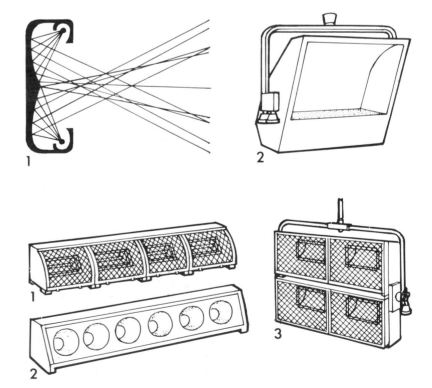

Fig. 9.15   Hard-light sources

1. *Fresnel spotlight* (100 W–10 kW, 8–38 cm (3–15 in) lens diameter). Sliding the lamp assembly to/from Fresnel lens adjusts light-spread – spot to flood. Adjusted by hand crank (crank or sweep lever), by pole (loop, ring, or T-fitting), or remote electronics. *Controls:* Focus, tilt, pan, filament-switch (where dual-filament lamps used). Barndoor may be permanently attached. Color-frame, French flags, etc., can be attached.

2. *Ellipsoidal spotlight* (profile spot) provides precisely-shaped hard-edged beams which are controlled by shutters, iris diaphragm, or metal plates (profiling blades). Shadow patterns can be projected, using an etched stencil plate of stainless steel (gobo, mask). Typical ratings 500 W, 750 W, 2 kW.

supported on floor stands, or rested on the ground, according to the design.

Adjustment of soft light sources is limited. Many can be turned or tilted, and any flaps (barndoors) can be used to restrict the coverage to some extent. Multi-lamp fittings can be switched to adjust the light output. Otherwise diffusers or dimmers are used to control their light intensity.

■ *Spotlights/Fresnel spots*   Focused spotlights with Fresnel lens and internal reflector are used as key lights, back lights, background/set lighting, and for effects (sunlight, broad decorative patterns, dapples). The light spread of the spotlight's beam is adjustable (*focusing*):

● By moving the lens and mirror assembly (in the Fresnel spotlight),
● By moving the position of the mirror (in lensless spots),
● Or, in some designs, by moving the lens alone (in 'ring-focus' spots).

Ideally, the beam intensity should remain even overall as the beam width is altered; but many designs develop hot spots or 'dark centres'.

The *external reflector/lensless spotlight/'Redhead'/'Blonde'* is widely used on location and for confined places in studio settings. Basically a bare tungsten-halogen bulb within a reflector, its design is compact, lightweight, and highly efficient. Its wide light spread (+ 80°, compared with a typical 60° Fresnel spot) makes it a valuable light fitting in confined spaces, although its beam is somewhat uneven. Power ratings range from 250 W to 2 kW.

■ *Effects/pattern projectors*   These include effects spots, projection spotlights, profile spots, ellipsoidal spotlights, and pattern projectors. They are used to project precisely shaped areas of light (soft or sharp-edged cut-off) for localized effects lighting, or to project patterns of stencils or slides (windows, tracery, leafy branches, decorative motifs).

■ *Follow spots*   Used for isolating static subjects or following moving performers (singers, skaters, dancers) in a confined pool of light. These large spotlights (e.g. 5 kW) are carefully balanced for continuous accurate handling and are usually stand or scaffolding mounted. The beam intensity is often shutter-controlled, and its circular spot area (hard- or soft-edged) is adjustable to suit the subject.

Lamp supports

Several methods have become standardized for supporting lamps.

■ *Ground lamps*   Lamp fittings may rest on the ground for certain purposes. *Ground rows, cyc lights, strip lights, troughs* are used to light backgrounds; *spotlights* can provide underlighting effects or be used to reach otherwise inaccessible areas.

■ *Floor stands*   Floor lights are mounted on telescopic three-castered stands. They have the disadvantages of occupying valuable floor space (perhaps impeding camera or sound-boom movement), casting shadows onto backgrounds, having trailing cables, and being vulnerable. But they do permit easily adjusted precision lighting.

In fact, most TV lighting is suspended, to leave floor space uncluttered by lamps or cables.

■ *Pipe grids*   Smaller studios frequently use a pipework lattice or ladder beams fixed below the ceiling. This piping (37–50 mm (1.5–2 in) diameter, at 1.2–1.8 m (4–6 ft) apart) enables lamps to be clamped or suspended as required. Catwalks may allow overgrid access.

■ *Battens/barrels/bars*   These are arranged in a regular parallel pattern over the staging area and individual battens may be height-adjusted (counterbalanced by wall weights or motor-winched) to allow lamps to be rigged, or related to staging requirements.

Fig. 9.16 Portable lighting
Typical portable lighting units include:
1. Small broad (600–1000 W).
2. Internal reflector lamp on plate (gaffer taped to wall, hung, hooked on bar) or fitted into clip-light.
3. Sungun (250 W) hand-held or clamped (gaffer-grip, or alligator clip). Powered from utility supply, or 30-volt battery belt (4).
5. External reflector spotlight, lensless spot, in lightweight stand.

■ *Ceiling tracks* Crossbars that can be slid along parallel ceiling tracks offer flexibility in lamp-rigging density. Power rails in single- or dual-track forms may support telescopic hangers or pantographs for individual or twin lamp arrangements.

■ *Lamp adjustment* When working from treads (stepladder) lamp adjustments are precise but time consuming. So many lamps are now designed with loop or 'T' controls to be operated from below by a long, extendable pole. Lamp adjustments by remote electronic control are quite practicable (focus, pan, tilt, barndoors) and invaluable for isolated lamp positions, but add to expense and maintenance complications.

Improvised lighting

Small mobile lamps are widely used when shooting under difficult conditions for news stories, documentaries, etc. where regular light fittings are impracticable.

Fig. 9.17 Lamp supports

Studio lighting is mainly suspended (from a pipe-grid in this example).

1. Clamped directly to the grid (with a C-clamp fitting).
2. Lowered from an extendable hanger (sliding rod, drop-arm).
3. A movable trolley holding a vertically adjustable spring counter-balanced pantograph (extension 0.05–3.6 m/2–12 ft).
4. Telescopic hanger (skyhook, telescope, monopole).
5. In confined space, a spring-loaded support bar (barricuda, polecat) wedged between walls or floor/ceiling.
6. Telescopic floor stand (0.45–2.7 m/1½–9 ft).
7. Clip-lamp (spring clamp) attached to scenic flat.
8. Scenic bracket screws to top of flat.
9. Camera light (headlamp, basher). Low-power lamp for eye-light or local illumination. Safety bonds (wire or chain) are fitted to all hung fittings and accessories.

Fig. 9.18 Lamp accessories

Various attachments control the light.

1. *Diffuser* consists of a translucent material (wire mesh, frosted plastic or spun-glass sheet). Diffuses light (overall or locally) and reduces intensity.
2. *Barndoor* has independently adjustable flaps (2 or 4) on rotatable frame; cuts off light beam selectively. Used to restrict light, shade walls, prevent backlight from shining into camera lens (causing lens flares).
3. *Flag* is a small metal sheet (gobo) preventing light spill or cutting off light beam.
4. *Cookie* (*cucaloris, cuke*) is a perforated opaque or translucent sheet that creates dappling, shadows, light break-up, patterns.
5. *Reflector* is a flat sheet (white or silver surface) reflecting light to re-direct or diffuse it.

- Compact quartz lamps such as small *lensless spots/external reflector spots* (e.g. Sunguns, omni-lights) are often attached to cameras (*camera lights*). *Hand-held*, they provide a mobile light source.
- *Internal reflector lamps*, or *PAR* fittings, may be clipped temporarily onto nearby structures or furniture (using gaffer grips, gator clips, sprung clip-lights). Lightweight telescopic standards (0.6–2.4 m (2–8 ft)), spring-loaded support bars are also used to temporarily position lamps.

Size and power are necessarily limited (e.g. 150–350 W) when using mobile supplies (e.g. a 30V DC battery-belt); but when household current is available (110/230 V AC) increased ratings may be used. Lamps are often overrun, so are relatively short-lived (perhaps 10–20 hours). It is important, therefore, not to leave them on unnecessarily, and to be aware of how long you have used the present bulb. Always carry spares!

Lighting control

Earlier methods of light control used several types of electrical dimming, including resistances, transformers, reactance dimmers, and magnetic amplifiers. But these have mostly been replaced by solid-state *SCR (silicon-controlled rectifier) dimmer/thyristor* devices. This system is extremely adaptable, and equally suitable for portable and complex computerized equipment. Control levers (faders) and channel switchers are grouped on a *lighting board (console)*, remotely controlling the actual dimmer units. Intensity adjustment is smooth, and proportional over their range, even for varying loads (consumption).

The SCR dimmer is a semiconductor device which controls lamp current according to the timing of a series of electrical 'gating pulses' applied to it. Earlier problems causing 'lamp sing' (filament vibrating at audible rates) or audio injection (mike cables picking up interference) can now be overcome by suitable suppression.

Dimmer board design

Every *lighting bar (batten, barrel)* in a studio has a number of permanent outlets fitted. These are numbered, e.g. Bar 22A, 22B, 22C, 22D. Each lamp on a bar is plugged into a separate outlet. This outlet is not itself a power supply. It is simply a tie-line, permanently routed to a corresponding patch cord (marked e.g. 22A) on the central *patch bay*. Any patch cord can usually be plugged into any power outlet receptacle or channel. Thus all the lamps lighting a cyclorama, for instance, wherever they are in the studio, can be patched into adjoining power channels; so that their dimmers are side by side for convenient operation.

Basically, you want to switch lamps (on/off) singly or in groups, and to adjust lamp intensities individually and/or in groups (to a chosen or variable level). Dimmers (faders) are usually scaled (10 = full, 0 = out) and normally worked around '7', to extend lamp life and permit 'above-normal' intensities when needed.

Fig. 9.19 part 1   Patching and control – basic patching
The *lamp* on the hanging bar/batten 'Bar 22' is plugged into a numbered *outlet* fixed to the end of the batten. All batten outlets are permanently routed to a central *patchboard*, where they appear as a series of numbered cables (*patch cords*), each marked with its bar/batten outlet number.

A patch cord is plugged (*patched*) into any one of a series of numbered power-circuit outlets (*channels*) – circuit No. 6 in this example. Each power supply incorporates its own *control dimmer or fader* and *channel switch*. Similarly, the lamp on bar 23 is being fed from power circuit outlet No. 7.

Each channel can be switched and dimmed independently. Avoid exceeding the power loading limit of a channel (e.g. 2 kW). Also switch off channels before patching lamps, to prevent burning contacts due to arcing.

Some installations use patch cords; others have permanent connections, switched patching, or miniature peg-board patching.

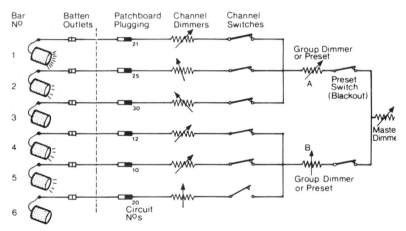

Fig. 9.19 part 2   Patching and control – group presets
A series of individually adjusted circuits can be grouped, to be dimmed/switched communally, e.g. fading cyclorama lighting up/down. Typical situation is shown here:

Preset A (fully faded up). Lamp 1 – Switched on, fully faded up (bright). Lamp 2 – On, faded down (dim). Lamp 3 – On, but faded out (out).

Preset B Faded down, reducing supply to all groups. Lamps 4 and 5 – On, individually faded up (but dim due to preset dimmer.) Lamp 6 – Channel switched off.

The simplest dimmer board comprises a row of channels, each with its separate switch and dimmer (fader). A *MASTER DIMMER* at the end of the row allows all the lamps to be *faded up/down together*. A *BLACK-OUT* switches them all on/off.

Many manual boards consist of two (or three) of these systems. Each group is then known as a *PRESET GROUP, PRE-SET, or BANK.*

Table 9.6   Changing the light intensity

When *light levels* are too low or too high they can be changed in several ways.
(INC = increase light intensity; DEC = decrease light intensity.)

● *Dimmers*. Alter dimmer settings to INC/DEC but check the picture for changes
  in color quality. Simple and immediate control, but can involve extensive
  equipment.

● *Diffuser*. Diffusers have the advantage that you can treat just part of a light beam
  if necessary. DEC: place a diffuser over lamp; add further diffuser material.
  INC: reduce/remove diffuser.

● *Spotlights*. INC: spot up the lamp slightly. DEC: flood the lamp slightly.
  Simple, but must be done manually, and affects the light spread.

● *Softlight sources*. Switch on/off sections of a multi-lamp softlight source. This
  does not affect color temperature. But the change in light level may be too great.

● *Lamp distance*. INC: move the lamp closer to the subject (now brighter, but its
  coverage will be reduced). DEC: move the lamp further from subject (light
  intensity falls, but its coverage will increase). Simple, but may not be
  practicable.

● *Lamp power*. Replace the lamp with another of higher or lower power. Except
  when lamp filaments can be switched (dual filament lamps), this involves rigging
  a new lamp.

● *Extra lamps*. INC: add more lamps. (Beware more shadows, or overlighting
  other areas.) DEC: remove lamps (e.g. switch off some of the soft light).

These pre-sets may be lettered (Pre-set *A*, Pre-set *B*), or be given colors
(*Red* pre-set, *Yellow* pre-set, *Blue* pre-set).

Each pre-set has its own *group dimmer* (*SUB—MASTER, GROUP
FADER, PRE-SET DIMMER, BANK DIMMER*) and its *PRE-SET
BLACK-OUT* switch. A *MASTER DIMMER* controls the overall
output from several pre-set banks.

You can switch any lamp channel to any of the pre-sets. Suppose you
have a series of lamps lighting a cyclorama. If you route those particular
channels to e.g. *PRE-SET A*, you will be able to fade the entire cyc
lighting up/down, just by operating that pre-set's group dimmer.

Like production switchers, there are many available designs. Smaller
dimmer boards are usually transportable – often as wheeled installations
on the studio floor. Very sophisticated computerized facilities are used in
larger studios. These can store considerable detail, including information
on lamp intensities and switching, gradual or instantaneous lighting
changes, cues, effects lighting, etc. These data can be recalled at the press
of a button (or automatically) from computer memory (solid state, floppy
disks, or cassette storage).

Basic lighting approach

Before lighting any production there are a number of preliminary
questions you will need answered. Whether you get these answers at a full
pre-production meeting with the director, set designer, audio engineer,
etc. or from a chat in the studio while looking around the set will depend
on the size and nature of the production.

What is going to happen?

● *The subject*. The main subjects in most programs are people. Even for a single person speaking to camera, or a seated interview, you must know where people are going to be positioned, and the directions they are facing. You will need details of the action. The answers will decide where you place *key lights*. If keys are badly angled, it can considerably affect portraiture. All subjects tend to have optimum directions for the main light direction.

● *The cameras*. Where are the cameras to be? Lighting must suit the camera's viewpoint. If the subject is to be shot from several positions the lighting has to take this into account – but that does *not* mean pouring light on from all directions!

● *The surroundings*. You will need to know about the general tones of the surroundings. Are they light-toned (then they could easily become overbright), or dark-toned (more light might be needed to prevent lower tones from becoming detailless shadows). Will the subjects stand out from their background, or tend to merge with it?

● *Atmosphere*. Are you aiming at a particular atmospheric effect (happy upbeat spectacle, cosy evening interior, intriguing mystery)? This will influence how you distribute light and shade in the scene.

● *Production mechanics*. These include such things as:
Sound-boom positions (to avoid casting shadows that will be seen in shot).
Lighting cues (e.g. someone apparently switching room lights on).
Lighting effects such as fire flicker, lightning, moonlight.

There will be times no doubt, when you have to light a setting without knowing any of these details. In those circumstances you can only provide a more general pattern of lighting, as in Figure 9.12, and check pictures during rehearsal, to see where 'first-aid treatment' can improve matters. Results under these conditions can be unpredictable.

Check out the facilities

You now know various production details; about the series of lighting changes needed at the start of the show, the spotlight that is to follow the singer, the effects the set designer would like to see on the cyc . . . But do you have the resources to do these things?

It is wise to check at this stage. If you find that you have not, inform the director immediately! Some relatively simple lighting treatments (e.g. multi-color changes on a cyclorama) can require a large number of lamps. Where equipment is limited, you may have to make do with another different lighting treatment instead (e.g. a single-lamp shadow effect).

Table 9.7   Preliminary facility checks

Now you know details of the production, you need to check the studio facilities before drawing a lighting plot.

- What is the light level required at a typical working *f*-stop? (For example, 805–2700 lux (75–250 fc) at *f*/4–*f*/8, 3000 K.)
- *Check out the lighting equipment.*
  What types of light fittings/luminaires are available?
  How many spotlights? (Sizes?)
  How many softlight sources?
  How many special-purpose lamps (effects projectors, follow spots)?
  What power is available?
  Is there likely to be sufficient spare cabling (e.g. to run to floor lamps)?
- *Check auxiliary fittings available.*
  Do you have sufficient diffusers, barndoors, color medium, etc.?
- *Check the various methods of lamp suspension available.*
  What are the safety arrangements for lamps?
  Are there safety wires or chains on hung lamps?
  Sandbags/stage weights to steady floor stands?
- *Check the lamp patching and lighting control facilities available.*

Even if you work regularly in the studio, a particular facility may not be available on the day of your show (broken, being serviced, being used on another production).

The lighting plot

Most people find the basics of lighting easy enough to understand, but are very apprehensive when it comes to the actual lighting process. How do you begin? Certainly, do not try to *imitate* 'standard plots'. They are, at best, only a general guide. Work out your lighting from first principles, to suit your own facilities. This is how to do so.

To start with, you need a scale plan of the studio, showing details of *scenery* and *main furniture*. If you just work from the back of an envelope, you'll get proportions and scale wrong. This *STAGING PLAN (FLOOR PLAN, GROUND PLAN, SETTING PLAN)* is usually provided by the set designer. It includes indications of the overhead lighting facilities, i.e. positions of lighting battens/barrels, power outlets, etc. If the main camera positions are also drawn, this becomes the *CAMERA PLAN.*

Fig. 9.20 part 1   Lamp stencil
A stencil with patterns for the main types of lamps used, to aid neat lighting plots.
Left column: Fresnel spotlight, lensless reflector spot, HMI arc.
Center column: Scoop, Softlight (internally reflected), small broad.
Right column: Cyc light/ground row, effects spot/profile spot, follow spot.

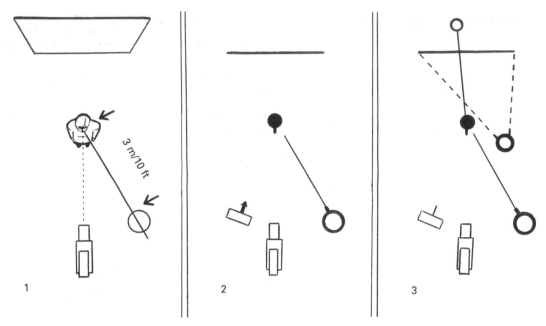

Fig. 9.20 part 2   Drawing the plot
1. The keylight direction is offset from the nose line, about 3 m (10 ft) away minimum.
2. Draw a symbol to represent the person (with nose direction), draw in the keylight. Fill light illuminates the shaded area of the subject.
3. A slightly offset backlight, and background lighting, complete the basic lighting.

Fig. 9.20 part 3   First assess the situation
The scene to be lit, showing the main light directions (compatible with daylight).

It is helpful to have a lamp stencil, which includes scale symbols representing each type of lamp you are using: e.g. spotlight, scoop, floodlight, projection spot, cyc light, etc. An accurate lighting plot will enable you to immediately identify every lamp during rehearsal. Without a plot, you will be left wondering which lamp is causing the boom shadow, or why there is hot spot on the cyc.

Work systematically, taking the project step by step. The art and craft of lighting cannot be reduced to a 'painting by numbers' routine! But it is possible to develop a regular procedure.

Let's assume that the lamps are positioned at around 3–3.6 m (10–12 ft) above the ground, and that people are standing or are on chairs at floor

Fig. 9.20 part 4 The lighting plot
After lighting the action areas
(chairs), the set is systematically lit to
simulate a sunny day. Lamps are
patched into supply channels (here
1–13) and each lamp's channel
number written within or beside it.

Keys 4, 10. Backlights 11, 13. Fill light
6, 8, 9. Sunlight through window 1.
Background lighting 12, 5, 7.
Backdrop lighting 3, 2.

○ 2 kW fresnel spot – hung

● 2 kW fresnel spot – on floor stand

▽ 1500 W scoop

▬ 1500 W striplight on floor

⌂ 4 kW softlight (internally reflected)

level (i.e. not on raised areas). A typical vertical lighting angle is around
30–40° (max) viewed from the subject's position.

When you are in the studio you can stand in the subject's position and
angle your stretched arm upwards to point at e.g. 35°. Generally, avoid
much steeper or shallower angles. You can judge a lamp's height by
comparing it with that of nearby standard flats.

In practice, to attain this angle, lamps hanging at 3.6 m (12 ft) should
be above a floor mark about 3–3.6 m (10–12 ft) away from the subject.
Lamps hanging at 3 m (10 ft) should be about 3–3.6 m (9–10 ft) away. If
lamps must be higher, they will need to be further away.

Now to the lamp plotting!

1. Draw a circle to represent the person, with a *nose line* showing the way
   they are going to face.
2. Draw a *key light* axis (i.e. the light beam) about 30° to this nose line. Do
   this on the side of the nose furthest from the boom, or on the upstage side
   of the camera (see Figure 9.20).
3. About 3–3.6 m (10–12 ft) away on the plan, draw the spotlight symbol.
4. Draw the spotlight axis *through* the head and beyond. At about two-thirds
   of the key light distance (say 3 m (10 ft) away), draw the small spotlight
   symbol for the *back light*.
5. Assuming that fill light is necessary (as it usually is), place a soft light
   source at about 3 m high, 3–4 m (10–12 ft) away on the opposite side of
   the nose from the key light. (A soft light source on a floor stand will
   probably get in the way of the cameras, and be seen in long shots.)

6. The relative intensities of the lights will need balancing while watching the picture. Typical ratios are: key light and back light of similar levels; fill light half that of the key.

7. What power ratings should the lamps have? That depends on the light levels your cameras need, how close the lamps are to the subject, and on the efficiency of the lamps. On location, a lensless spot (e.g. 1 kW) may provide a suitable key light. But in the studio, where lamps are further away, higher powers will be needed. Typically, a key light may be 2 kW, a back light anything from 1 kW to 500 W, and softlight filler around 1.5 to 2 kW. But it really depends on the area involved and the lamp distances.

   In larger studios, with lamps further away, or cameras working at smaller lens apertures, 5 kW keys will probably be necessary.

   This completes the lighting plot for that person. The result may not be art, but it will be along the right lines. With experience, you will get the feel of your particular light fittings and how they behave at various distances.

   If you have an interview to light, follow a similar process, with a separate plot for each person. Prevent one person's light falling on the other, unless they are deliberately sharing lamps (e.g. a shared key, or one person's key is also another's back light).

8. Check out each person's head-with-nose symbol, and consider possible key/back/fill positions. Some will result in shared keys, others may have to be compromises. But try to localize treatment as far as possible. If you do have to provide '*area lighting*' instead, pay particular attention to rehearsal pictures, and see whether results can be improved by extra treatment.

9. When all action has been lit, start to light the setting itself. Unless you are lighting a sky cloth or backdrop, do not light the walls of settings with soft light (e.g. scoops). The flatly lit or overbright tops to walls are unattractive. In some cases a single spotlight can cover a wall (barn-dooring off the top), in others a series of spots can light the wall in sections.

   These, remember, are only the basic mechanics of arranging the lighting plot; but they will certainly help you to light many regular types of production confidently and effectively. The techniques for coping with complex action, for creating and developing a particular atmosphere are another matter, and you will find these covered in *The Technique of Lighting for Television and Motion Pictures* (2nd edn.) and *TV Lighting Methods*, by Gerald Millerson, published by Focal Press.

10. The final stage of the lighting plot involves patching the lamps. Each lamp is to be plugged into an outlet on the lighting batten/bar and fed from a selected power channel. Write each *channel number* by the associated lamp. Only use the same channel for two lamps, if there is sufficient power (e.g. a 2 kW supply point for two 1-kW fittings); and remember, *they cannot be dimmed independently*.

   A *patching sheet* is necessary, so that someone can plug up lamps to correspond to the plot. You simply list the channel numbers and the batten outlets they feed. You do *not* need lamp descriptions on this list. A well-drawn plot is self-explanatory.

   If there are *lighting cues* during the show (i.e. lights to be switched on or off at certain moments) you may write these on the production *script* and/or in a separate *cue sheet*, with details of when various channel numbers or groups are to be altered.

Lighting rigging

Armed with the plot, you can begin to arrange lighting treatment in the studio. The process of selecting, positioning, plugging, and patching lamps is called *rigging*. You can approach the job in several ways:

1. *Select and redirect appropriate lamps* from those already hanging in the studio. A workable system with experience, but it depends for its success on there being sufficient suitable lamps from which to choose.

2. *Position lamps one by one*, lighting and setting each in turn as it is rigged. This can be a time-consuming piecemeal approach.

3. *Hang all the lamps required*, then when the rigging is complete, light and set each lamp.

4. *Have all lamps rigged and tested before the lighting session.* Here the lighting crew is given a detailed lighting plot, showing the position and type of each lamp required, and all accessories (diffusers, color medium), together with patching channel numbers.

This is a systematic approach, allowing lamp rigging to be carried out whenever convenient, and providing a valuable reference and record of events. The lights are set at a later session.

Setting lamps

The mechanics of setting lamps

Now we are about to adjust the lamps so that they cover the planned areas. Sometimes the most convenient method is to switch on one lamp at a time, set it, then switch it off and go on to the next. Its disadvantage is that you will not be able to see if any lamps are doubling, or areas have been missed. And you will need to have a clear mental image of the exact purpose of each lamp.

The best approach is a progressive one. Having set a lamp, you then *add* the next, and gradually build up the overall effect. Sometimes you will have to work with all the lamps switched on at the same time, and set each in turn; probably waving a hand over it to check its coverage. If all lit lamps are initially pointing in random directions, the result can be confusing and dazzling; but unavoidable, perhaps, where switching facilities are limited.

When setting lamps look out for *overlapping key lights* which can cause hot spots, and unattractive *multi-shadows*.

Finally, always be cautious about judging the picture quality from a monitor in the studio. Apart from any spill light diluting its screen, the monitor may not be set up correctly.

Table 9.8   The techniques of setting lamps

The subject

- Scrutinize the subject, and consider the particular features you want to emphasize or suppress.
- Will there be any obvious problems with that subject (e.g. a person with deep-set eyes or a peaked cap, who needs a lower key light)?
- Anticipate troublesome light reflections (e.g. on an oil painting). Will a carefully positioned key avoid bad speculars, or is dulling spray needed?
- How critical will the shots be? If revealingly close, will there be sufficient depth of field? Possible camera shadow problems?
- Is the subject stationary, or is it moving around?
- Is it being shot from several angles? If so, from which directions?
- Are shadows likely to fall on the subject from people nearby, or parts of the scenery (hanging chandeliers, arches, tree branches)? Lighting angles may need to be adjusted to suit the situation.

The key light

Arrange an offset key light, suitable for the camera position(s), subject direction(s), and action.

- Does the key light cover the subject? If the subject moves, will it still be unsuitable?
- Does the key need to cover more than one subject; an area perhaps?
- Does the light coverage need restricting? Is there any unwanted spill light onto nearby areas (people, setting)? Use barndoors, flags.
- Does that key suit the various camera angles? Will it be necessary to cross-fade to a second key for a different camera viewpoint?
- Check and adjust the key light intensity. (Adjust light level by slightly spotting/flooding; switching lamps; adding diffuser.)
- Is the key light likely to cause boom shadows?
- Is the key light position –
  Too steep (i.e. too high)? Look for dark eye sockets; long nose and neck shadows.
- *Too shallow* (i.e. too low)? It can dazzle talent; reflect in glasses; cause background hot spots; throw subject shadows onto the background; cast camera shadows onto people.
- *Too offset* (i.e. too far round to one side)? Causes a head profile on the person's shoulder; produces a half-lit face.
- Try to avoid placing people closer to the background than e.g. 1.8–2.7 m (6–9 ft) so that they can be lit properly, separately from the background.

The fill light

- Except for high-key or 'open-air' scenes, avoid high-intensity overall fill light (*base light*). It flattens modeling, reduces contrast unduly, and overlights backgrounds.
- Do not use high-intensity fill light to disguise the effects of badly positioned keys.
- Position the fill to illuminate the shadows; not to add illumination to the key light level.
- Avoid steep or widely angled fill light.
- Fill light must be diffused. If necessary, place diffuser over soft-light sources.
- Check that the fill light does not overilluminate items nearer the camera than the main subject. Are the back and side walls of the setting too bright, due to excess fill light?

Table 9.8 (cont.)

- Typical fill light intensity is around half key-light level.
- The more frontal the key light (i.e. the nearer to the camera lens axis), the less the need for filler.
- *Exceptionally*, in dark surroundings (e.g. a singer on a darkened stage) localized fill light can be provided by a dim, very diffused spotlight (despite the extra shadow it casts).
- Do not rely on light bounced from the floor to provide fill light. It is uncontrollable, and of low intensity.
- A lamp fixed to a camera can provide fill light, but its effectiveness varies considerably with camera distance. It is liable to be reflected in shiny background surfaces, glasses, etc.

The back light

- *Is the back light necessary?* It may not be needed for some subjects, or where edge lighting is used.
- Avoid *steep back light*. It becomes ugly 'top light' – flattening the head, and hitting the nose tip. If someone is close to a background and cannot be backlit properly, omit it. Do *not* use top light or side light instead.
- Avoid *very shallow back light*. Lamps come into shot. Lens flares may develop.
- Check that back light for one camera position is not creating *ugly side light* for another viewpoint.
- *Avoid excess back light*. Intensity is typically 1–1½ the key light level. (Excess creates unnatural hot borders to subjects, and overlights hair.)

Background lighting

- Is the background associated with a particular *style, atmosphere, mood*, that needs to be carried through in the lighting treatment?
- Will the background *predominate*, or is it an *incidental* behind mainly close shots of the subject? This may decide how much detail is put into background lighting.
- Is there any danger that the subject might *blend* into the background tones?
- Do any areas of background tone need *compensatory* lighting (i.e. too dark-toned, too light-toned, excessive contrast)?
- Does the background require *specific* lighting (e.g. a series of spotlit sections) or *broad* lighting (e.g. a flatly lit cyc)?
- Are there any practical lamps (e.g. wall lamps) that will influence the lighting treatment?
- Aim to *light the subject before lighting the background*. Any subject lighting falling on the background may make extra background lighting there unnecessary. Where possible, however, keep the subject and background lighting separate, for they usually require quite different treatment.
- Wherever possible, relate the light direction to the environment; i.e. visible windows, light fittings.
- Generally *shade off walls* above shoulder height to improve the subject's prominence.
- Check background lighting for distracting shadows, hot spots, patches, specular reflections.
- Avoid *bright* areas near the top of the picture.
- Take care not to exaggerate *tonal contrasts*.
- Avoid light *scraping along surfaces*, revealing and emphasizing surface blemishes, bumps, joins, etc. Look for spurious shadows from wall fittings.

Setting spotlights

Here are some hints on setting spotlights:

- Remember, when *flooded*, the spotlight's beam covers a greater area, but at lower intensity. The light coverage may not be *even*. *Spotting* the lamp reduces coverage, and increases light intensity considerably.
- Set a spotlight by *fully spotting* to position the center of the beam, then fully flood it to cover the required area. Or *wave over the light beam* (arm or lighting pole), watching the moving shadow to check its coverage.
- Avoid looking into lamps. After-images spoil your tonal judgement. Look at the scene through nearly closed eyes. It will help you to see tonal balance more accurately. (A 'monochrome' filter viewing glass can help, too.)

Lamp care and safety

- Avoid moving lamps when they are lit. *Filaments are fragile when hot.*
- Use gloves when handling hot lamps. (Preferably don't!) Never touch the new quartz lamp or HMI bulb (body acids destroy the envelope).
- Allow plenty of ventilation around lamps, to avoid overheating. (Drapes, cloths, cyc and other scenery can *burn* if too close to lamps) If you place diffuser material or color medium too close to a Fresnel lens you may crack the lens; so always use proper holders.
- Beware of overbalancing floor stands! Weigh the bottoms (weights, sandbags). Tidy away and secure cables, to prevent accidents.
- Have safety bonds (wire or chain loops) to secure all hanging lamps and accessories, in case they fall.
- Switch off lamps whenever possible, to reduce local heat, lengthen lamp life, and save power costs.
- Take great care when using ladders/steps. The main dangers are overbalancing (never lean over to one side to lift lamps), hitting suspended lamps and scenery, and dropping equipment from a height.

Lighting and camera rehearsal

Camera rehearsal is the moment of truth! Now you will see the results of your labors. Keep an eye on all preview monitors (even when cameras are off shot), and look out for lighting defects – e.g. distracting shadows, hot spots, unsatisfactory contrast, wrong light direction, unattractive portraiture, boom shadows, etc. If possible, readjust dimmers to improve the *lighting balance* (relative intensities) directly you see inaccuracies, for rebalancing could affect all subsequent shots.

The director will be arranging and readjusting his shots. Many will be as expected; some may be quite different, and could require total relighting. Whether you correct lighting problems as they arise (and miss continuing rehearsal pictures while doing so) or list them to be corrected during a break depends on the circumstances. You may have an assistant who can help. It is reasonable enough to adjust the odd barndoor quietly with a lighting pole during rehearsal, but diffusers and color media, or hung lamps, cannot be changed unobtrusively.

After production

When the production has been taped, and it is time to clear away equipment, remember that the next person to use it will welcome neatly stored lamps, tidied and looped cables, a de-patched board. To have to sort out a confusion of lamps and rigging left by others before beginning to light can be a very time-wasting and frustrating business!

TV lighting problems

Lighting treatment affects and is affected by the work of most other studio activities. Consequently the lighting director needs to cooperate closely with others to achieve maximum pictorial standards and minimum mutual frustration. So let us now take a look in some detail at the main problem areas.

Electronic problems

The technical needs of the camera-tube can frustrate your artistic aims. If a situation requires us to switch all lights off, or to provide very dim illumination, or to shoot against a very bright background, or have a scene lit by a single (usually unsuitable) source such as a candle, the camera would normally respond by producing inferior picture quality. So instead, the lighting treatment must necessarily be a compromise; a 'cheated treatment' aided by sympathetic video-control adjustments (Chapter 21). (In film making a similar subterfuge is used when labs adjust processing and the printer light for exposure and color balance control.)

Sound-boom shadows

Shot anticipation and coordination are necessary to prevent boom shadows falling across people and backgrounds. The normal trick is to throw the inevitable shadow out of shot by careful key-light positioning. Obviously, difficulties arise when this lamp position is artistically incompatible.

Fig. 9.21   Sound boom shadows
1. From Camera 1, mike shadow is out of shot and lamp provides backlight, but from Camera 2 lamp is now frontal throwing shadow on background behind performer.
2. Mike shadow (a) is caused by frontal key light being in line with boom-arm at A, whilst by placing frontal key at B, at a wide horizontal angle to the boom-arm, shadow (b) is thrown out of shot.
3. Floor lighting avoids mike shadows unless the boom-arm dips into the lamp's beam.
4. Boom shadows can arise when the boom-arm is parallel with a wall, (5) when the boom operator cannot see his boom shadows, and (6) when the performer is playing away from the boom. Where two booms pick up near and far action, the latter can shadow the closer source.

How settings affect lighting treatment

The layout, shape, and finish of settings necessarily affect how you can light them.

■ *Size*   Usually, the larger the setting, the broader will be the production treatment. Size alone is not significant since a series of small sets often require more lamps than one large set. Also, there are difficulties in providing precision lighting (e.g. for close ups) over a wide area, without overlaps.

■ *Height of settings*   Low-angle shooting usually necessitates higher sets (studio height permitting). This involves higher, steeper back and side lighting to ensure that lamps do not come into shot.

■ *Overhangs*   Appropriate lighting can be difficult for people or scenery underneath any overhanging feature such as ceilings, canopies, beams, branches, and chandeliers. This is particularly true when using hung lamps.

Table 9.9   Methods of eliminating boom shadows

	Method	Result
By removing the shadow altogether	Switching off the offending light.	This interferes with lighting treatment.
	Shading off that area with a barndoor or gobo.	Normally satisfactory, providing the subject remains lit.
		Shading walls above shoulder height is customary, to make the subject more prominent.
By throwing the shadow out of shot	By placing the key light at a large horizontal angle relative to the boom arm.	A good working principle in all set lighting.
	By throwing the shadow onto a surface not seen on camera when the microphone is in position.	The normal lighting procedure.
By hiding the shadow	Arranging for it to coincide with a dark, broken up, or unseen angle of background.	Effective where possible, to augment other methods.
	By keeping the shadow still, and hoping that it will be overlooked.	Only suitable when inconspicuous, and when sound source is static.
By diluting the shadow with more light		Liable to overlight the surface, reduce surface modeling, or create multi-shadows. Inadvisable.
By using soft light instead of hard in that area of setting		Occasionally successful, but liable to lead to flat, characterless lighting.
By using floor stand lamps instead of suspended lamps		Light creeps under the boom arm, avoiding shadows. But floor lamps occupy floor space; can impede camera and boom movements; can cast shadows of performers flat-on to walls.
By altering the position of the sound boom relative to the lighting treatment		May interfere with continuous sound pick-up or impede camera moves.
By changing method of sound pick-up	By using a low fishpole, hand-held shotgun (rifle) mike, slung, concealed, personal mikes, prerecording, etc.	These solutions may result in less flexible sound pick-up.

■ *Shapes of settings*   Deep narrow sets (e.g. corridors) and wide shallow sets restrict lighting angles, and can therefore frustrate good overall coverage.

■ *Surface tones*   Very dark backgrounds and furniture easily lose modeling on camera, causing foreground faces to appear unduly light. Extra lighting may improve reproduced tones, but can spill onto performers. Overlight surfaces appear glaringly hot on camera, often making faces look unduly dark. You can try to keep light off them, but even the

Fig. 9.22 Performer's positions
1. Mutual shadowing is often more easily remedied by repositioning people than by re-lighting.
2. Where people work too close to backgrounds, good backlight is impracticable. Side lighting or top-lighting (as shown) should be avoided.
3. Where action is in restricted or over-hung positions, lighting can be a compromise – or even impracticable.

illumination from distant soft light sources may leave them overbright. Darkening by spraying down with a lower tone (impractical over large areas) can inadvertently cause patchiness, ageing, or dirtying.

The illusion of depth requires good subject/background tonal separation. Contrast ratios of 1½:1 to 2:1 are typical. Backgrounds should rarely exceed 1½ times face brightness.

Shiny surfaces facing the camera can be particularly embarrassing, as lamps reflect in window glass, pictures, glossy walls, etc.

Overbright surfaces are a regular problem. Newspapers, scripts, table tops, light costume always require care; often having to be sprayed down (water-soluble color), dipped, or dulled down (wax dulling spray; anti-flare) to prevent excessive light bounce. A 'hot' back light can aggravate the situation. Shiny glossy surfaces inevitably produce bright specular reflections or glare, and each problem has to be treated as it arises (dull down, re-angle, cover up, relight).

Practical lamps

Under typical studio conditions the low-power table lamps, wall-lamp fittings, stand lamps, etc., used within settings, will seldom provide enough illumination to serve as light sources for action. Sometimes their bulbs can be uprated (e.g. using overrun lamps) to make them appear more realistic. But normally it is necessary to cheat their effect by adding supplementary lighting – e.g. a localized spotlight forming a light patch on the nearby wall.

Other factors affecting lighting

■ *Studio facilities* How elaborate lighting treatment can be is often influenced by facilities available. It can depend on the number and type of lamps, how they are suspended, the type of dimmer board and power-patching arrangements, time, and labor. Where many lamps are pre-rigged (*blanket rig*) for immediate selection this saves time; particularly with fast turnrounds between productions.

Clearly, problems become more acute if there are a lot of settings, with numerous camera angles and many lighting changes or cues.

■ *Space limitations* Most staging representing interiors has to be built in reasonably naturalistic proportions. So the working space available *within* the set for cameras, sound booms, and lamps remains pretty restricted. When action or treatment is complicated or continuous, lighting treatment becomes that much more of a compromise. Further lighting difficulties develop when, to conserve space, staging is located near a cyclorama (spurious shadows on cyclorama), or backings are positioned too close to windows for appropriate lighting.

■ *Multi-camera production* Multi-camera shooting does not necessarily frustrate good lighting. Much depends on shot duration, shot variations, and duration of takes. Often one set-up can light several viewpoints successfully. Otherwise you will have to introduce lighting changes (unobtrusive or direct) to solve the difficulties.

Lighting for color

Color adds another artistic dimension to the TV picture, enabling you to distinguish between planes more easily (for now there is *hue* in addition to *tone*), and to perceive visual effects that are totally lost in monochrome.

■ *Lighting methods and color reproduction* Many people associate color systems with 'flat lighting' and the extensive use of colored light. Neither is true. Flat overall lighting is as undesirable in color as it is with black and white systems. But reasonably *even* lighting is important for controlled results – with neither *hot spots* (paling out and desaturating colors) nor *underlit* (insufficiently illuminated) areas darkening and emphasizing hues. Remember, too, that under soft light, colors tend to appear paler; while under hard light, they can look brighter and purer (more saturated).

■ *Exposure and color* Exposure and lighting balance are more critical in color. If you stop the lens down to correct the exposure of a brightly lit subject its surroundings will reproduce darker as a result. Conversely, if you open up to expose an insufficiently lit subject correctly, other parts of the picture will look much brighter. So exposure compensations for unbalanced lighting can lead to brightness and saturation changes when pictures are intercut.

Face tones and color can become considerably modified by changes in exposure or color-temperature variations of the light. Caucasian faces look pallid or ruddy when over- or under-exposed, respectively. Brown skin-tones tend to become yellowish when overlit, and brown-black or terracotta in shadow. So a high lighting contrast (key-to-fill ratio) can create color-bisection effects. This situation is further exaggerated when lamps are being run at high and low color temperatures. In color, too, you become more aware of the blocked-off white highlights from skin shine, or perspiration.

Colored light

In fantasy or highly decorative situations anything goes. Faces may be lit with outrageous color mixtures in the most startling combinations. But for most productions, colored lighting (if any) must be confined to the backgrounds.

Sometimes even the subtlest changes of color temperature will be sufficient to tint light; for instance, when one uses low color-temperature lighting to simulate an oil lamp or candle-lit atmosphere. Occasionally you may deliberately alter the camera channel's color balance, or use an incorrect 'white balance'.

Usually, we clip a sheet of color medium in a *color frame*, in front of selected lamps. This material, bought in rolls or cut sheets, is of acetate, polyester, mylar, acrylic. Colored gelatin is cheap, but brittle, short-lived, and quickly changes color over hot lamps. Color medium is available in a wide range of hues and densities. But remember, deeper greens, blues, and purples can reduce the effective light output of a lamp to as little as one-tenth or less!

It is all too easy to misuse colored light. Certain treatments have been stylized to the point of cliché – blue to suggest moonlight; red-orange for fire; green for the uncanny. But when carefully introduced, colored light offers great visual opportunities. It enables you to ring changes on neutrally toned scenery and cycloramas. When combined with projected patterns, you can achieve impressive effects quite economically. However, take care that white lighting from other sources does not spill onto these surfaces and dilute the treatment.

Pictorial treatment

There are three broad styles of pictorial lighting through which we can depict the three-dimensional world on a flat screen: *notan, silhouette,* and *chiaroscuro.*

■ *Notan*   Emphasis is on surface detail, outline, and surface tones. Pattern rather than form predominates. The impression is flat (two-dimensional). Notan effects come from high-key, low-contrast treatments, an absence of modeling light, reduced back light, and widespread diffused light.

■ *Silhouette*   Here we concentrate on subject outline, suppressing all surface details. Apart from true silhouettes (black against a light background) used for dramatic, mysterious, and decorative effects; *semi-silhouettes* arise in contre-jour (against the sun) shots where back light predominates and frontal light levels are low.

■ *Chiaroscuro*   In this approach, light and shade conjure a remarkable illusion of solidity, depth, and space. The style is so familiar that we are liable to overlook that it is actually contrived. When well handled, this treatment possesses arresting, vital qualities, as the Dutch master painters found and depicted so convincingly.

Where subjects are set up before a totally black background (cameo), or a white background (limbo), the pictorial effect is more strictly a scenic design treatment than a lighting style, although commonly referred to as such. In *cameo* situations side light usually predominates (for maximum modeling); while *limbo* situations are often a notan treatment, avoiding shadows on a white background.

Unfortunately, terminology has too often become confused, so that *limbo* becomes used to indicate 'neutral backgrounds' of any tone. Similarly, for some people 'Rembrandt lighting' defines selectively localized lighting treatment, while for others it implies strongly modeled portraiture.

Table 9.10   Approaches to pictorial treatment

Illumination – overall (flat)	Main consideration is visibility. Lighting is almost entirely frontal and flat. Tends to *notan*. At its best, subjects distinguishable from each other, and from their background. At worst: flat, characterless pictures; ambiguously merging planes; low pictorial appeal.
Illumination – solid	By a careful balance of frontal and back light, subjects are made to appear solid. This and clarity are the principal considerations of this chiaroscuro approach. The lighting suggests no particular atmosphere.
Realism – direct imitation	*Direct* imitation of effects seen in real life, e.g. sunlight through a window imitated by a lamp shining through it at a similar angle.
Realism – indirect imitation	Imitation of a natural effect, but achieved by a *contrived* method, e.g. simulating sunlight by lighting a backing beyond a window and projecting a window shadow onto an adjacent wall, from a more convenient position.
Realism – simulated realism	An imitation of a natural effect, where there is no direct justification for it from within the visible scene, e.g. a window shadow on a far wall, that comes from an unseen (probably non-existent) window. (This may be a projected slide, cast from a cut-out stencil, or a real off-stage window.)
Atmospheric – 'natural'	A lighting treatment in which natural effects are not accurately reproduced, but *suggested* by discreet lighting. A pattern of light that highlights and suppresses pictorial detail selectively, to create an appealing effect. Suggesting realism in most instances, but seldom strictly accurate for that particular environment. A typical motion-picture approach.
Atmospheric – decorative	Associative light patterns, e.g. of leafy branches on a plain background.
Atmospheric – abstract	Light patterns that have no direct imitative associations, but create a visual appeal; e.g. a silhouetted unknown person, lit only by a rectangular slit of light across his eyes. A flickerwheel pattern cast over an exciting dance sequence.

Atmospheric lighting

Persuasive lighting treatment can considerably change the appearance and mood of a scene:

1. Concentrating attention – emphasizing particular features.
2. Revealing facts – showing form, texture, surface design, etc.
3. Concealing facts – preventing our discerning an object or plane; or seeing form, texture, detail, design, etc.
4. Associations of light – by light direction, intensity, distribution, recalling a particular atmosphere (firelight, sunset).
5. Associations of shade – shadow formations recalling certain subjects, environment, or mood (tree branches, prison-cell bars).

Mood lighting comes from selectively emphasizing and subduing. It is not enough to just imitate natural lighting, for under the camera's scrutiny true environmental illumination often produces ineffectual or ugly results; primarily hot tops, black eyes, half-lit faces, and steep harsh modeling. Instead, we must stimulate the imagination with light and shade – intriguing, hinting, evocative effects.

Fig. 9.23 part 1   Water ripple-tray
A spotlight shines through a water-filled glass tray, the rippling light being reflected on to the scene.

Fig. 9.23 part 2   Water ripple-trough
Light reflects from mirror fragments in water-filled trough.

Fig. 9.24 part 1   Shadow size, sharpness and intensity
Shadow size is always larger than the subject, increasing as lamp distance lessens. Close lamps give greater size changes, and exaggerated proportions. Shadow size increases with subject/background distance.
Shadow sharpness decreases with increased light source area, the lamp's closeness to subject, the subject's distance from background.
Shadow intensity depends on background tones and finish, and spill-light diluting shadow.

Fig. 9.24 part 2 Shadow distortion
Distortion arises when camera and lamp are not aligned, and not at right angles to background. Tilting the background or angling the lamp also creates distortion.

Fig. 9.24 part 3 Multiple shadow effects
These are produced when several lamps combine to light the same subject (particularly successful in color). If they rotate, the multi-shadows weave from side to side.

Fig. 9.24 part 4 Passing shadows
A rotating framework fitted over a lamp, and hung with a stencil cut-out, branches, etc., to create passing shadows. Patterns must not be obviously repetitive.

Fig. 9.24 part 5 To lose background shadows
This is achieved by displacing the subject from its background (e.g. on a glass panel), or by using a translucent illuminated panel.

Fig. 9.25 Reflected shapes
1. Reflective material (metal foil, plastic mirror-sheet) held in a sharply-focused light-beam, projects its image on to nearby surfaces. Bending the reflector distorts the reflected shape.
2. Spotlight focused onto *mirror-drum* faced with plastic mirror, produces 'passing-lights' effect for vehicle interior shots.

Animated lighting

You can introduce life and action into a scene by lighting. The movement of light may be used as a dominating effect, or as part of an environmental illusion. You will often meet examples of this technique:

Rain running down a skylight throws streaking shadows into the room below.
Fluctuating light and shade patterning the interior of a moving automobile.
A room lit by a rhythmically flashing street sign.

Lighting has the particular merit of *flexibility*, for you can change mood or significance in an instant, or imperceptibly alter contrast and balance. For example:

A prowler is suddenly illuminated by a passing automobile . . . and we see that it is not the person we expected.
During a brawl, the room light is broken . . . tension rises, as we no longer know who is winning.
Opening a window blind, the room's appearance is transformed by sunshine.
A happy atmosphere . . . becomes sinister . . . and finally horrific.
The high key lighting gradually becomes contrasty . . . until finally underlighting predominates.

Lighting effects

■ *Reflected shapes* Light can be reflected from metal foil sheeting or silvered plastic to throw decorative patterns. As the surface is moved or flexed, the pattern shapes and position change. Even stenciled symbols or lettering can be reflected to animate or distort titles.

Countless visual effects can be produced in this way (including nebulae, abstract and magical illusions), reflected directly onto backgrounds, front- or rear-projection screens, or superimposed.

■ *Firelight* To simulate firelight, move a stick with close linen strips gently before a floor lamp. Smoke or gas jets are generally less convenient and most automatic devices provide mechanical-looking results.

Fig. 9.26 Fire flicker
Narrow strips of rag attached to a stick are gently waved in front of a lamp to simulate firelight flicker.

■ *Lightning* You can achieve sheet-lightning effects simply by switching or uncovering a lamp for an instant. A group of lower power lamps (e.g. PAR lamps) may be more effective than a high-power tungsten source (e.g. over 2 kW), where the filament heating time slows the effect. Overrun lamps (e.g. photofloods) are liable to fail if switched on/off several times. Take care to avoid spurious shadows or unconvincing light patches on backgrounds, or gross overexposure during the flash.

Lighting on location

Varying conditions

When you are shooting away from the studio you will encounter a wide range of lighting conditions:

- *Day exteriors.* Varying from overcast skies to strong blinding sunlight with deep shadows.

- *Night exteriors.* Anything from pitch-black night to strong moonlight; from the odd street lamp to 'bright-as-day' surroundings.

- *Day interiors.* These can range from locations where sunlight through windows embarrassingly overwhelms any interior lighting to those where you need to provide a high-power lamp to simulate sunlight on a dull day!

- *Night interiors.* Conditions here can vary considerably; from total darkness to an extensively lit environment. Sometimes the interior lighting is quite unsuitable for the camera, and has to be switched off.

Lighting techniques on location

All the principles and practices of lighting we have discussed apply equally well on location. Faces still need key lights to be appropriately angled for the most attractive results, whether you are using the sun or a camera light to illuminate them.

Lighting on location is a matter of scale. Any given lamp fitting has its own 'dimension'. The intensity and spread of that light makes it suitable for a certain distance and coverage. Use a 10 kW lamp in a room, and it will be overwhelming; but used as fill light in a sunny exterior it might not be evident in the picture that it is there at all! Smaller lamps are useful for e.g. up to 6 m (20 ft) for fairly localized action. To light the inside of a large hall properly, bigger lamps at greater distances could be essential. Lots of small lamps would be difficult to position, and would probably come into shot.

A small production unit often has to light a location with a handful of lamps – because that's all they have! With modest facilities one's main concern is to make the subject *clearly visible* and as attractive as possible in the circumstances.

Given the option, one might well use a greater number of much larger fittings in order to achieve high-grade pictures from a number of camera positions, and create a more effective ambience.

Many factors can influence one's techniques. If, for instance, you were shooting during daylight in a hall with large ground-level windows, you might need few lamps, if any. But if instead, sunlight was shining in through windows located high up in the walls, you might need to introduce extra lighting to override its unattractive effects.

Much can depend not only on your resources but on how far you are able – even allowed – to modify conditions. Sometimes even a single lamp may considerably enhance the quality of the pictures. At other times only full-scale lighting treatment would really improve matters.

In Table 9.11 you will find a useful summary of typical equipment and techniques you can use when lighting on location.

Table 9.11   Lighting on location

Typical equipment

Lamps
- Camera light.
- Hand-held lamp.
- Lenseless spot (e.g. 250, 650, 800, 1000, 2000 W) with barndoor.
- Small broad (e.g. 600–1000 W).
- Floodlight bank/Minibrute (e.g. with four to nine 650 W PAR lamps).
- HMI arc (e.g. 200, 575 W; 1.2, 2.5, to 6 kW).

Accessories
- Lightweight lamp stands.
- Medium/heavy-duty lamp stands.
- Spring-loaded support poles ('barricuda', 'polecat').
- Gaffer grips/alligator grips.
- Wall plates (for PAR lamps).
- Gaffer tape.
- Sandbags.
- Diffuser/scrim/wires.
- 'Daylight' color medium (gels).
- Dichroic filters.
- Window filter material (rolls and sheets) – Wratten 85/light orange gel.
- Neutral density filter material (rolls or sheets). May be combined with color correction.
- Reflector boards or sheets.
- Mobile power supplies (e.g. battery-belt, 30 V DC battery pack).
- AC power adapter (DC from household mains).
- Power cables, multi-outlet cables/spider boxes.

Typical household supplies
110–120 V, 15 A wall outlets (1650–1800 W max.).
220–240 V, 13 A wall outlets (2860–3120 W max.).

Treatment

Exterior shots – DAY
Sunlight
- Avoid shooting into the sun, or having talent looking into the sun.
- Reflect sunlight with a hard reflector (metallic faced) as key, or soft reflector (white coated) for fill light.
- In closer shots color-corrected lamp can fill shadows.
- Bright backgrounds are best avoided, especially when using auto-iris.

Dull day; failing light
- Color-corrected light can provide key light or fill shadows.

Table 9.11 (cont.)

Exterior shots – NIGHT	● Quartz lighting can provide key, fill, and back lighting for most situations. For larger areas, higher-powered sources are necessary (e.g. HMI arcs).
	● Where necessary, either rebalance the camera to suit any local light sources (and filter your own lamps to match) or overpower them locally with your quartz light, and ignore background color inaccuracies. Extensive background lighting for night shots can require high-power lamps.
	● Avoid moving the camera around where possible (lag effects visible; comet tails from highlights). Large lens apertures are often unavoidable (producing shallow depth of field). Extra video gain may emphasize picture noise.
Interior shots – DAY	● The camera has to be balanced to the color temperature of *either* the daylight or the interior lighting.
	● Where strong sunlight enters windows: pull shades or blinds, put filter material over windows, perhaps plus neutral density media to reduce sunlight strength. Or avoid shooting windows. Alternatively, filter your lamps to match daylight.
	● Camera or hand lights (e.g. held 30–40° off lens axis) can serve as keys or fill light for nearby subjects, but: The light is very localized. (Very apparent in longer shots.) The very frontal lighting can easily dazzle people. The lamp casts adjacent shadows on a close background. A camera light flattens modeling. The light reflects in shiny backgrounds (e.g. glass, polished paneling). The light may be unsteady. The lamp may overlight close subjects, while leaving more distant ones underlit.
Interior shots – NIGHT	● Either supplement any existing lighting or replace it with more suitably angled and balanced lighting.
	● Where backgrounds are overlight, restrict main lighting to the subject. Overdark backgrounds may need extra lighting.
	Lighting arrangements may range from camera or hand lamps to three-point lighting. The most suitable form of lamp support depends on local conditions (on stands, clipped to structures or furniture, on telescopic poles from floor to ceiling, wall plates taped to structures, etc.).

Safety
On location it is important to take extra safety precautions in all aspects of lighting. For example:

Equipment condition	No frayed wires, loose parts.
Secure lamp fittings	Lamps should be firmly fixed and supported, and safety bonds fitted. All lamp stands should be secured or bottom-weighted to prevent overbalancing.
Power overloads	Keep within the power ratings of available sources. Remember, other nearby equipment may be sharing available power with your lamps.
Grounding/earthing	Have all lamp fittings individually fused and switched, and properly grounded/earthed.
Hot lamp fittings	Lamps can all too easily scorch or burn up nearby cables, drapes, paper, plastic, etc. In confined spaces, ventilation may be insufficient. Color medium can fume and smell. Overrun lamps can overheat fittings and nearby surfaces.
Floor cables	People can trip over cables, or inadvertently tug them and upset lamps. Tuck cables away, under rugs, near walls, hang them (gaffer tape or wire loops).
Water	Take great care when water is about! It can cause short circuits, or electrocute without warning. Water spray or rain on lamps will cause them to explode unless they are suitably designed for these conditions.

10 Scenery

Television settings – known variously as staging, sets, scenery – have to satisfy several requirements:

1. *Artistically*, settings must be appropriate to the occasion – the subject and the production's purpose.
2. *Staging mechanics* must be practical for the studio – its dimensions, facilities, and the production budget.
3. *Design* should provide suitable shot opportunities – operational freedom for sound, cameras, lighting, etc.
4. *The TV camera's characteristics* will influence the tones, colors, contrasts, and finish of settings.

Basic organization

Staging begins with the demands of the script and the aspirations of the director. Much depends on how effectively these can be related to the facilities, time, and budget available. As with all craftsmanship in television, optimum results come from a blend of imaginative perception and down-to-earth practical planning. TV set designers achieve minor miracles in making ingenious use and re-use of materials.

Planning begins with discussions between the director and the set designer. Using sketches, scale plans, and elevations, production concepts are transformed into the practicalities of man hours, costing, materials . . . For larger productions, there is close collaboration with various specialists, who consider:

Shot opportunities for cameras, performer action, and moves; the various lighting, audio pick-up, camera treatment, costumes, make-up and technical requirements.

In such an interdependent venture, teamwork is essential.

■ *The studio plan*   The basis for much of the organization is the standard printed *studio plan*, showing the studio's permanent staging area with such features and facilities as exits, technical supplies, cycloramas, service and storage areas, etc. A typical metric scale of 1:50, i.e. 2 cm = 1 m, is replacing the widely used ¼ in = 1 ft scale.

■ *The staging plan (floor plan, ground plan, setting plan)*   A rough plan of the staging layout usually begins with drawing potential scale outlines of settings, including their main features – windows, doors, stairways. By moving small tracing overlays around the studio plan you can make best use of available space, while ensuring maximum opportunities for cameras, sound booms, and lighting.

230

Standardized symbols representing scenic units, furniture, etc. are added until you have a mutually accepted 'bird's-eye view' of the entire staging area. Copies of a final plot are distributed to the production director, technical and lighting directors, scenic construction workshops, and anyone else who needs one.

■ *Camera plan (production plan)*   The importance of the staging plan becomes clearer when you bear in mind that in a closely planned complex production it is used by the director to evaluate or calculate his shots and devise a *camera plan* showing principal camera positions (Chapter 18).

■ *Lighting plot*   The lighting director overlays his *studio lighting transparency* (showing battens/barrels, lighting suspension points, lighting

Fig. 10.1 part 1   Staging – studio plan

**Fig. 10.1 part 2   Staging –
staging plan**

**Fig. 10.1 part 3   Staging –
elevations**

grid, rails, supply points, etc.), onto the staging plan. He then assesses the arrangements and types of lamps required for the effects he is seeking, bearing in mind the various production mechanics (Chapter 9).

■ *Furniture/props plot*   A series of larger-scale plans may show the disposition of all *set dressing* (furniture, drapes, etc.) and the main *props* listed on a props list.

■ *Elevations*   Devised concurrently with the staging plan and to the same scale, *elevations* provide a scale side-view of surface detail, treatment, and dimensions of all vertical scenic planes (walls, doors, windows, pillars, etc.). These not only guide construction and decoration but help us to imagine the three-dimensional staging in the studio.

If cut out from thin card, these elevations can be attached to a staging plan to create a simple *scale model*. This is particularly useful in complicated situations, to aid visualization of the final scene (for director, performers, specialists, staging crew). A miniature view finder will even show shots obtainable from particular camera positions.

Basic scenic forms

Staging is styled to suit each production's particular needs.

● *Neutral settings* offer the simplest and most economical backgrounds. Non-associative, they concentrate the audience's attention on the

subjects and the action. An open cyclorama or an arrangement of flats is
generally used; simply decorated perhaps with surface designs, graphics,
or lighting treatment.

● *Realistic settings* may represent a certain type of location (atmospheric
realism), an actual place (replica), or through selected details conjure up
a naturalistic impression (symbolic realism).

● *Decorative staging* takes several stylized forms, including abstraction,
silhouette, limbo, cameo, in which design is predominantly arranged to
delight the eye and stimulate the imagination.

Most studio settings are built from an assembly of prefabricated scenic
units. Carefully positioned to the staging plan (using wall/ceiling/floor
'footage' marks), they are fastened together and supported where
necessary and subsequently dressed or decorated to create the total scenic
effect.

Sectionalized units make transport, *setting up* (erection), *striking*
(dismantling), and storage much easier. Moreover, most of the component parts have been designed to be redecorated and re-used over
again, in different combinations, for many productions – as *stock units*.

The flat

Most scenic flats are made from fireproof burlap (hessian), plywood, or
prepared boarding (fiberboard, hardboard) on wooden frames. Although
canvas flats are lightweight, they are flimsy and lack rigidity. While
3.0–3.6 m (10–12 ft) high units are universal in larger studios, 2.5–3.0 m
(8–10 ft) are more convenient in smaller studios where the camera is less
likely to *shoot off* (*overshoot*) in longer shots. Widths from 0.15–3.6 m
(6 in–12 ft) are used, the commonest being 1.2–1.8 m (4–6 ft).

Fig. 10.2 part 1   Flat construction
1. Top rail.
2. Corner block.
3. Lash cleat.
4. Stop cleat (to align flats).
5. Brace cleat (brace eye).
6. Stile.
7. Frame (1 × 3 in pine).
8. Lash eye.
9. Diagonal brace (corner brace).
10. Keystone.
11. Toggle (stretcher).
12. Bottom rail.

Fig. 10.2 part 2   The box flat
A simple board frame structure that
may be bottom weighted or braced.
Bulkier and heavier than standard flats,
but provides a large flat surface (e.g. for
window backings).

Fig. 10.3 part 1   Setting flats – method of joining

1. Scenic flats lashed together by line (sash cord).
2. Adjustable cramp/clamp butts firmly together.
3. Pin hinge.
4. L-plate clip.
5. Securing nut (wing-nut).

Fig. 10.3 part 2   Setting flats – supports

1. The flat can be supported by extendable stage-brace (held firm with a stage-weight or sandbag), or braced to studio wall plate.
2. A triangular wooden jack (French brace) can be hinged or hooked onto flat rail (preferably bottom weighted).
3. Top bracing struts may secure unsupported settings. Suspension lines or bottom weighting are alternative arrangements.

Flattage can rise above 3.6 m (12 ft) but handling and safety problems increase. Tall flats are avoided where possible, for as lamps are forced upward to keep them out of shot their steeper angles cause coarser portraiture.

Surface treatments are legion. Cheapest are distemper or casein-prepared paints. Wall coverings (paper, vinyl) provide an extensive selection of patterns, tones, and textures. Finally, you can attach such materials as fabric or carpeting; or build up surfaces in relief with stuck-on forms or thin plastic-sheet mouldings.

Fig. 10.3 part 3   Setting flats – disguising joins

1. When flats are set edge-to-edge, their joins show. Butt joins may be covered with pasted-on paper or fabric (stripping), although this prevents later re-angling. Joins still remain visible in plain light surfaces.
2. Where possible breaks or returns are introduced, disguising joins, providing a more interesting effect, and improving acoustics.

Most flats are single sided (*single-clad*), but are made *double-clad* when you need to shoot them from either side. Curved flats are used for some applications (*sweeps*).

■ *Box flat*   The *box flat* takes a different form. Its simple board frame is faced with canvas, plywood, or 3 mm (⅛ in) masonite, and used mainly for large window backings.

Set pieces (built pieces, solid pieces, rigid units)

■ *Architectural units*   Although one can construct scenery complete with features such as doors, fireplaces, niches, the resulting units tend to be heavy, bulky, and less adaptable. So instead, it is often more practicable to use profile flats (frames), into which these details, made in the form of plugs (shells), can be bolted (Figure 10.4). Where features such as room doors, closet/cupboard doors are non-practical (i.e. unused), they can even be made in dummy form, and simply attached to the surface of a standard flat.

■ *Free-standing units*   A second, more extensive group of solid pieces provides not only such architectural features as stairways and arches but structures for general production applications such as *parallels* (*rostra, risers*) to create platforms or raised areas.

Fig. 10.4   Architectural units
Stock architectural features can be combined.
1. Contoured flat or frame (an example of a single-sided unit – viewable on one face only).
2. Door plug.
3. Fire-place plug.
4. Window unit (an example of a double-clad unit – viewable on both faces).

Profile pieces (cut-outs)

These vertical profiles of plywood, prepared board, etc. may be arranged either free-standing or attached to stock flats to modify their outline. Typical applications include:

1. Isolated decorative pieces – flat cut-out representations.
2. Wings – masking off the edges of an acting area.

Fig. 10.5   Solid pieces/built pieces

1. *Pillars:* cylinders or half-shells of 0.15–0.6 m (0.5–2 ft) diameter and up to 4.5 m (15 ft) high.
2. *Staircases (stair units):* groups of two or more treads, usually 0.15 m (6 in) risers, matching heights of stock parallels (rostra).
3. *Parallels (platforms, rostra, risers)* which are variously shaped level platforms on folding/dismantling frames with boarded-in sides.
4. *Ramp:* sloping plane surfaces.
5. *Arch.*
6. *Drape frame:* light framework in single or hinged units carrying draperies (otherwise suspended from batten or bar).
7. *Cove:* shallow sloping surface used to merge horizontal/vertical planes and hide cyc units.
8. *Step-box (riser block):* wooden shells from e.g. 0.15 m (6 in) to 0.6 m (2 ft) square. All-purpose unit that provides half-steps, display tables, for raising furniture, etc.
9. *Podium (drum).*

Fig. 10.6   Profiled pieces/cut-outs

1. Profiled flats painted in perspective, create a spatial illusion.
2. Profiled ground-rows suggest progressive planes.
3. Profiled flat supporting plastic-shell rock-face.

3. Ground rows – concealing background-to-floor joins.
4. Scenic planes – representing a skyline, and the intermediate terrain.

Profile pieces can provide cheap, very effective substitutes for elaborate scenic arrangements; for as the camera moves, parallactic movement between these planes can create a surprisingly convincing three-dimensional effect.

Although they may not deceive the camera in closer shots, profile units can appear very realistic at a distance – especially if cut from photo blow-ups. When shot from an angle, though, their flatness may become obvious – although this seldom matters with decorative units.

Cyclorama

Even the smallest studio makes full use of the cyclorama as a general-purpose background. The *cyc* (pronounced 'sike') is a suspended plain cloth; usually stretched taut by weights, battens, or tubular piping along its bottom edge where a totally wrinkle-free surface is required.

Fig. 10.7 The cyclorama
1. *Curved cyclorama*. A shallow C-shaped hung cloth background.
2. *Wrapround cyclorama*. A widely used form of cyc. Corners are gently curved, e.g. 2.7 m (9 ft) radius.
3. *Paper cyclorama*. A roll of *background paper* may be stapled to a run of flats, to form a continuous background.
4. *Merging coves/ground coves* can hide the join where the cyc meets the floor, and create a continuous plane.
5. *Cyc lighting* can be hidden behind a *ground row*.

■ *Cyc track*   The cyc is sometimes hung on straight or curved battens or scaffold tubing. But the most adaptable method is by gliders (runners) affixed to a permanent *cyc-track* (*cyc-rail*) round the staging area. Using this, the cyc can be repositioned, changed, and drawn back when not required. Sometimes a range of cyc tones is available for selection on parallel tracks.

■ *Materials*   Various materials are used – including duck, canvas, filled gauze, shark's-tooth scrim, and occasionally velours. Usual colors and tones include 'white' (60 per cent reflectance), black, light gray, mid-gray, light blue, dark blue, and chroma-key blue. Although permanent (*board*) cycloramas are now seldom used, as they restrict staging areas and cause sound coloration, small shallow C-curved flats sometimes provide backings for windows.

■ *Adaptability*   The plain light-tone cyc is extremely adaptable, for its smooth unbroken appearance can be considerably modified by lighting treatment. Its brightness and color can be changed; it can be shaded, or patterned, with projected shadows. With care, you can even attach very lightweight motifs to the cyc (double-sided adhesive tape, or pinned).

Backgrounds

Strictly speaking, any surface seen behind a subject is its *background*. Some people use the term *backing* synonymously, but that really refers to the planes beyond windows and other voids in the setting. These backings imply space and distance and prevent cameras from shooting off the set.

Neutral backgrounds

Neutral backgrounds are used wherever you want non-specific environments, e.g. for talks, *public* (*current*) *affairs* programs.

Because a setting is neutral it does not have to look plain and uninteresting; although to avoid distractions, any decorating is usually restrained. Surface texturing, uneven lighting (shading, dappling), decorative screens all have applications. Any drapes should avoid distinct patterning, for it easily becomes obtrusive and too recognizable for re-use.

Limbo (white) or *cameo* (black) backgrounds provide neutrality. Sustained viewing of either can be tiring, and similar subject or costume tones can inadvertently merge with them. The resultant effect easily vaccilates between naturalism, fantasy, and abstraction. Essential furnishings, props, and set pieces (doorways, windows) can be set up in front of the background – either symbolically or to form 'open settings'.

The somber gloom of black backgrounds can be inappropriate for certain subjects, and on many TV receivers may reproduce as gray. Foreground subjects may look overlight against these tones. On the other hand, white backgrounds can appear ethereal and infinite, although subject tones may appear darkened.

Fig. 10.8 Drapes
You can use drapes in many ways: to decorate a setting, to form parts of its structure, to provide the entire background. Drapes can be arranged:
1. Suspended from bars (battens).
2. Attached to a flat, or to a line hung across a flat.
3. Hung on a tubular *drape frame*.
4. Hung from a timber arm, hinged to the edge of a flat (*gallows arm*).

Fig. 10.9 Decorative screens
These take many forms. Stood or
hung in front of a cyclorama, they
provide a simple yet attractive
background. Typical designs include:
1. Decorated screens of expanded
   metal, wire mesh, perforated
   board.
2. Flats with contoured forms
   attached (e.g. of plastic shell).
3. Woven screens.
4. Open screens of stretched wire or
   cord, poles, slats, etc. They may be
   used to support motifs or profiled
   areas.
5. Curved flats (*sweeps*).
6. Flexible screens.

Pictorial backgrounds

Because it is difficult to distinguish in the two-dimensional TV picture
between distant objects that are flat and those that are solid, you can
simulate three-dimensional effects convincingly using a flat pictorial
background. Ideally, it would need to be free from blemishes, evenly lit,
and show no spurious shadows; its perspective, proportions, tones, etc.
should match the foreground scene; and it should be shot straight-on. In
practice, you will find that even quite blatant discrepancies can still be
very convincing on camera.

■ *Painted cloths (backdrops, backcloths, scenic cloths, canvas drops)*
Ranging from pure vaudeville to near-photographic masterpieces of
scenic art, these large painted sheets are used primarily as window
backings. Of canvas or twill, painted cloths are normally hung on battens
or pipes, or on wooden frames. In storage, a cloth may be rolled around
the pole that weights its lower edge, or *flown* (hung high above the
ground).

When used as backings, you may reduce a 'painted look' and suggest
distance (the detail loss of *aerial perspective*) by introducing a light overall
spatter or spray. Alternatively, you can stretch a black or white scrim over
windows to soften the effect.

■ *Photographic enlargements (photomurals, photo blow-ups)* Although
expensive, enlarged photographs represent the ultimate realism obtainable from studio pictorial backgrounds. Enlargements are made on
sections of photosensitized paper stuck onto a flat, or a canvas support.

Color is normally underplayed. Monochrome versions carefully
colored with aniline dyes are much cheaper, and can look much more
realistic on camera than high-quality color photographs.

A *photographic backdrop* of a location can prove to be a very worthwhile
stock item. It can be adapted and re-used by retouching or applying
stick-on overlays. It can be hung so that different sections of it are visible
on each occasion. Prominent parts may often be obscured by strategically
positioning a bush, a wall, or similar object.

You can also use photo-enlargements to provide decorative features
within a setting; as panels that are stood or hung within it.

■ *Projected backgrounds* Two systems are used: *rear projection (back
projection* – BP) in which a still or moving background picture is projected
onto the rear of a translucent screen situated behind the action; *reflex or
front projection* in which the image is *projected along the lens* axis, onto a
special beaded screen (see Chapter 21).

■ *Electronically inserted backgrounds (chroma-key, CSO)* By special
electronic switching circuits, foreground subjects can be inserted into the
background picture from any other video source (photograph, drawing,
miniature, TV camera, etc.), (see Chapter 21).

Surface detail and contouring

■ *Painted detail*   Because you can suggest solidity by suitable drawing and shading it is possible to create an illusion of brickwork, paneling, molding, etc. by brush alone. Realism depends on the scenic artist's skill, how closely the camera sees the effect, and whether oblique viewpoints or cast shadows reveal the true contours.

■ *Wallpapers*   Various photographic wallpapers of brickwork, stonework, wood graining, are easily struck to flattage – retouched or sprayed over where necessary.

■ *Molded pieces*   Ingenious lightweight imitations now exist for a diversity of subjects. Statuary, architectural features (beams, moldings), tree trunks, brickwork, roofing tiles, cobbled paving . . . are recreated with such conviction that they bear scrutiny – even up to fingernail scratching distance.

Earlier techniques with papier mâché and plaster or canvas on wire mesh have been largely superseded by fiber glass, molded rubber, and plastic forms. Solid items such as statues and rocks may be hand-carved by hot-wire cutters from lightweight styrofoam (expanded polystyrene foam blocks).

Most outstanding of all are the molded surfaces of thin plastic sheets (PVC). These are vacuum formed, up to about 2.5 × 1.25 m (8 × 4 ft) to produce realistic contouring shells depicting carved panels, rock face, stonework, brickwork, tiling, mullioned windows, as well as various wall furnishings (escutcheons, pistols, fish). These versatile panels are simply cut out, stapled onto stock scenic units, and painted. They have the merits of being low-cost, featherweight, adaptable. But they must be handled with care, to avoid compression damage.

Floor treatment

The studio floor's matte mid-tone surface serves as a neutral ground for most productions. But it can also provide some interesting staging opportunities.

■ *Painting*   Temporary floor treatment can be applied, using special water-soluble paints, either to change the overall tone or decorate the floor with realistic effects (floorboards, paving) or ornamental designs. Whether stenciled, hand-painted, or roller-printed, the treatment can be washed off after use. This means strictly avoiding spilled liquids for they destroy the treatment and make it treacherously slippery and sticky. Temporary adhesive floor tapes can simplify or augment painted designs.

Painted floors do not frustrate dolly movements as carpets and floor cloths can; but they are liable to become dirtied. Black floors all too readily show wheel and foot marks.

Table 10.1   Surface finish

Method		Purpose
Flat lay-in	Even-toned surface painting.	Textureless finish.
Dry-brush work	Overpainting a flat tone with a nearly dry brush. Sparse brush marks across the ground color.	Suggests metal, wood, stone, fabric.
Stippling	Series of small close dots of color on a different ground tone; using coarse brush, sponge cloth, wrinkled paper.	Suggests stone, cement, earth.
Puddling	Wet colors flowed together, intermixed for random variations.	Suggests ageing plaster, earth.
Daubing	Dabs of color with rolled rag, patted irregularly over a surface.	Varying density of tone.
Scumbling	Translucent coating, usually of darker tone over a lighter one.	Suggests surface undulations.
Glaze	Transparent dry-brush application of lighter tone.	Suggests highlight sheen.
Scuffing (dragging)	Skimming surface with brush, leaving textural depressions untouched.	Texturing a plain surface.
Wash	Thin coating of lighter or darker tone over background body color.	Suggests highlights or shadows.
Roughcast	Sprinkling material (sawdust, sand) irregularly onto freshly painted surface.	Random changes in tone or texture.
Spattering (dottling)	Mottling with random brush-thrown splashes.	Textural effect.
Stenciling	Applications of decorative motifs by stencils or rollers.	Decoration.

Where facilities allow, lighting may provide projected floor patterns; but these are very easily diluted by other lighting treatment.

■ *Scattering* Scattering innocuous materials much as peat, sawdust, leaves, cork chips, bark transforms a surface rapidly for naturalistic effects. However, material tends to stray around the studio (particularly when using wind machines) and must be confined. Avoid salt or sand – they foul up equipment!

■ *Floor coverings* The floor can be decorated by covering it with a *floor cloth* made of heavy duck, canvas, or tarpaulin (plain or prepainted);

Fig. 10.10   Floor treatment
1. The studio floor may be treated decoratively (painted, stenciled, stuck-on designs).
2. Painting simulates surfaces economically, leaving them flat for camera moves: (a) crazy paving; (b) paving slabs; (c) pavé bricks; (d) cobbles.
3. The floor surface can be covered by: (a) sawdust; (b)scattered peat; (c) dead leaves; (d) sheets of rubber/plastic cobbles, brickwork, etc.; (e) grass matting (surface contours changed by (f) sawdust sacks, or (g) sack-filled platforms).

photographic or patterned papers; or panels of prepared board. Thin materials may tear or ruck up under action or camera movements. Bulky materials such as turf or carpets can impede cameras.

■ *Adhesive patterns*   Adhesive colored tapes and designs in plastic sheeting can be stuck to the studio floor in decorative patterns. They wear reasonably well, and are easily removed after the production.

Basic forms of staging

Most TV staging follows a number of regular forms.

1. Scenic background

Here the action takes place in front of a flat background. This may be anything from a single decorated scenic flat or a painted cloth to a chroma-key inserted background. It may be augmented by a few foreground items or scenic pieces.

Extremely economical, the flat scenic background can be quite sufficient for fairly limited action. It is particularly useful in a small studio, where with a little ingenuity it can even be used to suggest extensive locations.

For example, suppose a person leaves their house and walks along a street. In a brief sequence, this could be shot as follows:

Person facing a street door flat, turns and walks towards the camera . . .
    (*STOP RECORDING*)
CUT to new shot Large brick flat with poster. They walk through the shot right to left . . . (*STOP RECORDING*)

Figure 10.11 Basic forms of staging
Scenic background. A single plain or decorated flat, a photo blow-up, or a painted scene provides sufficient background for limited action (particularly when chroma key inserted).

Area staging. Area staging is essential for broad action and widespread movement. Emphasis is on pattern and decorative effect.

Open sets. Economical and flexible, open settings are adaptable for stylistic and realistic situations.

Desk set ups. Modular units or custom-built desks are adaptable to many regular show formats.

Box sets. The traditional three-sided set convincingly simulates rooms while providing maximum operational flexibility.

Composite settings. A series of interconnected or conjoining sets makes maximum use of the staging area.

Audience shows. Sets are arranged to give the audience an optimum view of the action. The audience may be seen on camera or heard only as reactive background responses.

Two-tier staging. Very occasionally used where floor-level staging or subterfuges cannot be used. Requires well-designed scaffold framework for upper storey. Necessarily inhibits lighting, sound, and camerawork within the ground-floor setting.

1   2   3

Fig. 10.12   Skeletal settings
This form of scenic treatment is essentially decorative (unlike *open sets* that usually simulate a real environment). Isolated scenic elements are set up in front of an open cyc:
1. To create a symbolically realistic effect.
2. Decorative symbolism.
3. Abstract patterns.

CUT to new shot Same large brick flat (remove poster, insert lamp pole, leaf shadow on wall. They walk through the shot right to left . . . (*STOP RECORDING*)

Edited together, the few seconds of action are sufficient to create the 'environment' with just a couple of flats.

2. Area staging

This is the approach needed when presenting widespread action such as ballet, choirs, orchestras, bands, etc. To provide maximum space, area staging is usually based on the open cyclorama. In front of it are positioned a series of scenic units (e.g. pillars, arches, raised areas), hung screens, etc. to suit the occasion, without impeding the action.

Emphasis is usually on overall decorative effect, and, as we shall see, the cyclorama gives considerable scope for all manner of lighting treatment using light and shade, color, and projected patterns that can be changed at the flick of a switch.

3. Open sets

Basically, the open set simply consists of pieces of furniture or scenic units, set up in front of an open cyc. Yet on the screen the effect is remarkably convincing, and suggests a complete unified setting.

The result can be stylized or realistic, and against the dark cyc it can be hard to tell that cameras are not shooting a more conventional set. This low-cost arrangement is simple, extremely flexible, easy to stage, and allows cameras considerable freedom.

4. Desk set-ups

A wide range of productions use desk set-ups in one form or another as the central point for the action. As well as the newscaster's regular desk, we have desks used in discussion panels, quiz games, debates, demonstrations, displays, etc. The background to the action may be a regular three-walled box set; but a cyclorama is often used, augmented perhaps with a series of free-standing decorated flats.

The desks or benches used in these productions are usually demountable *modular* units. These consist of a metal or wooden framework to which decorative panels of plywood, prepared board, or plastic sheeting are attached.

5. Box sets (closed sets)

These are the traditional three-walled open-fronted arrangements used for many realistic room settings. It is not necessary to actually have *four* walls to an 'interior' setting to convey a convincing impression of completeness. You can even build various parts of a typical room around the studio, and, by careful intercutting, imply that they are part of the same room!

6. Composites

Here, instead of breaking an environment down into a series of separate settings the *composite* stages them interconnected as they would be in reality; part of a schoolhouse perhaps, with schoolroom and adjoining corridors, office, schoolyard. Where the camera *moves around* within this composite, passing from one section to another, the subjective effect can be completely realistic.

Most separate settings have a certain amount of wasted space around them, taken up with scenic supports (braces, jacks), through-ways, lamps, etc. By joining adjacent settings together as a composite, one can save the studio floor space that would normally be lost between them.

7. Audience shows

In this familiar situation a studio audience, on tiered seating faces a line of settings, a composite, an open set, or area staging. They have hung picture monitors and loudspeakers enabling them to follow the production while watching the floor mechanics.

8. Two-tier staging

Sometimes the story line calls for action to move upstairs or downstairs. Instead of actually building one set above another, it is far more convenient, and a lot cheaper, to 'cheat' the situation. You create the impression by intercutting between two sets at floor level.

Where the ceiling height of the studio permits, and two-tier staging is unavoidable, scenic construction can become a major project, for substantial scaffolding is usually necessary to support the upper floor with its scenery, furniture, performers, and cameras.

Fig. 10.13 The staging area
Locations are normally described in relation to a given camera's viewpoint.

1

2

Fig. 10.14 Typical sizes of settings
1. *Two-fold set* – 'bookwing, book flat'.
2. *Three-fold set* – 'box set'.

9. Enclosed sets

Another studio staging treatment that is avoided where possible. Here the action takes place within a complete four-sided room.

An actual four-walled room can be very restrictive to shoot, for the camera has difficulty in getting far enough away from subjects to provide wider (longer) shots. This occurs even when using wide-angle lenses or shooting in through doors or windows. Also, where several cameras are being used, they are liable to get in each other's shots if space is very restricted. On location, you just have to make the best of circumstances.

Where four walls are essential in a studio setting you may use intermittent videotaping to move in, or strike walls to shoot each viewpoint. Or you can actually build a complete four-walled set; arranging to raise, hinge, slide *wild walls* out when needed to give access to cameras and booms. In these situations lighting may become a compromise.

It may be simpler to provide peepholes for cameras – through doors, windows, fireplaces; *camera traps* as hinged wall flaps, e.g. behind pictures or camera-concealing drapes. When shooting a four-walled set you must particularly guard against *frame jumps* or disorientation by inadvertently cutting over the *imaginary (action) line*.

Size and shape of sets

Space and budget restrictions usually prevent you from building sets much larger than they need be. Instead, you can *suggest* space by scenic treatment. Where spacious effects are required, wide-angle lenses can exaggerate distance, so that even quite sawn-off versions appear impressive on camera. The kind and extent of action anticipated will influence set sizes. The smaller the setting, the more restricted will the camera and lighting treatments normally be.

Shooting off (overshoot)

Wherever you inadvertently shoot past the confines of the setting the solution is self-evident: readjust the shot, or add *masking* (intermediate planes, a screen, border, wall extension, drapes, etc.). Anticipation during planning can prevent needless last-minute rearrangements.

Shoot-off (overshoot) mostly arises when:

1. Cross-shooting on a shallow set.
2. Shooting downstage from an upstage viewpoint.
3. Windows or doors are inadequately backed.
4. Reverse-shooting into a set through a window or door.
5. Using low-angle shots.
6. Offstage areas seen in mirror/reflective surfaces.
7. Seeing through communicating openings (windows, arches) into adjacent sets.

Fig. 10.15 part 1   Proportions of settings – flat backgrounds
On flat backgrounds cross shots shoot-off easily.
1. The set lacks depth and solidity, but occupies little room (can be piled or nested).
2. Slightly improved, but setting looks disproportionately wide in cross-shots.
3. Very satisfactory proportions for general use.

Fig. 10.15 part 2   Proportions of settings – walls
1. Walls may be splayed slightly to improve camera access.
2. Right angled walls may restrict camera movement, but prevent exaggerated room-size in cross-shots.
3, 4. As sets narrow, little deviation from straight-on shooting is possible. Sound pickup may be 'boxy' and lighting tends to be steep.

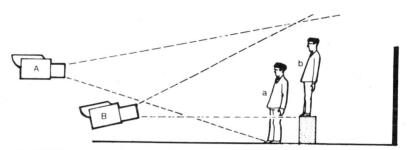

Fig. 10.15 part 3   Proportions of settings – staging height
The height necessary for staging depends on the longest shot to be taken (A), the lowest camera height (B), and the height of the subject (e.g. action on a staircase). A 3 m (10 ft) high flat is adequate for general use, a 3.6 m (12 ft) one being needed for larger settings. High backgrounds should be avoided to prevent steep lighting.

Fig. 10.16   Shooting off
1. Cameras can easily shoot past the edges of a set, and see the studio beyond. Solutions include (2) modifying the shot; (3) extending the set; (4) introducing appropriate masking pieces to prevent shoot-off (e.g. screen, wall, drapes).

Ceilings

Ceilings are introduced both to prevent cameras from shooting over sets into the studio beyond and to create environmental effects. However, unless carefully confined, a ceiling can frustrate the lighting treatment and produce boxy sound quality. Usually, the viewer simply assumes the ceiling, just as he does the non-existent fourth wall of a setting. Where ceilings are essential (in very low or long shots) and where high walls or a void (black drapes) would be unrealistic, various subterfuges are used.

Fig. 10.17 Ceilings
1. Complete ceilings over settings are feasible, providing appropriate lighting can be introduced (through windows, doors, lamps behind furniture, false returns, etc.). Translucent ceilings can help but light may be hot or patchy.
2, 3. Partial ceilings in corners or localized areas may prevent shoot-off.
4. Cutting pieces suggesting beams, vaulting; and suspended lamps (chandeliers) suggest a ceiling.
5. A scenic background (cloth, photo, chroma-key insert) may contain a ceiling.
6. A foreground camera matte simulates a ceiling on the studio setting.

Height and depth in floors

Vari-height platforms (parallels, rostra) are used where you need elevated floor areas. Any irregularities are built up with blocks, additional framework, tightly packed sawdust, or sandbags.

To create 'holes in the ground' (graves, bomb craters, trapdoors, wells) it is best to build up the overall floor level and leave the required 'hole'. This flooring must be suitably reinforced, and where heavy loads of scenery, people, or equipment are involved, tubular scaffold structures are essential. Where cameras are to move around on the elevated areas, surfaces must be level, flat, and non-skid.

To prevent unnaturally resonant flooring, platforms are best surfaced with felt, flexible urethane foam (foam-plastic sheeting), carpeting, or similar sound absorbants, plus internal packing where necessary.

Fig. 10.18 Height and depth in floors
Covered platforms (parallels, rostra) can be used to build up floor levels where height or depth are required.

Space economies

In most studios there comes a time when there is insufficient room for the sets you need in a production. Apart from cutting items, or restricting

Fig. 10.19 Space economies
1. Where congestion is acute, flats may be moved aside for camera access (hinged folds, wheeled, man-handled, or hung).
2. Settings' appearance may be changed by re-vamping (retain structure, alter dressing), rearranging scenery, and changing lighting
3. Nesting sets, where the inner unit is used and struck to give access to the second set.
4. Part of a setting can be built on a low wheeled platform (stage wagon, truck, float) and moved aside for access. Combined with chroma-key backgrounds (Chapter 21), considerable flexibility is possible.

action to smaller sets, one can often improve matters by imaginative mechanics such as those we see in Figure 10.19. They include move-aside flats, revamping sets, nesting sets, and wheel away sections.

Alternatively, you can record discontinuously (altering or striking sets during recording breaks), use prerecorded inserts (on videotape or film), or chroma-key processes to provide backgrounds.

Multi-plane techniques

Fig. 10.20 Multi-plane techniques
Foreground planes enhance the impression of depth.
1. They may arise naturally from the camera viewpoint.
2. Items can be deliberately positioned in the foreground.
3. Even an artificially introduced foreground object can appear natural in the picture.

Our impressions of *scenic depth* are comparative. They come from our relating the appearance of progressively distant planes, overlapping, scale, and a series of similar visual clues. The more planes visible between our viewpoint and the horizon, the stronger is the illusion of depth. When there are few spatial clues in a shot (e.g. an open stage), the picture seldom conveys a convincing three-dimensional effect.

These impressions of depth derive primarily from the foreground and middle distance. So you can arrange your staging techniques accordingly. Foreground pieces particularly enhance the feeling of depth and dimension. These can be such diverse objects as tree branches, furniture, tracery screens, and columns; all used to provide progressive scenic planes.

When carefully organized, foreground planes come into shot quite naturally as the camera moves around. But the effect can appear contrived, particularly when the viewpoint is unfamiliar. Overdone, this technique could leave cameras continually weaving among foreground obstacles, with the viewer failing to get a clear view of the action.

Partial settings

Why build more than the camera needs to see? Although some production situations require a total overall viewpoint or extensive construction, many shots need only a sectional view – a *partial setting*. Two deliberately restricted staging approaches are widely used. The first implies the whole by showing a *complete but localized part* – the doorway shot suggesting that the rest of the building is there – if we could see it. Audio effects help to create the illusion. The second method creates an impression by *judiciously placed foreground pieces* suggesting that the staging is more extensive than it really is, e.g. shooting through a foreground bookshelf, you imagine an entire library.

Fig. 10.21 The illusion of four walls
1. The fourth wall is usually assumed to be at the camera's position. Where the foreground wall must be seen, a mobile scenic piece (door, window) is often used. Designed as a *break-through piece* if camera dollies 'through' it.
2. Cameras can shoot over a low four-walled set for group discussions. (Beware of reverse cuts!)

Fig. 10.22 Partial settings
An environment can be implied by building a complete but abbreviated section.

Admittedly, such restrictions may not allow the director much latitude to change his mind, but the economies achieved in cost, space, and materials are considerable. The resultant effect can be totally convincing for short, relatively static scenes, and provide greater elaboration and scenic variety than would otherwise be practicable. Although, when unskilfully used it can lead to a cramped, restricted quality in the staging.

Realism

The artificiality of theatrical scenery is generally unacceptable in television wherever realism is intended. Yet paradoxically, where artificiality creates a genuine-looking effect, deception can go to any lengths. You may successfully use a fishline-activated curtain to suggest billowing winds, or have a leafy branch shadow indicate a nearby tree. Yet a genuine tapestry may look less realistic than a dye-painted canvas replica.

Realism can derive from quite subtle touches. A living room set must look lived in. Too tidy, too pristine, and it loses conviction. Surreptitious *dirtying up (antiquing, blowing down)* with a fine film of dark water paint can suggest wear, grubbiness, and discoloration around switches and door handles. Hand-sprays are useful for rapid localized treatment; although for large-scale effects (a slummy tenement) broad spraygun work becomes necessary.

Deception must be discreet. You must not expect photobackgrounds with foaming breakers that never move to fool anyone. Occasionally still backgrounds containing motionless trees, even static people, will be acceptable, but sooner or later they look suspiciously inert; particularly when accompanied by sounds of associated movement.

Sometimes the most convincing results come from using the real thing (e.g. real turf, tall grasses) while at others, grass matting (suitably discolored) and plastic flowers and foliage would be preferable to natural growth wilting under hot lights. Real water pools may be no more realistic on camera than clear plastic sheeting.

Fig. 10.23 Multiple use of units
Individual scenic units can be transformed.
1. Two glazed doors become a long window, or a ceiling light.
2. A low window can be turned into a throne.
3. An arch becomes book-shelves.

Scrim (scenic gauze)

Scrim or gauzes consist of thin cotton or synthetic net with a mesh of around 1.5–3 mm (1/16–1/8 in) diameter, in white, light gray, or black. Although it can be used in draped form, the material is generally stretched taut without visible seams or wrinkles. It needs to be of sufficiently open weave to prevent excessive light absorption or obscuring subjects beyond, yet robust enough to stand handling and stretching.

Fig. 10.24 Scrims/gauzes
Lit from the front alone (1), the scrim appears a solid plane. Surface painting or decoration shows up brightly against a plain white or black background. Unlit subjects behind the scrim are invisible.
By reducing brightness of front illumination (1) and lighting the subject (2) (behind scrim), the subject and setting are revealed with outlines and contrast softened, surface painting having almost disappeared.
A third lamp (3) added to rear-light the scrim, increases the mistiness over the scene, while silhouetting details on the surface of the scrim.

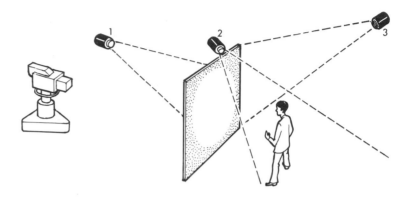

Stretched before a light-toned cyclorama, a scrim diffuses and obscures irregularities, and enhances the impression of spaciousness. Over a scenic background a scrim reduces contrast and artificiality. The material may be used as a glass substitute in scenery; it is safer, lighter, and gives no reflection problems. Lettering or decorative shapes can be attached to 'window panes' of scrim.

By adjusting its lighting you can alter the appearance of the scrim in several ways. When frontally lit, the scrim will look like a flat 'solid' surface. Lit from the rear, it becomes translucent with surface details silhouetted on it. Unlit, the scrim appears transparent, softening the distant scene.

Mobile scenic units

Mobile vehicles

To create a convincing illusion that a studio vehicle is moving you need to introduce a variety of 'clues': moving passing backgrounds; parts of the vehicle shaking; people being swayed or jogged; lights or shadows passing over them; perhaps wind, or dust clouds; sounds of progress (engine noise, hoofbeats, wheel noises, etc.); and the sounds of other passing subjects.

You have to interrelate these various features carefully, and above all ensure that there is compatible action between the subject and its background scene. If the vehicle stops, the background must stop too! This requires close coordination. Where moving film or videotape

Fig. 10.25 Movable units
1. The movements of a vehicle can be imitated by mounting it on a sprung platform or truck.
2. Using movable scenic sections, the large staircase splits to leave the soloist isolated, 3.

Springs
1

2

3

backgrounds are used (rear projection or chroma key) their timing and duration should be anticipated to prevent run-out or incompatibility.

A *sprung platform*, when suitably, handled, can provide realistic movements for a variety of applications – from rowboats, buggies, hansom cabs to automobiles.

For a large structure such as a ship you may need to imitate movement by gently tilting the camera, introducing moving light (e.g. a key light rising and falling), and even having people sway in unison.

Movable scenic sections

When you want to move around a subject and space is restricted, or to reposition staging to form new composition arrangements, you can often do this by using movable scenic sections. These may be flats or solid units on wheels, low wheeled trucks (floats, stage wagons), turntables, and similarly adaptable staging; see Figures 10.19(4) and 10.25(2,3).

1

2

3

Fig. 10.26 False perspective
The background can deliberately convey a false impression of space.
1. A flat background (photographic, painting, chroma-key) may contain an illusion of depth. But give-away shadows, wrong scale, or wrong foreground-background perspective can destroy the effect.
2. The whole setting may be built in false perspective (exaggerated size-reduction with distance), but then action must be kept downstage.
3. By deliberately arranging to have large objects in the foreground and progressively smaller items further from the camera, perspective can be cheated.

Fig. 10.27 Scale changes
1. Where the set is built with everything proportionately scaled down, people assume gigantic proportions.
2. If everything is scaled up, people are dwarfed.

Set dressing

Dressing is the process of furnishing and decorating the built setting . . . the arrangement of furniture, ornaments, drapes. This is the treatment that personalizes an environment.

These properties (props) are of several categories:

1. *Dressing props* used solely as decorative features.
2. *Action props* used in the course of plot action; e.g. a newspaper or telephone.
3. *Personal props* used or worn by specific performers; eyeglasses, wallet.

Where the item is *non-practical* it is not functional; for instance, a revolver that cannot fire or is simply not loaded. a *fully practical* article is completely working – the revolver is loaded, and used in the course of the action.

A setting soon acquires a filled-up look, cluttered with bric-à-brac that never registers on camera. So appropriate selection rather than profusion is the aim (Figure 10.28).

Where foreground space has been left clear for performers and cameras you may need to introduce (*set in*) extra props or furniture there for longer shots, removing (*striking*) them for camera moves. Although camera cranes can extend over foreground furniture to some degree, even slight obstacles impede pedestal dollies.

Furniture should not only be environmentally suitable but physically practical. Deep well-sprung armchairs, for instance, can encourage people to slouch, to look leggy when sitting, and to have difficulty in rising. Cushions may help where unsuitable design is unavoidable. So, too, seats that allow guests to swivel round, or that perch them uncomfortably, are best avoided.

If there can be said to be any specific tool for set dressing it must surely be the *staple hammer* or the *staple gun*, which can shoot wire staples through prepared board and soft wood up to 12.5 mm (½ in) thick. These versatile tools can attach pictures, drapes, posters, foliage, wall coverings, plastic moldings to flats; felting to flooring . . . A close runner-up is *double-sided adhesive tape*, which prevents articles from slipping or being moved out of position, attaches decorative motifs, holds arranged drapes in place, and fixes graphics. Adhesive gray *gaffer tape*, too, is a tough many-purpose plasticized cloth, sticking firmly to many surfaces yet removed without marking them. Its main purpose is to attach lightweight lampfittings or cables to walls on location.

Electronic and lighting considerations

Production treatment and the camera's idiosyncracies place a number of restrictions on set design. Occasionally you can disregard them – but only occasionally.

The final effect

It is important to remember that the audience only sees what the camera *shows*. Many a delightful skeletal setting has resolved itself into just a series of 'pole-through-the-head' shots as the director has concentrated on close viewpoints. Many a setting has looked fine in an establishing long shot but quite ineffectual in closer shots, or from other camera positions.

Color and tonal proportions in the picture can vary considerably with the shots selected. There may be only one small area of bright red in the set; but this could totally dominate and distract in a close-up.

Various hues are quite distinct in color, yet may merge indecipherably in monochrome; and for graphics (titles, graphs, maps) this can be a real embarrassment.

Tonal values

Marked tonal contrasts give a long shot a more definite emphasis than subtle pastel shades. But when you pan in closer shots over sharply contrasting background tones, or intercut between them, pictorial quality and visual continuity can be badly upset.

Conversely, if subject tones are too similar to their backgrounds the overall effect is unsatisfyingly flat or confused. So the tonal contributions of the setting, lighting, costume, and make-up need to be coordinated for optimum results.

To ensure good tonal reproduction it is best to work within a fairly restricted scenic contrast range for most purposes – around 10:1 to 15:1 (40–60 per cent reflectance) is sometimes quoted. Unless lighting is diffused, it will usually extend this effective contrast to the system's limits.

Surface detail

Plain surfaces, unbroken by detail or modeling, have limited pictorial appeal, but they can be considerably enhanced by lighting (shading, dappling, color variations).

Fig. 10.28 Visual detail
1. Excessive scenic detail is distracting, confusing, fussy.
2. If all but essentials are excluded, the result can be meager, cheap, empty; although suitably applied it becomes open, expensive.
3. Coordinated shape and line produce a stimulating arresting effect.

1   2   3

Bold details such as a strong pattern or elaborate motif are attractive as long as they do not draw attention from the action. They are most likely to do this if isolated within a plain background, or appearing unexpectedly in isolated shots.

Very small detail easily becomes lost in longer shots, or defocused where depth of field is restricted. So an attractive pattern that is quite clear in closer shots may dilute to an unexciting overall gray background at a distance. Consequently, where action moves to and from such a background we find pattern prominence altering as the focused plane changes.

Very close vertical or horizontal stripes are best avoided at all times – whether they derive from distant coarse patterns or close fine ones – for they can produce violent line beating (strobing).

Surface brightness

Bright surfaces leave the TV camera at a disadvantage where a full tonal range is to be reproduced. Even if no technical defects arise, the effect is generally distracting. So it is a good working principle to avoid overlight or shiny surfaces, unless for a specific effect.

Whereas in a *monochrome* system excessive highlights simply reproduce as white areas within grays, in *color* TV they block off to become white blotches on colored surfaces – and are therefore more prominent.

Highly reflective materials such as decorative aluminium foil or shiny plastic are notorious for causing troublesome hot spots, flares, or trailing. Providing any defects are not obtrusive, their attractive sheen can introduce vitality to a shot. But the borderline between pictorially attractive effects and disturbingly eye-catching blobs can be very slight.

'First-aid treatment'

Exposure is normally adjusted to achieve the most realistic *face* tones. If there are any disproportionally brighter surfaces in the shot they will block off to a detailless white. The result may be quite unobtrusive. But if it is unacceptable, the only solutions are to modify the lighting, remove the offending subject, or apply 'first-aid treatment'.

Although there are times when excessive lighting has aggravated the situation (as when strong back light burns out the shoulders of light-toned garments), such problems are more often due to high reflectance or smooth surface textures.

The obvious way to improve any overbright surface is to reduce or cut off the light falling onto it. But this may be impractical, especially where it robs adjacent areas of light. Flares or strong reflections (speculars) from a shiny surface can usually be cured by re-angling or tilting it, or changing the camera position slightly, or even by masking it with another subject.

Various aids can be applied to reduce such reflections (on automobiles, glossy paint, plastics), including dulling spray/anti-flare (wax spray), water paste, latex spray, putty, and modeling clay. Spurious reflections in glass or clear plastic can be similarly treated, although we may well obscure the surface by doing so.

Sometimes the only way to reduce overbright surface tones is to spray or spatter the surface lightly with black water-soluble paint or dye. Overdone, though, this can produce a dirty lifeless result, and destroy surface pattern.

Overdark surfaces may be improved similarly by light-toned treatment, picking out (edge painting) molding or detail, or perhaps by increased localized lighting.

Care is needed, too, in avoiding white or near-white set dressings; clothing, drapes, table coverings, papers, bed sheets, etc. You may substitute cream or light gray materials, or lightly dye them, or have them strategically sprayed or powdered down. Carefully done, the results on camera are well-modeled light-toned surfaces, reproducing as white. Overdone, though, you may finish up with people in dirty shirts reading gray newspapers!

Although modern camera-tubes can handle wider tonal variations it is best to avoid tonal extremes as far as possible.

Staging for color

Staging for color TV tends to fall into two broad categories:

1. Situations in which the excitement, vigor, and persuasive potentials of color can be fully exploited (singers, music groups, dance).
2. Situations in which color, unless carefully controlled, can inadvertently create false associations, appear tawdry, overglamorize, or provide an inappropriately vivid background to action (talks, newscasts, demonstrations).

In excess, color defeats its purpose and becomes visually tiring. Too subdued, and the picture lacks vigor.

For various psychological and physiological reasons, the TV screen can often exaggerate – even caricature – reproduced color. Certainly the general practice is to underplay color, rather than have color emphasis.

As a good working principle it is best to choose the surrounding décor to match the unalterable objects in the scene. Strong color is easily achieved; but subtle, sensitive color staging without simply resorting to gray-scale neutrals requires interpretive skill. Somber, slummy, drab surroundings can be particularly difficult to stage realistically in color.

Large areas of even, unrelieved color are best avoided, preferably being broken up with lighting, scenic elements, or set dressing.

Emphasis is generally achieved through the use of color in costumes, key props, and furnishings rather than in the set walls or drapes. Strong background hues easily dominate.

Costume (wardrobe)

Costume effectiveness is strongly influenced by its background. In larger TV organizations, performers' clothing (costume, wardrobe) is the responsibility of a specialist. But for many productions people wear their own clothing, and diplomatic guidance may be necessary to ensure that unsuitable attire is avoided.

You need to be sensitive to talents' feelings and taste when suggesting changes; particularly when you want them to wear an item from stock (off-white shirt, or a different necktie) to replace their own. Experienced talent may bring along alternative garments for selection on camera.

A costume that looks attractive full-length may be less successful when

Table 10.2   Costume problems

White shirts, blouses, etc.	Details and modeling lost where surfaces block off to white.
Glossy materials – satin, etc.	High sheen, especially from shoulders, blocks off to white or reflects color of incident light.
Light tones	These emphasize size, but if loosely cut, light garments can appear formless.
Dark tones	These minimize size, but modeling is easily lost in reproduction; particularly with dark velvets.
Strong, vibrant colors	Usually appear oversaturated and reflect onto neck and chin.
Fine stripes, checks, or herringbone patterns on clothing	Pattern strobes causing localized flicker, or produce blue-colored fringes (cross color), or color break-up. Color detail is liable to be unsharp and lost in longer shots.
Shiny, sequinned, or metallic finishes	Blocked-off highlights. Reflects onto nearby surfaces.
'Noisy' jewelry or ornamentation – e.g. multi-string beads	With a personal mike these cause extraneous clinks, rattles, or rustles.
Rhinestones and other highly reflective jewelry	Reflects bright spots of light onto chin, neck, face; and flashes obtrusively, especially when using star filters.
Very low necklines	In close shots can create a topless look.
Color fidelity	Certain colors can become emphasized or distorted (blues, magentas, deep reds) due to deficiencies in electronic or film processing.

Fig. 10.29 Costume problems
1. Avoid costume tones merging with the background.
2. Beware detailed or fussy patterns in both costume and background.
3. Close stripes and checks in costume flicker (strobe) at certain distances.
4. Low necklines appear topless in close shots.

seen as a head-and-shoulders behind a desk. Color matching that looks good to the eye, can reproduce quite differently; for example, 'reds' that differ due to their having dissimilar brown or blue proportions. Colors that have a strong bold appeal in long shots can seem harshly crude in closer views.

11 Make-up

Television make-up treatment follows three general forms: *straight*; *corrective*; and *character* make-up.

Straight make-up

Straight make-up is a basic compensatory treatment, affecting the performer's appearance to a minimum extent.

Skin-tone adjustment

This provides a good tonal balance in the picture: darkening pale faces and lightening swarthy complexions.

Routine improvements

These subdue blotchy skin tones, shiny foreheads; strengthen lips and eyebrows; remove beard-line (blue chin); darken overlight ears; lighten deep-set eyes; and lighten bags under eyes.

For many TV productions, performers require little or no make-up, with minimum correction and brief last-minute improvements often being sufficient. Regular performers may do their own.

Fig. 11.1 Make-up chart
Outline chart is used to record detailed notes of make-up treatment, materials, hairwork, etc.

Corrective make-up

Corrective make-up seeks to reduce less pleasing facial characteristics while enhancing more attractive points. Actual treatment can range from slight modifications of lips, eyes and nose, to strapping sagging skin or outstanding ears, or concealing baldness.

The general aim is to treat the person without their appearing 'made up'. Skin blemishes and unattractive natural color must normally be covered; preferably by using several thin applications of increased pigmentation, rather than trying to obscure with heavy mask-like

Fig. 11.2 Corrective make-up
Make-up can improve or disguise
various effects that may appear
emphasized on camera.
  1. Shiny bald head; untidy hair;
     scalp showing through thin hair;
     hair too light, dark, dense, to
     show well.
  2. Perspiration shine.
  3. Deep eye sockets; eyes appear
     too prominent or small; eyes lack
     definition.
  4. Shiny nose; nose coloration
     prominent.
  5. Beard-line prominent (blue
     chin).
  6. Neck scrawny.
  7. Lips need definition or shaping;
     normal lipstick too dark or light
     on camera.
  8. Age-lines; wrinkles
     over-prominent.
  9. Ears too prominent; different
     color from adjacent skin.
 10. Eyebrows barely discernible,
     over-prominent, untidy

coatings. Arms, hands, necks, ears may need blending to an even tone
(body make-up).

A person's skin quality will modify the make-up materials used. While
coarser skin textures provide more definite modeling, finer complexions
tend to reveal veining or blotches that the camera may accentuate. In
color, ears can appear reddish and translucent. Complexions become
flushed with exposure to heat (or hospitality). Make-up can become
disturbed in the course of action (e.g. lip colors 'eaten off'). Also,
bleached hair can exhibit alarmingly greenish shading, while blue-tinted
white hair can look startlingly overcolored, only improved by corrective
rinses.

Character make-up

Here, emphasis is upon the specific character or type that the actor is
playing. By facial reshaping, remodeling, changes in hair, etc. the subject
may even be totally transformed; for example, Frankenstein's monster.
But most character make-up involves less spectacular, subtle changes.
Theatrical make-up treatments appear rather too broad and crude under
the camera's scrutiny, except for such stylized characters as clowns,
ballet, pierrot.

Conditions of television make-up

The principles and practices of television make-up are almost identical
with those of motion pictures, except that in television the tempo and
continuous performance usually prevent the elaboration or shot-by-shot
changes that are possible in film.

A long shot ideally requires more defined, prominent treatment than
a close-up. A similar situation, in fact, to that found in lighting
techniques. But such refinements are seldom possible under typical
conditions. You may not even be able to do anything about such
distractions as perspiration, or disheveled hair, when the actor is on-
camera for long periods – except to correct them for any retakes, where
time permits.

For the very exacting demands of television drama, careful planning
and presentation are essential. At a preliminary meeting with the
program's director the supervisory make-up artist will discuss such
details as character interpretation, hair styling, special treatments, and
any transformations during the program (ageing, etc.). Actors who need
fitted wigs, or trial make-up, are then contacted.

Camera rehearsal

For camera rehearsal either of two approaches is common. In the first the
performers are made up beforehand as experience suggests. When seen
on camera this treatment enables the make-up artist to judge more exactly

the eventual detail work and tones needed. It also allows the lighting director and video control operator to assess tonal balance, contrast, and exposure.

While watching camera rehearsals on a picture monitor the supervisory make-up artist notes any changes that seem desirable, to guide the individual make-up artists handling the performers. The other make-up approach (especially for straight or corrective forms) is to see performers on the screen first, treating them as time and facilities allow.

Make-up treatment

Generally speaking, a straight make-up for men may take around 3 to 10 minutes; women require 6 to 20 minutes on average. Elaborate needs can double or even treble these times.

After a few hours, cosmetics tend to become partly absorbed or dispersed through body heat and perspiration. Surface finish, texture, and tones will have lost their original definition, and fresh make-up or refurbishing becomes necessary. Apart from on-the-spot retouching and freshening (mopping off and applying astringents), performers are normally treated in make-up rooms near the studio. Miracles of makeshift quick-changes have been achieved on the studio floor amidst the turmoil of production. But unless time limits or body position necessitates this (as with wounds), a more leisurely procedure is preferable.

There will always be problem occasions. Some performers cannot have make-up, owing to allergy or temperament. There are times when make-up has to be done immediately before air time, without any opportunity to see the performer on camera beforehand – a situation that the wise director avoids.

Varying conditions

Apart from artistic considerations, many technical factors affect make-up treatment:

1. Lighting – intensity, balance, direction, etc.
2. Scenery – relative face/background contrasts (simultaneous contrast effects).
3. Video adjustment (picture control) – exposure, gamma, black level, color balance.
4. Costume – relative to face/costume tonal contrast.

Such variations help to explain why the same performer's treatment may need to alter from one show to the next. Sometimes an astringent and light powdering may suffice, while at others more particular make-up becomes necessary.

Principles of make-up

The broad aims of facial make-up and lighting are complementary. Make-up can sometimes compensate for lighting problems, lightening eye sockets to anticipate shadowing cast by steep lamps. But whereas the effect of lighting changes as the subject moves, that of make-up remains constant. This distinction is important when we consider corrective treatment:

1. Large area tonal changes – making the entire face lighter.
2. Small area tonal changes – darkening part of the forehead.
3. Broad shading – blending one tonal area into another.
4. Localized shading – pronounced shading to simulate a jawline.
5. Drawing – accurately lineated lines and outlines.
6. Contour changes – built-up surfaces.
7. Hair work – mustaches, wigs, etc.

Localized highlighting by slight color accents will increase the apparent size and prominence of an area, while darkening reduces its effective size and causes it to recede. By selective highlighting and shading, therefore, you can vary the impression of surface relief and proportions considerably. But you must take particular care to prevent shading looking like grime!

You can reduce or emphasize existing modeling, or suggest modeling where none exists; remembering, though, that the deceit may not stand close scrutiny.

A base or foundation tone covers any blotchiness in the natural skin coloring, blemishes, beard shadows, etc. This can be extended, where necessary, to block out the normal lips, eyebrows, or hairline before drawing in another different formation.

Selected regions can be treated with media a few tones lighter or darker than the main foundation, and worked into adjacent areas with fingertips, brush, or sponge. After this highlighting and shading, any detailed drawing is done using special wax lining pencils and lining brushes. Lips are color outlined with a lip brush, then filled in with the lip color.

Make-up materials

The make-up media used in television and motion pictures include:

1. A dry matt cake of compressed powder (pancake).
2. A non-greasy base of creamy consistency, in small stick-containers (Pan-Stik) or jars.
3. A greasepaint foundation, contained in tubes.
4. Powder and liquid base.

Before applying a foundation (base) the skin is first prepared by thoroughly working it over with a cleansing cream or lotion (or cold cream) to remove any traces of existing cosmetics. Wiping this off with tissues, an astringent (e.g. eau de cologne) is patted on, to close skin pores, reduce absorption and perspiration, and generally freshen. On dry skins, a highly emollient cleanser/moisturizer (preferably oil based) is used to prepare a non-absorbent surface. This prevents oils in the make-up from being absorbed and causing a patchy finish. But for oily skins, a cleanser with an astringent freshener is needed to remove excess oils.

Following an after-transmission clean-off the skin is cleansed with special removers and washed with soap and water.

Which of the various make-up media is used depends on the effect required, the degree and nature of the treatment, and personal preferences. Each material has its particular features.

The pancake foundation

This base is worked up with water-moist sponge and applied thinly over the whole face. Its covering power (ability to overlay other tones, blemishes, etc.) is excellent. Its finish is predominantly matt. When too thickly applied, it can produce a mask-like appearance, flattening out facial modeling. Highlights and shading can be introduced with a sponge edge, using shades two or four tones different from the foundation color.

Cream base

This is dabbed onto small areas and worked by fingertips evenly over the regions being treated. Localized highlighting and shading with different tones is pat-blended or merged with flat-topped sable brushes. Surface finish depends upon any subsequent powdering to set the foundation. Unpowdered, the skin has a soft sheen. Powdering reduces shine leaving a smooth, satin finish. The cream has reasonable covering power and may be retouched easily. Leaving the skin's natural texture visible, it permits lighting to reveal more subtle half-tone modeling.

Greasepaint

This is similarly spread from small dabs. Although it has little covering power and may need refurbishing sooner than a heavier foundation, it is easily worked and retouched (by brush or fingertips). Powdering modifies its distinct shine to a silky gloss.

Such after-powdering, when applied to any completed make-up, softens contrasts and binds the materials. Any excess can be removed with a powder brush. A *beardstick* using a grease base can reduce a prominent beard-line.

Powder bases

These are supplied in compacts and resemble reinforced face powder. Applied with a puff, their covering power is moderate. They have general use for broad shading and tonal improvement, emergency repairs, shiny foreheads, and the like. Most liquid-type media have poor covering power, and tend to become streaky and patchy.

Fig. 11.3 part 1   Basic make-up techniques – general treatment

1. Hard hairline, forehead lowered by shading, face width reduced cheeks depressed.
2. Softened-off hairline, forehead width reduced by shading, deep-set eyes lightened, cheek and chin modeling increased.
3. Hairline reshaped and extended, forehead height reduced, chin made to recede, 'apple-cheeks' highlighted.

Fig. 11.3 part 2   Basic make-up techniques – nose treatment
Variations in nose shape achieved by shading (side shading, ridge highlighting).

Fig. 11.3 part 3   Basic make-up technique – eye make-up

1. Untouched.
2. Area above eye protrudes as a a result of lightening, eyebrows raised and thinned, making eye seem smaller.
3. Eyebrows thickened and lowered, and area above eye shaded. This opens up the eye and makes it appear larger.
4. Method of lengthening eyes.
5. Method of broadening eyes.
6. Distance between eyes reduced by shading.
7. Distance between eyes increased by shortening brows.
8. Detailed example of eye treatment: base of top lashes underlined thinly from center to just beyond outer corner, end being upturned. A short upturned line is occasionally drawn under lower lashes, but this tend to reduce the eye size. Eye shadow light towards the inner corners, slightly heavier at outer corners. A white penciled line along inside edge of lower lid.

Any powdering, whether to 'set' a foundation, reduce shine, or to absorb perspiration, must be applied judiciously. This is because the powder often tends to change color in use, or obscure base coloring.

Several accessory preparations are common to the beauty salon and the make-up room alike, e.g. mascara, eye shadow, and false eyelashes. A few, like rouge, have a less value on-camera and are better simulated by other means; while materials such as tooth enamel (to blacken or whiten teeth) or artificial blood capsules are more suitable to the television and film studios.

The make-up artist's tools range from brushes (for modeling, lining, applying lip color, etc.), sponges, wax pencils to palette knives. But for many workers their fingertips are their most-used aid, with which they blend foundation media into a homogeneously molded complexion.

The actual color tints and tones used for foundation powder, lipstick, rouge, and eyeshadow will vary according to personal assessment and the subject's skin tone. Some make-up artists work to a broad classification – e.g. fair, medium, dark complexion, but careful selection is necessary to avoid unwanted graying, dirtying, or the distortion of normal skin tones.

Refurbishing

With time, most make-up needs refurbishing, due to perspiration and wear. Blot up perspiration with tissue or a chamois leather lightly dampened with eau de cologne before powdering. Lip color may need renewing, as may localized highlighting or shading. To avoid hands appearing overlight, they may be treated with a darker pancake; which may also require fresh applications from time to time.

Surface modeling (prosthetics)

Manipulation of the subject's own skin or by sticking on new formations can change the physical contours of the flesh.

Manipulation

To produce scars, ridges, etc., *non-flexible collodion* may be brushed onto the skin. This mixture of proxylin, alcohol, and ether contracts the flesh; the painless contraction increasing with successive layers. Although readily removed, collodion can irritate sensitive skins. In such cases, quick-drying, liquid-plastic sealers may be preferable.

Fish skin can be used to contort the flesh within limits. The selected area of flesh is drawn into its new position, and the fish skin spirit gummed to hold it in place. Apart from imparting an oriental slant to eyes, this material is mostly used to emphasize or flatten out folds of superfluous flesh.

Surface contours

Surface contours such as warts, eye bags, wounds, nose modeling can be built up by several methods. Wax nose putty, mortician's wax, and modeling clay can all be molded into shape and stuck on. A latex rubber-base solution, *flexible* collodion (resin, caster oil, ether, alcohol), or various plastic equivalents, can be coated over a selected area until it is sufficiently extended. For larger protruberances, pads of absorbent cotton wool or sponge can be attached first by spirit gum. Surfacing is then carried out over this substructure. Because normal foundation media do not take to these surfaces, plastic sealers are finally brushed over to key them on and prevent any interaction.

For more drastic changes, partial or complete latex masks are molded and attached. They provide us with anything from double chins to grotesques. The advantage here is not only that more extensive alterations are possible but that they can be prepared beforehand, and the fitting/removal process is quicker and easier. All prosthetics are best camera tested to ensure color and textural suitability.

Hair

Hair may be treated and arranged by the make-up artist, or by a separate specialist. Such hair work includes: alterations to the performer's own hair; the addition of supplementary hair pieces; and complete wigs covering existing hair.

Hair alteration

In television, a certain amount of restyling, resetting, or waving may be carried out on the performer's own hair, but where extensive alterations such as cutting or shaving are needed, complete wigs are more popular. Hair color is readily changed by sprays, rinses, or bleaches. Hair whitener suffices for both localized and overall graying. Overlight hair can be darkened to provide better modeling on-camera, while dark hair may need gold or silver dust, or brilliantine, to give it life.

Supplementary hair pieces

Where the performer's natural hair is unsuitable for treatment, hair pieces or full toupees can be attached to the scalp, and unified with existing hair. Where staining of the scalp with masque cannot hide baldness, these made-up hair pieces may be necessary. For women, postiche work (pinned-on hair) may provide flowing tresses, buns, ringlets, etc., augmenting a short coiffure.

Beards, mustaches, side-burns (side-boards), stubble, and the like may be 'home-grown', preformed by using prepared hair goods, or built up from cut hair lengths. Prepared hair goods are, undoubtedly, most popular. These are obtained prefabricated by wig specialists. Here, hair has been tied strand by strand to a fine nylon silk or nylon netting (lace), and can be dressed to suit beforehand. This method is less demanding of the time and skill of the make-up artist.

On the other hand, treatment built up from cut hair is a lengthy and skilled business, but more versatile. Human and yak hair are the most-used materials. (Crepe hair has limited application.) Such hair may be laid in spirit-gummed sections until the required area has been covered. The result is trimmed, waved, and fixed (laquer sprayed), as necessary.

Wigs

These cover the performer's own hair entirely and are again formed from hair tied to a shaped foundation net. The front and sides of this net may be stuck to the forehead and temples and, where necessary, hidden by overlaying it with the base medium.

12 Audio

It is easy to take TV sound pick-up for granted. A desk stand, a tie-clip mike, or the ubiquitous baton microphone seem to meet most needs. We adjust audio amplification so that the reproduction is loud enough. Where is the problem? We can hear what people are saying.

The trouble with casual sound pick-up is that we often cannot. The audio quality alters so much it does not sound like the original. It becomes amazingly sibilant, muffled, distorted, volume varies, we hear random noise and distracting background sounds. The scale or proportions of the audio do not match the picture (close-up sound for a distant shot). Voices can become inaudible or confusingly jumbled together. The result is unrealistic and tiring to listen to. Little wonder that the professional audio man takes so much trouble to achieve the 'obvious'.

Sound quality

The simplest sound vibrates regularly in a sinusoidal fashion. Its oscillatory motion traces a *sine wave* of a certain frequency. Some sources (tuning forks, flutes, oscillators) can produce such pure tones. But most emit more complex sounds comprising a main note (the *fundamental*) accompanied by a mixture of multiple tones (*harmonics, overtones*). Their proportions alter with the source; e.g. the type of instrument, its design, how it is played. Sometimes, as with the oboe, these harmonics may even be louder than the fundamental note. Transient sounds, on the

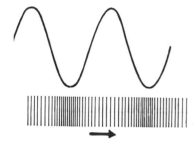

Fig. 12.1 Sound wave
When any material vibrates, its movement creates compressions and rarefactions in the surrounding air. In its simplest form, the air-pressure fluctuates at a sinusoidal rate. Sound in this pure form (*sine wave* tone) is emitted by certain sources.

Fig. 12.2 Defining sound
1. *Audio frequency:* The number of complete vibrations (cycles) made per second in hertz. The distance the wave travels while completing a cycle, is its *wavelength*. Its amplitude (strength) is measured in decibels (dB) or phons.
2. *Loudness:* Quiet sounds produce slight fluctuations, loud sounds, strong fluctuations.
3. *Pitch:* As the number of vibrations increases, the sound's pitch rises – from low to high frequency.
4. *Phase:* The relative time displacement between two sounds (in degrees. One cycle = 360°).

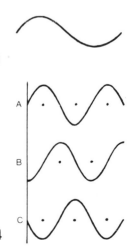

Fig. 12.3 Complex waveforms
The sounds from individual sources combine to form a single complex waveform. This is traced by the microphone, which generates a corresponding electrical waveform – the *audio signal*.

other hand (clicks, crashes, bangs), contain a broad random mixture of frequencies.

We come to recognize the characteristic ratios of fundamental and harmonics from various sources as their particular *quality*. Ideally we want to reproduce the original proportions exactly – but that is only possible within limits. Most audio systems modify quality due to their emphasizing or reducing parts of the audio spectrum, or adding spurious frequencies that are heard as various forms of *distortion*.

Paradoxically, while our brain is astonishingly tolerant and can interpret even wild travesties as substitutes for the original sound (as small radios continually demonstrate!), yet we remain quite critical of certain distortions – sibilance, overload distortion, severe loss of higher notes (top loss), strong resonances.

Reproduced sound

TV audio is predominantly *monaural* or '*mono*' (one-eared), and like a two-dimensional picture, lacks the ability to convey spatial information directly (although this is possible in stereophonic and quadraphonic systems). Mono sounds can only be segregated by volume, pitch, and quality differences.

Monaural problems

Our ears demand a wider frequency range for mono-sound reproduction than is necessary to achieve similar fidelity in stereo. Also, we become more aware of (and confused by) reverberation in monaural reproduction.

Fig. 12.4 Audibility
The ear's response to sounds varies noticeably with their volume and pitch. At lower sound levels, we are less able to hear the highest frequencies, and there is a considerable loss of bass.

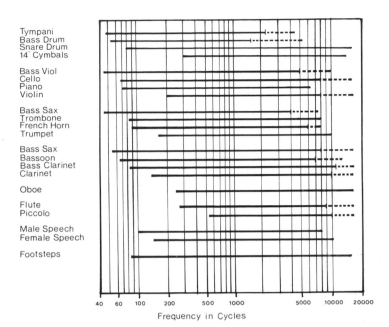

Fig. 12.5 Frequency range
Here the audible frequency range of
various sources are compared.

The mono microphone can give equal prominence to any sounds in its
pick-up range. So careful microphone positioning is often necessary to
avoid one sound masking another, or sources merging in reproduction, or
our overhearing extraneous noises.

Stereo sound

At best, stereo sound enhances the clarity of the audio, even though
TV receiver loudspeakers are invariably too close together, and have
performance limitations. Stereo sound overcomes certain mono problems
(e.g. source masking), and presents a dispersed sound image.

However, stereo sound pick-up requires more accurate mike location,
especially when subjects are some distance apart. It is liable to pick up
more background noises (e.g. ventilation, camera movements). The scale
and perspective of the stereo sound needs to match the impressions
conveyed by the picture. Close-ups of instrumentalists in the middle of
an orchestra, accompanied by a distant sound balance, are even less
acceptable in stereo than with mono sound.

The audio system

The *dynamic range* (volume range) that any audio system can handle is
limited. When too loud, sounds will cause *overload distortion*, producing
spurious discordant overtones. If too quiet, wanted sounds will become
merged with background noise of comparable level (volume), such as tape
noise, hum and ventilation.

So to avoid exceeding these limits it is essential that you do not overload the microphone itself (too near a loud source), or overamplify the signal (overmodulation, 'overmod'). Conversely, you must prevent the audio signal from becoming too weak (undermodulation, 'undermod') by placing the microphone close enough and using sufficient amplification. But at the same time, as you will see later, you must not destroy an impression of the dynamics of the original sound source.

Acoustics

Although acoustic design is the concern of the specialist, we are interested as users of the studio in how acoustic characteristics can affect audio quality, studio operations, and audiovisual matching.

Reverberant studios

A *live*, highly reflective studio would emphasize all sounds – wanted (speech, music) or unwanted (camera moves, cable drag, footsteps, ventilation, scenery movement). Even using close directional microphones, extraneous sounds would intrude; particularly during quiet scenes.

No staging depicting exterior scenes or small rooms can hope to be convincing if accompanied by echoing sound! It is always possible to *add* simulated reverberation to any sound, but not normally practicable to remove it to deaden the effect.

Strong acoustic reflections can mask the original sound, reducing intelligibility. And, due to quality changes caused by frequency-selective absorption, the overall effect may become hollow, hard, boomy, 'woofy'.

Dead studios

We can only avoid reflected sounds completely in free space, or in special highly absorbent, multi-surfaced *anechoic chambers*. But by using carefully positioned sound-absorbing materials we can suppress most acoustic reflections, and produce *dead* (non-reverberant) surroundings. Such conditions reduce the pick-up of extraneous noise, and make 'exterior' sets in studios sound more convincing. However, because sound waves do not carry well in such surroundings (reflections help to reinforce sound strength), they can be very tiring to perform in (especially for singers, musicians), and mikes need to be positioned closer as sounds seem weaker.

Practical acoustics

A certain amount of reverberation enriches and strengthens sounds, conveying an impression of vitality and spaciousness. Therefore most studios have quite carefully chosen acoustics; neither too live nor too dead.

———— Direct Sound
------ Reflected Sound

Fig. 12.6 Studio acoustics
As sound strikes surfaces a proportion is absorbed (frequency-selectively), or reinforced by structural resonance. The reflected sound, now modified, adds to the original (augmenting or partially masking it). Some coloration is artistically desirable. The time taken for the sound to die away (decay time; reverberation period) largely depends on room volume, surface materials, shape, and can range from less than 1 second up to about 6 seconds.

In practice, quality and sound absorption become modified by staging, equipment, audience, etc. Local acoustics within a setting can introduce considerable quality changes (sound becoming harsh, hollow, boxy), especially if there is a ceiling.

On location, the audio engineer has to contend with a wide variety of acoustic conditions and encroaching environmental noise, and must rely heavily on selective microphones and careful positioning to obtain optimum audio quality.

Where a performance is taking place in reverberant surroundings (e.g. a string quartet playing in a large empty studio) you can often improve the overall sound by placing *acoustic screens* around the subjects. The sound-absorbent tiles or padding on the screens shield the performers and their microphones from delayed sound waves reflected from the studio walls. Similarly, when an unseen group in the studio provides background music for action seen on camera you can use acoustic screens to prevent the action mikes from overhearing the musicians.

Microphone characteristics

The main thing you want to know before using a microphone concern:

1. Physical features,
2. Audio quality,
3. Sensitivity and directional properties,
4. Installation suitability.

Which aspects are most important to you depend largely on the type of sound pick-up involved and operating conditions. For example, ruggedness may be at the expense of fidelity.

■ *Physical features*   While *size* may be unimportant for a slung microphone it can matter where the microphone is to appear in shot or to be handled. *Appearance* then counts, too. *Ruggedness* is a consideration where rough or inexperienced usage is likely. *Handling noise* can also be a distraction for some sensitive microphones. *Stability and reliability* are features that only time and experience reveal, and most high-grade microphones can be relied on if given careful treatment.

■ *Audio quality*   Ideally a microphone should cover the entire audio spectrum evenly. Its *transient response* to brief sharp sounds (from musical triangle to jingling keys) should be impeccable. Audio should be accurately reproduced without coloration or distortion. Fortunately, such parameters are less critical in practice!

■ *Sensitivity and directionality*   A microphone's *sensitivity* determines how large an audio signal it produces for a given sound volume. Although audio amplifiers can compensate for even the least sensitive microphones, excessive amplification adds spurious hiss and hum to the audio signal.

Any microphone will normally have to work closer to quiet sounds than louder ones, but less sensitive mikes must be positioned that much closer. However, they are less liable to be overloaded or damaged by loud sounds, so that in certain applications (percussion) they may be preferable.

A sound-boom microphone needs to be pretty sensitive, or it would have to work too close to sources (casting shadows); and yet it must not suffer from *rumble* (when racking the boom arm in and out), or wind noise (as it moves through the air). So condenser or dynamic mikes are generally used.

The *directional properties* of the microphone (*polar diagram*) are simply its sensitivity pattern in space. Sometimes you will need an *omni-directional* response, that hears equally well in all directions. At others you require a very *directional* response, able to pick out a selected sound source and ignore or suppress others nearby. Certain microphones have adjustable directionality.

■ *Installation suitability*   When you connect together various pieces of audio equipment interfacing problems can arise. Inter-unit cable plugs are not standardized, and you must use the appropriate connectors or adapters. (Types include Mini, phono, RCA, Din, Cannon.) As with all audio equipment, the electrical *impedance* of your microphone must match the line or amplifier into which it connects. Although a low-impedance unit may sound fine in a higher impedance input, the reverse is less likely. Low-impedance mikes (50–600 Ω) are most versatile for you can use longer cable lengths without top-loss; unlike high-impedance mikes (2000–10 000 Ω), which are also susceptible to hum/electrical interference pick-up.

In European designs the amplifier input should be at least five times the mike's rated impedance (typically 200 Ω) to avoid high-frequency distortion.

■ *Choice of microphone*   All audio men have prejudices about the right mike for the job and exactly where to place it; for no two situations are *identical*. Listening to a piano performance, we find the instrument's tone varies considerably with its manufacturer, tuning, performer; and even changes with temperature, humidity, and acoustics. While most specialists would agree to use a condenser or ribbon microphone, its positioning is influenced by many subtle factors.

Where there is no 'universal' microphone type, one design may fulfil several different purposes. A certain condenser mike may well serve for a boom, floor stand, hung, or desk stand. But it would be unsuitable beside a boisterous drummer or as a hand mike at a remote, due to its susceptibility to overload.

Types of microphone

Dynamic (moving-coil) microphone

A very robust design, the dynamic mike is not sensitive to handling and has a wide range of applications: baton, fishpole, small boom, desk or stand, slung, and field (location) use. It is often used for less critical sound quality (close singer) or close loud sources (e.g. drums). Small versions are used as lavalier and clip-on personal microphones.

The microphone tends to be unidirectional to higher frequencies, but non-directional to low frequencies. Consequently there is a top fall-off as subjects move off-axis (center line). This feature is useful with sources that are shrill, toppy, or sibilant; when one deliberately positions them off-axis.

This type of microphone works by soundwave pressure variations vibrating a diaphragm which has a small coil of wire attached. Coil movement within a magnetic field generates audio currents. A typical frequency range is 40–16 000 Hz.

Condenser (electrostatic) microphone

The condenser microphone produces the highest audio quality (typically 20–18 000 Hz), and has an excellent response to transient sounds. It is used for high-grade pick-up (moving or static), especially when some distance from source (e.g. slung over an orchestra). It can be fitted to a boom, stand, fishpole, or slung.

The condenser mike has the disadvantages that it is relatively large, and, being highly sensitive, it is liable to input overload distortion by very loud nearby sources. In addition, the unit requires a polarizing voltage supply and an adjacent preamplifier.

In the condenser microphone a light flexible metallic membrane is stretched close to a flat metal plate and a polarizing potential (e.g. 60 V DC) is applied between them. Sound-wave pressure fluctuations alter the intervening space and hence their intercapacity. Varying current continually taken to recharge this changing capacitance constitutes the audio signal.

Electret capsule

The electret capsule is very extensively used as a personal or a concealed mike, providing good-quality pick-up. This relatively cheap miniature condenser microphone incorporates a plastic film diaphragm with an inbuilt 'permanent' electrostatic charge; thus eliminating the need for an applied polarizing voltage. A tiny associated amplifier (battery powered) is enclosed in the mike housing.

Performance deteriorates with ageing, resulting in a loss of higher frequencies (top, highs), reduced sensitivity, and increased background noise. Deterioration can be accelerated by high humidity, moisture, heat, and dust. Rapid unexpected failure is not uncommon.

A *pressure-zone microphone (PZM; boundary layer microphone)* is an unobtrusive low-profile, plate-mounted electret capsule with a hemi-spherical or a semi-cardioid pick-up pattern. Attached to e.g. floor, table, or wall surfaces near the sound source, the rugged PZM combines sensitivity and high-quality output, with considerable freedom from contact noise, or audio overload. It is, however, liable to emphasize ambient reflected noise from surroundings. (See Glossary: *Pressure-zone microphone.*)

Ribbon (velocity, pressure-gradient) microphone

This microphone is suitable for static pick-up of speech and music, and for stand and slung applications. It has an excellent transient response and produces the highest audio quality. The ribbon microphone has an even frequency response (e.g. 30–18 000 Hz) over its pick-up field – although there is some top-loss for pick-up oblique to its ribbon. Bass notes are emphasized when the source is very close. Its normal figure-of-eight directional response is often made unidirectional (asymmetrical) by internal design.

On the debit side, the ribbon mike is not generally robust or compact. It is not normally suitable for mobile boom use (or hand use), being susceptible to wind rumble and wind damage. Also it is subject to overload from close loud sounds.

In the ribbon microphone a thin corrugated foil strip held between magnet poles vibrates with air-pressure differences on either face, so generating an electric audio current in the foil.

Crystal microphone

Although very cheap, highly sensitive, and of small size, the crystal mike is fragile and its audio quality is restricted. Only adequate for less exacting use (field interviews), it is very suited to *contact* applications (electric guitar).

When sound strikes its diaphragm a small bimorph (two-sliced) crystal is twisted, and piezoelectric effect produces a corresponding voltage, the audio signal.

Directional characteristics

Whether a microphone responds equally well to sounds from all directions, or only to those over a limited angle, is determined by both its type (electrostatic, ribbon, etc.) and its construction. A microphone's *directional* or *directivity pattern* (*polar diagram*) is normally fixed, but some designs have *adjustable* characteristics that allow you to choose a directional response that suits a particular applicatioin.

Omnidirectional

An omnidirectional microphone is equally sensitive in all directions. Quality does not vary with the direction of the sound source. However, because the omni mike picks up all sounds in its vicinity it cannot discriminate between the subjects you are interested in and unwanted noise. It picks up speech, acoustic reflections, and environmental noises

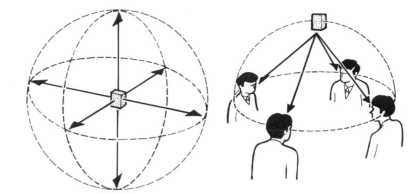

Fig. 12.7 Omni-directional response
Equally sensitive in all directions. Rugged, generally less susceptible to breath pops or impact shock.

equally well! It is useful, though, for group sound pick-up, or where subject moves are unpredictable.

Unidirectional

The unidirectional microphone is most sensitive in a particular direction and relatively deaf in others. This characteristic helps you to concentrate on certain pick-up areas and suppress background sounds, or to favor quieter sounds (weak voices) against louder ones. A boom microphone may be fitted with a unidirectional mike, so that it can work further away from subjects without extraneous pick-up.

However the microphone's response is not generally constant through the audio range. It is often more directional at higher frequencies than at lower ones. Consequently, if the mike is not pointed directly at the subject, or a person moves to one side, the audio can lose *definition* (*brilliance*, *highs*) as the high-frequency response deteriorates.

Cardioid

This broad, heart-shaped unidirectional pattern covers some 160°. Used for general-purpose sound pick-up, it readily accepts spaced sources,

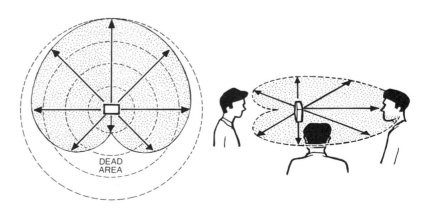

Fig. 12.8 Cardioid response
A broad heart-shaped pick-up pattern, insensitive on its rear side.

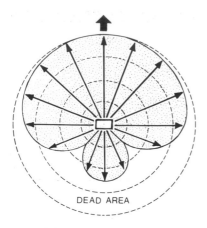

Fig. 12.9   Hypercardioid response
A modified cardioid response – more directional with a prominent rear sensitivity lobe.

unlike a half-eight pattern, which is more restrictive at close distances. Rear pick-up is limited; although some designs are more *omni*directional at lower frequencies.

Hypercardioid (supercardioid)

This has a modified cardioid response with a narrower frontal *lobe* (pick-up pattern) and a weaker rear pattern. Generally considered as providing the best balance between incident and ambient sound.

Bidirectional

Both faces of the microphone are live, providing a two-directional figure-of-eight pick-up patterns of about 100° each. To either side are two dead (deaf) areas. A typical traditional ribbon-microphone characteristic, this pattern is occasionally used for musical set-ups.

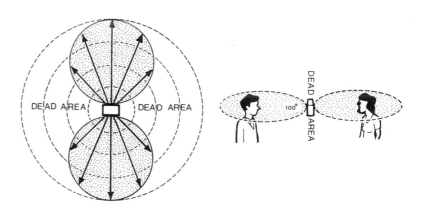

Fig. 12.10   Bidirectional response
Sensitive on either face, but deaf to sound pick-up at the sides.

Highly directional microphones

These have two applications:

● Wherever you want to pick out a particular subject from a group.
● In situations where subjects are some distance away, and increased audio amplification would make both the subject and environmental sounds much louder, the very directional pick-up reduces unwanted sound reflections and noise.

Line microphones use a slotted interference tube(s) with an attached electrostatic mike. The smallest version is the familiar *shotgun* or *rifle* microphone. This is around 0.54 m (22 in) long, and has a coverage of about 50°. It is very adaptable. It can be hand-held with or without its windscreen (windshield), fastened to the top of a camera to pick up atmospheric sound or single speakers. It can be used in a sound boom,

Fig. 12.11 Line microphones
A type of highly directional microphone. The popular shotgun (rifle) form is shown here, with and without its windscreen (windshield) of cloth, foam plastic, or artificial fur.

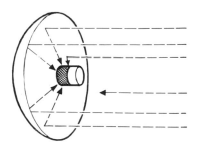

Fig. 12.12 Parabolic reflector
Extremely directional and sensitive, sound is focused by the reflector into the central microphone.

and can be fixed to a fishpole (fishing rod). The shotgun/rifle microphone is widely used for ENG and EFP applications and other work in the field.

The largest *machine-gun* versions, 2.5 m (8 ft) long, use combined tubes of varying lengths and are tripod mounted. Although rather cumbersome and producing inferior quality (particularly off-axis), the device is useful for isolating individuals in a distant group. Because directivity worsens below 2000 Hz, a bass cut is often introduced to reduce noise pick-up.

Parabolic reflectors provide a sensitive highly directional system (10–40°) in which a parabolic-shaped metal reflector 0.6–0.9 m (2–3 ft) in diameter focuses sound into a central cardioid microphone. Ineffective below about 300 Hz, the reflector is bulky and liable to wind rock unless firmly mounted. Whereas the *line microphone's* directionality is achieved by rejecting sounds outside its pick-up angle, the *parabolic reflector* actually concentrates sounds by acoustical reflection, and so has increased sensitivity.

Using the microphone

Personal microphones

One widely used approach to audio pick-up is to attach a personal microphone to the speaker. Audio quality is generally good, even under fairly noisy conditions. The main disadvantages are that: the mike can be muffled by clothing; loud noises can occur from contact with clothing (especially personal ornaments), or objects being demonstrated, or from handling; quality and volume vary as the wearer's head turns; and the mike may overhear other nearby sources.

Small windshields should be fitted for use outside the studio. And remember, leads and connections are particularly vulnerable and should be thoroughly checked.

Fig. 12.13 Lavalier (lanyard, neck)

This microphone is slung on a neck cord 15 cm (6 in) below chin.

Although less used today, this technique remains useful where a clip-mike cannot be fitted, e.g. where clothing is unsuitable or absent.

Fig. 12.14 Miniature capsule microphone

Known variously as a *clip mike, tie-tack mike* or confusingly as a *lavalier.* Both electret and dynamic versions are used. The mike is clipped to the necktie, lapel or shirt, in single or *dual-redundancy* form (live plus stand-by mike). Presence filters may improve sound quality. Plastic-foam windscreens/windshields can be fitted to reduce wind noise.

Clip mikes are often worn *upside down,* to reduce sound level variations caused by head movements, and to avoid breath noise, etc. Results vary, but there is some loss of top (reduced definition), and extraneous sounds from clothing, footsteps, etc., may be more pronounced.

Although a lavalier or a clip-on mike is itself unobtrusive enough its cable (visible, or unseen beneath clothing) usually connects the wearer via an audio plug to a long umbilical audio cable stretching away to a distant outlet. If a guest is seated you will have to link him up once he is in position. If he moves around he has to drag the cable along behind. Some people quickly accept the idea, others feel tethered, others foul up their cable on obstacles . . . In any case, this cable must be unplugged after program contribution, before the guest can depart.

Wireless (radio) microphone

This is simply a miniature mike operating into a small pocket or belt transmitter. Its signal is picked up by the nearby antenna (aerial) of a sensitive FM (frequency-modulated) receiver, and fed into the audio mixer. Although modern units are now reliable, transmission pick-up is not entirely predictable. Radio black-out (dead spots; drop-out), fading, distortion, or interference can arise from multi-path reception or screening due to metal structures or equipment. Diversity reception using multi-antennae arrangements can improve reliability. The system's range is often limited to around 400 m (440 yd) and the transmitter's battery should be regularly checked (life about 4 to 6 hours).

Each microphone needs its own transmitter/receiver system (at its own frequency), and there may be interaction. For long-distance reception a more sensitive antenna array may be essential. A preliminary site survey is generally desirable.

Earpiece

A technique that is widely used is to fit experienced commentators or presenters with an *earpiece*. This may be fed by a trailing cable or a small pocket receiver. A combination of wireless mike and earpiece can provide the wearer with considerable freedom of movement, while enabling him to have continuous contact with production staff for instructions, up-to-date information, editorial guidance, or prompting.

His earpiece can be fed with private line information, intercom (talkback), program audio, or remote sources (distant interviewees). This arrangement is known variously as *interrupted feedback (IFB), program interrupt, switched talkback (STB)*.

Hand microphone (baton mike, stick mike)

The hand microphone, which is usually of the omnidirectional type, must be rugged, permit free handling, and have an efficient *windshield (wind gag, blast filter, pop filter)*. This cloth or foam-plastic shield suppresses the rumbles and thumps from wind noise or close explosive sounds.

Many hand microphones are fitted with a *spherical ball mesh*. This permits very close positioning when used outdoors in noisy environments

Fig. 12.15 Hand microphone
The baton microphone is widely used for interviews. Directional response (cardioid) reduces extraneous noise pick-up. *Techniques:*
1. Held just below shoulder height. Pointing at speaker improves quality but can be daunting, and mike may then be too close. Avoid omnidirectional mike, which needs closer use (23 cm/9 in).
2. Avoid low mike position (it picks up background noises).
If visible microphone is unacceptable then use personal, fishpole, or rifle mike.

(to exclude extraneous sounds), or to avoid *howl-round* (*audio feedback*) where the mike feeds a PA system (public address, studio address loudspeaker) for a studio audience. It is a safeguard, too, where singers traditionally '*mug the mike*', holding it close to the mouth to add presence to their performance. A close directional mike exaggerates bass, so often needs filtering.

Although the sound quality from a hand mike is usually very satisfactory a lot depends on the skills of the person using it. There is always the risk of the mike being badly positioned. Some experience is needed, too, in handling the microphone cable. This is best held in one hand while directing the mike with the other. As it trails behind, the cable is liable to be caught up, stepped on, tripped over, unless the user takes care. The cable should never be pulled along by the mike or allowed to become knotted or kinked.

The cordless *wireless microphone* overcomes that particular hazard, for it incorporates a tiny radio transmitter, with an internal or 'hanging tail' antenna.

Lip mike/noise-canceling microphone

This specially designed hand-held mike is invaluable for off-camera commentaries in noisy surroundings. Its mouthguard is held against the upper lip.

Equalized for close speech (attenuating its normal bass excess), the environmental noise becomes inaudible. Because it obscures the user's face, the lip mike is seldom used in shot.

Stand microphone

Made in various sizes and of adjustable height (0.3 to 1.5 m (1 to 5 ft)) the stand microphone is used for soloists/speakers and for instrumental pick-up in orchestras, groups, etc. Various offset tubes (swan-necks) permit precision positioning and small slim fittings prevent the stand from being obtrusive. A quick-release top-clip enables the mike to be removed and hand-held where necessary.

The main disadvantages of the stand microphone are that the performer (talent) may kick it, causing loud resonant noises, or displace it, and its cable can prove a hazard (floor tape it if necessary). Remember, too, that it is essentially a *static* pick-up arrangement and people may easily move off-mike.

Fig. 12.16 Lip microphone
Used under high-noise conditions; the bar is held against upper lip to maintain constant mouth-distance. All noise-canceling mikes are susceptible to breath noises, and mike-to-mouth distance can be critical.

Desk microphone

Microphones can be clamped into small supports to enable them to stand on tables or desks. Formerly used to give an 'authoritative air' to a broadcaster, today the mike is small and unobtrusive, or sometimes hidden. A foam-plastic pad may prevent table-thump pick-up. Some audio engineers prefer to use stand mikes, hidden by a false table-front or through table-top holes, to circumvent this noise (Figure 12.18).

When audio pick-up is difficult a desk mike is sometimes used in drama productions to augment other microphones – hidden at a vantage point within staging, furniture props.

Desk discussions

Although clip-on personal mikes can be used for this situation, desk microphones offer better quality and are preferred by some audio engineers. Microphones should be positioned in the direction of head movement. Directional mikes reduce unwanted pick-up of acoustic and environmental noise or audience loudspeakers, but placement may be more critical. Do not intermix different types of microphone because quality will be inconsistent. Cables should be concealed, tidied, and taped (to desk and floor). Never run them alongside power cables and only cross them at right angles.

Prerehearsal checking includes: connections, microphone routing to the audio control board (scratch mikes, never blow on them when identifying), and *phasing* (connections). If mikes are not all similarly connected, the quality will change when their outputs are mixed together (bass loss).

Slung microphone (hung, hanging mike)

Where space is restricted, or other mountings cannot be used, you can suspend a microphone over the performance area. The slung mike is useful for broad group sounds such as sections of an orchestra, or to pick up audience reactions. It is less successful when used to pick up speech

Fig. 12.17   Stand microphone
Floor stands are height-adjustable and may be fitted with angled extensions. Microphone clips into quick-release head. Heavy base prevents instability.

Fig. 12.18   Desk microphone
1. For desk discussions, mikes in small fittings are often used.
2. Careful positioning is essential for good sound pick-up; typical distances D = 0.9–1.2 m (3–4 ft) and d = 0.3–0.6 m (1–2 ft).
3. Desk-top mikes may be vulnerable (desk thumps, displacement).
4. Alternatively the mike may be isolated on a floor-stand, either using holes in desk-top or behind false desk front.

Fig. 12.19   Slung microphone
Suitable for area pick-up or nearby sounds. Problems arise when people move, or are at different distances, or are seated.

from individuals within a seated group; especially when they are being shot in close-up. The mike is high above their heads, particularly when raised to be kept out of long shots, so that they are speaking across or away from the mike. The audio gain has to be increased, and the background noise can be very audible.

In a limited-access area (e.g. a narrow hallway) a slung microphone may be effective providing the performers play to the mike and there are not excessive reflections from nearby walls. Sometimes the microphone can be disguised as a light fitting.

If a *directional* microphone is used, you can reduce pick-up of acoustic reflections and environmental noise, but run the risk of people moving 'off-mike'. A non-directional (omni) pattern is less restrictive but needs to be closer to avoid reflected sound.

A slung microphone must be rigged securely with safety lines and placed to avoid distracting shadows or overheating by nearby lamps.

Fishpole (fishing rod)

Here a microphone is attached via a rumble-insulating cradle, to the end of an aluminium or bamboo pole (2–2.5 m (6–9 ft) long). The mike angle is fixed. Suitable for short-duration use under difficult conditions or to save a sound boom, the device is extremely flexible but tiring to operate. Fishpoles are widely used for sound pick-up on location, fitted with a shotgun/rifle microphone.

Fig. 12.20   Fishpole operation
The fishpole is fitted with the mike (preferably in shock proof cradle) at one end, and a counter-balancing audio cable connector-box (intercom to operator, audio to console) at the other. The fishpole can be held well-balanced above head or tucked under arm. 'Pole-in-belt' methods are unbalanced, particularly tiring, and hazardous.

Sound booms

Small sound boom (small giraffe, lazy arm)

Extensively used in smaller studios, this lightweight supplementary sound boom is used for static pick-up or limited movement over a smooth floor. Due to its fixed (preadjusted) arm length, the mounting must be pushed around to follow action; an operation that can be cumbersome and preoccupying.

As its central column height is raised the assembly becomes increasingly top-heavy and less stable (particularly during moves), so you normally tilt the boom arm for higher mike positions, keeping the column

Fig. 12.21   Small studio boom

The pre-adjusted telescopic arm (counterweighted) is pivoted on a column of adjustable height in a swivel-castered tripod stand. The boom arm can be tilted and panned, the stand wheeled around, and the microphone can usually be turned and tilted. Boom stretch is typically 3–4.5 m (10–15 ft).

Fig. 12.22 part 1   Fisher boom

1. Three-wheeled base (1.1 × 1.6 m/3 ft 9 in × 5 ft 3 in).
2. Brake and gear change.
3. Control to hydraulically raise/lower platform (moves with column), max column height 2.4 m (7 ft 10 in), pump handle to recharge cylinder. Operator's seat for stand-by periods.
4. Pan and tilt lock screws (pans over 360°).
5. Right-handed crank (max mike height 4.5 m/15 ft).
6. Script board.
7. Left hand-grip (squeeze for mike tilt, turn for mike turn).

Fig. 12.22 part 2   Typical boom operations

1. *Microphone position* is adjusted to suit shot, remaining just outside frame limits. Boom arm is raised/retracted as shot widens. Operator must anticipate cuts to longer shots.
2. *Head turn:* Either a swing and mike turn (slight arm-length change), or a static compromise position with mike turn.
3. *Reverse turn:* Extend and swing arm, with mike turn. Aim to avoid over-reaching subjects and turning mike back (any face shadows cannot be seen by operator).
4. *Ascending:* Boom arm tilts up and extends, mike tipping down during walk.
5. *Split sound:* Boom can accommodate separate sources up to about 2 m (7 ft) apart, by turning mike and/or swinging boom. Otherwise sources must move closer together, or use a second mike.

low. The boom's closeness to the subject makes it correspondingly more difficult to keep out of shot.

Cable guards on wheels prevent accidental cable overrun. Pushing over floor cables can be hazardous. The microphone's cable is laid along the floor away from cameras and lamp cables. The boom operator often plugs his headset into a nearby camera's auxiliary outlets for program and intercom.

Large sound boom (big boom)

Operationally, the large boom provides the most flexible method of audio pick-up, for you can easily follow movement and favor selected sources. This ensures optimum sound quality while keeping just out of shot and avoiding boom shadows.

The boom's microphone is held in a swiveling cradle at the end of its long, telescoping, tubular arm. This counterweighted arm is pivoted on the central vertical column of the wheeled boom perambulator (pram).

With his left hand the standing operator controls mike tilt and direction (gripping and turning respectively) and swings the boom arm, while extending/retracting the boom with his right (hand crank). The platform's

Table 12.1   Checking out the sound boom

Microphone	Speak to the audio engineer to identify mike and check audio quality. *Phase* the microphone if necessary, with others. Place the microphones close together. If there is a bass loss, reverse one set of connections. Check mike connector is secure (waggle cable end). Check mike cradle. Suspension OK? Free movement? Turn and tip mike. Operating strings taut and free moving?
Boom arm	Extend/retract boom arm (*racking* in/out). Any rumble? Controls and movement smooth? Is arm balanced throughout movement? (Adjust weights to suit mike weight.) Lock off the arm's pan and tilt.
Pram (perambulator)	Raise/lower platform (hand crank or hydraulic pump) Check wheel brake, lock, and steering. If steering mode is adjustable (steer/crab) check action. Tires OK? (Not overinflated, no stuck-on floor tape?) Check the seat.
Cable	Check plug into wall outlet. Is cable routing satisfactory? *Slung cable* – avoiding lamps, anticipating moves. *Floor cable* – not obstructing, sufficient available, free for boom moves.
Additional	Check intercom/talkback and private line (reverse talkback) to audio engineer. Check script board is secure and script available. Check picture monitor being used by boom operator (fixed to boom, or slung). If a loudspeaker is attached to boom (for *foldback* of effects, music, talkback instructions, etc.), check cables, connections, and reproducing levels.

Table 12.2   Sound-boom operation

Preliminaries
Check the boom is in the planned floor position relative to lighting treatment, and angle it to provide maximum use.

Check platform height to give good viewpoint over cameras, but avoid hanging lamps when operating.

Check boom arm at max/min reach relative to area coverage, obstructions, accommodating possible action spread.

Note key-light positions, look for potential shadow problems.

Operation

Mike position

Positioning depends on several factors: microphone sensitivity and directivity, acoustics, ambient noise, source loudness, and shot size. Closeness varies with the ambience required; a close mike minimizes studio acoustics, provides deader sound, and has better presence. It also avoids extraneous sounds. Very close mike positions coarsen sound quality, reveal breath noises, etc. Close microphones come into shot and cast shadows.

When the mike is further away, the distant sound quality and increased background noise may not be acceptable for the shot.

A steady boom

For a stationary situation, hold the boom arm still and the mike location steady towards the speaker. Avoid overhead positions – except when an omnidirectional mike covers random groups.

Swiveling the mike

A directional boom mike may be turned successively to favor each person speaking (gunning the mike), but someone can inadvertently be left *off-mike* unless the show is scripted. Benefits with closely positioned people are arguable.

Anticipate action

Lead rather than follow talent as they move around. Do not rely on script memory, or instructions alone, but watch people for preliminary signs (e.g. before they rise or sit).

Locking off

Beware locking off the boom arm (tilt and pan) except for a static subject, or when leaving or moving the boom. People may unexpectedly move away, get up, or sit!

Fully extended

Despite counterweighting, the boom arm becomes less manageable when extended. Swinging (arc) and raising the arm is less controllable, particularly when done quickly. By retracting during wide swings it is easier to move and avoids causing shadows.

Divide your attention between:

Performers

What performers are doing – are going to do.

Headset

The audio is 'split' on your earphones – one ear has *program sound*, the other has *intercom* from director and audio engineer. You can only judge audio quality and balance approximately, so be guided.

Shots

Be aware of picture monitors showing line (transmission) picture; check shot size. Camera tally lights show which is switched on-air. Monitors are usually too distant to detect whether your mike is appearing in shot. If in doubt, during rehearsal carefully dip it into shot; and when told of the shot limits remember these for subsequent mike positions.

Table 12.2 (cont.)

Boom shadows	Watch for mike shadows on people or backgrounds. Move the mike and check if sound quality is still acceptable. If not, indicate that it cannot be cleared. (Have the performer speak up, alter the shot, or relight.) During transmission (or a 'take'), hold the shadow still, or creep it out stealthily, or slowly raise the boom, or try to hide it, or wait until off-shot before repositioning.
Repositioning the boom	Boom moves to a new floor position may require a separate operator's aid (*tracker*) under instruction. Coordinate boom moves with cameras; watch for cable or boom arm catching in lamps. Take care when running over cables (damage, noise, instability).
Script or show format	Keep up to date on deleted or extra shots, or moves. Mark *take-over points* where action is to be covered by another boom.

operational height is adjustable – useful for seeing action past cameras. The microphone cable may be suspended or run along the floor to a wall outlet.

The large boom's main disadvantage for the smaller studio lies in its size. Also, unless the operator descends and moves his boom around a second person is needed to reposition it. Boom tracking (moving the pram while in use) is only normally necessary for large-area working, to follow widespread action, to move aside for cameras, or for fast relocation.

Efficient boom operation requires considerable skill, particularly where action is wide-ranging, and there is the danger of casting boom shadows across performers and the set.

Techniques and fashions change, and many types of productions that would once have used a boom regularly for sound pick-up now use personal mikes, wireless microphones (clip-on or baton type), and fishpoles with shotgun mikes instead.

Audio control

Located at his *audio control console* (board, desk, mixer panel) the *audio control engineer* (*sound mixer, sound supervisor*) selects and blends the various program sound sources.

His attention is divided variously between:

1. Selecting and controlling the outputs of various audio sources (mikes, discs, tape, film, VT).
2. Keeping the volume indicator within system limits by adjusting appropriate channel faders (amplifier gains).
3. Following the program audio and pictures (script, breakdown sheet), and the director's intercom (talkback) information.
4. Checking audio quality on high-grade loudspeakers.
5. Scrutinizing picture monitors showing line and preview shots, to check sound perspective, warn against mikes coming into shot, and boom shadows.

Fig. 12.23 part 1 Basic audio control

Microphone (1) plugs into studio wall outlet (2) and the audio is amplified (3). A side-chain *audition/pre-hear circuit* provides check-point before further processing. A pre-set *attenuator/pad* (5) adjusts channel amplification (*gain*) and a *channel fader* (slide, quadrant or knob) (6) controls it overall.

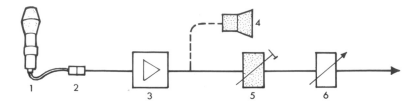

Fig. 12.23 part 2 Audio console

Pre-set gain. Adjusts audio channel gain (amplification) to compensate for variations in levels from sources.

Group selector. Switches a sound channel to a group fader (A or B).

Echo. Adjusts the amount of artificial echo added to an individual audio channel.

Equalizer. Adjustable tone filters altering sound quality by boosting/reducing/cutting high or low notes, or part of audio spectrum.

Channel fader. The main control adjusted to suit the volume of an individual source (e.g. quiet voice, loud instrument).

Audition/cue/pre-hear. A switch enabling the audio engineer to check-listen (earphones or loudspeaker) to a channel that is faded out; so not audible on the main audio output.

Group fader/group master/sub-master. All sources switched to that group (here labelled A or B) will be faded in/out simultaneously. The audio signal's strength (amplitude) is monitored by a local indicator.

Master fader. The outputs of the group faders are routed to this master control, which adjusts the overall program level, as shown on the master volume indicator.

Audio-control desks are made as completely integrated units, or in modular form as above (plug-in sub-units).
Additional facilities include: audio limiter/compressor; audio batons; echo devices; program monitoring level adjustment; control or audience address/foldback/playback system.

6. Guiding (and cueing) audio operators on booms, studio floor, audio disc, and tape repro.
7. Perhaps operating audio disc/tape equipment.
8. Liaison with other production team members.

Before rehearsal begins, the audio engineer plugs up the circuits he is going to use at a *patch panel*. Each of the various audio sources (e.g. Mic-1,

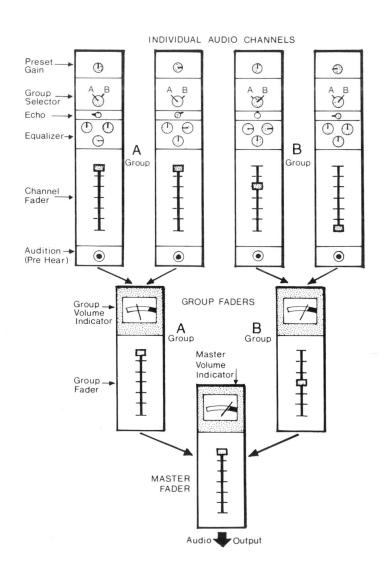

Mic-2, Mic-3, audio tape, disc, cart, VTR, film, etc.) has an outlet socket (*jack*) on the panel. Using *patch cords* (short cables with *jack plugs* at either end) he routes each source to an appropriate *channel input* socket on the patchboard, which is permanently tied to the audio console. Now each source is individually connected to an audio channel on the console, and can be separately controlled.

The outputs of audio equipment vary from a few millivolts (requiring a *low-level/microphone level* input system) to higher signals from audio tape or cartridge machines, film, and VT channels. Having already been amplified to e.g. 1 V, these are fed into *high-level/line-level inputs*. Each audio channel includes a *pre-amplifier* (*pre-amp*) to boost weaker sources and/or *attenuators* (*pads*) to reduce strong audio signals. Comparisons of average volume are made during rehearsal (*level tests*) to match their relative levels (volumes).

The gain (amplification) of the *program/channel amplifier* for each source is adjusted with a channel fader or 'pot' (potentiometer). This may be a rotating knob, or slider/quadrant control. (The latter has the advantages that several can be operated simultaneously with one hand, and their relative positions are obvious.) These channel faders can be used to fade individual sources in/out ('pot in/out') as well as control their average level. On some consoles you can switch to a pre-set pot setting (*keying in*); but there is always the danger of clipping the start of the incoming sound through a *late cut* (*upcutting*).

Having adjusted their relative strengths with individual *balance* faders, these sources (e.g. several choir mikes) can be linked to a single *group fader*, and are controlled simultaneously. The outputs of all group faders are controlled by a *master pot* (*line/main-channel control*). At selected points in the control chain, volume indicators show the strength of the audio signal there.

Dynamic range control

We need to control the system's amplification (gain) to keep the audio signal within its volume limits (*dynamic range*). This is done both manually and by automatic limiter/compressor circuits.

Manual control

Although our ears are tolerant of a wide volume range, tensing to very loud sounds and relaxing to receive quiet ones, straight audio systems do not have this property. If you keep audio amplification down to prevent peak overloads, quietest sounds will be inaudible. Increase amplification to hear these, and even fairly loud sounds now reach upper system limits and distort.

You can overcome this dilemma by imperceptibly altering the audio gain manually, to compensate for these volume peaks and troughs. Some sound sources need little or no control, while others (symphony orchestras) require continual sensitive readjustments. The trick is to

1

2

Fig. 12.24   Volume indicator
1. *Volume Meter (VU Meter)*. The upper scale, marked in decibels (dB), is for calibration and line-up purposes (using steady tone). The lower scale shows percentage modulation, where 100% is system's max limit.
2. *Peak Program Meter (European)*. Designed specifically to indicate sound volume *peaks*. The PPM has fast-rise/slow-return characteristics, so its needle fluctuates less than VU meter. Its easily read seven section logarithmic scale is akin to ear's loudness response (unlike VU meter).

anticipate, and to make any changes gradually, so that the listener is unaware of the subterfuge. You must not 'snatch back' peaks, or boost quiet passages, destroying dynamics completely through overcontrol (riding the gain).

VU meters and PPMs show the audio signal's strength relative to the system's available range (Figure 12.24). (See Glossary: *Volume indicators*.)

Audio processors

Automatic circuits can be used to adjust audio amplification; restricting the volume range, controlling unanticipated peaks, or wildly varying sound levels. They can substitute for manual judgement – but electronics make no artistic evaluation and can create unnaturally strangled crescendos, or inappropriately boost quiet sounds. Most audio engineers regard such equipment as a useful safety facility for the unexpected moment rather than an artistically viable control method (compressors; limiters).

While both variable gain systems prevent peak overloads above a selected volume the compressor also increases amplification of quieter passages, and can be used to compensate for unwanted volume variations, e.g. fading as a vocalist's hand-mike position changes. In radio, DJs deliberately use (misuse?) such facilities to make quiet background music surge in whenever they stop speaking. Similarly, the surging beat of *peak-limiting* is used as an audio effect. (See Glossary: *Ducker*.)

Sound balance

When you *balance* various sound sources you are adjusting their relative volumes, clarity, quality, scale, perspective, and the ratio of direct to indirect sound. The audio engineer is concerned in practice with two forms of program balance, that we can consider as *continuity balance* and *internal balance*.

Continuity balance

Here, the engineer controls a succession of sources; ensures that one person is not disproportionately louder or quieter than another; that the background music or effects are proportional to the dialogue; that other audio sources (film) match with studio sound. (Preliminary *level tests/ voice levels* assess typical audio control settings needed.)

Internal balance

Internal balance involves combining and blending a group of sound sources; e.g. arranging a microphone set-up for a musical group, an orchestra, or a choir. Actual techniques vary with personal preferences, the sound sources, acoustics, and the final effect required.

A *single microphone balance* places a single highly sensitive (often non-directional) mike at an optimum point for communal pick-up. At best, this method avoids the phase distortion created when several microphones pick up and blend a particular instrument and blur its attack. It avoids the variations in perspective and proportion we get when giving varying emphasis to selected instruments while backgrounding others. But its effectiveness depends upon acoustics, layout, and suitable positioning.

A *multi-microphone balance* uses a series of pick-up points. It is seldom possible in imperfect acoustic conditions to find one good mike position to suit a variety of instruments having different quality and attack. Distant pick-up of soloists when using one communal microphone can sound rather thin. The blending of a multi-microphone set-up offers better balance flexibility when rehearsal time is short.

Inappropriately used, however, multi-microphone pick-up can totally destroy the internal balance of a group. As sections or soloists are 'brought forward' and 'backgrounded' in various musical passages one loses any impression of layout and perspective. Instruments that normally provide an unobtrusive accompaniment can become disproportionately prominent.

Close balance techniques now widely used for musical group recordings are virtually a 'sound-processing' operation. Each instrument's (or subgroup's) output is recorded on a separate track of a multitrack audio tape (16, 24, 32 parallel tracks on a 2 in wide tape; 4, 8 tracks on 1 in tape). Instrumentalists or singers (using earphones) may perform together, or to prerecorded tracks. Individual tracks can be *lifted off* (*dubbed*), replaced, treated selectively (adjusting volume, quality, reverberation, pitch), synchronized, and blended with the others to achieve exactly the required combined sound. This complex *track-laying* or *mixdown* process can be computer assisted in the *dub-down* to a final track!

Sound perspective

At first it seems self-evident that the sound's proportions should match its associated picture. Close-up sound for a close-up shot; more distant sound for a long shot. This is a good working maxim. But there are exceptions where it is preferable to cheat this relationship and deliberately introduce nearer or more constant perspective than the actual shot suggests.

For example: the scene intercuts between shots of a bedroom where an old lady is dying, and shots of a street parade showing her long-lost soldier son's band returning from overseas. Audio cuts from the quiet death bed to the blaring military band. Should we avoid the rapid volume jumps that would actually take place – and either reduce the differences or spread the same sound over both scenes? The optimum treatment is a matter of taste, the effect you want to achieve, and the need to avoid ambiguity.

If a singer wanders around a spacious set, moving from close to long shots, do we really want the volume to vary? Can the mike maintain a constant relationship to the singer? It may be necessary to prerecord the song and have the performance mimed on camera to its playback.

We normally adjust sound perspective within a scene by altering the mike distance to suit the shot size by boom movement or intermicrophone mixing. As closer sounds tend to seem louder, with stronger bass and top than more distant pick-up, *presence filters (dialogue equalizers)* may be introduced to simulate or emphasize differences between close and remote sound quality.

Sound quality

Although high fidelity is our normal aim, there are good technical and artistic arguments for using audio filters to modify the system's frequency response when necessary:

1. Cutting low bass to reduce boom rumble, hum, improve speech clarity, improve the hollow or boomy quality in boxy scenery; reduce background noise/atmosphere (e.g. ventilation).
2. Cutting upper parts of the audio spectrum to reduce sibilant speech or S-blasting, quieten studio noise, reduce disc or tape noise.
3. Cut bass and top to enhance the illusion of exterior settings.
4. Slightly accentuate bass to increase the impression of size and grandeur of vast interiors.
5. Effects filters to simulate telephone (300–3000 Hz) intercom, public announcements. Phone filters (*distort*) are often controlled by the video switcher equipment, to provide automatic *audio-follow-video* switching as the picture intercuts between the two ends of a phone conversation.

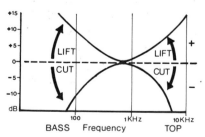

Fig. 12.25 part 1 Equalizers, audio filters, response selection amplifiers (RSA)
Filter for compensatory or dramatic effect. Progressive accentuation or reduction of top or bass. Bass and top roll-off are widely used, e.g. to remedy boomy reproduction, reduce air-conditioner noise, wind, traffic noise.

Fig. 12.25 part 2 High and low pass filters
Suppress rumble, hum, and high-pitched noises respectively.

Fig. 12.25 part 3 Audio baton, octave filter, shaping filter, graphic equalizer
A series of slider controls boost or reduce chosen frequency segments in the audio spectrum. Slider positions show effective response.

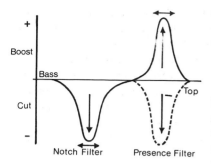

Fig. 12.25 part 4   Notch filter, presence circuits
Notch filter puts very steep localized dip into audio spectrum to diminish interference (e.g. hum) without substantially affecting overall quality. *Presence circuits* (*mid-lift*) provide boost or cut (up to 6 dB) around selectable frequencies (2 to 6 kHz) to improve clarity and audio separation, improve sibilants lost with distance, or bring sounds 'forward' (presence) from others.

6. By matching different types of mikes' frequency responses, we can reduce audible quality differences.
7. Quality matching between different sound sources (e.g. studio and film) can be improved.

Filtering can provide better audio continuity, and helps you to remedy such defects. Where the director is using *electronically inserted backgrounds* (e.g. by chroma key), or studio settings have inappropriate acoustics (e.g. a 'cave' constructed of timber and plastics), the audio quality can be made much more convincing by audio filtering and reverberation treatment.

Equalization

When disc or audio tape recordings are made, the frequency spectrum is automatically modified (top is boosted, bass is reduced). This anticipates or overcomes various technical difficulties such as background noise. There are several 'standards' in use. Strictly, therefore, a disc or tape should always be reproduced with compensatory equalization matching the standard used for recording (*Audio tape:* NAB, NARTB, CCIR, IEC, DIN. *Disc:* RIAA, Standard Spectra, ANSI, BSI, DIN, IEC, ISO, NAB, etc.). Some reproducers have selectable filters to suit a variety of standards.

Audio tape (recording and replay)

Operationally, audio magnetic tape recording is simplicity itself. You have only to avoid over- or undermodulation, and many recorders have automatic recording-level controls.

Audio tape

There are several types of audio recording tape: ferric, chrome (and 'pseudo-chrome', i.e. cobalt-treated ferric), ferrichrome, metal. For minimum background noise, least distortion, and best top response the appropriate bias setting and equalization should be switched in on the recorder/reproducer, to suit the type of tape used. Longer-play tapes are thinner, less rugged, and liable to print-through between adjacent layers (echo; pre-echo).

Recording

Before recording, the tape must be magnetically neutralized (wiped, erased). This can be done initially by a bulk electromagnetic eraser (bulked), but is usually a regular part of the recording process. In the recording mode the tape first passes an *erase head* where strong ultrasonic currents eliminate any previous recording. The result when played would be a barely audible rustling – *tape noise*. This *clean* tape passes against the *record head*, which is fed with the audio signal you wish to record. As each

Fig. 12.26 part 1   Typical layout of a reel-to-reel tape recorder
1. Supply spool.
2. Erase head.
3. Record head.
4. Replay head.
5. Capstan roller.
6. Pressure idler roller.
7. Take-up spool.

Fig. 12.26 part 2   Splicing audio tape
Play through to the *in* and *out* edit points. At each, stop the tape, and mark it with a felt-tip pen or wax pencil exactly at the *replay head* gap. Lay the tape in the splicer groove, with the recording surface downwards, and the marked tape at the editing groove.

Take the section of tape containing the other edit point, and lay it over the first tape (again face down). The marks should coincide.

With a sharp razor blade cut across at 45° using the splicer groove. Remove the unwanted tape ends, to leave the required sections exactly butted together. Fix a patch of special adhesive *jointing tape* to the splice (i.e. on the *back* of the tape). Cutting both edit points simultaneously produces a more accurate butt join than cutting the tape ends separately and pushing them together.

Editing audio cassettes. It is better to dub off passages, rather than try to physically edit 3.5 mm wide tape.

particle of the tape contacts the head's gap it becomes magnetized in proportion to the audio at that instant. The modulated magnetic pattern is invisible. To assist this recording process the record head is also fed with an ultrasonic *bias current*, which substantially reduces distortion and background noise.

Fig. 12.26 part 3   Audio tape tracks
Mono (monophonic) full track. The single track audio covers the full tape width. The tape is full after one pass.

Mono full track. The audio signal is recorded across half the tape width. During the first pass, the tape winds from the left-hand (supply) spool onto the right-hand (takeup) spool. At the end of the tape, the cassette is turned over ready to record/replay the second pass. In reel-to-reel systems, the full takeup spool is removed after the first pass, reversed, replaced on the supply spool and re-laced.

Half-track stereo. The audio from the left-hand channel is recorded on one half of the tape, while that from the right-hand channel is recorded alongside. The tape is full after one pass.

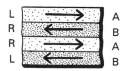

Quarter-track stereo. During the first pass (A), the left and right channels are recorded on tracks 1 and 3. After turning the tape over for pass (B), tracks 2 and 4 are used. Most stereo cassette systems use this format.

Multitrack systems. Using audio tapes up to 25 mm (1 in) or 50 mm (2 in)) wide, from four to 24 parallel tracks may be recorded/reproduced simultaneously.

Audio tape (like video tape) may be *bulk erased* with a large electromagnet to completely neutralize the tape's magnetic state.

Audio tape speeds are typically 7½ or 15 inches per second for reel-to-reel systems, and 1⅞ i.p.s. for audio cassettes.

Replay

The tape can be replayed (monitored) during recording and subsequently reproduced (and/or recorded on) several hundred times. To reproduce the tape, it is passed over a *replay head* (playback, reproducer); the tape's magnetic pattern inducing weak electric currents in the head, corresponding with the original audio. An interlock mechanism usually prevents your activating the recording circuit accidentally and wiping the tape during replay.

Audio cassettes (and also video cassettes) have a breakaway tag at the rear which, when removed, automatically prevents you from recording over the existing material. If you really want to record over the present recording, simply attach an adhesive tape strip to substitute for the safety tag.

Tape speed

The tape must be reproduced at the recording speed, or you will get a marked pitch change; fine for chipmunk effects, but otherwise to be avoided. Higher tape speeds provide a better high-frequency response, lower background noise, less obvious *drop-out* (momentarily silent gaps due to tape surface irregularities or damage), easier audio editing (the audio pattern is more spread out), but it uses more tape per minute.

Editing

You can edit ¼ in (6.35 mm) magnetic tape by physically cutting (45° diagonally, with an unmagnetized razor blade) and joining sections with an adhesive patch on the back of the tape. This quick, flexible process produces a silent joint but disrupts the original recording, particularly if it contains several parallel tracks. Instead, you can re-record (*dub, dub-off*) sections onto a new tape; but this can result in cumulative distortion, hum, background noise, etc. Colored non-magnetic tape is often inter-spliced as lace-up *leader*, or as mute *blanking* between sequences for identification.

Production use of audio tape

1. Providing a premixed track of music, effects, background, to simplify handling during the show.
2. Bringing back sounds from location shooting, to provide audio background to studio action.
3. To suggest that there is an unseen speaker (e.g. at the other end of a phone, outside a door).
4. Providing taped commentary while a lecturer moves to another exhibit, or is out of microphone range.
5. Providing total prerecorded commentary to film or videotape (voice over, voices off, VO; sound over vision, SOV).
6. Preselected effects or music dubbed from disc for cuing or treatment.
7. Recording atmospheric sounds (*room tone*), or other non-synchronized sound (*wild track*) for use when laying audio tracks during subsequent videotape editing. To provide overlays (bridging sound) between scenes.
8. Checking what was said during impromptu discussion (to guide editing).

Building the soundtrack

Most TV programs contain not only speech but also a proportion of music and effects. These vary with the type of program. While a chat show is only likely to have music at the start and end, to 'top and tail' the production, and give it a 'packaged' feel, a dramatic presentation may well be strewn with a variety of carefully selected atmospheric effects, and musical passages (bridges, stings, mood music).

While some sounds are prominently in the *foreground*, others are carefully controlled to provide an appropriate *background* to the action. Some may be crept in, and are barely audible, yet add an atmospheric quality to a scene (e.g. the quiet tick-tock of a grandfather clock). Others may be deafening, even drowning dialogue.

Some sound effects are continuous while others rely on split-second cuing to exactly match live action (e.g. the 'boing' sound as a clown's watch disintegrates).

Program audio

Program audio falls into several categories:

1. *Dialog* – Direct pick-up of people in shot.
2. *Voices off* – Someone out of shot is heard speaking (e.g. in the next room; loudspeaker announcements).
3. *Voice-over* – Commentator or announcer, explaining or making observations.
4. *Spot effects* – Effects made on the spot, such as door knocks, phone bells, car siren, baby cries, dog barks. Some can be made to order,

while others may not happen when you need them (e.g. a parrot's comment).

5. *Background effects* – General atmospheric sounds (e.g. wind, seawash, birdsong, traffic).
6. *Foreground music* – Someone playing (or miming) an instrument.
7. *Background music* – Mood music, nearby source (a radio playing, the music at a ball).
8. *Special effects* – Treated sounds (that may in fact be used in roles 3 to 7) to simulate robots, prehistoric animals, ray guns, phantoms . . .

Using recorded sound effects

Sound effects are used in many kinds of productions: drama, documentaries, newscasts, etc. They are introduced for a variety of reasons:

- To *add realism* to an artifice – e.g. the picture shows a dummy cart in the studio . . . we hear the sounds of a horse and turning wheels.
- To *supplement* location sounds – e.g. adding birdsong to a country scene (which was silent when shooting).
- To *reinforce* existing sounds – e.g. a small group in the studio appears to be part of a large mob when crowd noises are added to the shots.
- To *replace* the action sound because it is unconvincing – e.g. weak, poor quality.
- To accompany *mute* shots – where there was no sound pick-up during shooting; when mute *library shots* are used.

Catalogues of recorded sound effects include a fascinating range of subjects. Now available on vinyl disc, compact disc, and audio tape cassettes, they would seem to cover any possible occasion. However, there are points to look out for when making a selection. A lot depends on how you are going to use the sound effect:

Cued effect – i.e. the effect has to be played at a certain time. Some effects recordings cannot be used for spot cuing (e.g. a car horn effect that includes background traffic noise).

Synchronized effect – where a sound effect has to coincide with action in the picture; e.g. the sound of a bat hitting a ball to accompany a mute picture. It needs to be synchronized exactly, or the result is ridiculous. Where possible, it may be better to omit the effect altogether.

Foreground effect – i.e. prominent; loud environmental noises. The *scale* of sounds needs to be matched to the shot. As a shout does not become a whisper simply by playing it at low level, so the scale of backgrounds needs to be chosen appropriately. If the recorded sound was relatively quiet or distant it cannot be made to seem loud or close by amplifying it. The sound character will be quite different.

Background effect – i.e. sound that is only heard quietly as an incidental accompaniment. Again, we must consider the scale of the effect. While the quality of recorded sound can be important if it is used as a foreground effect, even a poor quality sound effect may be quite usable as part of the background. If you are adding sound effects to a mute library shot, picture and sound details need to match reasonably well. Where, for instance, we hear a crowd cheering as the troops march by, we may accept that there is an unseen crowd if the shots are pretty close. But if the shot shows us a distant isolated group of men this will stretch our credulity!

Forms of sound effect

Sound effects have several basic forms:

- *The single event.* When a sound effect is brief (e.g. a cannon being fired) it usually needs to be set up and cued very accurately. Check the channel gain beforehand to ensure that it is not going to overload the audio system.
- *Regular rhythms.* Where the effect has a pronounced rhythm take care not to interrupt it during editing. It requires patience and luck to match effects of e.g. footsteps to a mute picture of someone walking.
- *Repeated sound patterns.* Even when a sound effect is successful it may be too brief for your purpose. If you have only a few seconds' track of a dog barking you cannot usually repeat it conveniently more than a couple of times. Some sounds have distinctive recognizable features. It may be a shout from the audience during applause, someone coughing in a crowd, the toot-toot of a car horn within street noise . . . If you replay such an effect several times behind the action it will become recognizable, and seem quite false.
- *Continuous sounds.* Providing there are no easily recognized features, you can extend background sounds such as seawash, wind, applause, crowds, traffic by joining copies together without a break. Playing two copies of the effect can reinforce it, particularly if they are differently equalized.
- *Acoustics.* The surroundings in which an effect was recorded can limit their use. 'Footsteps', for example, come in endless variety; echoing, on pavements, gravel, squelching mud, moving through grass . . .
- *Extraneous sounds.* Many an effect has others intermixed with it. Birdsound may be accompanied by the other sounds of the countryside (e.g. sheep, tractors).
- *Defects.* It is wise to check sound effects recordings for defects; particularly discs, which may have high surface noise, clicks, and scratches.

Recorded inserts

Recorded sound has the particular advantage that it provides reliable material of a known quality and length. A sound effect produced live in the studio (*spot effect*) may not be as successful when repeated. As we shall see, recorded sound effects are not necessarily fixed and unchangeable. Sound quality, reverberation, and speed can be modified.

Particularly when mixed together, even the most critical listener would not recognize them as 'stock effects'.

Where you need to play a number of recordings at the same time (e.g. seagulls, sea, wind, thunder . . .) you can often simplify operations by 'mixing down' the separate tracks beforehand, dubbing them onto a single audio tape. It is best to omit any critically cued effects in case there are any last-minute changes! This technique is particularly helpful when your facilities are limited.

Music and effects (M & E track)

If a show is live, or live-on-tape, performance is continuous. The dialog, music, and effects are all introduced as you go.

But what happens if you decide to *edit* this videotape with its *composite soundtrack (married track)*? Suppose the program needs shortening, or you cut out some boring 'business'? On replay, you could find that there is a distracting change in the accompanying background music where you made this edit cut!

So where you anticipate detailed postproduction editing it may not be a good idea to add all music and effects during studio taping. Instead, to avoid these editing disruptions in the soundtrack you could record all the *dialog* on the videotape during performance, but add the *music* and *effects* later at a separate editing/re-recording (*dubbing*) session away from the studio.

When the action is shot in brief takes out of sequence you have no option but to build the program soundtrack in this way. Any effects or music played during individual takes would not carry through between the shots when they were edited together. There would be a poor continuity matching.

Another advantage of compiling the final soundtrack at the *postproduction stage* is that you can augment or modify the original track (e.g. remove or replace faulty material; insert censor bleeps) as well as adding title music. Where it was not practicable to perform a comedy show in front of a studio audience it would be legitimate to invite the public to watch a copy of the tape on large-screen replay, record their applause/laughter, etc., and add this to the final videotape soundtrack.

By keeping the dialog separate from the accompanying *music and effects (M&E) tracks* you have the additional advantage that it can make your program a very saleable product for foreign-language markets. They can add dialog or commentary in their own language based on the original script, and mix this with the M&E track.

Anticipating sound editing

When shooting on location you can make eventual editing and audio sweetening a lot easier if you habitually follow certain practices:

- *Level continuity*. Aim to keep the level and quality of successive shots in the same scene reasonably similar. Particularly in location interiors, you may find longer shots with lower sound levels and strong reverberation, while closer shots are louder and relatively dead acoustically.
- *Wild track*. It is good practice to make supplementary recordings of general 'atmosphere' (background noise) from time to time. Even in the studio, there is always a low-level background sound of air conditioning/ventilation. On location this 'atmos' may include wind in trees, passing traffic, etc. When editing the program there will be occasions where the soundtrack has been cut, or a sequence is mute, and this covering 'atmos' can be introduced to avoid distracting lapses into silence, and to give a feeling of continuity to the edited shots.

Incidentally, when recording on location keep an alert ear for any potential 'sound effects' that arise when you are not actually shooting yet might be integrated into the final soundtrack. Even unwelcome intrusive noises (e.g. passing fire wagon) might prove useful in your sound library for another occasion!

Extra audio taping is useful, too, when shooting *interviews* on location. Typically, the camera and microphone concentrate on the guest, and separate shots of the interviewer are cut in during editing. At the end of the interview the extra audio tape recording can be replayed to remind the interviewer, who repeats the questions to camera, or in an over-shoulder shot behind the guest.

Finally, this technique is widely used to ensure good speech continuity for *pick-up shots*. These are situations where you have someone speaking to camera, then the shot changes to show them continuing in another location. For example, the guide speaks to camera in a shot taken from a church tower ('She is buried down there beneath those trees . . .'): cut to a shot of the guide beside the grave ('. . . and you can see this inscription on the tombstone').

Audio sweetening

The process of working on the program sound after studio production is called *audio sweetening (dubbing session; track laying)*. Although it is obviously a lot cheaper to record a show *live-on-tape* and have a complete production ready for use at the end of the session, audio sweetening is both necessary and preferable where extensive videotape editing is involved.

Audio sweetening can be carried out at various levels:

1. *Additional material*. Adding extra material to the finished edited program; e.g. playing in title music, adding a commentary.
2. *Corrections*. Improving the sound within a scene. One might, for example, readjust varying levels between speakers' voices. Careful filtering could reduce sibilance, hum, rumble, ventilation noise, etc.

3. *Enhancement.* Modifying sound quality to improve realism or to achieve a dramatic effect; e.g. by adding reverberation, or changing its tonal qualities (equalizing).
4. *Blending.* Adjusting the relative strengths of effects and music tracks to suit the dialog and action.
5. *Continuity.* Ensuring that the sound levels, balance, etc. are consistent from one shot to the next when various shots are edited together.
6. *Bridging.* Adding bridging effects or music that will run between shots. An *overlay* track can be played throughout an entire sequence to ensure that the same background sound levels continue without level jumps or changes in quality. It may be kept down behind dialog and made more prominent during action.
7. *Added effects.* Where video effects have been introduced into a program after the studio action (e.g. laser beams, explosions, disintegrations) suitable sound effects can be added during sound sweetening.
8. *Overdubbing.* Replacing unsatisfactory sections of the soundtrack spoiled, for instance, by passing aircraft or other extraneous noise.

As you can see, there are very practical reasons to rework the soundtrack after production. Now that television makes increasing use of short takes and sophisticated videotape editing, it promises to become a regular part of the production process on complex shows, as in film making.

Typical postproduction methods

Let us assume that the videotape has been picture-edited. All shots are in their final order, with their transitions (cut, mixes, wipes, supers) and any postproduction video effects in place. But the soundtrack contains only associated *dialog.* The all-important sound element is incomplete. Music, effects, and any additional speech have yet to be added.

During the original studio recording session the precise time at which everything happened was continuously recorded along with the picture and dialog on the videotape. This *time code* serves as a reference for all editing and sound treatment.

The sound engineer now *lifts off* (re-records) the *audio track* and the parallel *time code track* from the videotape made during the studio session onto a normal ¼-in audio tape, to provide himself with a combined 'working tape' for the sound-sweetening session. (He could have made his own combined audio tape during the original taping session, but this would not, of course, coincide with the *edited* videotape used for the sweetening session. It would include all out-take material too.)

Using a *multi-track audio tape recorder* (typically 16 or 24 parallel tracks available), with a clean 2-in tape, he copies his working tape. The program dialog goes onto e.g. Track 1 of the multi-track and the corresponding time code onto e.g. Track 16.

Typically, he might reserve the empty Tracks 2–5 for *sound effects*; wherever possible, keeping them separate, so that he can intercut/mix/cross-fade between. Tracks 6–7 may be reserved for any *music* inserts, and Track 8 for any *additional dialog* (e.g. voice-over commentary, narration, etc.). The final *mix-down* can be dubbed onto e.g. Track 10.

The actual arrangements will depend on the complexity of the production. The idea, in principle, is to record the various missing sounds in their respective tracks so that their time slot coincides with the correct point in the picture/dialog sequence. If someone presses a doorbell in the shot at time code point 10h.30m.05s to 10h.30m.08s (3 seconds' duration), then this sound effect must be inserted in Track 2 at that position. Sound and picture will then be synchronized.

Each track on the multi-track tape can be independently recorded, reproduced, wiped. When we have finished *laying down* these tracks they will all be played simultaneously and blended together to be recorded on a new synchronized tape. This combined track is then dubbed onto the *master edited videotape*, exactly in sync with the pictures there.

If you wish, you can lay down just *one* track at a time. While the edited videotape is playing the picture sequence through, the multi-track is running in sync, ready to record on the selected track when you fade up the required effect or music at the right moment. (The effect or music comes from a separate audio tape machine, disc, cart, or CD player.) If the inserted sounds are to be *faded* in or out, you will need a long enough sequence to cover the head and tail fades. After rewinding, you can replay the videotape plus multi-track, to check that the result is successful.

However, this is a time-consuming method, and usually unnecessary. Instead you can adopt either of two methods: 'on the hoof' or 'laying tracks'.

The simplest technique is to treat the session as if it were a live show; cuing and controlling the dialog, effects, music passages, narration, etc. as you go. You run a copy of the edited videotape and, following the script, play in the effects/music at the appropriate moments, recording them on their respective clean (unused) multi-track tape channels. If any feature does not work first time (e.g. the bell effect was too loud) that particular track can be re-recorded at that point.

Another way of approaching the sweetening session is to work from a *track log*. You prepare this in advance. The log consists of a series of vertical columns (one for each multi-track channel), with the time scale running vertically. Watching a copy of the edited videotape with a *burned-in* time code visible at the bottom of the screen (Figure 12.3), the audio engineer, with the director, checks when the various contributions are required. He logs the bell effect, for example, and notes its in-and-out times – 10:30:05 and 10:30:08. Armed with this log, he records these contributions at the allotted points; at standard level (zero level), for they will be controlled during the next stage.

When all the tracks are complete with the various contributions on their respective tracks, it is time for the *mix-down*. The multi-track audio tape is run, and sounds from its tracks are mixed, balanced, equalized/

Table 12.3 Multi-track log

filtered, and any reverberation added, to produce a composite which is recorded as a *master soundtrack* on an unused track of the multi-track audio recorder (two, if the program is in stereo). This *master track* (*final mix-down*) is then *laid back* (*dubbed*) onto the soundtrack of the master edited videotape; and, thanks to the time code, will be exactly in sync with its pictures.

Where *computer-aided* dubbing systems are used, all variations of fader positions, equalization, reverberation you make during the mix-down rehearsal are stored. When you are satisfied, the system will run the VTR and audio multi-track, and perform all these adjustments exactly as rehearsed – unless you decide to override it at any point.

Playback (foldback)

By reproducing sound effects or music over studio floor loudspeakers (*playback, foldback*) performers can relate or synchronize their cues or action. However, this reproduced sound becomes colored by studio acoustics, and if picked up by the action microphones it often has a falsely hollow quality.

Miming and post-synchronizing

Good sound pick-up may not be possible where the action is very energetic, too distant, or taking place in very noisy surroundings. There are several solutions, although these may have varying success. You can prerecord the appropriate sound, and have someone synchronize their performance to its playback (*prescoring*). Or you can shoot despite poor sound quality, and have the performer (or someone else!) record the required song, dialog, later in the studio, in time with the reproduced pictures (*post-syncing*); a technique widely used in film making. With either method it can be extremely difficult to sustain *lip-sync*; any mismatch becoming distracting, even ridiculous. Really accurate synchronism is only possible by postsyncing short repetitive loops of a brief section, as when dubbing foreign language films (*dialog looping*), or by using *time-compression* techniques (see Glossary).

The simplest and cheapest solution, where it is possible, is to avoid shots that show clear mouth movements. Use more distant shots, point-of-view (POV), or over-shoulder shots, and reaction shots, which do not reveal any lip-sync errors, and add a separate voice-over track recording to the picture later!

Treating audio effects

You can modify audio quality in various ways to create or enhance a particular impact; for dramatic, environmental, or novelty effect.

■ *Filtering*   As we saw earlier, audio filters (equalizers) enable you to emphasize or reduce parts of the audio spectrum to any degree – either correctively or to modify quality. So you can make sounds seem shrill, edgy, thin, tubby, hollow, harsh, brittle, etc.

■ *Distortion*   To simulate the audio distortion from shortwave radio pick-up, public address systems, or intercom, you can hold a microphone near an earphone or earpiece, or small loudspeaker. You can alter tonal quality further by placing the assembly in a box, jug, or pipe.

■ *Acoustic feedback*   When a microphone's amplified output is fed to a nearby loudspeaker, and then overheard by the same microphone reamplified, a loud oscillatory howl-round (acoustic feedback) can build up. This situation is a hazard when using public address/sound-reinforcement systems. The cure is to reduce the loudspeaker output, move the mike or loudspeaker, use a more directional mike or loud-speakers; or even use digital processing, which moves successive repetitions away from the original frequency. As an *effect*, you may deliberately introduce controlled acoustic feedback to produce a hollow, echoing sound quality.

■ *Reverberation*   Artificial reverberation can be produced in several ways, and mixed with the direct, untreated ('dry') sound in appropriate proportions for the effect required. The *reverb* or *audio delay* units most commonly used are spring types, plate types, and, increasingly, analog/digital methods (see Figure 12.27 and Glossary: *Audio enhancement*).

Audio effects on tape

Audio tape provides a valuable range of sound-treatment opportunities.

■ *Feedback*   During recording, the tape output is controllably fed back to mix the replay sound with the input. The result can be varied from a drawn-out hangover effect, to distinct echo, or stutter effects (rapid multi-echoes – flutter echo).

■ *Speed change*   Replaying at speeds *slower* than the original recording lowers pitch and tempo, increasing reverberation. Most sounds take on a deliberate, sinister character. Xylophones, bells, thunder, gongs become strikingly powerful. Others are totally transformed (e.g. slow-speed wind or water) and can be used for 'synthetic' or atmospheric effects.

Reproduction at a faster than recording speed raises pitch and tempo. About one-and-a-half or two times, sounds become 'miniaturized', appearing perky and comic – the audioland of singing mice, insects, household utensils, etc. of cartoon. Reproducers with special rotating multihead turrets can provide pitch changes at normal tape speeds, or correct the pitch for tapes reproduced at the wrong speed.

Fig. 12.27 part 1   Echo room
Sound to be treated is reproduced over loudspeaker in echoing room (hard walls, baffle) – reverberant sound being picked up by microphone and mixed with direct original sound. Largely superseded by space-saving electronic methods, but a useful technique for improvized situations (e.g. using bathrooms, cellars, corridors, etc.).

Fig. 12.27 part 2   Magnetic tape delay
Time lag as audio tape travels from record to replay head can be used to produce a delayed reproduction of original – an echo when mixed with incoming sound. If this delayed reproduction is fed back into recorder input, *flutter echo* develops. The multi-replay head system shown here produces a succession of delays, which can be mixed with original sound or fed to series of studio loudspeakers to modify effective acoustics (ambiophony). The tape loop or magnetic disc records continuously, erasing each revolution.

Fig. 12.27 part 3   Mechanical spring delays
The original audio signal causes transducer head to vibrate the spring(s). The mechanical resonances detected by pick-up transducer head have a reverberant coloration and are converted into corresponding audio signal. The inherent coloration of spring systems ('twang') has been considerably improved to provide most realistic effects.

Fig. 12.27 part 4   Reverberation plate
A similar principle to part 3, using a suspended steel sheet as the vibrating medium. Adjusting the closeness of a parallel sheet of porous material modifies the reverberation time (1½–5 sec). Although effects are very realistic, temperature changes can affect performance.

■ *Reversal sound*   Tape reproduced backward (a normal recording fed in tail first) can modify the character of sounds. Sustained sounds tend not to change, but percussive or transient ones have a characteristic 'indrawn-breath' quality.

■ *Time compression and expansion*   See Glossary.

■ *Repeated sound*   A tape loop enables you to repeat a sound over and over again, for example to heighten tension, imply hysteria or mental derangement.

■ *Fading*   Slightly misguiding a tape during replay can simulate fading and top loss. Alternatively, two identical discs played slightly out of step produces fading and distortion.

Synthetic sound

There are many fascinating program opportunities for synthesized sounds, including abstract background noises, voices for the inarticulate or mute, newly created sounds for monsters and science fiction (see Glossary: *Audio enhancement*).

■ *Treated sounds*   You can use one audio signal to control another, modulating its volume or pitch by using voltage-controlled amplifiers, ring modulators, hybrid coils, etc. So you can articulate sound effects; a locomotive whistle cries 'All aboard', or an organ sings its own lyrics.

Taking fragments from existing recordings, you can modify their quality by juxtaposing them in any order (reversing, modulating, or repeating) to produce sounds quite dissociated from their origins. The resultant *musique concrète* may have a musical character (for jingles, title music) or provide imitative or humorous noises.

■ *Dissociated sounds*   Many sounds lose their identity when divorced from their original context. Some are unfamiliar anyway (straining pack-ice, roaring gas flames, insect noises). You can often transpose sounds for dramatic effect – jet engine noise to accompany typhoon scenes. Some take on an entirely new significance – a crushed matchbox simulating a collapsing barn.

Musical instruments can be used to produce a fantastic range of sound effects – disembodied waverings from a musical saw; squeaks, grunts, whines, and creaks from a violin. These noises can in turn be treated and modified. Such devices are more than audio stunts. They enable you to stimulate the imagination, often improve on available sounds, and to materialize the unknown or the impossible.

■ *Synthesized sounds*   Entirely synthetic sounds can be created electronically by an *audio synthesizer*, which enables a keyboard or interconnected control circuits to manipulate specially generated and processed sounds. Oscillations of various shapes, frequency, repetition rate can be selected and treated; volume can be varied (*vibrato, crescendo, diminuendo*); build-up and die-away adjustments can be used (attack and decay times); quality can be modified (selective filtering), and so on. The resultant synthesized sounds may deliberately simulate recognizable sources, or provide a new audio impression. Even quite modest home computers can now produce a wide range of sound effects that can be used (or further treated) for program applications.

Noise reduction

As you know, the audio engineer has to control the strength of the audio signal to prevent its exceeding the system's limits. (A loud sound can overload and create unpleasant distortion. A very quiet sound can be lost among background noise.) This control of the volume range flattens the sound's dynamics. Particularly where a sound is re-recorded several times in the course of preparing a program, relative dynamic ranges can be noticeably reduced.

This simplest method of reducing high-pitched background noise is to boost the upper part of the audio spectrum during recording (*pre-emphasis*) and reduce it correspondingly during replay (*de-emphasis*); but this is only partially successful.

A number of ingenious *noise reduction* (*NR*) circuits have evolved which considerably reduce background noise, permit quieter sounds to be reproduced, and so extend the effective dynamic range. Unfortunately these systems are not mutually compatible, and it is as well to realize this when reproducing a recording using a particular NR system.

Although designs differ, NR systems fundamentally aim to automatically compress the dynamic range during recording, and expand it (in a mirror image) during reproduction. The widest-used noise-reduction processes include Dolby A, B, C, HX; the *dBx*, the *Telecom* system. (See Glossary: *Noise reduction*.)

Table 12.4   Disc and audio tape reproduction

	Vinyl disc	**Audio tape**
Advantages	Lightweight, easily stored (vertically) and occupies little space.	With moderate care, not easily damaged (but rapid stop–starts can cause tape snarl-up!).
	Even brief sections are quickly selected from a disc, particularly if recorded in a series of *cuts/bands* (multi-cut/multi-band).	High audio quality, consistent throughout tape; permitting many replays.
	Extensive library sources available.	High reliability and durability.
	Two pick-ups can play one disc (for continuous repetition, echo effects, simultaneous play of different sections).	Tape length can be chosen to suit duration required.
		Recording can be revised, edited.
	Speed adjustment permits pitch change (for effects).	Audio tape can be erased and re-used.
		Background noise remains generally low.
	Two turntables provide continuous playing, mixing, crossfades.	Tape recording is a simple reliable process.
	Only two basic disc formats; 33⅓ rpm, 45 rpm (plus obsolete 78 rpm format).	Process can be automated.

Table 12.4 (cont.)

	Vinyl disc	Audio tape
Disadvantages	Surface noise (static attracts dust, fingermarks) worsens with use. Playing life limited (lightweight pick-ups are not robust, vulnerable), distortion and defects increase with use. Quality deteriorates towards disc center (waveform compression). Disc is easily damaged (scratches, blemishes, warping). Pick-up stylus is easily damaged; can ruin recording. Equipment may have speed instability (wow, flutter); and rumble. Unwanted sections cannot be removed. Disc recording involves precision processing (results vary); or *direct recording* onto lacquer/acetate discs (short life).	Larger reels are bulky and pose storage problems. Recording is damaged by magnetic fields, heat, humidity. Tape is susceptible to damage. Tape *drop-out* can disrupt the recording. Tape is not rapidly excerpted. *Unwanted* passages necessitate play-through, fast run-through, editing out, or dubbing onto another recorder. Tape has to be rewound before reproduction. Various incompatible tape formats. Recorder heads must be demagnetized with small electromagnet to obviate background noise build-up.
Cuing	Requires skill (monitor output at an audition/prefader/prehear point with channel faded out). *Methods:* 1 *Monitor.* Play silent up to cue point, then fade in channel. 2. *Back-cuing.* With a rapid-start turntable (0.2 second to full speed). Play to cue point. Switch off turntable with stylus in groove. Hand-reverse disc to cue point, then back a further e.g. half revolution (to provide run-up time at switch-on). When disc is required, switch on (microswitch on fader, or push-button start) and fade up. 3. *Slip-cue.* Use felt *slip mat* under disc. Find cue point as in 2, but do not reverse. Pinch-hold the mat, switch on turntable – disc remains still, turntable revolves. On cue, release mat and fade up.	Precision cuing is simple. (Check on monitoring system.) Equipment provides immediate start at any required points. *Methods:* 1. Play to cue point. Stop. Wind back by hand to exact cue point. (Rear mark tape at replay point for future cuing.) 2. Wind tape to footage indicator and check precise cue point. Cue point seeking can be automated: metallic cue tag; photostop (wipe off magnetic coating with solvent – clear backing-gap stops tape); microprocessor memory. Identifying color leader can be spliced in. Tape carts may use *cue-tones* (1 kHz) on an auxiliary track: to switch channels, fast run, or start the next cart in a stack.

Compact disc

120 mm (4.7 in) single-sided disc. See Glossary.

Advantages	Lightweight, easily stored (vertically), occupies little space. Even brief sections easily selected from disc. Rapid track selection. Fast forward/rev (skip), pause, repeat play, programmed playout. Precision cuing. Time indicator for precise location (elapsed time, remaining time). Highest audio quality, does not deteriorate with use. Process can be automated.
Disadvantages	Disc mechanically vulnerable (abrasion, scratches, heat, chemicals). Discs costly. Library material limited (sound effects, mood music).

Table 12.5 Audio tape and disc formats

Reel-to-reel tape

The supply spool is manually threaded through the tape path, to the take-up spool. The tape is easily edited, fitted with intersection color leader tape, and self-stop tape (foil or photostop).

Tape width	¼ in (6.35 mm) is universal. (½ in (12.7 mm), 1 in (25 mm), 2 in (50 mm), specialist versions are also used.)
Spool diameters and capacity (standard tape)	3 in (75 mm) with 175 ft; 4 in (100 mm) with 300 ft; 5 in (125 mm) with 600 ft; 5¾ in (145 mm) with 900 ft; 7 in (175 mm) with 1200 ft; 8¼ in (210 mm) cine with 1800 ft; 10½ in (265 mm) NAB with 2400 ft; 11½ in (290 mm) European with 3250 ft.
Tape speeds per second	15⁄16 in (2.35 cm); 1⅞ in (4.75 cm); 3¾ in (9.5 cm); 7½ in (19 cm); 15 in (38 cm); 30 in (76 cm).
Tape thickness	Standard play – 0.002 in (0.05 mm); Long play – 0.0015 in (0.04 mm). Double play – 0.001 in (0.025 mm); Triple play – 0.00075 in (0.02 mm). Quadruple play – 0.0005 in (0.013 mm).
Tracks	1 (full tape width); 2 (half-track); 4 (quarter-track) formats.
Running time (at 7½ in/19 cm per second)	1200 ft = 32 minutes; 1 minute = 38 ft (11.6 m); 30 minutes = 1125 ft (342 m). Other lengths and speeds in this ratio. For other tape thicknesses multiply duration by: Long × 1.5; Double play × 2; Triple play × 3; Quad play × 4.

Cassette

A small enclosed two- or four-track reel-to-reel system. Self-threading. Rapid loading and instant start (no wow or slur on run-up). End of track may not include auto-stop. Not readily edited.

Tape width 3.5 mm; speed 4.75 cm/second (1.7/8 ips). Cassette maximum durations: 30, 60, 90, 120 minutes (half-track, turning cassette over at end of first play-through); 15, 30, 45, 60 minutes per side.

Cartridge (cart)

Its container houses a single enclosed spool, holding an *endless* tape loop; feeding from its inside, and winding onto its outside.

Tape width ¼ in (6.3 mm); speed 7½ ips (19 cm/s). Self-threading. Auto-rewind by running on at normal speed to beginning of recording. Rapid loading. Instant start. Eight mono tracks, or four stereo.

Three NAB standard sizes (durations at 19 cm/s): A & AA = few seconds to 10½ minutes; B & BB = up to 16 minutes maximum; C & CC up to 31 minutes maximum. (Short-duration versions used for identification announcements, brief inserts of music, speech, effects.)

Widely used for automatic replay of spot commercials in a *carousel* playing, say, 24 carts in succession. Other equipment can play several carts simultaneously. Earlier design shortcomings now largely overcome (wow, flutter, stereo phase errors).

Disc formats

78 rpm	Obsolete. Coarse-groove reproducing stylus. Mono only.
45 rpm *33⅓ rpm*	LP fine-groove reproducing stylus (tip radius 0.0005–0.0007 in), in mono and stereo forms. For wide-hole discs (45 rpm) a special center adapter is needed.
Compact disc	120 mm (4.7 in) single-sided disc. See Glossary.

13 Film

Although video cameras are increasingly used for location shooting, film continues to have an important role in the television medium. It can be difficult at times to discern on the screen whether a program originates from film or television cameras, but there are very practical differences in their production mechanics. Paradoxically, as television/video systems become more flexible, the edges blur between these differing techniques.

Basic filming process

Film making involves a series of processes, each one hopefully taking into account later stages – the cameraman shooting in anticipation of the film editor's continuity problems, days or weeks later.

It is not possible to examine results while filming and you have to wait for proof prints (*dailies, rushes*) to show whether action, camerawork, lighting, etc. was successful. Occasionally, a small TV camera is fitted to the film camera (electronic viewfinder), providing an *approximate* monochrome check on a nearby TV monitor. Otherwise only the camera operator can know, for example, whether the mike dipped into shot – and he might have overlooked it while preoccupied with the action. As a result of retakes to correct faults or errors and selective editing, about 1/10 to 1/20 of the overall film exposed is finally used (a 10:1–20:1 *shooting ratio*). To save processing costs faulty takes (NG) are not printed.

Synchronized auidio may be recorded separately on a portable magnetic recorder; or in the sound film camera itself, on a magnetic strip alongside the picture. Entire scenes are often shot with a *silent camera*, the eventual audio track being devised later in the dubbing suite.

Scripting

There are several approaches to shooting a film, ranging from the hopefully empirical to the meticulously planned.

In *unscripted* off-the-cuff shooting, the camera tends to record available events: perhaps working from a rough outline (*shooting plan*). Material is selected during editing and compiled into a program format with added commentary. This technique is often used when shooting documentaries and news stories.

Fully scripted productions, on the other hand, are first broken down into their component shots or scenes, and the mechanics involved for each shot or group of shots are assessed. The staged action is then methodically shot out of story sequence (*shooting schedule/plan*) for maximum economy and efficiency. For example, if the story line requires a series of intercut shots between the heroine at the cliff-top and the hero below, you shoot

311

RAW STOCK
Exposed

AUDIO TAPE
RECORDER

Electronic Interlock

¼ in.
Audio
Tape

DUB TRANSFER

LABS

Negative
Master

Positive
Print

① LOGGING

Perforated
Magnetic
Tape

② SYNCHRONIZING

⑦

LABS
NEG
CUTT-
ING

Master Neg
Cutting
(Optical
printer
work)

Print
of Edit

③

Rough
Cut

Fine
Cut

REVIEW
SCREEN
(Projected)

Grading

④

EDITING PRINT

⑤

MAIN
SUBJECT

Audio
Tape

EFFECTS & MUSIC

Disc

Audio Tape

COMMEN
-TARY

⑧

TELECINE

Review
TARIF

Transmission

DUBBING
MIXER

FINAL PICTURE
PRINT
(Show Copy)

⑨

⑥

Magnetic
Sound
Track

Fig. 13.1 (opposite)   Basic sound filming process

Picture. Film is shot in a series of separate camera set-ups (re-takes, multi-versions); clapper-board being shown at head or inverted at the tail of each take (for identification and sound/picture sync mark). Potentially usable takes are processed and a *master negative* is obtained. An uncorrected positive check print is made (*rushes, dailies*). This is used for review and, later to devise editing *cutting copy*.

Audio. Location sound is recorded on ¼ inch magnetic tape. It is later dubbed selectively onto full-coat sprocketed magnetic film, to correspond with cutting-copy picture selections.

Editing development.

1. All information on material is logged (edge numbers, take numbers, descriptions, lengths/footages).
2. Picture and sound-track is then synchronized.
3. Sections are selectively assembled (rough cut, work print).
4. Revision, exact cutting prints and transitions are chosen (cutting copy, fine cut).
5. Various additional sound tracks are prepared or assembled (commentary, music, effects).
6. All sounds are then dubbed (using *dubbing mixer*) onto one mixed master soundtrack to match the edited picture.
7. Master negatives are prepared by the laboratory which correspond to editor's cutting copy (with his wax-pencil code marking the transitions required). Master negatives' edge-numbers are used for section/frame identification.
8. Specimen test-strip print-sections supplied by laboratories (timing, grading, cinex), for approval of processing color balance, exposure variations, corrections, etc.
9. Final print: This is either a *combined print*, which has the picture united with optical or magnetic sound track; or is *double-headed*, having separate picture and magnetic track, which are run synchronously.

---

all the sequences involved at one camera set-up, then move to the other viewpoint.

This 'out-of-sequence' shooting prevents unnecessary changes in camera set-up, location, relighting, resetting, and uses actors more economically.

Single-camera shooting

Single-camera shooting is the normal method of filming. Two or more cameras are only used for situations where repeat action would be impracticable or costly, or simultaneous multi-viewpoints are required; e.g. when derailing a train.

Shooting discontinuously out of sequence often requires performers to repeat their action for each change in camera viewpoint or shot length (and remember, their performance is probably out-of-story-sequence anyway). That introduces *continuity problems*. Action, gestures, expressions, costume, lighting, etc. must match in intercut shots and relate to the story development – although filmed at different times.

Fig. 13.2   Single-camera shooting

To achieve apparently smooth flowing action *with one camera*, a series of camera set-ups are often necessary.

Example.

A. Girl out walking (comes up to camera . . . which pans as she moves past).

B. Cut – she sees friend in distance (over shoulder shot).

C. Cut – CU of friend smiling.

D. Cut – friend's point of view. Girl arrives, speaking (LS to CU).

C/D. Intercut close-shots during conversation.

C. Girl says goodbye (MS).

E. Girl walks on.

The action taken for each camera set-up will be enacted/repeated out of sequence to suit each camera set-up in turn.

Flexibility of viewpoint

After a sequence is skilfully edited, the continuity appears so natural that one can easily overlook that it was originally shot as a *disjointed series of individual set-ups*.

In a typical filmed sequence we may find ourselves close to a person as he walks – yet an instant later see him from a distant viewpoint. The camera is often 'left behind' as he moves away – yet is at his destination as he arrives. Shots intercut from his viewpoint to that of the person to whom he is speaking.

The overall effect here is smooth-flowing and provides a variety of viewpoints. To do the obvious and shoot this entire sequence as *continuous* action would have required several cameras, spread over an appreciable distance – an approach that might not be practical anyway. Usually it would not provide the same effect.

Filmed shots tend to be of briefer duration than those in continuous TV production. Watching a well-made film, we see that most shots (the period between picture transitions) last only a few seconds (typically 3–15 seconds). A good serial film unit may achieve as many as 120 shots a day (about 18 minutes' running time), although this is untypical. A live TV production might last 25 minutes, and contain 100–200 shots, edited 'on the hoof'.

Production decisions

In film production the director works in very close proximity to his single-camera crew. He normally discusses shots, treatment, action, with the cameraman, who then interprets these instructions. The director will only see the results later, and must rely on his judgement and his crew. The brief action segment is rehearsed, shot; and then retaken if necessary. Additional cover shots (protection shots) may be taken, 'just in case'.

Positive prints are made of the good takes (checked as the *dailies/*

Fig. 13.3   Location filming
The location film team needs to be self-sufficient, anticipatory, well organized and adaptable.

rushes), which the film editor separates, examines, selects, relates, and interconnects. He uses a script or brief, cue-sheet, and *continuity-report* information (forms giving action detail, slate numbers, etc. identifying each *take*). So he forms the individual clips of film into a cohesive and appropriate continuity (the *cutting copy*). The editor evaluates processing and grading (print density and color quality). Having decided on shot relationships, cutting points, and suitable transitions, the editor submits his *rough-cut* for the director's approval. Subsequently he may modify the precise cutting points, tightening scenes, making final revisions to produce the final *fine-cut*.

Later the processing labs match the stored master negatives to his cut version, using the edge-numbers printed along the original film edge to guide them. An optical print is then made, using the transitions he has wax pencil codemarked on his cutting copy.

The soundtrack is compiled (*laying tracks*) and the *dubbing mixer* skilfully blends dialog, commentary, effects, and music. A *rock-and-roll* facility enables picture and sound tracks to be run synchronously forward/backward for rapid correction during dubbing.

There are opportunities to examine and reconsider at each step (time permitting!), and to remedy or improve results. Each stage in this exacting process paradoxically leads to a product with seemingly absolute freedom in time and dimension.

Library shots (stock shots) (See Chapter 15)

These are short film (or video) sequences of illustrative material, held in an organization's archives or rented from specialist libraries.

Library shots/stock shots are inserted into a program where it would be impracticable or uneconomic to shoot new material. These short clips cover a very wide field, including news events, location shots, manufacturing processes, natural history, personalities, stunts, etc., etc. They are widely used to illustrate talks, demonstrations, newscasts, and to provide atmospheric and environmental shots for drama.

Sound on film

Double-system

Using this method the picture and sound are recorded separately; so providing maximum editing flexibility. However, apart from general background sounds, close synchronization is normally essential between the film camera and its associated audio tape recorder; for speech we have to maintain exact *lip sync*.

To achieve precise synchronization, camera and recorder may be connected by a special sync-pulse cable, but this is physically restrictive. Instead, matched crystal controls can be fitted to independently maintain accurate motor speeds; or alternatively, wireless control interlocks or an edge time code may be used.

Table 13.1   Typical equipment for small-unit filming

16 mm camera lens	Arriflex, Eclair, Auricon Cine-Voice, Bolex.
	Zoom e.g. focal length 12–120 mm (hand-crank or rod-operated).
	'Normal' angle at 25 mm.
	Or turret lenses – 12, 16, 25, 50, 75, 100, 120 mm focal length.
Camera support	Body brace, shoulder brace, shoulder pad.
	Light tripod, with triangular spreader (spider).
	Sometimes a small lightweight dolly, for dollying (tracking) shots.
	Lens angles below 12°, i.e. focal length greater than 50 mm, require a firmly supported camera.
Shooting duration	Maximum 11 minutes with 400 ft (122 m) magazine.
	Battery-powered camera runs typically 1 ½ hours (3000 ft of film).
Lighting equipment	Small portable lamps on camera or hand-held (e.g. Sungun, Frezzi). Lightweight lamps, Red-heads, Lowell-lites, Colortran quartz lights; quartz broads, Mini-brutes; photofloods in small scoops; reflector boards.
	Lamp supports – hand-held, gaffer-tape attached, screw-clamps, gaffer-clamps (spring-jaw clamps), clip-lights, lightweight tripod stands, telescopic spring-loaded support poles (polecat, barricuda) fitted ceiling-to-floor or wall-to-wall.
Microphones	Lanyard, electret, or baton personal mike (cable connected, or wireless mike).
	Sound men with fishpole and/or shotgun (rifle) mike.
Sound recorder	Lightweight portable synchronized magnetic audio recorder (e.g. Nagra), earphone monitored.
	Synchronous sound using a camera-to-recorder sync connection (cable or wireless), crystal lock or time code.

As the start of each take, an *identifying head slate* is filmed, giving all reference details to aid eventual editing. By matching up the sound and picture at its small clapper-board closing (*sync marks*) we ensure that film and soundtrack are in step for that take. Automatic slating facilities are sometimes fitted – these 'flash' a frame and bleep the soundtrack simultaneously. Alternatively, a *tail slate/end board* (upside down) is shot at the end of a scene.

Fig. 13.4   Film sound
Optical track – combined (married) print:
1. Variable area track.
2. Variable density track.

Magnetic track:
3. Magnetic stripe. Balancing stripe facilitates flat, smooth roll wind.
4. Mute picture, separate 16 mm perforated magnetic film.

1   2   3 ↑   ↑   4
             Balancing   Magnetic
             Stripe   Stripe
                          (Sound Track)

Single system

This method, used for documentary and news filming, records the audio beside the picture on a magnetic *track*. However, the audio's 28-frame separation (in advance) from its corresponding picture (about one second difference) means that editing the picture will cut the audio too – but not at the same point.

An audible track may be recorded *optically* on film, using variable area or variable density light modulation systems. This optical track is printed

Fig. 13.5   Film formats
1. 35 mm gauze.
2. 16 mm.
3. Super-8.

1

2   SILENT (Mute)   OPTICAL TRACK   3

photographically along one edge of the released film, in a *combined (married) print*.

Many TV organizations keep picture and magnetically recorded sound separate throughout, and reproduce them in synchronism (*double-headed*) in the telecine equipment.

Most TV organizations use 16 mm film almost exclusively; a gauge that provides an optimum balance between running costs and good picture quality. Equipment is reasonably lightweight, especially when compared with costly, bulky 35 mm cameras. Editing, which becomes progressively difficult with smaller gauges, is still reasonably easy; although reliably unobtrusive splices require checkerboard (A/B roll) cutting. To simplify editing, the film may be transferred to videotape, the stripe soundtrack being dubbed onto a separate magnetic (sep-mag) film.

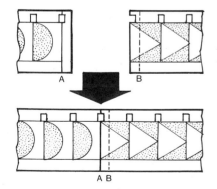

Fig. 13.6   Joining film
The two shots to be joined, are cut in the splicer and connected by: a *temporary splice* using translucent adhesive splicing tape (butt join), or a *permanent overlap weld* using film cement (scraping off film emulsion for overlap join), or a *heat butt-welded splice* along frame-line (used for negative editing).

Transmitting negative film

After the *negative stock* used for most filming is processed, a *positive print* is made. The original negative itself is generally considered too precious to risk damage through continual handling and projection, for any blemishes or dust (reproducing as white 'sparkle') can irremediably deface the picture.

However, to save the cost and time involved in printing, the negative film (electronically reversed) may be transmitted, e.g. for urgent news stories. The important compensatory color and exposure corrections (*grading*) normally made during printing have instead to be introduced

Fig. 13.7 Checkerboard and A/B roll assemblies

When printing narrow-gauge film, material is usually distributed between two rolls A and B, interspaced by blanking (black leader). By inter-switching/dissolving between rolls, optical combinations (dissolve, wipe, etc.) and invisible splices (not intruding into picture area) become possible. The system avoids intermediate duplication stages for combined effects.

1. For *checkerboard assembly*, the output changes between A and B rolls at each cut; except where an overlap is required for a combined effect (dissolve, wipe, etc.).

2. *For A/B roll assembly*, shots are spliced consecutively on one roll, until an overlap is required for a combined effect. The output then remains with the other roll for successive shots until the next combination is required. These techniques are also used for rapid excerpting from complete programs (film and VT).

operationally when the film is reproduced (on sight, or using programmed electronic correction).

Negative film is sometimes used when dark or dense scenes are to be transmitted from a vidicon telecine system; this method overcomes lag (trailing) problems otherwise arising from low-light conditions.

Reversal film

Film emulsions designed for *reversal* produce a normal positive image with natural colors and tones on the original camera film. There is no negative involved. No print is necessary, so processing is quicker.

The advantages of reversal film include higher available sensitivity (*speed*), finer grain, improved sharpness, and better color reproduction. Against this, the exposure range is very limited, which may produce crushed highlights and shadows. Also there is less opportunity to correct exposure and color errors. Most important, the original film is itself projected and is vulnerable. So a print may be needed, anyway, to provide a cutting copy for editing in order to preserve the master film.

Mechanics of film reproduction

We use film in television production in several forms:

1. As a *reel* of 1 minute to greater than 2 hours' duration.
2. As a series of brief-duration sections (*clips*) joined by opaque *blanking*, or *cue leaders*.
3. As closed *film loops*, joined tail-to-head to provide continuous repetition (mist, snow, rain) or repeated cyclic motion (e.g. to study machine movement) using a centerless spool or take-up pulleys.
4. As short *film strips* containing a series of different still frames.
5. As individual *film slides/transparencies* – televised by a transparency-projector (picked up by a TV camera) or a special slide scanner.

Fig. 13.8 Multiplexed telecine
A mirror or prism system enables one
TV camera to selectively shoot a slide
projector or either of two film
projectors. The assembly is mounted
on a film island.

Telecine

The European television picture rate is 25 pps (50 Hz power supplies).
If standard films (24 fps) are projected at this slightly higher rate (4 per
cent) there is no discernible speed-up. However, film shot specifically for
European TV is normally exposed at 25 fps instead of the motion-picture
standard.

■ *Camera-type telecines* This arrangement is extensively used in North
America. On a *film island* installation, a standard TV camera faces a
mirror or prism multiplexer system. Through this it can see, selectively,
the output of two film projectors or a 2 × 2 in slide (transparency) projector.

A storage-type camera-tube (vidicon, plumbicon) is used to produce
the video signals, coupled with a film projector exposing each film frame
for 2½ TV fields. This compensates for the discrepancy between the

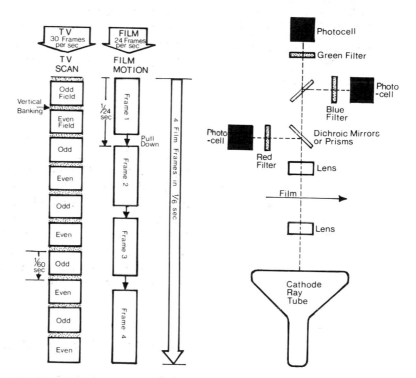

**Fig. 13.9 Picture-rate
conversion**
To relate the standard film projection
rate (24 frames per second) to TV
standards of 30 pictures (USA) per
second, several sampling methods are
used (e.g. project one film frame
3 times, the next twice; fast film
pulldown with light-source pulsing
5 times per film frame/4 times per TV
picture).

**Fig. 13.10 Color flying-spot
scanner**
A plain white raster traced on the
cathode ray tube focused onto the
moving film. This exploratory light spot
is focused through color filters into
corresponding photo cells. Their
outputs as each point is scanned,
constituting red, green, blue video
signals. To compensate for film
movement, twin displaced rasters,
twin-lens systems, or a rotating
polygonal prism are used.

standard film projection rate of 24 frames per second and the standard TV picture rate of 30 pps (related to 60 Hz power supply frequency) in the USA and Canada.

The intermittent projector moves the film in rhythmic 'pull-and-hold' jerks, to freeze each frame momentarily as it passes the picture gate, so giving the TV camera time to discern successive pictures clearly. The resultant video signals are then adjusted and processed.

■ *Flying-spot scanners*   These are widely used, and are capable of the highest-quality film reproduction. The film travels at a constant speed (*continuous motion*) through the telecine equipment. On a special picture tube a constant-brightness raster is scanned. The focused image of this scanning light pattern explores the moving film. The resultant fluctuations, as the varying film densities interrupt the scanning light beam, are picked up by photocells. Their modulated electrical signal forms the telecine's video output.

■ *Digital telecine systems*   These use three full-line sensors (RGB) to scan the passing film. These charge-coupled devices (CCD) analyze its light variations. The resulting charges are held in a digital frame store to be read out as the video signal. This system provides flicker-free slow motion, jog, and still frame pictures.

CCD telecine systems have the added advantage that special circuitry can be added to conceal dirt and scratches to a remarkable degree. A beam of infrared light passes straight through the film, unaffected by the color images, and falls onto a fourth CCD sensor. Any dirt, defects, scratches interrupt this beam, and cause circuits to switch momentarily, inserting previous picture information instead at that point (a form of *drop-out compensation*).

Video control for telecine

Film is capable of superb color reproduction, but it is not an entirely consistent material. We shall find some variations in color balance between different batches of the same film stock; and between different types of color film. Moreover when filming, exposure or color temperature may not have been accurate or consistent. Where film has aged, or is a copy of the original print (dupe), further changes arise. So in printing, film labs adjust the intensity and color balance of their printer lights to compensate empirically for discrepancies (grading).

However, when televising a film such errors are more apparent than in theater viewing, where eye adaptation and subjective effects tend to compensate. Consequently, a film that may appear satisfactory when theater-reviewed beforehand often requires further compensations when televised. Where the film has not been finely graded, these may be considerable.

By adjusting video gain, black level (sometimes gamma), color balance, and saturation considerable improvements become possible. Color correction may also be introduced by *electronic masking circuits*, compensating for film dye deficiencies and certain *analysis errors* arising when televising color film. Video gain and gamma adjustments to the RGB color channels ('TARIF' operation) provide good correction for various errors. Similar correction can be applied to slide (transparency) scanners.

Exposure and color-correction adjustments may be made 'on the fly' by an operator during replay; either empirically or to settings found during rehearsal. Some systems enable corrective settings to be filed, selected, and activated; automatically or by push-button.

Non-standard projection

Depending on design, telecine equipment may be able to provide several kinds of non-standard projection:

1. Hold a selected single frame (*still frame, hold frame, freeze frame*).
2. Dissolve slowly from one frame to the next (*inching*).
3. Run up from still frame to full speed (mute) without frame-roll or flicker.
4. Run at non-standard constant speeds (e.g. 16–60 fps) – forward or backward.
5. Fast wind-on (run-on) and rewind.
6. *Remote manual cuing* (from the production switcher), or *automatic cuing* using attached metalized cue tags or tape strip, or by microprocessor selection.

Cuing film

Telecine equipment cannot normally provide an instantaneous start for picture and audio. A brief run-up period is necessary for audio to stabilize. By attaching a time-scaled *sync leader* (e.g. SMPTE universal leader) to the head of a film you can ensure that the first picture frame with fully stabilized audio will appear a predictable time after switch-on. The required picture sync marker is positioned in the projector's picture gate, the director giving an anticipatory run cue 4 (or 8) seconds before cutting to film channel output. This avoids inadvertently switching to a stationary or unstable channel. To ensure that the film reproduction is neither clipped at its beginning nor runs out immediately after action finishes, a few *buffer (safety) frames* of the scene are included at the head and tail of each section.

Where several film lengths are conjoined, you can:

1. Use timed lengths of blanking between them; leaving the machine running while cutting away to studio (*roll-through*).
2. Introduce a series of sync leaders; recuing each section.
3. Cue the film at any time, switching to it when it appears.

Fig. 13.11   TV film sync leader
Several types of film leader are in use. In the American National Standard leader shown (35 and 16 mm motion-picture theater, and TV studios), a *start identification frame* ensures exact picture sync with the sound-head. A series of numbers from 8 to 2 (seconds) appear (a black background then a dark wedge moving clockwise in series of 15° steps) provide a visual count-down.

Fig. 13.12   Changeover synchronizing
At the appearance of a white (or black) circular dot in the top right corner of the picture area, the second projector is started (motor cue). After 7 seconds, a similar dot cues the changeover switch-point. This mark is printed or punched in the print (during processing, or editing).

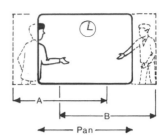

Fig. 13.13 Wide-screen films

Wide screen motion pictures do not use the TV screen's aspect ratio (4 × 3 shape; i.e. 1.33:1). If the picture is fitted to frame side-edges, so seeing all of film, overall picture size is small and areas are wasted at top/bottom of TV screen. If the *top/bottom* of the frame is fitted to the TV screen, then the sides of the film picture are lost. Solutions to this problem include zooming to full height, panning left/right to follow main action (top-fit) as shown (A to B). These operations involve scanning circuit adjustments (on-air or pre-coded), or compensated film prints.

Fig. 13.14 Cutting combined prints – problem

In a combined print (optical or magnetic stripe) the sound is displaced ahead of its corresponding picture (to suit the picture-gate to sound-head separation distance).

Physically cutting this combined print creates a dilemma: if the sound track is cut at a specific point (S), then over a second (26–28 picture frames) of unwanted picture is included in the selected film. When editing continuous speech, this can result in *lip-flap* before the wanted action, i.e. silent mouth movements left from the previous material, without any accompanying sound.

In the above example, cutting at the end of the picture sequence (P), will spuriously introduce sound from the next shot; while cutting after the explosion sound (S) will lose the picture of the event.

The problem can be overcome by intercutting a mute shot (e.g. cutaway), or re-laying the sound track.

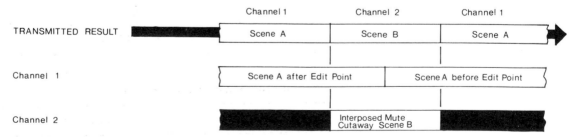

Fig. 13.15 Cutting combined prints – solution

A standard method uses a *double chain* or *A/B system*. A brief silent cutaway shot (reaction shot) is interposed to hide any lip-flap, jump-cut, etc., by strategically switching away.

Having previously ascertained the exact 'timing' (duration), the *in-cue* (first words) and *out-cue* (last words), precision insertion into the program becomes practicable. Occasionally, the exact entry/exit points for a videotaped film insert are determined during subsequent VT editing.

Recording color TV on film

Several methods have evolved for transferring video pictures to standard color film stock. Each has its particular advantages and limitations. At best, results are excellent. Film recordings have advantages in certain markets. They overcome incompatible TV standards that frustrate the world distribution of videotape recordings. Film prints permit large-screen projection, have wider educational and library applications, and are more convenient for certain field work.

Table 13.2   Film running times

		35 mm (16 fr per ft)				16 mm (40 fr per ft)				Super 8 mm (72 fr per ft)			
		24 fps		25 fps		24 fps		25 fps		24 fps		25 fps	
		ft	fr	ft	fr	ft	fr	ft	fr	ft	fr	ft	fr
Seconds	1	1	8	1	9	0	24	0	25	0	24	0	25
	3	4	8	4	11	1	32	1	35	1	0	1	3
	5	7	8	7	13	3	0	3	5	1	48	1	53
	7	10	8	10	15	4	8	4	15	2	24	2	31
	10	15	0	15	10	6	0	6	10	3	24	3	24
	30	45	0	46	14	18	0	18	30	10	0	10	30
Minutes	1	90	0	93	12	36	0	37	20	20	0	20	60
	5	450	0	468	12	180	0	187	20	100	0	104	12
	10	900	0	937	8	360	0	375	0	200	0	208	24
	15	1350	0	1406	4	540	0	562	20	300	0	312	36

		Seconds						
Feet	1	0.7		0.6	1.8	1.6	3.0	2.9
	3	2.0		1.9	5.0	4.8	9.0	8.6
	5	3.3		3.2	8.3	8.0	15.0	14.4
	7	4.7		4.5	11.6	11.2	21.0	20.2
	10	6.6		6.4	16.6	16.0	30.0	28.8
	15	10.0		9.6	25.0	24.0	45.0	43.2
	20	13.2		12.8	33.3	32.0	1 min 0.0	57.6
	30	20.0		19.2	50.0	48.0	1 min 30.0	1 min 24.0
	50	33.2		32.0	1 min 23.0	1 min 20.0	2 min 30.0	2 min 24.0

Table 13.3   Displacement of picture and sound

	35 mm	16 mm	Super 8 mm
Magnetic track	28 frames behind pic.	28 ahead of pic.	18 ahead of pic.
Optical track	21 frames ahead.	26 ahead.	22 ahead.

Several major films have been shot with video cameras and then transferred to film stock, for theatrical release. The main advantages here have included: the opportunity to monitor while shooting, immediate playback checks, more convenient and economical videotape editing, the opportunity to use digital video effects, and image enhancing. And all this has become possible due to the high image-transfer quality now available.

Image transfer

Several image-transfer methods are current:

1. A special film camera (using color film) shoots a color TV picture tube.
2. A similar set-up, filming a monochrome picture tube which displays in three successive runs the red, blue, and green component images from a videotape. The three separate monochrome recordings of the color information are combined to full color during laboratory printing.
3. *Laser beam* recording, in which three separate video-modulated lasers (RGB) combine optically on *color* film.
4. Electron beam recording (EBR) produces three separation negatives (RGB) on black-and-white film, scanned by electron beams akin to those in picture tubes. These records are combined during laboratory printing, using corresponding red, green, blue light sources.

14 Videotape

Videotape recording (VTR) is technically an extremely sophisticated process. But, happily for the user, equipment has become increasingly simpler to operate, more compact, and reliable.

The coming of videotape

In earlier days the TV program maker had just two choices: to shoot action *live*, as it happened, or to shoot it on film with a standard motion-picture camera, using telecine equipment to transmit it. The only method of *recording* the television image was to have a film camera shoot the TV picture displayed on a high-intensity picture-tube (*kinescope*). Results ranged from surprisingly good (suitable for archives or re-transmission) to abysmal (useful for program checks).

Various attempts were made to record video with sound on *magnetic tape*, and finally in the 1950s the Ampex Corporation's *Quadruplex* (*'Quad'*) system arrived, to become a broadcast standard for over two decades. This system is capable in its developed forms of recording/reproducing color television pictures that are virtually indistinguishable from the original. It brought new freedoms to the program maker.

With the passage of time, several other processes developed, until today we have a range of excellent but quite incompatible methods (see Table 14.2).

The advantages of VTR

Videotape recording has several important advantages for the program maker:

1. At best, the quality of the videotaped program is indistinguishable from the original video.
2. The recording can be replayed immediately, without any intermediate processing. Some equipment designs provide continuous off-tape monitoring (*confidence playback*) to check quality.
3. The videotape can be reproduced many times without deterioration.
4. The recording can be erased (*wiped*) totally or selectively, and new program material recorded in its place.
5. Videotape is easily edited, and faulty or unwanted sections can be replaced. The audience-impact of programs can be enhanced in various ways by selective editing. Performance can be improved by appropriate cuts (deletions), retakes. Long pauses, ineffectual material, or lagging pace can be corrected – usually by introducing

cutaway shots to disguise editing-out. Censor cuts (*continuity acceptance*) can be made unobtrusively; and any distractions, redundant shots, ambiguities removed.

6. Videotaping aids scheduling. Programs can be recorded when convenient, and replayed when required. This is particularly valuable where multi-time zones are involved; to suit training schedules; to facilitate study.

7. Taping can compensate for limited camera facilities, and provide apparent viewpoint mobility as separate recordings are edited together.

8. Various problems in staging can be overcome (e.g. moving wild walls, refurbishing sets, relighting, etc.) by stop–start taping, as can changes in costume, make-up, etc.

9. Any video effects can be taped, and checked immediately. This recording can then be replayed, and further electronic treatment added if required.

10. Within broadcast organizations, motion pictures are regularly transferred to videotape (i.e. telecine-to-VTR copying) to add identifying subtitles; for language translation; for optimum presentation of wide-screen prints; when adding music and effects to silent (mute) films; to preserve a valuable or damaged film print, or to edit Super-8 mm film records.

11. The director can make off-line editing judgements before the final postproduction editing session.

The videotape recording process

The amount of detailed information a magnetic tape can store as it moves past a recording head depends partly on the characteristics of the tape itself and partly on the *speed* at which the tape passes. In practice, there are not only mechanical problems when running tape at very high speeds but we finish up with large reels of limited playing time.

Instead, engineers developed a different approach. They put the recording heads on a fast-moving drum and passed the tape over this drum. As a result, the *effective speed of the tape past the heads* was now high, while the tape itself was being used at a very economical rate. The combined head and tape movement produces a series of sloping magnetic tracks across the tape. There are interruptions, of course, as each track reaches the tape edge and continues again on a new parallel path slightly further along the tape, but these gaps in information can be hidden. More of that in a moment.

This *helical scanning* (*slant-track*) process is used in all modern videotape recording systems and in digital audio tape (R-DAT) equipment. The term 'helical' is derived from the spiral-like path traced by the tape as it travels over the drum.

From the scanning principles, let's turn to the recording process itself. The tape travels from the supply reel, past a fixed *erase head* which

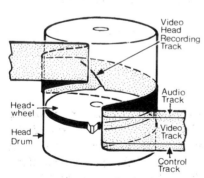

Fig. 14.1 part 1 Typical helical scanning arrangement
The tape is wrapped in a slanting path round a drum. Within the drum a disc head-wheel supporting recording (and erase) heads rotates, pressing heads against the tape at an acute angle as it slides past. (Designs include rotating upper drum, or slot scanner with narrow rotating center section.) Each head-drum revolution records one video track.

Fig. 14.1 part 2   Helical videotape tracks
Two incompatible helical 1-inch videotape formats are used professionally: the more popular *Type 'C'* and the *Type 'B'* system.

The type 'C' system (left) records a *continuous* or *non-segmented field*. Each head-drum revolution lays down a video track containing one complete field. This video track contains all picture information (active lines) *plus* any information introduced during the vertical interval (VITS, VIRS).

Separate heads on the head-drum simultaneously record and replay video (to allow picture monitoring during recording), and record a special sync track (or audio track 4). An automatic tracking-control head is optional.

Along the tape edge there are three longitudinal tracks: two for program audio, one for time-code, cue-track, or extra audio. Replay during *fast or slow motion, jogging, or freeze-frame* is achieved by adjusting the tape's travel speed, while the head-drum rotates as normal.

The type 'B' system (right) is a *segmented field* system. It records 52 television lines on each slant track. So five video tracks are needed to record one field, i.e. 262½ lines (NTSC). One complete picture requires 10 tracks (six tracks per field – 312½ lines – in a 625/50 system).

The head drum contains two video heads and a control head. Three more tracks are recorded along the tape edge: two *audio* for program, one for *cue-track* or *time-code*.

For replay at non-standard speeds, or freeze-frame, a *frame store synchronizer* is needed.

magnetically neutralizes ('wipes') its entire width during the recording process. It continues, guided in a helical path, to wrap around the cylindrical *head-drum/scanning drum*. From the surface of this drum protrudes a small video *record/replay head(s)*. As the upper section of the drum (or an internal disc holding the head) rotates, the head(s) on it turns, rhythmically pressing against the passing tape ('tip penetration'), and scanning across it. Due to the tape's slanting path, the head records an oblique video track on the tape.

We are not usually aware of the information loss at the end of each track, for it is arranged to fall outside the picture area on the TV screen. (The gap is made to coincide with the retrace period at the end of each field.) If, however, the *VTR tracking control* is not correctly adjusted on replay (particularly when playing tapes recorded on another machine) we shall be able to see the *noise-bar* or picture disturbances caused at each track end.

The magnetically recorded information on the tracks is read out as they are precisely scanned by the replay head(s) (or the recording head doubling for that purpose).

In addition to the slanting tracks across the tape, a series of tracks are recorded along its length at the upper and lower edges. The *linear* or *longitudinal* tracks are used to record *audio*, a *control track* for synchronizing the tape-scanning rate, and a *cue track* or Audio 3 track. These may be selectively recorded and wiped. (See Table 14.1 for details.) Again, there are associated replay heads that read off the information.

Table 14.1   Videotape tracks

Video track	A pattern of narrow tracks across the magnetic tape, recording the video signal in FM (frequency-modulated) form. (*Helical* – slant tracks; *quad* – transverse tracks.)
Audio track	A regular audio recording on a linear track along the tape edge (edge track). Up to three such tracks may be available. Audio quality is unavoidably limited on these longitudinal tracks; particularly at low tape speeds, as the tape performance is optimized for slanting video tracks (oblique grain orientation). For *depth multiplex* systems, see Glossary: *Consumer video formats*.
Control track	An edge track recording special regular pulses that accurately synchronize the tape movement and scanning rate, ensuring that the video heads re-scan the existing tracks correctly and aid color frame identification.
Cue track	An edge track, recording a special *address code/time code* to identify each part of the program for electronic editing. Otherwise the track may carry audio (of lower grade) for productional information, commentary, or a second language; or record cue tones.
Erase head	An electromagnet head that completely saturates, then demagnetizes the magnetic tape (across total tape width, or a track), leaving it neutral, ready for recording. Erasing (wiping) is carried out immediately before recording head scans the tape.

In the *non-segmented* or *continuous system* a single video head records one *field* on each track. (Remember, it takes two interlaced fields, odd and even, to form one complete TV picture.) This method has certain technical advantages (simple freeze frame, vari-speed), but unfortunately it omits several picture lines from each field, and all information during the vertical interval.

In the *segmented system* two video heads scan the tape in turn, each recording a succession of picture lines (e.g. 52 lines) on their respective tape tracks. Their outputs are interswitched to provide continuous, uninterrupted video output. Between them, the tracks record all picture and vertical interval information.

Tape formats

Today's various incompatible VTR tape systems use three basic tape formats:

1. *Open reel (reel-to-reel)*. Here the tape is unwound from a full supply spool, laced manually through the tape path/transport system, and secured to an empty take-up spool. The tape needs careful handling to avoid damage (creasing, scrape, edge crushing) or contamination (finger marks, grease, dust).

2. *Cartridge (cart)*. Often misleadingly called a 'cassette', the cart is an enclosed plastic box in which tape is held on a single reel in an endless loop. This arrangement reduces the overall volume of the package. As tape is drawn off, it is rewound onto the same reel. This format is often used for short-duration sequences (e.g. 6 minutes) – commercials, news inserts. In *carousel* equipment, a store of carts can be loaded and selected automatically, or by random access.

3. *Cassette*. A plastic box enclosing two spools (supply and take-up). Currently, cassettes may contain tape lasting from 5 minutes (ENG use of U-Matic) up to some 8 hours (domestic VCC system). Where a cart or cassette is used it is only necessary to plug it into the recorder, the equipment self-lacing the tape for recording or replay.

Picture defects

As you would expect, if you measure the performance of state-of-the-art broadcast equipment and low-price equipment intended for home use there will be wide technical differences. But picture quality is a remarkably subjective judgement.

Many defects are normally overlooked by the uncritical eye: picture noise, reduced texture, artificial edges to subjects (ringing, reflections), color distortions, spurious moiré-patterning effects (chroma-luminance interference), displaced color, edge jitter, crushing of highlights and shadows, flattened-out tonal gradations (cartooning), poor detail resolution . . . ! These are all visible on close inspection of your home TV picture! However, when the subject is really interesting, such defects seem unimportant if we *do* happen to notice them. Only when they distract us, or prevent our seeing clearly, are we normally aware of them.

For the program maker, though, these shortcomings must be reduced to a minimum, for they worsen considerably whenever the videotape is re-recorded (dubbed) in the course of editing or making further copies.

Combination video camera (VCR systems)

(See Glossary, *Combination cameras*.) The combination of a broadcast-quality video camera with its own inbuilt videotape recorder offers considerable production opportunities. Known variously as a *combo*, *VRC (videorecording camera)*, and *camcorder*, three incompatible formats have emerged. Mainly used in the field for ENG, EFP, they are based on the VHS, Betamax, and CVC (compact video cassette) techniques. (See Table 14.2.)

Table 14.2   Videotape systems

Broadcast standards

QUADRUPLEX (QUAD)

Open reel (14 in max.); cartridge;
cassette; 2 in tape

Quad 1: 38 cm/s (*IO*). Quad 2: 19 cm/s (*CDO*). Super high-band.
'Composite' signal recorded (i.e. in NTSC, PAL, SECAM form).

HELICAL SCAN (various incompatible formats)

Open reel (14 in max.),
1 in tape (CDO)

- *'B'-format.* Segmented field (i.e. 1 field = 5(6) tracks), two fields per
  picture. Component recording.
- *'C'-format.* Non-segmented field (i.e. 1 field = 1 track), two fields per picture.
  Component recording.

Cassette, ¾ in (9 mm) tape

- *U-Matic (standard U-format) (CDO).* Initially designed for industrial/
  commercial/educational closed-circuit use; subsequently adapted to broadcast
  use (especially ENG/EFP).
- *BVU-Matic (MP).* A high-band U-Matic system designed for broadcast use.
  Widely used in ENG/EFP production. Incompatible with standard U-Matic
  design. Two cassette sizes: 'portable short-play' and 'playback/edit'.
  Composite recording.

Digital videotape recorders,
¾ in (19 mm) tape

- *D-1 (CDO).* Mainly used for closed-circuit DVE. Video: three separate
  digital signals input.
- *D-2 (MP).* General broadcast use. Video: one analog composite signal input.

Cassette, ½ in (12.5 mm)

- *Betacam (Standard 'L-format').* Derived from 'Beta type' system running at high
  speed. Component recording.
- *Betacam SP(MP).* Developed form of Betacam.
- *M-II (standard 'M-format') (MP).* Derived from 'VHS type' system running at
  high speed. Component recording.
- *Super VHS (S-VHS)*

Broadcast combined camera/
recorder units ('combo; camcorder')

Broadcast-quality systems using ½ in and ¼ in cassettes. Several design
variations, including:
Betacam. Betacam-SP (Sony); *Hawkeye* (RCA);
M-II (Panasonic); *QuarterCam/Lineplex* (Bosch);
ARC (Ampex); *Recam* (Panasonic); *Camescope* (Thomson-CSF);
Super VHS (S-VHS) (JVC)

Domestic standard/consumer formats

Cassette, ½ in tape (CDO)

- *Betamax (Beta; 'G-format').* Linear soundtracks. Composite recording.
- *BETA-SP, BETA HI-FI, BETA HI-BAND, BETA-ED (MP)* Component
  recording. 'FM' and linear soundtracks.
- *VHS ('H-format').* Linear soundtracks. Composite recording.
- *VHS-Hi-Fi.* As 'H', with 'FM' and linear soundtracks.
- *Super VHS (S-VHS) (CDO).* Composite recording. 'FM' and linear
  soundtracks. Also *Super VHS-C* (compact form).

Cassette, 8 mm (¼ in) tape (MP)

Compact video cassette. Small cassette VCR format. Dual speed: 20.05 mm/s,
10.058 mm/s. 'FM' audio track (PCM stereo). Max. duration 1 ½ hours;
3 hours slow speed.

Domestic combined camera/
recorder units

An ever-increasing range of equipment, using 8 mm, VHS-C, standard VHS,
and S-VHS formats.

Audio systems include linear track, 'FM' multiplex, and digital sound (PCM).
Image pick-up devices include CCD and ½ in/⅔ in tubes. Weights from
0.9 kg to +2.5 kg.

Table 14.2 (cont.)

Tape types: IO – Iron oxide. CDO – Cobalt doped oxide. MP – Metal particle.
EM – Evaporated metal tape.

Abbreviations
SP: Superior performance (i.e. improved monochrome and color detail
   (resolution) and better color separation).
ED: Extended definition (i.e. performance improved by reducing interference
   between luminance and color, and improved detail).
CAV: Component analog video.
Composite recording: Luminance and color/chrominance signals share the
   same recording track.
Component recording: Luminance and color/chrominance signals recorded on
   separate tracks.

'FM' audio track, see Glossary: *Consumer VT formats (depth multiplex)*.
Linear sound track: Longitudinal analog soundtracks.

See Glossary: *Videotape standards, consumer videotape formats.*

The 'on-board' videotape recorder is detachable (*docking unit*), and
both camera and VCR can be used separately. The performance equals or
exceeds current ENG/EFP lightweight cameras.

Consumer video formats (domestic VCRs)

Narrow-format VCRs are increasingly used in domestic, educational, and
commercial fields. The two main systems are the incompatible *Betamax*
(*Beta*) and *VHS* formats. Both helical-scan systems use ½ in (12.5 mm)
tape cassettes.

The systems will record *direct* video and sound (e.g. from a camera and
microphone) or off-air (via an internal *modulator* unit). The output may
be a composite signal (e.g. NTSC, PAL, SECAM), video, or as separate
chrominance and luminance signals – to replay through a TV receiver or a
video monitor. (See Glossary: *Consumer videotape formats.*)

The original systems provide very acceptable picture quality for many
purposes (e.g. resolving 250 picture lines). Sound quality is normally
limited by the low tape speed. Developed versions, however, offer a
remarkably high picture quality and hi-fi sound. (Super VHS, for
example, can resolve over 400 vertical lines.)

Vari-speed replay

In many types of program, one wants to replay action in slow motion, or
as selected freeze frames, to demonstrate movement, to analyze, or to
provide an artistic effect. Both magnetic video discs and vari-speed VTRs
are used for this purpose. But there is an unavoidable problem here.

To capture really sharp images of fast action, individual pictures of the
event must be recorded at a comparable speed, and be of sufficiently brief
duration (short exposure). A standard TV system shoots at 30 (25)
pictures or frames a second, and this rate is not sufficiently rapid or brief

Fig. 14.2 Magnetic video disc
The magnetic video disc continuously records a mute 30 (36) second segment of the program video, progressively erasing and re-recording over the earliest material. The disc can be started/stopped instantaneously. Having captured the required piece of action (e.g. a high-jump), you have instant replay on cue at normal speed, slow, fast, vari-speed, reverse, freeze-frame.
The equipment contains one or two discs (16 in/0.46 m diameter) rotating at 60 rev/second (locked to vertical sync reference). The record/replay heads on either face, alternatively move inwards (later retracing outwards) in steps, to form 450 concentric video tracks total. Each track contains one video field. Increasingly replaced by multi-speed helical VTRs with a *slow-motion controller.*

to capture fast movements. A movie camera shooting at 24 fps has a similar problem (although its shutter opening may be reduced, light permitting, to reduce exposure and improve the sharpness to some extent). Reproduced at normal or fast rates, the eye does not usually notice this unsharp motion: but if we look at individual frames, we will see that faster movements appear quite blurred, while a transient such as a bursting balloon may even fail to register at all!

If a *film camera* shoots at a faster frame rate than normal (e.g. 64 frames/second) it records more separate versions of any movement (64 instead of 24), and correspondingly clearer images. But for really sharp individual frames of fast-moving subjects (humming birds' wings, bullets in flight), film cameras designed to shoot at e.g. 64–100 fps, up to 10 000, even 8 million fps are used. Special videorecording equipment can achieve up to 2000 fps.

Where a video camera using CCD sensors is fitted with an electronic *shutter* this effectively reduces the exposure time and allows you to capture faster movement. However, at the same time this reduces exposure, so that you need to open up the lens aperture to compensate – which reduces the depth of field. At briefer shutter speeds you may find that movements appear jerky and less realistic, and some disconcerting stroboscopic effects can develop.

Further applications

Video disc and tape can also provide:

1. *Still store* – A recording of a series of individual stills, which can then be selected in sequence, or at random (see Glossary: *Electronic still store*).
2. *Time-lapse effects* – Events are shot at a slow regular rate (e.g. 1 frame per hour), and replayed at normal speed to give a speeded-up presentation. Used to demonstrate traffic flow, plant growth, cloud formation.
3. *Time-controlled freeze frame* – A system in which a still frame is held for a selected duration during action replay.
4. *Animated graphics* – Creating animation of graphics by stop–start (stop–motion) recording; i.e. readjusting graphics between a series of very brief shots. Replaying the complete sequence at normal speed produces animation.

Videotape editing

As we saw in Chapter 8, there are a number of reasons why we need to edit a videotape recording:

● To correct or improve performance or treatment (e.g. to cut in retakes).

- To join together a series of separately recorded takes or sequences.
- To extend or reduce the program length (e.g. by introducing cutaway shots).
- To create a continuous, smooth-flowing presentation (e.g. introducing suitable transitions, improving visual continuity).
- To cut in material shot at a different time (e.g. library shots).
- To create a compilation from a series of productions.
- To create or enhance the viewer's emotional responses to the action (e.g. by fast cutting).

Methods of editing

You can edit a program in three ways: *in camera* as you shoot the action; by switching the VTR *during replay*; or by computer-controlled *copying* (*dubbing*).

Manual editing in camera

This technique is widely used with lightweight portable cameras. The VCR, which is connected to the camera by a short cable, can be controlled with a switch on the camera grip. Having recorded a shot, you operate the pause switch, arrange the next shot, and release it to continue recording. The result is a noiseless cut at that point.

On replay, you have (with luck!) a complete, continuous, edited program. But if you have misjudged, you will have some shots that run on too long, and others with clipped starts. The main drawback here is that you have provided little opportunity for any later editing corrections. This method of editing is inexact; but it may not matter if the edit points are not critical.

Its main advantage, perhaps, is that, unlike other methods, it produces *first-generation* recordings, so quality is optimum.

Manual editing during replay

In this arrangement you play a tape on one VTR, copying selected parts of it onto another. This is done empirically by watching the tape as it runs and making the editing switch 'on the fly' at the right moment.

- The MASTER VTR has the program tape to which the new scenes will be added.
- The SOURCE VTR has the videotape that includes the new scenes.

On a ½ in helical VHS VCR this simple editing approach is quite straightforward:

- Connect the SOURCE VCR to a suitable video input on the MASTER VCR recorder.
- Play the program tape on the MASTER VCR up to the edit point, and *PAUSE* the tape. (The tape stops moving, but the head-drum continues to turn.) You see a freeze frame.

- While still in 'PAUSE', you switch the MASTER VTR to the *RECORD* mode. You now see the source VTR's output.
- Next, you run the SOURCE machine, watching the new scenes, until you see the moment you want the copying to start. At the edit point you immediately release the 'pause' button on the MASTER VTR and the dubbing begins.
- On replaying the MASTER VCR, the picture on the original program tape should show a clean cut to the new shot.

Suppose that, instead of this maneuver, you simply play the MASTER program tape up to the edit point then stop. You run the SOURCE machine, and at the right moment you begin recording on the MASTER machine. What happens?

The probability is that when you press the *RECORD* button to begin recording, the MASTER VCR will automatically backspace for a few seconds, run forward, and, when up to speed, begin recording. If this happens you will lose the last few seconds of the previous program shot, interruption of the control track pulses will cause picture disturbance, and you will probably be slow cuing into the new shot. So be warned.

Using ¾ in U-matic machines you replay the program tape on a suitable *EDITING VTR*. When the tape is up to speed and stable (locked up) you switch it from 'PLAY' to 'RECORD' mode at the point where the new material is to begin, using the *Edit* or *Mode-change* button. Results can be excellent, but again, the editing point is approximate. (If you use this method with a non-edit U-matic there will be severe picture break-up at the edit point.)

Computer controlled copying

This is the regular method of editing videotape today. As in the second method, you replay tapes on one or more VTRs, while re-recording on another, to form a new compilation *Edited Master tape*. But this time, as you will see, operations are computer-controlled with precision.

The videotape editor

Comparison with film editing

Broadly speaking, a *film editor* runs through a *cutting copy* of his material on an editing machine, snips out wanted shots, and hangs them separately on nails over a bin (trim barrel). He then selects and joins these lengths of film, and reviews them. The separate soundtrack is compiled and matched up to the edited pictures later.

The *videotape editor* cannot cut the tape at all. Physical editing is impracticable with helical-scan systems. Apart from ruining the tiny video heads, any cut will interrupt several tracks, and at best produce a crude vertical picture 'wipe' at the join. Also the physical displacement of the audio and video tracks prevents their being cut simultaneously.

Instead, the VT editor has to *copy* (*dub-off*) each wanted segment onto a 'master tape' to build up the final program. Much or all of the program sound was recorded on an audio track on the original videotape, so may have to be dubbed off and handled separately.

The raw material

Videotape editors receive program tape in several different forms:

- A *continuous recording* in which most intershot transitions have already been made with a studio switcher. In this case the editor is mainly concerned with *corrective* work; removing faulty sections and inserting retakes, rearranging the sequence of scenes (e.g. from 'recording order' to 'program running order') adjusting the program running time, introducing detail shots that were recorded separately, making censor cuts, etc.
- A tape which has been recorded *discontinuously*. The scenes will probably have been shot out of sequence, the tape will include faulty takes, alternative versions, unwanted material, intermixed with the required takes.
- Several tapes recorded simultaneously on *dedicated VTRs*. Each has the output of a single camera. The required shots from that camera's tape have to be selected and joined to those from the other cameras shooting the same action.

Electronic splicing

We now come to some technical niceties that may appear only to concern the technician. In fact, there are real practical advantages in your knowing the differences between the two main editing processes.

When you record on a helical VTR a series of special pulses are generated and continuously recorded on the *control track*. These stabilize the motor system and ensure constant speed replay. If these pulses are interrupted for any reason, picture stability will be affected at that point.

When you are dubbing material onto a master tape you can use either the *assemble* or the *insert* mode.

- The *assemble* (or *assembly*) *mode*. This does the obvious thing, and adds the new picture sequence onto the end of the previously recorded shots. Using this method, the VTR records new video, audio, *and new reference pulses on the control track*.

  But there is a problem here! When you use the *assemble* dubbing mode these control pulses begin afresh *every time* you start to record. That's fine when making a fresh recording, but if you are adding another sequence to an existing tape there will be an interruption, however slight, in these all-important pulses. Consequently, on reproducing the master tape there could be a frame-roll or line tearing at each edit point!

Fig. 14.3 part 1 Electronic editing – assemble mode

Program is built up either (1) a scene at a time or (2) shot continuously, retaking any faulty scene immediately from its opening point. Assembly involves switching from replay (of Scene 1) to *record mode* at a chosen cue point (manually or automatically). As assemble mode automatically lays down a fresh control-track for each take, sync pulses change at joins, thus disturbing replay.

Fig. 14.3 part 2 Electronic editing – insert mode

If new material is to be inserted precisely between existing wanted shots, the 'in' and 'out' points must coincide with original, unwanted scene to avoid wiping wanted program. The original control track is not erased during the insert process, so no sync disturbances occur at the electronic splice.

Fig. 14.3 part 3 A/B dubbing

Here duplicate copies of the program are used on VTRs A and B to permit quicker search for sections, than by shuttling a single tape to and fro for selection. A simple production switcher can be used to cut/mix/super during transfer to VTR-C.

Fig. 14.3 part 4 Roll back and mix

Problem: Scene 1 has been recorded. You now wish to *mix* from Scene 1 to Scene 2 live in studio. Two VTRs available.
Solution: Roll back Scene 1 on VTR 'A' to convenient cutting point before mix. Recording on VTR 'B', replay VTR 'A' tape, mixing to studio when required. VTR 'B' tape now incorporates mix. Result can be inserted within original VTR 'A' tape at the earlier butt-join.

● The *insert editing mode* records in a different way. In this case the VTR only replaces the video and audio, but leaves the *original* references on the master tape's control track. So the control track is uninterrupted, and on replay there is no break-up at each edit point!

The original purpose of the *insert mode* was to allow the user to slot new pictures within an existing recording; to record the new scene in place of the old faulty section. It does that well – provided you position your insert *very accurately*! (Otherwise you will be left with a bit of the faulty scene, or clip an adjoining shot!)

To overcome this dilemma of an interrupted control track it is a common practice to use a little trick. You take the clean master tape before the session and record on it a *continuous control track throughout* – with a picture black and no sound (*assemble mode*). Then all editing is done using the *insert mode* (irrespective of whether you are actually going to add or insert pictures). The result is that you have a completely uninterrupted control track and optimum sync stability.

The disadvantage of this technique is that if you have an hour-long recording session ahead it takes an hour to prepare the tape's control track! So it is usual practice for VTR channels to stockpile a supply of prepared 'crystal-black' tapes for when they are required.

Postproduction editing

Let us turn now from the basic mechanics of editing to the realities of an editing session. The tapes invariably contain both wanted and unwanted shots, which can be in any order. They may be on several reels or cassettes. You now have to find the required material and dub it off onto the new master tape, in the right order, with the appropriate sorts of transitions between the shots.

Editing equipment provides straight cuts between shots. For mixes, wipes, supers you need to use a production switcher; while for more elaborate effects digital video effects (DVE) equipment of some kind is necessary.

Time code

(See Glossary: *Time code.*) If you are cutting together pictures of general action which have uncritical 'heads and tails' you may need no more than a general description, or a shot number, to identify sequences. But where a production is at all complex, or editing is to be precise, a more specific technique is necessary that allows you to identify *individual frames* in the recording. (In film making this is done by 'edge numbers' printed on the master negative.)

For precise identification, a *time code* system was introduced (*time address code, digital frame address system*). This is basically a continuous 24-hour digital clock showing the instant at which each moment of the videotape was recorded. This information is recorded on the tape's *cue track* or on a secondary audio track, in the form of binary pulses. A digital code provides four sets of figures: hours, minutes, seconds, frames (0–29 SMPTE, 0–24 EBU) plus 32 *user bits* of extra information. Although recordings made on different *days* will normally have similar coding, the time code allows you to identify any sequence at a glance, right down to the individual frame.

Normally this time code is laid down while recording. This is a particularly useful technique for you can look at a digital clock at any time

Hours Mins Secs Frames

Fig. 14.4 Time address code
Monitor display shows the precise
time at which the recording was made
– hours, mins, seconds, frames – to
facilitate identification, cuing and
editing. (For special applications such
as time-lapse recording – day, month,
year may be indicated.) Time-code
may be seen *burned in* to the picture
as above, or as a separate display.
Many studios time-code to actual
clock time, so that any notes made
during production can be coded
simply by glancing at an accurate
clock nearby. Some organizations use
zero start (*lapsed time*) coding, i.e.
zero time at the beginning of each reel
or session; using the hour digit
position to denote the reel No.

(or the time code readout displayed on a nearby monitor) and log when
something happened, how long it took, the available or elapsed time.
With this knowledge you can say 'We'll use the retake recorded at
15.25.30 not the one at 15.20.10' in anticipation of later editing.

If you are unable to include the real-time code while recording (e.g.
when on location) you can record code on the tape later to serve as
identification markers; although it will not, of course, be related to clock
times of the original taping session.

Some organizations do not use the time code in real-time but prefer
zero start (*lapsed time*) coding. They set the clock to zero at the beginning
of each reel or session and use the 'hour' digit position to denote the reel
number.

On-line editing

One approach to the editing session begins with carefully prepared
notes made when recording the program. These could, for example,
include a marked-up script and a *take sheet* showing the Reel No.; Scene
No.; Shot No.; brief shot descriptions; possible 'in-and-out points',
durations, etc.

You look through the recorded tape(s), choose the shots you want, then
dub each in sequence onto the master tape. However, for anything other
than the simplest situations this *on-line* editing approach usually proves to
be a time-consuming business.

Off-line editing

In a large organization *on-line* editing can tie up costly facilities and
personnel for considerable periods. So a far more effective method is now
universally used, called *off-line editing*. Here you make an *identical* copy of
the program tape(s) on a small-format VCR during the studio taping or
by transfer afterwards. This *copy-tape/workprint* has the program's
time-code/address code *burned in*, i.e. visible in picture (Figure 14.4), that
identifies every frame of the recorded material.

Referring to a *take sheet* or a detailed script made during the production, you can play this copy tape 'at leisure', running at normal or
slow speeds, freezing frames, to list the editing treatment you require –
the exact edit points, transitions, etc. Later, at an editing session, your list
of time-coded edit points will guide the VT editor, who uses it to develop
an *edit decision list*.

In certain circumstances, particularly when shooting on location, there
are advantages in checking through the copy tape at the end of each day
(*rough editing*) to judge whether any retakes or extra shots are needed to
improve final editing.

Fig. 14.5 part 1 Video tape leaders SMPTE standard
A video equivalent of the film leader, providing program identification details, technical alignment, and synchronizing information. The diagram shows the time sequence.

Fig. 14.5 part 2 Video tape leaders – typical British practice
Color bars and tone are recorded in prerecording line-up period. One-minute clock with seconds sweep-hand provides visual countdown. Retakes are identified by taped FM announcement (e.g. Retaking Shots 20–34, Take 3).

Fig. 14.5 part 3 The 'slate' and 'VTR clock'
An identifying *slate* or *board* is held in front of a camera during videotaping (after color bars and tone), to identify each take or scene, and provide information to assist editing. Erasable details may be added using chalk, china pencil (wax pencil) or dry marker. Some slates include a battery-powered stop clock. (TV slates are not fitted with clappers.)

Alternatively, an electronic 'slate' is often introduced at the start of a videotape recording. This also serves as a timed 'leader' and assists *preroll cuing* where the VTR requires several seconds to reach full speed on playback (e.g. 5 or 10 seconds). Many VTRs are now cued and run up from a freeze frame. Additional information may be included from a character generator.

Editing problems

How complex the editing process becomes is influenced, of course, by the number of takes involved, their lengths, their order, how many NG (no good) takes there are, etc. But much depends, too, on systematic note-taking while shooting, and on the editing facilities available.

Even routine postproduction editing is very time consuming. A typical finished half-hour program can involve some 150 to 200 cuts. You may find that you can make around six to ten straight cut edits an hour; but combined-shot video effects can slow you to only one to four. Even to run straight through a 1-hour tape on a ¾ in VTR can take about 12 minutes, so shuttling/searching for shots (especially with tape changing) and arranging the edit points can be quite a lengthy process.

Both in audio and video recording, the original tape made of a 'live' event is known as the *first-generation* take. If we dub that tape, the copy – which is the *second generation* – is inevitably somewhat inferior to the original recording (in an analog system). There will be imperfections, such as greater background noise, a loss of definition, distortions of various kinds. Hopefully, they are not obvious. But if we go on to make a copy of that copy (*third generation*) – for distribution perhaps – quality will be further degraded. Consequently, it is as well to keep such dubbing to a minimum; not going beyond the third generation if possible.

Unfortunately, there are times, particularly when creating special chroma-key effects, when one cannot avoid doing so, and has to accept any deterioration, for the sake of the effect.

One of the appeals of *digital videorecording* is that there is negligible deterioration of this kind at each dubbing, and copies of up to the twentieth generation may still prove satisfactory! But in the meantime most systems are analog, and care is needed.

Quality losses on *dubbing down* from larger tape formats (e.g. 1 in) to smaller ones (½ in) are less severe than when *dubbing up*, or when dubbing between *color-under* helical systems. You will find similar degradation when copying film (*duping*; e.g. library shots for program inserts). These copies of copies show increased graininess, color errors, and loss of definition that cannot be remedied.

The edit controller

Here, we come to the heart of the VT editing process – the *edit controller*, which provides a computerized control center for the entire system. It remotely controls the *RECORDING (Master)* VTR and the *SOURCE* VTRs. This control process involves not only switching them on and off at the right moment but allowing for the exact time they take to run up to speed (*run-up time*), stabilize, and synchronize. Having done this, the controller then makes the edit at precisely the right instant; copying the exact section you have chosen on the *SOURCE* VTR tape onto the correct section of the *MASTER* tape.

The edit controller does all this 'housekeeping' automatically, to your prearranged instructions! It counts off the tape's recorded control-track pulses (and/or time code) relative to your chosen edit point, and times operations accordingly.

Two monitors are used with the edit controller; a line monitor showing the input and replay of the *MASTER VTR* and a preview monitor showing the *SOURCE* picture.

Using the edit controller

Single-source editing

Let us look first at a *single-source editing system* using just two machines: the *MASTER* VTR to record, and the *SOURCE* VTR providing the shots to be edited in. If all the required program material is not on one cassette you will need to change the *SOURCE* cassette from time to time. You can, if necessary, introduce titling or graphics from supplementary sources (character generator, slide scanner) via a small switcher unit.

Designs vary, but typically you enter on a keypad the *time code number* or the *control track pulse count* – depending on which method you are using. The simpler process of counting pulses can be quite accurate, but it has the disadvantage that, unlike the precise time code method, the edit point can become displaced or lost during operations.

The keypad entry directs the system to a specific place on the tape. You can then use the handwheel/joystick to *shuttle* the tape forwards/ backwards at vari-speeds and examine the program material. *Jogging* will advance the tape frame by frame, and *freeze frame* allows you to stop temporarily to check an individual frame for precision editing.

Imagine that the shot on the *MASTER* tape shows someone opening the door of a safe (as in Figure 8.6). We see them walk up and reach forward to grasp the dial. Having roughly selected this *outpoint*, you can *frame trim* (i.e. add or cut frames to get exactly the right moment for a cut). You then cue in the indicated time code or pulse count. The new shot to be added after the one on the master tape shows a close-up of the hand about to turn the dial. Following the same search process as before, you run the *SOURCE VTR* tape and select the frame for the editing *inpoint* on the replay tape and enter that indicator reading.

You can then instruct the controller to *simulate* the edit without performing the actual dub-off. It will automatically back the master tape to its 'pre-roll' position, stop, roll, then switch the preview picture over to the *SOURCE* tape at the edit point. If you have second thoughts, the point is adjustable. If you accept this review, it will then repeat operations, and, making a real edit, go on to copy the *SOURCE* shot.

Multi-source editing

The most sophisticated computer-assisted edit controllers enable you to use two or more *SOURCE VTRs* from which to select material (usually identified as A, B, C). Even where scenes were shot out of order on different tapes, *multi-source editing* allows you to rapidly excerpt and copy them in sequence. And, of course, less time is lost in running tape to selected points, for while one sequence is being copied, another machine can spool to the next sequence.

This system allows you to choose edit points anywhere in the tape, and then, using a *list management* facility, to arrange these filed edits in a logical sequence. Your editing decisions entered at the keyboard can be displayed as an *edit-decision list* (*EDL*) either on a monitor screen or as a hardcopy printout sheet. This provides you with both a current guide and a record of how you have used the available material. You can remove all irrelevant or cancelled data with a *list-cleaning* program.

Advanced systems will check when you have accepted the workprint version of the editing and automatically create a *final edited master tape* to match (see Glossary: *Automatic assembly*).

You can edit the picture and its accompanying sound separately (*split edits*) using *layover/layback* techniques – i.e. dubbing off the soundtrack, treating it, then re-recording it on the VT soundtrack in place of the original audio. Audio mixing between soundtracks on the same tape may be possible.

At faster or slower speeds the sound can still be sufficiently identifiable for you to select sections. If the system is fitted with an audio *time compressor/expander unit* this will allow you to hear normal speech even when running tape above or below standard speed.

The system can be interfaced with:

● A production switcher – to make mixes, wipes, etc.
● Audio recorders – e.g. to add pre-recorded commentary on cue.
● Inserting photo stills from an electronic still store.
● Introducing video effects.
● Switching a character generator.

The entire dubbing process can be automated to follow prescribed editing instructions and produce a continuous, correctly assembled master tape.

A/B editing

In this dubbing system the program material to be copied is arranged on two or more separate *SOURCE* VTRs. The main benefit of doing this is to allow more rapid interselection of shots on the tapes, and to enable pictures to be combined for effects. There are several variations.

1. Two *SOURCE VTRs with identical copies of the program.*
2. One *SOURCE VTR* contains the main program, while tape on a second *SOURCE VTR has shots to be inserted into (or replace) those within the main program.*
3. Each *SOURCE VTR* has a collection of shots that are to be intercut or combined.

1. The first technique is used when e.g. excerpting shots from long-duration events, such as sports meetings, speeches, processions, where you have recorded the entire action yet only want to use highlights. While shots on reel A are being copied an identical copy on reel B runs on to the next high point. At an appropriate point you switch to reel B, and fast-run A on to the next excerpt. Using this principle you can even excerpt from tapes on-air! At a large sports meeting, for example, where several events are taking place concurrently, one VTR records continuously and two others record and replay highlights, which can be used to recap earlier action or show slow-motion replays. This may be combined with shots from dedicated VTRs, shooting other events.

2. The second technique is to have a main program (usually a talk or demonstration) on *SOURCE* VTR A, while on *SOURCE* VTR B a series of shots have been assembled, to be used as cut-ins, cutaways, illustrative inserts, etc. The audio from reel A is used throughout, while pictures from reel B are introduced at appropriate points.

3. If the shots to be copied are all on the *same* reel or cassette, the *SOURCE* VTR has to continually spool to and fro to find the selected sections. This can waste a lot of time; particularly if you are building up a rapidly intercut sequence, using shots near the start and end of the tape! When the shots are distributed within two or more replay tapes the whole process is speeded up; *and* you can now combine shots in supers, split screens, etc. This method is helpful where scenes are shot out of order on different spools/cassettes.

Editing ethics

Editing is a powerful tool. And we must not forget that the way a sequence is edited can strongly influence an audience's interpretations of what is happening. Editing can manipulate – sometimes unwittingly – and, particularly in factual programs (newscasts, documentaries), one needs to be aware of the underlying ethics of certain treatment. In the same way that unjustified canned laughter can be added to a poor comedy show, a sequence of pictures can be selective, and mislead an audience:

- One could deliberately avoid showing significant reactions – e.g. cutting out enthusiastic applause, or heckling during a speech.
- Omitting important action or dialog – e.g. a person rises, turns to another, bows reverently, and slowly leaves the room. This could be edited so that we see them rise, open the door and exit – apparently departing abruptly and unceremoniously . . . giving a very different impression of events.
- Introduce misleading or ambiguous action – e.g. during a speech, intercutting shots of people leaving or of a person in the audience yawning or sleeping.
- Introducing false material – e.g. showing enthusiastic applause . . . associated with a speech *different* from the one we have been watching.

Library shots taken from old newscasts may imply that action is occurring currently. (Such material should be subtitled as a 'library shot' and dated.) Particularly where the camera shows extreme behaviour or enthusiasm, one has to consider whether this is representative or just a small group playing to the camera.

Broadcast VTRs

The U-Matic standard

The *BVU* (high-band U-Matic) format provides a portable, robust, and relatively economical videotape recorder. Although developed from

Table 14.3   Anticipating editing
However good the pictures are, if they have been shot inappropriately they will not allow effective editing. Here are typical points to watch when shooting.

- Include *cover* shots of action wherever possible, to show the general view of the action.
- Always leave several seconds of *run-in* and *run-out* at the start and finish of each shot. Do not start taping just as the action is beginning or the reporter is about to speak; nor stop immediately action/speech finishes. Spare footage at the beginning and end of each shot will allow more flexible editing.
- Include potential *cutaway* shots that can be introduced when any sequence is to be shortened or lengthened; e.g. crowd shots, general views, passers-by.
- Avoid *reverse shots* (direction reversal). If it is unavoidable (e.g. when crossing the road to shoot a procession from either side), include head-on shots of the same action.
- Keep 'cute shots' to a minimum, unless they can really be integrated into the program. These include such items as reflections, sunbathers, silhouettes against the sunset, animals or children at play, footsteps in the sand . . .
- Try to anticipate continuity. If there are only a few shots taken in daylight, and others at night, it may not be practical to edit them together to provide a continuous sequence.
- Where there is going to be narration behind the pictures allow for this in the length and pace of takes; e.g. avoid inappropriately 'choppy editing' due to shots being too brief. (Editors sometimes have to slow-motion or still-frame a very brief shot to make it usable!)
- Aim to include longer shots and closer shots of action, to provide editing opportunities. For example, where the action shows people crossing a river bridge a variety of viewpoints can make a mundane subject visually interesting: e.g. *LS* – walking away from camera towards bridge; *MS* – walking on the bridge, looking over; *VLS* – shooting up at the bridge from the river below; *LS* – walking from the bridge to the camera on the far side; etc.
- Try to avoid sequences that are straight into the sun in one shot and against it the next. They do not intercut well.
- Remember that environmental noises can provide valuable bridging sound between shots when editing. They can be audio-taped separately as wild track (non-sync sound).
- Where possible, include features in shots that will help the audience to identify the particular location or terrain (landmarks, street names). Too often, the walls and bushes behind closer shots could be *anywhere*.
- Keep an accurate camera log giving relevant shot details that could help the editor (time, place, identify action, indicate if a take is faulty, etc.).
- Wherever possible, use an identifying *board* or *slate* at the start of each shot. Failing that, announce the shot number so that the soundtrack carries identification. If an 'intro-ident' is missed, put one at the end of a take (showing the board upside down).
- If there are pronounced background sounds during a take, in some circumstances they can be cut out (overlaid) during editing and replaced by neutral sounds (e.g. 'atmos' wild track).
   But this is not always possible. Suppose you have just shot a single-camera interview in quiet surroundings. Finally, you shoot the reporter's 'questions to camera', but now there is high background noise. When the shots of the guest and the reporter are edited together the noise will mysteriously cut and reappear during the sequence.
- Most one-camera interviews shot while speakers walk around, are taken in three sections: as (a) long-shots, (b) closer shots of the people speaking, (c) 'reaction shots/nod shots'. Make sure that mouths cannot be seen moving in (a) and (c). Check that the continuity of the action and positions in each version is reasonably similar.
- For the standuppers, check what is happening in the background behind the reporter. If the piece to camera is shot in several takes the background subjects could change noticeably between takes!

Fig. 14.6 U-Matic tracks
The ¾ inch tape has a *control track* at its top edge. Two *audio tracks* (*1 & 2*) run along the lower edge. Parallel with them is a *time code track* (*address track*).

the original low-band industrial grade U-Matic, its upgraded extended form is not compatible with it. Standard U-Matic ¾ in tape cassettes (1½ hours' duration) fit both older and later versions, but smaller cassettes are used in portable equipment.

There are several versions of the BVU format, including systems incorporating dynamic tracking, time code, etc. Larger machines are intended for use at base as play-off or editing facilities.

Of course, all systems have their associated limitations. The U-Matic format (like domestic VTRs) uses a *color-under* recording process (see Glossary), and picture quality can deteriorate noticeably if a sequence is copied and this dubbing re-recorded in the course of editing (multi-dubs).

When used in a precision broadcast chain (e.g. for ENG), a *time-base corrector* (TBC) must be used to stabilize replay. Because the resulting video signal is non-phased (out of phase), it cannot be mixed with other video (although individual monitors may cope with the irregular sync signals).

The equipment needs careful handling if you are recording while moving, as severe speed variations (gyro errors) can arise (e.g. a 30-lines error); although this can usually be compensated for by digital time-base corrector circuits.

This type of recorder is rather slow in running up to full speed from switch-on; a situation which could result in your losing a shot of unanticipated action during ENG. So a 'stand-by mode' is provided, in which the head-drum rotates at half-speed while the tape waits wrapped round it, ready to be cued.

Broadcast one-inch helical systems

Two high-grade broadcast standards have become established for 1-in helical-scan recording: the SMPTE *Type C* (*non-segmented*) and the SMPTE *Type B* (*segmented*) forms.

SMPTE Type C standard (non-segmented)

As each video track contains one complete *field* it is possible to stop tape travel and rotate the head-drum to continually reread the same track. The *still frame* this provides can be held for a while (tape wear develops). By adjusting the tape motion, you can reproduce a succession of complete pictures at various speeds; slow motion, fast motion, time-lapse (ultra-fast motion), and inching/jogging (frame-by-frame). Such facilities are invaluable for fast searching, selecting individual frames, analysis, etc., particularly when editing sequences. This format also permits continuous replay during recording (confidence playback), actually enabling you to monitor results *off tape* while recording. (Other methods only monitor the video signal within the equipment, but do not show whether it was successfully recorded.)

However, this system does not normally record all the picture information or data transmitted during the vertical blanking period.

SMPTE Type B standard (segmented)

Because this system records e.g. 52 picture lines on each track, it needs to read five (six) tracks to reproduce one field. So it is not possible to obtain a still frame simply by repeat-reading a single track. Instead, an electronic frame store/field store is necessary, to build up five tracks' worth of video (i.e. one field), which can be continuously read out from store. This can be done at a range of speeds, from slow-motion up to, say, 12 times normal speed; to facilitate rapid picture selection during editing.

Table 14.4   Videotape – before recording

Precautions	Regular equipment maintenance checks anticipate trouble before it happens.
	Always ensure that the tape heads, tape path (transport), and head-drum are clean (using suitable solvents), free from tape-dust clog, and regularly demagnetized (degaussed). After use, clean and cover equipment.
Tape care	Avoid touching the tape surface (skin oils). Also avoid smoking, dust, crumbs, etc. near the VTR as these all cause drop-out. Do not hand-stop tape, because it causes stretching.
	Cut off damaged leader on open-reel tapes, to avoid head damage.
	Check tape for uneven or loose winding (cinching, edge damage).
	Store tape upright in boxes and away from extreme heat, cold, dryness, humidity, magnetic fields.
	Allow tape and equipment to normalize after transit (e.g. from warm interior to cold exterior) to avoid condensation friction problems.
Pre-recording	Check audio and video levels are within limits. Check tracking and tension adjustments.
	Record and reproduce a test sequence at the start of tape (black level, audio tone, tonal step-wedge or sawtooth, and color bars) for alignment on replay.

Table 14.5 Videotape fault-tracing

No video	Check replay with a known good tape program. Check all units are switched on; correctly operated (facility switches and routing); connections OK. Check video input is OK. Is correct tape-type or system being used (compatibility)?
General noise	Adjust *tracking control* for maximum signal and minimum noise. Is head-tip penetration insufficient? Is head clogged? Is the record current/video level too low? Any head damage (chipped)? Adjust playback (replay) equalization for sharp undistorted pictures with minimum noise.
Noise band over top section of picture	If not corrected by tracking control, this may be due to an incompatible recording (misaligned tape path).
Horizontal noise bars across screen	Tracking control or control-track phasing incorrectly set. Capstan servo off lock.
Small black flashes on picture	Drop-out due to tape condition. Insufficient head-tip penetration. Ineffective drop-out compensator.
Close vertical bars (high frequency, RF pattern)	Incorrect adjustment of demodulator balance or limiter (interdependent effects).
Coarse beat-pattern across picture	Clogged erase head. Faulty tracking.
Picture flicker on playback	On a two headed machine, imbalance between head outputs.
Breakthrough of previous recording	Badly clogged or faulty erase head, or low erase oscillator output.
Rhythmical picture break-up	Faulty servo system (responsible for picture timing, speed, and synchronism). Other servo faults include noise or disturbance over a few horizontal lines (switching line fault), localized color loss, and inaccurate or noisy edit points. Audio speed variations (rapid flutter/slower wow).
Hooking (skew, flagging, broomsticking)	Vertical bending over at the top of the frame, in a random left/right motion. Adjust tape tension for minimum.
Edge scalloping	Regular horizontal displacement due to low-level video (undermodulation).
Audio playback low level (quiet, high background noise)	Tape recorded at low level. Clogged audio head. Bias too low.
Audio distortion	Damaged tape edge. Overrecorded (overmodulated). Poor head/ contact. Bias level wrong.
Buzz on audio	Video tracks are audible (poor erasure). Carrier frequency drift.
Wow or flutter	Dirty capstan or roller. Servo off-lock. Spool warped.
Tracking	On replay, video heads must exactly retrace the recorded tracks. Otherwise a horizontal band of video noise is seen across the picture. Use auto-tracking mode, or manual tracking control to correct.
Dropout	Small white or black segments appearing along picture lines, in place of picture information. Check tape (dirty, faulty surface). See Glossary.
Poor definition; smearing	Clogged record/replay heads.

15 Titling and graphics

First impressions are important! And the first impressions your audience has of your production come from the *opening titles*. They help to set the style and ambiance of the program, they inform, they guide. Well-designed graphics make a direct contribution to the success of any presentation. Poorly designed titles immediately discredit the production itself.

Titling and graphics today

In this chapter we are really concerned with two separate but frequently combined elements:

- *Titling*. The form and arrangement of lettering and numerals.
- *Graphics*. The diagrams, maps, charts, tables, decorative and pictorial illustrations.

At one time, even the simplest titles or graphics required the painstaking services of a skilled artist. Today various electronic devices are available that provide in a fraction of the time results that are far beyond human dexterity. Much of this equipment is costly for smaller studios, but even organizations working with a limited budget can make good use of low-cost models.

There are occasions where the traditional methods of creating graphics are more convenient or cheaper than sophisticated electronic equipment. It may, for instance, be a lot easier to base a graphic on a shot of an existing map than to draw a new one from scratch. Sometimes we combine the old and the new. Taking a library photograph or drawing of a subject, we can treat the picture electronically, to produce an entirely different image. We can combine and intermix a series of effects.

Good titling

The principles of effective titling are largely a matter of commonsense. Yet how often have you seen examples of overcrowded, barely readable credits on your TV screen?

Titling is there to *inform* your audience. They should be able to read it quickly, easily, and unambiguously. If they cannot, it has failed in its purpose. None of the lettering should be lost beyond the frame edge. This is particularly true of *subtitling*. How clearly lettering can be read will depend on its size, how elaborate it is, and the background against which it is seen. Readability will be affected, too, by the quality of the picture on the TV receiver, and how far away it is from the audience.

Fig. 15.1 Frame proportions
1. To fit the TV frame shape, graphics must have 4 by 3 proportions. The graph shows relative height-width proportions: e.g. if a card is 12 units wide, it should be 9 units high.
2. To avoid edge cut-off on the receiver screen, graphic information should be confined to the *safe title area*.

It is advisable to avoid lettering that is smaller than about 1/10 to 1/25 of the picture height. Fonts that look great on the printed page may not appear at all successful on the screen. Lettering should generally be bold and firm. Delicate, elaborate lettering with thin outlines or serifs is likely to break up, while closely patterned striping or cross-hatching is liable to strobe distractingly. If lettering is too condensed, with little space between its members, areas within it are likely to fill in, particularly if the lettering is electronically keyed into a picture, or given an electronic border.

Aim to keep titling information to a minimum, particularly if it is combined with detailed background. A screen full of 'printed information' can be daunting to most viewers, and tiring to read. People are easily discouraged from reading rapid titles. Leave information on the screen long enough to allow it to be read aloud twice, so that the slowest reader can assimilate it. If, for any reason, an announcer is to read out text that is clearly displayed, ensure that the reading is *accurate*!

Backgrounds to titles

Choosing a suitable *background* for your titling can be as important as the foreground lettering itself. Where you are using a scenic background, such as the closing shots of a drama, it may actually determine the style and weight of the lettering you can use.

Plain backgrounds can prove very effective, as they are unobtrusive and emphasize the lettering. But they can also be dull and uninteresting. Ornamental backgrounds, which include patterning, texture, abstract designs, may increase the graphic's visual appeal. But they can equally well look fussy and confused. Clearly, background selection requires careful choice.

Lettering against a multi-hue or multi-tone background is invariably harder to read. If you insert titles over location shots (e.g. a street scene) the eye may have some difficulty in discerning information, and may also be tempted to wander around the background instead.

In most cases, by using larger type in light tones (white or yellow) with strong borders (black edged), legibility is considerably improved. But even plain titling can be unclear in certain color relationships (red on green, or red on gray); or in monochrome when gray-scale of lettering and background are similar.

It is good working practice with all graphics work to consider what the result is going to look like in monochrome. Otherwise you are likely to find areas merging together – even disappearing within the surrounding tones!

As a general rule, avoid introducing lettering over backgrounds of similar tones or hues, or over printed matter (e.g. titles over a newspaper page). Obvious enough, but people do! Light lettering is usually more easily read than dark; and pastel or neutral backgrounds are preferable to saturated hues. Unless *superimposed* lettering has a black background (it then appears 'solid'), it is best keyed in (electronically inserted) from white-on-black title cards or slides; or in film, by *burn-through* using masking or controlled overexposure. Black lettering cannot be super-imposed on a white background.

Fig. 15.2 Methods of shooting graphics
1. Studio camera shoots graphic supported on easel or stand.
2. Caption projection unit; Slide is projected onto screen within box, via a mirror. Camera shooting via same mirror, sees and explores the picture.
3. Camera explores picture from rear-projected slides on translucent screen. Slides are usually transmitted using a multiplexed film-island projector (see Fig. 13.8) or a flying-spot scanner (see Fig. 13.10). Opaques may use similar systems.

If lettering on a title card proves to be too large, or needs to be offset, a larger black card placed behind it will enable the cameraman to take a longer shot or reframe without shooting off. Similarly, a chroma-key title card (usually white lettering on a blue card) can be extended with a large blue backing sheet.

Transparent plastic overlay sheets (cels) may be used for titling, which is then laid over background graphics. But there is always the danger of light reflections from the surface of the cel.

Although cameras can shoot titling on a foreground glass panel, depth of field is usually too restricted to obtain a sharply focused background scene at the same time. Instead, you would have to pull focus from the titling to 'dissolve' to the action.

Fig. 15.3 Title positions
Titling is normally localized for maximum impact, avoiding important subject areas (e.g. face).

Forms of lettering

Although lettering is usually taken for granted, nothing looks more amateurish than ill-proportioned, badly spaced, or poorly laid-out titles. Nowadays there are many short cuts to efficient titling:

■ *Dry-transfer (rub-on; instant transfer) sheets*   These offer a considerable range of rub-off lettering in many styles and fonts. (Some are unsuitable for television use.) Lettering and symbols can be appli   o various surfaces. Arrange the titling on a transparent acetate cell overlay, and it can be laid on a background graphic or photograph without damage. The position of the titling can be adjusted; even moved around in vision. And the same overlay can be re-used over different backgrounds.

■ *Hot-press lettering*   This system uses heated metal type to stamp through a pigment-faced plastic foil. It can provide black, white, or colored characters. Available styles are limited, and tend to become overfamiliar. This method has been used traditionally to prepare camera title cards and crawls (roller captions).

■ *Plastic letters*   Standard lettering can be stuck or clipped onto a background with double-sided adhesive tape, magnetic board, felt . . . There are many variations.

■ *Constructed lettering*   Arranged from toy bricks; formed in thumbtacks, toothpaste, rope; finger traced in sand or snow . . .

■ *Decorative effects*   Here lettering is seen as shadows, reflected, silhouetted, stencilled.

■ *Handwritten lettering*   However neat, handwritten titling tends to look crude, and is best avoided – even when lettering aids are used. It may be successful where results are meant to look inexpert; e.g. on walls, sidewalks, chalkboards, using chalk, crayon, aerosol paint.

■ *Photo-lettering*   In this system, titling is produced photographically by a machine fitted with a large disc, holding a single font (changeable). Letters are selected in turn, and printed onto a strip of photographic paper. Results are good but somewhat mechanical.

■ *Plastic labels*   This is the familiar technique in which the top surface of a two-layer plastic ribbon is punched out to reveal a white layer beneath. Available in several colors, the effect is mechanical.

■ *Computer-generated titling*   Personal computers can now generate a high standard of graphics and titling suitable for many applications. Both still titles and simply animated titling are quite practicable. You can make off-screen slides or, using appropriate synchronizers, feed the personal computer into the video chain.

■ *Character generators*   These small specialized computers are widely used to generate alphanumeric characters in a variety of styles and sizes. Lettering can be keyed directly onto the screen, or stored and electronically inserted on-cue.

Electronically inserted titling

Titling from any source can be either *superimposed* onto a background picture or *electronically inserted*. If titles are superimposed with the switcher (mixing the title and background source pictures together) there is, as with all superimposed images, an interaction between lettering and background tones and hues. Electronically inserted lettering appears to be 'punched solid' into the background shot. This can be done using *keying* or *non-additive mix* facilities.

The character generator

Character generators have become a regular graphics tool in TV production. In many studios where title cards and graphics are usually required for only a single TV program the character generator's rapidly produced low-cost display provides a valuable facility. Excellent quality titling and graphics can be achieved quite simply. The character generator is particularly useful where the information for the graphics is received only at the last minute, as in sports scores, contests, voting, news events, weather maps, etc.

Originally, the character generator simply generated alphanumeric characters (letters and numbers) for electronic insertion into TV pictures. But today, as in so many other areas, demarcations have become blurred, and some character generators have taken on part of the role of *graphics generators*, and *digital video effects (DVE)* equipment. Akin to a word processor, and using a standard typewriter/computer keyboard, the equipment is capable of producing a variety of lettering and basic designs (graphs, tables, charts) in a number of styles and sizes. It can generate such variants as Roman, Cyrillic, Japanese, Arabic with equal ease.

You can insert the character generator's output into a picture from any video source: a studio camera, slide store, VTR, film. So you can, for example, use a library slide of a logo, map, chart, etc. and introduce topical information to suit the current production.

Although you can display the titling as it is typed, it is usually preferable to store the information on floppy disk, or in computer memory (RAM – random access memory), or even on an audio tape cassette. The last is slow to file and access, but low cost. Once filed, you can recall a prepared *page* on cue, or keep it for later use.

Most character generators are used with a *preview channel monitor* on which to prepare the display, and a *line channel monitor* which shows the text being fed to the studio switcher for selection. Work usually begins by preparing the general formats of the pages you are going to need. For example, with a list of the names of the guests to be introduced as subtitles, you decide on the probable layout, fonts, background, decorative effects (e.g. borders), etc. These can be selected from a series of in-built choices; but in some equipment you can also design and store your own 'customized' treatments. (These can be derived from electronic graphic art, or from video stills.)

Using the planned layout, you select the elements in turn, and a movable *location cursor* helps position them anywhere on the screen. As with a word processor, you can correct or revise the information instantly, combining screens, selecting sections. There are facilities for autocentering, tabulation, size adjustment, and multi-page storage.

From then on, you may be able to do an almost endless number of things (see Table 19.5). As well as moving lettering around the screen, you can change its size, color, shape, texture, design. You can make it *roll* (vertical movement), *crawl* (sideways movement), *flash, animate, spin, flip, rotate, zoom, wipe, squash, tumble, fade, merge, zip* . . .

Using a *color synthesizer* you can selectively color the lettering and the background (these are normally black-on-white). Words or individual characters may be treated separately.

A *border generator* can introduce an outline or partial outline in black, white, or color around lettering to improve its legibility and impact. Borders are particularly effective when adding titling to multi-tone color picture backgrounds. There are several styles:

● All round the character, or along one edge.
● Along one side and the lower edges, to create a *dropped shadow* effect. This gives the characters a 'solid' look.
● The character is replaced with an electronically generated *outline* of itself.

Both the *color synthesizer* and the *border generator* facilities are also fitted to many production switchers to allow titling from *any* video source to be treated (e.g. camera title cards).

Fig. 15.4 Border generators
1. White solid lettering.
2. Black-edge border.
3. Drop shadow effect.
4. Outline.

Forms of graphics

Graphics in their various forms can make a valuable contribution to all types of TV program.

● *Statistical graphics in the form of bar graphs and charts* can show, in a moment, information that would be hidden in columns of figures. They enable you to simplify complex data, to compare, to show developments, to demonstrate relationships, etc.
● *Pictorial graphics* can be used to illustrate a children's story, to set the scene in a drama, to explain scientific principles, to provide an atmospheric background to titling, etc.

Graphic display

You can introduce graphics in several ways. The most obvious is to cut to a shot of a screen-filling graphic (e.g. a slide, or a title card). But, in many situations, it can be more attractive to have a graphic within a setting: on a display screen, as a desk chart, or a wall map, or a free-standing panel. Sometimes it may be best to keep a particular graphic out of shot or hidden until it is needed, to avoid it distracting the audience's attention.

You can even introduce titling or pictorial graphics as 'natural features' of a scene; a book title on a shelf, a wall poster, a street sign, a baggage label . . . even displayed on someone's sweatshirt.

You can show simple graphics on an in-shot picture monitor, but it is generally preferable to use a wall display screen (rear-projected, or electronically inserted), for the scale is more satisfactory. That method is particularly useful when you want to show a succession of graphics and VTR or film clips.

As in all aspects of presentation, there are vogues in the types of graphics used. It was once a familiar ploy for presenters to stand beside wall graphics adding and removing labels and symbols. Three-dimensional maps and graphs had their popularity. Many forms are left behind as others prove cheaper and easier to make.

Animated graphics

Animation can bring a graphic to life. Even the simplest movement, such as panning over it from one detail to another, zooming in/out on details, or intercutting between sections of it, can sustain interest in what would otherwise be a static display. Such techniques are an effective and economical way of illustrating children's stories, or a program that relies heavily on graphics or photographs (e.g. maps, photographs, paintings in historical sequences).

You can animate in a number of different ways. For instance, you can build up a graphic on-air by progressively adding details or sections (wipes, insets, supers). The most reliable method of animation is to videotape the sequence beforehand. You record a section, pause and add/remove/blank-out details, then continue recording, and so on. The result on replay is an animated graphic. This type of animation is best done by using overlay cels or attached sections, rather than by actually altering artwork, for if anything goes wrong it is far easier to reshoot the sequence!

Graphics have been enlivened with falling snow, swirling mist (obscuring one title, and clearing to reveal the next), falling rain, traveling light patterns . . . even by setting fire to them! Puppets have 'operated' them or pointed out information. Ingenuity knows no bounds!

Many mechanical animation devices that served well for decades, such as rotating boxes, drum titles, animated cards, have been superseded by electronic methods. But other 'old faithfuls' such as the *title card* have an ongoing value.

Table 15.1   Camera graphics

	Advantages	Disadvantages
Graphics on stand or easel	Simple method. Camera can zoom, select any section, adjust framing. The original artwork can be used (avoids extra copying stages). Graphics can easily be modified or updated.	Method ties up a studio camera. Graphics require an operator (opportunities for errors, wrong positioning, etc.). Graphics may shake during rapid; operation or changes. If graphics sizes vary, camera may have to refocus and reframe. Positioning may vary, causing glare, specular reflections, or revealing surface unevenness.
Front-projected graphics	Camera can zoom, select frame. Slides provide rapid, predictable changes.	Graphics must be prepared in a standard format (e.g. 35 mm slides). Spill light on screen may spoil image. Color quality variations are not easily compensated for. Apparatus usually requires an operator.
Rear-projected graphics	As above.	As above. Uneven illumination likely (central hot spot). Screen grain may be apparent in close shots.

Table 15.2   Graphics using special equipment

	Advantages	Disadvantages
Electronic still store (ESS)	No need to transport and sort slides. The equipment is very reliable. Stills can be selected instantaneously from a large library. Slides cannot become damaged through handling or use. You can 'browse-select' from available shots.	Any purpose-designed slides have to be shot and inserted into the general stills library for the occasion. Appropriate slides may not be available. Slides of the required subject may be overfamiliar from use in other programs It may not be possible to mix between slides.
Caption scanners	Designs vary considerably: slide transport by carousel or vertical drums; tray/box carriers, discs. Slide selection in sequential, random, or programmed order. Flexible color correction facilities included in equipment control. Can be remotely controlled.	Slides must be shot and mounted in proportions and framing required – position and size cannot normally be adjusted. Slides are not readily modified/corrected, and may acquire blemishes, dirt. Equipment reliability varies.
Rostrum camera	An adjustable overhead camera shooting horizontal artwork. Used to record a series of graphics (stills) on film or videotape; in order to simplify a rapid graphics sequence, to record a complex graphics presentation, or to animate a succession of shots. Sequence can be prerecorded, simplifying studio production.	Revision of individual segments requires editing or remake.

Table 15.3   Typical graphics sizes

Smallest size for convenient handling (smallest type size 24–36 pt)	30.5 × 23 cm (12 × 9 in)
Commonly used sizes shooting a 30.5 × 23 cm (12 × 9 in) area	43 × 35.6 cm (17 × 14 in) 40 × 30 cm (16 × 12 in)
Title cards – copy area 23.5 × 18 cm* (9.5 × 7 in)	35.6 × 28 cm (14 × 11 in)
Largest size for elaborate artwork	61 × 46 cm (24 × 18 in)
Thickness of support art board	2 mm (1/16 in) minimum

* Standard board is 71 × 36 cm (28 × 22 in).

Don't despise simple methods. Suppose you want to wipe in the letters of a program title, one by one. You could use a character generator, or a special effects generator, or a digital video effect . . . or you could simply place a sheet of black paper over a title card and move it to one side, to get the same effect!

Camera graphics

Title cards

The 'standard' *title card* is printed on a piece of thin plain black board, typically 35.6 × 28 cm (14 × 11 in). *Graphics* are mounted on a correspondingly larger sheet. The board is supported on an adjustable stand or an easel, and shot by the camera (Figure 15.5. and Table 15.1).

Title cards are used for show titles, performers' names, subtitles, and other credits. You can, of course, use many colors, tones, and textures for the lettering and background (although it is best to avoid white backgrounds). And for decorative titling, this is done. But many organizations regularly use title cards that are printed white on black.

These have the advantage that they are easily read, *superimpose* well on other shots, and the white lettering can easily be keyed into other pictures (*luminance keying*). In addition, you can *colorize* and *black-edge* (outline) lettering in the switcher. The background, too, can be colorized to suit.

It is good practice to use an acetate overlay showing the TV safe title area (Figure 15.1) when deciding on the layout of your title cards. Most titling is centered, but it is best to position lettering to suit its final purpose; i.e. slightly nearer the lower edge for subtitles, the upper edge for head titles. But leave sufficient space around for the cameraman to adjust framing to suit the shot. That, incidentally, is an advantage the title card has over a slide, which cannot be readjusted at the last minute to improve composition.

Try to avoid lettering smaller than about one-fifteenth of the card height, for it will probably appear too small on the screen and the camera will need to take a closer shot to improve proportions. This could emphasize any irregularities in the lettering.

Fig. 15.5 Graphics supports

1. *Caption stand* (tiltable shelf, adjustable height) suitable for title cards.
2. *Card-pulls* attached to edges make removal easier.
3. *Title card box* – Top card pulled out to reveal next title.
4. *Strap easel* used for larger graphics. Weighted webbing straps adjust to suit all sizes.
5. *Flat* displays various graphics of different sizes.

Aim to standardize your title card size. It makes them easier to handle, and the cameraman does not have to readjust framing to suit individual cards. Where you have a stack of title cards on a stand it is a good idea to attach numbered *card pulls* (*edge tags*), so that it is easier to remove cards quickly, to reveal the next beneath (Figure 15.5(2)).

Where you want to insert a multitone or colored title card into a picture the answer is to use a *chroma-key card* in which the lettering and decorations are against a background of chroma-key blue. If you use such a chroma-key card regularly (e.g. as opening titles over a live show, or an inserted logo) you can make it into a slide. This will avoid tying up a studio camera, which can be used for other shots.

Fig. 15.6 Symbols

Symbols enable information to be assimilated and compared rapidly. Several forms are available, having greater visual interest than a routine line-graph.
1. Multi-surface or strata graph.
2. Column graph.
3. Combined column graph.
4. Bar graph.
5. Sector, pie, or circle chart.
6. Volume chart, height chart, area chart.
7. Pictogram pictorial chart.
8. Pictorial symbols.
9. Flow chart.

Fig. 15.7 Shooting graphics
Only when shot straight-on, will the image of a flat plane be undistorted. Shooting off-axis produces *keystone* distortion, e.g. when the viewpoint is too high or shot from the side. In geometrical subjects (music, print, diagrams) the effect may be pronounced.

Normally, if you have a series of title cards you would need to use two (or more) cameras for the sequence. But, with a little ingenuity, you can show all the titles on one camera:

● Slide or lift the top card aside to reveal the next underneath (*pull titles*).
● Have the cards top-hinged on a ring binder or tape hinges (*flip-in/drop-in*), or bottom hinged (*flip-out/drop-out*).

The secret is to change cards smoothly without jerking them, and to take care that they do not become displaced.

The crawl (Figure 15.10)

Known variously as a *crawl, roller caption,* or *roller,* this one-camera alternative to a series of brief title cards has been around since the early days of television. Titling is hot-press or photo-printed onto a long strip of stiff black paper, which is moved continuously upwards or right–left across the shot. The *crawl title* enables a lot of printed information to be presented in an easily read form at any speed. The machine may be hand-operated or motor-driven at an adjustable rate to suit the production. Knowing, for instance, how long the end-of-show playout music lasts, the crawl can be timed so that the credits last for exactly that duration when cued in at the conclusion of the production.

The crawl can also be used in place of a series of separate graphics (e.g. to show a manufacturing process). And it is a much more controllable method than having a camera truck past long strip graphics (*pan cards*).

Fig. 15.8 Exploring graphics
A graphic can be 'animated' by exploring it with the camera, so creating continual visual change, e.g. from shot A, zoom out to include B, then to the full picture C, zooming in to select frame D, then E.

Unseen drawing

Seeing a drawing gradually form as we watch has a persuasive fascination. It is a useful method of introducing complex information piecemeal, or making a little material go a long way. However, its extended use can become tedious.

Fig. 15.9   Attached detail
Regular methods of attaching detail, labels, symbols, sections to graphics:
Flannelboard – Both the rear-strip behind shape and the background have surface of felt, baize, flannelette, PVC (plastograph).
Teazlegraph (Velcro) – Shape backed with small nylon multi-hook strip; background has multi-loop strip.
Adhesive strip – Double-sided adhesive tape behind shape; smooth background.
Magnetic – Magnetic plastic strip or small magnets, attached to steel-sheet background.

Methods of obtaining unseen writing include:

1. Rear writing in white paint on a clear glass sheet backed by black drapes. The performer is totally dressed in black.
2. Rear writing with a felt-pen on a paper sheet; the camera shooting the bleed-through on the reverse.
3. Drawing on a surface of chroma-key (CSO) hue (e.g. blue) for electronic insertion.
4. Writing on an overhead projector cel.
5. Special electronic 'remote-writing' equipment.

Electronic graphic art

Even modest personal computers can produce remarkably successful artwork today. Computer-aided design (CAD) is used to develop detailed drawings with ease. At this stage, the weakest feature of these low-cost systems is the unavoidable *aliasing* that causes diagonals and curves to appear jagged; although this can be overcome with greater computer

Table 15.4   Precautions with graphics design

Always work within 4 : 3 proportions.

Provide an adequate border for camera framing.

Use matt materials. Avoid spurious reflections from shiny or glossy lettering, paint, plastic tape, overlay sheets, pencil marks, etc.

Avoid buckling, wrinkles, and similar surface unevenness. Attach thin copy to heavy illustration board, which can be re-used.

A large graphic can look the same as a smaller one on the screen. But considerable side reduction will noticeably weaken thin lines; while magnification of small graphics coarsens detail.

Ensure that graphics are evenly lit, and shadows do not disrupt multi-plane captions.

Coarse tonal variations (for example, five spaced gray-scale steps between black and white) provide more dynamic reproduction than subtle half-tones.

Always consider how colored graphics will appear in monochrome.

Color impact in titling and graphics is important. A vibrant hue (red, yellow) may be arresting, forceful, giving emphasis, or disturbing, brash, tasteless, or aesthetically inappropriate.

Simplification of detail, clear symbolism, and unambiguous approaches have maximum effect.

Keep information detail to a minimum for rapid assimilation.

Choose simple structural forms for diagrams, particularly for comparative graphics.

Maps should contain only relevant main features, with good tonal and color contrasts; water areas (sea, lakes, rivers) being shown in darker tones. Name labels may be provided by a plastic overlay, superimposition, keyed in, or manually attached.

Comparative information on a single graph is preferable to a succession of graphics.

Table 15.5   Problems with graphics

Even quite simple graphics can reproduce badly on the TV screen if they are not prepared, shot, and lit carefully.

Graphic size	*If too small* Close-up details appear coarsened (e.g. texture looks crude, lines rough-edged). When close shooting with a narrow-angle lens, to get big enough detail, any camera movement is exaggerated.
	No room to pan around (explore or reframe) without shooting off. Camera may not be able to get large enough image due to limited minimum focused distance. Camera may shadow the graphic.
	If too large Camera may not be able to position far enough away to take in the entire graphic. If shot on a wide-angle lens, the graphic may appear distorted. Finer lines may be unclear or merge in a full shot.
Graphic shape	If a graphic is not roughly 4 by 3 horizontal format, it will not fit the TV screen shape. (See Figure 15.12).
Surface	*Tones too light* Light tones block off. Flare. Loss of detail/gradation in lightest tones and/or darkest tones.
	Tones too dark Picture usually lacks contrast. Lower tones merge. Muddy appearance.
	Black tones Various 'black' surfaces may have such different reflectances (shades, textures) that, when intermixed in a graphic e.g. black card, paint, ink, plastic tape), the picture cannot be set down to crush and unify black areas without degrading other picture tones.
	Texture Shiny surfaces appear either strongly saturated (bright color), or reflect light as unwanted white patches. Surface details and lettering become lost in the glare. (Tilting the graphic, or altering camera height slightly, may clear the reflection.)
	Distractions Graphics are easily defaced by surface wrinkles, finger marks, scrapes, scratches, lettering faults, adhesive, etc. that the casual glance overlooks but which stand out plainly on the screen.
Lighting	*Uneven lighting* Brighter towards the top, or to one side. (Lamp too steep, or far off the lens axis.)
	Central hot spot Lamp spotted; too close; filament image; lamp too close to lens axis.
	Multiplane shadows One surface can shadow another under it. (Centralize and soften the light; use Pepper's ghost device.)
	Camera shadows If lighting is at too shallow angle; or the camera is too close to graphic. (Use narrower lens angle.) Optimize lighting.
Camera angle	*Distortion* If camera is not straight-on to graphic (trapezium distortion); too high, off-center.
	Wide-angle lens distortion (barrel/pincushion distortion). Graphic not correctly positioned on its support.

Fig. 15.10 Crawl/roller-caption
This continuous strip display may be rolled up, or rolled horizontally. Varying the frame position of titling produces a *crawl title*. It may also be used as a traveling path display.

power. When we come to the outstanding 'photographic' quality of advanced computer graphics, the sky is the limit, as is demonstrated daily in television commercials!

You can use computer graphics (video art, graphics generators) systems in several ways:

● *Clean canvas*. Here, the artist works from a blank screen and builds up the final artwork.
● *Tracing*. Existing artwork or a photograph is laid on the graphics tablet and the required elements are traced over with the stylus. These tracings are used as the basis of the new design.
● *Grabbed frames*. A full-color or black and white picture from a video camera is *grabbed* and 'retouched'. The artist can add or reduce details, change textures, add or reduce shading, alter colors, combine picture segments, etc.

In most equipment the artist 'draws' with a pressure-sensitive electronic *stylus* (wire-connected to the equipment), on a special *graphics tablet*. The results of his movements appear on a color monitor screen.

The *menu* through which the artist instructs the system may be shown on the viewing monitor displaying the artwork or on a separate monitor. In other cases the 'palette' is arranged as a border around the tablet, to be selected at a touch of the stylus. So you have at your fingertips such features as:

● Various drawing 'instruments': pencil, brush, airbrush, spray; in variable thicknesses and densities.
● A wide variety of textures, tones, colors that can be added *specifically* (e.g. a brush using 'spotted paint') or to *fill areas* (e.g. a 'wash' of predrawn bricks).
● Automatically drawn lines and geometrical shapes.
● Color mixing and shading.
● Tonal changes such as posterization (a multi-toned image reproduced in coarse tonal steps).
● Insert lettering from selectable fonts (using an associated keyboard).

Fig. 15.11 Animation table
The mirror reflects operations on the glass-topped table. Sections can be moved, removed, added, animated (in vision or single-frame recorded). It can be used for unseen writing.

Glass Table-Top

Mirror

Fig. 15.12 Picture shape
1. Only a graphic in 4 by 3 proportions will fit the TV screen.
2. A tall narrow graphic can be shot as a whole, with black-sided borders.
3. Or it can be shot in selected sections.

- Erase, copy, paste-over (insert sections of other images).
- Invert, mirror (reflections), stretch, magnify, rotation.
- Icons (i.e. predrawn symbols and signs).

No list could ever suggest the visual opportunities opened up by computer graphics. One can simulate effects as diverse as charcoal drawings, pencil sketches, oil painting, cartoon cels, or engineering drawings. Each complete frame can be stored, and recalled in an instant. If you slightly alter features in a series of frames, and then play them in succession, you can create an *animated sequence*.

Although some equipment can *dump* screen images (using a hardcopy printer), to provide a paper printout for reference purposes, an off-screen photograph is usually more representative.

16 The background of production

As you would expect, organizations differ in their demarcations between various jobs. In some there are strictly observed distinctions, while in others, people gain by shared experience.

The director's job

The TV director's job can vary considerably within organizations, and the size and type of production. At one end of the scale there are those who initiate the program idea, write the script, even predesign the settings. They cast and rehearse the performers, guide the production team, and, having recorded the show, control the editing. Such all-round craftsmen are rare, but they exist.

At the other end of the scale, some rely heavily on specialists in the production team to provide them with workable staging treatments (settings, lighting, sound, camerawork). They themselves concentrate on directing talent, and on shot selection.

The director may have a *presentational* role. Here a number of separate program items (*stories*) are independently prepared by members of an editorial group (researchers/writers/editors). He or she visualizes production treatment that will coordinate these various contributions. We meet this situation in many magazine programs, newscasts, public affairs (current affairs) programs.

There is a place for all levels of expertise in the wide spectrum of television production. Like other craftsmen in the medium, directors become skilled in their particular field. Someone whose talent lies in drama production would probably lack the edge-of-seat intuition of a good sports director: an almost clairvoyant ability to anticipate action, and take off-the-cuff shot opportunities. On the other hand, someone specializing in sports would be lost in the world of drama. There the director, with painstaking shot-by-shot planning, guides performance and develops dramatic impact. Again, in presenting a symphony orchestra, one needs skills that are far removed from those involved in shooting a documentary on location.

For smaller productions the director may combine the functions of both director and producer. Having been allocated a working budget, he is responsible for the entire business and artistic arrangements: origination, interpretation, casting, staging, and treatment. He subsequently directs the studio operations and postproduction editing.

More often, a *producer* serves as the business head of a production. He is responsible for organization, finance, and policy, and may serve as artistic and business coordinator for several directors. As pro-

Executive producer
Producer
Assistant director   Associate director
Production assistant   Producer's assistant   Production manager
Floor manager/stage manager   AFM
Technical director   Technical manager   Engineering manager
Studio supervisor   Remote supervisor   Technical coordinator

Switcher/vision mixer	Talent/performers/actors/artistes
Set designer/scenic designer	Scenic artist Set dresser Props buyer
Make-up artist/make-up supervisor	Writer/scriptwriter Researcher Script editor
Make-up assistants Hair stylists	Announcer
Costume designer/costume supervisor	Film editor Telecine operator
Dressers Wardrobe handlers	Videotape engineer Videotape operator/VT editor
Graphics designer/graphic artist	Special effects designer Video effects
Lighting director	Electricians

The director

Video operator/shader/video engineer/vision control operator
Cameramen/camera operators   Camera assistants/dolly operators/pushers/grips
Audio engineer/audio control/sound supervisor   Sound crew   Boom operator
Set crew   Stage crew   Floor crew/floor men/stage hands/facilities men

Fig. 16.1   Production team
Studio production requires the services
and skills of a large number of people.
Their exact job functions and titles
vary between organizations.

ductions have become increasingly costly and more complicated, the workload needs to be spread. The director is then freed to concentrate on the program's interpretation, the staging and direction of the subject presentation.

Production emphasis

You can use picture and sound to report events simply, undramatically, and unobtrusively. For some types of production the best kind of staging and camera treatment provides a quiet, sympathetic background to the performance – a piano recital, an interview. However, there are program subjects that need as much 'hype' as you can offer: flashing, swirling light effects, arresting color, dominant, unusual sound quality, bizarre camera angles, unpredictable intercutting, to create an extravagant, sensational excitement.

While some productions have a relatively loose format, others require split-second timing, with accurately cued inserts coming from live remotes. There are effective programs based on a compilation of video-tape and film material woven together by commentary and music. Some types of production concentrate on action; others on reaction. Dialog may be all-important – or quite incidental.

Away from the studio, productions can be anything from a one-camera shoot trailing wildlife to a large-scale *remote* (*outside broadcast*), covering

Table 16.1   Production personnel

*Executive producer**	Overall organizational and administrative head of production group (e.g. a series of programs devoted to a particular field). He or she controls and coordinates the business management, including program budget, and may be concerned with wider issues such as funding/backing/coproduction arrangements.
*Producer**	Responsible to management for a specific production. Concerned with: choice of supervisory staff and crew; interdepartmental coordination; script acceptance; production scheduling. The producer may select or initiate the program concepts and work with writers. He or she assigns the production's director, and keeps a watching brief on deadlines, production planning, location projects, rehearsals, production treatment, etc. During rehearsal/recording also becomes involved in such specifics as retakes, overrunning scheduled times, craft or union problems, assessing postproduction treatment and the final program format.
*Director**	Responsible for interpreting and staging the production. This involves advising, guiding, and coordinating the specialists in the production team (scenic, lighting, sound, cameras, costume, etc.) and approving their anticipated treatment. The director may choose and hire performers/talent/actors (casting); envision and plan the camera treatment (shots, movements) and editing; and direct/rehearse the performers during prerehearsals. During studio rehearsals the director guides and cues performance (through the *floor manager*), and instructs the camera and sound crews, and switcher (vision mixer). He or she also evaluates the specialists' contributions (settings, camerawork, lighting, sound, make-up, costume, graphics, etc.). In some situations the director may operate the production switcher (e.g. on location), and guide and coordinate postproduction editing /audio sweetening. For smaller productions, the *producer's and director's* jobs may be combined.
*Assistant director, associate director (AD)**	Director's aide. Functions can depend on size of production. Supervises prerehearsals, location organization, etc. on director's behalf. During rehearsal in the production control room, lines up shots, checks special shots (supers, chroma key), gives routine cues (film and VT inserts), etc., while the director guides performance/cameras. Advises director of upcoming cues. May assist in off-line editing (timings, edit points). Checks program timing and progress. Helps director with postproduction editing routine.
*Production assistant (PA) – (UK)**	Director's aid. Supervises prerehearsals, location organization, etc. on director's behalf. During rehearsals/recording, functions similar to those of *floor manager*.
*Producer's assistant – (UK)**	Director's aide. General liaison/secretarial/coordinating helpmate. Checks performance against the script. Checks continuity. May line up shots, prepare inserts, etc. while the director guides performance/ cameras. Readies director, crew, VTR, and film channels re upcoming cues. Notes the durations/time code of each take. Keeps director's notes re changes to be made, retakes, etc.
*Floor manager (FM)/Stage manager (SM)**	The director's representative and contact on the studio floor. (May be allocated at planning stage, or only joins the production in the studio.) Cues performers. Checks and directs floor crew. Responsible for general studio organization, safety, discipline (e.g. noise), security. Assisted by AFM, who also ensures that talent are present.
*Production manager (UK)**	Responsible to producer/director for maintaining production within allocated budget. Also administrative functions relative to production.

Table 16.1 (*cont.*)

Technical director (TD)†	Crew chief. Coordinates and supervises engineering facilities. Evaluates technical quality. May instruct operational crew during production. May operate production switcher on director's instructions.
Studio supervisor (or Remote supervisor)/Technical coordinator†	Coordinates all technical operations, books facilities, checks technical feasibility, safety, etc.
Switcher/Vision mixer†	Specialist operating the production switcher (and perhaps electronic effects).
Set designer/Scenic designer†	Conceives, designs, and organizes the entire scenic treatment. (Perhaps including graphics.) Supervises scenic crew during setting, dressing, and striking settings.
Make-up artist/Make-up supervisor†*	Designs, prepares, and applies make-up treatment; aided by *make-up assistants* and *hair stylists*.
Costume designer†*	Designs or selects performers' costume (wardrobe). Assisted by *dressers/wardrobe handlers*.
Graphics designer/Graphics artist†	Designs and prepares all graphics and titles (studio cards, slides, displays).
Lighting director†	Designs, arranges, and controls all lighting treatment; both technically and artistically. (May be responsible for artistic picture quality.)
Video operator/Shader/Video engineer/Vision control operator†	Controls picture quality by adjusting video equipment. (Equipment alignment/line-up, exposure, black level, color balance, etc.) Operations are closely coordinated with lighting treatment.
Camera crew†	Led by a senior cameraman, a group of cameramen, dolly operators, etc., responsible for all camera operations on a production.
Audio engineer/Audio control/Sound supervisor†	Responsible for technical and artistic quality of program sound. Controls audio level, balance, tonal quality of all sound contributions, during rehearsals, recording, and postproduction audio sweetening.
Sound crew†	Supervised by the audio engineer. Audio personnel operating sound booms, positioning microphones; operating disc and audio tape equipment, etc.
Set crew†	Group of personnel responsible for erecting (*setting*) scenery.
Stage crew†	Group of personnel responsible for dressing sets (positioning furniture, props, drapes, etc.). Properties (props) may be arranged by a specialist property man.
Floor crew/Floor men/Stage hands/Facilities men†	Crew responsible for all action cues (e.g. rocking a vehicle), setting up camera title cards, operating crawl titles, and similar routines in the studio.
Electricians†	Crew responsible for rigging and setting lamps, and electrical apparatus (including electrical props).
Special effects designer†	Specialist designing and operating such mechanical illusions as fire, snow, explosions.
Video effects†	Specialist designing and operating various types of digital video effects.

Table 16.1 (*cont.*)

Videotape channel†	Engineers/operators recording and replaying videotape machines. Videotape editing may be carried out by a separate *VT editor*.
Film channel†	Operators reproducing film (telecine).
Announcer*	Concerned with off-screen announcements, commentary, continuity, etc.
Writer*	Person responsible for writing the script. May be freelance or staff. Producer or director may write material.
	May be assisted by *researcher*, who obtains data/information/references etc. for production team and/or writer.
	Further personnel operate other ancillary equipment, such as *prompters, character generator*, etc.

Performers/talent*
People appearing on the screen are termed variously:

Actors	Working to an established script, invariably play a role, create a character. Action/performance usually rehearsed before the camera rehearsal.
Performers/talent	Broad term for people appearing in front of the camera as themselves (interviewers, announcers, newscasters, anchor persons, emmcee, etc.), often addressing the audience directly through the camera. (May be scripted, semi-scripted, or unscripted material.)
	Sometimes *performer* refers to a person providing a specific act (e.g. juggler)
Guests	Invited 'personalities', specialists, or members of the public; usually without experience in front of the camera. (Interviewees, contestants, audience contributors, etc.)

* Personnel rated as *above the line* (non-technical) relative to program budgeting.
† Personnel generally rated as *below the line* for budgeting purposes.

a vast area with many cameras. Unforeseen problems are inevitable, and the restrictions of the environment and the weather must affect the director's opportunities.

Production approaches

There is no 'correct method' of presenting any subject. Directors have tried most approaches over the years. But certainly, if you choose an inappropriate technique you are likely to find your audience becoming confused, distracted, resentful . . . or simply losing interest.

Appropriateness

So what is *appropriate*? Well, in practice, it is largely a matter of custom, fashion, and convention.

- *Informal presentations* usually take the form of 'natural' situations. We chat with the craftsman in his workshop, or at the fireside, or while on a country walk.
- *Formal presentations* often follow a very stylized artificial format. We see people in carefully positioned chairs, sitting on a raised area in front of a cyc. They are often behind desks. There may be a chairperson, and 'rules of procedure'.
- *Display* is an unrealistic, decorative way of presenting your subject. Emphasis is on effect. We meet it in game shows, open-area treatment (e.g. choirs, music groups, dance), in children's programs.
- *Simulated environments* aim to create a completely realistic illusion. Anything breaking that illusion, such as a camera coming into shot in a period drama, would destroy the effect.
- *Actuality* is a revelatory style. We make it quite clear to the audience that we are in a studio by deliberately revealing the mechanics. On location, the unsteady hand-held camera and microphone dipping into shot supposedly give an 'authenticity' or 'veracity' to the occasion. We meet this approach in '*vox pop*' street interviews.

Routines

Some production techniques have become so familiar through convention or suitability that it could seem strangely unorthodox if we presented them in any other way – e.g. a newscaster sitting in a lounge.

Certain approaches have become so stereotyped that they enter the realms of cliché; routine methods for routine situations. The sheer extent and repetition of TV productions has thrown up a number of such formats: newscasts, studio interviews, game shows, chat shows, etc. If we analyze such productions we usually find that styles have evolved as the most effective, economic, and reliable ways of handling their particular subjects.

If we regard such a packaging as 'a container for the goods', then these routine treatments can free the audience to concentrate on the event. If, however, we consider the presentation treatment as an opportunity to encourage interest and heighten enjoyment, then any 'routine' becomes unacceptable.

Clearly, any dramatic or emphatic treatment would be quite gratuitous for many types of TV production. Instead, it is best to aim for pictorial variety, coupled with clear, unambiguous visual statements that direct and concentrate attention, rather than introduce any imposed 'style'.

Many non-dramatic subjects are *inherently* limited in their potential treatment. How many sensible meaningful shot variations can you take of people speaking to each other, or driving an automobile, or playing an instrument, or demonstrating an article? The range is small.

For certain subjects the picture is virtually irrelevant. What a person has to *say* may be extremely important; while what he *looks* like is immaterial to the message. It may even prove a distraction or create prejudicial bias. 'Talking heads' appear in most TV shows, but unless the speaker is particularly animated, the viewers' visual interest is seldom sustained. Changing viewpoint helps – but can appear fidgety.

Motion pictures inform us through continual illustration and commentary. Television's more economic but less enticing approach is for people to tell us about matters instead. They sit in the studio with graphics or film clips, or stand at the scene of activities and talk directly to us, instead of using the camera itself to demonstrate. Here the difference in approach is not inherent in the medium but the way it is being used.

Ambience

From the moment a show begins, we are influencing our audience's attitude to the production itself. Introductory music and titling style can immediately convey a serious or a jokey feeling towards what is to come.

We have only to recall how the hushed voice, quiet organ notes, slow visual pace, impart a reverential air to proceedings, or the difference between a regal and a 'show-biz' opening fanfare, to realize how our expectancy changes.

Surroundings can also directly affect how convincingly we convey information. Certain environments, for example, impart authority or scholarship: classroom, laboratory, museum, study. A plow shown at work on the farm will not only be more readily understood but will carry a conviction that is lacking in the studio demonstration.

Selective tools

The camera and microphone do not behave like our eyes and ears but substitute for them. Our eyes flick around with a knowledge of our surroundings, providing us with an impression of unrestricted stereo-scopic vision; in fact, we can only detect detail and color over a tiny angle (about $1\frac{1}{2}°$), and our peripheral vision is monochromatic and quite blurred. Also, our ears provide us with selective binaural pick-up, quite unlike the TV audio system.

In daily life we build up an impression of our environment by personally controlled sampling; concentrating on certain details while ignoring others. The camera and microphone, on the other hand, provide us with only restricted segments. And the information provided in these segments is modified in various ways, as we have seen, by the characteristics of the medium (distorting space, proportions, scale, etc.).

Selective techniques

As we saw earlier, if you simply set up your camera and microphone overlooking the action the viewer soon becomes overaware of the small restricted screen and limited detail. He is prevented from seeing whatever is outside the shot. Go closer for detail and he progressively loses the overall view. Show more of the scene and particular detail becomes indiscernible. In the choice of suitable viewpoint and shot size for a particular purpose lies the concept of guided selection; the beginnings of techniques.

Good production techniques provide *variety*: of scale and proportion; of composition pattern; of centers of attention and changing subject influence. You achieve these things by variation in shot size and camera viewpoint, by moving the subject and/or the camera, or by altering the subject seen.

Although you may sometimes encourage the viewer to browse around a shot, more often you will want him to look at a particular feature, and follow a certain thought process. The screen can all too easily become 'moving wallpaper', with our audience seeing – but not looking, hearing – but not listening!

The screen transforms reality

The camera and microphone can only convey an *impression* of the subject and scene. Whatever the limitations or inaccuracies of these images, they are the only direct information our viewer has available. And, of course, his interpretation must vary with his own experience and foreknowledge. Whether you are aiming to convey an accurate account (newscast) or to conjure an illusion (drama) the screen will transform reality.

You could fill the screen with a shot of a huge aircraft, or with a diminutive model. The pictures would look very similar. Yet neither conveys the subjective essentials; i.e. how you *feel* standing beside the giant plane or handling the tiny model. Introducing a person into shot would establish scale, but it would still not include our characteristic responses to such a situation: the way we would ourselves be overawed by size, or intrigued by minute detail.

Use your camera to select detail from a painting or a photograph and your TV screen puts a frame around it, to make this isolated area into a new complete picture; an arrangement that did not exist in its own right within the original; an arrangement that if sustained in close-up can become detached and dissociated in the audience's minds from the complete subject.

When you shoot solid sculpture its three-dimensional form becomes reproduced as a flat pattern on the TV screen. Planes merge and interact as they cannot do when we ourselves examine the real sculpture. Only on the flat screen can a billiard ball become transformed into a flat disc under diffused lighting. In practice, you can continually make use of this falsification of reality. The very principles of scenic design rely on it. But it is as well to appreciate that the camera and microphone do inevitably modify the images they convey; and that these images are easily mistaken for truth.

Interpretative techniques

It is one of those production paradoxes that although your camera can show what is happening, it will often fail to convey the atmosphere or spirit of the occasion. You can frequently achieve more convincing representative results by deliberately using selective techniques than by direct reportage.

Straightforward shots of a mountain climb impart none of the thrills and hazards of the situation. But use low camera angles to emphasize the treacherous slope; show threatening overhangs, straining fingers, slipping feet, dislodged stones, laboring breath, slow ascending music . . . and the illusion grows. Even climbing a gentle slope can appear hazardous if strong interpretative techniques are used.

Sometimes the audience can be so strongly moved by this subjective treatment that sympathetic bodily reactions set in when watching such scenes – dizziness, nausea. Even situations outside the viewer's personal experience (the elation of free fall, the horror of quicksand) can be conveyed to some degree by carefully chosen stimuli.

Making the contrived arise 'naturally'

You can introduce techniques *obtrusively* for dramatic effect, or so *unobtrusively* that the effect appears 'natural' and the viewer is quite unaware that the situation *is* contrived:

Obtrusive. The camera suddenly depresses from an eye-level shot to a low-angle viewpoint.
Unobtrusive. The camera shoots a seated actor at eye-level. He stands, and the camera tilts up with him. We now have a low-angle shot.

Where situations seem to occur accidentally or unobtrusively they are invariably more effective. For example, as an intruder moves towards camera he becomes menacingly underlit by a nearby table lamp.

Where an effect is blatantly contrived it often appears to challenge our credulity and we tend to reject it. A sinister figure is reflected in the victim's sunglasses; the camera whip pans to show him standing nearby.

As conventions become understood, and accepted by our audience, even flagrant changes become permissible: *flash cut-ins* (lasting ½-2 seconds) to convey 'recognition' or 'recall'; extreme viewpoint changes, close sound on long shots; exaggerated filmic time. But a director who deliberately misuses an established convention, trying to give it a new significance, treads a thorny path.

Many techniques have become so familiar that we now regard them as the normal and natural way of doing things. But they are really artifices that help us to convey particular concepts:

1. 'Chipmunk' voices (high-pitched through tape speed-up) for small creatures.
2. Echo behind ghostly manifestations.

3. Rim light in 'totally dark' scenes.
4. Background music.
5. Wipes, supers, etc.

Gratuitous techniques

Skilful presentation blends a carefully selected combination of visual and audio techniques to attract and persuade. But you can too easily use techniques for their own sake.

1. Rapid cutting in time with music – that provides a disjointed dissatisfying jumble of images.
2. Video effects – that leave us preoccupied with how it was done.
3. 'Clever' camerawork – focusing on irrelevant foreground objects while main subjects remain unsharp; shooting into lamps or specular reflections.

Such contrived methods have their occasional purpose, but they can quickly degenerate into imposed gimmicks.

Production pressures

Preoccupation with the organization and coordination of production mechanics leaves most directors little time to meditate on the medium's aesthetics. Rehearsal time is limited. The camera and sound crews are meeting the director's brainchild for the first time and need to be guided in his interpretation. If the treatment is elaborate and exacting there is greater opportunity for problems that require immediate solution. If the production is shot out of sequence it becomes that much more difficult to ensure that each segment is coherent, and will provide good continuity when edited together. In such circumstances there is an understandable temptation to substitute effective known mechanics for creative experiment.

Also, when you are closely involved with a production it can be quite difficult to estimate accurately the audience impact of pace, timing, tension, etc. Watching a film clip through *several* times, you will see how the stresses, emphasis, speed, and even its significance can change. A word or gesture can have more or less impact with repetition, while heavily pointed action may appear hackneyed or mannered.

17 Production practices

TV production groups all over the world follow surprisingly similar practices. This is partly due to the nature of the medium's mechanics, partly the result of sharing knowledge and experience.

Single-camera techniques

In the earliest days of television, multi-camera shooting soon became the established practice. It has many advantages. But as cameras and videorecording equipment have become lightweight and more flexible, an increasing number of productions are now being made on location with single-camera units.

As you will see, there are essential differences between single- and multi-camera production techniques.

Continuous single-camera shooting

Following camera

One approach when shooting *continuous action* 'live' or 'live-on-tape' is to adopt a *following camera* method. The single camera moves around to new viewpoints, following the performers, adjusting the shot size as the situation requires. If well done, the result can be a powerful subjective impression, in which the camera represents the audience's uninterrupted viewpoint. There are no transitions to distract them. Where closer shots are needed, the camera anticipates and moves nearer for that moment.

Continuous single-camera shooting can be so effective that entire plays have been shot live on a single mobile dolly. There are drawbacks to this approach, though. It requires skilled, well-controlled camerawork on a smoothly operated mounting. Mobile hand-held shots can only be sustained over a short period.

Working to the camera

Instead of having the camera 'work to the subject' in this way, you can arrange action and treatment so that the talent '*works to the camera*' instead. They move around to suit the shot; coming nearer the camera for close-ups and moving further away for long shots. This can be done naturally and unobtrusively, as we see in Figure 17.1. You can place larger subjects in the background, while smaller ones are closer to the camera. A turntable, or even a mirror may help to see an object from various angles. Occasionally, you might pull focus/throw focus from one subject to another to transfer attention.

Fig. 17.1 part 1   Subject movement and the single camera – equidistant positions
Items can be arranged equidistant from the camera, to provide a series of similar shots as the talent moves around.

Fig. 17.1 part 2   Subject movement and the single camera – movement in depth
Where subjects of various sizes are involved, the largest can be located furthest away; the smallest closest to the camera.

Fig. 17.1 part 3   Subject movement and the single camera – repositioned camera
Here the camera zooms out from a close-up, and arcs round to a new viewpoint as the talent moves to the new subject.

Even if your camera is on a *fixed tripod*, you can still create an impression of shot flexibility using this technique. Because you must simulate camera movement by zooming, aim to do so gradually and inconspicuously. Wherever possible, try to arrange zooming to coincide with subject movement. Zoom in as the talent turns to point at a wall chart. As they lift up an object we have been studying in close-up detail, zoom out to a mid-shot. Zooming in this way provides shot variety without becoming intrusive.

Stretched facilities

In a *multi-camera* studio you would assume that there would always be a camera or two free to shoot the subject from a fresh angle. Yet surprisingly often you will find that you have only *one camera* to work with! In a three-camera studio, for instance, if *CAM-1* is on-air, and *CAM-2* is set up on a title card, that leaves only *CAM-3* available to shoot the action at the start of the next scene.

If, during a demonstration, a geologist is showing us specimens on one camera, and the other two cameras are tied up with a combined illustration (e.g. a map graphic on *CAM-2* and superimposed titling on *CAM-3*), you are back to single-camera techniques.

When you are restricted to a single camera for any reason, you can often add variety and flexibility by cutting to insert material on slides, film, and

Fig. 17.2 Relocation
During an insert shot, the talent has unexpectedly moved to a new location and is discovered there; often disconcerting the viewer.

Fig. 17.3 Continuity
When retaking shots, inattention to detail can lead to poor continuity during editing; due to items having been consumed, moved, action or positions wrongly repeated, etc.

videotape. This may also give you the opportunity to reposition the camera, or change the shot size. Take care, though, not to create visual discontinuity. Inserts of this sort can show information that the studio camera itself might not pick up – such as hallmarks on silverware.

Discontinuous single-camera shooting

Shooting uncontrolled action

When using a single camera to shoot broad action over which you have no control you have the option of:

- Remaining at a fixed viewpoint and relying on the zoom lens to provide a variety of shots.
- Or moving the camera to a series of vantage points, changing viewpoint and shot size to capture the main features of the occasion.

Clearly, if you are shooting a public event such as a street parade on a single camera the first technique is very limiting. However, if you move around or stop shooting you are liable to lose some of the action, unless you can time your moves to fit in with a lull in the proceedings.

To assist subsequent editing make sure you have plenty of extra general material that can be used as *cutaway* shots. 'Cutaways' tend to be of two types; *active* and *passive*. The 'active' cutaway includes subjects that can only be edited into the program at a particular moment (e.g. shots of the town hall clock showing that the parade is about to start), or the crowd's responses to a particular event. 'Passive' cutaways, on the other hand, can be used at almost any time, and might include reflections, flags, sun through branches.

As with news events, you make the most of available opportunities. You may be able to plan exactly what you are going to do, checking out the route and your viewpoints beforehand. You may even be able to influence events a little; arranging for the beauty queen in the procession to turn and smile to camera as she passes. But, on the whole, you have to take things as you find them. There are no repeats!

Shooting controlled action

When shooting situations you *can* control (e.g. interviews, drama sequences) the situation is very different. Now you arrange the action, the camera set-up, and sometimes the lighting and staging (background, props, etc.) to suit each shot in turn.

If you want to repeat the same action so that you have long shots, medium, and close shots of it to intercut, that is usually quite practicable. Instead of having to select from whatever is happening at the location you may have the option to change things: to have a person leaning over the bridge to improve the composition; to wait for the sun to come out; to pause while loud aircraft pass over.

You will usually take the shots in the most convenient, rational order, then edit them together afterwards to suit the production sequence. If, for instance, you have a series of shots of people either side of a river it is obviously more sensible to shoot all the action on one side and then move to the other, rather than hop to and fro, shooting in script running order.

When shooting discontinuously you have to take care throughout that there are no obvious discrepancies that spoil the *continuity* between these shots when they are joined together. If in our example it happened to have been bright sunshine when shooting on one bank of the river, but pouring rain when shooting the other, the intercut shots could look pretty unconvincing, to say the least!

Segmented shooting

Shooting controlled action with a single camera, you will normally break the action down into a series of quite brief 'action segments'. If part of the action adds nothing to the situation you may deliberately *omit* it altogether. At other times, you may actually *emphasize* the action. Let's illustrate this with a simple situation:

Someone is walking along the street.

- If we are only really interested in what they do when they reach their destination we can omit the walk altogether.
- But perhaps we want to emphasize that they are lame, and every step is taken in agony. In that case, we might follow them in close detail . . . the heavy tread, the hesitant walking stick . . . the uneven paving, in a series of shots taken from different angles.
- On the other hand, suppose the story at that point aims to intrigue us. We wonder whether the person is being followed by the villain. We would probably shoot the sequence quite differently. The entire walk might be taken on a static camera, using a continuous panning shot. We

show them walking past the camera into the distance . . . and out of shot. We hold the empty frame . . . and their pursuer moves into the foreground of the shot.

Clearly, how you break up the action must depend on the dramatic purpose of the picture sequence.

As an exercise, run a videotape of any long action sequence from a motion picture or a documentary. It might be showing someone rock climbing, sailing a boat, in a car chase. Analyse the shots that make up this action sequence. Time them. Think carefully about the viewpoints.

In a car chase we might find that at one moment the camera is in the car beside the driver . . . in the next we see a front-on shot of it showing the driver alone in the car. *Cut*, and we are behind the driver's shoulder looking through the windshield . . . and now we are looking down from a high building as the car maneuvers a corner. It moves away into the distance and – *cut* . . . we see it coming up towards the camera.

When watching this treatment we never question the rapidly changing viewpoints, or query why the camera is suddenly located on a helicopter. When shooting in the desert we see the car vanish into the distance . . . without wondering if he is going to come back to pick up the cameraman!

Many types of action are, in reality, very drawn out and somewhat boring to watch. Shoot them continuously, and audience interest will wander. Break sustained action into continually varying viewpoints, and we create pace, and provide continuing interest.

One particular function of editing is that we can create an illusion of continuity between shots or situations where in fact none exists. This is not only a valuable dramatic facility but it enables us to develop action sequences which in reality we could not shoot.

Imagine a scene showing a bird on a branch . . . a close shot as it dives into the stream . . . an underwater shot of fish . . . a fish is caught by the bird . . . the bird sits beside the river eating its catch. These are probably shots of different birds, and of different fish, shot at different times. The separate shots are edited together to form a complete effective action sequence.

We have looked at these examples in some detail, for they epitomize the thinking and the techniques that underlie *single-camera shooting*. As you will see, they are noticeably different from multi-camera treatment.

Multi-camera treatment

Using two or more cameras gives you additional flexibility in the way you handle any situation. Without missing any of the action, or needing action repeated, you can intercut between different shots of the same subject, alter the camera's viewpoint, move to another area.

In an instant you can change the significance of a shot. You can provide fresh information, alter emphasis, point new detail, show reactions, shift audience attention, compare relationships, introduce visual variety. And all this while the action continues. Using a single camera, much of this effect has to be contrived.

Fig. 17.4   Two-camera treatment
Here shots are divided between two cameras. Cam 1 concentrates on long shots. Cam 2 takes close-ups of maps and speaker.

Cam 1   Cam 2

Using *several cameras*, you can arrange to have one covering the action and another ready to catch the audience's reactions. But if you are shooting with a *single camera* you are unlikely to turn away from the main event to see whether someone in the crowd is responding. You are more likely to shoot some reaction shots later (probably relating to entirely different action), and cut them in for effect at that point during editing!

Multi-camera treatment allows you to *combine* cameras; pictures – for supers, inserts, split screen, or other effects. You can fit one camera with a device (e.g. a periscope mirror), while other cameras provide normal pictures.

If you have only one camera you may need to alter a shot for purely mechanical reasons – e.g. widening a shot to accommodate an extra person. That recessive movement may be artistically inappropriate. It may be better to cut to a wider shot on another camera.

Visual variety

Fig. 17.5   Maximum use of cameras
1. One camera to each set is unnecessarily restrictive.
2. Near the end of a two-camera scene. Cam 2 pans to the next area.
3. Cameras move away successively. Cam 2 moves first (A to B), then Cam 1 joins it.

Static shots easily become a bore. So audience interest is encouraged by introducing movement and change. Although, if overdone, the pictures can become a strain to watch. Rapid cutting demands continual viewer concentration . . . that is not readily sustained. Ceaseless action and camera moves lead to pictures that fidget with movement. As always, the aim is a well-balanced blend with variations in pace, tempo, and emphasis.

Performer movement

Most visual variety stems from action within the scene, as people alter positions and regroup. Quite often more meaningful changes are achieved by performer movement than by camera moves or editing.

In a close shot the performer dominates. As he moves away from camera the audience becomes more aware of his relationship to his

Fig. 17.6   Visual variety
Depending on how a picture is arranged, its centre of attention, emphasis, and even the audience's interpretation can change.

Fig. 17.7 part 1   Subject/camera relationship

1. Here subject and action have been arranged to suit the camera's static viewpoint (playing to the camera).
2. Here the camera moves, relating to the static subject and action.

Fig. 17.7 part 2   Subject/camera relationship

Subjects may be arranged to provide shot opportunities, while cameras are moved or intercut to explore these arrangements.

surroundings. In long shots these surroundings may dominate. So by changing the length of shot you change emphasis and create visual variation.

These moves are motivated in various ways:

1. By *deliberately arranging* subjects (props, demonstration items) so that a performer is artificially 'motivated' to move to them in the course of the production.
2. By introducing a *gesture* (hand pointing) towards a subject – the camera pans over to see.
3. By a deliberate *turn* of the head or body – to initiate a pan, dolly, or zoom to a subject.
4. By a *verbal reference* ('The machine over there') providing a direct introduction to a shot change.

Fig. 17.8   Forming shots by isolation
By intercutting various shots of a group, you can introduce visual variety into a static situation.

Changes by grouping

Where people are seated (panels, talk shows) you can achieve visual variety by *isolation*; selectively shooting individuals, two-shots, sub-groups.

When people are mobile you can *regroup* them to provide freshly composed shots by introducing 'natural' moves (sitting, going over to pick up a book), or introduce visually motivated cuts (turning as a guest arrives). By varying emphasis and composition balance in this way the movement attracts attention and conceals the deliberate shift of interest.

Shooting static subjects

Visual variety can be introduced into your treatment of non-moving subjects (statuary, pottery, paintings, flowers) by the way you shoot and light them:

1. Camera movements alter the viewpoint.
2. You can selectively pan over the subject, interrelating its various parts.
3. Changing lighting can isolate or emphasize sections or alter the subject's appearance.
4. Small objects can be handled, turned to show different features, or turntable-displayed.

Fig. 17.9   Forming shots by subject movement
By introducing 'natural' moves you can form new groupings. Here *C* sits, *B* turns to him. *A* turns and exits, camera tightens to shot *BC*. A series of compositional changes have moved attention between the people.

Fig. 17.10 Composition change altering significance
By a single change in the picture's composition, you can alter its significance. The girl confronts her father (her frame position gives her strength, even in a rear view). He rises – the strength of his upward move and new position now make him dominant.

Variety by décor

The presentation of certain subjects is necessarily restricted (piano playing, singers). They are relatively static and meaningful shot variations are limited. You can prevent sameness between productions by introducing variations in the décor – whether by scenic changes or by lighting. The pictures *look* different, even if the shots and viewpoints follow a recognizable format.

Variety by effects

This is achieved by introducing various visual effects such as: combined shots, superimpositions, multi-images, split screens, decorative inserted backgrounds (using chroma key), and synthesized color.

The illusion of relationships

As we watch a succession of pictures we build up a mental image of where things are located within the scene. We form these judgements from various visual clues; comparing common features, movements, the relative directions in which people are looking, etc.

If, for instance, we see someone looking screen right and the picture cuts to another person looking screen left we tend to assume that they are facing each other. In reality they might be in quite different places. But we have interrelated and interpreted these shots. Subsequent shots (a more distant view, for instance) will confirm or correct our interpretation.

In a scene where someone says goodbye to their partner and walks out of the shot we usually assume that they have departed. If the camera cuts to another viewpoint, and shows them nearby speaking to somebody else, the audience is likely to be disconcerted.

The camera easily misleads, and unless you actually want to create ambiguity, to make a dramatic or a comic point, it is best to avoid such situations.

Sometimes we deliberately create a *false* impression. We have a close shot of someone speaking towards the camera, with their eyeline slightly to one side, to suggest that they are talking to a person seen in the previous shot. But they are really alone. It is a productional device – quite as much as the actor's earnest telephone 'conversation' with a prop phone.

It is very easy to confuse or destroy spatial impressions the audience has formed. When you change the camera's viewpoint some strange visual anomalies can take place. Something on the left of the screen in one shot . . . appears an instant later over to the right of the screen. Having established where someone is looking in one shot, their eyeline can appear to change direction on the cut.

As you can see in Figure 17.11, these disconcerting *jump cuts* and the loss of orientation arise whenever you *cut* across an *imaginary line* (*action line, action axis, center line*). This line has normally been established in

Fig. 17.11 part 1 The imaginary line – intercut facing shots

Shots can be intercut (cross-cut) between cameras located on the same side of the imaginary line; i.e. between 1 and 2, or 3 and 4. But inter-switching between cameras on opposite sides of this line, causes jump cuts (1 and 3, 1 and 4, 2 and 3, 2 and 4).

Fig. 17.11 part 2 The imaginary line – reverse-angle shots

1. Direction is reversed on the cut, for cameras have crossed the line.

2. A common scenic unit (doorway, window) usually makes reverse-angle cuts acceptable, providing cameras remain on one side of the line.

Fig. 17.11 part 3 The imaginary line – forward-facing positions

Whenever someone faces the camera (walking, sitting, singing, demonstrating) it is all too easy to interswitch inadvertently across the line to region X, and reverse direction.

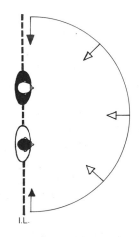

Fig. 17.11 part 4 The imaginary line – aligned positions

1. Where people are shoulder to shoulder (riding, walking) wide viewpoint changes are acceptable.

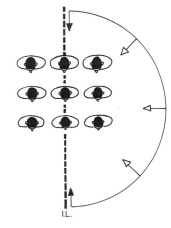

2. But for a larger gathering (audience, choir, parade) cameras should keep to one side of the front-rear axis when interswitching viewpoints.

Fig. 17.11 part 5   The imaginary line – curving path
Where action follows a curved path, only a head-on viewpoint is reliable if shooting is discontinuous. With continuous action viewpoint changes such as 1–2 are practicable.

Fig. 17.11 part 6   The imaginary line – three-way situations
If you assume that the direction of person A's look has established the axis AC, then you can intercut shots along the AC axis. Now, if he turns towards B, the axis is changed to AB (excluding C from shot) and shots can be intercut along the BC axis. Eyelines can be changed (even cheated) to permit inter-axis cutting.

Fig. 17.11 part 7   The imaginary line – exits and entrances
If during supposedly uninterrupted action a person exits beside camera-right 1, a straight cut showing action continuation should show him entering camera-right also 2.

our minds by previous camera viewpoints, or by eyelines (the 'direction of look'), or by performers' movements. If the camera *dollies* across the line, or you change the direction of the line by regrouping or moving people, or change the eye-lines, the effect does not arise.

Shot organization

It takes time to experiment, and production time is limited. So directors need a rational plan of campaign. You could distribute cameras around the scene and choose from shots the cameramen offered – but there would usually be little relationship between these pictures. Subject coverage would be patchy. There would probably be several near-identical shots of the pretty girl guest and none of the chairman! Perhaps several overall views or dramatic close-ups – but who could use them?

Shots have to be appropriately chosen and interrelated according to a coordinated plan, and only the *director* is in a position to do this.

Planned viewpoints

Using this technique, you begin with the action's mechanics (where people move, what they do there) and arrange strategic camera viewpoints from which to shoot it. Each camera position provides a series of shot opportunities and you select from these available shots as required.

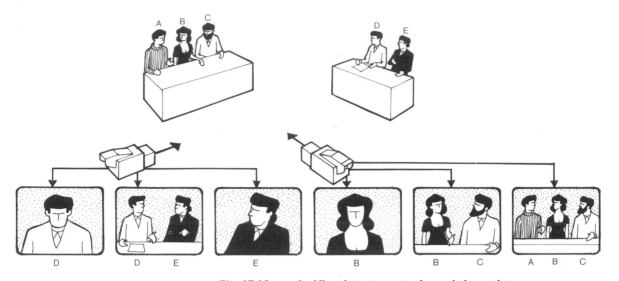

Fig. 17.12 part 1   Visual treatment – planned viewpoints
Cameras are placed at vantage points, from which appropriate shots can be selected and intercut.

Fig. 17.12 part 2   Visual treatment – storyboard approach
Following script analysis, treatment is visualized and broken down into key shots, which are sketched to show required camera treatment.

At sports events and other large-scale public occasions this is the only practical approach. Cameras are often widely dispersed, camera movement is restricted, and the director relies on cameramen to use their initiative to find appropriate shots. The director's knowledge of actual shot opportunities is mostly derived from what his cameras reveal and on-the-spot assistants. He guides selection, adjusts shot sizes, suggests desirable shots, and chooses from the available material.

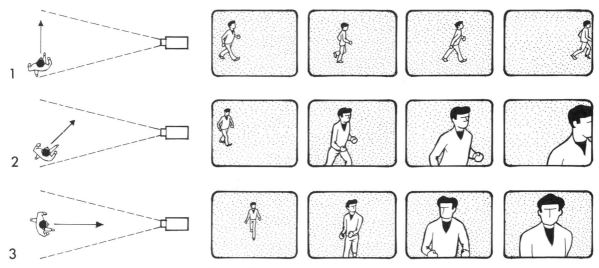

Fig. 17.13 part 1   The moving subject – direction of movement
1. A movement across the screen, quickly passes out of shot.
2. Diagonal moves are preferable, for they are visually more interesting.
3. Moves towards the camera from a distance are sustained longest, but can seem drawn-out.

Fig 17.13 part 2   The moving subject – widely spaced moves
Moves between widely-spaced points are best shot obliquely (Cam 1), rather than with a following pan (Cam 2).

Fig. 17.13 part 3   The moving subject – avoid decapitation
1. The cameraman must be warned of a 'rise' or 'sit', to avoid the bizarre effects of a delayed following tilt.
2. Equally ridiculous effects can arise if framing does not follow action.

You can use a similar strategy in *studio* production for certain types of shows with a regular format. For example:

Camera 1 – taking wider, *cover* shots (mid to long shots).
Camera 2 – primarily close-up shots.
Camera 3 – supporting close-ups, close detail, title cards, graphics.

This approach can be particularly useful for unscripted, off-the-cuff situations. But it is also valuable for a demonstrator, who consequently knows which camera to play to for close-ups at any time. However, you should resist any temptation to apply such a routine where more exploratory camera treatment is possible.

Storyboard approach (Figure 17.12, part 2)

Where systematic planning is practical a director may use a storyboard technique; sketching the required picture treatment for selected *key shots* or for scene-by-scene treatment. Here we are concerned with *shot significance*; ensuring that the shots have the appropriate dramatic value, attract attention to certain features, emphasize a particular point, and engender a mood.

Storyboard methods involve analyzing the script, deciding on composition arrangements, and then working out how to get them. You can use such planning as a general or specific guide. Accurate prerehearsal planning can achieve the highest standards; but it must be *realistic*, taking into account how one set-up needs to be developed from another. Most directors dislike the commitment of such planning methods and prefer a more flexible empirical approach. Although, where complex special effects are involved the storyboard may become essential.

Table 17.1   Arranging the shot

	In arranging a shot, you should be able to answer such questions as:
Broad objectives	What is the *purpose* of the shot? What is it aiming to *show*?
	Is it to *emphasize* a particular point or feature?
	Which is the *main* subject?
	Are we *primarily concerned* with: the subject, its relationship to another, or to its background/environment?
The actual picture	Is the shot *too close or distant* for its purpose?
	Is the *attention* reasonably localized – or split or diffused?
	Is the *composition arrangement* appropriate?
	Is the subject suitably *framed*? (Headroom, offset, edge cut-off, overcrowded frame.)
	Are subjects *clearly seen*? (Sharp, unobscured, good background contrast?)
	Is there any *ambiguity* or *distraction* in the shot?
The action	Are we aiming to show what a person is *doing* – clearly, forcefully, incidentally, not at all?
	Does action (movement, gestures) *pass outside the frame*?
	Are any *important features* or action accidentally excluded?
More specific objectives	Is the presentation to be *straightforward* or *dramatic*?
	Do we want to indicate subject *strength* or *weakness*?
	Do we aim to *reveal, conceal, mislead, puzzle*?
	What *effect, mood, atmosphere* are we seeking? (Businesslike, clinical, romantic, sinister.)
	Does the shot *relate successfully* to previous and subsequent shots?

Program opening

Establishing shots introduce the scene and the action, setting the mood, influencing your audience's frame of mind towards what you have to say and show. There are several familiar openings:

1. *The formal start*. Beginning with a 'Good evening' or 'Hello', introduces the show and gets on with it. Whether the presenter appears casual, reverent, indifferent, or enthusiastic can create an ambience directly influencing the audience's attitude.
2. *The teaser*. Showing dramatic, provocative, intriguing highlights from the production, before opening titles. Sometimes this inadvertently gives away the plot before the show even begins!
3. *The crash start*. Takes us straight into the program, which probably appears to have begun already. An automobile screams to a stop outside a store, a figure throws a bomb . . . which explodes, an alarm bell shrills, a police siren wails – the show has begun and titles roll over the chasing vehicles.
4. *The character introduction*. A rapid montage of symbols or shots of the hero in various predicaments provides an introduction to the characters we are to meet.
5. *The eavesdropping start*. The camera peers through a house window, sees a group round a TV screen, and moves in to join them.
6. *The coy welcome*. The camera dollies in to somone who is supposedly preoccupied. Realizing that we have arrived, his welcome of 'Oh, there you are!' provides informality – or nauseating artifice.
7. *The slow build-up*. The camera pans slowly round, arousing curiosity or suspense . . . until we reach a climax point (the bloodstained dagger). It is essential to avoid diminishing interest or anti-climax.
8. *The atmosphere introduction*. A series of strongly associative symbols establish the place, period, mood, or personality. On a mantleshelf: the brass telescope, ship in bottle, and well-worn uniform cap – the old sea captain is introduced long before we see him.

Subjective and objective approaches

You can use the camera either:
Objectively – in which the viewer becomes an *observer*, or
Subjectively – in which he finds himself a *participant* in the action.

In his *objective* role the viewer becomes an onlooker, eavesdropper, an invited audience at a vantage point, or a casual bystander. He sees what is going on but is never addressed directly.

Subjective approaches are a regular part of TV, as performers speak straight to camera, using the screen as a communicating opening to our home. The *subjective* role can be an extremely powerful one when the camera lens moves within the scene as our eyes – or those of a character. It goes up to see an object. It moves among a group of dancers. It follows a guide around a museum. The concept can be used forcefully, linking us closely with the action as the camera 'climbs stairs' or jumps out of a plane. Taken to extremes, it all becomes a visual stunt as we find ourselves punched, kissed, fired at, even drowned!

In *developing (development) shots* the camera moves from one viewpoint to another; helping us to build spatial impressions and to see varying aspects of the action. This requires carefully controlled camerawork, but

K

Fig. 17.14 The developing shot
Continuous camera movement may
explore the scene where intercutting
would disturb the sustained mood,
yet you wish to change the focus of
attention, reveal new information,
show various reactions, etc.

it can be most effective in *slow-paced* scenes involving tension,
expectancy, solemn or romantic occasions.

Providing the viewer realizes his intended relationship to the scene you
can change techniques between subjective and objective treatment. At
times, the distinction may be very nominal.

Focusing audience attention

It is as well not to overrate how much effort the audience is willing to
make to evaluate your picture. You can do a great deal to localize and hold
their attention by taking care how you arrange and present subjects.

Audience concentration easily lapses, so you need to continually direct
and redirect their attention to hold interest along particular lines. Such
redirection implies *change*. But excess or uncontrolled change can lead to
confusion or irritation. Pictorial change must be clearly motivated, to
allow the viewer to readjust himself easily to each new situation.

Varying concentration

You have to strike a balance between *sustained concentration* (where
interest soon flags) and *free association* (where minds wander):

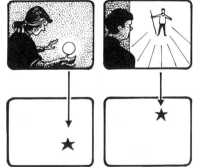

**Fig. 17.15 The center of
interest**
You can attract attention to a specific
place in the shot, by the way you
arrange and present the subject.

1. In some shots you will aim to concentrate attention on a particular
   center of interest.
2. In others you will encourage attention to move around, on ordered
   detectable lines.
3. Others of a more general nature encourage free ruminative inspection;
   concentrating perhaps on the audio (commentary, dialogue, music).

Fig. 17.16 Unifying interest
The eye should normally be led to (1) a single (2) unambiguous center of interest.

Fig. 17.17 Changing the center of interest
1. The eye-lines and attitudes of performers guide the viewer to a particular center of interest. If there are no visual clues, his attention is not readily transferred to another point. He must look around to see who is speaking.
2. By introducing eye-line and posture clues, the transference becomes obvious.
3. In moving interest around the picture, you must take care not to draw attention to a focal point where there is no real interest or create ambiguous centers.
4. Avoid leading attention out of the frame.

Although you cannot expect to direct an entire audience's attention with any precision you can do a great deal to lead them in their selection and influence their associated thoughts.

Shifting visual interest

It is just as necessary to be able to shift the viewer's concentration to another aspect of the picture as it was to localize his attention originally. You can do this by readjusting any of the influences listed:

1. Having a person stand up within a seated group.
2. Give the first person weaker movements (turn away), stengthening those of the new subject (face the camera).
3. Transfer the original emphasis (contrast, isolation, etc.) to the new subject.
4. Use linking action; first person looks to camera right . . . cut to new subject on screen right.
5. Weaken original subject, having him move to the new stronger subject.

Fig. 17.18   How to focus visual attention

1. Avoiding spurious centers of interest, e.g. prominent lettering, tonal contrast, etc., in supporting subjects.
2. Compositional lines (real or implied).
3. Tonal gradation. The eye naturally follows gradation from dark to light areas.
4. By deliberate unbalance (tonal or linear), with the subject in the heaviest position.
5. By isolating the main subject in depth.
6. By isolating the main subject horizontally.
7. By body position.
8. By height.
9. Using a stronger part of the frame.
10. With lighting.
11, 12. By similarity between the subject and its surroundings, although too great a similarity can pall or (13, 14) lead to confusion.

6. Alter the shot size, camera height, etc.
7. Pull focus from old subject to the new.
8. Change the sound source; new person speaks instead.

Creating tension

Tension in a dramatic situation derives partly from the dialog, story line, and interaction between characters; but it can also be considerably influenced by the way in which you present the subject:

1. Using progressively more powerful shots (intercutting closer and closer shots; lower viewpoints, gradual canting).
2. Using suspenseful music and effects.
3. Presenting ambiguous information – is the nocturnal shadow a bush . . . or prowler?
4. Presenting insufficient information – the audience sees the figure in the doorway . . . is it the villain?
5. Withholding information – have the pursuers arrived yet?
6. The audience knows something a character does not – he runs to escape . . . we know the route is blocked.
7. A character is suddenly confronted with an insurmountable problem – the stairway collapses as he reaches it.
8. We anticipate what is going to happen – surely someone will burst in through that door.

Table 17.2 Selecting camera treatment

	Mechanical purpose	Artistic purpose
Why pan or tilt	To follow action. To show a series of conjoined parts. To exclude unwanted subjects. To show an area that is too large to be contained in a static shot.	To join separate items. To show spatial relationships. To show cause/effect. To transfer attention. To build up anticipation or suspense. As an introductory move.
Why elevate? (ped up)	To see over foreground objects. To see overall action.	To reduce prominence of foreground. To look down onto objects. To reduce subject strength.
Why depress? (ped down)	To frame picture with foreground objects. To obscure distant action. To obtain level shots of low subjects.	To increase their prominence. To emphasize subject strength.
Why zoom?	*See Tables 6.1 and 6.2.*	
Why dolly (track) in?	To see or emphasize detail or action. To exclude nearby subjects. To recompose shot after one of subjects has repositioned or exited. To change emphasis to another subject. To emphasize an advancing subject.	To underline an action or reaction. To emphasize subject importance. To localize attention. To reveal new information. To transfer attention. To follow a receding subject. To provide spatial awareness. To increase tension. To create a subjective effect.
Why dolly back?	To extend field of view. To include more of subject(s). To include widespread action. To reveal new information. To include entry of a new subject. To accommodate advancing action To withdraw from action.	To reduce emphasis. To show relationship or scale of previous shot, to the wider view (whole of subject, other subjects). To increase tension, as more significance is gradually revealed. To create surprise (e.g. reveal unsuspected onlooker). To provide spatial awareness. To create a subjective effect.
Why truck (crab)?	To follow subject moving across the scene. To reveal the extent of a subject/ scene, section by section. To examine a long subject or series of subjects.	To emphasize planes in depth (parallactic movement).
Why arc?	To see subject from another viewpoint. without transitions. To exclude/include a foreground/ background subject. To realign or recompose subject(s) when it moves. To reveal new information or a new (extra) subject. To correct for inaccurate subject positions (actor off marks).	To change visual emphasis.

Table 17.2 (cont.)

Why follow a moving subject?	In *close shots* – to keep it in frame, while showing reactions or detail information. In *long shots* – to show subject progress through an environment, or its relationship to other subjects.	To spatially interrelate subjects. To avoid transitions or viewpoint changes; maintaining continuity.

The borderline between tension and bathos can be narrow. An intended climax too easily becomes an *anti*climax. So you have to take care not to emphasize the trivial, or unintentionally to permit an emotional let-down after an emotional peak.

Pace

We might define *pace* as the rate of emotional progression. While a *slow pace* suggests dignity, solemnity, contemplation, deep emotion a *fast pace* conveys vigor, excitement, confusion, brashness, etc.

A well-balanced show continually readjusts its pace. A constant rapid tempo is exhausting; while a slow sustained one becomes dull. Pace comes from an accumulation of factors:

1. *The script.* Scene length, speech durations, phrasing, word lengths. Sharp snappy exchanges produce a faster pace than lengthy monolog.
2. *The delivery.* Fast, high-pitched, interrupted sounds provide a rapid pace compared with slow, low-pitched ones.
3. *Production treatment.* The rate of camera movement, switching, performer moves.

The eye can maintain a quicker pace than the ear. While the eye can assess, classify, evaluate almost immediately, the ear has to piece together consecutive sounds to interpret their overall meaning.

While a fast *visual* pace is readily assimilated, it is usually at the expense of less attention to the accompanying sound; unless visual changes are so rapid that the viewer ignores their information and just listens! Where emphasis is to be on the sound, visual pace generally needs to be relaxed.

Timing

There are two kinds of timing:

Mechanically – timing refers to duration checks that ensure a program keeps to schedule.

Artistically – timing is choosing the right moment and duration for an action – exactly when to cut, the speed of a transition, the pause duration between a comment and a retort.

Fig. 17.19   Hidden areas of interest
If an implied center of interest falls outside the frame, or is obscured, you may either intrigue or frustrate the audience. Subtly introduced, the technique may make a change of viewpoint welcome.

Fig. 17.20   Eyelines
Sometimes a more attractive convincing shot is obtained by having an actor cheat his eyeline. Instead of looking at the other person, he turns his eyes/head along an axis roughly bisecting the centerline and the lens axis (using a distant marker). Cheated eyelines may also be used to intercut across the imaginary line (see Fig. 17.11).

Inept timing lays wrong emphasis. It can ruin a gag, overemphasize mechanics, and disrupt continuity.

Visual clarity

If a picture is to get its message over quickly and unambiguously your audience must be able to see relevant details easily and clearly. Aim to avoid confusion, ambiguity, obscured information, restricted visibility, distractions, and similar visual confusion.

Viewpoint

A poor viewpoint can make even the commonest subjects look unfamiliar. Occasionally you may want to do this deliberately. But you should generally aim at clear unambiguous presentation; even if, for instance, it becomes necessary for a demonstrator to handle or place items in an unaccustomed way to improve shot clarity.

Distractions

Poor lighting treatment can distract and confuse, for it can hide true contours, cause planes to merge, and cast misleading or unmotivated shadows (especially from unseen people). It can also unnecessarily create hot spots, lens flares, and specular reflections.

Strong tonal contrasts can distract, as can strongly marked detail. Where someone stands in front of a very 'busy' background the cameraman may inadvertently focus harder on the background (or seem to) than on the subject itself. Close inspection of eyes, necktie, hair, etc. will show us if this is happening.

Fig. 17.21   Viewpoint and subject attitude
While frontal viewpoints can suggest alliance, over-shoulder reverse-angle shots can convey conflict.

Fig. 17.22   Viewpoint and clarity
A good camera viewpoint can mean the difference between: (1) important parts of the subject being hidden, or (2) a clearly visible demonstration.

Fig. 17.23 Ambiguity

1. In a flat picture, visual ambiguity can arise whenever lines or tones in one plane merge into those of another; as when adjacent patterns of adjacent tones are similar or where scenic lines continue.
2. Take care to avoid items in the set becoming extensions of the performer.

Fig. 17.24 Background contrast

Hand held items are often shot against clothing. Ensure that this background is not similar in hue and tone, or too distracting. If necessary hold it against a more suitable background.

Slightly defocused details, particularly lettering that we cannot read easily, can sidetrack our attention. For similar reasons, strongly colored defocused background objects are best excluded from shot wherever possible.

Confusing and frustrating techniques

How often, when watching regular TV productions, do you experience total frustration or antagonism at the way the show is being handled? Here is a list of frequent annoyances:

1. Important subjects cannot be clearly seen – they are soft-focused, masked, or shadowed, or merge with the background.
2. Someone points to detail – it is too small or fuzzy to see.
3. An intriguing collection of items fills the table – we are shown only a couple.
4. The demonstrator shows the host a particularly interesting item – the camera never sees it in detail.
5. An item is promised us later in the show – but time runs short and it is eliminated.
6. Titling or graphics are shown – but too briefly for us to read or examine properly.
7. A demonstrator shows us how to prune a tree – but the camera gets a close shot just as he finishes.
8. We are watching interesting action – but it is cut short and now we watch a talking head instead.
9. We can hear the events taking place off camera – but the camera is still on this voluble announcer.
10. The speaker who says to camera. 'I'll be with you in just a moment' – why isn't he ready?
11. The interviewer who asks questions (quoting from notes) but is not really listening to replies.
12. The interviewer who gives the *guest* information about himself!
13. The interviewer who asks the guest questions which require only 'Yes' or 'No' replies.
14. A too-brief glimpse of a subject – followed by the commentator talking about it instead.

15. Someone speaks in a group – but the camera dwells on the previous person. (They have not yet lined up a shot of the new speaker!)

16. Wrongly cued performers – the action has already started, and we feel that we have missed seeing something important. Or the performer has finished, but the camera lingers. The performer with 'egg on the face' wonders what to do.

17. The shot that leaves us wondering what we are supposed to be looking at or where we are now.

18. The lost opportunities when the camera goes to a remote exotic location – but all we see are a few close shots against a nondescript background.

Interest or concentration patterns

Throughout any production audience interest and concentration will fluctuate; growing and subsiding. Tension and excitement build up and relax. The trick is to arrange these responses so that they come when you need them most.

Directors and writers rely on experience and intuition rather than analysis to blend the various contributory factors:

1. *Script construction* – the order and duration of shots, their dramatic strength, plot outline, etc.
2. *Interpretation* – the performance, its delivery, etc.
3. *Production treatment* – staging, camera treatment, editing, audio treatment, etc.

Fig. 17.25 Concentration pattern
Showing audience concentration throughout program.

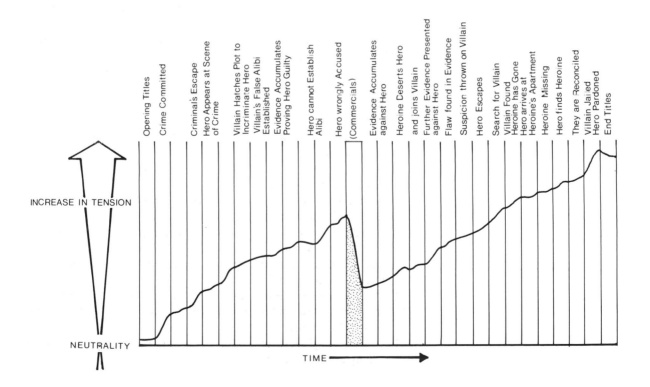

But by outlining this reaction pattern as a rough graph you can see how the overall impact changes throughout the production and how the separate factors combine.

In the well-worn storyline of Figure 17.25 you can see where one seeks to build tension; where it will be allowed to fall. You aim to grip audience interest at the start of the show, introducing suitable variations, and building to an encouraging peak just before commercial breaks. You can see the bid to recapture interest immediately afterwards . . . and so on to the finale.

Both strengthening and relaxing tension require some care. After a lull, a peak appears greater. But after a long relaxed period, a highly dramatic peak can be intrusive, so that the viewer becomes overaware of his own sudden reaction; responding with laughter rather than shock. A climax may even pass him by, unless he is emotionally preconditioned to receive it.

Fig. 17.26 Scene analysis
Various factors contribute to the effect of each scene.

Preferably, you build interest, concentration, or tension in a progressive series of peaks. But too slow a development can allow interest to wane. Too many climaxes eventually produce no climax at all.

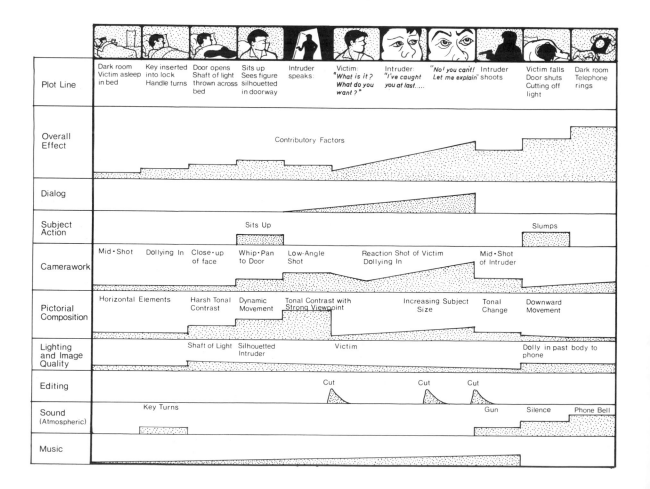

Relaxation after an interest peak can lead to indifference. Again, sudden tension release can precipitate amusement, after the nervous strain of concentration.

Where action or storyline follow a recognizable pattern the viewer may grasp the point before the director has time to finish making it! To avoid this happening you can disguise the obvious through careful treatment; or if this is not possible, at least bypass all superfluous detail (using filmic space and time).

Sometimes attention will wander, despite great visual activity. And when quickening pace or high mobility follow a slow episode (e.g. a fast-cutting film clip after slow-speed studio shots) the viewer often finds himself *inspecting* the fast scene rather than stirred by its tempo.

If you present an excess of information or provide facts too quickly the earnest student may feel frustrated and confused at his inability to note them. But a general audience is more likely to absorb a few random aspects and then relax when they have seen enough (not, as some believe, becoming bored when they have grasped its full import).

Table 17.3 Methods of focusing attention (Figure 17.18)

Exclusion	Taking close shots. Excluding unwanted subjects. Using neutral backgrounds.
Visual indication	Indication with a finger, inserted or superimposed marker (arrow, circle).
Aural indication	A verbal clue or instruction – 'Look at the black box'.
Color	Using prominent contrasting hues against neutrals or muted (pastel) colors.
Camera viewpoint	Avoid weak viewpoints (side or rear) or weakening angles (high or long shots). Concentrate interest by differential focusing or camera movement.
Composition	Using convergent line or pattern, picture balance, isolation, prominence through scale.
Contrasting the subject with its surroundings	Through differences in relative size, shape, proportions, scale, type of line, movement, association (e.g. elaborate with plain), disposition (e.g. seated with standing), etc. The area of interest might have the lightest tones or maximum contrast in the picture.
By movement	Movement attracts according to its speed, strength, and direction. Change direction during motion, or interrupt and resume, rather than maintain sustained action.
	According to how it is introduced, a movement can attract attention to: *itself* (a moving hand), the *subject* (person whose hand it is), or the *purpose* of the movement (what the hand is pointing at). Remember, when the camera moves (or zooms) it can virtually create the illusion of subject movement, so drawing attention to it.
	Synchronizing a movement *with* dialog, music, effects (especially the subject's own) gives it strength and draws attention to it. Having a person move on his own dialog emphasizes both action and speech.
By subject attitude	Having performers use strong movements – upward or diagonal, stand up, play to camera, move in front of others or scenic elements.

Visual padding

Although there are occasions when you can make effective use of silence, a blank screen is an anathema! Yet many subjects have no *direct* visual element. Consider discussions, poetry, music – the emphasis is on *sound*. What does the viewer gain from *seeing* people perform! He sees expressions, instrumental fingering, etc., but these are the mechanics. They have nothing intrinsically to do with the material itself, its significance or purpose (i.e. the argument or musical effect). In fact, the pictures may actually cause *distraction* as he watches the performers – becoming preoccupied with their appearance, expressions, and mannerisms.

The visual problem

For some programs, directly appropriate visuals are not obvious:

1. *Abstract subjects* – philosophical, spiritual, social concepts.
2. *General, non-specific subjects* – humanity, transport, weather.
3. *Imaginary events* – hypothetical, fantasy.
4. *Historical events* – before photography, or unphotographed events.
5. *Forthcoming events* – future projects.
6. *Filming is not possible* – photography is prohibited or subject inaccessible.
7. *Filming is impracticable* – photography is too dangerous, meaningful shots not possible.
8. *Concluded events* – event now over and has not been photographed.
9. *Appropriate visuals too costly* – would involve distant travel, copyright problems.

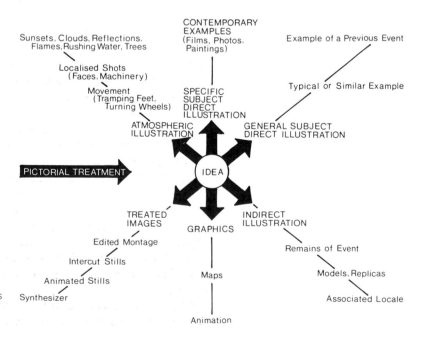

Fig. 17.27 part 1   Subject illustration – pictorial treatment
Where pictures are not readily available, or a more imaginative effect is required than the direct approach, various substitutes are possible.

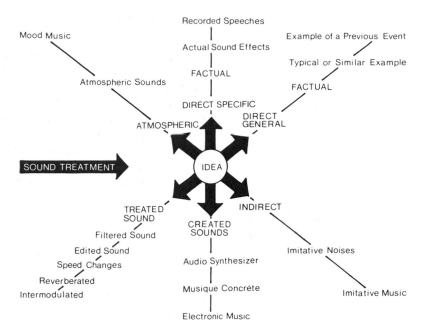

Fig. 17.27 part 2 Subject illustration – sound treatment
Some possible alternatives to direct sound.

Possible solutions

When the director cannot show the actual subject being discussed he often has to provide a suitable alternative picture – a kind of *visual padding* or 'screen filler' ('wallpaper shots').

The most economical solution, and the least compelling, is to introduce a *commentator*; who *tells* us about what we cannot *see*, as he stands at the now empty location (historical battlefield, site of crime, outside the conference hall).

Inserts in the form of photographs, film clips, VT excerpts, paintings, drawings (typically used for courtroom reports) can all provide illustrative material. Occasionally, a dramatic re-enactment is feasible.

When discussing future events you can show stills or library shots of a *previous occasion* to suggest the atmosphere, or show the principles (celebration days, processions).

You may show a *substitute* subject (not the animal that escaped but one just like it), hoping your audience does not mistakenly assume that they are seeing the actual subject.

Occasionally the camera can show the *absence* of the subject: the frame of the stolen painting; where the castle once stood.

Associated subjects are frequently used. We visit the poet's birthplace, often using stock tourist location shots. However, they may not be strictly applicable (wrong period), inaccurate (wrong part of city), or irrelevant (not architecture, but social conditions influenced his poetry). But, apart from family album snapshots or newspaper cuttings, nothing else is available!

When using library (stock) shots or stills there is always the danger that available shots will become overfamiliar through repeated use. This is

Fig. 17.28 part 1   Cheated substitutes – the desired sequence
A fugitive climbs a cliff to escape pursuers. The viewer sees the formidable cliff, and
his climb – but he dislodges a rock, and they look up.

Fig. 17.28 part 2   Cheated substitutes – the studio procedure
The studio set-up is simple: A gravel-strewn floor, a photograph of a cliff face, and a
surface-contoured flat over which the fugitive crawls (shot is canted to suggest
vertical climbing).

particularly likely with historic material, or unexpected tragedy (assas-
sination, air crash).

Some forms of visual padding suit a variety of occasions. The same
waving wheatfield can epitomize food crops, daily bread, prosperity,
agriculture, the war on insect pests . . .

Abstracts can be pressed into service at almost any time! Atmospheric
shots of rippling water, shadows, light reflections, into-sun flares,
defocused images, shooting up into a tracery of leaves . . . all have very
regular use!

The illusion of time

Motion-picture editing has long since accustomed us to concepts of filmic
space and time:

Filmic space – intercuts action that is concurrent at different places. As a
soldier dies . . . his son is born back home.

Filmic time – omits intermediate action, condensing time and sharpening
pace. We cut from the automobile stopping . . . to the driver entering his
apartment.

Table 17.4   Continuity (Figure 17.3)

	If you are shooting discontinuously, or out of sequence (for later correct-order editing), several kinds of continuity problems can develop.
Technical continuity	The quality of intercut shots of the same action should match: similar color, brightness, contrast, tonal balance; light direction; shot height; perspective.
Pictorial continuity	Atmospheric effect should be consistent: e.g. weather conditions – not raining in one shot, dry in a reverse shot.
Environmental continuity	The location should appear consistent from different viewpoints.
Spatial continuity	The audience can lose their sense of direction, e.g. on reverse cuts. Space and distance can change with varying lens angle.
Physical continuity	The appearance of people and the scene should not change noticeably between successive shots, e.g. clothing, set dressing, props, etc.
Performance continuity `Action continuity*	If you repeat an action sequence (to provide different shot lengths or viewpoints for intercutting) performers should have similar expressions and make similar gestures in each version. (Check VTR replay.)
Time continuity	There should be appropriate signs of time passing during scenes. Check how food, cigarettes, clocks, candles, etc. change.
Event continuity	Take care to avoid accidental jumps in time or place, when parts of continuous action are missing. (Use cutaways.) Avoid accidentally duplicated action. Avoid rediscovering people in a scene after they have apparently exited; or having a person unexpectedly relocated after an intermediate shot.
Relationship continuity	Avoid shot mismatches that jump-cut the subject around the screen.
Attention continuity	Make sure that centers of attention are reasonably related between shots.
Audio continuity (technically)	Ensure that audio volume and quality are compatible between successive shots.
Audio continuity (artistically)	Maintain similar atmosphere between shots in an edited scene: reverberation, background noises, effects, room tone, balance, etc.
Dialog continuity	Uninterrupted speech when shots change during dialog.

Where all the intervening action has no plot relevance the viewer would often resent a slow pace stating the obvious.

Time lapses

You can use several devices to indicate the passage of time. Explanatory titles are direct and unambiguous, but other subtler techniques are generally preferable. For short time lapses:

1. Slow fade-out, new scene slowly fades in.
2. Cutting away from a scene, we assume time has elapsed when returning to it.

3. A time indicator (clock, sundial, burning candle) shows passage of time.
4. Lighting changes with passing time (a sunlit room gradually darkens).
5. Dissolve between before/after shots of a meal, fireplace, etc.
6. Transition between sounds with time association – nocturnal frogs and owls, to early-morning roosters and birdsong.
7. Defocus shot, cut or mix to another defocused shot and then refocus.

For longer time lapses:

1. A calendar sheds leaves or changes date.
2. Seasonal changes – from winter snow to spring flowers.
3. Changes in personal appearance – beard growth, ageing, fashion changes.
4. New to old – dissolving from a fresh newspaper . . . to a yellow crumpled discarded version.

Flashbacks

A familiar device, the *flashback* turns back time to see events before the present action for reminiscive, explanatory, or comparative purposes. Typical methods include reversed time-lapse conventions (e.g. the old becomes new again) or explanatory dialogue during 'mist', edge diffusion, ripple, or defocus dissolves. Nowadays, a very brief *flash cut-in* (½–2 seconds long) conveys recognition or moments of memory recall.

Interscene devices

As well as the usual editing transitions (cut, dissolve/mix, wipe) and their derivations (defocus and ripple dissolves), you can use various interscene devices to link sequences.

1. *Blackout.* A performer moves up to block out the lens. He (or another subject) moves away, revealing a new scene. A balloon is used similarly, being burst to show the new scene

Fig. 17.29 Crowds
Crowds can be simulated by selected viewpoints:
1. Showing part of the crowd.
2. Using foreground (real, dummy, cut-outs).
3. Inserting people electronically into a recorded scene.

2. *Pan away*. The camera turns from the action area to a nearby subject. Panning back, we now see different action (or appearance), for time has passed.

3. *Bridging subject*. Associative material interconnects two scenes: shots of wheels turning to imply travel, swirling mists to form an atmospheric transition.

4. *Decorative bridge*. Abstract forms in light or shadow between scenes. Moving patterns – kaleidoscope, spirals, whip pan. Digital video effects are increasingly used here: mosaic tile, posterization treatment, explosions, etc.

5. *Matching shots*. The close-up ending one scene (wristwatch) dissolves to a matching shot (bus station clock) in the next.

Deliberate disruption

The idea of deliberately cutting away from the main action to look at incidental happenings nearby may seem somewhat incongruous. Yet, if appropriately introduced, this disruption offers valuable production opportunities. Providing the viewer does not feel that he is missing vital information or is robbed of exciting action, the technique can heighten interest and enthusiasm.

Cutaway shots (intercut shots)

By cutting from the main action to *secondary activity* or *associated subjects* (e.g. spectator reactions), you can:

1. Join shots that are unmatched in continuity or action.
2. Remove unwanted, unsuccessful, dull or excess material.
3. Suggest a time lapse, to compress or expand time.
4. Show additional explanatory information (*detail shots*).
5. Reveal the action's environment.
6. Show who a person is speaking to; how another person is responding (reaction shots).
7. Show what the speaker is seeing, talking about, or thinking about.
8. Create tension, to give dramatic emphasis.
9. Make comment on a situation (cutting from a diner to a pig at trough).

Interviews can be shot using a continuous intercut multi-camera set-up or as a one-camera treatment. A separate series of cutaway shots (*cutaways, nod shots*) are often recorded *afterwards*, in which the interviewer and interviewee are seen in singles or over-shoulder shots, mutely smiling, nodding, 'reacting', looking interested. When edited in (to disguise cuts, continuity breaks, or to add visual variety), the subterfuge appears quite natural. Without such intermediates, any continuously held shot would *jump frame* when edited (dissolves may improve the disruption).

Cut-in or *inserts* may also be used when reshooting parts of the action from another camera set-up (different shot size, or angle).

Reaction shots/partials/cut-in shots

By skilfully concealing information you can prime the imagination and arouse curiosity. Instead of showing an event, you demonstrate its effect.

1. *Reaction shot*. The door opens . . . we see the victim's horror-stricken face, not the intruder.
2. *Partial shot*. A switchblade opens . . . is moved out of frame . . . we hear the victim's cry . . . then silence.
3. *Cut-in shot*. We watch the victim's cat drinking milk . . . to sounds of a fight and a body falling . . . the victim's hand comes into frame, upsetting the milk dish.

This technique can provide maximum impact with minimum facilities, conveying information by implication rather than direct statement. It aims to intrigue and tantalize. Ineptly introduced, though, it can frustrate.

The recorded insert

Occasionally during a studio production we may cut away from studio cameras' pictures to show film or videotape instead. There are several reasons why we might want to do this:

- *To illustrate a lecture, demonstration or talk*; e.g. shots of a trip down the Amazon.
- *To imply that the studio setting is in a particular location* (showing stock shots of moorland 'outside the house').
- *To 'authenticate' a setting*. We see a small boarded room in the studio. A stock shot of a ship is inserted, so we accept that this is a ship's cabin.
- *To show environments that could not be re-created effectively in the studio* (e.g. a typhoon).
- *To extend action*. You can have a person walk through a door in the studio set (an apartment) out into the street (on film).
- *To extend settings*. Shooting a *partial setting* in the studio (e.g. a shop doorway) we cut to the complete street location in the film insert.

Fig. 17.30 Staging distractions
Various distractions can appear in shot. Here is a particularly disastrous collection!
1. Unexplained, distracting object in shot.
2. Cable in shot.
3. Visible surface damage on flat.
4. Shadow of someone out of shot.
5. Wall-picture not straight.
6. Light reflection.
7. Camera reflection visible in table picture.
8. Multiple shadows from lamp fitting.
9. Distracting light patch.
10. Wall mirror appears as 'halo'.
11. Wrinkle in background surface.
12. Shooting off the set!
13. Obtrusive foreground prop.

- *Reducing the number of studio settings.* Where studio space is too limited for the required number of settings, additional scenes can be insert-filmed.
- *Once-only action.* Prefilming or videotaping is essential where action might prove unsuccessful in the studio (for example, involving animals); or take too much time during the videotaping period (an elaborate make-up change); or is too dangerous (fire); or is non-repeatable (an explosion); or is very critical (an accurately thrown knife).
- *Visual effects.* To produce time-lapse effects, reversed action, transformations, etc.
- *Animation sequences.* These may be cartoon or animated still-life.
- *To include performers not otherwise available.* Filming persons who could not attend the taping session (e.g. overseas guests).
- *Situations where effective studio staging is impractical.* Recording location exteriors, spectacle, etc. where studio replicas would be impractical or less effective.

Library shots (stock shots)

These are short film (or video) sequences of illustrative material, held in an organization's archives or rented from specialist libraries. *Library shots/stock shots* are inserted into a program where it would be impracticable or uneconomic to shoot new material. These short clips cover a very wide field, including news events, location shots, manufacturing processes, natural history, personalities, stunts, etc. etc. They are widely used to illustrate talks, demonstrations, newscasts, and to provide atmospheric and environmental shots for drama.

The picture quality of library shots can be variable in color, blemishes, and definition – they may not cut into studio shots unobtrusively. Also, available library shots can become too familiar, particularly when they are the only record of an event.

Where only monochrome shots are available and the program content is appropriate, these clips may be tinted (sepia, blue, red-orange). This is achieved by using a color synthesizer, by adjusting color balance, or using 'tarif' controls. Snow scenes and night shots may still prove convincing in black and white, although transmitted in a color system.

Library shots are often run mute (silent), and new effects or music substituted for any original soundtrack.

The illusion of spectacle

Budgets do not generally permit lavish staging. Yet occasions arise when you want to create an impressive illusion of space, grandeur, and spectacle. Several methods are available.

■ *Library shots (stock shots)*   By intercutting existing filmed library shots with limited studio action (often close shots) it is possible to build up extremely convincing illusions. Where highly dramatic spectacle is required, as in battle scenes, hurricanes, volcanic eruptions, mobs, earthquakes, floods, this is usually the only solution.

However, available library shots may not be exactly suitable for your purpose (contents, quality, viewpoint, time of day, unwanted or spurious aspects included). It might even be necessary to reorganize the studio treatment to suit the library shot!

■ *Direct imitation*   A complete or *partial* replica of part of the scene (e.g. a stone wall) is intercut with location material or library shots (the actual castle).

■ *Indirect imitations*   Here an environment provided by electronic insertion (chroma key, CSO), rear projection, photo backings, or glass shot, etc. is conjoined with a localized studio setting. For example: an automobile in the studio is inserted into a filmed shot of a highway; an impressive ceiling (a graphic) appears to be part of a studio set.

■ *Cheated substitute*   Montage can create an illusion by intercutting small representative parts of the action to convey a composite impression. Ingenious, imaginative, and most effective if properly handled, you must ensure that the component parts are completely integrated. For instance, you can build up a dramatic impression of a battle simply by rapidly intercutting close shots of details in war photographs to an audio background of battle noises.

18 Production organization

How any director organizes his show varies with local procedures, the nature of the production, and his own experience and temperament. Consequently, there are approaches ranging from the 'spontaneous' to the meticulously planned. Much depends, too, on the artistic and operational standards you demand, and the production crew's experience.

Unplanned productions

Total unpredictability is not adventurous. It creates needless stress and haphazard results. Television necessarily involves teamwork. If people do not have a clear idea of what is happening you must not be surprised when there is no chair for the extra guest, the film insert is not ready, lighting is inappropriate, the camera has a wrong shot, or you cannot hear the speaker.

The amateur often collects material, then considers how to use it. The professional invariably starts with a plan of campaign, however broad, and obtains or arranges material to these concepts; modifying as necessary.

Unrehearsed formats

Even where you cannot rehearse a production you will usually find that the situation fits some familiar format. So you can arrange suitable staging and camera positions, and allocate probable shots. It is possible to precheck potential shots and lighting, using available people as stand-ins. Then, when talent appears, you can quickly preview them to check over voice levels, make-up, lighting, and costume.

If the format is less definite (e.g. a dance troup arriving just before air time) it is a matter of choosing typical strategic viewpoints (front and cross shooting), then allocating cover shots and close shots to cameras for a defined working area (not forgetting to tell the performers of any necessary movement limits!). The show itself largely involves recognizing effective shots as they are offered; taking action detail and group shots in a balanced ratio.

Regular formats

There are a number of regular formats: interviews, panel discussions, piano and instrumental performances, singers, and newscasts. These are usually familiar to the production team and meaningful shooting varia-

407

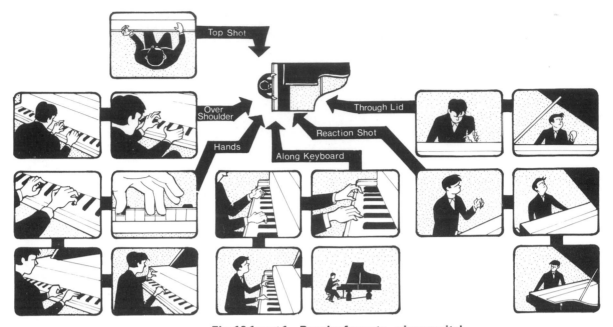

Fig. 18.1 part 1   Regular formats – piano recital
The basic range of pictorially attractive shots is limited when presenting a piano performance.

Fig. 18.1 part 2   Regular formats – formal interview
In a formal interview, the number of effective shots is relatively few.

tions are limited. What the performer is saying (or playing) is more important than straining to achieve new and original shot development. Consequently, such productions follow recognizable lines, so that the director often starts off with planned viewpoints and then introduces a particular treatment as it becomes desirable.

Planning for regular productions may largely be a matter of co-ordinating staff and facilities, ensuring that film or VT inserts are available (with known timing and cue points); graphics, titles, etc. are prepared, and any additional material organized. The production itself may be based upon a series of key shots and spontaneous on-the-fly decisions.

Complex productions

Whether you are shooting in the studio or on location, time is money and must be used efficiently. While smaller shows may get by with a

Table 18.1 The production process

Program concepts	Idea potentials, objectives, potential audience, market, saleability, probable duration.
Executive decisions	Selecting *above-the-line* personnel (production: director, writer, etc.). Budget allocation. Production scheduling (deadlines). Preproduction publicity.
Scripting	Theme, coverage, style, research/advisor. Script editing (evaluating content and practicability). Script conference/rewrites. Director's visualization.
Organizing talent	Contacts, auditions, interviews, casting, contracts. Organization/preparation of performers. Read-through, rehearsals, costume/make-up preliminaries.
Organization of inserts	Any *pre-studio* photography, filming, taping. (Arrangements for shooting these: copyright clearances, facility fees, access permissions, permits, insurance, scheduling, staffing, editing, etc.) Selection of illustrative inserts (film clips, VT, stills. Graphics and titles. Musical inserts (on disc, on tape, performed live). Any equipment for demonstrations (construction or hire).
Staffing	Coordinating services of *below-the-line* personnel (technical, operational, facilities).
Production paperwork	Requisitions. Scripts (draft, rehearsal, and camera script). Rundown sheet, camera cards, etc.
Organizing artistic services	Staging, costume/wardrobe, make-up.
Organizing technical services	Cameras, lighting, audio, telecine, VTR, special effects.
Organizing facilities	Loan/hire of equipment. Storage, transport, catering, accommodations (dressing rooms). Prompters, audience arrangements (tickets, seating, warm-up).
Pre-studio rehearsals	Rehearsal of dialog, moves, action; treatment preparation.
Studio rehearsals	Camera rehearsals (finalization of action, video, and audio treatment).
Videotape recording	Straight-through, discontinuous, or compilation recording.
VT editing	Off-line selection, organization, and editing of video recording. Audio sweetening.
Review and transmission	Evaluation of recording.
Postproduction activities	Logs/reports. Publicity/billing/promotion. Correspondence, ratings.

Table 18.2   Typical considerations in technical planning

Talent	Cast discussed, re costume and make-up requirements (styles, fitting, etc.).
Staging	Style, treatment of sets. Staging plan: details of set structures, scenic changes, storage, audience seating. Special visual effects (physical, video, lighting). Special props. Safety precautions, regulations, etc.
Action	Director indicates possible performer positions, action, business.
Cameras	Number of cameras, types of mountings, main positions for each scene, probable moves. Any camera accessories (special lenses, etc.). Specialists estimate feasibility of anticipated treatment (checking sufficient working space for cameras/booms, time for moves, cable routing, etc.).
Lighting	Discussion of lighting treatment feasibility, relative to: scenic design, action, sound pick-up, time/equipment/manpower availability. Discussion of pictorial effects, atmosphere, etc. Discussion of picture matching to inserts (film or VT).
Audio	Similar discussion to *'Lighting'*. Considering audio pick-up methods, potential problems. Audio inserts discussed (prerecorded library effects, spot effects, music).
Effects required	Special effects, staging effects, lighting effects, optical effects, chroma key (CSO), DVE, special sound effects, etc.
Artwork/graphics/titles	Displays, graphics, maps, charts, models, etc.
Further technical facilities	Equipment organization, re filming or pre-studio videotaping. Technical resources required: telecine, videotape, video disc, slide scanner, picture monitors, prompters, cuing facilities, etc.
Scheduling	Pre-studio/recording. Experimental sessions.
Pre-studio rehearsals	Read-through, block action, dry run (technical run).
Studio rehearsal/recording	Production approach: live, live-on tape, rehearse/record, scene-by-scene, etc. Camera rehearsal (times and arrangements, meal breaks). Technical periods (camera line-up, relighting, resetting scenery). Recording schedule.
Editing	Scheduling and facilities. Audio sweetening. Postproduction video effects.

preliminary talk-over a few days before the production date, for more complex projects comprehensive planning is essential. The team must be briefed and organized, and this requires discussive agreement; for there are sundry factors to consider, such as time estimates, costing, manpower, safety, union agreements, etc.

Planning preliminaries

Planning begins with *script study*; the director reading and visualizing with his budget, facilities, and personnel in mind.

Some directors rely on the set designer to produce an environment for action and then arrange performers within this setting. Others indicate the strategic features or staging format they require, and from that briefing the designer interprets and builds workable arrangements.

After preliminary discussion, the designer produces a rough scale plan of the various settings; often on separate pieces of overlay (tracing) that can be moved around the studio staging plan for optimum layout. He may include sketches, reference photographs, and preliminary elevations.

Those responsible for studio operations, including technical organization, cameras, lighting, audio, make-up, costume, etc., may be involved at these early stages.

Treatment breakdown

Clearly, there are many ways in which the director could set about devising his production treatment. So much depends on individual experience, methods, and the kind of show involved. A typical approach is to closely analyze the script, and within the staging format to visualize potential treatments for each situation. The director then systematically blocks out movement and camera shots, to build up a continuous, effective presentation. The same situation can often be tackled in various different but equally successful ways. Let us look at an example for a dramatic production:

Returning husband enters door, wife has unexpected guest.

This could be broken down as:

1. Husband enters door, hangs up hat . . . MLS shows who it is, yet orientates audience.
2. Wife looks up, greeting him . . . Medium two-shot showing her with guest.
3. Husband turns and sees guest . . . CU of husband's reaction.
4. Guest rises, walk to greet husband . . . From medium two-shot; pans with guest, dollying in for tight two-shot of guest and husband.

The interpretation could have been simpler. Its impact would have been different.

1. Husband enters door, hangs up hat . . . Over-shoulder long shot between wife and guest, showing entrance. Watch husband's reactions, tightening shot as he walks to guest.

Shot 1 = Cam 1
Shot 2 = Cam 2
Shot 3 = Cam 1
Shot 4 = Cam 3

Fig. 18.2 Action treatment
The plan summarizes the camera treatment for a brief scene (see text).

ABOVE THE LINE COSTS
Writing, Performing, Production Elements

Cast
Performers
Music · Script
Floor Manager
Writer · Script Editor
Choreographer · Musicians
Production Personnel
(Producer, Director, Assistants)
Insert Materials (Stock Film, etc.)
Offices · Rehearsal Room
Announcer · Office Services

BELOW THE LINE COSTS
Physical Elements Involved in Mounting the Production

Make-Up · Costumes · Graphics · Prompters
Titling · Transportation · Storage · Labor
Scenic Design · Scenery · Construction · Properties
Studio Servicing · Engineering Personnel · Filming
Editing · Videotape Recording · Remote Pick-ups (O B s)
Special Effects · Sound Effects · Stage Manager
Studio Facilities & Personnel (Technical Operations Crew, Cameras,
Sound, Video, Lighting)
Additional Technical Facilities Etc. Etc.

Fig. 18.3 Budget
Accurate cost estimation and accounting are essential in TV organization, despite the great diversity of the various contributions. Budgets are usually related to the concepts of 'above' and 'below' the line. These differentiate between the 'writing, performing, and production elements', and the various 'back-up' services and physical elements involved in mounting the production.

2. As guest stands . . . Cut to frontal two-shot of guest and wife greeting him. Zoom in to guest. Intercut CU of guest and husband.

Having decided on a particular treatment the director now arranges camera and audio coverage for these shots. He will often use a 'shot plotter' (protractor or transparent triangle) showing the lens-angle coverage, estimating and marking the camera positions needed (1A, 1B, 2A, etc.), and locating a sound boom (A1). The resultant rough production plan (camera plan), together with his script margin action notes or sketches, form the basis for all rehearsals. Even the biggest productions can be analyzed into shots or sequences in this way.

Production planning meeting

Once a complete provisional floor plan has been prepared by the designer, the specialists involved in studio operations meet with the director and the designer. They examine the staging proposals and production treatment; evaluate, discuss, anticipate practical problems, and so on. They outline their own proposed contributions – lighting treatment, audio effects, costume details, etc.

Following this meeting, they then carry through their own organizational procedures (documentation, costing, manpower, scheduling, equipment selection), and the designer issues the agreed *staging plan (floor plan, ground plan, setting plan)*.

The production planning meeting forms the basis for efficient economic teamwork. Problems anticipated and overcome at this stage prevent last-minute compromises. Camera cable routing, for example, is

Fig. 18.4 The Camera Plan
Position of cameras 1, 2, 3, 4 are successively marked (1A, 1B). Positions of sound booms A, B, are successively marked (A1, A2).

a typical potential hazard. Cables get snarled up, can impede other cameras, or drag around noisily. So directors may move around scale card cutouts of cameras (perhaps cord-attached to simulate cables) when devising their camera plans.

Much depends, of course, on the type of show you are considering, how it is to be recorded, elaboration of treatment, any special set-ups (chroma key), rehearsal time, editing facilities, etc.

In a *live* or live-on tape show you must allow time for people, cameras, and sound booms to move between situations; time to cover any costume or scene changes, and to reposition equipment or furniture. Discontinuous shooting overcomes such problems; although continuity and editing factors then arise.

The script

Semi-scripted show

For ad-lib shows, discussions, interviews, variety, compilation shows, and demonstrations it is normal to use *outline scripts*. This script lists the talent involved, facilities being used, graphics (slides), film and VT

Table 18.3   The rehearsal script

SCENE	INT./ EXTR	LOCATION	TIME OF DAY
3.	INT	LOUNGE	NIGHT

(GEORGE ENTERS. WALKS TO TABLE SWITCHES ON LAMP.)

GEORGE: (CALLS) The lights are OK in here.
It must be your lamp

(GEORGE TAKES GUN FROM DRAWER.)
SLIPS IT INTO HIS POCKET: PULLING OUT TELEGRAM. HOLDS IT UP.

'SORRY CANNOT COME WEEKEND. BRIAN SICK. WRITING . . . JUDY.'

(HAND SCREWS IT UP AND THROWS INTO FIRE.)
(DOOR OPENS: EILEEN ENTERS.)

EILEEN: Really, these people are too bad. They promised to be here tonight.
Look how late . . .

GEORGE: It's probably the storm that has delayed them. They'll be here all right.

(EILEEN SITS ON COUCH: GEORGE JOINS HER.)

EILEEN: If Judy knows you're here, it'll take wild horses to keep her away.

GEORGE: How many more times do I have to tell you . . .

EILEEN: Why do you keep pretending?

/ LIGHTNING FLASH /

GEORGE: I've warned you. You'll go too far.

Table 18.4   The camera script

SHOT	CAM.	(POSITION)	SCENE	INT./ EXTR.	LOCATION	TIME OF DAY	F/X
			CAMS. 2A, 3A, 4B.		SOUND BOOM B1		
			3.	INT.	LOUNGE	NIGHT	
							TAPE:
	F/U						WIND
10.	2.	A					RAIN
		LS PAN/ZOOM on GEORGE to MS			(GEORGE ENTERS. WALKS TO TABLE. SWITCHES ON LAMP.)		
					GEORGE: (CALLS) The lights are OK in here.		
11.	3.	A	It must be your lamp. /				
					(GEORGE TAKES GUN FROM DRAWER.)		
12.	2.	A			/		
		MS			SLIPS IT INTO HIS POCKET: PULLING OUT TELEGRAM. HOLDS IT UP.		
13.	4.	B			/		
		BCU of telegram	'SORRY CANNOT COME WEEKEND. BRIAN SICK. WRITING . . . JUDY.'				
		PULL FOCUS on fire as he throws.			(HAND SCREWS IT UP AND THROWS INTO FIRE.)		
14.	3.	A			/		
		LS			(DOOR OPENS: EILEEN ENTERS.)		
			EILEEN: Really, these people are too bad. They promised to be here tonight. Look how late . . .				
			GEORGE: It's probably the storm that has delayed them. They'll be here all right.				
		DOLLY IN to MS as EILEEN X's to couch.			(EILEEN SITS ON COUCH: GEORGE JOINS HER.)		
			EILEEN: If Judy knows you're here, it'll take wild horses to keep her away.				
			GEORGE: How many more times do I have to tell you . . .				
			EILEEN: Why do you keep pretending?				
					/ LIGHTNING FLASH /		
15.	2.	A			/		
		CU	GEORGE: I've warned you. You'll go too far.				DISC: THUNDERCLAP

inserts (identifying sections, giving durations). Dialog is only included in detail for introductory announcements, and commentary containing cue-lines (for cuing inserts, editing breaks, or redeploying cameras).

Fully scripted show

Here the script develops in several stages:

1. *Preliminary script/draft/outline script/writer's script.* Initial submitted full-page script (dialog and action) before script editing.

2. *Rehearsal script.* Script prepared for TV and used for pre-studio rehearsal. Script details the locales (settings), characters, action, talent directives, dialog (Table 18.3).

3. *Camera script.* A revised script for camera rehearsals, augmented with details of production treatment: cameras and audio, cues, transitions, stage instructions, set changes (Table 18.4).

TV scripts follow several 'standard' layouts. The preferred version uses two vertical columns, with picture treatment (cameras, switching) on the *left*, action and dialog on the *right*, together with stage instructions and lighting/effects cues. Some studios prefer a *single-column* cinematic format, with transitions in a left margin, and all video and audio information in a single main column. Directors often hand-mark this version with their own instructional symbols indicating transitions and shots. But for more complex productions this is less easily followed than a two-column format.

The *full script* is not, as some people believe, an artistically inhibiting document that commits everyone concerned to a rigid plan of procedure. It can be modified as the need arises. It simply informs you about what is expected at each moment of the production. Studio rehearsal time is too precious to use up explaining basic mechanics as you go. Far better to have a detailed script that shows the exact moment for the lighting change, to cue the film, or introduce the superimposition. The full script is a plan of campaign, that has details added to it as the production develops.

For some types of show the outline script is quite sufficient; in fact, any attempt to include 'pseudo information', such as the entire dialog for a film insert, would usually be pointless. (The duration and 'in and out cues' would suffice.)

When is it necessary to fully script a production?

1. When the dialog is to follow a prescribed text, that is to be learned, or read from a prompter or script.

2. Where action is detailed, so that people move to certain places at particular times and do specific things there. (This can affect cameras, sound, and lighting treatment.)

3. When there are carefully timed inserts (film, videotape) that have to be cued accurately into the program.

4. When the duration of a section must be kept within an allotted time bracket, yet cover certain agreed subject points. (The speaker might otherwise dwell on one point, and miss another out altogether.) Even where postproduction editing is available, it is not always possible to remedy uneven subject coverage.

5. Where there are spot cues, e.g. a 'lightning flash' and an effects disc of thunder at a point in the dialog.

So you will find fully scripted approaches in newscasts, drama productions, operas, comedy shows (situation comedy), documentary-type presentations, and major commercials. Where dialog and/or action are spontaneous, there can be no script; only an outline of routine (e.g. discussions). A formal talk is scripted.

Table 18.5   TV script abbreviations

Many organizations duplicate the *rehearsal script* on white paper. Operational information is added to the original stencil to provide the *camera script* on yellow paper.

All *camera shots* are numbered in a fully scripted show. *Inserts* are not numbered (film, slides, VT, titles, graphics), but are identified in the audio column. Where possible, cutting points are marked in the dialog with a slash mark _____ /
underlining back to the camera number.

Various abbreviations are widely used:

Equipment	CAM	Camera.	CG	Character generator.	
	MIKE; MIC	Microphone.	Title; TC	Title card.	
	BOOM	Sound boom.	G	Graphic.	
	F/P; FISH	Fishpole.	PIC	Pictorial graphic.	
	VT; VTR	Videotape.	PIX	Photo-caption (on camera).	
	F	Film.	ESS	Electronic still store.	
	TC; TK	Telecine.	SL	Slide.	
	PROJ	Projection unit.	CP; CAP	Caption.*	
	RP	Rear projection.	BP	Back projection.*	
	DVE	Digital video effect.	ROLLER	Roller caption (crawl).*	
			CPU	Caption slide.*	
			TJ	Telejector (type of slide scanner).*	
Position	L/H, R/H	Picture left-hand, right-hand	B/G, F/G	Background, foreground	
			X	Move across.	
	C/S	Center stage			
	U/S, D/S	Upstage, downstage	POV	From the point of view of person named.	
	P/S	Prompt side (RHS facing stage)	O/C	On camera.	
	O/P	Opposite prompt (LHS facing stage)			
Cuing	Q, I/C, O/C	Cue, in cue, out cue.	ROLL; RUN	Start cue for film (telecine) or VT.	
	Pull, flip, animate	Graphic (caption). animation.	C/S	Change slide.	
	S/B	Stand-by.			
	FX	Cue effects.			
Cameras	BCU, CU, MCU, MS, MLS, LS, LVS (*see Chapter 6*).		D.I.	Dolly in.	
	2–S, 3–S	Two-shot, three-shot.	H/A, L/A	High angle, low angle.	
	AB	As before, i.e. shot as previously.	N/A, W/A	Narrow angle, wide angle.	
	O/S, X/S	Over-shoulder shot.	P/B, D/B	Pull back, dolly back.	
	FAV	Favor (make the named subject more prominent than another).	FG/BG	One person foreground; another background.	

Table 18.5 (cont.)

Switching (vision mixing)	CUT	Not marked, but implied unless other transition marked.	LOSE 2	Cut out Cam. 2 from a super or key.
			FI, FO	Fade in, fade out.
	MIX (DIS)	Mix (dissolve).	T	Take. (Moment for a transition.)
	WIPE	Wipe.		
	SUPER (S/I)	Superimpose.	S/S	Split screen.
	KEY (INSERT)	Electronic insertion (chroma key, CSO).	CK	Chroma key.
Audio	F/UP	Fade up audio.	Spot FX	Sound effect made in studio.
	FU	Fade audio under.	STING	Cue strong musical chord emphasizing action.
	P/B	Playback.		
	FB	Foldback (audience address).	OS; OOV	Over scene; out of vision (audio heard where source not shown).
	DISC CART CASSETTE S/TAPE; A/TAPE GRAMS	} Recorded audio insert	REVERB	Reverberation added.
			B/G	Keep audio in background.
			OPT; MAG	Film audio: optical; magnetic.
			SOF	Sound on film.
	ANNCR	Announcer.	SEP MAG	Separate magnetic track.
	ATMOS	Atmosphere (background sounds).	SOT	Sound on tape.
			SIL	Silent.
General	TXN	Transmission.	POS, NEG	Positive negative.
	SEQ	Sequence.	MON	Monitor.
	P/V	Preview.	ID	Station identification.
	ADD	An addition (to a story).	MOS; VOX POP	Man-on-street; interview
	PBU	Photo blow-up.	EXT	Exterior.
	PRAC	Practical.	INT	Interior.
	PROP	Property.	LOC	Location.

* UK term.

The more fragmentary or disjointed the actual production process is, the more essential is the script. It helps everyone involved to *anticipate*. And in certain forms of production (rehearse/record; total chroma-key staging) anticipation is essential for tight scheduling.

In a complex production that is videotaped out of sequence the production crew may be unable to function meaningfully without a full script, which makes it clear how shots/sequences are interrelated, and reveals continuity. The lighting director may, for example, need to adjust the lighting balance for a scene so that it will intercut smoothly with a different viewpoint shot yesterday.

So the full script can be a valuable coordinating document, enabling you to see at a glance the interrelationship between dialog, action, treatment, and mechanics. During planning, of course, it helps the team to estimate how much time there is for a camera move, how long there is for a costume change (perhaps a recording break will be necessary), whether re-arranging shooting order will give the necessary time for a make-up change, the scenes during which the 'rain' should be seen outside the windows of the library set (i.e. the water spray turned on and the audio effects introduced) . . . and the thousand and one details that interface in a smooth-running show.

The full script is used differently by various members of the team. The director uses it to develop his treatment, control timing, etc., and to demonstrate to the rest what he requires. Thoroughly familiar with it (hopefully!), he refers to his script for certain treatment and cuing details. His assistant(s) follows it carefully, checking dialog accuracy, noting where retakes are needed, timing sections (durations), perhaps cuing contributory sources from the script, as well as 'calling out shots' on intercom ('Shot 24 on 2, coming to 3'). The switcher follows the script in detail, preparing for upcoming transitions, superimpositions, effects.

Others (such as the cameramen, boom operators, electricians) may use the script as a detailed reference point when needed, but use simplified outlines (breakdown sheet, camera card) as they memorize their operations.

Auxiliary information

In addition to the script, various supplementary summaries may be necessary.

■ *Synopsis*   An outline summary of characters, action, plot. Appended to a dramatic script; particularly when shot out of sequence, or to coordinate a series.

■ *Fact sheet/run-down sheet*   Summarizes information about a product or item for a demonstration program; or details of a guest for an interviewer. Provided by a researcher, editor, or agency for guidance.

■ *Breakdown sheet/show format/running order*   Lists the events or program segments in order, showing allowed durations, participants' names, cameras and audio pick-up allocated, setting used, video and audio inserts, etc. (Sometimes ambiguously called a run-down sheet.)

Invaluable for unscripted, semi-scripted, and scripted shows that contain a series of self-contained segments (sequences, scenes). Also as a summary of a complex dramatic script to show at a glance: shot numbers for each scene, operational details, inserts, VT breaks for major resetting (clearing props, redressing set, moving scenery), costume/make-up changes, etc. (See Table 18.6).

■ *Camera card/shot card*   A sheet provided for individual cameras, showing their successive floor positions (perhaps with a layout sketch)

Table 18.6   Breakdown sheet/show format/running order

EXAMPLE 1: DRAMA PRODUCTION

Page	Scene (sequence)	Shots	Cameras/audio (layout across set)	D/N Day/night	Cast
1	FILM – 1 (40 sec) OPENING TITLES (20 sec)		SOF (SEP. MAG.) 4A. S. TAPE (RAIN)		
1	1. INT. DINING ROOM	2–9	1A. 4A	N.	GEORGE EILEEN
3	2. INT. LOUNGE	10–27	4B, 2A, B1, 3A.	N.	GEORGE EILEEN
	RECORDING BREAK				
10	3. EXT. GARDEN	28	B2, 3B	D.	JUDY GEORGE
10	4. EXT. STREET	29	1B. Slung.	D.	BRIAN
11	5. INT. CAFE	30–43	2B, 4C, A2	Eve.	BRIAN JUDY GEORGE

ETC . . .

EXAMPLE 2: DEMONSTRATION PROGRAM   (TOTAL DURATION: 15 MINS.)

Sequence no.	Item (sequence segment)	Cameras/F/VT	Seq. dur.
1	OPENING TITLES – SIG. TUNE.	4A, 1A.	07 sec
2	PROG. INTRO.	2A, 3A.	30 sec
3	TIMBER FELLING.	VT.	24 sec
4	PREPARING WOOD.	1B, 2B.	2 min 30 sec
5	CARVING DEMO.	1C, 4B, 3B.	8 min 00 sec
6	TIMBER IN BUILDINGS.	FILM.	2 min 58 sec
7	CLOSING LINK.	3A.	22 sec
8	END TITLES – SIG. TUNE.	4A, 1A.	09 sec
			15 min 00 sec

and their allocated shots (shot numbers, type of shots), camera movements, action.

The camera card is not to be confused with a *shot sheet*, which carries brief details of *all* cameras' shots and is used as a summary list when preparing a treatment framework for an unscripted show. (See Table 18.7.)

■ *Requisition forms* Essential for interdepartmental organization, requisition forms are legion. There are no standard approaches. Each station has its own procedures for booking studios, equipment, facilities, services, manpower, etc. The director may become involved directly in

Table 18.7   Camera card

CAMERA THREE		'DEATH COMES ONCE'	STUDIO B	
SHOT No.	POSN.	(LENS ANGLE*)	SCENE/SETTING	
11	A	13°	SC. 2.	LOUNGE
				CU GEORGE pockets gun from drawer pulling out telegram.
14	A	35°		LS EILEEN enters DOLLY IN to MS as she X's to couch.
19	A	20°		BCU GEORGE'S eyes.
23	A	13°		BCU EILEEN screams.
25	A	20°		CU GEORGE puts gun in drawer.
		QUICK MOVE TO GARDEN		
28	B	35°	SC. 3.	GARDEN
				MLS follow GEORGE carrying body: tightening, depressing to L/A shot: ZOOM IN to hand as he stops.
		MOVE TO RHS LOUNGE		
44	A	50°	SC. 4.	LOUNGE
				LS DETECTIVE enters. PAN with him into MS as he goes to phone.

* *Optional*

ordering props, graphics, titles, etc., or simply inform specialists. Various requisitions concerning costume, make-up, staging, lighting, video, audio, VTR, filming, editing are normally handled by the specialists.

Calculating shots

Many directors prefer to work empirically, from mental concepts, rough notes, and experience. They make 'guesstimates', or wait until they can guide the cameramen and see which shots are practical. They improvise instinctively and draw inspiration from the occasion. This is fine, as long as time is available to experiment, improvise, and coordinate the production team. But as a general practice it is preferable to plan as fully as possible; modifying, correcting, and improving during camera rehearsal and subsequent editing.

Why measure?

Preliminary planning can provide you with the answers to a lot of your camera problems long before even preliminary blocking:

What shots are available on this immobile camera?
Am I going to shoot off the set?

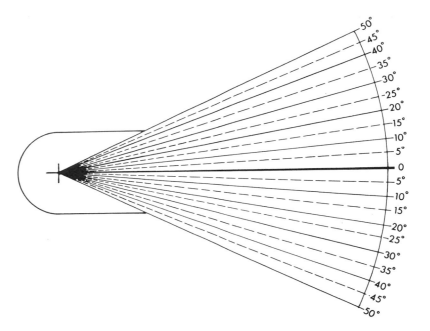

Fig. 18.5 The 'shot plotter'
The horizontal lens angles are marked
on this protractor. Laid on a scale floor
plan, they show the shot coverage for
any angle. (Vertical angles for use on
elevations, are ¾ horizontal angle.)

20° coverage, for example, is
between the 20° markings either side
of the central axis (0).

Can I get the shot from here?
What will relative sizes (proportions) be?
How large must we make the graphic in this setting?
Where do I position people for this chroma-key effect?

Why *guess* whether it will work on the day when you can check it out now?

The tools are simple enough: a scale floor plan and a transparent triangle or protractor representing the horizontal lens angle. Wherever you place this 'shot plotter' on the floor plan it shows what the camera sees from that viewpoint. If the angle falls outside the marked-out setting you are shooting off (Figure 18.6).

Shot proportions

The edges of the lens angle represent the left- and right-frame edges. Any object that touches both lines fills the screen width – whether a small close item or a large distant one.

To make a subject fill one-third of the screen width just mark on a paper strip a length *three times* the subject's width. At the distance this marker fits across the angle the subject will exactly fill one-third of the screen width. Conversely, if a subject is a known distance away, measure the scene width there and divide this by the subject width to find proportions.

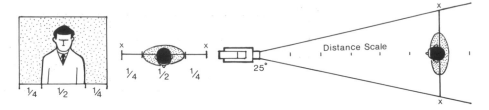

Fig. 18.6 part 1   Shot planning – required camera distance
You can find shots by *trial and error* or calculate them from a *graph* (Fig. 18.7), or *measure* the set-up needed as follows.
Q:. What camera distance is needed on a 25° lens, to have a person fill half the screen width?
A: Person is ⅜ in across on a ¼ in = 1 ft scale (1 cm across on a 1 cm = 0.5 m scale). So draw a line × 2 this length (i.e. person is now *half* the line length). Fit this line exactly across the lens angle, and check the distance on scale from camera to subject.

SHOT	BCU	CU Head & Shoulders	MCU Chest	Mid- Shot Waist	¾ Shot Knees	Full Length
Meters	1.0	1.25	1.75	2.0	4.0	+6.0
Feet	3.3	4	5.7	6.5	13	+20

Fig. 18.6 part 2   Shot planning – shots available from a particular layout
First measure the person's distance. In the example he is 4 m (14 ft) away. (A 25° lens would provide a ¾ shot/knee shot – see table.) Draw a line across the lens angle at that point and you see that he occupies about ⅛ screen width. The object behind him is 1.5 m wide at Y–Y (shot width 2.5 m) = ⅗ of screen width. So now you have the shot's proportions.

In Figure 18.6 you have a quick shot-check table showing the distances for 'standard' shots on a 25° lens. For other lens angles, distances are inversely proportional:

$50° = {}^{25}\!/_{50} = \times 0.5$ table distance.
$10° = {}^{25}\!/_{10} = \times 2.5$ table distance.
$40° = {}^{25}\!/_{40} = \times 0.6$ table distance.

For a useful formula that you can apply to your particular zoom lens system, multiply its maximum focal length (in millimeters) by the corresponding horizontal lens angle at that setting (e.g. 110 mm × 5° = 550).

Then, when you want to find the lens angle given by a particular focal length (e.g. 55 mm), simply divide this 'standard factor' by that figure (e.g. 550 ÷ 55 = 10°). When you need a certain lens angle (e.g. 25°), divide the factor by 25, and you will find that you need a focal length of 22 mm.

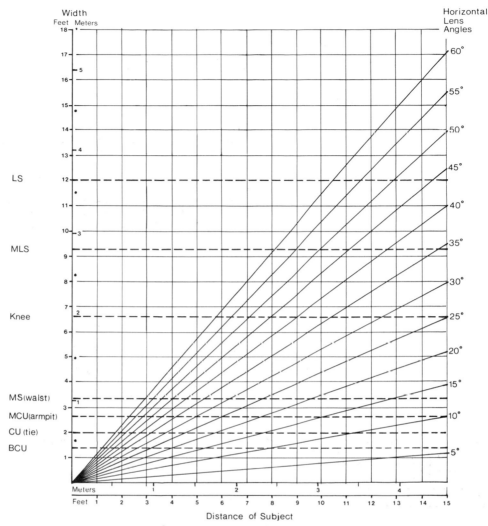

Width — Feet — Meters

Horizontal Lens Angles

LS — 12

MLS

Knee

MS(waist)

MCU(armpit)

CU (tie)

BCU

Meters / Feet — Distance of Subject

Fig. 18.7 Camera set-up graph

The graph shows how much any lens sees at various distances. (The *height* of the area seen is ¾ of the *width*.)

1. **How far away does the camera have to be, to get a certain type of shot?** Select type of shot you want on vertical scale . . . look across to the lens angle you are using . . . then down to the *distance scale*.

2. **What lens angle is needed for a certain type of shot?** Trace a line across graph, from the *shot* you want (vertical scale) . . . draw another line, up from camera's distance on the bottom *scale*. Where they cross, shows the best *lens angle*.

3. **What type of shots will I get from here?** Draw a line up from the *distance scale*, to the *lens angle(s)* you have available (max and min zoom angles). Then across left, to the *shot scale*.

4. **How much will the camera see from here?** As 3, but read the scene *width/height scales*.

5. You can get the **same shot size at different distances,** by altering lens angle. Trace a line right from the shot needed (e.g. CU) and note the distances at which it cuts various lens angles.

6. **To make a subject fill a certain proportion of screen width** (e.g. ⅓). Measure the subject width; multiply this by 3 for ⅓ width (4 for ¼, etc.). Look up this screen width on the left vertical *width scale*. Trace across to the *lens angle* used, then down to the *distance* needed. The subject will now fill ⅓ screen width.

Lens Angle

Horizontal	Vertical
5°	3·75°
10°	7·5°
15°	11·25°
20°	15°
25°	18·75°
30°	22·5°
35°	26·25°
40°	30°
45°	34°
50°	37·5°
55°	40·25°
60°	45°

1

2

Fig. 18.8   Equipment stencil
Scale stencils are used to mark the floor
plan, with equipment positions.
1. Camera/Sound boom stencil.
2. Typical furniture stencil.

19 In production

Any production benefits from some kind of rehearsal prior to recording or live transmission. These rehearsals take several forms.

Pre-studio rehearsal

Complicated productions particularly gain from pre-studio rehearsal. Even a table demonstration can be discussed, practiced, and checked beforehand; perhaps in a *preparation room* near the studio.

For larger shows (drama, comedy) it is essential to work out mechanics, practice dialog and action, and coordinate performance. So these productions are often rehearsed in halls (outside rehearsal rooms) some two or three weeks before studio date. Meanwhile, the studio is scheduled for other programs.

Prerehearsals begin with a *briefing, read-through, or line rehearsal*, in which the director outlines his interpretation. The cast becomes familiar with the script, the other actors, and the required characterizations.

The rehearsal hall floor is taped or chalked with a full-size layout of the studio setting. Doors, windows, stairways, etc. are outlined. Stock rehearsal furniture substitutes the actual studio items and action props (telephone, tableware) are provided. Rehearsing in this mock-up, actors become accustomed to the scale and features of their surroundings; vertical poles, chairs, dummy doors marking the main architectural limits.

The director arranges performers' positions, grouping, action, to suit his treatment. He rehearses in sections: the cast learning lines, practicing performance, moves and business; until the entire show runs smoothly, ready for its studio debut. Segments and overall timing are checked (and controlled) throughout, allowing for subsequent non-action inserts – titles, film, VT, graphics, announcements, etc.

During rehearsals, the director scrutinizes action through his view-finder from potential camera positions, adjusting details as necessary.

A few days before the studio date the specialists concerned with technical operations watch a complete rehearsal (technical walk-through/ technical run), checking and anticipating problems, envisioning camera and boom treatments. Following this meeting, facilities are finalized and the lighting prepared.

Studio rehearsal

Before a studio rehearsal the staging crew, supervised by the set designer, erects and dresses the settings. Lamps are rigged and adjusted under the guidance of the lighting director, to cover their plotted areas. Camera and

Table 19.1   Prerehearsal blocking hints

Timing	A preliminary read-through gives only a rough timing estimate. Allow time for business, moves, recorded inserts, etc. Anticipate potential script cuts if an overrun is evident. Many productions include sequences that can be dropped, reduced, or expanded to trim timing.
Briefing performers	Ensure that performers have a clear idea of the program format, their part in it, and their interrelationship with other contributions.
	Ensure that performers have a good notion of the setting; what it represents, where things are.
Props	Provide reasonable substitutes where real props are not available. Sometimes only the actual item will suffice. Where unfamiliar costume is to be worn (cloak, hoop skirt, space helmet), a rehearsal version is preferable to dummy motions.
Directing performers	Maintain a firm attitude towards punctuality, inattention, background chatter during rehearsals, to avoid time wastage and frustration.
	Check that performers' positions are consistent and meaningful (they do not stand 'on' a wall).
	Avoid excessive revisions – of action, grouping, line cuts, etc. Wrong versions can get remembered, new ones forgotten.
	Warn performers where they are in close shots, to restrict their movements; perhaps indicating which camera to play to.
Shot arrangement	Use a portable viewfinder to arrange shots. Even a card cut-out frame or a hand-formed frame is better than unaided guesses.
	Always think in terms of *shots*, not of theatrical-styled groupings, entrances, exits, business. At script stage, form ideas about shots rather than arranging 'nice groups' and trying to get 'good shots' during rehearsal.
	When setting up shots in a rehearsal hall do not overlook the scenic background that will be present in the studio. Check shot coverage with plans and elevations.
	Consider depth of field limitations in close shots or deep shots (close and distant people framed together).
	Think in terms of practical studio mechanics. You may rapidly reposition your viewfinder, but the move may be impossible for the studio camera.
Audio and lighting	Try to bear audio and lighting problems in mind when arranging positions and action. For example: where people are widely spaced, a sound boom may need time to swing between them, or have to be supplemented.

sound equipment are positioned. The performers arrive, seeing the staging for the first time. The show is ready to begin.

Directors organize their studio rehearsals in several ways, according to the complexity of the production, available time, performer experience, and criticality of results. Given the opportunity, you might like the luxury of:

1. *Dry run (walk-through)*. Actors perform, familiarizing themselves with the studio settings, etc., while the studio crew watch, learning the format, action, and production treatment.
2. *Camera blocking (stagger-through)*. Initial camera rehearsal, co-ordinating technical operations, discovering and correcting problems.

Table 19.2   Effective studio rehearsal

Unrehearsed or briefly rehearsed studio production

Director's assistant checks that available production information is distributed (breakdown sheet/running order). Also checks that contributory graphics (titles, slides, floor graphics) and film/VT inserts are correct. The assistant has details of all word cues, for inserts, announcements, etc., and their timings.

Director with floor manager, technical director, lighting director, cameras and sound crew, arranges basic performer and camera positions (floor is marked). Even a basic plan aids coordination. He outlines action or moves, and shot coverage. Lighting is set.

If talent is available, line up shots and explain to them any shot restrictions, critical positions, care needed in demonstrating items, etc. (Otherwise use stand-ins for shot line-up and brief talent on arrival.)

Check that performers, crew, and contributory services (prompter, film channel, etc.) are ready to start.

If full rehearsal is impractical, carry out basic production checks: rehearse 'tops and tails' of each segment with intermediate links (e.g. announcer's in-cues/out-cues, to cue film or VT inserts); check any complicated action or treatment. Check any errors or problems.

Intercom and the director

Remember that the production team is interdependent. A quiet, methodical, patient approach is as infectious as an acrimonious one. Be firm but friendly. Avoid critical comments on intercom.

How detailed intercom instructions need to be depends on the show's complexity and crew experience. Aim at a balanced information flow, avoiding continuous chat and comment. (A mute key cuts the circuit when necessary.)

Preferably call cameras by numbers, guiding all camera moves (and zooms) during rehearsal, warning the crew of upcoming action and movements.

Examine each shot. If necessary, modify positions, action, movement, and composition.

Consider *shot continuity*. Alterations may affect earlier shots, too.

Remember, the crew and performers are *memorizing*. Their aids are the production paperwork and your intercom reminders/instructions.

Do not be vague. Make sure that your intentions are understood. In correcting errors, explain what was wrong and what is wanted. Not 'Move him left a bit' but 'He is shadowing the map'. Do not assume performers will see and correct any problems.

Avoid excessive changes or revisions, or there will be hesitations and mistakes.

Correct operational and performance errors, even in early camera rehearsal. Misjudgements and inaccuracies should be noted directly they occur (e.g. camera in shot, shooting off, late cue, wrong lines, wrong shot, wrong mike). But avoid an overinterrupted rehearsal, or timing and continuity will be lost.

If a cameraman offers alternative shots (e.g. to overcome a problem), briefly indicate if you accept or disagree, and why.

Where practicable, at the end of each sequence ask if there are any problems, and whether anyone wants to rehearse that section again.

Remember, various staging and lighting defects may be unavoidable in early rehearsal. Certain details (set dressing, light effects) take time to complete. Some aspects need to be seen on camera before they can be corrected or finally adjusted (overbright lights, lens flares). Shot readjustments during rehearsal often necessitate lighting alterations.

Never repeat a segment without indicating whether it is to be *changed* (move faster next time), or is to correct an *error* (late cue), or to *improve* the performance/operations.

(*continued over*)

Table 19.2 (cont.)

Ensure that everyone knows when shots have been deleted or added (e.g. Shot 2A, 2B, 2C).

At the end of rehearsal: check timings, give notes to performers and crew on any errors to be corrected, changes needed, problems to be solved. Check whether they have difficulties that need your aid.

At least one complete uninterrupted rehearsal is essential for reliable recording/transmission.

At the end of videotaping, give details (including shot numbers) and reasons for any retakes.

3. *Predress run-through* (*continuous run-through*). 'Polishing' rehearsal, proving corrections.
4. *Dress rehearsal* (dress-run). Hopefully, fault-free 'on-air' quality performance.
5. *Videotaping/transmission*. Final optimum performance.

In reality, many productions have little more rehearsal time than the show's running duration, and the second and fifth stages have to suffice. So a continual watch on progress, relative to available rehearsal time, is essential.

Rehearsal procedures

As we saw earlier when looking at *videotape editing*, there are several different ways of organizing and recording a program. Now we consider the situation from the director's viewpoint.

In many types of production we want to prepare and rehearse the entire action and treatment until it reaches a peak, then record the polished performance. In others, we rehearse each small section and record it before going on to the next.

Camera blocking/stagger-through/first run/stopping run

Here, the director controls operations from the production control room, only 'going to the floor' when personal on-the-spot discussion is essential. Otherwise, his eyes and ears are the picture monitors and loudspeaker. All communication with his crew is via the *intercom* (*production talkback*) system; the *floor manager* cuing and instructing the talent through his intercom guidance.

Many directors use the *whole method*, and go straight through a sequence (segment, scene) in camera rehearsal, continuously guiding until a serious problem arises to require stopping and correction. The director discusses problems, solutions, and revisions; then reruns the sequence with corrections. It should now work.

This method gives a good idea of continuity, timing, transitions, and operational difficulties. But, by skimming over the various shortcomings

Table 19.3   Methods of videotaping productions

'Live-on-tape'	Multi-cameras (e.g. 2–4). Single videotape recorder.*
Advantages	● Program is ready for transmission immediately after taping. ● No lengthy postproduction editing is needed. (Saves cost, equipment, staff, time.) ● Recording period needed is only slightly longer than the length of the show. ● No loss of pace or interaction, which can occur when action is continually interrupted. ● Performers and team are all keyed up to give their best performances.
Disadvantages	● All shots and transitions are normally unchangeable. ● There are no opportunities for second thoughts or alternative treatment. ● The production includes any less successful material, errors in performance and treatment (editing, camerawork, sound, lighting). ● All costume, make-up changes, scene changes, etc. have to be made in real time during the show. ● Any editing is usually nominal, unless insert shots are taped afterwards (e.g. cutaway shots or brief retakes inserted).
Shooting in segments/scenes/ sections	Multi-cameras (e.g. 2–4). Single videotape recorder.*
Advantages	● Opportunities for corrective retakes, alternative treatment, experiments, etc. ● Editing within the sequence can be made with the switcher. Where necessary, further editing decisions can be left to a postproduction session. ● The performers and production group can concentrate on each segment and get it right before going on to the next. ● Recording breaks can be arranged to allow costume, make-up changes, scene changes, etc. ● Scenes can be shot in the most convenient time-saving order; in sequence or out of sequence. ● Peformers who are not required for later scenes can be released (actors, extras, musicians). This can save costs and reduce congestion in the studio. ● If a setting is used at various times throughout a show (e.g. a classroom) all scenes with action there may be shot consecutively and the scenery struck to make room for a new set. This technique virtually extends the size of the studio, and makes optimum use of available space. ● Where a set appears in several episodes of a series, all sequences there can be shot in succession to avoid the need to store and rebuild the set over and over. ● Similarly, where a program consists of a series of brief episodes (e.g. a story told in daily parts) these can all be recorded consecutively during the same session.
Disadvantages	● Much more time is needed to tape the show. Time lost during breaks can become greater than anticipated. ● Retakes and revisions can take so much time that the session falls behind schedule (overrun). This can result in economic and administrative problems. There is a continuing pressure to save time and to press on. ● Extensive postproduction editing is essential. At the end of the taping session you have no show until the separate segments are sorted and edited together. ● All extended transitions between segments (mixes, wipes, video effects) must wait until postproduction. Similarly, music/effects/dialog carrying over between segments must be added during audio sweetening. ● In a complicated production, recording out of sequence can lead to confusion and to continuity errors in a fast-moving taping session.

Table 19.3 (cont.)

Multi-camera with ISO camera	All cameras are fed to the switcher, and program taped by the main VTR.*
Advantages	A separate ISO VTR can record continuously the output of any chosen camera:
	● Provides slow-motion replay for inserts into the program.
	● Provides extra shots for postproduction editing.
Disadvantages	● The arrangement ties up another VTR.
	● Most of the material on the ISO recording is not used.
Multi-cameras with dedicated VTRs	Action is shot: live-on tape, or in segments/scenes/sections.
Advantages	● All material from all cameras is recorded.
	● No shots are missed.
	● Alternative shots are available throughout the show.
	● No irrevocable editing was carried out during the performance.
	● Unexpected action, unrehearsed action, is recorded and available.
	● Postproduction editing can be adjusted to suit the final performance.
	● Camera treatment can need little planning.
	● Normally ad lib unplanned shots can upset planned production treatment (e.g. may delay a camera from moving to a new position). This is less likely when using dedicated VTRs.
Disadvantages	● The entire show requires total postproduction editing.
	● The total program sound may need to be recorded separately from the pictures and laid down, with effects, music, applause, during postproduction editing.
	● The arrangement can lead to poor mechanical production treatment; off-the-cuff shooting. Concentration on action rather than visual development.
	● Camerawork may degenerate into semi-static cameras zooming in and out to vary shots.
Single camera	Single videotape recorder.* Taking brief shots or continuous sequences.
Advantages	● An extremely flexible, mobile method.
	● One camera is easier to direct than a multi-camera crew.
	● There are advantages in working with a small unit.
	● The director can concentrate on the action and treatment.
	● No switching is involved.
	● No cuing of film or videotape inserts.
Disadvantages	● All the strain of camerawork falls on one operator.
	● The production process is much slower than multi-camera treatment.
	● There is a temptation to shoot retakes for better performance, or extra 'just-in-case' shots that might be used. These extra shots can absorb allotted shooting time.
	● All material requires sorting and detailed editing.
	● Production flow is continually interrupted (unlike multi-camera treatment).
	● Away from the studio, various extra problems arise when shooting on location (weather, traffic, public, etc.).
	● All film or videotape inserts in the program have to be introduced during postproduction.

* Usually with backup VTR, in case of recording faults.

before the 'breakdown point', quite a list of minor corrections may develop.

Other directors, using the *stopping method*, stop action and correct faults as they arise – almost shot by shot. This precludes error adding to error, ensuring that everyone knows exactly what is required throughout. For certain situations (chroma-key treatment) this may be the only rational approach.

However, this piecemeal method gives the impression of slow progress, and can feel tedious and nit-picking. The continual stopping makes checks on continuity and timing more difficult. Later corrections are given as notes after the run-through.

Floor blocking

Using this method, the director forsakes the production control room and works from a studio picture monitor. Guiding and correcting performers and crew, he calls out required transitions to the switcher in the control room, watching results on his monitor screen. This is the luxury of delayed decisions!

This technique is often used by directors who find visualizing difficult, feel remote from operations in their orthodox position, and prefer direct contact to relaying instructions.

The director often returns to the control room to run each floor-rehearsed scene. During videotaping, the show may be shot as segments, scenes, or continuous action.

Where a set-up is particularly complicated or discontinuously recorded, the system may have some advantages. But it has all the weaknesses of the 'stopping method' plus low crew cohesion. When they *all* hear the same intercom instructions, crew members can coordinate more effectively. At worst, this method wastes a great deal of time, and because the director has not been watching channel previews or listening to audio while on the floor, continuity and video/audio relationships may be below optimum.

Rehearse/record

This is really a form of 'floor blocking', in which the director sets up a sequence, rehearses it, then immediately records the corrected result. Each sequence may need to be relit, cameras repositioned, and scenery reset or cheated. The separate videotaped sections are later edited together with appropriate transitions and bridging sound.

Ideally, this pseudofilmic technique could provide optimum results for each shot. But in practice, the process can be extremely frustrating and time consuming. Normally the effectiveness of lighting, scenery, make-up, costume, etc. is checked on camera, and improved or corrected while another scene is being rehearsed or during a studio stand-down. In a *rehearse/record* situation such changes have to be made immediately, so that the scene can be shot – and this leads to many compromises. To save time, a director may even record the first camera rehearsal with all its imperfections, in case it can be used! A videotape channel is continuously tied to the studio. Themes and variations are shot for later selection, and repeat action may be necessary to ensure editing continuity. Considerable post-studio videotape editing is necessary. Audio sweetening becomes a major consideration.

Rehearsal problems

During the course of rehearsal various problems regularly arise. Here, in summarized form, are typical situations.

The shot

1. *Subject detail not sufficiently visible.* Move subject/camera closer. Zoom in. Shoot subject in a series of close detail shots or localized insets (magnified view within longer shot). Is greater detail available? (Very close shots of some subjects are confusing or reveal no further information – e.g. close-ups of unsharp photographs.) Is detail defocused? Is the subject shadowed or obscured?

2. *Extreme close-ups of details required.* Problems can arise from the limited depth of field, an unsteady camera, the subject moving in/out of frame. So where possible, locate the item on a firm surface (use position marks). Use higher light levels (intensities) to permit stopping down. The camera may be able to focus closer on a wide-angle lens (closer MFD). Use the *macro* position on the lens. Use a photo-enlargement of detail.

3. *Subject's shape does not fit screen aspect ratio.* Take a long shot of total subject, then pan/tilt over detail or intercut closer shots. If a series of items are involved do similarly or recompose the shot (move them together, arrange in depth, or shoot more obliquely).

4. *Unsatisfactory framing.* Subject cut off by frame edge. Shot too tight or loose. Subject too high in frame or off-center (unbalanced). Unsuitable headroom.

5. *One subject masks (obscures) another.* Reposition subject and mark floor. (Check that this does not spoil earlier shots.) Reposition camera (e.g. arc or truck/crab).

6. *Subjects appear too widely spaced apart.* Move subjects closer together, shoot obliquely, or intercut single shots.

7. *Subject appears too large or small relative to others in shot.* See Table 6.3.

8. *Subject appears too prominent.* Reduce shot size, alter composition, or increase camera height.

9. Background objects or scenic lines 'grow out' of subject. Reposition camera or subject. Move, cover, or remove background items. Reduce their prominence by lighting or defocusing.

10. *Unwanted distortion.* Adjust lens angle to nearer 'normal' (25°) and change camera distance accordingly, reposition subject or change viewpoint.

11. *Colors have similar monochromatic values.* Lighten/darken areas concerned. Change hue or materials (surface texture). Put black outlines round areas of similar tone.

Performers

1. *Out of position.* Check if they have toe marks or location points. Move them and re-mark floor (instructing performers). Reposition camera.
2. *Performer working to wrong camera.* Floor manager signals. Draw attention to tally (cue) light on camera. Switch over to the 'wrong' camera.
3. *Dialog errors (cuts lines, dries/fluffs, or freezes and needs prompt, wrong lines).* Use prompter, cue cards, etc. Give audible prompt. Is prompter working, script OK? Misunderstanding? Retake sequence, or insert cutaway shot and dub audio retake into audio track of VT.

Scenic problems

1. *Check staging for distracting features.* Overbright surfaces or reflections. Can relighting cure? Re-angle, use dulling spray, repaint, cover over, scrim over or remove.
2. *Colors or tones unsuitable* (e.g. subject merges with background). Modify background, lighting or subject (e.g. change costume).
3. *Background blemishes* (dirty marks, tears, scrapes, wrinkles, etc.). Rectify, refurbish, cover over, or relight.
4. *Ugly or distracting shadows on background.* Performers or scenery too close to background? Relight or modify shot.

Operational hazards

1. *Camera shooting off set.* Modify shot, extend scenery, or add foreground masking.
2. *Lens flares.* Raise camera viewpoint, improve lens shade (hood), shield off camera, or raise lamp height. Alter shot.
3. *Unwanted subjects in shot.* Have their positions changed since last rehearsal? Alter framing, camera position, or lens angle. Rearrange shot, remove unwanted items. Mask/cover items. Leave items unlit.

Fig. 19.1 Guiding the performer
Show them where to stand: using (1) a locating point, or (2) toe marks. (3) Keep other action and monitors out of their eyeline.

4. *Boom mike in shot.* Check whether boom operator is aware. Warn him before cutting from close to distant shot. Tighten (reduce headroom) or recompose shot. Alter sound pick-up method.

5. *Boom shadows.* Check with audio/lighting personnel if avoidable. Consider modifying shot – tighter shot or change viewpoint. Alter sound pick-up or lighting.

6. *Cables in shot.* Check for distracting cables in shot – audio, lighting, monitors, cameras.

7. *Graphics/captions/titles.* Check they are straight, level, and undistorted. Can all be seen (no cut-off) and read? Time to read?

Editing/video switching/vision mixing

1. *Transitions appropriate*? Suitable type? Timing and rate of transitions OK?

THE PRINCIPLES OF FILM CUEING

The film is laced up, projecting the chosen sync number. This represents a known run-up time.

At the cue point in the speech 4 secs. before it is due to finish, the film channel is cued to run.

The film machine runs up to speed . . .

Precisely 4 secs. later, the film pictures begin. Buffer frames allow for slight timing errors.

As the speech ends, we cut to film, and its picture is transmitted instead.

STUDIO CAMERA

CUE POINT IN DIALOGUE

". . . places, where this type of flower grows in profusion today."

CUT TO FILM

FILM LEADER SYNCHRONIZING NUMBERS

Film Standby — Run Film — 3 secs to go — 2 secs to go

TIME

1 sec

FIRST FILM FRAMES

Safety Buffer Frames — Transmitted Picture

Fig. 19.2   Cuing a film channel
Although some telecine channels provide an 'instant start' from a still frame, many take a few seconds to run up to normal running speed and stabilize. A film leader (marked in seconds) is spliced onto the start of the film, and provides an accurate, predictable run-up time when the film is cued.

Some VTR systems similarly require time to reach normal speed, and an equivalent *leader* is recorded at the start of a sequence (a numbered count-down, or visible clock; see Fig. 14.5).

2. *Any distractions?* Any reverse cuts, jump cuts, position jumps, instant changes in size, direction, frame height? Any loss of orientation or direction on cuts? Any image confusion during supers or mixes?

The floor manager

The *floor manager* (FM) is a person of many parts. On larger productions, he or she may, with an assistant (AFM), join the show at its onset and assist with organization, local liaison, location shooting, and sometimes substitute for the busy director at pre-studio rehearsals. Alternatively, the FM may join the production in the studio for camera rehearsals.

During studio preparations for camera rehearsal the FM checks all *non-technical* aspects of the show, confirming the team's readiness. Progress checks ensure that there are no staging hangups (i.e. action props work, scenery and furniture are in planned positions, doors do not stick . . . etc.); that no fire, safety or union regulations are being contravened. He guides the floor crew/stage hands, relative to operating graphics, studio/title cards, cue cards, scenic moves, effects cues, etc.

Around this time, arriving performers may need to be welcomed, checked in, and accommodated; and told when and where they are required. Ensuring punctuality and the observation of scheduled times are important aspects of the FM's duties; whether for rehearsal starts, *turnarounds* at the end of a rehearsal (returning equipment, props, scenery, to opening positions), or studio breaks (meals).

Rehearsal

As the director's contact man on the studio floor, the FM, wearing earphones, listens to the director's intercom (talkback) and then passes this information on to the talent. He anticipates problems, rearranges action and grouping, furniture positions, etc., as the director indicates, marking the floor where necessary. He supervises staging and property changes.

Normally, the FM alone will cue and stop all action in the studio on the director's instructions. The director only exceptionally uses the *studio-address loudspeaker (public address, studio talkback, loudspeaker talkback)* to talk directly to performers. (Loudspeaker announcements can be quite disrupting!) The FM talks back to the director over studio mikes, his own miniature 'reverse-talkback' transmitter, or by gestures in front of preview cameras. Being on the spot, he can often correct problems not evident to the director in the control room.

A good FM combines calmness, discipline and firmness with diplomacy and friendliness; putting talent at ease. Always available yet never in shot. He maintains a quiet studio, yet appreciates that various last-minute corrective jobs must progress. He investigates any delay, aiming to clear it; or if rehearsal is likely to be halted, suggests an alternative sequence that is ready instead. Later, the FM may welcome and guide any studio audience, relative to the show format and their contributions.

Taping/transmission

In checking and making ready for 'air time' or videotaping, the FM confirms that all studio access doors are shut, talent and crew standing by in opening positions, the ident slate has accurate details (which he reads during the VT countdown), studio monitors are showing pictures, etc.

During the show he is cuing talent, keeping a wary eye on all about him, listening to intercom guidance, anticipating hazards, and generally smoothing proceedings. At the end of taping he holds talent and crew until results have been checked; announcing and preparing any necessary retakes, finally 'releasing the studio' (performers and crew). He checks on safe storage of any valuable or special props or equipment and ends his duties with a logged account of the production.

Guiding performers

How much guidance performers need varies with their experience and the complexity of the production. But you must always ensure that talent realizes exactly what you want them to do and where to do it. A preliminary word may be enough, or a painstaking rehearsal may prove essential.

Inexperienced talent

Having welcomed talent, put them at ease, and outlined their contribution, they are best supported by an experienced host who guides and reassures them. Have them talk and demonstrate to the host rather than the camera, for he can steer them by questions and ensure that subject positions suit the shots.

We all feel daunted by unfamiliar conditions, mechanics, and disciplines; self-confidence is essential for good performance. So keep problems to a minimum, with only essential instructions to talent. Avoid elaborate action, discourage improvisation, and have minimal rearrangements.

Even slight distractions may worry inexperienced talent. Sometimes a small cue card or a list of points held beside the camera may strengthen their confidence. However, few inexperienced people read scripts or prompters 'naturally'; but instead have a stilted, ill-at-ease delivery.

The balance between insufficient and excessive rehearsal is more crucial with inexperienced talent. Uncertainty or overfamiliarity can lead them to omit sections during transmission. Sometimes the solution lies in either taping the item sectionally or compiling from several takes.

Professional talent

You will meet a very wide range of experienced professional performers in TV production – actors, anchormen, hosts, link men, commentators, introducers, presenters, and MCs (Master of Ceremonies).

Familiar with studio routines, they can respond to the most complicated instructions from the FM, or an earpiece intercom (*program
interrupt, switched talkback*) without the blink of an eye, even under the
most trying conditions – and yet maintain cool command of the situation.
Comments, feed questions, timing and continuity changes, item cuts,
ad-libbing padding are taken in their stride.

The professional makes full use of a prompter displaying the full script
– this means that cameras must always be within reading distance. His
performance (action and positions) is accurately repeatable and he will
play to particular cameras for specific shots, making allowances for
lighting problems (e.g. shadowing) or camera moves.

Cuing

To ensure that action begins and ends at the instant it is required, precise
cuing is essential. If you cut to performers and then cue them you will see
them waiting to begin or watch action 'spring into life'. Cue them too
early before cutting and action has already begun. So '*cue and cut*' is
normal practice.

Wrong cuing leaves talent bewildered. If they have finished their
contribution and you have not cut away to the next shot they may stand
with 'egg on the face', wondering whether to ad lib or just grin! Wrong
cuing can mean that film or VT runs out to a blank screen, or we see
run-up leaders flashing by on transmission. VT editing may compensate
for poor cuing and disguise sloppy direction.

Methods of cuing (See Figure 19.3)

1. *Hand cues.* Given by the FM (or relayed by the AFM), these are the
   standard methods of cuing action to start or stop. Sometimes a
   performer cannot watch for cues (during an embrace) and a tap on foot
   or shoulder may be used instead. Remember, some stations have their
   own variants on the signals in Figure 19.3 and it is advisable to use
   these. But make sure that your signals are going to be understood by
   the talent. Explain any basic cue to them if necessary. Do not assume –
   especially with inexperienced performers! If you use a hand over the
   mouth to indicate 'You are speaking too loudly' they may interpret it
   as a sign to 'Stop talking'! People have been known to *turn round* or
   speed up, instead of *winding up* when the FM rotated an upward-raised
   arm!
2. *Word cues.* An agreed go-ahead word or phrase during dialog,
   commentary, or discussion may be used to cue action or to switch to an
   insert. We note *out cues/out words* (last spoken words) at the end of a
   recorded insert (VT or film) to ensure accurately timed switching to
   the next item.
3. *Monitor cues.* Commentators and demonstrators often watch recorded
   inserts on a nearby picture monitor, taking a go-ahead cue from certain

Fig. 19.3 Floor manager signals

1. Stand-by . . . go ahead.
2. Speed up, faster pace, quicker tempo (speed according to increase required).
3. Slow down, slower pace, stretch it out (indicated by slow 'stretching' gestures).
4. OK, you're all right now, it's OK (confirmation signal).
5. Keep talking (open/close beak movement).
6. We're/you're on time, on the nose.
7. FM TO CAMERA. Are we on time? How is the time going?
8. You have . . . time left (illustrated – 2 min and ½ min).
9. Wind up now, conclude action. Some use this sign for *speed up* ('Go faster'), and hold the arm vertically, moving the hand or arm in circles, to indicate *wind up.*
10. Cut it, stop, finish, omit rest of item.
11. You are cleared. You are now off camera, and can move or stop action.
12. Speak more loudly.
13. Volume up, louder.
14. Volume down, quieter (sometimes preceded by 'Quiet' signal).
15. Quiet, stop applause.
16. Get closer to mike.
17. Come nearer, come downstage.
18. Go further away, go upstage.
19. Stop, keep still.
20. Turn round (in the direction indicated).
21. Move to camera left.
22. Tighten up, get closer together.
23. Open up, move further apart.
24. You're on that camera, play to that camera (sometimes with turning head gesture).
25. Play to the light indicated. (When actors are shadowing, point to light source and to area of face shadowed.)

26. Commercial break (brush right hand over left palm – spreading butter on bread).
27. FM TO AUDIENCE: You can applaud now (may be followed by louder sign).
28. Stop. (For applause, widespread action, etc.). Some use this sign ambiguously: slow to stop; fast to increase.

Additional signs include:
VTR or film is running – hand turning an imaginary crank.
Walk to the next position – walking movements with index and middle fingers, while pointing direction with other hand.

action. Alternatively, they may use a *time cue*, counting down (e.g. from 10 seconds) from a cue point. Most inserts have a few seconds without strong action or speech as *run-in* (*top*) and *run-out* (*tail*) to cushion/buffer the cuing.

4. *Light cues.* Performers can take a cue from the *camera tally* (*cue*) *light* (illuminated as the camera is switched to line). For announce booths or when cuing actors behind scenery, small portable *cue lights* are often used, where the stand-by 'flick' is followed by a steady 'action light'.

5. *Intercom cues*. These are given direct to a performer (newscaster, commentator) wearing an earpiece – interrupted feedback, program interrupt, switched talkback.
6. *Clock cues*. A go-ahead at a specific time.
7. *Buzzer cues*. Used in some organizations, for intercom between film/videotape areas and the production control room. (One buzz; 'Yes' or 'Start': two buzzes; 'No' or 'Stop'.)
8. *Electronic cue dots*. Used by networks at program change points, these small black/white squares in corner frame cue program out time, or give the next source a go-ahead cue.

Prompting

Relatively few performers can be expected to learn a script accurately and deliver it at a repeatable speed. Even the most experienced are liable to deviate from the written script, 'dry' (forget), or 'cut' lines. Whether this is a problem largely depends on the show format, whether live or taped, and if it is spontaneous or strictly scripted.

Fig. 19.4 part 1   Prompting – direct methods
1. Handwritten prompt cards usually held near the camera, may contain dialog or reminder notes. (Cue-cards, idiot board, goof sheet.)
2. Camera flip cards usually carry brief reminders.
3. A roller-script (speed remotely controlled) may be attached to the camera, or floor-located.

Fig. 19.4 part 2   Prompting – video prompters
1. Video prompters use a 45° clear glass sheet at the camera lens, reflecting a picture-tube display of the script: from a nearby script-scanner (monochrome TV camera shooting a miniature roller script), or a computer-stored script. Simpler prompters reflect a wide paper roller script with 'jumbo' type.
2. The camera lens shoots through the glass sheet at the subject. The reader appears to be looking straight at the lens and the audience. (Other systems can result in an off-camera stare.)
3. Where the speaker does not need to speak directly to the camera, the prompter-script video may be fed to floor video prompters or monitors.

While a quiet verbal prompt may suffice (perhaps using a muting key to temporarily kill the mike), more sophisticatea methods are generally needed. There are generally two types of prompters – *reminder notes* (*aide-mémoires*) that give data, subject heads, or show format; and *continual references* giving entire script or lyrics.

Reminders

These have been written on shirts cuffs or nearby scenery, but more orthodox methods range from small hand notes to the clip boards used by many interviewers, commentators, and anchormen. These boards carry their notes, questions, and research information.

For brief information, cards can be held near the camera by floor crew (cue card, goof sheet, idiot card), or smaller *flip cards* (*flippers*) suspended under the camera head.

Script

A talking head reading a desk script does not make good television. It is dull and lacks 'spontaneity'. But a regular script ensures accurate timing. Consequently, many shows use a *roller prompter* (mechanically or electronically operated) that provides a continuously rolling copy of the script at or near the camera lens.

The vari-speed display is remotely controlled (by the talent or an operator) and typically has some 20 words visible in an eight-line frame. To disguise eye movements or a fixed stare, the performer 'casually' changes his head position while reading. Off-camera prompters can lead to a 'shifty-eyed' presentation, for the speaker has to continually glance away from the lens axis.

Prompters may inhibit shot variations because cameras carrying prompters need to be close enough for comfortable reading. Where only selected cameras have prompters, you must ensure that one of these is always near the speaker.

Earpiece prompts

In a daily soap opera the cast has little time to learn new lines. So some organizations fit actors with earpieces attached to small receivers. As they perform, the actors hear each line in turn being read from the script, which they repeat aloud. This is done so skilfully that the audience is quite unaware of the technique. The actor is completely mobile, and does not have to read prompters.

Production timing

Whereas a *closed circuit* program needs only approximate timing, a *live transmission* must fit its allocated time slot exactly. Overruns can result in end cut-off or cause scheduling problems. In live *composite productions*,

Table 19.4 On-air intercom

Intercom (talkback) instructions reveal the split-second teamwork involved in efficient TV directing. Although local terminology and personnel vary, the following intercom talk from an actual show certainly reflects the spirit of the occasion.

Director's assistant	*Director*
Stand-by studio. Going ahead in 1 minute . . .	(FM alerts studio and gives countdown.)
Stand-by film. (Acknowledging buzz from film channel.)	Start VT. Show slate (identifying board) on 4.
Stand-by announcer.	
Roll film . . . 4–3–2–1–Zero.	Fade up film. Music (on audio tape).
On film for 1 minute . . . Stand-by 1.	Super 1.
Shot 1.	
On 1 . . . Stand-by 2.	Take music under. Cue Announcer. (Cue light in announce booth.)
Coming to end of film. Counting down . . . 30 seconds – 20–10–5–4–3–2–1–0.	Bring up music. Cue Peter (FM cues talent). Take 2 (cut to Cam. 2). Take music under.
On 2. Shot 2 . . . 1 next.	He's going to sit. Go with him . . . Dolly in slowly to CU . . . Hold it there . . . Super slide title (guest's name) . . . take out super. Steady 1 . . . a bit tighter . . . good . . . take 1.
On 1. Shot 3 . . . 2 to graphic.	
Inserting 2 . . . Stand-by disc (grams).	Wipe in 2 . . . fine . . . take 2 out.
Clear 2 (after combined shot).	Go disc. Stand-by Joan (FM alerts talent).
Stand-by 3 . . . Coming to 3.	Music under. Cue her on and cut. He'll exit left.
On 3. Shot 4 . . . Stand-by 2 . . . Extra shot 4A.	
On 2 . . . We're 15 seconds over (overrun).	Coming to 2 . . . Mix to 2 . . . She's going to open the box . . .
On 2 . . . Shot 4A . . . Stand-by VT.	Cue Joan to open it (FM cues) . . . we're tight for time . . . Drop Shot 5.
Shot 5 is *out* (to be omitted).	Give her a wind-up . . . run VT.
Coming to VT . . . 4–3–2–1–0.	Cut to VT.
On VT for 2 minutes 7 seconds.	
1 minute left on VT . . . Coming out of VT in 30 seconds.	
Out words . . . 'on the road'.	
Stand-by 2 for Shot 6.	
Stand-by studio. Coming out of VT. 20–10–5–4–3–2–1–0.	Hold it 2. Cut to 2.
On 3. Shot 60 . . . Clear 1 to crawl (roller titles).	He's going to move to the door and wave. Give him ½ minute.
Stand-by tape (audio). Stand-by 1 for Shot 61.	(FM signals talent) Wind him up . . . go crawl, go tape.
On 1 and 3 . . . Off the air.	Super 1. Take out 3 . . . Go to black at end of phrase.
Stand-by for retakes.	Right everyone. That was great. We'll just check VT (VTR spot-checked). OK. Thank you very much. We have a clear.

where various contributory sources '*opt-in*' or '*opt-out*' (temporarily join or leave) the main presentation to insert their own material accurate timing is imperative.

Scripts may be roughly timed by reading aloud and allowing for any mute action, business, or inserts. Many run at around a minute a full page. During rehearsal each segment or scene is timed, and subsequently adjusted to suit a timed show format/running order (estimated, permitted or actual).

Types of timer

Time can be checked in several ways:

- By referring to an *analog wall clock*. It is often quicker to calculate an 'out time' by envisioning the repositioning of the clock's hands than to add figures (e.g. 1527 to 1545 = 18 minutes).
- Using a *digital timer* for *forward timing*. The clock counts forwards, showing *real-time* ('clock time'). Or it starts from zero, and shows *elapsed time*. This can be a desktop display or superimposed on a preview monitor.

Fig. 19.5 Forward and back timing

1. *Forward timing* (*front timing*): duration timing (estimated and real) as the show proceeds.

Desired durations	Running stop watch reads (from prog. start)	Clock start time	Clock end time	Item running times (actual duration)
Intro 30″	30″	19.15.00	19.15.30	30″
Item A 10′	10′ 33″	19.15.30	19.25.33	10′ 03″
Item B 8″	18′ 30″	19.25.33	19.33.30	7′ 57″

2. *Back timing:* a 'remaining time' measurement, showing the amount of time before the production ends.

Item duration	Clock time (item starts)	Remaining time
Item X 1′ 0″	20.23.00	2′ 0″
Item Y 30″	20.24.00	1′ 0″
Item Z 30″	20.24.30	30″
End titles, Out time	20.25.00	00.00

- Using a *digital timer* for *back timing*. A similar facility, in which the scheduled duration is entered, and the clock counts down to zero. Any *minus* reading represents an overrun of the allotted time.
- Two hand-operated stopwatches, checking overall running time, and running time of individual sections, items, or scenes.

Timing methods

■ *Intermittent timing* When rehearsal is halted for any reason the stop clock time is noted. Rehearsal recommences at a point *before* the fault and the timer is restarted when the fault point is reached. A videotaped production can usually be edited to reduce excess; its associated *time code* providing duration or elapsed time checks throughout.

■ *Shortening inserts* A live transmission needs continual timing surveillance to obviate over- or underrunning – particularly with unscripted material. If one segment *overruns* (*spreads*), another may have to be shortened. Where prerecorded inserts (film or VT) are involved, their durations and *out words* should be precisely known. However, they offer little time flexibility, particularly if accompanied by recorded dialog. We can only shorten them on the air by omitting their start (a *late-in*) or end (an *early-out*), or even omitting an insert entirely (*dropping*).

To assist cuing when excerpting from existing material (e.g. a complete speech), we should note both the *run-in* (pre-cue) dialog and the *in-cue* (in-words).

■ *Back-cuing* To ensure that recorded play-out music finishes precisely at program fade-out, time the music from a recognizable cue point to its conclusion (say 1 minute 35 seconds). On transmission we start the music from that cue point at 1 minute 35 seconds before program out-time, fading it up when required. (Dead-pot/backtime.)

Table 19.5   The director's instructions

To cameras	Opening shots please.	Cameras to provide initial shots in the show (or scene).
	Let's line up Shot 25.	Adjust that camera's shot and subject, for composition required in Shot 25.
	Ready 2: Stand-by 2.	Stand-by cue for Cam. 2.
	Give me a single; two-shot; three-shot/group shot/cover shot.	Isolate in the shot the single, two or three persons specified./A shot including a group of people./A wide shot taking in all likely action.
	Zoom in (or out).	Narrow (or widen) zoom lens angle.
	Tighten your shot.	Slightly closer shot (slight zoom in).
	Get a wider shot.	Get the next wider standard shot, e.g. from CU change to MS.
	2 match to 3.	Cam. 2 relate to or fit into Cam. 3's shot (using viewfinder 'mixed feeds').

Table 19.5 (cont.)

More (or less) headroom.	Adjust space between top of head and top of frame.
More (or less) offset.	Adjust space between angled or profile face and side of frame.
Center (frame-up).	Arrange subject in picture center.
Lose the hands.	Compose shot to avoid seeing hands.
Cut at the hands.	Frame to just keep hands in shot.
Pan left (or right).	Horizontal pivoting of camera head.
Tilt up (or down)/pan up (or down).	Vertical pivoting of camera head. (Strictly, *'pan'* should apply only to *horizontal* action, but term's misuse is very widespread.)
Dolly back/pull back/track back.*	Pull camera mounting away from the subject.
Dolly in/push in/track in.*	Push camera mounting towards the subject.
Creep in (or out).	Push in (or pull out) very slowly, imperceptibly.
Truck left (or right)/crab left (or right).*	Move mounting to the left (or right).
Arc left (or right).	Move mounting round subject in an arc.
Ped up (or down).	Raise (or lower) column of pedestal mounting.
Crane up (or down)/boom up/ (sometimes elevate or depress).	Raise (or lower) crane arm or boom.
Tongue left (or right)/crane/ slew/jib.	Turn crane boom to left (or right).
Tongue in (or out)/crane/ boom in.	Crane positioned across the scene, move boom to and from subject.
Focus up 3.	Warning to a camera 'standing by' that is defocused.
Lose focus on the boy.	Let the moving boy become defocused, remain sharp on other subject(s); *or* deliberately defocus on the boy.
Pull focus on the girl.	Change focus deliberately from previous subject, to the girl.
Follow focus on the boy.	Maintain focus on moving boy.
Split focus.	Focus equally sharply between main subjects.
Focus 2/two, you're soft.	Criticism that Cam. 2's shot is not sharply focused.
You're focused forward (or back).	Focused at a point too near the camera (or too far away – e.g. background sharp while nearer subject is unsharp).
Rock focus 2. (Focus check.)	Focus to and from the subject to check optimum sharpness.
Stand-by for a rise (or sit).	Person is about to stand up (or sit down).
Follow him over/hold the boy.	Keep subject in shot (well composed) as he moves.
Let him go.	Do not reframe. Let him pass out of shot.
Lose him.	Recompose (or tighten shot) to exclude him.
Cam. 2, you're on lights.	Cam. 2 has lamps or strong reflections in shot (liable to damage the camera tube).

Table 19.5 (cont.)

	Clear on 3/you're cleared 3.	A 'clear', usually after a combined shot (super, chroma key); Cam. 3 can move to its next position.
	Release 3 to captions.	A 'clear' directing camera to next position.
To the floor manager	Opening positions please.	Performers (and equipment) in position for start of show (or scene).
	Stand him by/give him a stand-by.	Alert him in readiness for a cue.
	Cue action/cue 'Bob'	Give sign for action to begin (perhaps name person or character).
	Hold it.	Stop action/performance; to correct an error.
	Freeze there.	Stop movement exactly at that point; hold it quite still.
	Back to the top/take it from the top.	Begin again at the start of the scene; repeat the rehearsal.
	Pick it up from Shot 20.	Recommence rehearsal from Shot 20.
	Would they just walk it?/Go through it?	Without dialog or performance, actors move through their various positions.
	Clear 2's shot.	Something/someone is obscuring Cam. 2's shot.
	Tighten them up.	Move them closer together.
	Move him downstage (upstage).	Move him toward (away from) the camera.
	Move her camera left.	Move her to *left* of the camera's shot (i.e. stage *right*).
	Give him a mark.	Draw a toe mark to show him a location point.
	Give her an eyeline.	Show her the direction in which to look.
	He'll take a word cue.	He will begin action on hearing certain dialog.
	Give him a light/flash him.	Operate a cue light.
	Have him take a beat (or two) before he moves.	He should delay for a silent count of one (or two) before moving.
	Have him play to his key.	He should face his main light (key light).
	Show David 3/he's on 3.	Indicate to him which camera is shooting him.
	He's to work to/play to 3.	He should face Cam. 3.
	Ask him for more (less) voice.	To speak louder (more quietly).
	Show him the mike.	Indicate the mike picking him up.
	Speed him up.	Tell him to go more quickly (i.e. time is short).
	Stretch him/tell him to spread.	Tell him to go more slowly (i.e. there is time to spare).
	Tell him to pad/keep talking.	Tell him to improvise until next item is ready. (Often a hand signal, thumb and extended fingers touch and part.)
	Give him 2 minutes . . . 1 minute . . . 30 seconds.	He has 2 minutes left (followed by countdown on fingers).

Table 19.5 (cont.)

	Give him a wind/wind him up.	Signal him to finish.
	Give him a hard wind/quick wind.	It is essential for him to stop immediately. (Faster signal.)
	Kill him/cut him.	He is to stop immediately.
	Give him a clear.	We have left him. He is free to move away (or relax).
	Lose the flowers.	Remove (kill) the flowers (for the shot or scene; or take them away entirely).
To audio (sound mixer)	Fade up sound/fade up boom.	Fade up from zero to full (general or specific source).
	Stand-by music (disc/grams, tape, effects, etc.).	Warning before cue.
	Cue music/go music.	Go-ahead for music (live, disc or audio tape).
	Creep in music/sneak in music.	Begin very quietly, gradually fading up audio.
	Down music.	Reduce volume (level) of audio.
	Music under/music to background.	Keep music volume low, relative to other sources.
	Hit the music.	Begin music, at full volume.
	Up music.	Increase volume of music, usually to full.
	Sound up (or down).	General instruction to increase (or decrease) overall volume.
	Kill (cut) the music.	Stop the music.
	Fade sound.	Fade out all program sound.
	Fade tape (disc, film sound, etc.).	Fade out specified source. Usually leaving other sources.
	Cross-fade; mix.	Fade out present source(s), while fading in the next.
	Segue (pronounced 'seg-way').	One piece of music immediately follows another without a break.
	Cue tape.	Start audio tape replay.
To switcher (vision mixer)	Take 1/cut to 1/cut 1.	Switch to Cam. 1's picture.
	Fade up 2.	Bring Cam. 2's video-fader from zero to full.
	Stand-by to fade 2/ready to fade 2.	Prepare to fade Cam. 2's picture out.
	Fade/go to black/fade out.	Fade selected camera's video fader down to zero.
	Stand-by to mix (dissolve) to 3.	Warning before mixing cue.
	Mix (dissolve) to 3.	Mix from present camera(s) to Cam. 3's picture.
	Supering 3/ready to super 3.	Warning before super cue.
	Super 3/superimpose/add 3.	Fade Cam. 3's picture up, adding to existing sources.
	Take 2 out/lose 2.	Remove (usually fade) Cam. 2's picture, leaving the rest.
	Wiping 3 over 2.	Stand-by for wipe.

Table 19.5 (cont.)

	Wipe to 3.	Using prearranged pattern, Cam. 3's picture obliterates present picture.
	Ready black . . . go to black.	Stand-by . . . fade picture to black.
To graphics (captions)	Flip, animate (de-animate). Change caption. Go crawl (roller).	Cuing animated graphics. (De-animate indicates 'return to pre-animation position'.)
To other source	Cue telecine/roll film/run TK.	Start film projector (similarly for *videotape*, although some organizations ROLL film and RUN VT).
	Go ahead PARIS.	Start cue to remote source in PARIS.

* *British/European terms.*

20 Imaginative production

Pictorial function

Most pictures are factual, showing subjects in a familiar undistorted fashion, without any predominating emotional appeal. Yet, by judiciously arranging these same subjects, by careful composition, and a selective viewpoint you can modify their entire impact and give them quite a different implied *significance*. You *interpret* the scene.

You can deliberately distort and select reality so that your presentation bears little direct relationship to the actual situation; you may do this to create a dramatic illusion . . . or to produce an influential force (advertising, propaganda).

Abstracting further, you can stimulate emotions and ideas simply by the use of movement, line, form, etc., which the viewer personally interprets.

Most TV production aims at the direct reportage of events. But there are occasions when we seek to stimulate the audience's imagination; to evoke ideas that are not conveyed directly by camera and microphone. In this chapter we shall examine these concepts and how they can be used.

Picture usage

The purposes for which pictures are employed are, of course, extremely varied. Some of the more common uses are:

1. *Factual*. Conveying information directly.
2. *Environmental*. Establishing location. (Big Ben suggests London.)
3. *Interpretative*. Visual associations, conveying ideas, thoughts, feelings. (Plodding feet suggest weariness.)
4. *Symbolic*. Symbols associated with people, events, etc. (Old Glory to symbolize USA.)
5. *Imitative*. Imitating appearance or action. (The camera 'staggers', as a drunk reels.)
6. *Identifying*. Features associated with particular people, events, etc. (trademarks, logos.)
7. *Recapitulative*. Recalling subjects met earlier.
8. *Coupling*. Linking events, themes, etc. (Pan from toy boat . . . to water . . . to ship at sea.)
9. *Montage*. An interplay of successive images, or a juxtaposition of subjects.

Productional rhetoric

Rhetoric is the art of persuasive or impressive speech and writing. Unlike everyday conversation, it stimulates our imagination through style and technique, by inference and allusion, instead of direct pronouncement, by appealing to our inward ear and eye. The rhetoric of the screen has similar roots that film makers such as Alfred Hitchcock have explored over the years to great effect.

The analysis that follows is more than a concise list of facts. It is a distillation of production techniques with exciting persuasive potentials, techniques that have moved audiences to tears, of laughter and of pity; that have held them in tense expectation. Translate these principles into living illustrations and we see how the camera can, without a word of dialog, convey the whole gamut of human responses.

An example. A veteran performer ends his brave but pathetic vaudeville act amid gibes and cat-calls. He bows, defeated . . . we hear hands clapping . . . the camera turns from the sad lone figure . . . past derisive faces . . . to where his aged wife sits applauding.

Summary of devices used

Regard this analysis as a series of fingerposts, pointing the opportunities to build up original situations of your own. The summary outlines the principles involved. The examples that follow show those principles in action.

1. Making a *direct visual contrast*.
   (a) Of the picture quality – brightness, clarity, tonal contrasts.
   (b) By editing, contrasting the shot duration, transitions used, cutting rhythm.
   (c) Contrasting camera treatment – shot sizes, viewpoint height, camera movement, composition.
   (d) Through the subject itself. Creating a change that reveals new information, altering the picture's significance, e.g. by introducing a subject movement (the blonde turns . . . to reveal it is a man in drag); by cutting to a new viewpoint (the formally dressed butler . . . is wearing sneakers); by lighting. Contrasting the movement of one subject with another (contrasting energy with langor). Contrasting subject associations, i.e. the mood, qualities, properties, state of one subject with another (new with old). Contrasting subject form (building construction with its subsequent demolition).
2. Making a *direct audio contrast*. Contrasting the sounds' relative volume, pitch, quality, reverberation, speed, rhythm, duration, methods of transition, composition, sound movement, association.
3. We can *directly contrast the picture and its sound*. By comparing any aspect of (1) with another in (2) (e.g. a picture of starving children singing *Pennies from Heaven*).
4. Similarly, we can make a *direct comparison* between two ideas, situations, etc. for visual comparison, audio comparison, picture and sound compared.

5. Showing identical subjects with *different associations*.
   (a) Identical or similar subjects having different purposes, values, significances, etc.
   (b) The original purpose (or associations, etc.) of a subject has become changed.
6. Linking a variety of subjects, through *common association*.
7. *Juxtaposing apparent incongruities*.
8. *Implication*. Hinting at a situation without actually demonstrating it. Examples range from filmic time to censorable innuendo.
9. *Unexpected outcome*.
   (a) Climatic build-up to an unexpected outcome.
   (b) Anticlimax, following a build-up.
10. *Bathos*. A fall in significance; from the sublime to the ridiculous.
11. *Deliberate falsification or distortion*. 'Accidentally' causing the audience to misinterpret.
12. *Imitative interpretation*.
    (a) Between subjects.
    (b) Between mechanics and subjects;
13. *Associative selection*.
    (a) Direct, using part of a subject to represent the whole.
    (b) Recalling a subject by referring to something closely associated with it.
    (c) Symbolism – using a symbol to represent a subject.
14. *Deliberate overstatement*. Excessive emphasis on size, effort, etc. for dramatic strength.
15. *Deliberate understatement*. Preliminary underemphasis, to strengthen the eventual impact of size, effort, etc.
16. An *unreal effect* seeming to evolve naturally.
17. A *natural effect* introduced through *obviously contrived* means.
18. *Repetition*.
    (a) Of sound.
    (b) Of picture.
19. *Sequential repetition*.
    (a) A series of sequences, all beginning with the same shot, associations, etc.
    (b) A succession of similar circumstances.
20. *Successive comparison*.
    (a) Showing the same subject in different circumstances.
    (b) Showing the same subject in different manifestations.
21. *Pun*. Play on a subject's dual significance.
22. *Irony*. A comment with an inner sardonic meaning, often by stating the opposite.
23. *Modified irony*. An ironic modification of the real significance of a subject, situation, etc.
24. *Dramatic irony*. The audience's perceiving a fact that the character involved is unaware of.
25. *Personification*. Representing an inanimate object as having human characteristics.

26. *Metaphorical transfer*. Transferring the properties of one subject to another.
27. *Flashback*. Jumping back in time, to a point earlier than the narration has reached.
28. Referring to *future events* as if *already past or present*.
29. Referring to *the absent as if present*. Usually relating concurrent events by montage.
30. Referring to *the past as if still present*.
31. *Cutaway*. Deliberately interrupting events to show concurrent action elsewhere.
32. *Fade-out on climax*. Fading at the crucial moment in action:
    (a) To leave the audience in suspense.
    (b) To prevent the climactic peak being modified by subsequent action.
33. *Double take*. Passing by a subject casually . . . then returning to it quickly, having suddenly realized its significance.
34. *Sudden revelation*. Suddenly revealing new information that we were not previously aware of . . . immediately making the situation meaningful.
35. *Incongruity*. Where a character:
    (a) Accepts an incongruous situation as normal.
    (b) Exerts disproportionate effort to achieve something.
    (c) Displays disproportionate facility (i.e. exaggerated speed, etc.).
    (d) Is unable to perform a simple act.
    (e) Imitates unsuccessfully.
    (f) Does the right thing – wrongly.
    (g) Caricature.

Examples of productional rhetoric

These are, of course, only the bare bones of opportunity. You can take any of the devices listed and apply them in many quite different ways. For example, let us take (10) *Bathos*. Here is the basis of the 'banana-skin' and 'custard-pie' jokes, and our reactions when the tattered hobo dusts off the park bench before sitting. In the following examples you will see how readily these ideas can be introduced.

1. (a) A sudden mood change, by switching from bright gaiety . . . to macabre gloom.
       Contrasting a soft-focused dream-like atmosphere . . . with the hard clear-cut state of harsh reality.
       Contrasting the airiness of a high-key scene . . . with the restrictiveness of heavy chiaroscuro treatment.
    (b) Contrasting the leisurely pace of prolonged shots . . . with fast-moving short-duration shots.
       Contrasting the peaceful effect of a series of fades . . . with the sudden shock of a cut.
       Contrasting the jerky staccato of rapid cutting . . . with the deliberation of a slower cutting rhythm.

(c) Contrasting the size of a giant aircraft . . . with its diminutive pilot.

Contrasting an individual's dominance in close-up . . . with his relative insignificance within his surroundings.

Contrasting the subject strength from a low-angle shot . . . with its inferiority from a high-angle viewpoint.

Contrasting a forward aggressive move . . . with a backward recessive move.

Contrasting the restriction of limited depth of field . . . with a spacious deep-focus shot.

Contrasting the normality of a straight-on shot . . . with the instability of a canted shot.

(d) The only refuge on a storm-swept moorland is revealed by a lightning flash . . . as a prison.

2. Contrasting the busy crowds' noise by day . . . with the hush of the empty street at night.

Contrasting realistic . . . with unreal sounds.

3. A hippopotamus lumbers along, in step with delicate ballet music.

4. A pair of lovers embrace . . . and the camera tilts up to show a pair of lovebirds.

A soprano's high C . . . merges into the scream of a factory siren.

A helicopter hovers . . . to the sound of a bee buzzing.

5. A favorite record which has been played at a party is later used to cover the sounds of a murder.

6. Shots of sandcastles, rock pools, beach ball; sounds of children's laughter, sea-wash, suggest the seaside.

7. Shots of a massive French locomotive . . . end with the shrill, effeminate toot of its whistle.

8. Suspecting that he is followed, a fugitive leaves a café . . . the sound of feet joins his own in the empty street.

9. A thief grabs a valuable necklace . . . it breaks . . . the pearls scatter.

It is spring. Migrant ducks arrive and land on a lake . . . but skid on its still-frozen surface.

10. After ceremonial orders, a massive gun is fired . . . producing a wisp of smoke and a pop.

11. South American music, a striped blanket on sun-drenched stone, a bright straw hat, cactus . . . but only a sunbather in a suburban garden, listening to the radio.

12. Someone is speaking to a deaf person . . . we see his lips in close-up, but without sound.

An upward movement . . . accompanied by rising-pitch sounds.

13. (a) The name on a ship's life-belt identifies the vessel – *Titanic*.

(b) The guillotine used to epitomize the French Revolution.

(c) A shot of the Golden Gate bridge to represent San Francisco.

14. A close shot of an auctioneer's gavel descending.

15. A smoker casually throws aside a cigar-butt. A fire starts . . . which develops into a devastating forest blaze.

16. As we watch a moving picture . . . a large hand appears and turns it over like the page of a book.

17. Watching a street fight as a distorted reflection in the chromium wheel-trim of a nearby automobile.
18. A searcher shouts the lost person's name . . . it echoes and re-echoes. An angry crowd closes round a central figure. Close shots cut alternately between the accused and individuals in the crowd.
19. A successful concert tour is symbolized by the artist taking a series of similar curtain calls.
20. A succession of shots show the same policeman in a variety of situations; directing traffic, guiding a sightseer, rescuing a would-be suicide, making an arrest . . .
21. A parrot at an open window whistles for food . . . a passing girl turns at the 'wolf whistle'.
22. It is a power blackout. The lost traveler strikes a match . . . and sees a poster – 'Save Energy'.
23. A newspaper advertisement shows extraordinary bargains . . . then we see it is an old copy, used to line a drawer.
24. A mountaineer climbs . . . unaware that his rope is fraying.
25. An animated coffee-pot describes the great coffee it makes.
26. An elephant that flies ('Dumbo').
27. An old woman tells of her childhood . . . brief shots showing her life as a girl.
28. Looking at the projected plans of a ship . . . we hear the launching festivities.
29. A superimposed montage showing a missing man surrounded by headlines; radio announcers telling of his disappearance.
30. A derelict ballroom echoing to the sounds of bygone dances.
31. The fugitive escapes down a side alley. But just as we see that his way is blocked the shot changes to show his pursuers.
32. A little man arrogantly challenges a person sitting nearby . . . who stands and towers over the challenger. The picture cuts to another scene.
33. Walking past a poster of a wanted robber, a man suddenly stops, reacts, and returns to it. He realizes that its picture looks like himself.
34. Entering a room, we see someone reading . . . a close viewpoint reveals the dagger-hilt protruding from his back.
35. A man takes off his hat . . . and eats it.

Imaginative sound

Although the aural memory is less retentive it is generally more imaginative than the eye. We are more perceptive and discriminating towards what we see. Consequently, our ears accept the unfamiliar and unrealistic more readily than our eyes, and are more tolerant of repetition. A sound-effects recording can be re-used many times, but a costume or drapes design may become familiar after a couple of viewings.

In many TV shows the audio is taken for granted, while attention is concentrated on the visual treatment. Yet without audio the presentations can become meaningless (talks, discussions, interviews, newscasts, music, game shows, etc.): whereas without video the production would still communicate.

Audio can explain or augment the picture, enriching its impact or appeal. Music or effects can suggest locale (seashore sounds), or a situation (pursuing police heard), or conjure a mood (gaiety, foreboding, comedy, horror).

A non-specific picture can be given a definite significance through associated sound. Depending on accompanying music, a display of flowers may suggest springtime, a funeral, a wedding, or a ballroom.

Sound elements

■ *Voice*   The most obvious sound element, the *human voice*, can be introduced into the presentation in several different ways:

1. A single person addressing the camera, formally or informally.
2. An off-screen commentator (voice-over) providing a formalized narrative (e.g. travelogs); or the spontaneous commentary for a sports event.
3. We may 'hear the thoughts' of a character (reminiscive or explanatory narration) while watching his silent face, or the subject of his thoughts.
4. Dialog – the informal natural talk between people (actual or simulated), with all its hesitance, interruptions, breaking off, overlapping; and the more regulated exchanges of formal discussion.

■ *Effects*   The characteristic sound picture that conjures a particular place or atmosphere comes from a blend of stimuli: from action sounds (e.g. footsteps, gunfire), from environmental noises (e.g. wind, crowd, traffic), and from the subtle ways in which sound quality is modified by its surroundings (reverberation, coloration, distortion).

■ *Music*   Background music has become near-obligatory for many programs. It can range from purely melodic accompaniment to music that imitates, or gives evocative or abstract support. You can even use musical instruments to create audio effects (creaks, clicks, whines, etc.).

■ *Silence*   The powerful dramatic value of *silence* should never be underestimated. However, silence must be used with care, for it may too easily seem to be just a loss of audio.

Continued silence can suggest such diverse concepts as: death, desolation, despair, stilness, hope, peace, extreme tension (we listen intently to hear if the marauders are still around).

Sudden silence after noise can be almost unbearable:
A festival in an Alpine village . . . happy laughter and music . . . the tumultuous noise of an unexpected avalanche engulfing the holiday makers . . . then silence.

Sudden noise during silence creates an immediate peak of tension:
The silently escaping prisoner knocks over a chair and awakens the guards (or did they hear him after all?)

Silent streets at night . . . then a sudden scream.

Dead silence when the audience has been following action that would logically lead to a tremendous noise can give a scene a taut unreal quality:
To a crescendo of sound, intercut shots of two locomotives traveling towards each other at speed on the same track . . . they crash in silent slow-motion.
The explosive charge has been set . . . the detonator is switched . . . nothing happens . . . silence.

Sound emphasis

You can manipulate the relative volumes of sounds for dramatic effect; emphasizing particular sources, cheating loudness to suit the situation. A whisper may be amplified to make it clearly audible, a loud sound held in check.

You may establish the background noise of a vehicle and then gradually reduce it, taking it under to improve audibility of conversation. Or you could deliberately increase its loudness so that the noise drowns the voices. Occasionally you may take out all environmental sounds to provide a silent background – for a thoughts sequence, perhaps.

You can modify the aesthetic appeal and significance of sound in a number of ways.

For *factual sound* you can use:

1. *Random* natural pick-up (e.g. overheard street conversations).
2. *Selective pick-up* of particular sources.

For *atmospheric sound:*

1. By choosing certain natural associated sounds you can develop a *realistic* illusion. (Cockcrow suggests it is dawn.)
2. By deliberately distorting reality you create *fantasy* to stimulate the imagination. (A Swannee whistle's note suggests flight through the air.)
3. By *abstraction* the pitch and rhythm of sounds can evoke ideas and emotions without direct reference to naturalistic phenomena. (Film music, cartoon soundtracks, musique concrète.)

Sound usage

As with picture usage, this can be extremely varied:

1. *Factual.* Conveying information directly (normal speech).
2. *Environmental.* Establishing location (traffic noises imply a street scene).
3. *Interpretative.* Of ideas, thoughts, feelings (a slurred trombone note as a derisive comment.)
4. *Symbolic.* Of places, moods, events (air-raid siren denoting an attack).

5. *Imitative*. Of a subject's sound, character, movements (music imitating a cuckoo's call).
6. *Identifying*. Associated with particular people or events (signature tunes, leitmotif).
7. *Recapitulative*. Recalling sounds met earlier.
8. *Coupling*. Linking scenes, events, etc. (Musical bridges between scenes.)
9. *Montage*. A succession or mixture of sounds, arranged for dramatic or comic effect. (A bassoon and piccolo duet.)

Off-screen sound

When someone speaks or something makes a sound it might seem logical to show the source as a matter of course. But it can be singularly dull if we do this repeatedly: she starts talking, so we cut and watch her.

You can use *off-screen* sound in many ways, to enhance program impact:

1. Having established a shot of someone talking, you might cut to see the person they are speaking to and watch their reactions, or cut to show what they are talking about. The original dialog continues, but we no longer see the speaker. So you can establish relationships, even where the two subjects have not been seen together in the same shot.
2. Background sounds can help to establish location. Although a mid-shot of two people occupies the screen, the audience interprets that they are near the seashore, a highway, a sawmill.
3. Off-screen sounds may be chosen to intrigue us, or arouse our curiosity.
4. A background sound may introduce us to a subject before we actually see it, informing us about what is going on nearby or is going to appear (e.g. the wheezy spluttering of an approaching jalopy).
5. Tension can build as a character recognizes and reacts to a sound that the audience cannot interpret. Again, tension grows when a character hears a sound (that we also hear) but cannot understand its significance. Alternatively, we may realize the significance of a sound that the character has not heard or understood.
6. Off-screen sounds can exaggerate or emphasize our impressions of a scene (a crowd, traffic); perhaps indicating them even where none exists.
7. By deliberately *overlapping* sound you can create a linkage between scenes; introducing the next scene's audio before you cut to it. For example, an old man reminiscing at dinner: 'In those days, Vienna was a city of wonderful music.' While watching him, we hear a waltz in the background . . . the picture dissolves to show a soirée.
8. The background sound may create audio continuity, although the shots switch rapidly. Two people walk through buildings, down a street . . . their voices are heard clearly throughout at a constant level.
9. An audio montage of several different sources, may be used to suggest thoughts, dreams, etc.

Substituted sound

Surprisingly often, instead of reproducing the *original* sound we shall deliberately devise a substitute to accompany the picture. There are several reasons for this approach:

No sound exists. As with sculpture, painting, architecture, inaudible insects, prehistoric monsters.

Sometimes the actual sounds are *not available, not recorded* (mute shooting), or *not suitable.* For example: absence of birdsong when shooting a country scene; location sounds were obtrusive, unimpressive, or inappropriate to use; a location camera may obtain a close shot of a subject (using a narrow-angle lens) that is too distant for effective sound pick-up.

The sounds you introduce may be just *replacements* (using another lion's voice instead of the missing roar), or *artificial substitutes* in the form of effects, music, synthesized or treated audio.

Background music and effects should be added cautiously. They are easily:

1. Disproportionate (too loud or soft).
2. Hackneyed (too familar).
3. Over-obvious (imitating every action – 'Mickey Mousing').
4. Obtrusive (surging into slight gaps of silence).
5. Out of scale (overscored music).
6. Inappropriate (have wrong or misleading associations).

Controlling sound treatment

Various working principles are generally accepted in sound treatment:

1. The scale and quality of audio should match the picture (appropriate volumes, balance, audio perspective, acoustics, etc.).
2. Where audio directly relates to picture action it should be synchronized (like movements, footsteps, hammering, other transient sounds).
3. Video and audio should normally be switched together. No audio advance or hangover on a cut.
4. Video cutting should be on the beat of the music, rather than against it; preferably at the end of a phrase. Continual cutting in time with music becomes tedious.
5. Video and audio should usually begin together at the start of a show; finishing together at its conclusion, fading out as a musical phrase ends.

Audio analysis

We all recognize that some sounds seem exciting, martial, happy . . . while others are melancholy, soporific, wistful. Is this entirely fortuitous, or are there working principles to guide our audio selection? Experience suggests that there are.

If you analyze a series of sounds creating a particular emotional impact you will find they have many common features. Table 20.1 shows some

Table 20.1   Analysis of sounds and their effect

	Sound characteristics	*Associated with*
Volume	1. Loud sounds	Big, strong, assertive, powerful, energetic, rousing, earnest.
	2. Soft sounds	Small, soothing, peaceful, gentle, subdued, delicate, little energy.
	Against a quiet background	Alerting, persuasive.
Pitch	3. Pitch	Often suggests physical height.
	4. High-pitched sounds	Exciting, light, brittle, stirring, invigorating, elating, attractive, distinct, sprightly, weak.
	5. Low-pitched sounds	Powerful, heavy, deep, solemn, sinister, undercurrent, depression.
Key	6. Major	Vigor, brightness.
	7. Minor	Melancholy, wistful, apprehensive.
Tonal quality	8. Pure, thin (e.g. flutes, pure string-tone)	Purity, weakness, simplicity, sweetness, ethereal, daintiness, forthright, persuasiveness.
	9. Rich (possessing strong overtones, harmonics)	Richness, grandeur, fullness, complexity, Confusion, boisterous, worldly, vitality, strength.
	10. Edgy, brassy, metallic	Cold, chill, bitter, snarling, vicious, forceful, hard, martial.
	11. Full, round tone (e.g. horn, saxophone bowed basses)	Warm, rich, mellow.
	12. Reedy (e.g. oboe, clarinet)	Sweetness, nostalgic, delicate, melancholy, wistful.
	13. Sharp transients (a) High-pitched (e.g. xylophone, breaking glass)	Thrilling, exciting, horrifying.
	(b) Low-pitched (e.g. timpani, thunder)	Dramatic, powerful, significant.
Speed and rhythm	14. Slow	Serious, important, dignified, deliberate, ponderous, stately, somber, mournful.
	15. Fast	Exciting, hopeful, fierce, trivial, agile.
	16. Simple	Uncomplicated, deliberate, regulation, dignity.
	17. Complex	Complication, excitement, elaboration.
	18. Constant	Uniformity, forceful, monotonous, depressing.

Table 20.1 (cont.)

	19. Changing	Vigorous, erratic, uncertainty, elation, wild.
	20. Increasing (accelerando)	Increasing vigor, excitement, energy or force; progressive development.
	21. Decreasing (rallentando)	Decreasing vigor, excitement, energy or force; concluding development.
Phrasing	Repetition of sets of sounds:	
	22. Regular repetition	Pleasurable recognition, insistence, monotony, regulation, coordination.
	23. Irregular repetition	Distinctiveness, personality, disorder.
	24. Strongly marked accents	Strong, forceful, emphatic, rhythmical.
	25. Unaccentuated sounds	Continuity, lack of vitality.
	26. Interrupted rhythm (syncopation)	Character, vigor, uncertainty, unexpectedness.
Duration	27. Brief, fragmentary	Awakening interest, excitement, forceful, dissatisfaction.
	28. Sustained	Persistence, monotony, stability, tiredness.
	29. Staccato	Nervous vitality, excitement.
Movement	30. Movement pattern	Movement pattern of sound suggests corresponding physical movement, e.g. upward – downward – upward – glissando pitch changes suggesting swinging movement.
	31. Upwards	Elation, rising importance, expectation, awakening interest, anticipation, doubt, forceful, powerful.
	32. Downwards	Decline, falling interest, decision, conclusion, imminence, climatic movement.
Pitch changes	33. Sudden changes	
	(a) Rise	Increasing interest, excitement, uplift.
	(b) Fall	Force, strength, decision, momentary unbalance.
	34. Slow changes	
	(a) Rise	Increasing tension, aspiration, rising motion.
	(b) Fall	Saddening, depression, falling motion, reduced tension.
	35. Well-defined pitch changes	Decision, effort, brightness, vitality.
	36. Indefinite pitch changes (e.g. slurs, glissando)	Lack of energy, indecision, sadness.
	37. Vibrato	Instability, unsteadiness, ornamentation.
Volume changes	38. Tremolo	Uncertainty, timidity, imminent action.
	39. Crescendo	Increasing force, power, nearness, etc.
	40. Diminuendo	Decreasing force, power, nearness, etc.
Reverberation	41. Dead acoustics	Restriction, intimacy, closeness, confinement, compression.
	42. Live acoustics	Openness, liveliness, spacious, magnitude, distance, uncertainty, the infinite.

42 sound characteristics and typical associated responses. These effects can, of course, combine in various complex ways. For example, from Table 20.1, it is obvious that a sound containing the features 1, 4, 9, 10, 13, 15, 19, 20, 23, 24, 26, 27, 31, 33a, 35, 39, 42 must necessarily produce an exciting, vigorous impact. On the other hand, one containing features 2, 5, 8, 11, 14, 16, 18, 21, 22, 28, 32, 34b, 36, 41 must be a sad, peaceful, sound.

The effect of combining sounds

When we hear two or more sounds together we shall often find that they *interrelate* to provide an emotional effect that changes according to their relative loudness, speed, complexity, etc.

Overall *harmony* – conveys completeness, beauty, accord, organization.

Overall *discord* – conveys imbalance, uncertainty, incompletion, unrest, ugliness, irritation.

Marked *differences* in relative volume, rhythm, etc. – create variety, complication, breadth of effect, individual emphasis.

Marked *similarities* – result is sameness, homogeneity, mass, strength of effect.

Focusing attention

Audience attention is seldom divided equally between picture and sound. One aspect usually dominates. However, you can transfer concentration between ear and eye. For example, a movement will emphasize a remark made immediately afterwards. Dialog before a move gives it emphasis.

The ear is particularly drawn to certain types of sound:

1. Loud sounds, increasing volume.
2. High-pitched sounds (around 1000 to 4000 Hz).
3. Sounds rich in overtones (harmonics); edgy, metallic sounds; transients.
4. Fast sounds, increasing speed or rhythm.
5. Complex rhythms.
6. Briefly repeated phrases, syncopation, strong accents.
7. Short-duration or staccato sounds.
8. Aural movement.
    (a) Especially increases in volume, pitch, etc.
    (b) Clear-cut, unexpected, violent, changes.
    (c) Interruption, vibrato, tremolo.
9. Reverberant acoustics.
10. Marked contrast.
    (a) Between the principal and background sounds.
    (b) Between the sound and the picture (i.e. their associations, composition, etc.).
11. Marked similarity.
    (a) Between sounds (e.g. one source echoing another).
    (b) Between sounds and picture (e.g. simultaneous upward movements in both).

We can transfer aural attention to another subject by:

1. Giving the original subject's sound pattern (rhythm, movement, etc.) to the new source.
2. Weakening the original subject's attraction and strengthening the new source.
3. Linking action, e.g. having the pattern of the original sound change to that of the new subject, before stopping it.
4. Transferring aural movement through, e.g. by carrying over a solo sound while changing its background.
5. Cutting to a shot of the new source alone.
6. Changing the original composition lines, e.g. whereas upward sounds lead attention towards high notes, downward sounds lead attention towards lower notes.
7. Dialog attracting attention either to its source or to its subject.

Selective sound

In recreating the atmosphere of a particular environment the trick is to use sound *selectively* if you want the scene to carry conviction, rather than try to include all typical background noises. You may deliberately emphasize, reduce, modify, or omit sounds that would normally be present; or introduce others to convey a convincing sense of location.

The selection and blend of environmental sounds can strongly influence the interpretation of a scene. Imagine, for example:

The slow, even toll of a cathedral bell accompanied by the rapid footsteps of approaching churchgoers.

In developing this scene, you could reproduce random typical sounds. Or, more persuasively, you might deliberately use audio emphasis:

1. Loud busy footsteps with a quiet insignificant bell in the background.
2. The bell's slow dignity contrasted with restless footsteps.
3. The bell's echoing notes contrasted with the staccato impatience of footsteps.
4. The booming bell overwhelming all other sounds.

So you can use the same sounds either *environmentally* or *atmospherically*; to suggest hope, dignity, community, domination . . . simply through selection, balance, and quality adjustment.

As you saw earlier (*substituted sound*), instead of modifying a scene's natural sounds you might augment them or replace them by entirely fresh ones.

Fig. 20.1   Interaction between sounds
1. Towards a common focal point – suggesting conflict, concentration.
2. Away from a common focal point – suggesting divergence, broadening.
3. Contrasting sound movement – suggesting diversity, variety, interdependence.
4. Parallel sound movement – suggesting similarity, unanimity.

1   2   3   4

Table 20.2 Selective sound treatment

Scene: After a long hopeless day seeking work, a cripple returns through emptying streets.

Sound selection	Interpretation
All sounds audible – of subject and background.	His footsteps sound amidst traffic and crowd noise.
The subject alone is heard.	His stumbling footsteps echo through quiet streets.
The subject plus selected background sounds.	His slow tread contrasts with the brisk steps of passers-by.
General background sounds alone.	Traffic noises. Passers-by.
Significant background sounds alone.	The laughter and gaiety from groups he passes; contrasting with his abject misery.
Interpretative sounds, not directly originating from the scene.	His echoing footsteps become increasingly louder and distorted. By progressively filtering out the higher audiofrequencies his labored tread becomes emphasized.
Significant selected sounds from another scene (providing explanation or comment).	Voices of people refusing him work echo in his brain.

Audiovisual relationships

The picture and its audio can interrelate in several distinct ways:

1. *The picture's impact may be due to its accompanying audio.* A close shot of a man crossing a busy highway . . .
    (a) Cheerful music – suggests that he is lighthearted mood.
    (b) But automobile horns and squealing tires – suggest that he is jaywalking dangerously.
2. *The audio impact may be due to the picture.*
    (a) A long shot of a wagon bumping over a rough road . . . and the accompanying sound is accepted as a natural audio effect.
    (b) But take continuous close-ups of a wheel . . . and every jolt suggests impending breakdown!
3. *The effect of picture and audio may be cumulative.*
    A wave crashes against rocks . . . to a loud crescendo in the music.
4. *Sound and picture together may imply a further idea.*
    Wind-blown daffodils . . . birdsong, lambs bleating . . . can suggest spring.

21 Visual effects

We use 'effects' to create an illusion. They may be simple and un-obtrusive, or elaborately impressive. In more extreme applications our audience will realize that there must have been some subterfuge, but many effects are subtle and their methods undetectable.

'Effects' are used for very *practical* reasons too: for convenience, economy, safety, reliability – and when a particular visual impact is not possible in other ways.

Pictorial effects are achieved by various means:

1. *Special effects* such as fire, explosions, fog, are a specialist craft, and best left to the expert. In amateur hands the results can be uncertain, unconvincing or dangerous.
2. *Staging effects* include scenic illusions such as false perspective, scale changes (Chapter 10).
3. *Lighting effects* range from environmental impressions such as sunsets to illusory effects – passing vehicles, water ripples, firelight.
4. *Mirror effects* to reposition the camera viewpoint or multiply images.
5. *Projection effects* using front- or rear-projection images.
6. *Camera effects* using optical attachments.
7. *Foreground effects* in which the camera shoots through a foreground device.
8. *Electronic or video effects* resulting from manipulating or controlling the video signal.
9. *Temporal effects* involving the speeding, slowing or freezing of time.

Mirror effects

Mirrors are a simple straightforward way of creating certain illusions. Although vulnerable to marking, surface-silvered mirrors are preferable to rear-silvered types, which produce a tinted, less sharp image. Mirror-plastic, ferrotype, or chromium sheeting are successful for less critical applications where distortions can be tolerated or are required.

Mirrors are mostly used for overhead shots (demonstrations, piano, dancers) and for low-angle (periscope) shots. They can be time consuming to adjust and usually permit little camera movement. The mirror size needed increases with the camera/mirror distance and when using oblique mirror angles. Large mirrors are heavy and expensive items.

Having adjusted any mirror set-up during rehearsal, ensure that camera, mirror, and performer positions are clearly floor marked.

Where the lateral reversal (mirroring) is unacceptable a further intermediate mirror or reversing prism can be introduced to correct the effect. While monochrome cameras can be either laterally or vertically reversed

Fig. 21.1 Basic laws of reflection

1. Light is reflected at an angle (R) equal to the angle of incidence (I). The *normal* is a line perpendicular to the mirror surface and starting from where the beams meet. The *incident* and *reflected* rays and the *normal* lie in the same plane.
2. The reflected image appears laterally reversed and as far behind the mirror as the subject is in front. The camera focuses on the subject image, not the mirror surface.

electronically, only the latter is possible directly with most color cameras. (Digital video effects systems, where available, may provide lateral or horizontal reversal.)

Pepper's ghost

An old theatrical device, the camera shoots through an angled sheet of clear glass or semi-transparent mirror (pellicle), which reveals the direct scene and/or a reflected scene, according to their relative lighting intensities (see Figure 21.8).

Fig. 21.2 part 1 Changing the viewpoint with mirrors – using a single mirror

1. Overhead (top) shot – image inverted and laterally reversed.
2. Reverse-angle top shot.
3. Very-low-angle shot (inverted).

Fig. 21.2 part 2 Changing the viewpoint with mirrors – using two mirrors

1. Overhead shot.
2. High-angle shot.
3. Low-angle shot.
4. Low-level shot (mirrors may be mounted separately, fixed in a portable periscope stand, or attached to the camera mounting).

Fig. 21.3 Area seen in a mirror
The easiest method of planning a mirror position and judging what it reflects, is to cut out a paper triangle of the lens angle (e.g. 25°), folding it at the anticipated mirror position and placing this on a scale floor plan. This indicates mirror size and distance required. (The smaller the mirror, the closer it must be to the camera.)

Fig. 21.4 Mirrors to extend space
The camera's effective distance can be increased, to obtain a longer shot than studio space permits.

Fig. 21.5 Multiple images
For multi-reflections, you can arrange mirrors:
1. Angled – the smaller the mirror-angle, the more the images (number = 360/angle).
2. Parallel mirrors.
3. Triple mirrors.

Fig. 21.6 Split screen reflection
A horizontal reflector (foil, mirror, clear glass) across the lens can provide reflected images, mirage or water-reflection effects.

Fig. 21.7 Mirror shot
Here a subject is shot together with a background mirror. The result is a combination of the direct and reflected images.

Fig. 21.8 Pepper's ghost
The out-of-shot person (B) is reflected into the lens as a transparent ghost within the main subject picture. Depending on the relative illumination, you can see A or B, or both (B ghostly).

Fig. 21.9 One-way mirrors
The thin reflective coating on this one-way mirror makes it appear transparent (with a considerable light loss) from the rear unlit side (Cam 1); but as a normal mirror in the brightly-lit scene (Cam 2).

The idea is widely used with display dioramas in museums (comparing before and after conditions). In television, we find it in *shadow boxes* which present a series of graphics simultaneously to one camera; cuts, superimpositions, dissolves between them being achieved by lighting changes.

The device is a useful aid to shadowless lighting for multi-plane animated graphics. It also provides the background image for *reflex projection* systems (see Figure 21.14).

Rear (back) projection *(see Figure 21.10)*

Here the camera shoots action against a translucent screen of 'frosted' plastic; a film or slide being projected onto its rear side.

Once used extensively in motion pictures and monochrome TV, rear projection has been largely replaced in film by process work (matting during optical printing), or reflex projection; and in color TV by electronic insertion (chroma key, CSO).

However, rear projection still has some useful applications in TV studios. As well as being used for pictorial rear projection, the translucent screen can be used to display silhouettes, shadows, or pattern effects.

Front projection

We can project still or moving images directly onto a light-toned background, or even onto action for decorative or scenic effect.

Basic light patterns (from metal stencils) are most effective, but under typical full-lighting conditions subtle half-tones and low-key images are

Fig. 21.10   Rear projection
1. A slide or film image is projected onto one side of a matte translucent screen. On the reverse side, a camera shoots action for which the screen image provides a background.
2. The rear-projected image can be used as a complete scenic background with foreground set-pieces, furniture, etc.; or (3) used to supplement a built set (e.g. window backing); or (4) to extend a built set.

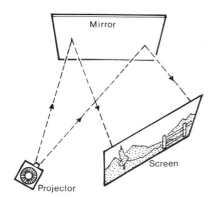

Fig. 21.11   Folding the light path
By folding the light path with a mirror, floor space can be saved. Using a second mirror even greater compactness is possible, but with a further loss of clarity.

Fig. 21.12   Image distortion
Unless the studio camera is perpendicular to the flat two-dimensional background picture, distortion occurs. Similarly, the projector must be dead square to the screen to avoid distortion. In some situations, of course, distortion is a natural effect (e.g. from a skylight).

disappointing. Geometric patterns and shapes, clouds, etc. are regularly projected onto cycloramas, and used to simulate natural light and shadow effects (window shadows). Scenic projectors can provide certain moving images (flames, sea-swell, snow) that are effective enough under favorable conditions. See Figure 21.13.

Given *sufficiently sensitive* cameras and no spill light to dilute the image (so reducing its clarity and contrast), further interesting effects are possible, e.g. an announcer with newsprint projected onto his face, dancers against black drapes who are illuminated only by striped lighting.

Fig. 21.13 Scenic projector
An enclosed glass disc with painted or photographed patterns is rotated at an adjustable speed by a small motor. This device is attached to a projector spotlight and focused onto a background to simulate moving clouds, snow, water patterns, etc. The low image-intensity usually restricts the usable image-size.

Reflex projection

In this system (also called *front axial projection* or simply *front projection*) the background is projected directly along the TV camera's lens axis via a half-silvered mirror onto a special background screen material. The secret lies in this *highly directional* surface, comprising millions of minute glass beads, each reflecting nearly 92 per cent of the projected background image back to the camera. (The principle of this Scotchlite sheeting is identical to that used in many reflective traffic signs and night-safety clothing strips.) See Figure 21.14.

Normal subject lighting cannot dilute the background image (unless placed near the camera) thanks to the screen's directionality. Where the front projected *background* image falls onto the performer or foreground subjects it is swamped by action lighting and so is not visible on camera. Shadows from it are cast directly behind subjects and so are unseen by the camera, providing the system is accurately aligned and the lens angles of the camera and projector are comparable.

Although not a foolproof system, it can provide near-miraculous effects for both film and TV cameras. Its limitations include: mirror light losses; light subject tones can be reflected in dark screen areas, causing edge haloes; the system must be aligned to avoid dark subject edges; and the studio camera must be *static* in most applications.

If pieces of reflex screen material are cut out and positioned to match objects or planes in the background picture (e.g. wall, tree, couch, archway) the studio performer can seemingly walk 'behind' them very convincingly.

Fig. 21.14 Reflex projection
1. In Reflex (axial) Front Projection, the background scene is projected along the lens axis, via a half-silvered mirror, onto a highly directional glass-beaded screen. Actors' lighting swamps the image falling on them.
2. People appear *in front* of the background scene.
3. If people move behind a surface covered with beaded material, they will appear *behind* corresponding areas of the background scene (walls, trees, etc.).

Table 21.1   Rear projection/BP

Advantages	The system is adaptable and simple to use.
	The background image is visible to performers.
	Compact screens can provide backgrounds outside small scenic openings (e.g. automobile windows).
	Rear projection can provide display panels in settings to show graphics, titles, microscope shots, film clips, etc.
Disadvantages	Studio space is wasted due to the projector-to-screen distance (*throw*) required, especially for large screens.
	Projectors occupy floor space.
	Projector noise may be audible.
	Subject illumination may spill onto the screen, diluting its image. (A black scrim layer over the screen may improve matters.)
	The projected image may be: insufficiently bright, have a central hot spot or edge darkening.
	Only slides or film can normally be projected. (Film is susceptible to vertical *hop* and horizontal *weaving*.) Projected TV images are seldom of suitable quality when shot by the studio camera.
	The rear-projected picture's apparent sharpness will vary with the studio camera's focusing and depth of field
	Matching of the projected background and foreground subject/scene may pose problems: perspective, scale, light direction, contrast, color quality, etc.
	Problems can arise in matching audio perspective and quality to varying projected backgrounds.

Camera lens filters

Filters of various kinds can be clipped over the front of the lens or inserted in a *filter-wheel* holder within the camera.

■ *Neutral density filters* These have various light transmissions (Chapter 4) and are used to prevent gross overexposure when working under strong sunlight.

■ *Corrective filters* When there are changes in the color temperature of light sources these filters can be used to compensate, e.g. when moving from daylight to tungsten-lit areas.

■ *Star filters* These are clear discs with closely scribed grid patterns. Diffraction effects produce multi-ray patterns (typically 4, 6, 8) around highlights from flames, specular reflections, and lamps. Sunburst versions may have some 60 rays! The rays' directions change as the filter is turned.

■ *Diffusion discs* Available in various densities, these filters provide general image softening through fine surface scratches or dimpling on a clear disc. Nylon or muslin net or hose may be similarly used. Sharp detail is reduced and highlights develop glowing haloes. To produce localized softening or distortion, a clear glass disc can be lightly smeared with grease or oil where required – usually round the edges. The effect can be ethereal, or woolly and irritating. But never treat the actual camera lens, for this would damage its special surface coating!

■ *Low-contrast filters*   When used, these desaturate and mute colors, while softening contrast.

■ *Fog filters*   Made in different densities, these create image diffusion from slight mist to dense fog, with strongly haloed highlights.

■ *UV (haze) filters*   When used on daylight exteriors these help to reduce haze blur due to ultraviolet light.

■ *Night filters*   These are graded neutral density or blue-tinted filters (denser at the top) used to simulate night or evening scenes. By heavy filtering (particularly the sky areas) and considerably reducing overall exposure it is possible to shoot 'night scenes' during daylight ('day for night' shooting) – thereby saving money and avoiding lighting problems.

■ *Color filters*   These are rarely used on *color* TV cameras, as hue changes can be introduced electronically. In monochrome, they facilitate lightening/darkening the tonal reproduction of parts of the spectrum.

■ *Polarizing filters*   These are occasionally used to reduce strong reflections or flares from smooth or shiny surfaces such as glass or water. (They have little effect for rough materials.) Polarizing filters can be used to darken an overbright sky without affecting overall color quality; although light loss is inevitable (e.g. 75 per cent loss). The filter's properties derive from its crystalline structure, which enables it to discriminate against light reflected at around 35°. By rotating the filter, you can selectively reduce or suppress particular reflections.

Lens attachments

A variety of add-on devices can be attached to the lens to modify the image:

■ *Multiple images*   These can be produced by prismatic or multi-faceted lenses. One form splits the screen into a series of repeat-image strips. Another has a static central image facet surrounded by a series of repeat versions, while a further form provides a ring of merging images. Their image patterns can be repositioned or rotated about the center by a small handle (or motor control), the images remaining upright; unlike those from the simple *kaleidoscope* mirror tube.

Fig. 21.15   Prismatic lenses
The number and position of images is determined by the facets on the lens. The peripheral images move round as the lens is turned but remain upright.

Fig. 21.16   The kaleidoscope
1. Shooting through a three- or four-sided mirror-tube produces an upright central image surrounded by angled reflections, which move round as the tube turns.
2. Two angled mirrors provide multiple converging images. (Number of images equals 360 divided by angle of mirrors.) Surface-silvered mirrors are needed to avoid spurious ghost images.

■ *Image distortion*   Methods available for distorting the image include shooting through molded ripple or patterned glass, via a flexible mirror, or water dish, or a foil tube giving peripheral effects. Fisheye lenses cover a wide angle of view (e.g. 100–360°), providing extreme geometrical (curvature) distortion.

■ *Image rotation*   Several mirror or prismatic attachments enable you to rotate, invert, or tilt the picture. Apart from ceiling walking, you can simulate floating in free space, flying, cliff climbing, and other feats – the easy way. The most frequent use, however, is for *canted (dutch angle)* shots in which the picture is horizontally tilted for dramatic effect. If the image is to be rotated continuously this must be done smoothly and at a suitable speed. Digital video effects allow images to be tilted, reversed, inverted, or rotated.

■ *Split-field close-up lenses*   These are used to overcome extreme depth-of-field problems, for they can provide sharp images of both close *and* distant subjects simultaneously (Figure 21.19).

Fig. 21.17   Ripple distortion
1. The camera shoots into a shallow mirror-bottomed water tank, giving an inverted ripple image.
2. The camera shoots into a mirror periscope containing a water-filled glass tray. Ripples can be made to flow across the picture, finally breaking it up altogether. If an opaque liquid is poured into the tray, the picture blots out with a fluid wipe.

Camera mattes (gobos)

For many years, solid or transparent foreground devices have been used in motion-picture making to create composite visual effects. Although often replaced in TV by electronic insertion methods, they still remain a useful facility. These *mattes* (masks) or *gobos* ('go-between') take several forms. The term *gobo* is also used for a black surface that masks off lights or cameras appearing in shot; *and* for the metal stencil used in effects projection lamps.

Fig. 21.18 part 1   Tilting the picture – using mirrors
Tilted shots can be obtained from (1) elevated or (2) depressed angles using canted mirrors. Shooting via a 45° mirror (3) attached to the lens system, causes the scene to cant as the camera tilts.

Fig. 21.18 part 2   Tilting the picture – using prisms
1. The Porra prism (a pair of reversing prisms). Rotating one of the prisms causes the image to rotate. A similar device can be constructed from two sets of double mirrors.
2. Image inverter prism (straight-through reversing prism). Rotating the assembly causes the picture to revolve.
3. A device similar to 2 uses a three-mirror assembly. Lateral reversal takes place.

Fig. 21.19   Split-field close-up lens
A half-lens (½ to 3 diopters) provides a sharp image of a close object, although the main lens is sharply focused on a distant subject; so simulating a considerable depth of field. The broad band of confused focus at the border, is arranged in a subject-free area.

Foreground matte

At its simplest, this is just a plain surface with a hole in it, through which distant studio action is seen. Painted black, it provides a soft-edged isolating *vignette* (stencil) selecting part of a scene for example:

To superimpose or insert somebody's head into another shot.
To create a shaped border, simulating a telescope, binoculars, keyhole. See Figure 21.20.
To provide localized *chroma-key insertion*, a colored foreground matte board (e.g. blue) is used. See Figure 21.37.

The foreground matte may be used to introduce a *decorative border*, or a *framed opening* (picture frame), or a *realistic* scenic effect (window). Often the camera dollies forward and 'enters' the scene as it loses the matte. *Cartoon gobos* are 'funnies', where the performer appears behind the cut-out section of a comic drawing, or pokes his head through a hole.

Insertion matte

Sometimes the foreground matte is intended to merge imperceptibly with the background scene, e.g. a foreground photograph with a cut-out area, or a painted *glass-shot* putting a matching ceiling 'onto' a studio setting. The scale, perspective, lighting, colors, tones, etc. of 'foreground' and background must be matched accurately to be really convincing and action must not normally move behind the matte opening (or it will disappear). When using insertion mattes, we must have considerable depth of field or overall sharpness may not be feasible.

Fig. 21.20 Foreground mattes
This is a foreground surface (plain or
decorated), through part of which the
distant scene is visible. It has several
purposes:
1. Selectively isolating an item, e.g.
   for localized superimposition.
2. A pattern vignette, e.g. keyhole
   effect.
3. Scenic foreground, e.g. a window
   through which camera shoots.
   A breakthrough frame parts to
   enable the camera to dolly
   'through' the foreground.
4. *Camera matte.* A studio subject is
   apparently inserted into an area
   within a foreground graphic.
5. A glass-shot, e.g. positioning a
   foreground painted ceiling 'on' a
   studio setting.

Foreground miniatures (models) are occasionally used to extend the
scene, but these are usually rudimentary – foliage, saloon swing doors,
drapes, pillars, arches. *Transparent mattes* can provide a decorated
foreground plane showing titling or graphics (a world map, show window
sign, patterns, etc.); the camera throwing focus from the foreground to
the background scene.

Electronic effects

The pictorial opportunities that electronic effects can provide are endless.
The more you use them, the more will you discover fresh applications for
both realistic and abstract picture treatment. They combine practical
economies with fascinating magic that never palls.

Superimpositions

As we saw in Chapter 8, when two picture sources are faded up together their pictures intermix. The relative strengths of their images are *additive* and can be adjusted, but:

1. Where *black* appears in either shot, the other shot's detail appears firm and solid.
2. Where *white* appears in either shot, the other shot's detail appears diluted, paled out. A peak white can burn through another shot's detail.
3. Where different hues appear in both shots, they form a new color mixture (e.g. $R + G = Y$).

Black level adjustment

By electronically darkening the lowest picture tones until they crush to a solid overall black (batting down on blacks, sitting down) you can:

1. Ensure that 'black' materials (black drapes, black title cards) reproduce as a firm black without wrinkles or shading.
2. Prevent slight tonal variations and construction being seen in hand-animated graphics – e.g. to make a black strip (with white titling) merge with its black background card.
3. Make parts of a subject disappear – e.g. a black-gloved hand against black drapes will disappear while light-toned objects that are held, remain visible.

To make a near-*white* tone merge with a white area you increase exposure so that lightest tones merge (burn-out, clip off) at white-clipper video limits.

Picture weave (electronic ripple)

Many switchers include a device that introduces a sideways ripple into a picture. Its rate and strength are adjustable. Straightforward picture weave is used to simulate flashbacks, or in transformations. But combined with multiple wipe patterns (Figure 8.12, part 4) you can break the picture up to provide a variety of undulating, decoratively shaped transitions.

Normal   Weave

Fig. 21.21   Electronic weave/ripple effects
An S-distortion (of variable strength and speed) is created electronically by varying the line-trigger pulse.

Negative picture

Electronic switching enables you to reverse picture *tones* (reverse polarity) so that they become *negative*. White reproduces as black, black as white. This is a useful facility for changing standard white-on-black titling to black-on-white (to improve clarity on light backgrounds). It can also be used to produce negative images or to reproduce negative monochrome film.

Complementary picture

Color can be transformed into its complementary hues – red, green and blue become cyan, magenta, yellow. This system enables us to directly transmit negative color film. Reversal can be used dramatically, too: transforming smoke, clouds, steam; creating black highlights glistening in a white sea; black lightning in a white sky.

Camera channel adjustment

The color TV camera channel requires careful adjustment for optimum picture quality. But, by making certain changes from standard line-up, you can obtain some interesting visual effects:

1. Reduction of the camera tube's beam current (*beam limiting/debeaming*) causes light tones to lose sharpness and intensity, and wash out (*puddle*).
2. The *video gain* or the *black level* controls of the RGB channels can be altered to give or correct a color cast in light or dark tones, or overall. So you can provide color effects that would otherwise require extensive colored lighting (suggesting moonlight, firelight, candlelight).

Video feedback

TV cameramen soon discover that by shooting a picture monitor showing their own output they can obtain interesting repeat-image effects. When you mix this camera's repeat-video with that from *another source* (in the studio switcher) and feed this combination back to that picture monitor, all manner of interesting multi-effects develop. (Two or more cameras can be used.) This technique can produce a variety of dynamic patterns, transformations, and surround images.

Interesting effects are obtainable, too, if you take a defocused shot of a subject on a picture monitor and superimpose it on the original picture. The resultant halo creates a convincing aura round 'supernatural' beings.

If positive and negative images of a subject are intermixed, a strangely 'solarized' image results that can be further processed by video feedback.

Fig. 21.22 Video feedback
Point a camera at a monitor showing a picture of its *own* output, and a random feedback pattern develops if you momentarily interrupt the shot (wave a hand over the lens, pan the camera, snap-switch a picture onto the screen).

For a more elegant controlled effect, mix the picture into the feedback loop, using a switcher.

Keyed insertion (electronic matting)

Electronic insertion processes can provide in an instant, illusions that in film making involve costly expertise, laboratory apparatus, and time. Nowadays TV production switchers have many of these associated effects facilities ready at the touch of a button! They have become an everyday tool, offering challenging opportunities.

How it works

Electronic insertion is an ingenious interswitching process used to selectively combine different picture sources. It is virtually a process of 'cutting a hole' in one picture and inserting exactly a corresponding piece of another picture. (Seldom putting one picture *over* another.)

As you know, a TV picture is normally formed by scanning the scene's image in a series of horizontal lines. The switcher selects which source is sent to line. However, suppose we had an instantaneous electronic switch available, so that the system switches itself between sources *during* this scanning process. We might, for instance, begin *each* scanning line by showing Cam. 1's picture but half-way through that line switch to Cam. 2's shot instead. (Switching back to Cam. 1 at the end of each line.) Because of this interswitching, the resultant transmitted composite would show the left half of Cam. 1's picture and the right half of Cam. 2's picture. (You will recognize this particular example as a split-screen effect.)

Fig. 21.23   Inter-source switching
1. If an electronic switch changes from Cam 1's picture to Cam 2's output halfway through each line period, the resultant *split screen* combines those parts of the shots.
2. If the switching moment is earlier in the line, the division is displaced left.
3. Occurring later in the line, the division is displaced right. The shots may be composed to suit the division being used; or the division located to suit the composition.
4. If the apparatus is arranged to select the top half of Cam 1's picture, switching to Cam 2 for the remainder of the frame, the result with these particular shots is nonsensical.

Altering the exact switching moment repositions whereabouts the division appears in the frame. If we *gradually alter* the switchover moment, a *moving* division (a *wipe*) is produced; in this example, horizontal wipe movement. So by carefully controlled switching we can create a combined or composite picture, selecting parts of two or more separate shots.

This automatic switching process is called *keying* or *matting*. The voltage that triggers the switching can be produced by

- A *separate* piece of equipment, in which case we call the process *external keying* (this is sometimes called a 'separate key mode'),
- Or by tones or colors within the subject picture itself. Then the process is termed *internal keying* or *self-keying*.

External key

Whenever you use *external key mode* for creating composite pictures you have to prepare the system in some way; to select a stored pattern, or to make a matte or mask. Let us look at several regular ways of using external keys.

Special effects generator (SEG)

The most familiar form of external key is the *wipe* facility with which most switchers are fitted. As we have just seen, wipes are produced by an electronic switch. This particular switching device is called a *special effects generator (SEG)*.

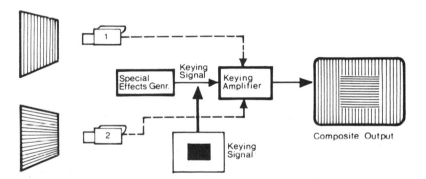

Fig. 21.24 Special-effects generator (SEG)
The SEG provides voltages of variable waveforms (square, parabolic, triangular, etc.). These control the exact switching pattern of the keying amplifier, so producing a series of geometrical matte shapes.

The SEG produces a series of voltage shapes (waveforms) to interswitch sources. Depending on the shape and frequency of the waveform used, so the picture divisions (i.e. the wipe pattern) will vary. If the switching waveform repeats over and over, the wipe pattern appears stationary. If it gradually alters, the pattern will move or change shape. The effects produced are independent of the pictures involved.

The picture divisions produced by this interswitching are invariably *geometrical*, but you can alter them in several ways:

- You can adjust the pattern's *size*; expanding or contracting it.
- You can adjust the pattern's *shape*. A square can be made rectangular, a circle can become an ellipse.
- The pattern can be moved around the frame; up/down, left/right, diagonally.
- It can be moved to a fixed position within the frame; e.g. to form a static *insert* (*inset*).

Fig. 21.25 Wipes
Wipes can be controlled in various ways: (1) direction; (2) position; (3) symmetry; (4) edge sharpness. Changes can be made at any speed.

- You can control the *speed* at which the pattern changes or moves, using a fader lever, or *autowipe* button.
- The *symmetry* of the pattern can be adjusted.
- The pattern *edges* can be made hard (sharp) or soft (diffused). If sources are interswitched *instantaneously* there will be a sharply defined division. If the insertion circuits *mix* between the two sources they will merge at their borders, to provide a soft-edged effect.
- A border can be placed around a pattern insert; in black, white, or color.
- The pattern can be made to *weave* or *ripple* at adjustable speed and strength.
- A spotlight pointer, or magnifying glass effect, can draw attention to a particular feature (Figure 21.34).

There are literally dozens of wipe patterns, but some typical examples are shown in Figures 8.12 and 21.25.

Physical mattes

The SEG has inbuilt prepared patterns, but for other forms of external key you have to make your own physical *mattes* or masks of some kind beforehand to suit the situation. A matte may be painted or cut out of card.

Camera matte

Here a studio camera shoots a graphic with the required matte shape (mask, key), e.g. a black silhouette on a white background (or vice versa).

Fig. 21.26 Camera matte
The graphic in front of the matting camera (3) results in a video signal which interswitches Cam 1 (flowers) with Cam 2 (girl) in a heart-shaped mask form. Wherever complex, non-geometrical matte shapes are required (e.g. tree-branch patterns, flower shapes, decorative screens, etc.), camera mattes are used.

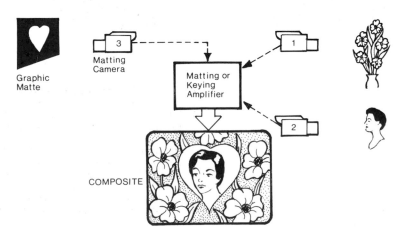

The video from this masking camera is used solely to operate intersource switching (via a *keying amplifier*). Its picture as such is not used. Even if the matte is of a complicated shape (a map silhouette), it will key a corresponding area from one chosen picture into another.

The key could equally well be derived from a static matte in a *slide scanner*:

Cam. 1 shooting a brick wall photograph.
Cam. 2 shooting a striped surface.
Matting slide – Title slide.
Matted result – Lettering in striped paint, on a brick wall.

Moving camera mattes are also possible:

Cam. 1 – A cloud scene.
Cam. 2 – Glittering reflections (defocused tinsel).
Cam. 3 – Silhouette of dancer in studio, used as a matte.
Matted result – A glittering shape dancing among clouds.

The rostrum camera

Some studios use a separate *rostrum camera* instead. Here again, a silhouette matte is used and the rostrum camera's video actuates the switch (Figure 21.27). This method saves tying up a valuable studio camera just to provide a 'camera matte'.

Where a studio has a separate monochrome *video prompter* camera (Figure 19.4, part 2) this could be utilized instead to serve as a rostrum camera.

Fig. 21.27 Rostrum camera (inlay desk)
Using this external keying apparatus, even elaborate masks are practical.
1. TV camera – the overhead monochrome TV camera shoots a back-lit white panel. Cut-out card, inked or painted shapes, provide a matte for the keying signal.
2. Picture tube – the matte is placed or drawn on a *cel* (clear plastic sheet) or glass, over a picture tube displaying a plain white picture (raster) – a flying-spot scanner. The phototube picks up a constant scanning output (i.e. peak white video) except where interrupted by the matte. Adjustment of the scanning width or height alters the effective matte shape. Zooming produces matte size changes.
3. Keying signal – this is fed to the montage amplifier, where it inter switches between the cameras' outputs.

Finally, we can use a *recorded matte* as the external key. Here the matte shape has been filmed or videotaped beforehand. This idea is particularly useful if a show has regular opening titles on film or VT. They can include a matte shape (e.g. a chroma-key blue patch), in which we insert the current studio opening shot.

Internal key (self-keying, self-matting, common key mode)

In this process the matting signals are derived from the *Master* (*Subject*) picture itself. This sophisticated method of keying requires no prepared mattes or waveforms. Instead, it continually examines the video from the

Table 21.2　Keying methods compared

	Advantages	Disadvantages
External key (using SEG, camera matte, slide matte)	Simple to operate and adjust.	Complex scenic mattes (ceiling insert) may require accuracy in construction and adjustment.
	Reliable and definite in action.	
	No spurious breakthrough between pictures.	*The camera set-ups for recording must usually be identical to rehearsed version.
	Any tones/colors usable in foreground subjects *and* background shots.	*Normally, foreground and background cameras should remain static. Any film must be free from hop or weaving in static scenes.
	Only the matted area is inserted into the composite.	
	No mutual degradation of picture quality (unlike *superimpositions*).	*In pictorial insertions, foreground and background shots should match in perspective, proportions, scale, lighting, etc.
	Studio area required for insertion may be confined.	*The *whole* of one picture source cannot normally be inserted into *part* of another shot (*see Figure 21.31*).
	Sharp matte edges keep edge ragging to a minimum.	But appropriate or accidental cut-off or disappearances can arise.
	Subjects disappear behind matted areas. Appropriate when moving *behind* walls, objects . . .	
Self-keying/self-matting (using chroma key, CSO)	Operation is automatic.	Similar to *external key* disadvantages marked*.
	No mattes/masks have to be prepared.	The keying/matting tone or color must only be present where 'background' is required. Shadows or reflections may cause spurious breakthrough.
	Subject movement is not confined (but may need restriction, to suit background scene).	
		Edge ragging and color fringing arise.
	Various tones or hues can be used, for differential keying.	When inserting into long shots a large studio area may require chroma-key background and floor unless keying foreground matte/gobo is used.
	Foreground subjects always move *in front* of background and cannot be cut off by matte or inadvertently disappear . . .	But the effect may not be appropriate and foreground matting flat or external matte may also be necessary.

master shot, and wherever it detects the *keying tone* or the *keying color* – depending on the system you are using – it switches from the master shot to a separate *background* picture in that area.

If you are using a particular *tone* for the automatic switching process – *luminance keying (insert key)* – wherever that chosen tone appears in the foreground shot (usually black or white) a corresponding part of the background is seen instead in the composite picture. So areas of the

Fig. 21.28   Self-keying/self-matting
Wherever a selected *tone* (or *hue* if you use *chroma-key/CSO*) appears in the *master shot* (the subject or foreground shot), a corresponding part of the background shot is seen instead. The system switches back to the master shot for all other tones (or hues) in that scene. *Background* scene tones or hues do not affect keying in either system.

Fig. 21.29   Choice of system

External key. Here switching is controlled by a separate matte. It does not normally allow foreground subjects to move *in front of* features in the background picture. The subject disappears when it moves outside the matted area.
1. This is appropriate when people are to move behind walls, trees, etc.
2. But it is incongruous if, for example, they get out of a car matted in by external key. *Any tone or color* may be used in the foreground and background scenes.

Self-keying. This relies on hues (or tones) within the foreground shot (master shot/subject) to operate the keying. Chroma key is the commonest form of self-keying used in color TV. Subjects cannot normally moved *behind* background features.
3. The process can at times produce incongruous effects. People may appear to stand or sit in mid-air!
4. Where appropriate, self-keying is completely convincing. The *subject and foreground scene* should not contain or reflect the keying color. The background scene may contain *any* colors or tones.

keying *tone* must only appear in the *foreground scene* where you require insertion; otherwise you will see spurious breakthrough. This *tonal keying* can be used with monchrome or color TV/video systems.

When *color* is used to key the insertion, the process is called *chroma key* or *CSO – color separation overlay*. (There are additional allied processes, too, such as *Ultimatte*.) Wherever the selected keying/switching *hue* appears in the foreground or master scene the background is switched into that area instead. This technique can only be used in a color system. Because chroma key is such an important facility in television today, we will examine it in detail shortly.

Using keyed insertion

Inserting titling

In Chapter 15 we mentioned the idea of electronically inserting *titling* into a picture for various purposes; e.g. subtitles, credits, data information, etc. Now we can look at title insertion in greater detail. The titling itself can come from camera title cards, a character generator, or photo-slides, and be inserted in several ways:

- *Superimposition*. This is only really successful against a dark eventoned surface. Where the background tones or hues vary, the lettering may be locally affected, or appear 'transparent'.
- *Non-additive mix (NAM)*. Using this facility, the source with the lightest tones (usually white titling) inserts 'solidly' into the other picture (Table 21.3).

Fig. 21.30 Title insertion
1. Titles introduced by *superimposition* are satisfactory against plain backgrounds (preferably white letters against black), but otherwise mutual interaction reduces evenness and clarity.
2. *Inserted* letters cut through all picture tones; but for titling against similar tones (white on white, gray on gray) black-edging is desirable.
3. Sometimes an *inset area* (mid-gray presenting black or white titling) is more distinctive. It does not require a border. But the overall effect may be intrusive.

1   2   3

Table 21.3 Electronic insertion terms

Background	The picture into which the foreground subject (master shot) is electronically inserted. It can usually contain any tone or color.
Black edge	Facility putting an artificial black border round titling, to improve readability. Border generator.
Blink; flasher	Blinks keyed-in titling or symbols at an adjustable rate.
Border generator; edge key; black edge generator; outline	Facility introducing a black, white, or color border around a keyed-in subject. It may also derive outlines.

Table 21.3 (cont.)

Character generator	Computer-generated lettering, numerals, signs, widely used for inserted titling and graphics.
Chroma-key process	Facility for inserting a subject with a single-color background (e.g. blue) into another video picture. Several systems exist, including: 1. Fast-switching chroma key, using *encoded* composite video signals (e.g. video coded into NTSC form with syncs). 2. Similar system using direct RGB (decoded) video signals. More precise, less noise or spurious switching. 3. *Ultimatte*, which derives separate black matted images that are then superimposed in an additive mix.
Chroma keyer	Equipment controlling chroma-key operations. 1. Selects hue of the keying color. 2. Selects the input for chroma-key treatment. 3. Selects edge switching (hard, soft, color).
Clip control; clipper; clipping level; key level; threshold level	Adjusts the precise brightness (luminance) level at which switching takes place, when keying in a subject. Adjusted on preview to suit each shot. If incorrect, tearing or spurious breakthrough occurs.
Color synthesizer; colorizer; color field generator	Equipment generating color synthetically by applying proportional voltages to the RGB channels. Can be used to artificially color black and white pictures, either with an overall hue or with different hues for selected tonal values. Can also substitute different colors in a color picture.
Cycling	Facility for progressively changing the hue of synthesized color through the spectral range. *Also* to flash the luminance level (brightness).
Digital video effects	Images produced by storing color and detail information about a picture in digital form, then selectively reading out those data to produce visual effects.
Downstream key; title key	A facility that allows titling to be inserted when the main effects banks are already in use (e.g. for chroma key). It inserts *titles* or an *external key* into the switcher 's' *line output*. It may also be used to fade a program to black.
Drop shadow	An artificial black contour added to the side and lower edge of lettering, to create a pseudo-three-dimensional effect.
Double re-entry; cascade re-entry	The output of one *mix/effects bus amplifier (A/B)* can be re-entered into another *M/E bus (C/D)*. So we can mix to or from *combined shots* (e.g. keyed-in titles, split screen, supers, chroma key). *Also*, a key from an external matte source may be used to create a matted area in one shot that is filled in by another camera's background picture.
External key	A matte shape, from a camera matte or SEG, that virtually punches a hole in the background picture and inserts the corresponding part of *another* picture source in the matted area. (E.g. creating silhouetted lettering, and filling it with a shot of texturing.)
Foreground	The subject inserted into the background shot. In chroma-key set-ups it contains the keying color.
Hard key	Keying process *switching* from foreground to background, producing sharp-edged matting. Imperfections (tearing, crawling, jitter) can be very visible at subject edges (see *Soft key*).

Table 21.3 (cont.)

Hue control	Control adjusting the actual color used or chroma-key insertion (usually blue, sometimes green or yellow).
Insert in/out	Switches selected matted picture in/out of the program picture.
Insert key	Where the key source exceeds a particular brightness level (selected by clipper adjustment) its subject is inserted into the background picture. Used to insert white-on-black titling into pictures; from camera title cards, slides, character generator.
Insert program fader	Control used to fade inserts in/out of program picture.
Insert source	Selects which picture source fills in the matted area, produced by the *key source*.
Internal key; self-keying, self-matting	A particular *color* or *tone* in the foreground shot actuates an automatic switch, which inserts a corresponding part of another source picture in that area instead. (E.g. *TONE* to insert white lettering; *COLOR* for chroma-key insertion.)
Key fill	Selects the source or color of infill for insert titling.
Key invert	Allows the output of a *mix/effects bus (M/E)* to fill external key subjects, and pre-set wipes.
Key mode	Mattes in lettering, giving it black edge, drop shadow, or border/outline treatment.
Key source	Selects the picture source used to matte out part of the background picture (see *insert source*).
Linear keying; transparent matte, proportional keying	Circuits controlling the keying amplifer gain, for chroma-key insertion. It allows *transparent materials* (e.g. glass, smoke, water) or *finely edged* subjects (e.g. feathers) to be inserted while permitting the background to be seen through them. The linear keying mode can also be used to transform a normal picture input – to provide *color to monochrome mixes, tinting effects* (e.g. sepia tints), and negative pictures.
Luminance	Control adjusting the brightness level (in monochrome) or saturation (in color).
Luminance key; tonal key; inlay	A self-keying/internal-keying process in which a selected tone (black or white) in the foreground/master shot is replaced in the composite picture by a corresponding portion of the background shot.
Matte; mask; key	A specially generated signal supplied to a keying amplifier, causing it to switch from one source to another in the matted area. It can be derived from a silhouette (painted, inked, or cut in card) as in a *camera matte* or *rostrum camera*, from a picture, from titling (e.g. character generator), from specially generated waveforms (wipes, SEG).
Matte key	A system for infilling keyed outlines with tone or color (e.g. titling, maps).
Mode	The *bank fader lever* on some switchers can be made to do several quite different things, so avoiding the need for separate controls. 1. *MIX/LAP DISSOLVE* between banks/buses. Its regular purpose. 2. *MASK KEY* to move wipe patterns. 3. *MIX KEY* to fade in a matte (key) signal. 4. *PATTERN TRANSITION* to provide a pattern transition between A and B buses.

Table 21.3 (cont.)

Non-additive mix (NAM); peak mix mode; insert key; white insert mode	A circuit facility in which the lightest tones of one picture are inserted solid (opaque) into another picture. Used for title insertion.
Overcut	Switching in which the *main subject* is changed, appears or disappears, while the *background* picture remains constant throughout (see *Undercut*).
Pattern direction	Selects the direction in which a wipe/pattern moves when the control lever is operated.
Pattern edge	Adjusts pattern's edge sharpness (hard, soft) or width.
Pattern generator	Control selects interswitching patterns used for wipes and insets.
Pattern limit	Pre-sets the final size or extent of a wipe pattern; e.g. limiting a rotary wipe angle.
Pattern modulator; pattern weave	Causes the wipe pattern or the overall picture to ripple from side to side (adjustable rate and extent) to create a dynamic decorative effect.
Polarity; key reversal	Reverses the picture's tonal scale, so producing a negative image. *OR* it toggles (alternates) whether white or black tones actuate the keying.
Position	Joystick positioning a pattern in the frame.
Preview (P/V) bus key	The source selected on the *preview bus* mattes a hole in the picture on *Bus A* and fills it from the picture on *Bus B*.
Quad split	The screen is divided into four sections, simultaneously displaying separate images. The proportions of the divisions are adjusted with *VAR* or *SPLIT* controls.
Sequential effects amplifer	Matting carried out in a series of steps to produce a complex composite.
Shadow keyer	In chroma-key systems, subject shadows falling on the blue keying surface are normally not seen in the composite, and cause spurious 'tearing'. Special shadow-keying circuits can insert apparently 'natural' shadows.
Soft key	The keying system virtually mixes between the keyed subject and the background shot, producing diffused-edged matting (adjustable softness). Keying imperfections at edges are less visible. Images can be blended together at borders.
Special effects generator (SEG)	Equipment generating a series of electrical waveforms (e.g. square wave, sawtooth, triangular, parabolic) at line and field rate. From these waveforms, switching patterns are derived to provide wipes and inserts.
Spotlight	The background brightness is darkened around a disc matte (joystick positioned) to give a spotlight effect.
Undercut	Switching in which the main subject picture is retained while the background picture is changed; a performer's background switches to a new scene while we watch (see *Overcut*).

- *Keyed insertion*. This technique allows lettering of any tone or hue to be solidly punched into a background picture without interaction effects. (It may be done through *external luminance keying* or lettering on a *chroma-key* blue backing.)

A *clip control (key level)* adjusts the brightness level at which the titling is keyed in. If set too low, the outline will be unsharp or show tearing. If set too high, finer parts of the lettering are liable to become lost.

Even well-inserted titling cannot be read if its tone or color proves to be similar to the background. If you are faced with this dilemma there are several solutions:

- *Border generator*. Here edge keying electronically creates an edge shadow outline around lettering. This can be black ('black edge'), white, or of any selectable color. The width of this border may be adjustable. It is usually possible to switch to a *drop shadow mode* or an *outline mode* in which the border replaces the original lettering (Figure 21.30).
- *Infill*. The lettering tone or color can be altered by infilling it with a separate source. A *colorizing generator (color synthesizer)* produces color signals artificially, which can be used to color lettering and/or backgrounds. A *cycling* mode can make the coloring self-change throughout the spectral range.
- *Double re-entry*. This switcher facility enables you to introduce texture or patterning into lettering (see Table 21.3).
- *Negative switching*. White lettering may be switched to black, or black lettering to white, if you find them coinciding with background tones. For example, when using standard white lettering on black camera titles they can be 'phase reversed' to insert them into a snow scene.
- *Flashing/blinking*. It may help at times to flash the lettering rhythmically, to draw attention, or make it more visible against its background.

Display screens

Surprisingly often, we want to accompany a shot of a person speaking to camera with a supplementary background picture showing what they are talking about. We find this regularly in newscasts, where the display screen introduces pictures of the upcoming story, or shows us the person the newscaster is speaking to. In talks, the screen can show us illustrations, photo-enlargements, maps, etc.

The most obvious way to obtain a screen of this sort is to bring a large picture monitor into the shot. If you have a rectangular hole in a flat the monitor can be placed behind it and appear as a wall screen. This can work quite well, especially if the monitor has a tinted screen. (Sometimes a neutral gel or black net over the screen helps.) But there may be problems with lights reflected from its screen.

In addition, you will usually find that when you switch from the direct picture of the display subject, to the studio shot showing it on the monitor screen, the display subject's color quality changes. You can usually improve matters by altering the color balance of the studio monitor (reducing blue), so that it looks right on camera.

1

2 Subject Cut Off

3

4

5

6

Fig. 21.31   Display screen
1. A 'wall display' screen can be simulated by self-matting (chroma key).
2. External keying can only be used when nothing moves into this area.
3. A 'screen' may be used to include a distant guest in a studio interview.
4. This is achieved by using a corresponding chroma key area in the main shot.
5. Care must be taken that the person to be inset is in proportion and position for the display screen.

To insert the whole of one picture into part of another, a picture monitor must be used (or a digital effects unit). Monitors should be shaded from reflected or spill light, color-adjusted (yellow bias), preferably using a dark screen (black matrix) tube. Quality unavoidably deteriorates.

An alternative approach to display screens is to have an opening in a flat behind the subject covered with a translucent sheet. You can then *rear project* slides onto this screen.

Another regular method is to use electronic insertion, to *simulate* a screen in the background:

● Use a *box wipe* or a *camera matte* to insert a picture of a monitor screen. Performers must not move in front of the matted area or parts of them will disappear!
● Have a blue panel or blind, or a patch of blue light on the background, and chroma key the display into this 'screen' area. People in the foreground will not be cut off if they move in front of the 'screen', but edge-ragging problems can arise.
● Using digital video effects, you can reduce the size of the display subject's picture and insert it into the background of the main shot. Again, performers must not move into the matted area.

Localized inserts

■ *Insert/inset*   You normally introduce a *detail insert* into a wider shot by wiping in and holding the required shape (e.g. to show a close-up soloist within a full orchestra long shot, a box or iris wipe is positioned in the selected part of the screen). A hard-edged inset is usually preferable, to prevent image confusion – perhaps with a colored border to emphasize

Fig. 21.32   Inset
To introduce close-up detail while retaining the main shot, an inset can be used (created by any method).

Main Scene

Detail Shot

Composite

Fig. 21.33 Surround matte
Mattes can be used: (1) to mask off unwanted material in the shot, or (2) to simulate a vignette.

demarcations. Occasionally a soft (diffused) edge is unobtrusively effective – for a dream montage or a 'think' bubble (Figure 21.25).

■ *Vignette/surround matte*   You can use keyed insertion to provide decorative surrounds or borders to an insert subject, or to form symbolic shapes (keyhole, telescope, binoculars, heart). Geometrical patterns are available on the SEG.

By blanking out parts of the shot you can exclude unwanted subjects. The support stand of a world globe could be matted out, so that it appeared in 'free space' – perhaps inserting a skyscape into the now-black surround.

■ *Indicators*   Many switchers include facilities for inserting indicators that draw attention to specific information – in maps, charts, diagrams, photographs. Arrows, surround-rings, spotlight effects (a lightened disc on darkened background) are widely used, and located by joystick positioning; often with a 'blink' option.

■ *Appearance/disappearance*   This is simply achieved, by switching or fading the insertion in and out.

Fig. 21.34 Indicators
Visual indicators in the form of an arrow, ring, spotlight (devised electronically or by any matting method), can identify specific detail.

Multi-split screen

This is a method of showing information from several shots simultaneously, by dividing the screen into two, three, four or more sections (with or without border lines).

Individual segments may show:

1. *Different views* of the same situation (reactions and prize giving at a game show).
2. A *montage* of concurrent events (different rescuers moving to the disaster area).
3. *Sequences* (steps in the development of a product).
4. *Groupings* of subjects with a common significance (all members of the team).

This multi-split screen effect (Figure 21.35) can be achieved by:

1. *Sequential insertion* (quad overlay). The switcher treats pictures in turn; matting out a chroma-key area, passing the matted result on to combine with the next source (with its chroma-key area), matting from this combination, and so on. (Each insertion could use a different keying hue if required.)

Fig. 21.35 part 1   Type of split screen
Several forms of divided screen are widely used:
1. Split screen.
2. Triple split.
3. Quad split.
4. Multi-split.

Fig. 21.35 part 2   Methods of creating split screen effects
Several methods are used: *sequential switching* – the system selecting each source in turn for a certain period. *Sequential insertion* – after the first picture has been treated, part of a further picture is matted in. The next source is inserted into that composite . . . and so on. Other techniques include VT build-up (see Fig. 21.43), or digital image-processing.

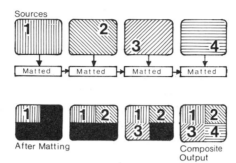

2. *VT build-up*. Recording a split screen pattern; then reproducing the tape and matting in a further segment(s).
3. *Digital video effects*. Capturing a frame, reducing the image size, and positioning it beside other frozen images, in a multiframe store.

Chroma-key insertion techniques

Chroma key has endless applications; especially when combined with other video effects. You can simulate total reality or create magical, stylized, decorative displays. The opportunities are endless, the economies considerable. But you need to apply chroma key carefully, keeping in mind its problems and limitations, if you are going to achieve convincing, accurate results. Forethought and careful planning can save a great deal of rehearsal time. So we shall look in some detail here at many of its potentials and its pitfalls.

Setting up chroma key

Although chroma-key insertion can seemingly perform miracles, it does have important restrictions that we cannot ignore.

The fixed camera

Normally, the camera itself must hold a fixed shot. If you truck (crab) or pan the camera, the inserted subject will slide across the background shot. If you dolly or zoom, the subject will grow or shrink. Intriguing effects, but usually to be avoided!

There are exceptions to this rule. If foreground and background cameras can move in exact synchronism, realistic pan/tilt/zoom changes are often possible. In simpler situations, skilled cameramen have managed to do this effectively. But the most reliable synchronism requires special equipment, such as in the *Magicam* process, where foreground and background cameras are ganged by electronic servo systems. Here the foreground camera can pan/tilt/zoom and the background camera shooting a photograph, graphic, or model will move proportionately.

In the *Scene-Sync* process the background derives from a static camera shooting a servo-controlled graphics stand or a rear-projection device (slide or film). Results can be extremely convincing as the foreground camera follows action and adjusts shot length. However, the background camera must turn on a correctly adjusted pivot center, and its displacement rate must match the relative lens angles used. So it, too, needs expert adjustment. Where possible, it is advisable to avoid critical situations with strong perspective or parallactic changes (Figure 21.40).

Check the chroma-key area

When you are preparing a chroma-key set-up, begin by checking that the chroma-key area and subjects are suitable.

- Is the color of the background appropriate? Ideally, the blue background (and floor if necessary) should be of an even overall tone and cobalt blue. Some systems are more color-critical than others. Check that blue-painted chroma-key flats have a dull, even finish. Blue background or floor cloth should be stretched, without folds or wrinkles.
- The blue keying surfaces should be evenly lit. If they vary in brightness, it will be difficult to adjust clipping levels correctly. Shadowy areas can cause poor clipping. So look out for *deep shadows* falling on the chroma-key blue surfaces (particularly from the performers or furniture).
- Spurious breakthrough will occur if there are any *accidental* blue areas in the foreground subjects. So check clothing, objects, props, furniture, scenery, etc.
- Check that there are no shiny surfaces (e.g. mirrors, glasses) likely to reflect nearby chroma-key color from the blue floor or backdrop.

Fig. 21.36 Background insertion
1. **Internal keying.** The person stands in front of a chroma-key blue surface, and a new *background* is inserted. This can be plain tone or color from a color synthesizer, black level, pictures from any video source.
2. **External keying.** Using a matte from a camera or rostrum camera, part of the studio scene is matted out, and a background picture inserted in its place (from a graphic, slide, VTR or film).

Chroma-Key Backing   Studio Scene   Camera Matte   Background Scene

Composite

1   2

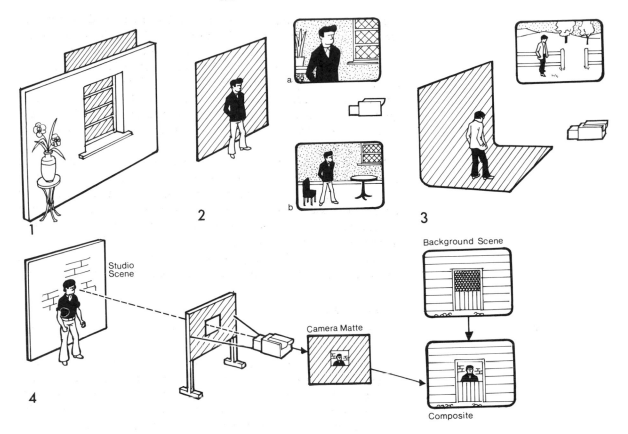

Fig. 21.37 Typical chroma-key set-ups
1. You can insert a photographed 'exeterior' outside the window, by using a chroma-key blue backing.
2. Only a simple chroma-key blue flat is needed, if (a) the floor is not in shot, or (b) if the studio floor will appear natural in the composite.
3. When people are to appear *within* the background picture, or where the studio floor would look incongruous in the composite, you must use a *continuous* chroma-key blue surface, behind the subject and on the floor.
4. Here the camera shoots through the hole in a blue matte-board. Particularly useful for long shots, this camera matte masks off most of the studio, so prevents the camera shooting off into lights etc. It also avoids the need for large keying areas in the studio. All blue keying surfaces must be evenly lit to a similar level, free from shadows, etc., to give good overall clipping.

Clipping level

Adjust the *clipping level* to obtain firm, clean edges around inserted subjects. There should be no tearing, ragged edges, or bleeding around edges.

You will need to adjust the clip control continuously for optimum effect. If the clipping levels are set too low the inserted subject will show severe edge ragging around its borders. Set too high, and you will lose parts of the inserted subject itself.

How critical this adjustment is in practice will depend on the system design, how it is set up, and the subject to be keyed in. If lighting is uneven, or there are odd shadows, you will find clipping is successful in some parts of the insert but not in others. Overall firm clipping may not be possible.

At best, the insert will be perfect and undetectable. At worst, there will be discernible tearing, breakthrough, edge ragging within and around the subject.

Technical note: Ideally, for clear-cut insertion one should use the *separate* red, green, and blue signals from the keying source to actuate the chroma-key circuits (*RGB keyer*). However, this is often impracticable, and you will have to use a *composite* video signal from the keying source instead (i.e. the complete NTSC or PAL signal: video waveform plus all color and syncs information). Some sources only output a composite signal; e.g. VTRs, telecine, ESS, external sources and remotes, and some studio cameras. Chroma-key inserts using this *encoded keyer* are more difficult to adjust; edges are less clean as switching is not so accurate. Some chroma-key systems can be switched to either *RGB keyer* or *encoded keyer* to suit the incoming keying source.

Aiding performers

● In a total chroma-key situation (blue backdrop and floor) place blue discs on the floor to give talent *location marks*.
● If action requires an actor to look directly at something in the background shot (which he cannot see!) place a dim colored lamp in a corresponding position in the studio to give an *eyeline* to work to.

Matching

For *pictorial* inserts the foreground and background usually need to match reasonably well. The scale, perspective (lens angle, height, eyeline), color quality, contrast, light direction, etc. should be compatible.

Original Scene   Background Film Camera

Studio TV Camera

Fig. 21.38 Matching camera height
The height, angle of tilt, and lens angle, of the studio camera should be identical to that used to photograph the background scene, if distortion is to be avoided. Often the errors are not obvious.
1. Unmatched viewpoints.
2. Matched viewpoints.

Fig. 21.39   Matching eyelines
1. The foreground subject matches its background's perspective only when the television camera's eyeline coincides with the eyeline of the background.
2. Background eyeline *above* subject eyeline.
3. Background eyeline *below* subject eyeline.

So when a person is to be inserted into a background picture we must take care to check proportions, and use a camera height that suits the background viewpoint.

- Check that the person's feet are rationally placed within the background; that he does not appear to be standing in mid-air, or in an incongruous position (e.g. on a pond).
- Check that the person can move across the screen, and a short distance forwards/backwards, without creating visual problems. If an actor is apparently to 'walk around within the background', the scale and perspective should appear to be consistent throughout the action.
- People should not seem to grow taller or shrink as they move nearer or further from the camera (wrong lens angle).
- Nor should they rise or fall (wrong camera height).

Much depends on whether there are many visual clues to perspective in the shot. In open background scenes (beach, landscape) even gross errors may not be obvious. But scenes including architectural subjects (rooms, buildings, streets) can be very critical.

Adjusting scale and perspective

Lacking detail of the lens angle and height of the original camera shooting the background photograph, you can use the following empirical technique to avoid strange scale or perspective effects:

- Display the shot of the background picture on a monitor. If you are using a background photograph set up in front of a camera, lock off that camera's panning head. (If a drawing or painting is used as a background, its perspective might not be correct, so adjustments are a matter of luck!)
- Check the background shot on the monitor and choose points where you can make reasonably accurate guesses about the sizes of subjects; e.g. doorways, cars. (Avoid choosing indefinitely sized objects such as bushes or fences.) At these points, using a wax pencil or a felt-tipped pen, mark vertical lines to scale on the picture-tube, representing the performer's height. (If there are no true clues you will have to make guesstimates.)
- Take a long shot of the studio chroma-key area on a normal lens angle. Insert the performer into the scene. Adjust the clipping level.
- Position him to coincide with the 'nearest' marker in the background picture. Adjust the camera distance to fit the person's height to the marker.
- Holding that camera and lens position, move the performer further away from the camera to coincide with a 'distant' marker position in the picture. If perspective is correct, he will appear reasonably similar in height to the distant marker. If he looks disproportionately shorter, zoom in a little and

Fig. 21.40   Ganged backgrounds
By using a servo-controlled interconnection ('ganging') between the subject (master) camera and the background (slave) camera, the latter pans, tilts, and zooms automatically as the subject camera follows the action. Alternatively, the background graphic itself may be moved vertically/horizontally by servo systems using a static slave camera.

dolly back to compensate. If he looks too tall at the distant point, zoom out and dolly in. A reasonable compromise is usually possible.
- If the subject camera is now overshooting the chroma-key area, or seeing cameras, boom, lights, place a chroma-key matte in front of the camera (blue card with a 4×3 rectangular central hole). Otherwise use a localized wipe pattern to cut off unwanted areas.

Further practical problems

Having set up the chroma-key shot, there may be two obvious defects:

- Depth of field.
- Color fringing.

If the depth of field is limited in the foreground scene, yet depth appears limitless in the background, you have a problem. Occasionally, slightly defocusing the *background shot* will help. Otherwise, more light will be needed on the *foreground scene* so that the subject camera can stop down.

Blue color fringes can develop round the borders of keyed-in subjects. Chroma-key blue lighting may have spilled onto it, or be reflected onto it. It may be due to optical flare. It can be due to the system's inherently poor color detail (restricted bandwidth). The often-recommended 'remedy' of using yellow backlight (minus blue) may occasionally alleviate the problem but is more likely to tint the subject yellow!

Some systems are more susceptible to color fringing than others. Soft-edge keying can diminish the effect, but for total suppression, special circuits (*hue suppressors, fringe eliminators, exclusive hue matrix*) are often necessary. Unfortunately, these may modify the reproduction of certain color mixtures.

When inserting finer detail (e.g. hair, lace, fur, feathers) or vague, unsharp subjects (e.g. smoke, glass, water, steam) edges will normally tend to break up or become noticeably blue-fringed, due to indecisive switching action. You can often improve the situation by using *soft-edge keying*. But the real solution is to use *linear keying* (transparent matte; proportional keying) which allows such subjects to be inserted without any visible side-effects.

Keying surface and hue

Strictly speaking, the color you use in the foreground scene to key the chroma-key insertion should closely match the color for which the system is designed. This is usually a highly saturated blue (approximately *cobalt blue*); chosen because it is chromatically most distinguishable from flesh colors and least likely to arise in foreground scenes. If you try to key with a greenish blue, a fairly dark blue, or some impure mixture you may find it difficult or even impossible to achieve clean sharp keying. Some systems are much more critical than others.

In practice, chroma-key set-ups often deviate from the ideal. Using a variety of colored cyc cloths, cycs lit with blue light, blue-painted flats, stretched blue-painted cloths, blue-painted floors, the brightness and spectral distribution of these various sufaces can vary considerably! Although the system usually works, clipper adjustment can be unreliable.

Chroma-key systems can be adjusted to key on *any chosen color*, but, as you know, this color must not be present (or reflected) in the foreground or master shot. Otherwise there will be serious breakthrough at that point. When using blue keying hue, for instance, any performer wearing blue slacks would appear legless when keyed into the background shot! Similarly, the background would be seen through a hole in the chest when wearing a blue tie!

Where you cannot avoid having blue in the foreground subjects, the system can usually be adjusted to key on *green* or *yellow* instead. Then, of course, you have to prevent this new keying hue appearing in the subjects.

Special circuitry can be so precise that it only responds to a very limited band of the spectrum. When this is used even close colors or color mixtures do not trigger spurious switching. There are also systems that rely on *color comparison* processes rather than the direct color-keying method of chroma key (e.g. Ultimatte), and these are less susceptible to break through problems.

Shadow chroma key

One of the main weaknesses of the normal chroma-key process is that any shadows falling onto the blue keying surfaces are lost. (Not only that, but if they are dense enough they will spoil the clipping.) If you are using a blue floor then the inserted subject will appear to stand without the natural floor shadows, apparently *suspended* above the ground. The result is very artificial.

This happens because the chroma-key process removes *all* blue and near-blue areas from the picture. As far as the system is concerned, any subject shadows falling on the blue keying surface are normally removed with the rest of the blue areas.

Without floor shadows, however, inserted people may appear to 'float' and the illusion is spoiled – particularly where shadows are evident in the

Fig. 21.41 Shadows
1. Chroma-key insertion relies on color to actuate switching, but does not normally differentiate between different intensities of the keying-hue (i.e. shadows on the chroma-key surface). So subject shadows are not inserted.
2. Special extra circuitry permits 'shadows' to be produced (actually luminance-derived mattes), but the shadow falls along the floor and may be inappropriate.
3. If a carefully-positioned matting flat is used in the chroma-key set-up, so as to coincide with planes in the background picture, the subject shadows falling on it seem to be on the photographed wall.
4. The inserted shadow's sharpness must be comparable with that of the photo background.
5. Given compatible shadow direction, contouring and hardness, a totally convincing illusion is possible.

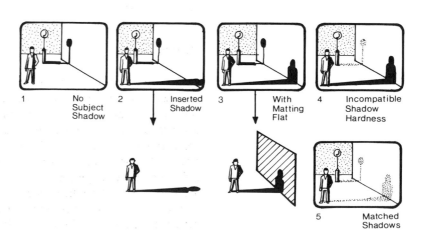

background scene. With shadow-key circuitry a natural shadow can be *simulated*. It detects the lower brightness (luminance) of the shadow on the keying surface, deriving a matte from it of adjustable sharpness and density, and introduces it transparently over the background scene. Extremely convincing, even its position can be relocated to match the background by including keying surfaces in the foreground scene.

Moving backgrounds

Where a photostill is used for the background scene you should avoid any 'frozen' features (waves, smoke, people) drawing attention to the falsity. When keying into moving backgrounds from film or VT you should make sure that sequences last long enough for the foreground action and are suitably synchronized (e.g. a 'moving' automobile's background).

Foreground pieces

With care, you can arrange the foreground subjects in the studio chroma-key set-up so that they appear totally integrated into the background scene. Furniture, pieces of scenery (pillars, walls, bushes) blend with the overall effect. If there is an unwanted feature in the background shot (perhaps a hovering seagull in a beach-scene photograph!) you might hide it with a foreground tree-branch.

Complex insertion *(see Figure 21.42)*

Moving 'behind' background subjects

When you want people in the foreground scene to 'move behind' subjects in the background picture you can use either *keying areas* or *external mattes*. If you exactly align an area of keying hue (e.g. blue) in the foreground scene, with a subject in the background shot, you effectively 'detach' that item in the background picture. Make a blue matching flat in the studio correspond with a wall in the background photograph and a performer can paste a bill on it, or walk behind it in the chroma-keyed composite! Wherever there are features in the background, such as stairs, platforms, rocks, you place an equivalent-sized blue-painted structure in the foreground scene.

Where your performer is to move behind fine detail (tracery, open screens, foliage, fences) in a background photograph you can use an *external matte silhouette* that inhibits the chroma-key insertion, letting the background through instead. A suitable silhouette can be traced from the background picture or the projected image of a background slide. As this inhibiting matting signal can be switched in or out, a person can walk behind (matte in) or in front of (matte out) the background feature at choice.

Fig. 21.42 part 1   Foreground mattes – matting flat
A flat of chroma-key hue can be positioned within the chroma-key set-up to coincide with a wall in the photo background, so enabling a performer to 'move behind' it.

Fig. 21.42 part 2   Foreground mattes – camera matte
Normally, when subjects are chroma-keyed into a scene, they appear in *front* of the background. But by introducing an *additional matte* (e.g. a silhouette camera matte as an external key), to suppress the chroma-key insertion in that area, you can make subjects 'move behind' parts of the background scene. Such matting can be switched in and out to allow moves in front and behind background objects.

Fig. 21.42 part 3   Foreground mattes – relating to background objects
By appropriately positioning suitable items in the chroma-key set-up (blocks, parallels, stairs, etc., painted in the keying hue), people can apparently sit, lean, climb, or put objects on features in the background shot.

Video build-up

You can key a person into a background, replay the composite, and then key him into that. So far, he has become twins! You could then continue inserting into composites (with quality deteriorating at each dubbing) to provide any number of different insertions of the same performer; thus generating a barber-shop quartet, choir, or orchestra! One ingenious

Fig. 21.43   VT build-up
1. Using chroma-key, extra subjects can be inserted into videotape to provide action build-up e.g. a series of separate recordings (passes) using the same person in different costumes.
2. Multi-camera shooting can be integrated to produce simultaneous multi-images of the same subject.

Fig. 21.44   Mirror effects
1. A demonstrator stands before a 'magic mirror' displaying a series of changing images. In fact, the mirror reflects a cloth of keying hue, so turning it into a self-matting area, into which subjects are inserted (from slides projected on obliquely-angled screens).
2. A person walks through a mirror. In fact, an opening in a blue flat is hung with a curtain of thin blue strips and corresponds to another camera's mirror flat.

example showed a man sitting beside himself, taking a tiny figure (of himself) out of his pocket . . . and so on!

You can even insert subjects from videotape (or video disc) played in fast or slow motion, freeze framed, or reversed, and integrate real-time action and changed time *in the same shot!* (See *Temporal effects*.)

Multi-level synthesis

This keying process switches in a chosen synthesized color wherever a particular tonal level appears in the treated picture. So, for example, in a two-tone system a white-on-black slide can be reproduced as a red-on-yellow picture. Both economical and adaptable, this is a regularly used facility in many studios; titling being prepared in monochrome and then video processed.

Using *multi-level digital synthesis*, greater elaboration is possible. The picture is analyzed into perhaps eight tonal levels, each of which can be colorized to a different hue or tint. So a multi-tone graph becomes transformed into a multi-hue display. A normal vari-toned picture (monochrome or color) becomes strangely posterized in synthetic colors; akin to a colored contour map. The same device may be used to produce *tonal coarsening*, reducing half-tones to three or four gray-scale levels (*posterizing*). It can even reduce the picture tones to solid areas of black and white.

Fig. 21.45   Sequential keying (sequential insertion, cascade insertion, quad overlay)
Each picture is keyed in 'on top of' the previous combination, to build up an overlapping composite; a layering process.

Digital video effects

The current TV camera produces a fluctuating voltage (the video signal) which is a direct *analog* corresponding to the scene's light and shade. However, there are many technical advantages in transforming the video into a different form through digital analysis. To the engineer, this provides exciting opportunities using digital picture processors to improve picture quality (image enhancement), reduce picture noise (snow removers), improve apparent definition (edge enhancement), stabilize picture synchronism from mobile recorders, build switchers (vision mixers) that accept non-sync and synchronous sources, permit multi-generation dubbing without quality deterioration. Also to provide more compact higher quality equipment such as standards converters, teletext facilities, electronic still stores, time-base correction, etc., etc.

Digital analysis is remarkably simple in principle. It checks the strength of the video signal at regular intervals and stores away these samplings in numerical form (binary digits – i.e. an on–off pulse code representing numbers). Now, instead of fluctuating video, we have a store of numbers representing the brightness and color of each tiny area (element) of the picture. These 'quantized' stored digitally coded signals can be recalled (or replaced) at will and reconstituted into the original picture.

The particular advantage of what otherwise seems a tortuous transformation is that we now have random access to each stored element of the picture! Normally, picture information would be taken from the store in its original order. But the equipment can now manipulate the video according to the rate and order in which it reads this information: repeating parts of the picture, sampling in reverse order, skipping information, changing the sampling rate . . . and here lies the magic of digital effects!

As you can see from Table 21.4, an increasing range of visual effects is available. Some have a direct productional value, some add an interesting new (for now) dimension to presentation, and others are just fun! Like wipe patterns, some are rarely used, others have become a regular part of productional techniques.

Fig. 21.46 Multi-hue chroma-key
Several keying hues are used in turn, each keying in a particular video source. So different pictures appear on this rotating multi-colored block.

Table 21.4 Digital video effects

DVE systems manipulate the visual image in many ingenious ways. Terms are not universal, and like the effects themselves, are continually being invented. Many results are obtained by combining several separate effects.

1. *Aspect ratio*	The picture height and or width can be changed independently, to alter the picture shape. Images are deformed, being correspondingly squashed or stretched.
2. *Aspect ratio change*	Picture holds its non-standard shape, as it is zoomed or positioned.
3. *Audio activation*	Effects change at an audio rate.
4. *Auto freeze*	Picture freezes at selected frame intervals, producing a strobe effect.
5. *Auto key tracking/key follow*	Automatic adjustment of the keying area's size and position in a chroma-key insertion as the foreground subject picture is adjusted. (Zoom on a camera shooting a simulated wall screen, and the amount of the background picture visible in the insert would alter. Using auto tracking, it remains constant.)

Table 21.4 (cont.)

6. *Auto sequence*	Stores a selected effects sequence on floppy disk, to run automatically on cue.
7. *Border*	This puts a color border around a small picture that has been inserted within the frame.
8. *Bounce*	Combined 'flys, zooms, swings'.
9. *Breakthrough/videomelter*	One picture dissolves (in tonal order) into another.
10. *Burns*	Feedback (output back to input) creating swirling, flaring, multi-layering, etc.
11. *Composite*	General term for a picture created by electronically inserting one or more separate images to provide an overall effect.
12. *Compression*	While the picture shape remains constant, the picture contracts from a full-screen size down to a point. This can be done as a continuous movement to provide shrinking, or to readjust the image to a different size for insertion. (See *Expansion*.)
13. *Cover*	One picture moves over, or overlaps another.
14. *Crop*	Moves picture frame edges in selectively, to mask the picture.
15. *Cube*	Rotating cube with different picture on each face.
16. *Curves*	A plane surface (e.g. a flat picture) is made to appear concave or convex.
17. *Cylinders*	The pictures wraps round to form a cylinder. It may have another picture on the reverse side.
18. *Decay*	Picture contrast/brightness reducing at adjustable rate.
19. *Drop shadows*	Transparent drop shadows trail behind the moving object.
20. *Echo*	Multiple-layered repeats of an image.
21. *Effects dissolve*	Smooth vari-timed transitions between two dissimilar effects.
22. *Elastic sheet*	Differential shape changes.
23. *Expansion*	While the picture shape remains constant, the picture expands from a point to full-screen size. This can be done as a continuous movement to provide growth or to readjust the image to a different size for insertion. (See *Compression*.)
24. *Explosion*	Picture breaks into many diverging fragments.
25. *Flip/flip-over*	Vertical or horizontal reversal. Used to compensate for the image having been reversed when shooting via a mirror. Or to provide more satisfactory composition (lateral reversal). Or reversal may be carried out in vision, as a dynamic effect (rate adjustable).
26. *Fly*	Picture zooms up from nothing to any position on screen while spinning.
27. *Fold*	The left and right edges of the picture fold inwards until the image becomes a vertical line. It may fold out again to reveal a new picture.
28. *Freeze frame*	A single picture selected from a sequence and held.
29. *Globe*	The 4 × 3 picture contracts to form into a globe shape. (Still or turning.)
30. *Glow*	A glow effect created around key signals.
31. *Hall of mirrors*	Repeated overlapping images of diminishing size, resembling the repeat images seen in facing mirrors.
32. *Image positioning*	Places the image anywhere in the frame.
33. *Image size changes*	Overall image compression, expansion.
34. *Image trail freeze ('Teletrak', 'Action Trak')*	Composite shot, showing path of subject movement, by freezing images at regular intervals.
35. *Key pattern*	Picture shape changes to conform with an external matte; e.g. a star.
36. *Layering*	A process in which a series of separate framed pictures are presented, one on top of the other, each slightly overlapping the image beneath. They may appear to grow smaller with 'distance'.
37. *Magnifying glass*	Localized area of picture enlarged; 'false zoom-in' effect.
38. *Matrix wipe*	The picture resembles a jigsaw puzzle of square sections. As pieces are removed *at random* corresponding parts of the new picture 'beneath' are revealed until it is finally complete.
39. *Mirror image*	Horizontal and/or vertical reversal, inversion.

Table 21.4 (cont.)

40. *Mosaic*	The screen is divided into a pattern of small equal-sized squares. (Similar to a crossword puzzle.) In each square the tones and colors of the original picture are averaged. The more squares are used (adjustable), the closer the image's resemblance to the original picture. This technique is often used to prevent a speaker's face being recognized.
41. *Motion decay/motion smear*	The moving image trails a smearing image behind it.
42. *Multi-move*	Series of segments or frames moving.
43. *Multi-image freeze/multi-freeze*	Array of frozen images from one input.
44. *Multi-segment*	A checkerboard of frames showing different subjects, or different stages of the same subject's action.
45. *Negative polarity*	Luminance or color, changed to negative version.
46. *Non-linear movement*	Slow start . . . accelerate . . . slow down.
47. *Ooze*	Change picture frame to amorphous shapes; e.g. circle creates fisheye effect.
48. *Orbit*	Circular, elliptical, corkscrew image movement around the screen.
49. *Page turn*	Picture appears to turn over like a page.
50. *Pan/tilt*	Total picture moves horizontally/vertically around screen.
51. *Perspective changes*	Pseudo perspective effect, introducing trapezium distortion along horizontal and/or vertical axes.
52. *Pong*	Reduced frame bounces around as it reaches screen edges.
53. *Posterization/solarization*	Picture tones are coarsened and reduced to just a few levels (adjustable). Tonal gradation is lost and areas appear even toned. (See text: *Multilevel synthesis*.)
54. *Push-off*	Frame moves off the screen.
55. *Push–pull wipe*	A new frame pushes the present picture off the screen.
56. *Roll-up*	Picture curls to form a tube (right edges to left edge). Perhaps another picture revealed on 'reverse face'.
57. *Rotate*	Image appears to turn around X, Y, Z axes.
58. *Shape*	Forms the flat picture into a geometrical shape (still or revolving); e.g. sphere, cylinder (barrel roll), cone, cube. Perhaps with a different image on each face.
59. *Skew*	Partial rotation.
60. *Slide*	Push-off, push-over wipe.
61. *Snapshotting*	A combined display of a succession of four to 16 reduced freeze frames; progressively updated.
62. *Sparkling trail*	A cloud of small dots ('stars', 'sparkles') trails behind moving objects. (Random pixels.)
63. *Spin*	Continuous rotation clockwise or anti-clockwise at variable speed.
64. *Split*	Splits the screen into segments, which independently wipe to new sources.
65. *Split wipes*	Picture breaks into two, three, four segments, wiping them off the screen (horizontally, vertically, diagonally).
66. *Squeeze/compression*	Vertical or horizontal reduction of image size, compressing the image.
67. *Star trail*	Moving subject is followed by a trail of 'stars' (random pixels).
68. *Strobe title*	Flashing image.
69. *Swing*	Image moves to and fro in a curved path.
70. *Swoop/scoop*	Curved path movement.
71. *Toroid*	The picture wraps round into a doughnut shape.
72. *Trail*	Moving video frame passes over a frozen frame, creating a three-dimensional effect.
73. *Tumble/roll*	Similar to continuous flip.
74. *Video outline*	All luminance values changed to e.g. white, with all edges black.
75. *Zig-zag*	Series of reduced pictures move around, collide, overrun, explode from frame center.
76. *Zoom*	Image expands/contracts from full frame to zero on screen.

Fig. 21.47   Outline effects
The outline of a girl dancer transforms into the outline of a tree. To obtain this: Camera 1 shoots a white on black silhouette of the dancer, gradually zooming in until the white shape fills the screen; while Camera 2 is close on the white tree silhouette, gradually zooming out. The combined effect is fed through a border generator and the outline transformation develops.

It is not always obvious that an *effect* is being used. You might, for instance, use a digital effect to fill the screen with just a section of a photo-slide, or to trim off the edges of its picture. A perfectly normal-looking map could be a DVE composite. A 'graphic' showing a series of portraits could be displaying slide images from an ESS, combined by digital effects. A high-angle shot might actually be a digitally reversed mirror shot.

Although terms are still developing, and there may be several names for the same action, most are evocative of the effect they describe.

Technically speaking, when describing movement –

● Horizontal movements (left/right; right/left) are along the X axis. Anything rotating around the X axis is said to *tumble* or flip over and over.
● Vertical movements (up/down; down/up) are along the Y axis. Anything rotating around the Y axis is said to *spin* or *rotate* round and round.
● Where features appear to be moving towards and away from the viewer they move along the Z axis. (The illusion of depth actually comes from their growing larger/smaller; from expansion and compression.)

Temporal effects

Once *real time* has been recorded, you can control the speed at which this action is reproduced; using film, VT, video disc, or digital processing.

■ *Fast motion*   Fast-motion effects can be introduced for various reasons:

1. Speeding up subject movement and time scale.
2. To exaggerate energy for comic effect, pixillation, or dramatic force (fast-moving clouds).
3. To shorten an action's normal duration.
4. To reveal the development of a slow process – time-lapse shots speeding plant growth.

In film this is achieved by shooting at less than 24 fps and reproducing at normal projection rate of 24 fps; or by regularly omitting frames.

■ *Slow motion*   The uses of slow motion include:

1. Slowing subject movement and time scale.
2. To exaggerate movement, form, or pattern.
3. To allow rapid movement to be discerned (humming-birds' wing-beats).
4. To emphasize movement, giving it force and importance (emphatic body movements).

In film, slow motion is achieved by shooting at more than 24 fps and reproducing at normal speed, or repeat printing alternate frames (stretch/skip frame). In television, slow motion is achieved by magnetic video disc or by slow replay of helical VTRs.

■ *Freeze frame*   Stopping action during its course to show development or prevent completion. Achieved by still-frame VTR, magnetic video disc, digital effects processing, or by repeat-printing the required film frame.

■ *Reverse motion*   Reproducing action backwards for comic, magical, or explanatory effect – a demolished building reforms, articles wrap themselves up, scattered lettering arranges itself. There are several regular methods of obtaining reverse motion:

● Magnetic video disc.
● VTR with reverse-play facilities.
● Some telecine equipment will provide normal pictures while running backwards at standard or adjustable speeds.
● Certain telecine machines will allow you to feed the film in tail first and electronically invert the picture.
● Film labs can *reverse-print* the selected sequence.

■ *Animation (single frame, stop frame)*   Achieved on film or VTR by recording a single frame at a time and changing the subject a little for each. When reproduced in quick succession, the shots develop a group significance – usually creating apparent movement. Thus you can animate cartoons, puppets, still-life.

Photo-animation uses a series of photographic prints as the basis for treatment, rephotographing them after progressively adding titling, retouching, sectional movement, etc. Thus various process effects can be achieved economically, including complex wipes, spins, phantom sections, and explosions.

Video rostrum cameras are increasingly used for animation treatment (often combined with digital video effects) for promotion material, advertisements, graphics.

■ *Cyclic motion*   Recurrent repetition of an action; achieved by a film loop or conjoining a series of identical copies of a sequence.

■ *Extended and contracted time*/space   By editing-in a repeated part of an action sequence (from another viewpoint, to avoid an obvious jump cut) we create the impression that space or time are extended. Similarly, by editing-out action (with a viewpoint change or cutaway shot) we contract space and time.

■ *Transformations*   By animation; or by stopping action during recording (with locked-off cameras), then modifying the scene and continuing recording. When the sections are joined together we can, for example, make trees burst into bloom and a man turn into a mouse!

22 On location

Today, the program maker has choice. It may be cheaper and quicker to send a single-camera unit out to shoot an interview on location than to set up a production in the studio. Television production has long outgrown the confines of the studio. You can now use the television camera virtually anywhere.

Shooting on location

There are important differences between making a program on location and using a regular TV studio; differences that directly affect productional opportunities and techniques. Whereas a television studio provides the director with an established package of facilities, and back-up close at hand, the production team on location can have to face many kinds of difficulties, ranging from weather to crowd control. The crew on location has to be very self-sufficient, and to anticipate needs to a degree that their colleagues in studios are spared.

Instead of a convenient overhead lighting rig from which to select any lamp from any angle the lighting director on location may have difficulty in finding anywhere to place light fittings without either damaging the surroundings or having a lamp come in shot. A cameraman may need weatherproof clothing as he stands for long periods isolated on a rain-swept camera tower. The audio engineer often has to cope with unsuitable acoustics and intrusive environmental noises.

Even the best-organized shoot on location involves a deal of anticipation and improvization – and an element of luck. So it is not suprising that a high proportion of TV shows are still made in the controlled conditions of a studio.

Most program making away from the studio takes two forms:

- The single- or two-camera unit with a small production team.
- A multi-camera crew with full production facilities; using a mobile control center or converting the location point into a 'studio' for the occasion.

On location with the single camera

Even a brief list reminds us of the flexibility of the single television/video camera on location.

1. *Electronic field production (EFP)*
   Drama. From isolated shots or scenes to complete drama productions.
   Program inserts. To record short sequences for insertion into studio-based programs; e.g. illustrating talks, children's programs.

Documentaries. Material ranging from dedicated (one-topic) nature programs to multi-topic science magazine programs.

Training. On-site surveys of jobs and processes.

2. *Electronic journalism (EJ)*. An increasingly widening field, including investigative journalism, background material to current news stories.
3. *Electronic news gathering (ENG)*. News features over a wide spectrum, from planned public events to unforseen disasters.
4. *Electronic sports gathering (ESG)*. To supplement a regular camera crew, e.g. at a sports event.

Portable camera techniques

Typical set-ups

There are two kinds of single-camera unit. In the first, the cameraman has an assistant who handles a portable videotape recorder, looking after sound levels and holding a hand light. In the second, the cameraman who maybe unassisted carries a small VCR cabled to the camera, or a combined camera/VCR (*combo*) which incorporates its own microphone and camera light.

Fig. 22.1   Portable cameras
Mobile camera designs include:
1. Shoulder-mounted (battery belt supply).
2. Hand-held camera cabled to a back-pack. Cameras with microwave transmitters may work up to e g 1500 meters from the base unit.
3. Body-brace support for camera cabled to control equipment on a trolley-pack (transmitter or VTR).
4. Small hand-held camera attached to shoulder pack VTR.
5. Combo cameras.

In most set-ups an on-the-spot director/reporter guides the cameraman. On occasions a cameraman may be given a 'brief' (an outline of what is required), and is left to his own initiative to bring back the material (e.g. environmental shots).

Sometimes sound and picture from the portable camera are sent back to the base vehicle by a small microwave unit, and either transmitted live or taped for later editing. Radio intercom helps to coordinate camerawork.

Camera care on location

The old scouting motto of 'Be prepared' is certainly apt when you are working with a portable video camera on location. A moment's oversight can ruin a day's shooting. There is usually no video engineer to provide aid and advice. You are on your own.

When you have been working for some hours, particularly under trying conditions, it is very easy to lay your camera to one side, forgetting what a vulnerable bit of equipment it really is. Any list of dont's is really a matter of common sense. The odd thump, jolt, or vibration may seem nothing at the time, but careless handling stores up trouble.

It is pretty obvious that rain, dust, sand, grit, seawater, snow, strong sunlight, heat, strong magnetic fields can ruin your equipment. But under typical conditions you may well find yourself shooting in the rain, by a waterfall, beside the sea, or where wind-blown sand is unavoidable. Then all you can do is to keep its exposure to a minimum and use waterproof protective covers – even if you have to improvise. But take care, for excess wrapping can cause overheating. Check regularly that your lens is clean and dry.

Unexpectedly high tempertures can build up in strong sunlight, and enclosed places such as the trunk (boot) of a parked car are to be avoided. Make sure that you do not leave spare batteries, tapes, etc. stored there. Nickel–cadmium batteries lose their charge rapidly in hot surroundings.

Cold weather, too, brings its problems – apart from slippery ground underfoot. Condensation can form in the lens and within the equipment when it is brought into warm surroundings. (Internal circuitry includes moisture checks that prevent a VCR from functioning.) In cold weather, batteries are less efficient, and some cameramen shoot with their NiCad battery-belt worn underneath a jacket to keep it warmer.

Whenever you stop shooting make it a practice to put the lens cap on your lens to protect its coated surface. At other times, to protect the camera-tube against bright light (sunlight, strong specular reflections) it is advisable to turn the filter-wheel to a blank cap-up position. With certain lenses a '*cap*' position entirely closes the iris, but do not rely on this.

A shoulder-mounted camera appears to get heavier and heavier through the day. (A good reason for using a tripod where practicable.) Mind how you put it down to rest. It is best kept horizontal to avoid damage to the camera-tube, viewfinder, microphone, etc.

Damaged cables or connectors are a regular source of trouble, and if you are using a separate VTR there will be less wear and tear if you leave them connected.

From time to time, look over your gear and recheck the security of cables, battery, microphone, etc. so that all is ready to use.

At intervals, and whenever changing location, reset the white balance. Point the camera at 'standard' white-level material you carry with you. (Roll, do not fold it.) Cards are cumbersome and easily damaged. They can, however, be double-sided (white on one side, metal foil on the reverse) and used as a reflector. Never use just any 'white' that comes to hand on location (e.g. handkerchiefs, tissues, scarves)! Results will vary. With some cameras you clip a white translucent cover over the lens and point it towards a light source to adjust the white balance.

Power supplies

The video camera normally requires a 12 V DC power supply. This can come from:

● An on-board camera battery-pack (internal or clip-on unit at the rear).
● A worn battery-belt, containing rechargeable nickel–cadmium or silver–zinc cells.
● The battery used to power the VTR.
● A heavy-duty battery in a shoulder-pack.
● A heavy-duty battery in a trolley or cart (trolley-pack).
● The battery fitted to a car (using the cigar-lighter socket for a connection).
● An AC power adapter used when working near regular utility supplies (mains supplies). It converts the supply voltage (e.g. 120 V AC to 12 V DC).

On many occasions you will be relying on batteries to power your camera. Don't take batteries for granted. Carelessly used, they can be unreliable. Correctly used, they will give excellent service. In Table 22.1 you will see typical points to bear in mind. Always have spare batteries with you. How many depends on the nature and duration of your project and your opportunities to recharge exhausted cells.

The single camera in action

So the equipment is working, you have set up the camera, and are ready to shoot.

Handling the camera

If you are using the camera shoulder-mounted make sure that it is comfortably balanced before you begin. Try to use the camera as an extension of your body; turning with a pan, bending with a tilt. With your legs comfortably braced apart, turn to follow movement – preferably from a midway position between the start and end of the pan.

Learn to shoot with one eye looking through the viewfinder and the other *open*, seeing the general scene. (With practice, it's not as difficult as it sounds.) You stand a better chance of walking around without accident than if your attention is glued to your viewfinder picture.

Even though its image is magnified, you need to look carefully at the viewfinder picture to detect exact exposure adjustments. You can overlook something intruding into the frame that will be very obvious on a large-screen TV receiver. Distracting brightly colored items can pass unnoticed in the black-and-white viewfinder.

Keep walking to a minimum while shooting. If you must move, slightly bent legs produce smoother results than normal walking. (Practice to see what you find comfortable and effective. And critically examine the resulting tape.)

Table 22.1   Battery care

A lot of dos and don'ts here, but remember, when batteries fail, everything may come to a halt!
Batteries power your *camera viewfinder*, the *VTR, lamps*, and *picture monitor* . . . So switch off (or use the stand-by mode) and conserve power whenever possible. If you are not careful, time taken reviewing tapes and lighting can leave you with low power for the take.

- Handle batteries carefully. Dropping, or excessive flexing of connections (particularly interwired cells in power belts), can cause breakdown.
- Always check a battery's voltage while it is actually working.
- Do not leave equipment on until a battery is completely exhausted. This can ruin a new battery.
- Recharge batteries as soon as possible.
- A battery-pack or battery-belt is made up of several cells connected in series. Its poorest cell will limit the battery's overall performance, so never mix old and new cells.
- Avoid storing batteries in very cold or hot places.
- Stored batteries tend to discharge themselves to a noticeable extent.
- If you partly discharge a battery for e.g. half an hour then recharge it fully; it can develop a 'memory'. Instead of delivering its full charge, it will regularly drop after half an hour. (It requires a careful charging/discharging cycle to remedy this state.) To avoid this, use a battery fully but not to exhaustion. Rather than leave it partly charged, discharge it periodically with a lamp and recharge fully.
- *Portable lamps* are typically 30 V; 150, 250, 350 W; and fed from a battery-belt worn round the waist. (Do not sling the belt around your neck or shoulder; it damages connections.) The voltage of a freshly charged battery is higher than normal, and may burn out a bulb. Let the battery-belt stabilize for a while before use.
- In addition to the main battery that powers the camera, there may be 'keep-alive' batteries for memory circuits within the camera and VCR system that should be checked regularly. The camera microphone is probably an electret type, using a small pre-amplifier battery.

Table 22.2   Be prepared – the system check-up

As with the studio camera, preliminary checks before shooting can anticipate and prevent problems later. If you do not have access to a color picture monitor as you shoot, you are relying on the small black and white viewfinder for all picture checks. So if, for example, you forget to white-balance the camera it will not be apparent until the picture is reviewed at base!

The camera
- *Viewfinder.* Check controls, and adjust for a good tonal range. Check over the various indicator lights, and *always* be guided by them when operating the camera.
- *Lens.* Lens cap fitted? Lens clean? Lens firmly attached?
  Focus: check both manual and auto-focus systems over the full range.
  Aperture (f-stop): manually adjust over range, and check exposure changes in viewfinder. Check auto-iris movements on panning over different tones.

Table 22.2 (cont.)

- *Zoom.* Operate manual zoom over full range; checking focus tracking. Operate power zoom in and out over full range.

- *Microphone.* Test camera microphone (shotgun) and hand microphone. Check cable and sockets by gently shaking and listening for crackles, breaks in sound. Check the audio output through an earpiece (left ear). The sound is not off-tape but confirms that the mike is working. Replay the tape to confirm the audio recording. Some cameras have an inbuilt loudspeaker against which your right ear presses while shooting. (Useless when supporting the camera in other positions!)

- *Genlock.* For multi-camera operation, check genlock system (communal synchronization).

- *Subsidiary controls.* Looking at a color monitor, check filter-wheel positions, white balance, black adjust, video gain, etc.

VTR	Make *check recordings* of camera test chart and multi-tone scene. Examine playback in viewfinder and on a color monitor.
Power supplies	Check all batteries. Confirm that all *spare* batteries are fully charged. Are AC cords/mains cables, AC adapter, car-battery adapter, etc. OK?
Cables	Don't leave cables attached to equipment during storage. Never be casual about cables; they have a will of their own, and tangle easily. Loop-coil them neatly, and secure them with a quick-release plastic cable fastener or tie.
Lamps	*Examine any portable camera light or hand lamp.* Check the condition of its bulb, lamp reflector, cable, plug, while powered from a battery
Separate audio recorder	Used for continuity checks; to record wild track, sound effects, background, etc. Check its tapes and operations. Monitor all audio on an earpiece or headphones.

Spares	Always a personal choice. There are unarguable essentials, though, such as spare lamps, batteries, cassettes, audio tapes.

- Examine all VTR cassettes. Are they the *right types*? Do they have protective tags intact? (Otherwise you cannot record on them.) There should not be excess tape slack within the cassette. If there is, run and rewind the tape. Beware tightening by hand-turning the reels; it leaves the tape under tension. Have fresh labels for all cassettes.

- Are the spare *lamp bulbs* and *fuses* good ones? (Broken versions can inadvertently be left as 'spares'.) Take a spare microphone. Include diffuser material and dichroic filter or color medium for the hand-lamp.

- Avoid field maintenance and cleaning unless you are experienced and equipment is in need. 'Helpful cleaning' often makes things worse, and can clog heads! Protective covers prevent problems. If it ain't broke, don't mend it!

Tools	Small and medium screwdrivers and pliers; electrical insulating tape; masking tape; gaffer tape; cord . . . Head-cleaning fluid (isopropyl alcohol), cotton-tipped cleaning sticks. Compressed-air can.
Accessories	Flashlight (with spare bulb and batteries). White material (or card) for checking 'white balance'. Small reflectors (white, silver foil).
	Again a matter for personal preferences. There are circumstances where mosquito repellant, sunscreen preparations or waterproofs can be more essential than a comprehensive tool kit! Much depends on where you are working.

Lens angles

Generally speaking, avoid extreme lens angles. A wide-angle lens makes camerawork easier, and slight jolts are less noticeable. But everything looks so far away. Closer subjects appear distorted. You imagine that you have much more space to maneuver than you actually have, and are liable to trip or walk into things in the foreground.

Narrower lens-angles produce unsteady shots, and focusing can be difficult. On hand-held cameras they are only suitable for brief stationary shots, while holding your breath. A little wider than 'normal' is probably the best compromise.

If you have an assistant, walking around while shooting can be guided by a hand on your left shoulder; particularly when moving backwards. Walking backwards unguided is at best hazardous, at worst foolish, unless you are on an open flat area without obstructions. People can move towards you a lot faster than you can hope to walk backwards.

Low light levels

In the studio, light levels are controlled. Elsewhere, you have to adapt to local conditions. Your camera lamp will provide you with a limited main light source (key light), or reduce tonal contrast in nearby subjects, but don't expect too much of it.

Shooting under low-light conditions, the picture will probably be underexposed; i.e. dim and showing signs of lag and smearing, with pronounced picture noise. The real remedy is to open up the lens to a larger aperture (smaller f-stop number; e.g. $f/1.8$) to try to expose the shot more accurately. Unfortunately, this inevitably reduces the depth of field, and makes focusing more difficult.

Switching in extra *video gain* will not compensate. It will result in a *brighter* but still underexposed shot. It cannot correct for underexposure defects, and video noise will usually increase. Nevertheless, this is the only solution when working under conditions where one cannot improve the lighting.

Automatic controls

Automatic controls such as *auto-focus* and *auto-iris* are a 'safety net' when you do not have the opportunity to control your camera accurately by hand adjustments. But remember, automatic controls are far from foolproof.

Audio

Audio circuits can be either manually or automatically controlled (*AGC: automatic gain control*). When you set the audio gain adjustment *manually*, so that audio peaks reach the upper operating limit, if anything louder comes along it will exceed the limits, and distort. Use *AGC* circuits; they protect against unexpected overloads but may bring up weak background sounds and make them over-prominent.

Cables

If you are working with another person, whether he is handling a microphone, a lamp, or a VTR, always be aware of the cable between you. Forget for a moment, and you are likely to find yourselves either side of a lamp-post or with a fully stretched cable, or caught up on an obstruction. Fast moves can be particularly hazardous.

Shooting from vehicles

When shooting from vehicles, resist the temptation to rest the camera on anything. If possible, shoot through an open window. With tinted windows, white-balance through the glass for optimum results, and make sure that the glass is as clean as possible.

Logs

Always keep an accurate log with information about all shots: times, observations, tape-indicator reading, etc. Give each video and audio tape an identifying label as it is used. If you are not using *time code* for shot identification (see *Glossary*), written details now may save hours later when editing. If your camera has a built-in title generator this can be used as a 'slate' to identify shots (with clock time, date, location, shot number).

Clearing up

When you have finished shooting, camera care comes first: cap up the lens (lens cap, filter wheel, close iris).

Switch off all equipment. Remove camera light, camera mike. Remove and wind up cables.

Disassemble and store the camera in its case.

Remove video and audio cassettes and store safely (insert fresh ones if necessary).

Later clean off and check all items at base before storing. Replace burned-out lamps or fuses, any worn or damaged items. Check and recharge batteries. Check over the log to augment or correct it if necessary while details are fresh in your mind.

Multi-camera units

The single-camera team has some important advantages. It is extremely mobile and is easily relocated. It can be surprisingly unobtrusive. It is largely independent of its surroundings. It is economical.

On the other hand, there are many productional situations where a single camera has little hope of capturing much more than a glimpse of events, and multi-camera treatment is the only answer:

● Where coverage from different viewpoints is to be continuous and comprehensive.

Fig. 22.2 Field camera mountings
Some typical methods of mounting the TV camera in the field.
1. Roof-top tripod at vantage point.
2. Camera on frame or tower.
3. Lightweight pneumatic pedestal.
4. Lightweight tripod. (3 and 4 may have wheeled bases.)
5. Portable cameras.
6. Van with hatch, roof, rear-platform cameras.
7. Hydraulic platform.
8. Helicopter.

● Where action is spread over a large area; e.g. a golf course.
● At a public event, where there is no time or no opportunity to move cameras around to different viewpoints.
● Where there is to be a 'once-only' event (e.g. demolition of a bridge).
● Where the location of action continually changes; e.g. between various parts of a sports field.
● Where cameras could not move to new viewpoints; e.g. because of obstructions.
● Where cameras must be concealed, or located in fixed places.
● Where rapidly intercut viewpoints are essential (e.g. at a horse race).
● When you cannot accurately anticipate where action is to take place.

Location vehicles

The facilities one needs will depend partly on the scale of coverage and partly on the nature of the event. For example, a 'treasure-hunt' program that dashes around the countryside searching for clues may be based on a couple of helicopters; one to house a single-camera unit that 'hops, lands, and explores', while the other provides a communications support and relay facility. For a museum visit, the same crew could carry their equipment in a car.

Large mobile control room (location production unit)

The biggest vehicles used for remotes usually take the form of a large custom-built truck or trailer. The unit provides a full broadcast standard production control center, with complete video and audio facilities. As well as a stack of preview monitors, line monitor, associated switcher, etc., equipment can include comprehensive audio and lighting boards, audio and videotape recorders, character generator, special effects unit, multi-speed VTR for inserts, full intercom (wires and radio), etc. The unit also carries a range of cables (camera, audio, lighting), camera mountings, microphone mountings, etc.

The unit may be used in several ways:

● Parked *within* the action area (e.g. in a public square) with cables extending to cameras at various vantage points.
● As a *drive-in control room* parked outside a temporary 'studio' (e.g. a public hall, theater, large tent).
● Control equipment may be removed from the vehicle and installed within a building. This is often done at major indoor events (e.g. at a conference center, or a sports stadium).
● Sometimes a small mobile studio or stage is taken with the unit to the location site and serviced from the mobile control room.

The program may be recorded (and edited) on board the control vehicle. Or it may be relayed to base by microwave links (telescopic mast, or parabolic dish) to be transmitted live, or recorded and edited at base.

For large-scale telecasts in which on-site control is essential this traditional *remotes (outside broadcast)* approach has considerable merits.

Remotes van

A more compact system uses a small control room in a lightweight van. This contains full broadcast-standard equipment for one or two lightweight cameras. Basic switching, monitoring and audio facilities are provided. The program material may be videotaped (1 in helical or U-Matic) for subsequent editing at base; or microwave transmitted to base.

Typical applications include EFP (for documentary and drama inserts), ESG, and some ENG.

Lightweight truck (small van units)

Fitted with one or two *broadcast lightweight cameras* and a helical-format VTR (1 in, U-Matic, or ½ in format VCRs). This type of mobile vehicle has proved highly adaptable for ENG, EFP, ESG, and commercials. Versatile designs often include arrangements for roof-mounted cameras, a cab hatch, and/or a rear platform for flexible camera viewpoints.

Program material is recorded on the internal VTR, and/or microwave transmitted to base.

The vehicle may also be used as a *satellite unit*, transmitting back to a mobile control room, e.g. traveling at speed around a horse-race track, cycle-race circuit, etc.

Station wagon (small van units)

Designed to meet the demands of rapid news-gathering techniques, this unit carries one or two 'broadcast ENG' cameras and a small-format helical recorder. The cameras may feed audio/video to the support vehicle by cable or small microwave transmitter. The program is videotaped and/or transmitted to a central relay station (at a high vantage point) from which it is retransmitted to the news center. There the signals are processed (time-base correction, image enhanced, color corrected, noise reduction) and videotaped.

Program handling

Program material (audio and video) can be handled in several ways for field production:

1. Videotaped in the field and delivered to base by courier or when the unit returns. A growing technique involves single- or two-camera shooting with a VTR per camera and without a switcher; all editing being a postproduction operation.
2. Videotaped on site and transmitted to base via a suitable relay station. In remote areas, where local topography prevents a line-of-sight transmission path (dead spots due to hills or ridges), it may be necessary to drive to a known good transmission point to replay to base. For an ongoing event a courier may continually rush videotapes to a mobile microwave transmitter unit, sited at a vantage point, where they are relayed to base.
3. Transmitted live to base over microwave links (occasionally via helicopter or satellite stations) for live broadcast.

While some mobile units are essentially self-contained, others such as ENG teams maintain continuous two-way VHF communication with base for engineering and production control. When the team is remote from their vehicle it serves them as a repeater station (receiving and transmitting) for their program audio/video and control.

Most organizations videotape the incoming material (after time-base correction and image enhancement) onto 1 in helical VTRs for subsequent editing.

News techniques

Techniques can vary, according to the occasion. Some news situations are predictable, even routine, while others are unexpected and have to be tackled off the cuff. It may take a great deal of persistence to get good coverage of a news event; as well as the knack of being in exactly the right place at the right time.

Production teams develop regular approaches to particular situations. In broad terms, news stories fall into the three time categories of 'Before', 'During', and 'After' the event. Obviously, when the camera is able to be present *during* an event it will usually have the best visual opportunities – whether it is covering a highway-opening ceremony or a volcanic eruption.

Fig. 22.3 Field transmission

1. *Camera* may be hand-held or tripod mounted, its video being fed to a 'window unit'. Local mike connects to camera's audio pick-up socket.
2. *Window-unit* is a lightweight battery-operated transmitter. Range 1–8 km (1–5 miles) in line-of-sight contact with support vehicle (13 GHz).
3. Coaxial or fiber-optic cable from camera to support vehicle.
4. Portable VTR.
5. Portable dish reflector of 60–120 cm (2–4 ft) diameter, or microwave antenna (telescopic mast) transmits audio/video from support vehicle to central relay station. Range is 16–24 km (10–15 miles).
   (Transmitter 10–20 W. 2–7 GHz, circular polarization.) (In certain situations a helicopter may serve as a relay point.) Satellite up-links are increasingly used between the remote unit and production center for live ENG.
6. Remote signal is picked up on 4-horn remotely controlled 360° dish antennae system on a distant high building. The signal from the uplink receiver is up-converted to 7 GHz, for transmission to news center.
7. At news center, signal correction is introduced (digital timebase correction, image enhancer).
8. Two-way communication system from news center (program and engineering coordination) to field unit (450 MHz).

Remote pickup broadcast frequencies. FCC: 150–170 MHz (VHF); 450–456 MHz (UHF); 2, 2.5, 7, 13 GHz. Europe: Also 66–73 MHz, 76.5–108 MHz.

But there are those other occasions where there is little to see; either because the actual event has not yet taken place or because it is all over by the time the cameras arrive! Many subjects do not lend themselves to visually interesting treatment. Quite often, there is nothing significant to shoot. We can only look at the outside of the bank that has been robbed or the water in which the ship sank.

On such occasions news reportage has to speculate, rather than recount. Quite a lot of news coverage resolves itself into shots of the location, followed by a reporter providing 'sound bits' to camera (*stand-upper*), some cutaways to allow for later editing, and interviews with witnesses or victims.

Routinely, location interviews consist of continuous shots of the interviewee, with later cutaways of over-shoulder 'nod shots' (mute) and frontal shots of the interviewer (perhaps asking the questions).

ENG editing

The production demands of ENG are considerable, and special organization has evolved to meet its particular needs. In some systems, the mobile crew (reporter/director, engineer/operator) is closely coordinated from the news center through two-way ratio communication. The center provides news evaluation, late-breaking information, updating, talent cues, production timing, and interrupted feedback. The editorial coordinator serves as field producer, continually examining story progress and giving editorial guidance.

The program material is transmitted from site to the base news center (via a relay point), where it may be continuously taped; both as a 'work-print' copy for editorial purposes and a master reference copy storing the material.

Although time code is widely used for editing (single-frame accuracy), some organizations count VT control track pulses instead (6–8 frame accuracy) for technical convenience.

In one system, an *editor* reviews the 'work-print' copy, assessing edit-decision points, logging in-out times, and audio cues. An *assembler* using this edit decision list enters the precise frame numbers into the VT editing equipment. Computer-controlled VT equipment locates these points in the master reference tape, dubbing off the selected sequences for broadcast – perhaps with a corresponding back-up version. During this

Fig. 22.4 Typical ENG organization

1. The *News Coordinator* controls/advises the ENG unit, and scrutinizes the incoming program material.
2. The incoming pictures and sound are videotaped on both a *master VTR*, and a separate VTR making a *time-coded workprint*. The latter will be used for off-line editing decisions.
3. In a decision booth, an *Editor* (with writers, reporters) examines the workprint, logs in/out times of shots (time-code), selects the excerpts required, notes audio cues for edit points, etc.
4. An *assembler* dub edits from the master tape, to the editor's instructions. Commentary, graphics, slides (ESS), titles are added. (Computer-controlled selection may be used.) The assembled 'show copy' recording may be arranged on one or more VTRs for stop/start cuing during the newscast, or as a series of separate cassettes that can be loaded into an automated cassette player: 1 in, 19 mm (¾ in), and 12.7 mm (½ in) systems.
5. Automated cassette player with edited stories (segments).

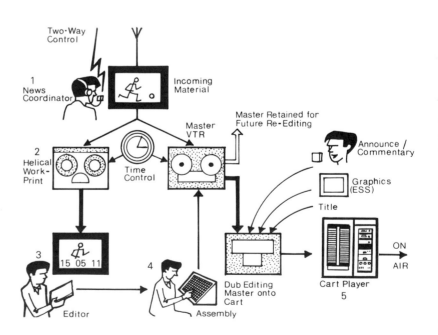

dubbing session commentary may be added from an adjacent announce booth; titles can be inserted (character generator); stills or graphics can be added (ESS, rostrum camera); video effects can be introduced (e.g. insets, split screen).

These edited copies of the stories may be videotaped on reel-to-reel or cassette systems. Cassettes offer greater flexibility for they can be loaded into an automated player for push-button selection in any order. This allows items to be revised, updated, or dropped during transmission.

The original *unedited master reference tape* remains unaffected, and is available for any revised editing or revamping for later newscasts or archives.

23 Video engineering

For many program makers, video engineers are the less familiar backroom figures, who shade pictures, adjust the equipment, and keep it working – and use inexplicable technical terms. Here we will look at a few of their 'mysteries'.

Behind the scenes

The video engineer is generally involved in three kinds of activities:

- *Servicing (maintenance)*. Ensuring that all video equipment is fault-free.
- *Set-up (line-up)*. The performance of video equipment tends to gradually alter with use ('drift'). Camera channels vary; monitors develop color bias and color fringing (registration faults); switching between sources can produce differences between brightness levels of pictures, etc. So the video engineer has to check and adjust performance.
- *Picture control ('shading')*. Cameras need to be adjusted to produce optimum picture quality as shots change. Without appropriate *matching* there would be color, brightness, or contrast changes on interswitching between them. The quality of different picture sources (cameras, film, slides) needs to be continually compared and adjusted.

The camera chain

Camera set-up (line-up)

If you want consistent high-quality pictures it is necessary to keep camera channels adjusted to within very close technical limits. Even top-grade systems drift to some extent during use, and it is advisable to make periodic checks both before rehearsals begin and before videotaping. Drifting picture quality may not be obvious when working with a single camera (until intercutting various shots during editing!), but in a multi-camera studio, differences can be very evident.

Set-up/line-up involves readjusting pre-set controls within the camera channel's circuitry. How often the camera chain needs checking and correcting depends on its design and stability. Two types of camera systems are in use today:

- *Non-digital* equipment, which follows traditional analog design. All adjustments to the camera channel are made manually. This can prove to be a time-consuming process (perhaps 20–30 minutes per camera) and results may depend on individual skill.

- *Digitally controlled* systems, on the other hand, include a computer-aided facility which allows circuit adjustments to be made automatically. Current such systems are quire costly, and their sophisticated electronics require skilled specialist maintenance. But set-up takes a fraction of the time (e.g. 2 minutes), and requires less experience.

Manual set-up

In non-digital camera systems each *camera head* is cable-linked to its *camera control unit/CCU*, where most of the circuitry involved in generating and processing the picture video and its associated sync pulses is centralized. The CCU houses the main electronic adjustments for the camera. At a master console, which contains equipment for precise video checks and measurements (e.g. waveform monitors, vectorscope), the CCU's circuitry can be adjusted to conform with specific standards.

Using a series of geometric patterns and tonal step wedges (placed in front of cameras, or in slide diascopes) all circuit adjustments are made directly by the video engineer while examining and measuring waveforms.

Digitally controlled equipment

As technology advances, and more compact reliable low-cost microprocessor circuitry becomes available, digital techniques are increasingly applied in all areas of television production – lighting control, video effects, switchers, audio systems, remote control mechanisms, camera design . . .

Digital systems have very practical advantages over traditional 'analog' designs (see Glossary: *Digital techniques*):

- They can be used to transmit video or speech, remotely control equipment, send numerical or alphabetical information.
- When varying electrical signals (analog) are converted into digital coded pulses they are far less likely to become irrevocably distorted by the time they reach their destination. They can be transmitted accurately over long distances by cable or radio, unimpaired by electrical interference or background noise.
- Compact 'converters' can transform signals from analog form to digital form, and vice versa (A/D and D/A converters) wherever necessary.
- A number of different digital signals can be sent over the same cable or radio link in rapid succession (time-division multiplexing), and separated without interaction at their destination.
- Data representing numbers or letters can be stored in digital form and read out or altered quite easily. This information can be checked and updated instantaneously, many times a second. If conditions vary, the digital system can check against stored data and bring circuits back to prearranged settings.

- Provided a piece of equipment is fitted with a battery power supply, it can be set up with operational data from a master control, disconnected, and then used independently elsewhere ('scramble').
- Digital data can be stored in various forms (e.g. floppy disk, magnetic tape, microchip) and inserted into equipment when required.

Digitally controlled cameras

These digital techniques have been applied directly to television camera design.

The camera receives continuous instructions in digital form from the camera control unit – now called a BSU (base-station unit) or CPU (camera-processing unit). These signals include: remote-control adjustments by the shader/video engineer, camera circuit corrections (set-up), lens-distortion corrections, sync pulses, intercom, program sound, viewfinder feeds of program or other video sources, prompter video, etc. Control information and data are continually updated or corrected. The camera's video and audio (intercom, sound mike) are relayed digitally to the base station. The base station also includes genlock facilities, cable-length compensation, and power supplies.

There are several configurations for camera control:

- A *remote-control unit (RCU) for each camera* provides standard operational controls (Figure 23.1) as well as controls for auto set-up.
- A multi-camera *set-up control unit* with operational channel controls.

Press for preview

Fig. 23.1   Video control
The main operational controls for each camera channel can be centralized at a video control (vision control) position. A single control knob is used to adjust:

- *Exposure* (to and fro). The iris/diaphragm varies ± ½ stop.

- *Black level/lift* (rotate knob). This raises/lowers all picture tones simultaneously.

- *Preview.* Pressing the knob allows the channel's picture to be compared with the shot currently on line from the switcher (to match picture quality).

Further sets of controls may provide:

Gain adjustment (amplification) for the camera's red, green and blue channels. (To adjust color bias.) This may be in the form of separate knobs, or a combined *'paintpot'* joystick control.

Gamma variation. This adjusts tonal coarseness or subtlety. It allows lightest and/or darkest tones to be modified. You can improve their clarity or merge them, to adjust the overall effect.

- A removable set-up panel applied for single or multiple set-up. The video engineer has the choice of either making checks and adjustments by hand or using the *auto-set-up* facility.

In an extended multi-camera system when more than e.g. six cameras are used, arrangements become rather more complex, and additional units are needed.

Each camera head contains a memory system (powered by an internal battery) which retains all the correct adjustment settings; even when the camera is switched off or disconnected. During operation, self-checking circuits ensure maximum stability of crucial synchronization and timing.

Because the camera cable no longer has to carry as many as 80 separate conductors for the different circuits, its thickness and weight can be greatly reduced for digitally controlled cameras. Consequently the cable is less bulky and easier to handle, and longer reels can be carried on remote trucks. As effective cable losses are low when using digital systems, the camera can work further from the CCU than with large analog multi-core (e.g. 1.8 km (1.1 miles)).

Adjusting picture quality

Although scenery and lighting can build up an atmospheric effect, how successfully this is conveyed by the camera will depend on the video equipment and how it is adjusted.

It is really a matter of standards. The very act of producing pictures *at all* may be sufficient for some purposes – e.g. surveillance. But to produce pictures that are consistently attractive and persuasive requires fore-thought, skill, and patience. To obtain optimum picture quality you must do more than just point a camera at a scene. Appropriate control is necessary, otherwise shadows can become clogged and detailless; the lightest tones may merge; successive pictures may jump in brightness; and some shots may look 'washed out' while others are overcontrasty.

In the studio you can help to ensure good picture quality by carefully selecting tones, and lighting, wardrobe, and so on. But on location, where the situation is less easily adjusted, it may be necessary to avoid shots that produce unacceptable results, such as an overexposed exterior seen outside the window of a room. Alternatively, you may be able to introduce compensatory lighting.

'Picture processing' in the form of video control (shading) is necessary to get the most from the TV system. Ideally, all video sources (cameras, film slides, tape) should be continuously monitored and their pictures suitably adjusted. But this is often neither practical nor economic, so three basic approaches to the control of TV picture quality have evolved:

- *Pre-set adjustments.* Here the system is adjusted and left.
- *Automatic control.* With this method we rely on auto-adjustments.
- *Manual control.* An operator monitors pictures and adjusts picture quality.

Pre-set adjustments

In this arrangement the equipment is *set-up (lined up)* manually or using *auto-set-up* to adjust its working limits. Thus the lens aperture has been set for a typical working *f*-stop exposure checked against a standard tonal chart, black level set.

From then on, it is up to the production team to adjust lighting, setting tones, costume and make-up for optimum results. They must work within the system's limits.

Lighting under these conditions does not *have* to be *flat* and uninteresting, but it generally needs to be consistent and of low contrast. This technique can be quite adequate for simpler presentations (e.g. newscasts) and where staffing is kept to a minimum.

Automatic control

In this method, after aligning the video equipment, the cameras are switched to *auto-iris, auto black*. During production they will self-adjust, avoiding over-exposure by stopping down and ensuring that the blackest area in the shot is reproduced as 'picture black' (*black level*).

Although this control approach avoids gross errors it has inherent weaknesses. As we saw earlier, automatic systems can be fooled.

A person's face should appear of similar tone when seen on intercut cameras. But automatic controls react to *all* picture tones, whatever their significance. With light backgrounds in one shot, and dark backgrounds in another, face tones would not match. Have another person move into shot wearing a much darker or lighter costume, and the picture may change as the lens opens up or stops down.

Even if the lowest tones in the shot are not really black, but of some dark value, the system can electrically *set down* the tonal scale so that they appear black, and shadow detail could be lost.

Dynamic contrast compression circuits can help to control highlights and to stretch blacks, so that we can see tonal gradation in shadows. But their performance is necessarily arbitrary, and can modify other picture tones.

When we adjust a camera channel's controls manually we can anticipate, and make allowances. We can make artistic judgments.

Manual control

Way back in the early days of television, the TV camera-tube (the iconoscope) was a particularly temperamental device. Its pictures were marred by spurious light and dark patches which continually changed with picture tones. Patient and dexterous video engineers sought to cancel out this shading with specially generated electrical waveforms ('tilt and bend' in Britain) and earned for themselves the title *Shader*, which has been used ever since.

There are two approaches to manually controlling picture quality. In the first, the video engineers who service and align the camera channels sit at the *camera control units (CCUs), remote-control units (RCUs)*, and adjust them to suit each shot. Adjustments include:

- *Lens aperture/f-stop* (remotely controlled).
- *Black level (lift; sit)*.
- *Video gain*.
- *Color balance*.
- *Gamma*.

In the second system all the camera's operational controls are extended to a central console (usually near the lighting board). Here a *vision control operator*, who is continually in touch with all video sources (cameras, film, ESS), can control picture quality.

Each channel has a combination control knob:

- Forward/backwards to adjust lens aperture or 'iris'.
- Twist to adjust black level.
- Press to compare the channel's picture with the shot on-line at that moment.

The operator also has a set of controls which independently adjust the *gain* (amplification) and the *black level (lift; sit)* of the red, green, and blue channels of each source. A *TARIF* control adjusts the color balance of pictures from telecine film and slides.

Why is video control necessary?

Many TV production groups rely entirely on pre-set adjustment or auto-control methods. It might be reasonable to ask, therefore, how necessary manual control really is today. The answer is a qualitative judgement; rather like comparing the results of automatically processed color film with those achievable by a specialist film laboratory.

Exposure control

As we saw earlier, 'correct exposure' can be very subjective. The exposure suitable for one camera position will not necessarily be appropriate for another. Subtle changes in the *lens aperture* or *iris* can readjust all picture tones.

- Unless a surface is rough its brightness can alter appreciably as we shoot it from various angles.
- Flat lighting produces uninteresting pictures, and skilled lighting directors avoid it. However, the light and shade that create depth and atmosphere can emphasize tonal contrast and produce uneven light levels for multi-camera viewpoints. Skilled vision operation can control and enhance these variations.
- Similarly, where scenic tones exceed the system's limits, by carefully adjusting exposure, gamma, and black level they can often be accommodated. It is a lot easier (and cheaper) to adjust the system than to change the staging.

- Where we want to see detail or tonal gradation in very light or very dark-toned subjects appropriate video adjustments can show them more clearly. When taking a close-up of a page in a book, for instance, a combination of reduced exposure and lower black level can improve clarity. Otherwise the page would probably block off and appear blank!
- Video is usually adjusted so that the peak whites in the picture meet the *reference white level*, while the blackest tones in the shot meet the *reference black level*. This makes full use of the system's tonal range. Beyond these limits, any tones are 'clipped off' electronically, and reproduce as solid white or black.

  But there are times when we *deliberately* allow white or darkest tones to be clipped off for artistic effect; to make a cyc appear totally white, or a black background to merge into solid black tone. (A regular practice with black-background title cards.)

  To lift *all* picture tones we can 'set up/sit up' the video (raise black level). The darkest shades will 'gray out' and can help to simulate a misty day, or enhance an ethereal effect. (You cannot use this idea to reveal any more detail in shadows. Only increased exposure, extra lighting, or reduced gamma will improve shadow detail.)
- Deliberately 'undermoding' (undermodulating) a shot by *under*exposing it will help to suggest a dull overcast day, or improve a dingy scene. Controlled *over*exposure, on the other hand, can simulate dazzling sunlight.
- Our impression of a subject's brightness can vary considerably with the background tones; particularly where these are very light or very dark. In these circumstances intercut shots can appear mismatched, as the amount of background tone varies. Again, judicious control can compensate for this subjective effect.
- Distant shots generally appear more dynamic if tones are strongly contrasted. Closer shots appear coarsened by excess contrast. When shooting is continuous it can prove more practical to emphasize tonal values in the long shots by setting down the picture a little rather than by lighting adjustments.
- Slight changes in a camera's color balance can help to compensate for unwanted subjective color effects; e.g. for the way faces can appear warmed or paled against strong background hues.

  Sometimes a slight color bias will enhance an atmospheric effect: a warmer cast for fireside or sunset scenes; a colder bluish cast for moonlight, or gaslight effects. You would normally achieve this color shift by adjusting the RGB channel gains.

  But in a camera that is fitted with *compensatory color filters* (used to match the camera to different lighting color temperatures) you can use a false Kelvin setting to give the picture a color cast. A filter setting that is too high will warm the picture, while a setting that is too low will cool it.

Camera-tubes and image sensors

Although the electronic intricacies of your TV camera are really only the concern of the video engineer its performance can directly influence staging practices and productional techniques. Today's camera-tubes are capable of producing pictures of the highest quality, and certain performance weaknesses have now been reduced (Table 23.4). Camera-tube sizes range from 12 mm (½ in) ENG/EFP), 18 mm (⅔ in) (ENG/EFP), to 25 and 30 mm (1 and 1¼ in) (studio and field).

The vidicon (antimony trisulphide target)

This forerunner of today's family of camera-tubes proved to be a cheap, reliable, long-lived, simply adjusted device. It has been widely used in closed-circuit TV systems as well as in the film and slide scanners. Its low sensitivity necessitated high light levels, and it suffered from pronounced *lag* (image smearing on movement). Its spurious background shading (uneven picture brightness across the frame) was also troublesome.

The lead oxide camera-tube (Plumbicon – Philips; Leddicon – EEC; Vistacon – RCA)

The pick-up tube that pioneered high-quality color TV, it has a higher sensitivity than the vidicon, a more constant tonal response (unity gamma), and much less spurious shading. Its poor response at the red end of the spectrum is now improved in 'extended red' versions, but picture noise is generally 'high in the reds'. It has a tendency to *lag*, but this is improved where *bias light* is fitted (internal illumination of the target). The tube overloads on highlights, and creates grossly enlarged white blocked-off areas in overbright regions such as skies (*blooming/puddling*). Disturbing *comet tails* trail behind moving speculars or lights.

Various design features improved these limitations: *highlight overload protection (HOP), anti-comet-tail guns (ACT), automatic beam-optimizer circuits (ABO)*. Similarly, *separate target mesh tubes* have improved detail resolution, highlights, and geometry. *Diode-gun* designs have improved resolution and reduced lag. To the director these technicalities mean better pictures under difficult shooting conditions.

The saticon camera-tube (Hitachi/NHK; RCA)

This has been increasingly used. Its target layer of selenium arsenic tellurium is more stable and long-lived than the lead oxide target. It provides higher resolution of detail (definition) and has a more even color response. Its performance in 18 mm (⅔ in) form has proved comparable with larger cameras using 25 mm (1 in) camera-tubes. It exhibits less image lag, and comet trails tend to be white rather than the usual red or green. Under low-light condition, however, lag can be more troublesome than with lead-oxide tubes.

CCD image sensors

The *CCD (charge coupled device)* is a solid-state image sensor that uses a small silicon chip containing thousands of individual elements,

Table 23.1   The CCD image sensor

The CCD image sensor has many advantages over the camera tube:

- Small. (Therefore smaller lightweight cameras are possible.)
- Rugged. (High resistance to vibrations, shocks and bumps.)
- Consumes low power. (So battery life is effectively extended.)
- Rapid start-up (½ second). (No warm-up time is needed.)
- Does not suffer from image *burn-in*.
    (So no 'stuck-on' after-images of lights or specular.)
- No comet tailing behind moving lights.
- Less image retention.
- No geometric distortion.
    (So straight lines cannot lean, or become bent.)
- Low lag under low-light conditions.
- Free from magnetic field interference.
    (So no glitches in pictures shot near radar or radio transmitters.)
- High sensitivity (30 Lux).
- Long life compared with camera-tube.
- Greater dynamic range.
- Less blooming.
- Better resolution of moving detail.
- Does not suffer from *drift* (i.e. performance change during use).

But it has certain disadvantages:

- It is liable to have background blemishes (holes, spots, uneven background).
- It has limited resolution, e.g. 574 elements per line.
    (Effectively improved by offsetting the green sensor.)
- Its color response is good but inferior to camera-tubes (especially at red end of spectrum).
- There is more noticeable smear.
- Slightly more picture noise than the ⅔ in *saticon*.
- A vertical smear on excess highlights.
- It is flicker sensitive.
- Excellent quality fully corrected lenses are essential for high quality.
    (Circuits can dynamically correct lens errors in camera-tube systems.)
- Strobing effects can be pronounced on fine line structures.
- Poor vertical resolution.
- It can have image-patterning problems.
- Noise from CCD sensors may form a fixed background at low light levels.
- Small formats (12 mm/½ in) with an *f*/1.4 standard lens provide greater depth of field, making differential focusing difficult.

There are two systems for transfering information from the CCD sensor: FT – frame transfer; IT – interline transfer.

FT system
- Requires a mechanical shutter to prevent smear. (This can be genlocked.)
- Inherently less sensitive.
- Pseudo-interlaced fields (image area cleared every field).
- Larger formats are difficult to manufacture.

IT system
- Slight smear; mechanical shutter cannot be used.
- Choice of true interlace and improved vertical resolution (but poor definition on movement, and interframe 'twitter'). Or pseudo-interlace, as in FT system.

Typical sensor size: 6.8 × 8.8 mm (same as 18 mm (⅔ in) camera-tube, or 6.4 × 4.8 mm (½ in)).

Table 23.2   Inherent picture defects

Line beating (strobing)	Localized flickering regularly encountered with close horizontal stripe patterns in clothing, fabrics (checks, stripes), line engravings, close mesh, etc. Can be reduced by altering the shot size or by slight defocusing. Effect is due to subject lines coinciding with picture scanning lines. Interference effects (cross-color) can arise too, producing a color-fringing effect on fine stripes (Table 23.4).
Stroboscopic effects	When the movement of rotating wheels or pulsating light coincide with the TV picture scanning rate of 60 per second USA (50 per second Europe) they will appear stationary. Slightly faster or slower speeds can cause wheels to apparently rotate forwards or backwards.
Interlace break-up	When viewed closely, a TV picture's interlaced line structure breaks up as we look up or down the frame. Line structure becomes coarser and vertical definition halves. Evident on fast crawl titles and extensive titling ('panning-up') shots.
Horizontal break-up	During panning or fast horizontal movement, strong vertical lines or detail break up into displaced sections. Due to the inherent time lag between scanning the odd and even fields of the picture (1/60 or 1/50 second).
Highlight flicker	Sometimes visible on very bright highlights, particularly when viewed in dark surroundings; although the picture repetition rate is too fast to be detected under normal conditions.

each independently charged by light from corresponding parts of the lens image. CCD sensors have many advantages for ENG work (see Table 23.1) and are increasingly used in lightweight camera systems. Currently, however, camera-tubes with ever-increasing refinements would seem to produce higher picture quality under controlled conditions.

Synchronizing the system

As we saw in Chapter 3, the TV scanning process is kept in step from camera- to picture-tube by specially generated *synchronizing (sync) pulses*. A color system is particularly critical, and requires stable precise sync pulses (for scanning accuracy), and *color burst* signal (for hue accuracy) for optimum reproduction.

Complete synchronism is essential if TV pictures are to be transmitted and reproduced without color errors: or even total loss of color and picture displacement.

A master SPG (sync pulse generator) supplies these pulses to the entire video equipment in studio or station. So all the equipment is *synchronous* (scanning in unison). Your switcher can accept any synced source (camera, film island/telecine, caption machine), and intercut, mix, superimpose, insert, chroma key between their pictures.

External video sources (remotes) on the other hand, operate from their own synchronizing generators. Although these are producing identical types of pulses they will not be exactly in step with the station's pulses

Video engineering

Table 23.3 Camera set-up (line-up): basic electronic adjustments

While the camera shoots special geometric charts and tonal step wedges, picture and waveform monitors are scrutinized to check the following:

Electronic focus	Focuses the camera-tube's scanning beam for sharpest picture detail.
Beam current	Controls the scanning beam strength. This is set to prevent lightest picture tones blocking off to detailless white areas (i.e. to discharge target's white elements). Too high a beam loses picture clarity, giving excess video noise. Too low a setting and no video is generated.
Target volts	Set for optimum tonal contrast. If too low, camera needs more light (larger *f*-stops or higher illumination) to compensate for weaker video – but image lag (trailing) is less. In the *vidicon* target voltage adjustment is used as manual or automatic sensitivity control – instead of continual aperture adjustment.
Black level (sit)	Adjustment relating darkest picture tones to system's video level representing black. May be automatically and/or manually maintained. Virtually moves all reproduced picture tones up or down the tonal scale.
Video gain	Ensures video amplification similar for each camera channel (1 V overall).
Alignment	Camera-tube beam's scan pattern adjustment (geometry).
Scan width and height	Adjust scan limits on camera tube and obtain 4 : 3 aspect ratio.
Vertical/horizontal shifts	Enables tube's scanned area to be centralized.
High peaker/aperture correction	Circuitry enhancing apparent picture sharpness by emphasizing higher video frequencies. (But increases video noise.)
Neg/pos switch	Picture tones (hues) as in scene, or 'phase-reversed' for negative effect.
Local/remote switch	Switches lift, black level and target controls from CCU to remote control point.

Table 23.4 Spurious visual effects

Certain picture defects are created or aggravated by unsuitable staging, lighting, and video operation; while others are inherent.

After-images (sticking, image retention)	Faint well-defined image remaining on the screen after the subject has moved away; especially of light-toned areas and highlights. Particularly bad on ageing camera-tubes and under cold conditions.
Background	Blemish, spot, patch, on a particular camera-tube. May be due to target damage or deterioration, or a low-grade camera-tube. Also a general unevenness over the light-sensitive area. In solid-state arrays (CCD) isolated spots are difficult to avoid.
Blooming (puddling)	Camera-tube overload causing overbright areas to be reproduced as grossly enlarged areas of blocked-off white. Reduced by tube design: anti-comet-tail gun (ACT), diode gun, highlight overload protection (HOP), or automatic beam optimizer (ABO) circuits/dynamic beam control circuits.

Table 23.4 (cont.)

Burn-in	Spurious after-image of light or bright reflection, temporarily (sometimes permanently) 'stuck on' to all of a camera's subsequent shots. Vidicon and plumbicon tubes are *not immune*, so avoid sustained shots of strong highlights. The effect worsens as the camera-tube ages.
Color response	Ideally, reproduced colors should be completely accurate. However, apart from design compromises, inaccuracies inevitably arise (analysis errors, unbalance, drift), throughout the system, from camera-tube to picture-tube. Many are corrected during line-up process.
Comet tails	An intense bright afterglow trailing behind moving highlights, lamps, specular reflections. Seen when either the subject or the camera moves. (See *Blooming*.)
Cross-color	A 'rainbow' interference effect seen on fine stripe or check patterns caused by luminance information intruding into chrominance signal. Inherent in the NTSC, PAL, SECAM systems. Prominent in helical scan VTR systems, but noticeably reduced where luminance and chrominance are recorded separately.
Cross-luminance	Bands of crawling dots seen at sharp color transitions. This is due to chrominance information intruding into luminance signal.
Definition (resolution)	Maximum resolution of detail is not generally possible over the entire picture area, on camera-tubes or picture-tubes. It deteriorates away from the frame center; although in broadcast equipment it still remains well within required standards.
Doming	An effect found in all 'spherical' shadowmask color picture tubes. In bright areas of the picture, the tube's shadowmask deforms temporarily (overheating), causing misalignment. Spurious color patches develop, destroying local color fidelity. More evident on large *flat square tubes* (*FST*). Significantly improved in nickel-iron/invar shadowmask designs.
Edge effects	With plumbicon and vidicon tubes, circuits compensating for definition fall-off (*aperture correction*) can produce false black edging round high-contrast borders – even crispening distant detail that would naturally be soft focus. Does not sharpen low-contrast borders.
Exposure time	The inability of the system to capture fast movement accurately; reproducing it instead as a blurred image. An *electronic shutter* on CCD cameras results in sharper images of moving subjects.
Lag (trailing)	Smearing or trailing seen behind movement, particularly on high-contrast subjects in low-key scenes. Evident on vidicon film channels during night scenes. In color systems, colored trailing or hue changes may be seen. Reduced by *bias lighting*. (See Glossary.)
Flare	*Optical:* Overall reduced contrast; graying (set-up) of picture; spurious light-streaks or patterns, due to internal reflections (light scatter) within lens system, and camera-tube face-plate. Caused by light shining directly into lens (backlight). *Electronic:* Excess highlights in the scene causing localized blooming around this area of the picture (charge redistribution effect).
Geometric distortion (non-linearity)	Cramping, stretching or bending of picture due to electronic (scanning/sweep circuits) or optical shortcomings. Includes S-curvature, trapezoidal, barrel, and pincushion distortions.
Microphony	Strong horizontal streaks arising when the camera is jarred, vibrated, or near strong sound sources (explosions, gun shots, singers, trumpets). Susceptibility to microphony depends on camera-tube and camera design.

Table 23.4 (cont.)

Performance stability	Most camera systems (like picture monitors) take some time to warm up and become stable (drift, color balance, etc.). To avoid/reduce cold start-up problems, cameras may be left on 'standy-by' (i.e. camera heaters kept warm); but this consumes battery power.
	Performance variations may only be obvious on comparing several monitor displays or cameras showing the same subject, and when editing together shots taken at different times (!).
Picture noise ('snow')	Overall fluctuating grain due to random electronic disturbances. Always present in the TV picture: it becomes particularly noticeable in dark scenes. At worst, develops into a 'snowstorm' overall. Chroma noise varies with hue.
Registration	The red, green, and blue picture images should coincide exactly over the entire frame area. In practice, *registration errors* arise (mainly at edges/corners); known as *convergence errors* on the picture-tube.
	Note: If error disappears on cutting to another source, it is faulty camera registration. If the same error is visible on all sources' pictures in same part of picture, it is a convergence error on the monitor.
Sensitivity	When light levels are below optimum, and lens aperture has been fully opened, video gain may have to be increased (often switchable on camera). This will improve video signal strength, turning a dim flat picture into a brighter contrasty one (with increased video noise!), but cannot compensate for any picture defects arising from the lack of sufficient light to the camera-tube (e.g. lag, smearing).
Shading	Localized lightening/darkening or color shading of parts of a camera's picture (electronic or optical causes). Most noticeable on plain light-toned surfaces. Reduced by corrective electronic shading signals.
Streaking	Black or white streaks extending across the picture beside high-contrast subjects (stair treads, venetian blinds). Usually due to overload or low-frequency losses in video channel.

(*out of phase*; wrong *timing*). If you feed such a *non-sync source* into most production switchers you will get totally unacceptable pictures (having displacement, tearing, break-up, roll, extreme color errors).

Where the production switcher design permits, you can *cut* to non-sync sources (*hot cuts*), but still cannot mix or combine their pictures with other local video sources. Only certain switcher designs (digital systems) allow you to combine 'sync' and 'non-sync' sources.

Synchronizing systems

To match two independent video sources' synchronization, several ingenious electronic systems have evolved. The earliest and simplest was *Genlock*; which adjusts the timing of the local pulses to get them into step with the remote (non-sync) source. This system of slaving works well as long as the remote's syncs are not interrupted or distorted, for then, *all* local equipment run from these genlocked pulses would 'lose syncs'.

VTR sources present another allied problem. Although the original sync pulses were recorded along with the picture, on replay these syncs become irregular and distorted. This is particularly true on small-format VCRs, due to minute random speed fluctuations arising from tape travel and mechanical imperfections. Although pictures will appear quite satisfactory on a picture monitor (which adjusts itself to varying sync pulses), if we tried to use such an unstable source with a precisely synchronized TV system it would cause color loss and image break-up. Particularly when editing or using picture combinations (supers, insertions), some form of synchronizer is needed that will accept these randomly changing syncs and adjust them to match local pulses.

Table 23.5 Picture monitor checks

Picture quality can only be judged on correctly adjusted, high-grade monitors, without spill light or reflections diluting the picture. Here are general methods of checking performance. Allow time for warm-up before adjustments.

Gray scale (all picture monitors)	Feed a *gray scale* (from camera, slide, or electronic generator) to all monitors. Adjust BRIGHTNESS (BRILLIANCE) to ensure *black* merges with blank screen-face. Adjust CONTRAST for maximum white brightness without line defocusing and good half-tone reproduction. Ensure all monitors' pictures are similar. Replace gray scale (tonal step wedge) with a monochrome picture containing good tonal variations. Compare all monitors' gradations and highlight brightness.
Color monitors	As above. Examine gray-scale reproduction for traces of color cast throughout tonal range. They should be neutral grays (good color tracking). Circuit adjustments may be necessary. Recheck using same color picture on all monitors. The picture should contain facial tones and pastel hues (desaturated) and not primary colors, or color bars.
Picture size/shape	Check that the screens show *all* of the TV picture (no edge cut-off) in correct 4 × 3 proportions.
Focus	Scanning lines should be sharp over entire picture, reproducing maximum detail on camera test chart.
Linearity	The picture should not show serious geometric distortions (cramping, stretching, bends). Check the linearity with a cross-hatch generator (grille). This produces a lattice of thin white lines on a black background.
Color defects	Check reproduction of cross-hatch for color fringing (*convergence errors*) along pattern. In practice some spurious color edges may be unavoidable. Check overall for: *color balance* (warm or cool?), *desaturated color* (washed-out, low contrast?), *oversaturated color* (overstrong color, high contrast?), hue shift (predominant overall color), and color shading (*purity* errors).
Black level	Picture *black* should be constant; not varying with picture tones, or reproducing as gray in low-key scenes or when faded to black. (Variations are due to equipment design or fault condition.)
Off-air pictures	Probably appear noisier and less sharp than direct off-line pictures. They may have displaced multiple images (ghosts, reflections) and ringing, due to multi-path reception of transmission; and/or interference patterns (herringbone, stripes, edge tearing).

A range of *time-base correction* equipment is available that provides automatic compensation for synchronizing inaccuracies on replay or imperfect sync pulses from mobile cameras.

Digital time-base correctors store up the video information from the VTR (notwithstanding the incoming variations) and clock it out of store again at precisely timed intervals in perfect synchronism with the station sync-pulse rate. (If the incoming video is interrupted the system may hold a still frame of the action, and recommence when the signal is re-established; so preventing picture break-up on air.) These units often offer additional facilities, such as: freeze frame, digital enhancement, drop-out compensation, noise reduction, color correction . . .

Standards converters (transcoders), which are used primarily to convert TV signals from one system to another (e.g. NTSC to PAL), may also be used to ensure source synchronism.

Composite signals – and switcher operation

A *composite signal* consists of the total video (picture) information together with inserted sync pulses at the end of each scanned line and field. Depending on local facility design, the video system may be supplied with either a full composite signal or a *non-composite* version (video information only, no sync pulses).

Certain production switchers are self-compensatory, accepting composite and non-composite inputs. Others only permit you to *fade to black* by sliding split A-B faders to out, when controlling *non*-composite video. If this fade-out is attempted with *composite* signals the switcher loses color. In such designs, you must select a *black-level button*, and mix to this 'non-channel' to simulate a fade-out.

Some switcher designs present severe video overloads when peak-white or light-toned areas are combined through mixing or superimposition. If your switcher does not incorporate protective circuits (processing amplifiers), you must avoid fading up channels fully in such circumstances.

Table 23.6   Video engineering terms

Synchronizing pulses	
	Sync pulses from the master control sync pulse generator (SPG) keep the entire TV system in step – from camera to receiver (preventing picture tearing, roll, etc.).
Line (horizontal) drive pulses	Synchronize the *line* scanning rate (horizontal sweep). At 525 (625) lines per second.
Field (vertical) drive pulses	Synchronize the *field* scanning rate (vertical sweep). At 60 (50) lines per second. Two *fields* provide one complete interlaced *picture* (*frame*) at 30 (25) lines per second.
Mixed syncs	The total, combined sync pulse information used to synchronize the system

Table 23.6 (cont.)

Composite video signal	The complete video waveform, together with synchronizing pulses.
Blanking	Special pulses used to suppress video output from the camera to enable sync pulses to be inserted. The scanning process retraces to the beginning of the line or field during blanking.
Timing	Video signals take a measurable time to travel along distribution cables within a building. If various sources (e.g. film, VTR, ESS channels) are at different distances from the studio (or master control) their pictures would arrive at slightly different times. Any attempt to combine these sources' pictures (e.g. mixing/superimposing/insertion) would show some pictures horizontally displaced (or cut off) due to their different path lengths. To avoid this situation, each route needs suitable compensation to ensure identical *timing* at the destination.

Color information

Color subcarrier	A constant carrier frequency that is modulated to encode information.
Reference color burst	A brief burst of the above subcarrier, introduced into the synchronizing information to stabilize color reproduction.
Coder (encoder)	Circuitry (matrix) converting a camera's red, green, and blue video signals into a single luminance/chrominance encoded form (NTSC, PAL, or SECAM) for distribution and transmission.
Decoder	Circuitry (matrix) converting the coded video back into separate RGB video to drive the receiver or monitor circuits.

Equipment

Distribution amplifier (DA)	Video amplifier used to isolate and distribute video signals. (Zero gain, or amplifying signal strength to compensate for subsequent losses.)
Processing amplifier/stabilizing amplifier	Corrects errors developing in the video signal. Used to reshape, reinsert, or separate sync pulses from the composite signal (i.e. video plus syncs).
Image enhancer (IA)	Circuitry used to improve apparent picture definition, reduce video noise. (*See* Glossary.)
Termination	To match a picture monitor to its video cable a termination resistance is introduced at its video input. This avoids signal losses, distortions, and reflections. Only *one* termination is required for a succession of looped-through monitors.
Color bar generator	An electronically generated color test pattern, comprising vertical bars displaying white, yellow, cyan, green, magenta, red, blue, and black. Used for video system checks.
Standards converter	Electronic equipment used to enable pictures televised by one TV system (e.g. 525-line NTSC – USA, Japan) to be reproduced by another incompatible system (e.g. 625-line PAL or SECAM).

Glossary

The digests in this glossary aim to help you by

- Explaining or defining points that would otherwise interrupt the flow of the main text,
- Including additional technical details for those who are interested,
- Providing additional terms.

Acoustics (*see Figure 12.6*) Higher frequency sound waves travel in straight-line paths. So they are easily deflected and reflected by hard surfaces; and are absorbed by porous fibrous materials. Lower frequency sound waves (below 100 Hz) spread widely, so are not impeded by obstacles and are less readily absorbed.

  As sound waves meet nearby materials they are selectively absorbed and reflected; the reflected sound's quality being modified according to the surfaces' nature, structures, and shapes. Studios are carefully proportioned and their walls covered with suitable absorbent materials (fiber panels, rockwool, mineral wool, seaweed quilting) to prevent unwanted sound coloration and to reduce reverberation (small TV studios 0.3–0.5 second; larger TV studios 0.7–1 second). The acoustic characteristics of scenery, furniture, drapes, people, further modify audio quality.

Animation Creating an illusion of movement – by intercutting stills, using graphics with movable sections, using step-by-step changes in a static subject (objects, models, drawings, photographs, etc.), or control-wire activation.

Aperture correction Electronic correction to compensate for the loss of definition due to inherent spread of the scanning beam in the camera-tube.

Audio enhancement Thanks to developments in semiconductor technology, sound signals can be treated in a number of ingenious ways: processed either by *analog* (charge transfer capacitance devices) or by *digital* systems. These convert and selectively retrieve the stored result. Each has its advantages.

  Various effects can be achieved, including: variable reverberation, echo, doubling/double-tracking (close repeats), delays, chorus, chords, tunneling, phasing, Haas effect (shifting stereo images), hollowing, sweep effects, Doppler effect (pitch changes), arpeggio, vibrato, spin (feedback), flanging (original with delayed version of changed strength and phase), time compression, expansion.

Audio synchronizer A facility for computerized automatic editing of audio tapes and VT soundtrack. An audio stereo tape is prepared with *time code* on one track (from a *time-code generator* or the *cue track* of a videotape), and program audio is recorded (in mono) on the other. The push-button programed unit can automatically stop/start and synchronize both audio tape and VT machines. It can locate edit-point addresses, and then

(1) dub-off code-selected sections from one audio tape onto another, or (2) transfer sound segments from audio tape to VT soundtrack.

Automatic assembly   The VT editing process is time consuming, and several methods have developed to assemble the program automatically from instructions. In *auto assembly* the computer-aided editor, guided by time code, files edit decisions, translates, and carries out edits and effects, in sequence.

Linear assembly (Mode A) performs the edits in the order of the *edit list*. As the unedited material is usually shot out of order (execution order), this can involve several reel changes and VTR set-ups.

In *reel sequential assembly (Mode B)* the edit list is scanned, and those sections available in the reels currently loaded on the VTRs are carried out (no overlaps or overlays are permissible).

In *look-ahead assembly* any VTR not actually being used readies itself (i.e. finds the next edit point, pre-rolls ready to run-up and record), so saving preparation time.

Automatic tracking   A system on some VTRs for ensuring that the replay head (which is mounted on a deformable piezoelectric element) accurately retraces the recorded video track when replaying a helical recording; particularly when replaying a tape recorded on another machine of the same type. This avoids picture quality variations (of detail, chrominance, saturation), noise bars (due to playing guard tracks), or disturbed synchronism. Video playback head position is automatically adjusted as the recorded track is sampled for maximum signal. This arrangement also allows full color at varying tape speeds; avoiding picture break-up during stop action, jogging, fast/slow motion. (*Ampex* – AST: automatic scan tracking. *3M* – ATF: automatic track follow. *Sony* – dynamic tracking.)

Azimuth   Magnetic recording/reproducing systems (audio and video) use heads that scan the passing magnetic surface with a fine slit. In audio systems the head's slit is at right angles to the tape edge. If the slit of the reproducing head is not at exactly the same angle to the track as the original recording's (i.e. the same *azimuth*) there will be a corresponding reduction in the audio output. Azimuth checks (like cleaning and demagnetizing) should be a regular part of recorder maintenance.

Helical VTR systems deliberately *angle* a pair of video heads (e.g. $\pm 6°$) so that two separate tracks can be recorded on the same portion of tape without mutual interference. Neither head reproduces the other's track signals, because their azimuths are different. This principle has been taken further in a VHS system with hi-fi audio (*depth multiplex recording* – *see Consumer video formats*). Here high-quality stereo sound (in FM form) is recorded along exactly the same track as the *video*, with $\pm 30°$ heads, angled at $120°$ to the video record, so providing independent outputs! (The standard audio edge-track is also recorded; lower-quality mono sound.)

Backing track   A prerecorded track providing musical accompaniment for a performer who, listening on earphones (or a playback loudspeaker), is recorded on his individual mike.

Banding   Can occur on quad or segmented-head recorders, dividing the picture into a series of wide horizontal bands if head responses are uneven (e.g. a head clog) or are not automatically compensated.

Bands In a videotape recorder an FM carrier is generated which is then modulated with the video signal. It is this modulated carrier that is recorded on the tape; the video component itself being recovered during replay. However, spurious interference effects can arise in the process (close bands or stripes, noise effects) depending on the FM carrier-frequency band being used. A *low-level* 2.5 MHz is suitable only for monochrome. A *high-band* 3.58 MHz is suitable for color, but liable to a fine moiré pattern in colored areas, especially red. *Super high-band* 8 MHz considerably reduces the problem.

Batteries Several types of battery are used with video equipment. The *NiCad* or *nickel–cadmium cell* is popular, small, rugged, long-lived, and easy to charge – but relatively costly. It delivers 1.2 V per cell max. falling to 1.1 V per cell min. A NiCad cell works best at 65–75°F (18–23°C). It should be stored at 68° to 22°F (20° to −6°C). The cell retains its charge well in cool storage; but loses it rapidly in hot surroundings.

Sealed lead-acid cells are cheapest and toughest, but bulky and heavy. They tolerate extreme temperatures, but are liable to top leak (2 V per cell max. falling to 1.65 V min.).

Silver-zinc cells provide high storage capacity for their size (three times the NiCad cell) but are less tolerant of high temperatures and misuse, and have a shorter life.

The capacity of a battery is indicated by its rating in *ampere-hours* (*Ah*). The higher the rating, the longer the battery will function before recharging. A typical 'in-board' battery of 2 Ah may last for e.g. an hour, while a battery-belt (power-belt) of 4–7 Ah could last 2–3.5 hours.

Beam splitter An optical device used to derive three identical images from the camera lens's image. The natural-color lens image passes through a pair of dichroic mirrors that split it into its red, blue, and green light components, respectively. The color images are reflected onto their corresponding camera-tubes via compensatory relay lenses. Additional 'trimming' color filters exactly adjust the spectral spread of each light path.

An alternative method uses a glass prism block instead of dichroic mirrors (less light loss, more stable, but more costly).

Beeper An identification audio signal sometimes used at the start of a recorded section (videotape, audio tape, or disc band) to aid sound cuing.

Bias current An ultrasonic current (e.g. 75–120 kHz) is combined with the audio in the record head; this effectively linearizes the tape's magnetic characteristic. Its strength is adjusted to suit particular tape materials. The bias setting is a compromise between distortion and high note response.

Bias light Many camera-tubes suffer from *lag*, which creates movement blur, and ectoplasmic smearing (*trailing, beam lag*), and color fringes behind moving high-contrast subjects under low-light conditions. This effect is considerably reduced by internally illuminating the camera-tube target (e.g. with a miniature pea lamp) when working under low-light conditions. A similar lag effect can occur when a camera-tube is slow to charge (*build-up*) during movement from low tones to a bright surface area.

Blooming A transparent microscopic anti-reflection coating is deposited on the surface of lenses to reduce light scatter, internal reflections, and flare within the lens system. The result is improved light transmission and overall contrast in the picture. The coated surface must be treated with care to avoid scratching, pitting, or wear. You should use special lens-cleaning tissue, or a soft lens brush to clean the lens surface, and, exceptionally, special lens-cleaning fluid.

Bridge Words or music introduced to tie together two dissimilar items. *Also* the shorting together of RGB channels on a picture monitor to produce a black and white picture.

Bulk eraser A large electromagnet which demagnetizes an entire tape spool, ensuring that any previously recorded program is completely wiped.

Camera cables TV cameras can be connected to video equipment by various means: coaxial cable, triaxial cable (coax plus outer screen), multi-conductor/multi-core cable, fiber-optic cable, radio mini-link, laser link, infrared link. Each method has its advantages, but typical factors to be considered include: cost, bulk, weight, damage vulnerability, interference pick-up. Whereas *multi-core* may have a length limit for a particular camera of e.g. 1800 ft (550 m), with *triax* the camera could be 6500 ft (2000 m) from base, and with *optical fiber* 7000 ft (2150 m) away. Fiber-optic cables weigh only around 5 lb per 1000 ft (2.3 kg per 300 m). Switchable *cable compensation* circuits correct for the definition losses that increase with cable length.

Camera control unit (CCU) Although portable/compact cameras are self-contained, in multi-camera systems cameras are normally cabled to a central control point. Here each camera may have a separate *camera control unit – CCU*, or be routed to a *master control console (remote-control unit – RCU; base-station unit – BSU)*. This is usually located adjacent to the studio or in a central apparatus room serving several studios.

   The CCU centralizes most of the circuitry involved in generating and processing the picture video and its associated sync pulses. It has the main electrical adjustments and operational controls for the system, and equipment for measuring and checking technical parameters. System adjustments (*lineup; set-up*) can be made using either automated or manual methods (See Table 23.3.) Operational controls may be extended to a vision operator's position near the lighting control console, so that picture quality and lighting treatment can be coordinated.

Camera lens The camera lens is a precision optical system, so it is extremely important to protect it from water, shocks, grit, moisture, heat, etc. if it is to maintain performance. The lens system consists of a series of individually designed lenses (*elements*) exactly set within a tubular metal barrel. Various optical inaccuracies can arise that cause the lens image to have uneven brightness, varying sharpness, distortions, color fringes, etc. These *aberrations* can be reduced by including extra compensatory elements within the system. However, each element causes additional light losses. (See *Blooming*.) If these overall losses are too great, the image reaching the camera-tube is weakened, and stronger lighting is needed on the scene, or a larger lens aperture, to compensate. An insufficiently bright image results in an *underexposed* shot.

A variable diaphragm or iris within the lens system adjusts the overall amount of light passing through it. So the image brightness can be altered for exact exposure. Its adjustment also affects the *depth of field*.

In a zoom lens selected elements are moved within the lens system to change the overall focal length, and hence the lens coverage (field of view; camera angle).

To adjust the focused distance a *fixed-optics* lens system is moved to and from the camera-tube. In a *zoom* lens, elements are repositioned.

The regular methods of attaching the lens system to the camera head are the screw-type *C-mount* and the quick-release *bayonet lock mount*, where the barrel fits into a slotted keyway in the camera head.

Cinching (windowing) Slippage between tape layers on a loosely wound spool, causing physical distortion and even tape damage.

Closed circuit Production being recorded, reviewed, etc. *locally*; as opposed to programs being *broadcast* for public viewing (off-air, or cable). Closed-circuit television (CCTV) is the general term for non-broadcast TV.

Coding Electronic process of encoding RGB video signals into NTSC, PAL, SECAM, color systems. (*Decoder:* circuitry for transforming the encoded signal into its RGB components.)

Color bars Video test signal presenting a series of vertical bars of fully saturated color: white, yellow, cyan, green, magenta, red, blue, black.

Color definition The eye cannot readily detect fine color detail. Therefore, to save bandwidth in color TV systems, full detail is transmitted in *luminance* only – 4.2 MHz; i.e. 320 lines horizontal resolution – NTSC 525/60 (5.5 MHz. PAL. 625/50). Color information is deliberately restricted: I bandwidth (orange to cyan) 1.6 MHz; Q (green to magenta) bandwidth 0.8 MHz. The effect is of lower definition color 'overprinted' with tonal detail. Colors are transmitted in the proportions 30 per cent red, 59 per cent green, 11 per cent blue, to produce a suitable monochrome tonal balance.

Color synthesis Any color can be simulated in a TV system by supplying appropriately proportioned voltages to the red, green, and blue video channels. The color produced by the *color synthesizer/colorizer/color-field generator* may be switch-selected or controlled by a roller-ball or joy-stick control ('paintpot'). Its central position produces white, but the controller can be moved anywhere within a red, green, blue triangle. The synthesized color can be used as a source for electronic insertion: titling, title backgrounds, decorative effects, substituting picture colors or tones.

Color temperature Although all 'white' light includes colors of the entire visible spectrum (red, orange, yellow, green, blue, indigo, violet), the actual *proportions* of the spectral colors vary. We are unable to detect such variations because the brain compensates. But pictures from video and photographic systems reveal a color cast if they are used with lighting that does not color-match their particular color balance.

Because 'white' light is a very arbitrary term, a system is used, based on the Kelvin scale, to classify and compare the 'whiteness' of light sources. This system is based on the following concepts. If a hypothetical 'black body' is heated (actually tungsten filament or carbon) it will emit light. The color quality of the light changes throughout the temperature scale. (0 K = −273°C, i.e. the temperature at which molecular movement, causing heat, ceases.) At lower temperatures it will be predominantly red. But as the temperature is increased, the radiated light covers more and more of the spectrum, and includes an increasing proportion of blue.

Because the color quality of the light changes along the Kelvin temperature scale we can use these readings purely as *labels*; each figure corresponds to a particular light quality. Let us suppose that we measure the light from a candle with a pocket spectroscope, and check the proportion of each spectral color (its 'spectral distribution'). If we find that it has a color quality similar to that of 1930 K on the Kelvin scale, we say that it has a *color temperature* of 1930 K. That does not imply that this is the *actual* temperature of the candle! It is just a convenient method of classifying its overall color rating. Some light sources, such as fluorescent lamps, do not correspond very accurately to the Kelvin spectral coverage, but their quoted 'color temperatures' are a useful enough guide.

Knowing the color temperature of the light source, and that of our system, we can adjust either the light or the system, so that they match, and avoid a color cast in the picture.

Color temperature meters compare the proportions of red and blue light coming from any source, and this is transformed into a corresponding Kelvin reading.

Color film is designed to be used with a particular type of light (daylight 5500+ K; tungsten light 3200–3400 K). Under other conditions, a compensatory filter must be fitted.

Television systems are immediately adjustable to accept prevailing conditions ranging from a *clear sky* (10 000–20 000 K) to tungsten lighting (3000 K). Although studio lighting has a color temperature of about 3200 K, the lamps are usually slightly dimmed (under-run) as this improves lamp life. Cameras are lined up to this lower color temperature – around 2850–3000 K. Dimmer variations of 200 K are not generally noticeable as color changes in the picture. But where several lamps are lighting a light-toned surface, even 50–100 K differences may be detectable as bluish or orange-yellow variations.

Many video cameras contain switched compensation to adjust them to 'daylight' (5600 K) or 'tungsten light' (3200 K). Although these are arbitrary settings, they suit most conditions.

Color terms:

Achromatic values (gray scale). Progressive scale of brightnesses (luminance), from black through grays to white. Usually expressed as steps in a reflectance scale (Figure 3.8).

Brightness. Our *impression* of the amount of light received from a surface. The term is often used to indicate *luminosity* (US).

Chroma. See *Saturation.* (Term used in the Munsell system.)

Complementary colors. In *light*: two colors which, when added together, produce white light; e.g. blue and yellow; cyan and red; magenta and green. In *pigment or dye*: complementary colors produce black.

Hue. The predominant sensation of color; i.e. red, yellow, orange, etc. (Term used in the Munsell system.)

Lightness. Our impression of the brightness of surface colors.

Luminance. The *true* measured brightness of a surface. Snow has high luminance (reflecting 93–97 per cent of the light falling on it). Black velvet has a low luminance (reflecting 1.0–0.3 per cent of the light falling on it).

Luminosity. Brightness. Our impression of the amount of light received from a light source, or reflected from a surface.

Minus colors. If the visible spectrum is filtered, to hold back one primary color (e.g. red), the result is a 'minus red' mixture. 'Minus red' = blue + green – i.e. cyan. Similarly, minus green is magenta (red + blue); minus blue is yellow (red + green).

Monochrome. Generally refers to 'black-and-white' (achromatic) reproduction. Strictly means varying brightnesses of *any* hue.

Primary colors. Three colors (usually red, green, and blue) which, when mixed in correct proportions, can produce any other color of the spectrum.

Saturation (chroma, intensity, purity). The extent to which a color has been diluted with white (paled out). If a hue is pure and undiluted, it has 100 per cent saturation. As it becomes diluted, its saturation falls; e.g. 100 per cent red desaturates to pink (e.g. 15 per cent).

Secondary colors. In light, the hues resulting from the additive mixture of a pair of primary colors. (In printing, the orange-red, green, and purple-blue colours produced when pairs of *subtractive primary* colored inks are superimposed).

Shade. A hue mixed with black.

Spectral colors. The series of color bands seen when white light is diffracted by a lens, prism, or diffraction grating. Merging continuously from red (longest wavelength; lowest frequency) through orange, yellow, green, blue, indigo, violet (shortest wavelength; highest frequency).

Tint. A hue diluted with white; i.e. a desaturated color.

Value. Subjective brightness (Term used in the Munsell system.)

Color-under Several different techniques are used to record color information on videotape:

1. Recording a *composite* signal (which includes a chrominance-modulated subcarrier).
2. *Color-under recording.*
3. *Component recording*, in which luminance and chrominance (actually, *color difference signals*) are recorded separately.

The detailed information in a fully encoded color TV signal (i.e. NTSC, PAL, etc.) cannot be recorded accurately at the slower videotape speeds of small-gauge VTR systems (U-Matic, VHS, Betamax, etc.). Instead, an ingenious *color-under* system is used. In principle this involves recording brightness (luminance) and color (chrominance) information simultaneously on two adjacent carriers (FM, AM), using filters on replay to distinguish between them. However, there are problems in differentiation, and various visible defects arise: detail loss (above about 2 MHz), chroma noise, moiré patterns, edge sparkle, color displacement, ringing (edge repeats), 'cartooning' (plain areas lack texture). Such interference may be reduced, and definition increased, by raising the carrier frequency of the luminance signal (as in S-VHS).

Combination cameras Various incompatible forms of camera systems incorporating a VTR are available (called 'combos; VRCs; camcorders'). Based on the VHS system, but with different electronics, are the *ARC* (Ampex), *Hawkeye* (RCS), *Recam* (Panasonic), *ProCam* (JVC), and Ikegami versions with Matsushita-design recorder. This system is widely referred to as *M-Format* (*M-wrap*) due to the tape path shape, or as *Chromatrak*.

Sony's *Betacam* system or *CTDM-format* uses a Betamax-type cassette (used also in Thompson-CFS *Camescope*). The Bosch Fernseh produced *QuarterCam* (*Lineplex*) system uses ¼ in CVC tape (allied versions by Hitachi and Philips).

Although based originally on domestic recorder formats, broadcast quality has been achieved by: faster tape speed (hence better detail, lower noise), separately recorded encoded color components (chrominance) and luminance; which avoids the spurious patterning/cross-color effects of color-under systems. Although tapes carry luminance track, color track, two audio tracks, control and timecode tracks, their arrangements and form differ considerably between formats. Typical tape duration is 20 minutes. Performance approaches 1 in C-Format VTRs.

BetacamSP format, and *M-II* format: using ½ in metal particle tape, record luminance on a 'Y' track (FM) and color difference signals on a 'C' track (FM). (The color difference signals are compressed and time-division multiplexed into a single signal.) A special reference *burst* on the Y and C signals improves jitter and phase errors. There are four audio channels (two longitudinal/linear analog audio tracks; 2 FM depth-multiplex recordings).

Compact disc Digital audio disc (DAD) recordings use a universal format on 4.7 in (120 mm) single-sided discs (79.8 minutes max. duration). Audio is digitally recorded as a pattern of shallow depressions (pits) along a fine-groove spiral track. (These correspond with regular samplings of the original fluctuating audio signal/analog signal.) This track is replayed by a contactless laser/optical pick-up system. Audio quality is exceptionally high, a wide frequency range, virtually without rumble, flutter, wow, background noise; a high dynamic range > 90 dB); low distortion (< 0.05 per cent peak).

Track information begins with coded data on the playing time and the number of tracks. Scanning from in to out, the disc begins rotating at 510 rev/min, reducing as the diameter increases, to 210 rev/min, with a constant linear speed of 1.25 m/s. Track width is roughly one-eighteenth that of a standard LP disc groove.

Compatible   When video or audio signals are generated by one system or piece of equipment and reproduced effectively by another the second is said to be *compatible*.

Consumer videotape formats   A wide range of features are available in these low-cost helical-scan VTRs, including: off-air recording; with channel selection and programming (auto-record timer); video input (for cameras or dubbing); tracking control (adjusts replay for best track-following); audio dub (change or add audio track); noise reduction; cue/review controls, shuttle search (fast picture search forwards/backwards); pause/still (freeze frame); remote control (cable, infrared); timer (auto switch on-off); auto rewind at tape end; auto program marker (signal locates starts or cue points); tape-used/elapsed time indicator; tape-left indicator.

Dual-speed VHS models are available (lower quality on half-speed). Some recorders have stereo sound capability. Typical maximum duration at normal speed 3 hours 35 minutes (Beta) to 4 hours (VHS).

The *Beta* and *VHS* provide very comparable results. Certain design features are similar; color-under processing, tilted-azimuth heads. Others are quite individual: e.g. the tape path (U-form in Beta; M-form in VHS), and tape handling (tape remains laced up during all operations in Beta; but retracts for fast winding in VHS). Advanced forms (S-VHS) offer enhanced picture quality (+ 400 lines horizontal resolution, compared with VHS (250 lines)).

VCRs with *depth multiplex recording* (*FM*) audio systems provide very high-quality stereo sound output. Here two audio heads lay down an FM signal of relatively low frequency, deeply penetrating the tape. The video heads immediately follow them along the same track (different azimuth), erasing and replacing the top level of the FM audio recording with a higher frequency video signal. This creates a 'two-layer' effect, with virtually no interference between recordings.

Crossed gray scale (chipchart)   A standard test graphic comprising two opposed horizontal nine-step tonal gray scales (from 3 per cent to 60 per cent reflectance).

Cut-back   During editing, returning to the main scene after a series of interpolating close shots.

Date   A system of sound distribution used by PBS (Public Broadcast Service) network, in which audio is digitally encoded for distribution and decoded at the local receiving station. Usable for stereo simulcasts (simultaneous TV and high-fidelity FM stereo radio transmission), the system can relay four audio channels in addition to the mono TV sound.

Decibel (dB)   A logarithmic unit indicating ratios of powers, voltages, or currents, and used to express transmission levels, gains, and losses. The human ear (like the eye) does not respond proportionally to changes, but follows a 'power law'. A decibel represents the smallest perceptible change in audio level.

Degaussing   Demagnetizing. Tape recording heads must be periodically degaussed to prevent magnetic build-up from increasing tape hiss. Videotape is usually bulk erased before re-use.

Dichroics   A dichroic mirror reflects one color band while letting others pass through it. When a series of extremely thin semi-transparent layers of material are deposited on a glass surface, light waves are interreflected there, creating interference effects. (Similar to colors reflected when oil floats on water.) The exact effect varies with the wavelength (hue) of the light. Treatment can be selective, to allow only e.g. the blue-green part of the spectrum to pass, while e.g. the red region is reflected. Carefully controlled color light filters can be made using this process.

In *beam splitters* this principle is used to convert the lens image into three identical color images (R, G, B) of the scene. (See *Beam splitter*.)

In lighting, *dichroic filters* are placed over tungsten-halogen lamps to change their color temperature from the warmer 3200 K to the bluer color of daylight (5600 K).

Diffuser   A sheet of wire mesh, spun glass, or opaque polyester placed over a light fitting: either to diffuse (soften) the illumination or to reduce the light output, without affecting the color temperature. If the fitting is insufficiently ventilated, overheating can result, reducing the life of the lamp.

Digital techniques   The output of many *transducers* such as camera-tubes or microphones takes the form of a continuously fluctuating voltage. These fluctuations are comparatively slow in the case of audio; e.g. 15 to 20 000 vibrations a second. For picture information (video) they may be up to e.g. 4–8 million vibrations a second. These are termed *analog waveforms*, as their form follows that of the original source.

Unfortunately, as *analog* signals pass through the system they can easily become deformed in various ways. So by the time they arrive at their destination they often present a distorted version of the original picture or sound. We may accept or overlook these shortcomings, but they are there.

Instead of handling the original vulnerable analog signal, a *digital* system converts it into a different form. It measures the strengths of the original analog waveform at rapid regular intervals, and these values are sent through the system as a series of numbers (digits). Each number takes the form of an 'on–off' code of eight pulses. So for instance, the *binary code* for 1 is **00000001** and for 2 is **00000010**.

This technique sounds very cumbersome, but it stems from the fact that, like the dot–dash system of Morse code, it has proved to be a very 'robust', accurate method of sending information (data). Even when it becomes distorted or is accompanied by noise, the basic binary on–off pattern is usually still quite discernible. So it can be converted back into analog form at its destination and accurately reproduce the original signal.

Microtechnology allows information in 'on–off' binary form to be transmitted and stored accurately in a number of ways, and new low-distortion techniques have developed in several television/video fields: *digital disk systems* storing sound and picture (e.g. CDs, LaserVision), *videotape systems* (e.g. D-1, D-2), *audio tape systems* (e.g. R-DAT, DASH), *digital video effects* (DVE), etc.

Diopter   A *diopter lens* is a simple supplementary lens placed over the main camera lens to alter its effective focal length. Mainly used for close-ups of small objects.

The *diopter* is the measurement of the power of a single lens; 100 divided by its focal length in centimeters. So a lens of power + 15 diopters has a focal length of $100/15 = 6.66$ cm (66.6 mm).

+ indicates that the lens is converging; − that it is diverging.

Drop-out Magnetic tape surface defect or damage causing momentary disturbance of reproduced video, resulting in small localized information gaps in a line (black flash, color loss). To disguise this brief loss of FM signal pick-up from the tape, a *drop-out compensator* can insert stored picture information from a corresponding part of the previous line. (This term is also used for the information loss, *noise* band at end of line/frame scanning in helical recording.)

Ducker/voice-over ducker An audio-fader circuit that automatically reduces the volume of e.g. music ('backgrounds' it) to enable an announcement to be heard; its level being restored as the speech stops.

Dupe neg A duplicate negative prepared from a positive print – when the original negative is not available, or to protect the original negative, or for special-effects work. By using *color reversal intermediate film*, duplicate negatives of the original color negative can be prepared, so eliminating one printing stage (reduced grain, improved color reproduction and sharpness).

Electronic cinematography (EC) Video cameras designed to produce typical 'film look' picture quality. Used for shooting 'motion pictures' that will subsequently be transferred to film for screening. These cameras are intended to handle and perform like 35 mm cine cameras. They have the merits of both media, i.e. the advantages of videotape over film stock, continuous monitoring, with interchangeable lens systems (prime and zoom), T-stops, the familiar angles of film camera lenses, and facilities for a separate focus-pulling operator.

Other design features include extended dynamic range, soft clip (i.e. a *knee* in the exposure curve, instead of the hard/sharp cut-off of highlights in the normal TV white clipper/white limiter). The inherent characteristics of TV camera-tubes remain, of course.

Electronic still store (ESS) Photographic slides are costly, vulnerable, bulky, need manual sorting and loading, etc. So magnetic video disc stores of various designs are increasingly used that provide a library of still video pictures. These pictures can be 'grabbed' from any video source (cameras, slide scanners, videotape, film, computer graphics) and range from artwork to photo-stills or titles.

Storage capacity may range from a few hundred to several thousand frames. Sometimes a number of work stations can load from one central library store. Individual stills are coded and may be selected at random, or arranged to play through in a programmable sequence.

As stills selection from store can be almost instantaneous, several can be shown in rapid succession to create animated effects. An index of descriptions/titles can be displayed on a monitor screen, and may enable a simultaneous multi-segment picture (e.g. 64 'slides') to be displayed (*browse mode*).

Exposure curve (transfer characteristic) Only where a picture system's output is directly proportional to the light input (unity gamma) will tonal reproduction be strictly accurate. Most systems have a linear (straight line) portion to their characteristics, but are less responsive to changes at exposure extremes. Lightest tones are therefore progressively compressed at the upper end of the exposure curve (knee, shoulder), while shadow detail merges at the lower end (toe).

Fiber optics   A cable of fine glass filaments conveys intensity-modulated light from light-emitting laser diodes in a miniature transmitter to light detectors, which transform these light pulses into corresponding electrical signals (video and audio).

The advantages of optical fibers include: lightweight, small-diameter cable, no electromagnetic interference, no crosstalk between fibers, low losses, no radiation, no picture degradation, no equalization needed, wide bandwidth, independent of line-of-sight and weather conditions (unlike external radio links), rapidly routed, very robust (withstands vehicles, trampling, wet, mud, sand, snow, etc.).

Filter wheel   Most cameras have an internal multi-position filter wheel fitted between the lens and the beam splitter. A control at the side of the camera rotates the wheel to select from the available filters. Usually, one of its openings is left clear. Another is blanked off, to allow the lens to be 'capped up', preventing any light from falling on the camera-tube or CCD. The rest of the wheel is used for three kinds of filters: neutral density, color correction, and effects.

Neutral density filters are an alternative to having to stop the lens down to avoid overexposure; particularly when you do not want to increase the depth of field. These gray-toned filters reduce all colors equally.

Color-correction filters compensate for the color quality of the prevailing light. Instead of readjusting the camera's *white balance* circuits on moving to light of a different *color temperature* (e.g. from artificial light to daylight), a color-correction filter can change it to suit the existing color balance.

Effects filters of several types may be fitted. The commonest are four- or six-point star filters (starburst) and diffusion discs.

Flash cutting   A sequence structured from a series of very brief shots, each lasting only a few frames.

Flying erase head   In a standard helical scan VCR a fixed erase head wipes the entire tape width. Thus it erases parts of *several* video tracks simultaneously. It cannot erase one complete video track at a time. This precludes precision picture editing. To overcome this problem, recorders designed for *insert editing* have an auxiliary *flying erase head* fitted just before the record head, on the head drum. In some recorders there is also a *flying reproduce head* (*confidence head*) which immediately follows the record head; so allowing simultaneous off-tape monitoring during recording.

Forced processing   When a film is developed at a higher temperature or for a longer period than normal its effective *speed* (sensitivity) is increased; although contrast, graininess, and fog are emphasized. Reversal films 'push' more successfully than negative film material. This technique is resorted to when light levels are too low for normal exposure.

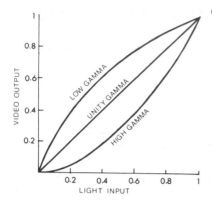

Gamma
The *gamma curve* reveals how a video system reproduces tonal gradation. Where a device is linear (gamma of 1) its output is proportional to the input. A *low gamma* device accepts a wide contrast range, compressing it into the system's limits, resulting in reduced tonal contrast (thin). A *high gamma* device accepts only limited subject contrast, expanding it to fit the reproduction limits, giving exaggerated coarsened tonal values.

Gamma   *Gamma* is a logarithmic measurement that compares the tonal values in the scene with the way they are reproduced on the screen. If reproduced tones correspond with those of the subject (i.e. are directly proportional), the system is said to have *unity gamma* (*gamma = 1*). In fact, various parts of the television system may have gammas other than the ideal (e.g. a color picture tube with a gamma of around 2.2); but gamma-correction circuits can compensate for deviations.

We can alter the subtlety or coarseness of tonal gradation in a picture by adjusting *gamma* controls. A *low gamma* results in thin, reduced tonal contrasts. A *high gamma* produces coarse, exaggerated tonal contrast. By readjusting the gamma, we can often provide greater clarity in shadows or lighter tones. However, there is the drawback that picture noise can become more pronounced with increased *gamma* correction. Occasionally one deliberately uses a higher gamma to emphasize tonal contrasts for dramatic effect.

High-definition television (HDTV)   Today's broadcast color TV standards were conditioned largely by the need to provide systems compatible with existing black-and-white (monochrome) services. Far higher picture quality is achievable, and NHK/Sony have demonstrated a high-definition color system using 1125 lines, 60 field-scanning rate, with a picture of 5:3 aspect ratio, interlaced 2:1, with the video bandwidth increased from the present 4.5 MHz to 30 MHz.

Although the process is incompatible with existing TV systems, it has been used effectively in closed-circuit and 'film-making' applications. Definition is higher than 35 mm motion-picture film, and scanning lines are not discernible at ×3 picture height.

Currently other high-definition systems are also being considered, including 1050 line (59.94 frames) and 1225 line (50 frames) formats.

Highlight overload   Camera-tubes are liable to block off on bright areas, the edge overspill of charges affecting darker picture tones nearby. Spurious *comet tails* also develop behind moving lights or speculars.

Special camera-tube design reduces these problems by enriching the scanning-beam density (during line blanking/retrace periods) to discharge extreme highlights on the target. The camera-tube's exposure curve (light transfer characteristic) develops a *knee*.

Automatic beam-optimizing circuitry is variously termed *highlight overload protection* (*HOP*), *anti-comet-tail gun* (*ACT*), *dynamic beam control* (*DBC*).

Hyperfocal distance   When the lens is focused at infinity (∞), focus remains sharp from infinity to a plane near the camera. When focused at this *hyperfocal distance* (*H*) the scene is sharp from about distance ½*H* to infinity:

$$H \text{ in meters} = \frac{(\text{focal length in cm})^2 \times 100}{\text{lens } f\text{-stop number} \times 0.05}$$

Image enhancement   Electronic correction and improvement of video signals by a *video processor*. This includes corrections such as crispening edge sharpness (high-frequency synthesis), edge color-fringe removal, color-displacement correction (chroma/luma delay), reduced noise ('snow remover'), suppressing 'ringing' at edges, and improved small image detail, sync regeneration.

Lens angle   The horizontal field of view of the camera lens; from frame left to frame right. The horizontal angle is:

$$2 \times \tan^{-1} \frac{\text{Diag.}}{2 \times F}$$

where Diag. = the diagonal of the image area on the pick-up tube (in inches) and F = focal length of the lens (in inches). (See Table 4.2 for typical diagonals.)

In practice, this angle also varies with camera alignment and with the distance at which you focus the lens.

You can estimate the width taken in by a shot at a certain distance from:

$$\frac{W \times \text{focused distance (ft)}}{\text{Focal length of lens (in)}}$$

where W = width of scanned area on target (e.g. 0.35 in (8.8 mm) for ⅔ in (18 mm) tube; see Table 4.2).

Light measurement:

Lumen. A unit of light output (luminous flux).

Lux, foot candle. Units of incident light intensity falling on a surface (illumination).

Nit, foot lambert. Units of surface brightness; reflected light intensity (luminance).

Nanometers, micron, angstrom. All units specifying wavelengths of light (e.g. identifying spectral colors) and other electromagnetic radiation.

Kelvin. A unit of color temperature. (See *Mired.*)

Linear matrix masking   When the color camera analyzes the scene into red, green, and blue images their relative proportions must be accurate; otherwise color values in the final picture will be incorrect. Certain unavoidable errors that arise in the camera system (e.g. due to the pick-up tubes' color response, imperfections in filters and dichroics) may be compensated by special electronic circuitry; a process known as *linear matrix masking*.

Lock-up time   The time taken from starting a VTR (or telecine) for it to reach a stable running speed. Some helical recorders use *stand-by idling* (for recording) and *timebase correctors* (on replay) to reduce start-up time and picture instability.

Low-frequency extender (line extender)   Audio equipment permitting regular phone lines to be used for 'broadcast-quality' commentary speech by suitable frequency shifting, filtering, etc. to remove clicks, pops, hum, and compensating for limited audio bandwidth.

Mired (microreciprocal degrees)   Unit derived to classify a color filter, or the color temperature of a light source. It enables easy calculation of the color shift required to modify a light source's color quality. Mired value equals one million divided by the Kelvin value, e.g. 2500 K = 400 mired.

Mixed-minus (clean feed)   A commentator often needs to be able to monitor pictures and sound of the program to which he is contributing in order to suit the shots, and avoid speaking while others are on-air. If he listened to the complete program sound he would hear his own voice fed back into his earphones/earpiece as he speaks. Instead, he can be supplied with a special source-selective feed of the program sound, termed *mixed minus* or a *clean feed*. He hears all program sound *except* his own contribution. Video *clean feeds* are also used.

Multi-vision (multi-screen)   A large presentation using an assembly of adjoining TV or projector screens to form an extensive composite single or multi-image display. Sometimes indicates several images appearing simultaneously in the same frame.

Munsell color frame   System of notation defining color through a set of charts showing *hue* (five principal and five intermediate hues), *value* (brilliance) in a scale of 10 steps from black to white, and *chroma* (saturation).

Noise reduction (NR)   (See Chapter 12.) The major audio background noise-reduction systems are incompatible. Audio recorded with a given system must generally be reproduced by the same method; although some can be played satisfactorily, through suitable equalization adjustments on any reproducer (Dolby B). Each system has its associated compromises (e.g. need for careful alignment, or performance limitations).

In the complex *Dolby A* system used for professional recording the audio-frequency spectrum is filtered into four sections (bands). Each is individually treated, boosting very quiet signals, while leaving louder ones virtually unaffected. When decoded on replay, the original relative audio levels are restored, and background noises correspondingly reduced.

The *Dolby B* system is widely used for audio-cassette recording. It is level-selective, but operates only on the high-frequency end of the audio spectrum. So tapes recorded with *Dolby B* noise reduction are subjectively compatible when played without correction.

Dolby C offers improved noise reduction. Widely used for audio-cassette recording, it uses pre-emphasis; the frequency at which the boosting begins depending on the volume at that moment. There is corresponding de-emphasis on replay.

During audio taping the strength of the fixed bias current applied to the recording head is normally a technical compromise. (Lower bias improves high notes but worsens bass distortion, modifying the system's overall response.) The *Dolby HX* (*headroom extension*) adjusts the tape bias automatically, according to the high-frequency energy content of the program, to produce lower distortion levels overall.

The relatively straightforward *dBx* system does not split the audio spectrum, but applies routine pre-emphasis/de-emphasis to the program. The Telefunken *Telecom* and *High-com* systems have features similar to Dolby A, but with a constant compression.

The newest *Dolby SR* (*Spectral Recording*) process combines aspects of the A, B, and C systems, the playback complementing the recording process. During recording, quiet sounds are selectively raised above tape noise. Loud sounds are reduced below distortion levels, according to their energy content at different frequencies, so as to suit the ear's characteristics. A further Dolby system *ADM* is used with high-quality *digital* stereo sound systems.

Further facilities for reducing unwanted background noise include *noise gates* which selectively suppress low-level signals; and *notch filters* which reduce a narrow selected part of the audio spectrum (e.g. hum reduction).

One and a half heads (1.5 heads) principle   A separate head records the vertical interval information near the lower edge of the tape, thus retaining VIRS, VITS, teletext.

Optical printer   A special film-printing machine in which a filmed image is projected onto the film stock rather than printed by contact with it. The projected image can be independently exposed to provide optical transitions, superimpositions, size changes, freeze frame, step printing, speed and direction changes, skip frame, multi-image, traveling matte, image-position changes, image distortions, etc.

Overlapping sound   An introductory editing treatment used when flat cuts join two dissimilar scenes. The sounds of the next scene are heard before the vision switches.

Overscanning   If a picture on a monitor is expanded so that its edges are lost beyond the surround mask it uses the full picture-tube screen, and appears subjectively to be larger. But in fact all the picture information around the edges is being lost – sometimes including subtitles. In any production areas, monitors should be *underscanned* to show the entire TV frame (*raster*) including corners; for this will reveal when any unwanted subjects are peeking into shot (mikes, another camera, distracting items); and also display certain technical defects more clearly (e.g. sync problems shown by ragged picture edges).

Padding (fill)   Improvised action/dialog introduced when a program is underrunning, or *stretching* available material to fill the allotted time.

Panning head (camera-mounting head)   Several designs are widely used. The cheapest and simplest is the *friction head*. For lightweight cameras, it relies on surface friction (stiction) between parts to steady pan/tilt movements. But it is not easily controlled, due to excess friction at the start of movements, and vertical balance cannot be adjusted.

The *fluid head* is an excellent all-purpose mounting head for light- to medium-weight cameras. Layers of high-viscosity silicon fluid dampen head movement and produce very smooth action, unaffected by temperature changes. Pan and tilt friction can be adjusted. For very fast movements, damping can be switched off. A spring element compensates for imbalance during tilting. The head often incorporates a leveling indicator.

The *cradle head* is often used for heavy cameras. Large and cumbersome, its balance is fairly good, as the camera's center of gravity is distributed, but its tilt range is limited. Friction settings (drag) tend to be unreliable, and change in use.

Cam heads overcome these problems. These incorporate cams or cylinders on either side of the head to control pan and tilt movements. Drag is adjustable, and the head can be locked in chosen positions. Particularly suitable for heavier cameras, control is extremely smooth.

Perspective distortion Perspective effects strongly influence interpretation of space. Where the camera's lens angle and your viewing angle to the screen are comparable you see 'natural perspective', showing proportions and spatial impressions similar to those of everyday life. When a *camera moves* towards a subject to obtain a larger image (i.e. a closer shot), perspective remains consistent, the proportions of subjects are compatible, their relative positions and spacing changing as you approach.

Zooming, on the other hand, simply alters the overall magnification of the lens image, so these natural effects do not result. Although by reducing the lens angle you can fill the screen with a distant subject – so suggesting that it is close – the resultant image is generally dissimilar from the impression you would actually get at a close viewpoint. Instead, subjects show characteristics you normally associate with *distance*: depth in the picture appears foreshortened, and there is often considerable overlapping. Sizes do not diminish naturally with distance. You interpret such incompatibilities as *spatial compression*. A *spatial exaggeration* effect arises when a very wide camera lens angle is used. (The illusion of natural perspective can be restored by changing your viewing distance proportionally to the lens angle used.)

Pick-up A loose term for any separate shots recorded after the main program to be inserted during VT editing. They may be *corrective* (e.g. to enable action, dialog, technical errors to be removed) or *detail inserts* (e.g. showing close-ups, location action, reactions, etc.) that could not be shot during the original take.

Picture monitors One's opportunity to assess picture quality and video equipment performance largely depends on the standards and adjustment of the picture monitor. Where monitor performance drifts (loses focus, convergence alters, color balance changes) or reproduction varies with picture content, judgement is very arbitrary.

Various types of picture-tube are used (Figure 3.5). While delta-gun dot-mask (shadow mask) tubes provide generally superior pictures, their convergence drifts with time (so subjects seem to develop color fringes). PIL tubes have improved convergence stability, but coarser resolution.

In black matrix screens the phosphor dots are laid down on a low-reflectance black background, so that less light is reflected from the screen surface. The picture-tube's resolution depends on the closeness and size of the screen's dot: from typical broadcast tubes (pitch of 0.47–0.63 per in), to high resolution (0.43), and ultra-high (0.31).

Typical picture-tube performance is around: white 25 fL (max.) to black ½ fL (minimum limited by flare and dispersion in glass). Maximum contrast of 50:1 is possible, but 15:1 in a lighted room is more typical.

Picture quality A subjective grading scale may be used to assess video or audio quality (CCIR/CCITT).

Quality	Grade	Impairment
Excellent	5	Imperceptible defects
Good	4	Perceptible, but not annoying
Fair	3	Slightly annoying
Poor	2	Annoying
Bad	1	Very annoying

Pilot tone VTR development in which a special frequency is recorded (1.5 times the color subcarrier) to provide constant monitoring and correction of the system's chrominance, as well as checking scanning synchronizing errors for improved time-base correction.

Pixillation Jerky fast motion effect created by regularly omitting frames from film shot at normal speed. *Also* an animation effect obtained by conjoining a series of still frames.

PLUGE Electronically generated image used to adjust picture monitors to a uniform standard. Picture comprises a vertical white bar, an area of reference black, and two reference tones slightly higher and lower than the reference by 2.5 IEEE/IRE units (Institute of Electrical and Electronic Engineers). The monitor is adjusted so that the darker patch merges with reference background, the brighter patch still remaining visible.

Post-syncing The process of recording sound (speech, sound effects) to synchronize with an existing picture – as when replacing original dialog with a different language, closely following the original lip movements; or when fitting convincing new sound to a mute print.

Pressure zone microphone A form of high-quality electret mike. Its flat baseplate contains a narrow slot through which sound reaches a diaphragm. Reflected and direct waves are in phase in the *pressure zone*, so that when the mike is placed against a large reflecting surface it becomes non-directional.

Program interrupt (switched talkback) Many shows use a central performer to introduce and link items, interview, provide commentary, etc. This person can wear an earpiece through which he receives instructions/guidance from the director or program associates, unheard by the studio microphone (typically, suggesting interview questions, explaining last-minute changes or emergency situations). This intercom circuit remains silent until activated by a switch in the production control room. Or alternatively, the earpiece circuit may carry program sound, which is interrupted and replaced by intercom whenever the director needs to contact the performer; who can acknowledge silently with a gesture, or speak over a local microphone.

Quadruplex (quad, transverse) VTR Now obsolescent, this high-quality system uses a 2 in wide magnetic tape moving at 38 cm/s. A full-width erase head demagnetizes the tape, which passes a transverse headwheel with four recording/replay heads. Mounted 90° apart, these scan across the tape in turn recording a series of parallel transverse video tracks (effective writing speed 3800 cm/s or 1500 ips). Each track records 16 lines in 525 systems (20 lines, 625 systems). Interhead switching ensures continuous recording/replay. The audio, control, and cue tracks are located along the tape edges (see illustration on page 552).

Rostrum camera Two basic forms are used. (1) A vertical TV camera shoots an animation table, where successive drawings (or cels) are displayed on a horizontal surface; top lit, or illuminated by a light-box underneath. The results are recorded on a VTR or magnetic video disc. (With *two-frame animation*, changes are made after every other exposed frame.) In sophisticated designs, camera movement, zoom, table position changes (N/S, E/W), exposure rate, etc. are computer-activated.

Quadruplex system
The 2 in/50.8 mm wide magnetic tape passes over an *erase head* that demagnetizes (wipes) its full width. The four record/replay heads on the headwheel press against the tape, recording across it in a series of parallel transverse tracks, each covering a 16-line segment of the picture (20 lines in European 625-line system). Heads are switched successively to provide a continuous video signal, recording or replaying the tape. The video heads are upstream of the corresponding audio heads (by 23.5 cm/9.25 in). Recording is checked by replaying random selections (spot checks). The Quad II system uses the track format: audio 1, cue/code track, audio 2, video, control.

(2) Another system projects a video recording of live action (a frame at a time) onto a glass screen, where it is traced on a cel to derive an animated cartoon.

Simultaneous contrast (spatial induction) A visual illusion in which the apparent tone, color, and size of an area is modified by its background. A light-toned area appears lighter and larger against a dark background; a dark area even darker against a light one. Similar interaction arises in color, where an area may look cool (bluish) against a dark background and warm (red/yellow) against light tones. A colored background may modify the appearance of the foreground subject, often biasing its color towards a complementary hue. Juxtapose red and blue, and the red will seem quite orange while the blue has a greenish tinge. A strongly colored subject may similarly influence a neutral background tone.

Single-system sound Audio recorded directly onto film soundtrack (or integrated VTR), using a mike on top of the camera. Automatic gain circuits control audio levels. In *double systems* a separate camera and synchronized audio recorder are used; picture and sound being combined during editing, or reproduced in sync on separate equipment (*double headed*).

Single-tube color camera Simpler color TV cameras reduce cost and weight by using only *one* camera tube or image sensor instead of the three in high-grade designs. The natural-color lens image is split into the three component colors R, G, B by attaching a striped color filter to the front of the camera-tube target (external or internal). This filter may have red, green, blue stripes overall, or a combined pattern of cyan/clear stripes and diagonal yellow/clear stripes.

In the latter type the red component of the scene is recovered from the clear (luminance) stripes and the cyan (minus red) stripes. The blue component is recovered from the yellow and clear (blue is 'minus yellow'). The green signal is derived from the other components. The result is ingenious, but inevitably of lower color quality and definition than more complex optical systems.

Slate (clapperboard, clapstick) An identification board used during filming. Shown before a shot; or inverted if taken at its end. The hinged top section is brought down quickly to produce a loud noise, which enables the separate picture and soundtrack (double system) to be synchronized during editing. Electronic *time code* systems of synchronizing are increasingly used.

An electronically generated '*slate*' with a time-remaining clock is widely used as a VTR 'slate'/leader.

Slides

Standard 35 mm slide format.   Mount 50×50 mm (2×2 in); aperture 36×24 mm; aspect ratio $3:2$.

Superslide format.   Similar mount size; aperture 40×40 mm (1.6×1.6 in).

Slide scanner   An optical projector or flying-spot scanner used to televise transparencies. Plastic-mounted slides are fitted into pairs of drums, discs, or trays (typical capacities of 36–40). Selection may be sequential (instantaneous) or random (delayed) from the production switcher position. Scanners do not usually permit size and position adjustments of the image. (See *Electronic still store.*)

Slow-motion controller   This device provides instant slow-motion replay on a 25 mm (1 in) helical VTR. A cue-mark is added while recording. When cued, the system rapidly rewinds the tape, ready to replay at variable slow speeds, with freeze-frame options. This facility is gradually replacing the magnetic video disc for slow-motion replays during programs.

Sound in syncs   A system in which audio is digitally encoded, and introduced into the composite video signal, during the line syncs period. Thus both video and audio can be transmitted on one carrier instead of requiring two separate transmission systems.

Staging   The design and arrangement of scenic elements (scenery, furniture, props) to create a practical and artistically suitable working environment; permitting appropriate action, shots, sounds.

Staircase (step wedge)   Video test signal generated to provide a series of distinct brightness steps from black to white.

Standards converters   Used primarily to convert composite picture signals originating from one TV system (e.g. NTSC) to another incompatible system (e.g. PAL).

Conversion problems include: motion judder/blur, color errors, horizontal edge-flicker. Various degrees of design sophistication exist, but six-field storage equipment provides more accurate movement rendition, is free from drift, and includes such operational features as freeze frame, noise reduction, technical corrections (blanking errors, head-switching, frame break-up).

Teletext (Oracle, Ceefax, Antiope, Telidon)   Systems for the digital transmission of written information and diagrams during vertical interval period – for selective display of data on visual display units or home TV receiver.

Television systems   All color TV pictures are distributed or transmitted in coded form (not as separate RGB signals).

NTSC (National Television System Committee). The three primary color video signals (RGB) are transformed by a coder into a *luminance* (brightness) signal conveying the tonal values and two special *chrominance* or color difference signals (I and Q). I and Q signals are used to simultaneously modulate the chrominance subcarrier; its strength (amplitude) varying with a color's saturation at that moment, and its phase changing with the hue (quadrature modulation). The resultant complex transmitted wave therefore contains both chrominance and luminance information. Color errors can arise in the path from transmitter to receiver (phase errors). Corrective receiver circuits increasingly use *VIR* signals to regulate these errors. Overall bandwidth 4.2 MHz. Color subcarrier 3.58 MHz.

PAL (*Phase alternating line*). Basically a similar system, but one of the color difference signals is reversed in phase on alternate line, so that slight color errors due to phase shift are averaged out. (Greater errors become visible as *Hanover bars*.) Overall bandwidth 5.5 MHz. Color subcarrier 4.43 MHz.

SECAM (*Sequential color and memory*). Similarly derived, but here the chrominance signals are transmitted one at a time sequentially, on alternate lines of each field to average out phase errors. (A delay line stores and reinserts color information.)

All three systems can exhibit 'herringbone' (moiré) or 'crawling dot' patterns.

Time-base correction Any disturbance of synchronizing pulses in a color system can cause such picture defects as jitter, frame roll (vertical), skew or hooking at the top of frame, scalloping at edges, hue and saturation errors. (Helical scan recorders are very susceptible to such irregularities.) Ingenious circuitry can reduce such scanning errors by using delay lines (as in analog *time-base correctors*, TBC), or by digital storage of a full frame of video information (as in *frame synchronizers*). Sophisticated digital correctors have overcome certain problems in video switching and remote source synchronizing, and in satellite transmission.

Time code This is a specially generated digital code based on the 24-hour clock; recorded with a video or audio program, to provide continuous shot identification. The original standard time code (*longitudinal time code – LTC*) is widely used, in NTSC and EBU forms.

Where time code is recorded on an edge track (*longitudinal time code – LTC*) the tape must move past a replay head at over one-fifth normal speed to be read reliably. On stopping the tape motion (for a still frame), code readout ceases altogether, although the video replay heads continue to scan, reading out the *picture information*. But during VT editing, tape motion varies considerably: fast search, slow motion, jogging (frame by frame). To overcome this dilemma, another time-code format was introduced (*vertical interval time code – VITC*) in which the code is recorded in the vertical interval (retrace) period, and read out by the video heads, so is always available with the picture at all tape speeds.

Whereas the LTC format codes at *frame rate*, decoded at the end of the video frame, the VITC format is a *field-rate code*, decoded at the start of each video field, and odd/even fields are identified. Unlike the LTC format, where picture and its corresponding time-code pick-up points are displaced along the tape (offset), the VITC is read with its picture.

Because the NTSC system scans at 59.9 Hz, using a 60 Hz power supply, there would normally be a progressive difference between the time code reading and clock time (3–6 seconds' error per hour). To compensate for this, a couple of frames are dropped from the time-code count for 9 minutes out of every 10–108 frames per hour. This *drop frame* convention has been widely adopted. Where time code is used in *zero start mode* this error is unimportant, and correction may not be used. But it is essential that computer facilities are not presented with a mixture of 'drop-frame' and 'non drop-frame' tapes.

Simpler editor systems often count control track pulses (deriving 'user bits') to aid frame identification during editing. However, this process has several disadvantages compared with time code, when editing is at all complex. Reading errors arise while shuttling tape to and fro, so that frame counts are only approximate. Unlike time code, this method cannot locate specific tape points. Nor can it be used for precise control of other equipment during editing, such as multi VTR playbacks, audiotape replay, switchers (for transitions between shots), digital video effects.

Time compression Circuitry that strategically adjusts the length of pauses on replay of a taped program, by just a few milliseconds, enables the overall duration to be adjusted automatically by e.g. 3–6 minutes in a 30-minute show (10–30 per cent contraction). Tape-transport speed is guided by a digital controller, which speeds up the tape very slightly, without obviously changing the audio pitch or showing perceptible visual disruption. This facility allows precise program-duration adjustment to a fixed time slot without having to edit the tape unduly.

Translator Equipment used to extend the service area of a TV station by receiving the transmitted signal, boosting it, and retransmitting at increased power.

Transmission numbers (T) The *f*-stop number is based on physical aperture size, and disregards light-transmission losses and reflections between lens elements. *T-stops* are based on the actual amount of light passed by the lens system. In practice, these systems are comparable.

Traveling matte A film-printing process in which a matte or mask silhouette is derived from a subject image to block out a selected area of another picture. This permits the subject (or other material) to be introduced into that area.

Traveling shot Any shots from a moving camera (e.g. tracking shot).

UHF Ultra-high frequency. TV transmission band *above* Channel 13, 470–890 MHz. (UK bands IV, V.)

Vertical interval reference signals (VIRS) As you know, the TV system scans each complete picture in two separate 'fields'. After scanning each field there is a brief *retrace* period when the system returns from the bottom-right corner of the screen to the top-left, ready to scan the next. During this brief *vertical interval/field blanking period* no picture information is transmitted. So the broadcaster takes the opportunity to introduce encoded data instead – (*VIRS, VITS*) and perhaps *teletext* information.

These inserted data are transmitted just before *picture* information begins, and are visible on the receiver screen as a dot pattern within the first few lines at the top edge of the frame. However, as most home receivers are overscanned (i.e. the picture is expanded to overlap the screen edges), the lines fall outside the normal viewed picture area.

VIRS can be used to provide identification of the program source, the point of origination, time and date of the original broadcast, etc. Technically, reference data can be included that automatically adjust the screen color balance to levels specified at the source, compensating for any signal distortions arising between the transmitter and the receiver. But this practice is not widespread.

Vertical interval test signals (VITS) are used for technical measurements, monitoring, and performance correction of transmission systems.

VHF Very high frequency. TV transmission band covering Channels 2–13, 54–216 MHz. (UK bands I, II.)

Video discs Following similar principles to the audio *compact disc*, the video disc format permanently stores picture and sound information digitally on a metalized disc surface in the form of a pattern of pits on a fine spiral. These are read optically by a reflected laser beam.

The video disc has unique storage merits, for it offers: continuous replay (e.g. an entire motion picture); *selective replay* (frame search, freeze frame, vari-speed); *still store* (thousands of individually selectable still frames); *interactive routing* (user-selected sequences from a menu); *disc/computer interfacing* (computer-selected stills, sequences, animation).

Although non-erasable, the video disc has the particular advantage over videotape systems that information is instantaneously selectable.

Video signal The video signal is a voltage in analog form of light and shade in the scanned image. During the retrace periods after scanning a line any picture information is suppressed (*blanking*), and a horizontal (line) synchronizing pulse is inserted. This ensures that the entire TV system scans in step. In addition, a brief burst of subcarrier frequency provides a color reference signal to ensure color accuracy.

In a 525-line TV system the system scans the lens image in 262.5 lines in 1/60 second. When this *odd field* is complete, the system retraces to scan between the first set of scanning lines, to provide the *even field*. The odd and even fields are *interlaced* to form one complete *frame*. Thirty of these frames (i.e. 15 750 lines) are scanned each second. Of the 525 lines, 485 actually contribute to the picture information (are *active*). Others are scanning during the blanked-out vertical retrace period.

In a 625-line system the respective figures are: 312.5 lines per field, scanned in 1/50 second; 25 complete frames per second; 15 625 scanning lines per second.

At the end of each complete field a further synchronizing pulse is introduced for vertical stabilization (*vertical sync pulse*). Additional signals may also be included (*VIRS, Teletext*).

The illustration shows details of one complete scanning line, together with the names of its various features: 1 Peak white (peak modulation); 2 Peak black. 3 Color burst; 4 Front porch; 5 Horizontal (line) sync pulse; 6 Back porch; 7 Synchronizing level (sync level); 8 Blanking level; 9 Set-up (pedestal); 10 Reference black (black level); 11 Reference white (white level).

Videotape standards (see *Quadruplex VTR*)

SMPTE Type C (*non-segmented*). The videotape wraps round most of the split head-drum. The upper drum, with a single record/play head mounted on it, rotates at field rate (60/50 revolutions per second). This rotating head loses tape-contact at the end of each scan, so misses 10 picture lines (12 in 625/50 system), which are either replaced by a time-base corrector store, or recorded on a separate track by an additional *sync head* just in front of the *record head*. (The 16 or 19 lines this head records overlap the missing segment, so compensating for changes in tape tension, slow motion, and still-frame modes.)

Where broadcast-quality slow motion or a still frame is required, an extra video head is included, mounted on a piezoelectric element, to ensure optimum tracking accuracy (*auto scan/dynamic tracking*). Along the tape edges are located three (four) audio and one control track. Full information in the TV vertical interval (blanking) period can be recorded where it contains control and logging data (e.g. for activating auto opt-out, advertisement logging). In Europe an extra head can be fitted to record the vertical interval information, or an extra high-quality fourth audio track.

In general, audio tracks 1, 2 are used for main program sound (for stereo: *SMPTE* record sum and difference signals; *EBU* record left- and right-hand channels). Gyroscopic errors that may arise (due to the large head-drum) if the machine is moved violently while recording may not be within the range of a time-base corrector on replay; but scanner servos do help to reduce replay errors.

SMPTE Type B (*segmented*). The videotape wraps round 190° of the small-diameter low-mass head-drum. Its two heads together record the *total* picture information, without loss or disturbance during the line-retrace/blanking period. The small mass of the head-drum enables lighter, more compact design, high-speed stability, and immunity to shock or gyroscopic effects if recording while mobile. Simple tape threading (lace-up) reduces tape friction. The high writing speed makes tape quality less critical. The shorter track length (80 mm) provides more accurate tracking and interchange compatibility. However, there is less room for confidence heads on the head-drum, and the possibility of head-switching problems (banding). Along the edges of the tape there are four independent longitudinal tracks: audio (two); time code; control track. (There are differences between the SMPTE/NTSC and EBU/PAL formats.)

Viewing conditions Preferred viewing conditions recommended by CCIR include – viewing distance four to six times picture height; peak screen luminance 60–80 cd/m^2; blank screen 0.02 of peak white.

Volume indicators (*see Figure 12.24*) Our ears have a *logarithmic* response, i.e. they can detect slight changes in quiet sounds, but at higher volumes even quite large variations do not seem very different. So our subjective impressions of volume changes are not very accurate. They vary with the frequency (pitch) and the strength of the sound.

Audio equipment, on the other hand has a direct *linear* response to increases in sound level. The audio becomes distorted when it exceeds the system's limits; but our ears cannot accurately judge when it is about to reach that point. So we need some kind of volume indicator to show when to reduce the system's gain (amplification) in anticipation.

Several forms of volume indicator are used to guide our judgement and prevent accidental *overmodulation* (*overload distortion*) or *undermodulation* (as weak audio becomes intermixed with random background noise).

The widely used *VU meter* is a cheap, simple indicator of program *loudness*, i.e. how strong the sound appears to the *ear*. It has 'decibel' and 'modulation' scales (*volume units*) showing the audio system's limits. The continual rapid needle movement can be confusing and tiring to watch. The indicated readings for steady sounds (tone) are accurate but much less reliable for fluctuating audio, and very inaccurate for loud transient sounds (e.g. percussion), that can read low, so that the sound system overloads and distorts. Normal range used: −20 to 0 dB. Speech. −14 to 0 dB. True undistorted maximum modulation reading is around 50 per cent on the meter.

A *peak program meter* (*PPM*) responds to the audio signal's *peaks*, so gives a better indication of system overload. Readings are accurate for steady sounds, transients, and for complex audio, so reveal any possibilities of overload distortion. However, unlike the VU meter, the PPM's readings do not necessarily relate to the impression of loudness we actually hear. Normal range used: 2 to 6 (each scale step is 4 dB).

Various forms of *visual display* are becoming popular as peak-volume indicators including: bargraphs of LEDs (light-emitting diodes), gas-discharge devices, plasma displays, and light patterns on video monitors.

Wall outlets (distribution boxes) At intervals around the studio walls various supplies are centered at combined outlet points. These can include:

AC outlets ('household current'/general service supplies) to power electrical equipment for demonstration apparatus, musical instruments, loudspeaker amplifiers, etc.

Camera cable outlets (to studio engineering area/apparatus room/master control). Outlets carry supplies to cameras, video from camera.

Audio outlets (tie lines from studio to sound control room): audio signals from each studio microphone (boom, personal, radio mike).

Audio feeds (tie lines from sound control room to studio): to feed studio monitor loudspeaker(s) (e.g. sound effects; playback; foldback).

Sound-monitoring outlets (for earphone monitoring – studio sound output; selected sound sources; sound cues; incoming telephone calls; private line; 'mixed-minus'/'clean feeds').

Intercom outlets carrying production intercom/talkback. Also, switched intercom ('interrupted feedback' (IFB)/interrupted talkback). Only activated when keyed in production control room; for selective cuing (as opposed to general intercom/general talkback).

Video outlets (tie lines from engineering area) carrying studio video output to feed picture monitors; or providing a selected video source such as film channel, VTR output, video effects to picture monitors. Remote monitor switching (monitor display can be switched in production control room).

Cue-light circuits (push button cuing, from control room, of attached cue lights in studio).

Private wire outlets: tie lines for individual cuing/instruction of boom operators, floor workers, electricians, special-effects operators, etc.

Telephone to production control area (e.g. lighting).

Additional services such as water, compressed air, steam are provided elsewhere as wall outlets, away from distribution boxes.

Waveform monitor (WFM) A small oscilloscope tube displaying a fluctuating line which traces the variations of the video signal, sync pulses, and insertion pulses. Individual picture lines can be selected and examined (line strobe).

Zoom microphone A specially designed camera-mounted microphone, containing electret capsules, which combine to provide adjustable coverage. This ranges from 'omni-directional' (equal sensitivity in all directions) to 'ultra-unidirectional' (narrow-angle). The apparent closeness of the sound can nominally be adjusted to match different zoom-lens settings: i.e. 'close' sound for close-ups, 'distant' sound for long shots. The arrangement is very arbitrary, but a useful compromise for a one-camera unit.

Further reading

If you want to explore further aspects of television/video production the following companion books by Gerald Millerson, published by Focal Press, are available.

Video Production Handbook
This realistic practical guide to low-cost video program making explains how to achieve professional standards with limited facilities and a restricted budget.

Effective TV Production
This is a 'succinct but thorough overview of the production process' (*American Cinematographer*) distilled for rapid study into a single volume.

Video Camera Techniques
A quick, lucid guide to the essentials of handling video cameras.

The Technique of Lighting for Television and Motion Pictures
An internationally established sourcebook, discussing in detail the principles and techniques of the art of lighting.

TV Lighting Methods
A rapid guide to practical lighting techniques in television and video production.

TV Scenic Design Handbook
A study in depth of the art, the mechanics, and techniques of scenic design for television and video production.

Index

Major references are indicated by **bold** type.